RELIGION IN AMERICAN CULTURE

A Sociological Interpretation

THE DORSEY SERIES IN ANTHROPOLOGY AND SOCIOLOGY

EDITORS

Robin M. Williams, Jr.
Cornell University

William Foote Whyte
Cornell University

Argyris *Understanding Organizational Behavior*

Adams & Preiss (ed.) *Human Organization Research* (Published for the Society for Applied Anthropology)

Hsu (ed.) *Psychological Anthropology: Approaches to Culture and Personality*

Bell (ed.) *The Sociology of Education: A Sourcebook*

Hagen *On the Theory of Social Change: How Economic Growth Begins*

Bell *Marriage and Family Interaction*

Barnouw *Culture and Personality*

Gottlieb & Ramsey *The American Adolescent*

Jacobs *Pattern in Cultural Anthropology*

Johnson *Crime, Correction, and Society*

Salisbury *Religion in American Culture: A Sociological Interpretation*

RELIGION IN AMERICAN CULTURE

A Sociological Interpretation

by W. Seward Salisbury, Ph.D.

Professor of Sociology
and Chairman,
Social Science Department
State University College
at Oswego, New York

1964

THE DORSEY PRESS

HOMEWOOD, ILLINOIS

First Printing, July, 1964

Library of Congress Catalogue Card No. 64–22110

PRINTED IN THE UNITED STATES OF AMERICA

To
my wife, RUTH
and our sons
WILL, RICHIE, *and* BOB

INFORMATION ABOUT RELIGION is necessary and useful for an understanding of the culture in which the citizen lives. This book seeks to provide this information by interpreting the American religious culture within a social science frame of reference.

This work is not, however, a sociology of religion text. There are several well conceived and well executed sociology of religion texts on the market to which the interested student or teacher may turn.

The sociology of religion deals with the general principles concerning the relation of religion to society. The sociological analysis of religion seeks to understand a particular religion or patterns of religious behavior by applying sociological principles to the analysis of the religious phenomena under observation. The sociology of religion and the sociological analysis of a particular religion or a religious culture are by no means mutually exclusive or dichotomous categories. One tends to shade into the other.

This presentation is a sociological analysis of religion. Students, the author has found, need first to have some basic knowledge of the substance and content of religion and religious behavior before they can theorize meaningfully about religion.

Although the analysis of the religious culture is central and the sociology of religion more peripheral to the major objectives of this study, considerable knowledge of the principles that constitute the content of the sociology of religion can be acquired by a close study of the materials offered within these pages.

The book is divided into logical parts, each of which includes two or more chapters on specific subtopics. Each part is preceded by a foreword identifying and defining the theoretical tools and concepts that are used in the more descriptive chapters that follow. Each part is followed by a few theoretical observations based upon the substantive and descriptive materials that precede. The forewords and concluding observations are designed to stimulate the thinking of those who are particularly interested in social analysis.

Religion is almost as universal as people and personality. The anthropologists remind us that religion is one feature of the universal culture pattern—it is found in every culture. Every religious person in being religious, therefore, does have something in common with every other religious person. Every religious person is like some other religious persons: Catholics are like other Catholics. Methodists are like other Methodists, Jehovah's Witnesses like other Jehovah's Witnesses, and so forth. But every religiously oriented person is in some respects unique, unlike any other religious personality. Religion is a complex phenomenon; personality is a complex phenomenon. The possibilities for variation in any given religious personality are infinite. The uniqueness of religious experience and religious behavior is underlined in this treatment of the religious culture by the frequent use of autobiographical case study material.

The author wishes to recognize the debt he owes to the various students whose autobiographical accounts of their own religious feelings and experiences appear in these pages. No autobiographies were required; all were voluntarily submitted. Each reader has to decide for himself the validity or the uniqueness of the various biographical accounts. If these accounts are useful, if they offer any helpful insight into the nature of religious feelings and behavior, the credit is due those students who sincerely and effectively shared their experience and feelings with their instructor.

Credit and appreciation is due the clergymen and religious leaders who so graciously gave of their time and talents that students in various sociology classes might become acquainted with religion as it is conceived and practiced at the parish level.

The author wishes to acknowledge his indebtedness to Robin M. Williams, Jr. for the theoretical framework which provides the basis for the organization and presentation of the data and materials of religious behavior which follow. Sociologists will recognize the framework and numerous theoretical references as primarily derived from William's excellent study *American Society, A Sociological Interpretation*, which is now in its second decade as a standard theoretical guide for American sociologists.

Religion in American Culture is planned to interest a wide range of persons and groups. The general citizen will become informed concerning the nature and significance of pluralism in religion. Clergymen and laymen of particular churches can find here factual information about their faith and their church objectively reported and evaluated. Through this analysis members of the three faiths—Protestants, Catholics, Jews—may view themselves in the light of the cultural perspective. They will find themselves alike in many aspects of structure and process that should provide the basis for meaningful dialogue and the increasing tolerance and understanding that follows.

This organization of materials may serve as a text with or without collateral readings for a variety of social science and religion courses. It is the hope of the author that its study will stimulate an ongoing interest in religion and the religious culture.

Oswego, New York   W. SEWARD SALISBURY
April 1, 1964

Table of Contents

PART I

Introductory

Chapter I

Introduction

THE PUBLICATION OF THIS BOOK is a reflection of the increased interest in religion throughout American society and of the widespread feeling that religious institutions can now be studied scientifically. This book also recognizes the growing belief that the objective study of religion deserves a place in the curriculum of general education.

The interest of the American people in religion has been demonstrated by the steadily increasing percentages who have identified themselves with the various denominations sinceWorld War II. Although the growth has leveled off and may have become stabilized in the neighborhood of 60 percent of the population, this still represents the highest proportion of religious identification and affiliation in the history of the American people. This is a social fact of considerable significance even though the involvement of many may be minor, and the motivation of others may be nonreligious in nature.

The Communist challenge to democracy contributes to the quickened interest and concern that Americans show for their religious institutions. The antireligious and atheistic image presented by Communism keeps American religious institutions in sharp focus. Many Americans feel that freedom of religion and religious pluralism would be lost should Communism win its struggle to make the Communist ideology the basis for universal cultural forms. This threat to their institutions has stimulated some Americans to study religion and religious institutions: how it functions and what its place is in the total cultural pattern.

The publication and cordial reception of Herberg's *Protestant-Catholic-*

Jew[1] is convincing evidence of the academic interest that Americans have in their religious institutions. Herberg chose to present his stimulating and provocative interpretation of the religious culture within a sociological frame of reference.

Scientific Study of Religion

Two groups devoted to the scientific study of religion have developed and flourished during the post–World War II period. The Society for the Scientific Study of Religion was organized in 1950. It seeks to bring together students and scholars from all the disciplines interested in the scientific study of religion for the interstimulation and cross-fertilization of their thinking and research. Theologians and Biblical scholars, as well as sociologists, psychologists, anthropologists, psychiatrists, and historians, present papers at the various meetings and participate in the activities of the Society. Although organized in the Northeast with its first meetings held on the campuses of Harvard, Yale, and Columbia, the Society is now national in scope, has regional representation, and holds meetings in Chicago, Minneapolis, San Francisco, and Los Angeles. The Society publishes the *Journal for the Scientific Study of Religion* biannually, and issues a newsletter six times a year.

Another organization, the Religious Research Association, is likewise devoted to the scientific study of religion with a major focus upon research—its methods and its findings. The Association is national in scope. In the winter of 1962 regional meetings were held in Atlanta, Dallas, Los Angeles, Minneapolis–St. Paul, and Princeton, with the annual meeting in Chicago in June. The Association sponsors an H. Paul Douglass Lecture given each year by an outstanding writer and researcher before the annual meeting. Its journal, the *Review of Religious Research,* is published three times a year.

The interest in the study of religion by sociologists has grown to the point where two or more sections of the annual meeting of the American Sociological Association are given over to papers on some phase of the sociology of religion.

Social Science Publications in Religion

A number of social science studies and monographs have appeared in recent years. Some of the greatest contributions to an understanding of religious phenomena have arisen out of the research sponsored by the churches themselves. Organized religion no longer looks upon the scientific study of religion with suspicion, but rather looks upon research as the means by which the work and services of the church may be improved and strengthened.

Catholic Studies. Catholic scholars have been leaders in subjecting the

---

[1] Will Herberg, *Protestant-Catholic-Jew: An Essay in American Religious Sociology* (Garden City, N.Y.: Doubleday & Co., 1955).

religious institutions to empirical analysis. Studies sponsored by the Catholic Church have led to a better understanding of the Catholic religious culture as well as contributing to the sociology of religion. The pioneer work of Joseph Fichter, S.J., makes him the most productive scholar in the sociology of religion among American sociologists. His analysis of the representative Catholic parish, published as *Southern Parish, Dynamics of a City Church*,[2] and *Social Relations in the Urban Parish*,[3] stands as the classic of parish research. This was followed by *Parochial School*,[4] a sociological study of the Catholic parochial school. Fichter then subjected the Catholic religious vocations to a scientific analysis. This was published as *Religion as an Occupation, A Study in the Sociology of Professions*.[5]

Nuesse and Harte edited a volume of selected studies and essays on the Catholic parish under the title, *The Sociology of the Parish*,[6] and Schuyler has studied a representative urban parish in the North analyzed and published under the title *Northern Parish*.[7] A number of sociologists have studied the Catholic family. Several monographs and textbooks have been published, of which Thomas' *The American Catholic Family*[8] is one of the most widely known and used.

Jewish Studies. There are always numerous studies of Jewish religion and Jewish culture. In every generation the Jewish emphasis upon education and learning has brought forth a number of scholars who chose to make their contribution to learning in terms of historical descriptions of the Jewish people. During the post–World War II period several students of Jewish religion and culture have turned to a sociological frame of reference for their analyses. The work of Sklare is outstanding in this field. His *Conservative Judaism*[9] is an empirical work of high quality that submits to scientific analysis the Jewish denomination that most clearly reflects adaptation to the American cultural milieu. Sklare has also edited *The Jews, Social Patterns of an American Group*,[10] a collection of essays by different scholars on various facets of Judaism, written for the most part in terms of the sociological idiom.

---

[2] Joseph H. Fichter, S.J., *Dynamics of a City Church* (Chicago: University of Chicago Press, 1951).

[3] J. H. Fichter, S.J., *Social Relations in the Urban Parish* (Chicago: University of Chicago Press, 1954).

[4] J. H. Fichter, S.J., *Parochial School* (South Bend, Ind.: University of Notre Dame Press, 1959).

[5] J. H. Fichter, S.J., *Religion as an Occupation: A Study in the Sociology of the Professions* (South Bend, Ind.: University of Notre Dame Press, 1961).

[6] C. J. Nuesse and Thomas J. Harte (eds.), *The Sociology of the Parish* (Milwaukee: The Bruce Publishing Co., 1951).

[7] Joseph B. Schuyler, S.J., *Northern Parish: A Sociological and Pastoral Study* (Chicago: Loyola University Press, 1960).

[8] John L. Thomas, S.J., *The American Catholic Family* (Englewood Cliffs, N.J.: Prentice-Hall, Inc., 1956).

[9] Marshall Sklare, *Conservative Judaism: An American Religious Movement* (Glencoe, Ill.: The Free Press, 1955).

[10] M. Sklare (ed.), *The Jews: Social Patterns of an American Group* (Glencoe, Ill.: The Free Press, 1958).

Jews in Suburbia[11] by Gordon submits the Jewish aspect of the great post-war movement to the suburbs to sociological analysis. An earlier work of Gordon's, *Jews in Transition*,[12] also deals with the theme of the adaptation of Judaism to a dynamically changing culture. *American Judaism*[13] by Glazer is a brief and concise summary of the Jews in America. Some attention is given to the historical development of American Judaism but the emphasis is upon Jews in contemporary culture.

Protestant Studies. Protestantism has an active research program. Protestant groups are investing an increasing amount of time and money in the scientific study of their own institutions. Research is recognized by the National Council of the Churches of Christ in the United States of America (NCCCUSA) by its Bureau of Research and Survey. Various theological seminaries include one or more staff members trained in the social sciences and assign them to research and its interpretation.

Liston Pope's study of the religious structure of Gastonia, North Carolina, which was published as *Millhands and Preachers*,[14] includes a much-quoted interpretation of the sect-church typology. Blizzard, at the instigation of NCCCUSA, made a comprehensive study of the Protestant clergy, their training and their work.

Most of the major denominations have their own research staff and office to provide the data and information on which the denomination may be organized or reorganized to better discharge its mission. One such researcher, Yoshio Fukuyama, as a result of his work for the Congregational–Christian Church, made a notable contribution to theoretical sociology in his refinement of the concept of the dimensions of religiosity.

Other Studies. The growing literature of scientific studies of religion includes several useful and informative monographs on certain of the smaller sects and denominations. Eister's study of the Oxford Group Movement and Moral Rearmament came out as *Drawing Room Conversion: Sociological Study of the Oxford Group Movement*.[15] O'Dea's *The Mormons*,[16] is an excellent historical and scientific study by a sociologist who has made the Mormons and the sociology of religion the focus of his research interests and activities.

In the area of interfaith relations, Underwood's *Protestant and Catholic: Religious and Social Interaction in an Industrial Community*[17] is one

[11] Albert I. Gordon, *Jews in Suburbia* (Boston: Beacon Press, 1959).

[12] A. I. Gordon, *Jews in Transition* (Minneapolis: University of Minnesota Press, 1949).

[13] Nathan Glazer, *American Judaism* (Chicago: University of Chicago Press, 1957).

[14] Liston Pope, *Millhands and Preachers* (New Haven, Conn.: Yale University Press, 1942).

[15] Allan W. Eister, *Drawing Room Conversion: A Sociological Account of the Oxford Group Movement* (Durham, N.C.: Duke University Press, 1950).

[16] Thomas F. O'Dea, *The Mormons* (Chicago: University of Chicago Press, 1957).

[17] Kenneth W. Underwood, *Protestant and Catholic: Religious and Social Interaction in an Industrial Community* (Boston: Beacon Press, 1957).

of the best analyses of interfaith contact and conflict within a community context. Lenski's study of the effect of religion upon selected aspects of social behavior, published as *The Religious Factor: A Sociological Study of the Religious Impact upon Politics, Economics, and Family Life*,[18] is generally considered by critics to be a substantial contribution to both religious and sociological knowledge.

New data and insights concerning religion have arisen out of the numerous studies of values that have flourished on college campuses during the post–World War II period. The values studies of Gordon Allport[19] of Harvard and his students, and the comprehensive intercollege study carried on by the Cornell Department of Sociology and Anthropology, have produced a great deal of information useful and relevant for the sociology of religion.[20]

Religion in Public Education

The widespread interest of the layman in religion has led to proposals for the study of religion at the elementary and secondary as well as the college level. This interest is found in both public and private institutions. In public education, however, the question of instruction is complicated by the current interpretation of the principle of separation of Church and State. In many states and municipalities all references to religion, whether in the form of opening ceremonies or within a course of study, are forbidden. The same strict interpretation of the principle has been applied to a number of public colleges where baccalaureate services, prayer, courses on religion and the Bible have been eliminated.

This avoidance of religion and things religious has even extended in some colleges to include the religious aspects of courses in the humanities and the social sciences. However, the strict interpetation of the separation principle has led to a counter movement in the public colleges. The feeling is widely held that the general education of the student is in short measure when the curriculum does not give some attention to the reciprocal relations that exist between religion and the culture (wherever such materials are relevent to the discipline).

Studies have been made and programs have been constructed that incorporate religious materials into the curriculum wherever such are relevant to the discipline. The method involved is termed the "objective" study of religion. Apologists for this approach find legal justification in constitutional decisions that distinguish between instruction "about" re-

---

[18] Gerhard Lenski, *The Religious Factor: A Sociological Study of Religion's Impact on Politics, Economics, and Family Life* (Garden City, N.Y.: Doubleday & Co., 1961).

[19] James Gillespie and Gordon W. Allport, *Youth's Outlook on the Future* (Garden City, N.Y.: Doubleday & Co., 1955).

[20] Rose Goldsen, Morris Rosenberg, Robin Williams, Edward Suchman, *What College Youth Thinks* (Princeton, N.J.: D. Van Nostrand Co., Inc., 1960).

ligion as compared to instruction that involves "commitment." "About" is proper and legal, while "commitment" violates the separation principle.

One of the most ambitious of these programs is the Danforth Teacher Education and Religion project.[21] The project was initiated to enrich the general education of the teacher-in-training. Those responsible for the project assumed that unless the teacher-in-training acquired the fundamentals of religious literacy he would fail to reflect the necessary depth and breadth of a liberal education which the public and parents have a right to expect.

The objectives of the project were sought by means of action-research carried on by a number of selected pilot institutions. The experiment extended over a five-year period. A wide range of activities and curricular modifications and innovations was recommended to colleges that wished to provide religious literacy within the framework of general education. The project was financed by the Danforth Foundation and sponsored by the American Association of Colleges for Teacher Education for the benefit of its 300 member colleges and universities that have a program for the training and certification of public school teachers. The curricular and extracurricular recommendations of the project have received wide acceptance among both public and private institutions of higher learning.

Sociology of Religion Texts

The growing interest in religion as a subject for study and analysis as an integral part of the curriculum is reflected in the publication within the past few years of five social science textbooks. These are the first social science books written especially for use at the college level. Their publication is a recognition that the scientific study of religion is an appropriate subject for the college curriculum, and that sufficient empirical data and theoretical formulations have accumulated upon which such a course could be based.

The trail-blazing text was Yinger's *Religion, Society, and the Individual*,[22] brought out in 1957. The interdisciplinary nature of the book is implicit in the title. The following year Hoult's *The Sociology of Religion*[23] was published. Benson's *Religion in Contemporary Culture: A Study of Religion through Social Science*,[24] appeared in 1960. Two texts were published in 1962: Vernon's *Sociology of Religion*;[25] Moberg's *The Church*

---

[21] A. L. Sebaly (ed.), *Teacher Education and Religion* (Oneonta, N.Y.: American Association of Colleges of Teacher Education, 1959).

[22] Milton Yinger, *Religion, Society, and the Individual* (New York: The Macmillan Co., 1957).

[23] Thomas Hoult, *The Sociology of Religion* (New York: The Dryden Press, 1958).

[24] Purnell Benson, *Religion in Contemporary Culture: A Study of Religion through Social Science* (New York: Harper & Bros., 1960).

[25] Glenn M. Vernon, *Sociology of Religion* (New York: McGraw-Hill, Inc., 1962).

as a Social Institution.[26] Moberg indicates the sociological orientation of his work by giving it the subtitle *The Sociology of American Religion.*

Plan of Book

The plan of this book follows Williams' outline for the proper study of a social institution. Williams[27] suggests that the normative structure of the institution be surveyed first, then the nature and extent of social change, and finally case studies of individuals in their relation to the institution. The cultural dimension is brought out in the study of the normative structure; the sociological dimension is involved in the normative structure and in the processes of change, while the psychological dimension receives some attention in case study analyses.

Social change is reflected in the various social processes: cooperation, competition, conflict, accommodation, assimilation, and the like. Both structure and change involve interrelations of institutions.

Although case studies are illustrative rather than demonstrative data, they are relevant and proper for adequate understanding. Considerable autobiographical data are used to illustrate varieties of religious behavior. Although autobiographical data do not lend themselves to quantification and may be atypical rather than typical, their mere existence constitutes a social fact which thereby gives them validity. The validity of any single item of subjective data is further established whenever a reader can duplicate the feeling or the experience reported in his own experience. We suspect that in the variety of religious experience included in the section Religion and the Individual, each student can find some bit of case and autobiographical material which will strike a responsive chord.

Parish Clergy as Resource Persons. A great deal of the religious fact and substance reported and described in these pages was secured while the author was teaching the course Religion in American Culture over a period of some ten years. Much of the basic materials of Protestantism, Catholicism, and Judaism herein reported was secured from lectures upon the beliefs and practices of their religion given by a large number of different clergymen from each of the three faiths.

This has particular significance in that we are getting here the belief and practice of religion at the grass roots level. Most of the books written from within one of the faiths are written by specialists-publicists, professors in the seminaries, and other authorities. What is believed, what is taught, and what is practiced on the parish level is sometimes quite different in thought and concept from what is taught at the seminary level. It is "operational" rather than "conventional" religion.

Rather than depend upon books and publications, or more formal inter-

---

[26] David O. Moberg, *The Church as a Social Institution: The Sociology of American Religion* (Englewood Cliffs, N.J.: Prentice-Hall, Inc., 1962).

[27] Robin M. Williams, Jr., *American Society: A Sociological Interpretation* (New York: Alfred A. Knopf, Inc., 1960), p. 34.

pretation by the instructor on the Catholic religion, we ask a community priest to give us his interpretation. Furthermore, the lecture is given not in the college classroom but within the sanctuary of the church that is being described. When the priest talks about representative ritual and symbolism he can point to the altar, the stations of the cross, the confessional, and the like. Sometimes the priest-lecturer will illustrate symbolism and ritual by formally vesting himself and explaining the meaning of not only the vestments but the ritual that goes along with the act of vesting.

In like fashion, information about Judaism is received directly from a rabbi lecturing to a class of students within the synagogue or temple. Students not only hear the rabbi give his interpretation of what the Jews believe, but they see an Ark, a Torah, and hear them described and interpreted. Students see the prayer shawl, a shofar, and hear the rabbi explain the history and meaning of the various rituals and symbolic practices.

In this class it has been our practice to suggest the variety within Protestantism by having a pastor from both a high—or liturgical—church and from a low—and non-liturgical—church give lectures. The differences found between the sanctuaries—the altar, the pulpit, the divided chancel— are revealing.

A number of clergymen from all three faiths have given these lectures upon their respective faiths over the years, speaking as practicing clergymen who hold charges in the Oswego, Syracuse, Rome, and Utica areas of upstate New York, and in Ashland, Oregon, and Fresno, California (where the author has given this same course to college students). This course has also been given for officers and enlisted men at various bases in Germany as one of the offerings in the University of Maryland Overseas College Program. Chaplains representing the Catholic, Protestant, Jewish, and Mormon faiths participated in the overseas lecture program of the course.

Lay clergy and leaders of the more atypical sects and denominations have spoken to these classes, and have been the authority for some of the information that is included in this analysis. Christian Science readers, the Company Servant for local congregations of Jehovah's Witnesses, young Mormon missionaries, officers presiding over local Salvation Army Corps, pastors of Seventh-Day Adventist Churches have appeared before classes contributing statements and interpretations that appear in these pages.

The Community Laboratory. A representative cross section of the authoritative social science studies of religion is included in this interpretation of the religious culture. Although many excellent research studies of religion have been published in recent years, many areas are untouched and much remains to be done. It is not assumed that social scientists have provided the last word in religious data and analysis.

Students in our Religion in American Culture classes are encouraged to attend the services of various churches and religious groups and to analyze the respective "action systems" in terms of sect-like characteristics, church-type characteristics, and other distinguishing features.

Religious items in the newspapers provide an open and readily available laboratory, giving a running account of the growing edge of religion, points of conflict, areas of tension, and the like. Religious news is so pervasive and of such interest to the American public that a special wire service —the Religious News Service (RNS)—is transmitted throughout the country and extensively used by newspapers and periodicals. Clippings of various items of religious news appearing in the various papers and current periodicals, properly categorized and classified, constitute a good working analysis of the religious culture.

Attendance at various religious services, interviews with religious leaders and laymen, and the selection and classification of current news items concerning religion, are experiences and exercises by which the student becomes his own social scientist and his own most meaningful analyst and interpreter of the religious culture.

Religion as Theory and Substance. This analysis of the American religious culture falls into several logical sections. Each section is prefaced by a brief description of the social science tools and concepts that provide the theoretical framework within which the succeeding substantive data and information are presented.

Preceding the section dealing with the individual and religion is a survey of some of the social psychological terms and concepts which psychologists employ to provide a meaningful frame of reference for the scientific analysis of individual religious behavior. Preceding the section devoted to the normative structure of religion is the sect-church outline, a conceptual tool that is commonly used in the interpretation of the structure of religious systems.

The section on religious change is introduced by a discussion of the concept of social process and by definitions of the various social processes that are frequently used to show the extent and nature of social change. A brief explanation of the theory of functional analysis introduces the section dealing with the interrelations of religion and other social institutions. At the conclusion of each section are offered some theoretical observations concerning the meaning of the content and substance of the preceding section.

THE MULTIDIMENSIONAL NATURE OF RELIGION

The scientific study of religion calls for an interdisciplinary approach to the investigation of religious phenomena. Parsons has been a leader in the movement to study religion scientifically through his translations and interpretations of the work of Durkheim[28] and Weber.[29] Parsons and his students maintain that the study and understanding of society involves three levels of abstractions which are roughly synonymous with anthropology, psychology, and sociology.

Anthropology contributes the concept of culture, which is conceived to be a system of norms and usages designating proper behavior for the members of any given society. Culture serves as the "blueprint" of behavior. Psychology offers the theory and concept of personality—an organized system of tendencies. Personality constitutes the raw material of the various social systems of which any given society is composed.

From sociology comes the concept of social system. Social systems are networks of interactive relationships. Social systems as currently conceived comprehend the more traditional concepts of group and of social institution, and are different only in the greater emphasis they place upon the functional aspect—interaction.

Although emphasizing the group aspect of religion, sociologists recognize that the phenomenon has other dimensions. Wach[30] identified three universal expressions of religion: the theoretical, a system of beliefs; the practice, a system of worship; a sociological, a system of social relationships. The system of beliefs and the system of worship might be found with both personal and group overtones. The incorporation of the psychological dimension into a sociological frame of reference is by no means the unique achievement of Parsons. A number of outstanding sociological figures have argued for the inclusion of data on inner and psychic experience as a necessary prerequisite for sociological understanding. Blumer, Cooley, Ellwood, and Weber have stressed this aspect of the psychological dimension in their writings.

Religion Defined and Conceptualized

Anthropology. The scientific study of religion owes much to the work, concepts, and theories of anthropologists. Tylor collected substantial amounts of ethnological data to illustrate his concepts and hypotheses about culture and religion. In his studies of primitive societies Tylor found widespread beliefs in human spirits inhabiting the body and surviving after death. It was believed also that spirits might dwell in natural objects or move freely throughout the universe. Tylor called this belief *animism*[31] and maintained that any definition of religion should include the belief in

---

[28] Emile Durkheim, *The Elementary Forms of the Religious Life*, trans. Joseph W. Swarin (London: George Allen & Unwin, Ltd., 1915). Reprinted by The Free Press, 1947.

[29] Max Weber, *The Protestant Ethics and the Spirit of Capitalism*, trans. Talcott Parsons (London: George Allen & Unwin, Ltd., 1930).

[30] Joachim Wach, *Sociology of Religion* (Chicago: University of Chicago Press, 1944).

[31] E. B. Tylor, *Religion in Primitive Culture* (New York: Harper & Bros., 1958), p. 8.

spiritual beings. Lowie found ample support for animism in his account of the religion of the Crow Indians.[32]

The important common denominator of primitive religion to Frazer was *magic*. All peoples, but primitive peoples more so, were concerned with magic. The presence and uses of magic were the basic ingredients of religion. "By religion, then, I understand a propitiation or conciliation of powers superior to man which are believed to direct and control the course of nature, and of human life."[33] Malinowski, like Frazer, finds magic an important ingredient of primitive religion.[34] He sees another dimension of religious behavior, ritual, consistently associated with magic. Magic and ritual step in, he maintains, where knowledge fails.[35]

A number of anthropologists have seen the core of religion to reside in the "feeling" experience. Feeling was emphasized in the early writings of Marett.[36] Goldenweiser found the feeling element the outstanding characteristic of religion, and wrote in terms of the religious "thrill" which accompanies experiences with the supernatural.

One of the great figures in the theological development of liberal Protestantism, Schleiermacher, put the emphasis upon the emotional element. Schleiermacher maintained that the heart of religion is not found in the intellect (in science or metaphysics) nor in the type of action represented in ethics, but rather in the realm of "feeling." Religion belongs to the sphere of "feeling," which is distinct from and prior to knowing and doing.[37]

Power is the leading component of religion, according to a number of other anthropologists. One form of power is *mana*. Mana is the special power, over and beyond the natural, which the individual possesses to give him victory over his enemies, or which the husbandman possesses which makes his gardens flourish over those of his neighbors. Herskovits belongs to this school of religious definition. Herskovits sees religion as a "belief in, and identification with, a greater force or power. . . . Religion implies the emotional response to the power that rules the universe, however it may be conceived."[38]

Psychology. The scientific study of religion owes much to psychology, for religion indisputably has a psychological dimension. Psychologists have been and are concerned with the religious dimension of personality

---

[32] Robert H. Lowie, *Primitive Religion* (New York: Liveright Publishing Corp., 1952).

[33] J. G. Frazer, *The Golden Bough* (New York: The Macmillan Co., 1941), p. 50.

[34] Bronislaw Malinowski, *A Scientific Theory of Culture and Other Essays* (Chapel Hill, N.C.: The University of North Carolina Press, 1944), p. 198.

[35] Bronislaw Malinowski, *The Foundations of Faith and Morals* (London: Oxford University Press, 1936), p. 34.

[36] R. R. Marett, *The Threshold of Religion* (London: Methuen, 1909), p. XII.

[37] Friedrich Schleiermacher, *Speeches on Religion* (London: K. Paul, Trench, Trubner & Co., Ltd., 1893), p. 36.

[38] M. J. Herskovits, *Man and His Works* (New York: Alfred A. Knopf, Inc., 1951), p. 377.

and, as we would expect, their definitions of religion are primarily in terms of the personal aspect of religion. A number of books have been written on the psychology of religion by American psychologists. These books represent varying schools of psychological thought. William James, the first major American psychologist, wrote the first psychology of religion: *Varieties of Religious Experience.*[39]

In 1912, Leuba[40] brought out a second book on the psychology of religion. Some twenty-five years later Wieman and Wieman published *Normative Psychology of Religion.*[41] In 1945 Johnson brought out the first edition of his *Psychology of Religion*[42] in which he found there were at least three major ways of defining religion—as there were of looking at the mind. Religion could be subjectively defined and determined. This approach would include the introspective interpretation of human behavior such as represented in the writings of Hume, Titchener, and Locke; the dynamic psychology of James, Thorndike, and Woodworth; the depth psychology of Freud, Jung, Adler, and Rank.

It was also posited that religion could be objectively defined and determined. This approach includes the behaviorism of Pavlov and Watson, and the functional psychology of Dewey, Angell, and Mead. The third approach to religious analysis would be found in the synoptic school where the mind is viewed in perspective. This approach would include the *Gestalt* school as represented in the work of Wertheimer, Koehler, and Koffka; the personalistic approach of Gordon Allport; the interpersonal emphasis of Sullivan, and the field theory of Lewin.

Regardless of the particular emphasis—whether religion arises from within or is imposed from without, or is some combination of these forces—psychologists are in agreement in defining religion in terms of the individual. This was explicit in the work of William James. James conceived of religion as the "feelings, acts, and experiences of individual men in their solitude." Wieman and Wieman gave a similar emphasis to the personal aspect of religion when they defined religion as "devotion to what one holds to be supremely worthwhile not only for himself but for all human living."[43]

Psychologists are not alone in conceiving of religion in terms of what is "supremely worthwhile for the individual." Nathaniel Schmidt, for many years a distinguished professor of oriental history at Cornell University, used to define religion for his students as "striving for the highest."

---

[39] William James, *Varieties of Religious Experience* (New York: Longmans, Green and Co., 1902).

[40] J. H. Leuba, *A Psychological Study of Religion* (New York: The Macmillan Co., 1912).

[41] H. N. and R. W. Wieman, *Normative Psychology of Religion* (New York: Thomas Y. Crowell Co., 1935).

[42] P. A. Johnson, *Psychology of Religion* (Nashville, Tenn.: Abingdon Press, 1945).

[43] Wieman and Wieman, *op. cit.,* p. 29.

Both psychologists and historians here find themselves in agreement with the theologian, Paul Tillich, who is well known for his delineation of religion in terms of the things of "ultimate concern."

A more recent interpretation of religious phenomena from a psychological frame of reference is that of Walter H. Clark. Clark maintains that religion can be most characteristically described as the "inner experience of the individual when he senses a Beyond, especially as evidenced by the effect of this experience on his behavior when he actively attempts to harmonize his life with the Beyond."[44]

Contemporary psychoanalysis is largely the product of Freud's insights and the subsequent attempts of his students and others both to support and to modify the theories that he advanced. Religion to Freud was one of man's greatest illusions. Freud arrived at this position through his interpretation of the evolution and development of the human species.

Modern man, according to Freud, is largely a product of his animal and instinctive nature. In a state of nature man would behave in terms of his instincts, satisfying his *id* (animal desires rooted in his primeval past) by taking his pleasures as he willed: killing, robbing, and sexual conquest without restraint. Culture develops to protect man from himself, but culture is "unnatural."[45] The communal life, dictated by culture, is built upon coercion and the renunciation of instincts, and stands in opposition to the destructive antisocial tendencies present in all men.

Religion, according to Freud, is a key cultural tool that both protects man from himself and compensates for his weaknesses. Religions have a threefold task: they must "exorcise the terrors of nature," they must reconcile the individual to the "cruelty of fate—particularly as shown in death—and they must make amends for the sufferings and privations that the "communal life of culture" has imposed upon man. [46]

Religion is an illusion, Freud maintains, because it is derived from man's wishes. In this respect it approaches the psychiatrist's concept of a delusion—an essential conflict with reality. Religious doctrines are an illusion, according to Freud, because they do not admit of proof, and some are so inconsistent with reality (as ascertained empirically) that they are, in fact, delusions. Furthermore, Freud maintained that the idea of God is nothing more than wishful thinking within the personality system: man's childlike need for a father image. The idea of God, likewise, is at best an illusion—if not an outright delusion.

Not all psychoanalysts follow Freud's pioneer work in psychoanalytic theory. Jung, one of his early students, broke away from Freud's interpretation of the origin and significance of religion. To Jung, religion is a

---

[44] Walter H. Clark, *The Psychology of Religion* (New York: The Macmillan Co., 1958), pp. 21–22.

[45] Sigmund Freud, *The Future of an Illusion* (Horace Liveright and The Institute of Psycho-Analysis, 1928), p. 22.

[46] *Ibid.*, p. 26.

reality, not an illusion.[47] Religious experience is absolute; it cannot be disputed. The most the skeptic can say is that he never had such an experience, but this does not deny the fact that many individuals do have such experiences and proceed to follow very definite patterns of behavior, religious in nature, because of such experiences. Religion to Jung was a positive good, not an irrational or illusory crutch.

Jung's concept of God was psychic in nature, but where Freud saw God as a fictitious idea created out of wishful self-seeking, Jung viewed God as emerging out of a context of idealistic motivation. Psychoanalysis conceives of religion in terms of man's psychic nature, but whether religion is a positive good or at best a useful crutch is a question upon which psychoanalysts are in hearty disagreement.

Sociology. Sociological definitions of religion emphasize the group dimension of religious origins and religious behavior. It is important to note, however, that current sociological thought involves an integration of anthropological, psychological, and sociological data and theory, and that nowhere is this integration more apparent than in the sociology of religion.

One of the leaders of this sociological school of thought is Talcott Parsons. Much of Parsons' published works is concerned with the theoretical implications of religious phenomena.[48]

In his substantial and insightful contribution to the sociology of religion, Yinger poses the question: Can religion be private? and responds by stressing the importance of the social dimension. He sees religion as a shared experience taking on its most significant aspects in the interactions of the group. Even death represents a group crisis, requiring reorganization and reorientation of the family and of the community.

According to Yinger the refusal to capitulate to death, to give up in the face of frustration, as well as the refusal to allow hostility to tear apart one's human associations, are functions of religion which the individual can best meet within a group context. Religion, because it spreads the "burden of one's fears" has been described as serving as a sort of "psychic insurance policy." Yinger defines religion as a "system of beliefs and practices by means of which a group struggles with the ultimate problems of human life."[49]

Hoult,[50] Moberg,[51] and Vernon[52] in their recent sociology of religion

[47] Carl G. Jung, *Psychology and Religion: West and East* (New York: Pantheon, 1958), p. 104.

[48] Talcott Parsons, *The Social System* (Glencoe, Ill.: The Free Press, 1951), and *Religious Perspectives of College Teaching in Sociology and Social Psychology* (New Haven, Conn.: The Edward W. Hazen Foundation).

[49] Milton Yinger, *Religion, Society and the Individual* (New York: The Macmillan Co., 1957), p. 9.

[50] Thomas Hoult, *The Sociology of Religion* (New York: The Dryden Press, 1958), p. 9.

[51] David Moberg, *The Church as a Social Institution* (Englewood Cliffs, N.J.: Prentice-Hall, Inc., 1962), p. 3.

[52] Glenn M. Vernon, *Sociology of Religion* (New York: McGraw-Hill, Inc., 1962), p. 46 ff.

texts have constructed working definitions of religion which are in general agreement in their emphasis upon:

1. Beliefs—concerning supernatural or ultimate power;
2. Values of transcendental importance that become
3. Systematized into social institutions with emotional attitudes dominating, and,
4. Characterized by ritual and symbolic activities,
5. Group-oriented beliefs and values shared and expressed within a group context.

Other provocative and useful formulations are those of Glock[53] and Fukuyama[54] which center attention upon the "actor"—the religiously behaving personality. Their formulations deal with "religiousness" as a concept in terms of its respective dimensions. Their formulations include:

1. The *cultic* or *ritualistic dimension* encompasses religious practices: attendance at worship services, participation in church activities, and so on.
2. The *creedal* or *ideological dimension* deals with what the individual believes about his religion as distinguished from what he practices.
3. The *devotional* or the *experiential dimension* deals with emotional feelings and experiences as distinguished from practices and beliefs. Religious sentiment is internalized as inward feeling rather than externally articulated as creed.
4. The *cognitive dimension* of religiousness deals with what the individual knows about religion. The well-informed religious personality is the "knowledgeable church member." He is well informed about the Bible and religious matters, and derives substantial satisfaction from the intellectual stimulation which sermons and religious discussions offer.
5. The *consequential dimension* is concerned with what the religious personality does as a result of his religious beliefs, feelings, and practices. For example, it was found in one study that the personality scoring high on the cultic, creedal, and experiential dimentions of religiosity tended to reflect secular behavior that was more ethnocentric and in-groupish than the less religiously oriented personality.

Objectives of This Study

This book has two objectives: to understand the religious culture in which the American student finds himself, and to use the analysis of American religion as the means by which the student may become familiar with the sociological way of thinking—its system of analysis. The latter objective requires attention to the sociology of religion.

The sociology of religion is the scientific study of the ways in which society, culture, and personality influence religion and, conversely, how religion affects society, culture, and personality. The above definition suggests that religion creates or modifies society, culture, and personality,

---

[53] Charles Y. Glock, "On the Study of Religious Commitment," Research Supplement to *Religious Education*, July-August, 1962, pp. 98–110.
[54] Yoshio Fukuyama, "The Major Dimensions of Church Membership," *Review of Religious Research*, Vol. 2 (Spring, 1961), pp. 154–61.

and on the other hand is also the product of society, culture, and personality.

Thoroughgoing determinism accepts the second proposition and would argue that religion merely reflects society and culture. Under these circumstances religion would be a dependent variable arising out of and relying entirely upon the nature and structure of society and of culture. Religion would be an independent variable to the extent that it tends to create or to modify the cultural norms and expectancies, and the groups and the personalities of which society is composed.

The answer to the above is neither the one nor the other, but rather both. The Catholic Church has influenced American society, American culture, and American personalities, but it has also been modified by the cultural norms, and influenced by American groups and personalities. Out of the above dichotomy, Hoult[55] constructs the theoretical orientation of his analysis of religion and the religious culture.

He terms the first operational rule the principle of *sociocultural determinism*, or compatibility. According to this principle, religion is the product of the culture in which it functions, and is of necessity integrated with and related to the other features of the cultural pattern: family, government, community, and the like. This would be an implementation of what anthropologists have called the "strain for consistency."

Hoult's second guiding principle is the concept of *interaction*. This term includes interaction between one group and another and between personalities and groups. The concept of interaction implies both cause and effect for no person or group can interact with another person or group without both influencing and being influenced to some degree.

Paul Tillich, outside a strictly theological frame of reference, has dealt with the religion-culture controversy by suggesting that religion gives content and dynamic thrust to a culture, whereas culture provides the form for religion.[56]

The Scientific Method

The scientific study of religion requires that the empirical data on which religious analyses are made be acquired by means of the scientific procedure. The scientific point of view is *amoral* in approach. Science is not concerned whether a social structure—an experience, a relationship, a value—is *good* or *bad*, but rather with *what* it is. The value judgment—the goodness or badness of something—is not a concern of science but rather of religion.

American sociology was handicapped in its early years by teachers of sociology who were more concerned with what society *ought* to be than with what it actually *was*. This nonscientific point of view was frequently associated with the teaching of social institutions, including religious in-

---

[55] Hoult, *op. cit.*, pp. 10–13.
[56] *Christian Century*, April 25, 1962, p. 522.

stitutions. Consequently the sociology of religion came into disrepute in academic circles because it was so frequently taught and interpreted in terms of religious commitment. Only recently, with the development of the scientific study of religion, has the sociology of religion received the attention it deserves in the teaching of sociology.

The Research Design. The data upon which the sociology of religion is grounded was acquired through the use of the scientific method. The social scientist begins with a problem. A representative problem in the study of religion could be the testing of the proposition that Methodists represent a higher social class level than do Presbyterians. The next step would be the selection of the method by which the proposition or hypothesis might be tested. The method selected would be the research design.

The research design is very important. The value of the data secured depends upon how it was selected and gathered. If the problem sought to compare American Presbyterians and American Methodists, it would obviously be impractical and too costly to get the necessary social class data on all Presbyterians and Methodists in the United States.

Social scientists have discovered that a sample, scientifically chosen, will provide information that is representative of the universe (in this case all Presbyterians and all Methodists). The techniques of determining and selecting a scientific sample are well known and accepted. The researcher has a familiar and dependable pattern to apply.

Collecting the Data. The next step is the gathering of the relevant data from the sample which has been selected. The researcher's task is eased when the data he seeks are objective and tangible, such as census data already gathered and listed, or tax assessment data which are a matter of public record.

Data having to do with human relations pose more of a problem. Data that must be obtained through the *interview* or *participant-observer* techniques are demanding and often difficult. Skill and training are required on the part of the interviewer and the participant-observer to insure that the data acquired will meet the standards of scientific objectivity.

In our hypothetical sample it would be much less difficult to secure reliable information on the occupation of any unit of our sample (that is, a Presbyterian or a Methodist) than it would be to analyze and report some of the nuances and intangibles of social class behavior by means of the interview or participant-observer techniques.

Analysis of Data. After the necessary and appropriate data have been gathered it is evaluated. (Social scientists and sociologists place great stress upon measurement.) Are the revealed differences between Methodists and Presbyterians statistically significant? The social scientist must apply the rules of statistical analysis to his data to secure the answer. The data may support, or reject, his hypothesis that Methodists represent a higher social class level than Presbyterians. The researcher may argue that his data are sufficiently convincing to give the hypothesis the credibility of an established generalization.

Verification. Verification is an important step in the scientific procedure. A hypothesis, a theory, a law should be subjected to verification. Verification requires that the problem be attacked again; that the various steps in the scientific procedure—the formulation of the research design, the selection of the sample, the gathering of data, the evaluation of the data in terms of theory and concepts—be done over again. If similar research projects support the hypotheses and theories, the theories achieve the stature of a law and become a recognized part of the reservoir of scientific knowledge.

"Laws" are also proper subjects for verification, according to the scientific point of view. In the fields of physical and natural science, research and discovery have progressed so rapidly that what was assumed to be immutable law twenty-five years ago has been discarded or drastically reformulated in the light of revolutionary discoveries and developments.

Although nothing quite so radical has developed in the social sciences, both the accumulation of empirical data and the rapidly changing social scene makes verification of laws equally relevant. There are instances within the social sciences where the reassessment of "immutable truth" has resulted in truth quite different from its original formulation.

Intuitive Knowledge. Whether the scientific study of society can accept information secured by insight is a question about which social scientists differ. Insight is the power to see into a personal or social situation with or without conscious reasoning. Intuitive knowledge is insightful knowledge acquired without conscious reasoning. Insightful knowledge is that reported by the individual who claims the power to make such judgments.

Insight is synonymous with *verstehen* or understanding. Both the word and the concept of *verstehen* have been borrowed from German sociology. The case against insight as a source for scientific formulation is that knowledge secured by insight does not lend itself to objective analysis or verification. Insightful knowledge is no better than the perceptive skill of the reporter.

In competent hands, however, insight can make substantial contributions to knowledge. Through insight Archimedes hypothesized that floating bodies are buoyed up by a force equal to the weight of the displaced water. He was subsequently able to prove his theory, which future generations came to know as the Law of Archimedes. Social scientists are generally suspicious of knowledge insightfully derived unless it can be empirically verified. Nevertheless, some of the greatest contributions to social science received their original impetus from the insights of gifted persons.

If insightful knowledge were excluded from interpretations of human behavior, Freud's contributions to an understanding of human nature and psychoanalysis would have been lost. Freud's conceptualization of personality in terms of the *id*, *ego*, and *superego* was based upon his study of fewer than twenty cases. Although these cases were studied in depth, Freud's data did not lend itself to objective or statistical verification. Freud himself despaired of finding reliable evidence on the nature and complexity of neuroses in the statistics collected by psychiatric clinics. It is better "to examine one's own individual experience," he wrote, than to rely upon mass data from clinics.

Other landmarks in the accumulation of social science knowledge arose out of the insights and perceptions of other gifted men and women. Cooley's concept of the "self," a bench mark of social psychology, was insightful and perceptive in origin. Both insightful hunches and objective data statistically measured and analyzed are appropriate sources of social science knowledge and the prudent student will ignore neither in his quest for the most complete understanding of religious phenomena.

Some Basic Concepts

A great deal of recent empirical research in religion has been conducted under the direction of sociologists and written with the use of sociological terms and concepts. Some understanding of these terms and concepts is required to understand the empirical findings.

Group. A group is any number of persons interacting with each other with some continuity and in some patterned manner; who share one or more common interests and carry on some social activity; who recognize themselves as a distinct social entity (and are usually so recognized by others) because of their particular meaningful reciprocal behavior.[57]

Society. A society is a group with the following characteristics:[58]

1. Definite territory.
2. Comprehensive culture.
3. Independence.
4. Norms for the regulation of marriage and reproduction.

Social System. The concept-social system is currently a popular theoretic convention among American sociologists. A social system is a group which is usually comprehensive enough to include subgroups. Groups and social systems both have *structure*. Structure is the pattern of relationships that exists between the various entities of which the group or social system is composed. Structure implies an appreciable degree of regularity in the relationships of the entities.[59] While *structure* implies relationship and position, *social system* carries an operational connotation. It brings the dynamic, processual, and action aspects of the group into focus.[60]

---

[57] J. O. Hertzler, *American Social Institutions* (Boston: Allyn and Bacon, 1961), p. 17.

[58] Harry M. Johnson, *Sociology* (New York: Harcourt-Brace & Co., 1960), p. 10.

[59] Williams, *op. cit.*, p. 21.

[60] Hertzler, *op. cit.*, p. 46.

The *structure* of the social system includes:

1. Subgroups of various types, interconnected by relational norms.
2. Roles of various types within the larger systems and within the subgroups, each role system interconnected with other role systems through relational norms.
3. Regulative norms governing subgroups and roles.
4. Values.

Any one of these entities—subgroup, role, social norm, value—is known as a "partial structure."[61]

Thus in any given religious system there are normative codes and beliefs: worship practices that include rituals and symbolisms. A religious system is composed of "actors" (people or collectivities) which interact in approved and expected ways. Most of the religious "actors" are communicants, but some are functionaries (the clergy for example). Every religious system has formal organization and is characterized by values.

Social Institution. Social institution is conceptualized at the cultural level of abstraction and analysis. A social system is institutionalized in a society when its norms are widely approved and accepted—or sanctioned. A social insitution is, then, a complex of obligatory norms for conduct. The main individual and social needs of a society are met by the several major social institutions: family, religion, government, and education. But there are different operational family systems (subcultures), educational, religious, and other systems that also contribute to the overall institutional blueprint.

The religious institution is an abstract term or ideal, whereas particular groups in concrete situations are extensions of the technical meaning of the term. The Methodist Church in Fulton, the Church of Christian Science in Oṣwego, the Catholic Church in Ithaca, are all operational religious systems and subject to the recognized norms for a social institution at the theoretical level.

The social institution, like the social system, has its structure. The entities ("partial structures") of the religious institution include:[62]

1. Systems of ideas and beliefs concerning the nature of man, the cosmos, and the supernatural.
2. Systems of rituals and symbols.
3. An organized religious community which may—but need not be—a "church," and in which leadership may take many forms and be of many different types.
4. Ethical norms and values.

Social Control. Social control is conceptualized as all the ways in which the group makes the individual conform.

Community. Community is another concept which social scientists find

---
61 Johnson, *op. cit.*, p. 51.
62 Williams, *op. cit.*, p. 327.

useful for an understanding and interpretation of religious systems and religious behavior within the common culture. Communities differ, have changed, and are changing. Religious systems and religious behavior are influenced by the type of community in which the religious system is located and where religious behavior takes place. Community is an organization of all the different kinds of groups within a more or less limited and jointly inhabited area. Community is a special "grouping of groups" on a territorial basis. American society is a sort of community of communities because it is made of separate but intersecting communities that share some features of a common social life.[63]

Communities have been conceptualized as a continuum with the simple preliterate, the medieval manor, and peasant village at one pole, and the highly urbanized metropolitan community of contemporary technological society at the other pole. German sociologists[64] have given the names *gemeinschaft* and *gesellschaft* to these two types of societies—terms derived from the kind of groups and personal relations that predominate in each.

The *gemeinschaft* sort of community is dominated by primary groups and face-to-face relationships. Primary groups are small, natural groupings that reflect the spontaneous expressions of the social nature of human beings. In the *gemeinschaft* community communication is face to face and direct, relationships are primary and personal, and members consistently exhibit strong feelings of identification and belonging. Division of labor is limited and leadership is personal. The *gemeinschaft* community (the traditional community of rural America) tends to be small and self-sufficient, both economically and socially. Kinship groups, neighborhood groups, the local church, and mutual aid groups—which developed informally to discharge some simple task—are of primary importance.

The traditional community of rural America was a milieu of intimacy: everyone knew everyone else. Experience was in terms of the total personality and social control was informal in nature. There was such great pressure to conform to the mores that gossip and ostracism were effective agencies of social control. Deviation and diversity were penalized with the result that the community was marked by homogeneity and conformity. There was little variety and little choice, and solidarity was based upon consensus.

The *gesellschaft* community is characterized by its secondary groups and associations. This type of community is sometimes spoken of as the "associational" or "mass" society. Contemporary urban society tends to be an associational society in which formal secondary groups organize work, religion, politics, and even leisure. The milieu of the associational society is impersonal and removed, and experience is segmentalized.

Although there is great variation in the social relations patterns of

---

[63] Hertzler, *op. cit.*, p. 25.
[64] Ferdinand Tonnies, *Fundamental Concepts of Sociology* (New York: 1940), trans. by C. P. Loomis from *Gemeinschaft and Gesellschaft* (1st ed., 1887).

urban areas, it is a mistake to assume that *gesellschaft* relationships dominate urban living. Recent studies show significant differences in the nature and extent of social interaction between areas of high urban and low urban structure.[65]

The highly urban areas are *gesellschaft* oriented, while the low urban areas are oriented towards *gemeinschaft* relationships. In the highly urban areas are found the greatest concentrations of single persons, multiple dwelling units, and married couples without children. More married women are gainfully employed. People depend more upon widespread social groups for social contact and relationship although such contacts are more removed, less binding, and more transitory.

The low urban areas are quite different, and are frequently—but not necessarily—suburban. Just as social life is family centered, the community itself tends to be autonomous in that its people depend primarily upon immediate associates for their essential human relationships. The organizations to which family members belong are located in the low-urban area.

Heterogeneity and variety of choice is characteristic of the high urban areas. This environment tends to produce the atomistic personality who may both experience, and suffer from, *anomie*. *In "mass society"* no one seems to care what one does or how one behaves. Social control is formal and removed (and largely reserved for the "other-regarding" catastrophic act). Order results from the functional interdependence of differentiated groups: teachers need farmers, and farmers need teachers. Solidarity within groups leads to dynamic relations between them.

Bureaucracy. The associational society is increasingly dominated by a large-scale formal organization which is known as bureaucracy. Bureaucracies appear when a society's development has reached the stage where division of labor, purposive planning, and hierarchic regimentation have become necessary in order to accomplish all the tasks that need to be done.[66] Four factors—specialization, a system of rules, a hierarchy of authority, and impersonality—are the basic factors of bureaucratic organizations.[67]

A bureaucracy is structured in the form of a pyramid and is composed of horizontal layers of administrative, technical, and operative personnel. The policymakers are at the top; the intermediate executives, technical experts, and managers are next, and, at the bottom, is the mass of workers with various levels of skill. Each level of organization has an assigned pattern of tasks and responsibilities and of rights and privileges.

The effective performance of the bureaucracy's tasks demands depersonalization in both internal and external affairs. It is expected that the

---

[65] Scott Geer, "Individual Participation in Mass Society," in *Approaches to the Study of Politics*, Roland Young, ed. (Evanston, Ill.: Northwestern University Press, 1958), pp. 329–43.

[66] Hertzler, *op. cit.*, pp. 22–25.

[67] Peter M. Blau, *Bureaucracy in Modern Society* (New York: Random House, Inc., 1956), p. 19.

necessary tasks will be performed according to established rules and procedures, and without regard to person.

The division of labor sees that complex patterns of specialization are organized into separate and manageable parts, and that each part performs its special and interrelated function in total operation.

The parts, processes, and personnel are fitted together in an orderly and integrated whole so that overall goals will be attained. This requires proper centralization—and decentralization—of authority at various levels among the several departments.

An effective bureaucracy standardizes procedures and routinizes operations. It tends to retain its structure, functional identity, and direction. Personnel may come and go, but the organization lives on. And religious groups and institutions in contemporary society have frequently found themselves drawn into the web of bureaucratic trends and tendencies.

Summary

The publication of this book is a reflection of the increased interest of the American people in religion, of the growing feeling that the scientific study of religion is both appropriate and feasible, and of the belief that the objective study of religion is a necessary ingredient of general education.

A number of good studies of their own religions have recently been brought out by representatives of the Catholic, Jewish, and Protestant faiths. Religion has become an increasingly large area of interest and investigation for anthropologists, psychologists, and sociologists.

On the ground that the study of religion might violate the principle of separation of Church and State, public institutions of higher learning avoided the subject for years. Now, however, they are showing marked interest in the "objective" study of religion.

Religion has so many facets and dimensions (cultural, group, and personal are just a few) that its objective study demands materials and analyses that are secured by strict application of the scientific method.

This book seeks to enlighten American religion by (1) presenting an overview of the normative structure of the various American religions (with emphasis upon the three basic faiths), (2) a consideration of the substance and processes of religious change, (3) case study and autobiographical materials which indicate characteristic religious reactions in representative individuals.

Chapter II

The Historical Development of the Three Faiths

Religion and the Church in Colonial America

Religious Freedom: A Motive for Colonization. Freedom of worship was an important reason for the immigration of a great many Europeans to the New World. It was a basic motive in drawing the Pilgrims to their settlement at Plymouth, the Puritans to Boston, the Quakers to Pennsylvania, the Catholics to Maryland, the German Lutherans to the Mohawk Valley and various parts of Pennsylvania, the Anglicans to Virginia, the Scotch-Irish (mostly Presbyterians) to the frontier, and the Jews to New York and Rhode Island.

Many of these first immigrants represented minority religious groups which had been persecuted in their homelands. The desire to practice their religion without hindrance was strong enough to uproot them from their past and bring them to the New World. They were willing to undergo a long and uncertain voyage and to settle in a wilderness because of the promise of freedom of religious expression and belief.

But of course there were other motives for settlement in the New World. Many Europeans were attracted by the hope for better economic opportunities or political freedom, and the economic was probably the decisive factor for most people. The settlers in general came from the lower social and economic levels of Europe. They had little chance to improve their status at home, and moved to America in the hope that in a new and undeveloped country they would have a chance to "get ahead in the world."

26

Whether an individual settler came to America for religious, economic or political reasons, it was generally true that religious freedom, political liberty, and economic opportunity went hand in hand. If the settler had one, he very probably had all, and if he was restricted in one, he very likely was restricted in all.

Limitations on Religious Freedom. Colonial America did not enjoy the full freedom of religion which is characteristic of American society today—even though the promise of religious freedom had been an important motive in the founding of most of the colonies. Many of the groups which settled in America denied freedom of worship to other religious sects who arrived after them, and in most of the colonies the church of the dominant group was made the official religion and given special privileges.

The Puritans, who settled in Massachusetts, had left England because of persecution suffered at the hands of the King and the Anglican Church. However, Massachusetts was neither a safe nor a pleasant place in which to live if you did not agree with the religious beliefs or the political policies of the Puritan leaders of the colony. Roger Williams and Anne Hutchinson were exiled because of religious beliefs, and in 1692, about twenty eccentric but harmless residents of Salem were accused of witchcraft by their fellow citizens and burned at the stake.[1]

Although the charter of the Dutch colony of New Netherlands granted freedom of worship to all citizens, Peter Stuyvesant, the last Dutch governor, refused to extend this right to Jews and Quakers. He caused a Quaker in Flushing to be arrested for holding services in his home. Twenty-four citizens of Flushing, who were not themselves Quakers, protested this arbitrary action of the governor in the famous *Flushing Remonstrance*. When word of the incident reached Holland, the officials of the Dutch West India Company (which controlled the colony) reprimanded Stuyvesant, ordered him to free the persons arrested, and to extend freedom of worship to every citizen in compliance with the charter.

In 1664 the city of New Amsterdam was captured by the English. The colony of New Netherlands became English and was renamed New York, and a few years later the governor of the colony issued the Charter of Liberties which, among other rights, guaranteed freedom of religious worship.

Maryland and the Toleration Act. In 1634, Lord Baltimore founded the colony of Maryland chiefly as a refuge for English Catholics, who at that time had no religious or political rights. (Catholics, however, were always a minority group in the colony, and in ten years constituted less than one-quarter of the population.) In order to protect them, Lord Baltimore induced the provincial assembly to pass the famous Toleration Act of 1649, which provided that "no person in this province professing

---

[1] Gustavus Myers, *History of Bigotry in the United States* (New York: Random House, 1943), p. 36.

to believe in Jesus Christ shall be in any way troubled . . . for his religion." Since the Act excluded non-Christians it represented something less than full religious freedom,[2] but it was a notable step forward and was better than what was to follow.

In 1692 the province was taken away from the Baltimores and put under a royal governor. The Anglican Church was established as the official church with the effect that Catholics, who then constituted about 10 percent of the population were deprived of their political rights and again became second-class citizens.

Union of Church and State. By the time of the Revolution, and in most of the colonies,[3] the leading religious group had an established church, which, as the official church of the colony, had special privileges and powers. Its main advantage over other churches was that it was supported by taxes that were paid by all residents of the colony. Members of the established church usually enjoyed other rights—the right to vote and to hold public office—that were denied to nonmembers.

In Massachusetts the clergy of the established Puritan church, working closely with the political leaders, was able to gain virtual domination of the colony and to form what has become known as the New England Theocracy. The Puritan Church attained a similar position throughout New England, while in New York and the southern colonies the Anglican became the official church. Rhode Island and Pennsylvania were the most notable exceptions to the general rule of the union of church and state.

Roger Williams and Religious Freedom. Roger Williams, a young pastor of Salem, incurred the wrath of the Massachusetts leaders by taking a firm stand against the exclusive prerogative of church members to elect colony officials. Neither did he think these officials had any right to interfere with an individual's religious beliefs. But Williams' views were considered intolerable by the Puritan authorities and in 1635, by order of the General Court, he was expelled from Massachusetts. After spending the winter with some friendly Indians at the head of Narragansett Bay, Williams and a few followers founded the settlement which became Providence, Rhode Island.

Another courageous soul who was exiled from Puritan Massachusetts because of religious beliefs was Anne Hutchinson, who also founded a settlement in Rhode Island—at Portsmouth.

All the settlements around Narragansett Bay were united in 1644 under a patent which Roger Williams secured from the King of England. Church and state were completely separated and it was decreed that men of whatever belief might "walk as their conscience persuaded them, every one in the name of his God." Because he stood firmly for the principles

---

[2] Theodore Maynard, *Story of American Catholicism* (New York: The Macmillan Co., 1954), p. 58.

[3] William Warren Sweet, *Religion in Colonial America* (New York: Charles Scribner's Sons, 1949), p. 28.

of freedom of conscience and religious toleration—principles which were to become fundamental in the American way of life—Roger Williams is regarded as the father of religious liberty in America.

The "Holy Experiment." Another colony which separated church and state was Pennsylvania, founded in 1682 by William Penn primarily as a refuge and haven for the Quakers, who were ridiculed and persecuted in England. But, people of all nationalities and creeds were welcomed, the functions of church and state were separated, and religious freedom was extended to all. At a time when scores of crimes in England were punishable by death, Penn decreed that murder and treason would be the only capital crimes in the colony. Pennsylvania also was the first colony to oppose slavery.

Penn treated the Indians fairly and lived up to his treaties with them, thereby sparing the colony the horrors of raids and massacres. Germans, Finns, Irish, Welsh, Scotch-Irish, and many others flocked to the colony to try what Penn called his "holy experiment." Within twenty years the colony had become the largest and most prosperous in America.

The Protestant Churches of Colonial America

The great reformers—Luther, Zwingli, Calvin, and Cranmer—were conservative leaders, and the parties they led were composed of upper-middle-class people. All during the colonial period Protestant state churches, with elaborate forms of polity, dominated the European scene and retained the familiar state-church relationships.

In spite of the many shades of Protestant doctrine and practice represented by the immigrants and colonists, their churches tended to fall into two broad classifications which have been termed *conservative* or *right-wing* churches—similar to their European counterparts—and *radical* or *left-wing* churches.[4] The leading conservative churches were the Anglican, the Congregationalist, and the Presbyterian; the Reformed and Lutheran churches were also conservative in doctrine and practice, but not as numerous or as influential. The leading radical churches during the colonial period were the Methodist and the Baptist.

The Conservative Churches. All the conservative churches had an approved interpretation of the Bible, practiced infant baptism, and supported an accepted set of beliefs that was known as the "official confession of faith."

The conservative churches furthermore required that their clergy be college-educated, and Harvard, for example, was founded a few years after the settlement of the Massachusetts Bay Colony primarily for the training of Puritan clergymen. College-trained men were at a premium and few could be induced to settle very far from the seaboard where

----

[4] William Warren Sweet, "The Protestant Churches" *Annals of American Academy of Political and Social Science*, March, 1948, p. 43.

the population was greatest and more advantages and conveniences available. The conservative churches therefore were strongest in the coastal areas.

The theology of the Congregational Church, the descendant of the colonial Puritan Church (along with Presbyterian and Dutch Reformed theology, which differs from Anglican—or Episcopalian—theology) is based largely on the teachings of John Calvin. Calvin's was an aristocratic theology that divided mankind into classes of which only one—the "elect" class—was predestined for salvation.

The conservative churches never surpassed the influence they had during the colonial period. They were administered and supported by community leaders who favored aristocracy in government and in society. Because of this support from the well-to-do and influential, the conservative churches exercised far more power in the community than their numbers warranted. And, by virtue of education alone, conservative clergymen assumed a strong position of leadership in colonial America.

The Radical Churches.   The radical or left-wing churches were in the spirit and tradition of the Anabaptists. Because their strongest appeal was to humble people, they received their greatest support from the ranks of the "common man."

The Methodist and Baptist were the leading churches of the radical or left-wing group in their championship of a democratic gospel of "free" grace. For both these churches the most important act of religious behavior was the individual's decision to join the church as an independent and rational being, and for the Baptists this called for a "believer's baptism"—at or after the age of reason.

Both churches also emphasized individual interpretation of the Bible rather than reliance upon an official confession of faith. They did not require their ministers to be college trained and usually the Methodist and Baptist ministers were rank-and-file parishioners with no special training who, simply, received the "call" and possessed the "word."

One knew he had received the "call" when he felt divinely inspired to preach the Gospel and spend his life in religious work. A man who could preach with enough conviction to bring about conversions was said to possess the "word." In contrast with the conservative congregations, the services and sermons in the radical churches tended to be expressive and emotional rather than restrained and doctrinal.

Because the radical churches maintained that religion was primarily a personal matter, they emphasized freedom of conscience, resisted all church-state relationships, and insisted that the state should have no control over ecclesiastical affairs. With this background it was only natural that radical churches came to be associated with individualism and democracy in both government and social institutions.

The Revolution and Religion.   The American Revolution was a movement for democracy in religion as well as in government. As each state wrote a constitution to replace its old provincial charter, it either disestablished its church outright or took the first steps which would eventually lead to complete separation of church and state.

Thomas Jefferson, who was the governor of Virginia when its new constitution was written, believed that his part in bringing about the separation of church and state in Virginia ranked with his writing of the Declaration of Independence and founding of the University of Virginia as the three most important and significant acts of his public life. His epitaph, which he wrote himself, bears this out.

During the Revolution, which cut across church lines, each of the American churches severed its ties with its mother church in the Old World. A large number of Loyalists—or Tories—were Anglicans, but many of the great patriot leaders were also Anglicans. Most of the Methodists and Baptists were patriots—or at least sympathetic to the revolutionary cause —yet John Wesley and other Methodist leaders remained loyal to England.

The Revolution not only marked the widespread acceptance of the principles of religious freedom and the separation of church and state, it was also responsible for the incorporation of these ideas into the Federal Constitution a few years later.

RELIGIOUS DEVELOPMENTS IN THE NINETEENTH AND TWENTIETH CENTURIES

The Protestant Churches

Religion and Democracy. At the outbreak of the Revolution the leading churches in numbers and influence were, respectively, the Congregational, Presbyterian, Baptist, Episcopalian, Lutheran, Reformed (Dutch and German), Quaker, various German sects, and Methodist. But great changes took place in the relative influence of the Protestant denominations between the Revolution and the Civil War. By 1860 the largest denomination was the Methodist, followed, respectively, by the Baptist, Presbyterian, Congregational, Lutheran, Disciples of Christ, and Episcopal.[5]

The Methodist and Baptist churches gained (at the expense of the more conservative groups) largely because they represented democracy in religion and in the community. During this period democracy was everywhere triumphant in America—in government, in economic life, and in social relationships. It is not surprising, therefore, to find the democratic, or "radical," churches forging to the front.

Several factors contributed to the spread of democratic concepts and the democratic churches. As the first arrivals, the Puritans and Anglicans were able to establish their churches along the seaboard and in the tide-

---

[5] *Ibid.*, p. 45; also Willard Sperry, *Religion in America* (New York: Macmillan Co., 1948), pp. 71 ff.

water areas. The succeeding waves of immigration—Quakers, German and Pietists sectaries, Huguenots, Scotch-Irish—were repelled by the formality and conformity demanded by the established churches. These later groups defined religion more in terms of an inner personal experience than in terms of doctrine and convention. They felt more at home with the Methodists and Baptists.

The "natural rights" philosophy of John Locke was written into the Declaration of Independence by Jefferson and his collaborators. According to Locke's interpretation of this theory, religion was a personal affair and the church a voluntary association.

Decade by decade, as the frontier pushed westward across the nation, the democratic religious sects moved in with the first settlers and became the prevailing churches in the newly settled communities.

The Methodists and the Baptists were particularly successful in making converts and organizing new churches in the frontier country. No small part of their success may be credited to the diligence and determination of the Baptist farmer-preacher and the Methodist circuit rider. There was a saying in the old rural culture on severe winter days that "there is nothing out today but crows and Methodist preachers."[6] The typical circuit rider was a lay preacher who worked his farm during the week and carried the Gospel on horseback to frontier settlements on Sunday and during the slack farming season.

The Methodist and Baptist theology and service was equalitarian and individualistic, stressing personal salvation and making greater use of revivalism than the conservative churches. Revivalism, by its very nature, cuts across class lines and tends to put all people on the same footing. The Methodists and the Baptists flourished because in organization and in religious practices they were best suited to the environment of the frontier and to the psychology of the men and women living there.

Liberalism and Neo-orthodoxy. The late nineteenth and early twentieth centuries witnessed developments in Protestant patterns of belief and worship, and changes in the relation of Protestantism to the total cultural configuration: the rise and ultimate dominance of liberalism, followed by the development of neo-orthodoxy as a competing theology and social and spiritual orientation. After the Civil War the differences that distinguished most left-wing from right-wing churches became less marked and conspicuous.

Cultural change was reflected in religious behavior. Like the conservative churches, the radical churches now were also served by an educated clergy and boasted of an increasing number of educated laymen. Education, refinement and dignity especially characterized the ministry and worship of the Methodists and the Baptists. Methodists once again made use of their gowns and prayerbooks, which had been put aside in the

---

[6] George M. Stephenson, *The Puritan Heritage* (New York: Macmillan Co., 1952), p. 76.

pioneering period. The doctrinal and theological differences between the various Protestant churches, that had once seemed so important, were no longer emphasized and a general class of religion which was commonly characterized as Liberal Protestantism began to emerge. Liberal interpretation of the Bible was stressed and great emphasis was put upon the "social gospel."

These changes have continued into the present. Sermons in the various Protestant churches sound so much alike that one can seldom determine the denomination of a Protestant church on the basis of the message from the pulpit. And traditional churches have lost so much of their former "aristocratic" orientation that in any village or city today the church with the most social prestige and influence is as likely as not to be Baptist or Methodist.

Liberalism reached its peak as the dominant expression of Protestantism in the decade immediately following World War I when Protestantism was swept by a wave of optimism. Liberalism was confident that man, with science, and under the inspiration of God, would conquer evil and bring about the Kingdom.

The great evils besetting mankind—sickness, poverty, war—could be eliminated, it was felt, through the application of science and reason. Theologically, the liberal movement sought to replace the religion "about Jesus," a religion of dogma and creeds, with the religion "of Jesus," a religion of justice, love, and cooperation. The religion "of Jesus" was thought to center upon the social gospel, and liberal Protestants were united in their emphasis upon this centrality and importance. Liberalism was the product of many forces and the expression of leaders such as Walter Rauschenbusch, a forceful and convincing publicist for the social gospel, who was a key force in the rise of liberal Protestantism.[7]

In the early 1930's the neo-orthodox protest that liberalism was unrealistic and inadequate began to attract more attention as it became evident that man and science could as easily destroy the world as "redeem" it. The rise of Hitler was convincing proof to many Protestants that evil was not entirely social in nature: that it included personal attributes as well.

In Reinhold Niebuhr the social gospel found a climactic critic.[8] Niebuhr rediscovered orthodoxy and defined its doctrines in terms of contemporary knowledge: grace, a God-given saving power that is beyond science, society, and politics, opens the way for the soul to save itself; man's greatest

---

[7] Rauschenbusch's thought was widely disseminated through his books: *Christianity and the Social Crisis, Christianizing the Social Order, A Theology for the Social Gospel* (New York: The Macmillan Co., 1907, 1912, 1917).

[8] Between 1927 and 1943 Reinhold Niebuhr contributed eight books to the religious dialogue that were widely read and provoked widespread debate; two of them are *Moral Man and Immoral Society* and *Reflections on the End of an Era* (New York: Charles Scribner's Sons, 1932 and 1934). Other American theologians made substantial contributions to the neo-orthodox movement in publications, sermons, and lectures, notably Paul Tillich, H. Richard Niebuhr, H. P. Van Dusen, John Bennett, and Ernest Johnson.

sin is pride and selfishness; and man is "saved" from sin by realizing his limitations and inability to achieve an absolute perspective on life.

Neo-orthodoxy did not make social action irrelevant for either the individual or the church because, according to Niebuhr, religious fulfillment in God "beyond" history includes the activities of men "within" history. Christian experience must remain in politics and attempt to achieve the best possible expression of the ideal.

Observers do not agree on how or to what extent theological positions, whether liberal or neo-orthodox, have been a significant influence upon the practice of religion at the parish level.[9] Even at the peak of the liberal movement the social gospel direct-action ministers still formed a minority of all Protestant pastors and few congregations were completely committed to the revolutionary doctrine of salvation within history. Even today, neo-orthodoxy is largely confined to the seminaries. For practical purposes, neo-orthodoxy is a return to a theology that most Protestants never left in the first place.[10]

New Churches Arise. Although the majority of Protestants showed various degrees of commitment to liberalism, not all of them were influenced by it. A considerable number continued to cling to a literal interpretation of the Bible and to reject the changed orientation and emphases of liberalism. These groups, known first as "fundamentalists" now prefer to be known as conservatives because of their conservative theology. They should not be confused with the conservative or right-wing churches of the colonial period nor with the theology and world view of neo-orthodoxy.

Other Americans joined one of the newer sects and denominations that have appeared on the American scene within the last century and a half; notably the Mormons, Christian Scientists, Salvation Army, and Jehovah's Witnesses.[11]

At the same time that the majority of American Protestants were grouping under the liberal banner, the two other great contemporary religious traditions—the Roman Catholic and the Jewish—were taking firm root in America and growing rapidly in strength and influence.

The Roman Catholic Church

Catholics comprised a small minority of the population during the colonial period. Religious intolerance was typical of the age, and the few who came to the English colonies found themselves victimized by prejudice and anti-Catholic sentiment. Most of Europe, in fact, had been devastated by a series of bloody religious wars during the century that preceded the settlement of the English colonies.

---

[9] This period is extensively dealt with in Donald B. Meyer's *The Protestant Search for Political Realism: 1919–1941* (Berkeley: University of California Press, 1961).

[10] See Chapter VI for a more extended discussion of liberalism, conservatism, and neo-orthodoxy in contemporary Protestantism.

[11] See Chapter IX, "Creative Innovation."

Because the great majority of Englishmen (and therefore the great majority of early settlers) were both Protestant *and* strongly anti-Catholic, the colonial governments promptly imposed numerous civil disabilities on Catholics and interfered in various ways with the free practice of the Catholic faith. By the beginning of the 18th century there were only two colonies (Rhode Island and Pennsylvania) where Catholics enjoyed a large measure of civil rights. Even in Maryland, which had been founded as a refuge for Catholics, rigorous anti-Catholic measures were in force.[12]

The Vatican has estimated that there were fewer than 20,000 Catholics in the colonies before the Revolution. There were approximately 10,000 English Catholics in Maryland and 5,000 German Catholics in Pennsylvania. The balance, including many French, was scattered throughout the other colonies.

Catholic Support for the Revolution. The most common charge against Catholics was that they could not be loyal citizens of the new country because of their religious allegiance to a "foreign potentate," the Pope. But events proved that there was no basis for this fear; few Catholics were found among the Tories when the Revolution broke out. The Carrolls of Maryland, a leading Catholic family, produced great patriotic leaders. Charles Carroll was one of the signers of the Declaration of Independence, and two other Catholics, Daniel Carroll and Thomas Fitzgibbons, were signers of the Constitution.[13] Furthermore, had Catholic France not come to the assistance of the colonies with men, money, and arms, the Revolution probably would have failed.

Although the Revolution was a great landmark in the movement towards religious freedom, only Pennsylvania, Delaware, Virginia, and Maryland granted Catholics absolute equality with other Christians in their new constitutions. The last political disabilities were not removed from the fundamental state laws until 1790 in South Carolina, 1798 in Georgia, 1806 in New York, 1818 in Connecticut, 1833 in Massachusetts, and 1835 in North Carolina.

Father John Carroll. Before the Revolution Catholics in America were under the Vicar Apostolic of London, who held jurisdiction for the Church of Rome over all the British colonies and islands in America. There was almost no connection between the church in America and the authorities in Europe during the Revolution, and thus the church in America began to develop its own native leadership. A succession of able and liberal churchmen rendered valiant services in the long struggle of American Catholics to adapt their church to American conditions and to convince the Protestant majority that it was possible to be both a good Catholic and a good American.

At the close of the Revolution no Catholic official in the colonies was

---

[12] Maynard, *op. cit.*, p 62.
[13] Anson Phelps Stokes, *Church and State in United States* (New York: Harper & Bros., 1950, Vol. I), p. 285.

vested with the authority to administer confirmation and to carry on other important religious and administrative functions of the church. The church resolved this dilemma by the appointment of an American Catholic, Father John Carroll, as "Superior of the Mission" in the United States. Father Carroll was given the powers of a bishop, although without the title. American Catholics were reluctant at this time to have a bishop named because they were afraid the mere appointment to this high office would fan the anti-Catholic feeling and make their position even more difficult.

Father Carroll proved to be an excellent choice for this key position. He was respected and trusted by George Washington, and his prestige and unimpeachable conduct, both as a religious leader and as a citizen, did a great deal to allay anti-Catholic feeling. In 1788 it was possible to vest him with the title of bishop, and in 1815 he was raised to the office of archbishop.

Immigration and Catholicism. The nineteenth century was a period of rapid growth for the Catholic Church in the United States, made possible largely by vast numbers of Catholic immigrants from Europe. The great exodus of Irish from southern Ireland to the United States, which reached its peak following the potato famine in the 1840's, was almost entirely Catholic in religion. The German immigration equalled and soon surpassed the Irish in numbers. The Germans were about equally divided between Catholics and Protestants.

Anti-Catholic Feeling. Anti-Catholic bigotry, which had largely subsided by the close of the eighteenth century, erupted again as the stream of Catholic immigrants began pouring into the country during the 1830's.[14] The feeling against the newcomers, however, was only partly due to religion. It was also, in good measure, an "antiforeign prejudice" that arose from the unwillingness or inability of some Americans to understand and appreciate people who represent a culture different from their own.

Most of the immigrants came from the lower economic and social groups of their native countries and naturally became the chief source of low-wage labor which was needed to construct the canals and railroads and to work in the new factories. Native American workingmen felt that this supply of cheap labor represented a threat to their living standards and, as has happened so often since, many of them expressed their economic grievances in animosity toward racial and religious minorities. Antiforeign and anti-Catholic sentiment became one of the leading political issues of the day. The chief support of the Native American Party in 1845 and the Know-Nothing Party in 1850, for example, came from such antiforeign and anti-Catholic groups. However, the reaction against extremists in these factions led to the election of Pierce as president in 1852—with Catholic support.

---

[14] Myers, *op. cit.*, p. 140.

Later Catholic Immigration. Toward the end of the nineteenth century the leading sources of immigration shifted from Western and Northern Europe to Eastern and Southern Europe.[15] With the Italian and Polish elements especially numerous, this immigration was almost entirely Catholic. And because the vast majority of these newcomers did not speak English, foreign-language and national parishes soon became as numerous in many parts of the country as English-speaking Catholic parishes.

It was now the turn of the Eastern and Southern Europeans, stigmatized as "foreigners" and "undesirables" and as a source of "cheap" and "anti-union" labor, to occupy the lower rungs of the social and economic ladder. Often the subjects of derision and discrimination, they sometimes suffered outright persecution. Many of them lived in "Little Italys" and "Little Polands," and never succeeded in adapting themselves to all the conditions of American life.

Such a situation, naturally, had an unfavorable effect on the status and prestige of the Catholic Church. The problem, however, virtually disappeared as the "second generation Americans" (children born and raised in America) grew up and succeeded their parents. These descendants of Italian and Slavic immigrants, the vast majority of whom have retained their Catholic faith, are today an important and highly respected element of the population of the United States.

The decade from 1900 to 1910 was the peak period of immigration into the United States. World War I brought immigration to a virtual halt and it has been severely restricted since then. The American Catholic Church, like the other denominations and sects in our country, is therefore in a position where it can grow in numbers and influence only by maintaining the allegiance of its followers and by proselytizing members of other churches and persons who belong to no church.

Judaism

Comparatively few Jews found their way to America during the colonial period. As a minority group they, too, suffered a number of disabilities, which varied in severity from colony to colony. In general, however, they fared better in the New World than they had in the Old.[16]

Like other religious minorities, they were treated most generously in Rhode Island and Pennsylvania, but they also enjoyed fairly good conditions in Massachusetts, South Carolina, and New York. The connection of the Jews with New York began as early as 1654 when a group of twenty-three Hebrews entered the colony (then New Amsterdam) from Brazil.

---

[15] John Tracy Ellis, *American Catholicism* (Chicago: University of Chicago Press, 1955), p. 82 ff.

[16] Hyman B. Grinstein, *Rise of the Jewish Community of New York: 1654–1860* (Philadelphia: Jewish Publication Society of America, 1945); Albert I. Gordon, *Jews in Transition* (University of Minnesota Press, 1949); Oscar Handlin, *Adventure in Freedom: Three Hundred Years of Jewish Life in America* (New York: McGraw-Hill Co., 1954).

By the time of the Revolution, the Jews had increased considerably in numbers, although their total population did not reach 10,000 until some years later. Their leading settlements were in Newport (Rhode Island), New York City, Philadelphia, and Charleston (South Carolina). Francis Salvador was elected to the First Provincial Assembly of South Carolina in 1774. He is believed to have been the first Jew in modern times to serve in an elective public office.

Gains during the Revolution. Jews were well represented and active in the Revolution: more than 100 are known to have served in the colonial army and navy. Haym Salomon, broker and banker, gave generously of his wealth and talents to help finance the Revolution. He was a leading advisor and coworker of Robert Morris, and both James Wilson and James Madison were onetime pensioners of his.

Jews received full legal rights for the first time in the new state constitution of New York (adopted in 1777), but other states had clauses in their constitutions which prevented Jews from rising to a position of full citizenship. Maryland's constitution required a "declaration of belief in the Christian religion" as one qualification for "any office of trust or profit." North Carolina forbade any person to hold public office "who shall deny the Divine Authority of both Old and New Testaments." The struggle to win complete equality by the elimination of every discriminatory clause in constitutions and statute books was not won until 1867 in Maryland and 1868 in North Carolina.

Immigration of Jews. There are approximately 5 million Jews in the United States today, most of them the descendants of Jews who immigrated to America in three major movements.

The first movement, in colonial times, was made up of Sephardic groups with their background of Spanish and Portuguese culture. Then, from 1830 to 1870, German Jews streamed into the United States by the thousands. The last great Jewish immigration was from Eastern Europe.

Between 1881 and 1924, 2,388,000 Jews entered the United States from Eastern European countries. More than two-thirds of these came from Russia (which then included most of Poland), and the remainder came from the Austro-Hungarian Empire and Rumania. Jews in all of these regions had suffered from discrimination, persecution, and even *pogroms* (organized massacres) which were encouraged or at least winked at by the governmental authorities. The New World was a beacon of hope to these unhappy people.

Largely because of the quota restrictions of the Immigration Law of 1924, only 352,000 Jews immigrated to the United States between 1925 and 1943. They were, largely, refugees from Nazi and fascist anti-Semitism. They came at first from Germany and Austria, and later from Italy, Hungary, and Czechoslovakia.

The peak of Jewish immigration at the end of the last century coincided with the peak of Catholic immigration from Eastern and Southern Europe so that the anti-Catholic and antiforeign sentiment of this period had another counterpart in the rise of anti-Semitism. During the first quarter of the twentieth century the Ku Klux Klan was revived in various parts of the North (as well as the South) to exploit anew the prejudices and hatreds which some of the more ignorant and prejudiced segments of the community have always felt towards "outsiders." Originally anti-Negro in its motivation, the Klan now expanded its hate program to include Jews, Catholics, and indeed anyone who was not "White, Anglo-Saxon and Protestant."

Summary

Freedom of religion brought many Europeans to the American colonies but in most colonies the dominant religious group enjoyed privileges that were not available to the minority groups. Pennsylvania under William Penn and Rhode Island under Roger Williams extended freedom of religion to all groups and maintained complete separation of church and state.

Although Maryland was organized as a haven for Catholics, Catholics never constituted a majority of its settlers and were even at one time denied full rights of citizenship. Sephardic Jews, a product of Portuguese and Spanish cultures, settled in small numbers in the seaboard cities of Newport, New York, Philadelphia, and Charleston.

In terms of their practices and social structures the Protestant churches fell roughly into two categories: "conservative" and "radical." The conservative churches required a college-trained clergy, had an official confession of faith, and practiced infant baptism. The radical churches were led by a "lay priesthood," left the interpretation of the Bible to the individual, and practiced "believers' baptism." The conservative churches were dominated by the ruling classes whereas the radical churches were strongholds of the common man. The Anglican, Puritan, Presbyterian, and Reformed churches were conservative in practice and structure; the Methodist and Baptist originally were radical.

The American Revolution stimulated the movement for the separation of church and state in those colonies that had an established church. During the first half of the nineteenth century the Methodist and Baptist churches, being most attractive to democratic and frontier sentiment, forged ahead of the conservative churches. During the latter half of the century the differences between the conservative and the radical churches became less marked. A general type, known as Liberal Protestantism, with an emphasis upon the "social gospel," gradually became the dominant expression of Protestantism in the first quarter of the twentieth century. Then, in the 1930's, neo-orthodoxy arose to challenge the theology and worldview of liberalism.

Through immigrating waves of Irish and Germans from Western Europe in the middle of the nineteenth century, and waves of Italians and

Slavs from Southern and Eastern Europe during the latter part, the Catholic Church in America grew in numbers and influence from a minor to a major religious group. The Jewish religion developed in the United States through immigration from Western Europe during the middle of the nineteenth century (primarily Reform Jews from Germany) and from Eastern Europe during the latter part of the century (primarily Orthodox Jews from Poland and Russia) to rank as the third major faith.

PART II

Religion and the Individual

PART II OF THIS STUDY will focus upon various aspects of the individual in relation to his religion. As has been noted, one dimension of belief religion is the emotional-feeling or experiential dimension.* The religious-feeling dimension is of special interest to psychology. Many new studies that deal with some aspect of the feeling or experiential dimension of religious behavior are now available for study and analysis, and some of them will be considered here.

A second aspect of the relation of the individual to religion, to which some attention will be directed, deals with the involvement of the individual in his local parish religious system. This aspect will be illustrated through a discussion and summary of some of the typologies of parishioners. Typologies are available which indicate the nature and degree of involvement of individuals in religious systems such as the typical Catholic parish and a representative Protestant congregation.

In this section attention also will be directed to relevant studies that deal with the individual as a "religious statistic." There are important studies by the respective churches and denominations of membership and affiliation, studies of religious preferences based upon responses to public opinion and other objective fact-gathering bodies, and studies of per capita contributions by members and affiliates of various churches and denominations, of age and religion, and sex and religion. These statistical and empirical studies all contribute to a more complete understanding of an individual's religious nature and behavior.

---

* See Chapter I, p. 13.

THE SOCIAL PSYCHOLOGY OF INDIVIDUAL BEHAVIOR

Tools of Analysis

Social psychology is the discipline that is concerned with how groups influence, create, and modify the behavior of the individual, and with how the individual can influence and modify the group of which he is an interacting entity.

Personality. Personality may be defined as the sum total of the individual's habits, attitudes, and feelings, or as an organization of reacting tendencies. Any given person (personality) is the produce of his experiences, many of which are acquired in the various groups to which the individual belongs and with which he is identified.

Interaction. Personality tendencies are acquired through interaction. The individual interacts within the family group; the pupil interacts with his teacher and his classmates within the classroom group, and the student interacts with his fraternity brothers within the fraternity group. Each interactive experience adds to the total of experiences which forms the warp and woof of personality.

The individual is an *actor* in the group-interactional arena. The quality of the interactive experience in any given group situation determines how much impact the given experience may make upon the individual's existing pattern of attitudes and feelings. An interactive experience of depth and intensity can have either a constructive and integrating—or a negative and disintegrating—influence upon the personality structure of the individual.

The Group. The quality of the interactional experience depends upon the nature of the group in which the experience occurs—groups which may be conceptualized as primary and secondary.[1] Primary groups are the most important sources of interactional experiences in depth and therefore have the greatest influence upon the development and modification of personality. Primary groups are intimate, face-to-face groups, in contrast to secondary groups where intimacy and face-to-face relationship is limited or lacking. Primary groups are generally small; secondary groups tend to be large.

The family, the play group, and the work group are primary groups. Membership in a political party, in a teachers' association, or in a church is for many persons a secondary group relationship. The degree and amount of interaction in the latter case is mild and limited—often only nominal.

Status and Role. In any particular group the actor occupies a *status* and plays one or more roles, a status being the position or place that the actor occupies in the group. Since the group has significance for the actor primarily in terms of interaction, it is more informing to say that a status is

---

[1] J. O. Hertzler, *American Social Institutions* (Boston: Allyn and Bacon, Inc., 1961), p. 17.

the position or place that an actor occupies in a set of relationships. A status relationship is polar or reciprocal, such as mother-child, leader-follower, preacher-congregant.[2]

A status carries with it a set of rights and duties. The mother is expected (has the duty) to protect the health and well-being of her children, but also has the right to demand respect and obedience from her children for her efforts in their behalf. The Protestant minister is expected to deliver a weekly sermon but he enjoys the right—within the limits established by custom—of preaching what he wants to preach in whatever way he chooses.

In a particular group the actor not only holds a status but plays one or more *roles*. A role, technically, is a set of expected, approved, and demanded behaviors which are socially considered to adhere to a status,[3] and it can be easily illustrated in the immediate family group.

The male plays a number of roles—in his relations with his wife, for example, the role of husband. His interactional relations with his children constitute the father role. The breadwinner role is composed of the activities the husband and father engages in to bring to the family the means by which it may be maintained as a family unit within the culture.

These are the traditional roles, but the representative suburban father and husband has acquired a new role: that of homemaker—doing a number of things about the house and for the children that were traditionally the duty and responsibility of the wife and mother.

The woman, likewise, has a number of roles. Her interactive relationships with her husband constitute her role as wife; her relationship with her children her role as mother; what she does for the family within the home her homemaking role. But wives also have often acquired a new role by being gainfully employed outside the home for wages which they contribute to family needs and welfare. They thereby assume a breadwinner role.

Role Conflict. Because the individual is oriented towards, belongs to, and interacts with a number of groups within the context of his total interactive behavior, he frequently experiences *role conflict*. This conflict may involve psychological stress: anxiety, guilt, or frustration arising out of the incompatibility of differing values of the varied groups with which the individual is associated or seeks identity. Role conflict may be "objective" in nature, or an "overload" in terms of available time and resources.

Objective conflict is a frequent experience of the working mother. Her occupation requires that she be out of the home and on the job at fixed and regular hours—demands of her occupational role which often conflict with her role of mother. Most working mothers arrange for normal care and supervision of their minor children while they are away on the job, but if the child becomes ill the mother feels impelled to be with her child for

---

2 Robin Williams, *American Society* (New York: Alfred A. Knopf), p. 35.
3 *Ibid.*, p. 36.

comfort and succor; she is torn between the demands of her job and her responsibilities as mother. Many individuals become involved in similar unhappy role conflict situations when they find that the norms of their religious value system are inconsistent with their pleasure goals.

Pivotal and Peripheral Behavioral Activities. The goals and aspirations of the individual lead to various kinds of interactional relationships in various types of groups. Some group interactive relationships are *central* and *pivotal* in terms of the individual's hierarchy of goals and values, while other interactional relationships tend to be *marginal* and *peripheral*. A number of recent studies have shown that the typical college student expects the satisfactions that arise from family and career activities to occupy the central and pivotal positions in his hierarchy of goals and values, and the satisfactions that arise from religious and community service activities to be only incidental—or marginal and peripheral in his scheme of values.

Role Differentiation. Role differentiation is an integral component of the interaction system of more complex groups (social systems) whose social relationships both permit and require considerable division of labor in role behavior. In a typical school there are not only the pupils (who play the role of student and learner) but the specialist-functionaries of the educational interactional system: teachers, administrators, school board, and custodial staff.

Role differentiation is a significant factor in the personality development and structure of many members of a social system.

The "Significant Other." The behavior of individuals is often influenced by the "significant other"—the person from whom the individual takes his cues for behavior in various situations: the small boy who imitates his father's speech or the adolescent girl who takes her cues for dress, conduct, and mannerisms from a movie star. A baseball star is also a "significant other" for many an adolescent boy during his hero worshipping stage of development. Or the "significant other" is sometimes a person who belongs to one or more of the same groups and interactional patterns as the individual for whom he is significant.

The "Reference Group." Similar to the significant other in its impact upon individual personality is the "reference group." A person may be influenced not only by the group in which he is interacting but also by his conception of other groups of which he is *not* a member; that is, apart from any direct interaction. Any group is a reference group for a person if its conception is part of his frame of reference for appraisal of himself or of a group to which he belongs. The United States Military Academy at West Point might well be the "reference group" for a military school cadet who hopes for an appointment.

Anomie. Social organization provides the individual with predictable interpersonal relations so that individual conduct becomes regularized with the behavior of others in the various arenas of interacting relationships.

The individual feels secure when he "knows what to expect." Rapid shifts in social organization, and particularly in the primary groups with which the individual has been identified, lead to disorientation and personal disorganization which is often made evident in erratic and disturbed behavior.

The individual does not know what to expect when he has no patterned norms that can guide his behavior. To the extent that regularity disappears in his circle of personal relationships, he lives in a milieu of normlessness and a state of *anomie*. The behavior of adolescents, delinquents, divorced persons, "marginal men," displaced persons, and highly mobile persons frequently shows the consequences of having to interact in interpersonal relationships in a milieu of low predictability.[4]

Functional-Dysfunctional. An experience is functional for a person if it contributes to the adjustment, adaptation, or integration of the individual with his environment. An experience is dysfunctional if it decreases adaptation, stimulates maladjustment, or has disorientating or disintegrating results for the individual.

Courtship has been described as the process in which the individual selects a mate and leaves his family of orientation to establish his own family of procreation. In American society it includes several stages: group and random dating, going steady, pinning, engagement. The individual's experience in any one of these stages is functional if he gains greater insight about himself (the sort of person that he appears to others), or about the opposite sex and appropriate heterosexual behavior. It is functional if he moves constructively towards the moment when he will select from among the available choices the person who can best meet his needs for effective married-pair living.

The experience in any one of these stages is dysfunctional if it sets him back on the path—away from effective heterosexual behavior—so that he is less well prepared to select a mate adapted to his needs and personality.

A child's religious training and indoctrination likewise would be functional if, not minding the duties or the restraints which the practice of his faith required of him, he also found the training an enjoyable and happy experience from which he gained a sense of peace and security. A child's religious training and indoctrination would be dysfunctional if he resented the duties he had to perform or the activities in which he could not participate because of his religion, or if the experience was a continued source of conflict and disagreement between the child and his parents or religious teacher—all of which left him with a sense of fear and frustration rather than one of peace and security.

"Other-Directed" Personality. Riesman has advanced a theory of personality types and structures in terms of cultural determinism that has attracted widespread attention among social scientists.[5] The "tradi-

---

[4] *Ibid.*, pp. 561–67.
[5] David Riesman, Reuel Denney and Nathan Glazer, *The Lonely Crowd* (New Haven, Conn.: Yale University Press, 1950).

tion-directed" personality was the product of the feudal age and feudal society, according to the theory. People were born into an estate which was, in effect, a caste: into the second estate as a noble, or into the third estate as a peasant. A peasant acted in the prescribed ways that custom dictated for peasants, and a noble acted as custom dictated a noble should act. The tradition-directed personality was essentially a predestined personality.

Although American society arose out of a tradition-directed background, the American scene brought forth its own peculiar personality structure which was, according to Riesman, the "inner-directed" personality. The inner-directed personality was the product of the interplay of independence, individualism, and the frontier. The typical American was a transplanted peasant, upwardly mobile and success-oriented. He disciplined himself to work and sacrifice, and, to use the folk expression of the frontier, he literally pulled himself up by his own bootstraps. Although he was always subject to the informal social control of a *gemeinschaft* community, he had internalized the Protestant ethic and was primarily motivated by his conscience and therefore basically "inner-directed."

Contemporary "associational" or "mass society" has, according to Riesman, brought forth a new and different personality type: the "other-directed" personality. The contemporary American lives and works in a milieu of organizations and bureaucracies, and his experience is no longer focused and total but rather segmentalized and fragmented. The typical American achieves success and enhances his ego by his skill in adapting himself to the various groups—home and neighborhood, work and professional, play and recreational—that constitute his round of life. Since a premium is placed upon his adjustment to varieties of groups, he becomes a typical "other-directed" personality.

Social critics see in the "other-directed" personality a twentieth century counterpart of the sophists of Socrates' Athens, who boasted of their skill in being all things to all people. With Socrates the critics search contemporary society in vain for the universals of truth, virtue, and integrity, which they claim to have found in the youthful, unsophisticated, and "inner-directed" society of the frontier.

Riesman's theses are stimulating and provocative, but they have been challenged because personality is neither so simple nor "determined." His theses are, however, useful devices by which contemporary religious behavior may be investigated and they must be considered by careful students of religious culture.

Chapter III

Religion and Personality

UNTIL RECENTLY, scientific studies of religion avoided the investigation of the motivating forces that attract and hold the individual to his particular religion—partly because of the difficulty of submitting subjective religious feelings to objective and statistical analysis.

This reluctance no longer holds true. No religious group could long survive without the personal feelings and emotional experiences which individual personalities find within organized systems of worship. Psychologists, sociologists, and anthropologists have given subjective religion considerable attention in recent years.

The Psychology of Religion

Psychology's contribution to the understanding of subjective religious behavior is suggested in its definitions and conceptualizations. Clark's definition, which includes the "inner experience of the individual when he senses a Beyond,"[1] has already been noted.

A representative of the phenomenological school ("self-image") of psychological thought comes to grips with religion as a psychological concept when he conceives of religion as the area of personality development by which the individual seeks oneness with the universe and thereby gains a deep feeling of value and belonging.[2]

---

[1] Walter H. Clark, *The Psychology of Religion* (New York: The Macmillan Co., 1958), p. 22.

[2] Donald Snygg, "The Psychological Bases of Human Values," *Goals of Economic Life*, E. D. Ward (ed.), (New York: Harper & Bros., 1953).

In any event, beliefs represent attempts to gain wholeness, and are not blind responses, neuroticisms, or the like. These feelings, values, beliefs vary according to the individual's conception of himself and of the situation. Self-conceptions and situations are so varied, in fact, that a psychologist can say that the subjective religious attitudes of every individual are unlike those of any other individual.[3]

Allport has been as much concerned with religion as an area of investigation—and recognized for his publications in this field—as any contemporary psychologist. He sees religious "sentiments" as integral facets of the individual's struggle in the process of "becoming," and the struggle to "become" is, according to Allport, a progression towards a mature religious faith. Implicit within his conceptual schemata are distinctions between a mature and an immature religion.

Allport thinks that the error of the psychoanalytic theory of religion lies in locating religious beliefs exclusively in the defensive functions of the ego (as a fortification against the inroads of anxiety, doubt, despair) rather than in the core and center and substance of the developing ego itself. The healthy and mature person seeks to cure his own "partialness" by finding something more convincing than partialness itself. Therefore the developed personality will not fabricate his religion out of some emotional fragment, but will seek a theory of being in which all fragments are meaningfully ordered. Although the progression towards "becoming" requires the intellect to exert itself, intellect alone is not enough. The mature faith requires faith and love as well as reason,[4] and Allport does not leave us in the dark about the characteristics of the mature faith:

To feel oneself meaningfully linked to the whole of Being is not possible before puberty. . . . Becoming has been much more thoroughly studied for the years preceding puberty than for adolescent and adult years. It is, therefore, understandable that the factors influencing the religion of childhood should loom large in our present view familism, dependence, authority, wishful thinking, and magical practice.[5]

The psychological frame of reference has provided us with several "tools" for the study and interpretation of religious behavior. We have found, for example, that the psychological dimension of religion is characterized by:

1. An "inner experience" with a supernatural referent (the "Beyond").
2. A "feeling and experience" of individual men in their solitude.
3. "Beliefs" that vary according to the individual's perception of himself and according to the situation.
4. Any given individual's religion, which may include cognitive and volitional as well as affective attributes.

---

[3] Gordon W. Allport, *The Individual and His Religion* (New York: The Macmillan Co., 1952), p. 26.

[4] G. W. Allport, *Becoming: Basic Considerations for a Psychology of Personality* (New Haven, Conn.: Yale University Press, 1955), p. 94.

[5] *Ibid.*, p. 95.

Belief Dimension of Religiosity

The belief dimension of religion has been the subject of considerable analysis and conceptualization by a number of psychologists. Clark has conceptualized belief in terms of several levels of understanding and comprehension.[6]

The first level of belief is *stimulus-response verbalism*—the same level that Allport has designated as "verbal realism"[7]—which originates in the developing life of the child. Saying religion is the same as religion: the child's beliefs are bound up with a magical reliance on the power of words. Many adults, moreover, hold to this verbal level long after childhood.

The second level of belief is *intellectual comprehension*. Beliefs of thinking personalities do not remain in a vacuum, and religious persons who think at all are bound to use some degree of logic and reason to establish their beliefs on a rational ground. "Mature beliefs grow out of the conflicting doubts and affirmations that characterize productive thinking."[8] The intellect receives the truth, questions the truth, and validates a new truth through the process of synthesis, antithesis, and a new synthesis.

The third level of belief is *behavioral demonstration*. The religious personality's actions reflect his real beliefs much better than his verbalisms. This is truth in the Socratic sense: one knows, and is known to, the truth only insofar as the truth is reflected in one's actions. The Good Samaritan is the classic illustration of this level of belief.

The fourth and final level of belief is *comprehensive integration*. This is found in the religious personality who has so internalized his beliefs that they are reflected in all of his behavior; Fichter's nuclear parishioner is this kind of a man.[9] His beliefs are an integral part of his personality. He has internalized the Christian values and tends actually to think and act as a Christian is taught to think and act. He is in fact an integrated Christian and has gained the final level of belief: comprehensive integration. The saints—Albert Schweitzer or St. Francis of Assisi—are the ultimate illustrations of comprehensive integration.

In his latest conceptualizations, Allport views religious faith at this level as *intrinsic* and *extrinsic*, and includes this view in a hypothesis of social behavior: extrinsic faith makes for prejudice, intrinsic for absence of prejudice. The religious, intrinsically oriented person has internalized the values of his faith; its moral and ethical values are thoroughly interwoven into the fabric of his personality: he lives his religion. Humanity is the center of intrinsic religion, and human-heartedness is as essential as belief.

The religious, extrinsically oriented person is often, but not necessarily, an average or irregular church attender. The church group and not hu-

---

[6] W. H. Clark, *op. cit.*, p. 220 ff.

[7] G. W. Allport, *The Individual and His Religion, op. cit.*, p. 122.

[8] *Ibid.*

[9] Joseph H. Fichter, *Social Relations in the Urban Parish* (Chicago: University of Chicago Press, 1954), chap. 3.

manity is the center of his interest. Religion serves him, but he does not serve it. His religion confers status, offers sociability, gives pleasant excitement at Christmas and Easter, is a comfort in crisis and bereavement, but nowhere requires a surrender of prejudice.[10]

The Orthodox Personality

A recent study of belief as a dimension of religiosity showed considerable variation in behavior between those who ranked high on a scale of orthodoxy and those who ranked lowest.[11] Twenty-one hundred schedules composed the universe from which the sample was drawn. About half of the schedules were from students at a state college in the Deep South and the other half from students at a state college in the Northeast. The Orthodox were those who took the orthodox position on each of the following points of Christian belief: the Deity, the Person of Christ, immortality, and the nature of the Bible. The Unorthodox were those from the remaining schedules who failed to take the orthodox position on any one of these points of belief.

Only those schedules were used in which the respondent identified himself with one of the established Protestant denominations. The greater proportion of the southern sample reported a Southern Baptist or Methodist preference, while all of the major Protestant denominations were well represented in the northern sample. Twelve percent of the sample met the Orthodox test, and 22 percent the Unorthodox test.

Comparisons were made between the most belief-oriented Protestants (the Orthodox) and the least belief-oriented Protestants (the Unorthodox). The study showed that the Orthodox were differentiated by religious behavior that was both more extensive and intense than that of the Unorthodox. Because the Orthodox attended church services at a significantly higher rate than the Unorthodox, their religiosity also included the cultic dimension. The Orthodox were also found to experience a crisis type of religious awakening at a higher rate than the Unorthodox, so their religiosity, also included the *experiential* dimension. When asked from what activities they expected to derive the greatest satisfaction, the Orthodox cited religion and religious activities at a significantly higher rate than the Unorthodox.

The study found the Orthodox personality ranked high in each of the conventional dimensions of religiosity. He believed—and behaved—religiously, and religion likewise ranked high in his hierarchy of values. There was consistency and continuity in his religiosity.

This study was also concerned with the consequences which Orthodoxy in belief might have for nonreligious behavior. It was found that the

---

[10] G. W. Allport, "Prejudice: Is It Societal or Personal?" *Journal of Social Issues*, Vol. XVIII, No. 2, 1962.

[11] W. Seward Salisbury, "Religiosity, Regional Sub-Culture, and Social Behavior," *Journal for the Scientific Study of Religion*, Vol. II, No. 1 (Fall, 1962), pp. 94–101.

Orthodox were more determined to marry within their own faith and to send their children to a segregated school. They were less willing to send their children to an interfaith school and less willing than the Unorthodox that women should have full pastoral responsibilities and privileges, but the Orthodox found less conflict between religion and science than the Unorthodox did.

School segregation is a clear violation of the Christian ethic. The internalization of the Christian values, such as those embodied in the Golden Rule, was less evident in the behavior of the Orthodox Protestant than of the Unorthodox Protestant. The Orthodox had certainly not reached the comprehensive integration level of religious belief and behavior, and whether they had gone beyond the verbal comprehension level was open to question.

The study concluded that the Orthodox personality is typically ethnocentric and in-groupish; he tends to be conservative, conventional and traditional, and he resists innovation. Even the Orthodox from Protestant denominations that have admitted women to full pastoral rites and status hesitated to accept this official policy.

The study also concluded that the Orthodox personality tends to compartmentalize his religion. The key and pivotal role which religion plays in his life is in a personal rather than social context. He pursues a truly "separated Christian life" and is self-oriented within an intragroup instead of in an intergroup environment. The science-religion conflict is less of a problem for him because he can reject "unacceptable" science from his frame of reference.

Emotional-Feeling Dimension of Religiosity

The emotional-feeling and experiential dimension of religiosity has been subjected to empirical analysis in a number of studies by psychologists and sociologists. Several of the studies have centered upon the conversion experience.

A significant early study of 2,174 autobiographical cases[12] identified three types of religious awakening:

1. *Definite Crisis.* A real crisis is reached and passed in which a definite change in attitude seems to have taken place. This type corresponds to what is commonly considered as a distinct religious conversion.

2. *Emotional Stimulus-Awakening.* The emotional upheaval is much reduced in intensity—or even entirely absent—but the subject looks back to some event which served to stimulate or awaken the religious consciousness. Joining a church, going forward in an evangelical meeting or standing in a Sunday School decision-day service were illustrations of this type of awakening.

3. *Gradual Awakening.* No single, specific occasions are as decisive as those above because the religious sentiment develops gradually. In this third category fall all persons whose religious life has flowed onward like a stream,

---

[12] Elmer T. Clark, *The Psychology of Religious Awakening* (New York: The Macmillan Co., 1929).

enlarging and growing, but striking no obstructions and forming no cataracts.[13]

Seven percent of the cases showed the definite-crisis awakening, 27 percent the emotional-stimulus awakening, and 66 percent no definite awakening of any kind. More males than females were found in the crisis category, and individuals who were reared in a theology that emphasized total depravity, damnation and eternal punishment were more inclined to experience the crisis awakening than individuals who had been taught to believe in a forgiving and kindly God and a loving Christ.

Individuals, furthermore, who were brought up in a religion that emphasized confirmation were less likely to report a crisis-awakening experience. Persons with little religious training in the home and limited Sunday School experience, from rural areas, and either in a religious vocation or planning to enter one, were more likely to have had a crisis experience.

Zetterberg has conceptualized the emotional-feeling experience in terms of social relationships and changes in the social role. His analysis was based upon a study of youth groups of a revivalist church in Sweden, the Swedish Mission Covenant Church. Out of 276 cases 16 percent reported a definite crisis experience, 56 percent the emotional-stimulus experience, and 28 percent a gradual awakening. The definite-crisis experience was significantly more common among rural than among urban residents, among men than among women, and among those with limited than among those with higher education.

The definite crisis type of experience, according to Zetterberg, leads to a *sudden change of role*. The individual leaves an established pattern of habits and attitudes to become an entirely different personality, interacting in new groups with different attitudes and different goals.

The emotional-stimulus awakening leads to *sudden role identification*. The individual becomes deeply involved in a group in which he was previously only a nominal member.

Gradual awakening represents *role assimilation*, a learning process that continues without sudden changes in role or role identification. It may begin in childhood or later on in life.[14]

A recent study of the emotional-feeling factor of religiosity of Protestants showed that more men than women experience the crisis type of religious awakening, and persons who live in the South as opposed to the North.[15]

Summary of Emotional-Feeling Dimension

Psychological. 1. Some personality types tend to react emotionally to various stimuli and to give this reaction a religious interpretation.

---

[13] *Ibid.*, p. 45.

[14] Hans L. Zetterberg, "The Religious Conversion as a Change of Social Roles," *Sociology and Social Research*, Vol. 36 (January–February, 1952), pp. 159–66.

[15] W. S. Salisbury, *op. cit.*, p. 99.

2. Some personality types are predisposed to an emotional response in depth and will react in such a manner when presented with the appropriate cue, depending upon the situation, the person's conception of the situation, and his relation to it.

Sociological. 1. The emotional-feeling response depends upon the religious environment to which the individual has been conditioned. Liturgical Protestantism (Episcopal and Lutheran churches, for example) emphasize confirmation and do not encourage overt emotionalism. It is the confirmation experience, rather than the conversion experience, to which the novitiates' attention is directed.

Liberal low-church Protestantism, constituting the great majority of Baptist, Methodist, Presbyterian, and Church of Christ congregations, no longer promotes the traditional revival service as an attraction for membership and a renewal of faith. Preparatory classes for new members—especially young people—is the chief recruitment device, and is very similar to the confirmation pattern of the liturgical churches. Overt emotionalism is neither expected nor desired.

The conservative Protestant churches and the new sect-type churches still put the emphasis upon the emotional-feeling and conversion experience as the most appropriate path to membership and fellowship. The revival service is also the accepted avenue for renewal or reaffirmation of faith, but even in the conservative churches the emotional element tends to be watered down.

The author has in recent years attended several evangelistic services in conservative churches where the concluding plea to come forward to make decisions for Christ is satisfied merely by members raising their hands while the entire congregation stands in silent prayer; the public character of the decision is conspicuously underplayed. Many observers at the Billy Graham revival meetings have found both the appeal and the atmosphere to be less emotional and more rational than in the revival meetings of more traditional Protestantism.

2. The nature and degree of emotional-feeling varies according to the regional subculture and a different type of Protestantism, accordingly, appears to flourish in the South. An informal "attendance imperative" seems to operate so that "good Protestants" attend weekly church services at almost as high a rate as Catholics.[16] Southern Protestants were also found to experience the crisis-religious awakening at twice the rate of their northern counterparts. This differential reflects the traditional nature of the South where religious and other institutions have been less affected by the winds of change than those of the North: Southern Protestantism is different only in that it has changed less. The Southern Protestant is expected to respond to religious stimuli in a crisis manner and he tends to give overt expression to this expectation.

---

[16] *Ibid.*

3. A persistent sex differential in the incidence of the crisis-experience appears in various studies. Males consistently show a higher rate of crisis-experience than females, but whether the cause factors are primarily social or psychogenic is not clear. It is possible that there are intervening variables which have not yet been identified.

William James and Religious Behavior

Any discussion of the individual and religion within the context of American culture would not be complete if it did not recognize and pay tribute to William James whose thoughts and insights have relevance even for students of contemporary religious culture.

In his classic *The Varieties of Religious Experience*[17] James analyzed religious groups and needs in terms of personality types. He held that the religious sentiment is expressed and can be conceived in terms of two widely separated personality types, a thesis he developed in two well-known chapters, "The Religion of Healthy-Mindedness" and "The Sick Soul."

The religion of "healthy-mindedness" is optimistic and happy, and its "adherents"—literally and figuratively—can cry out "Hurrah for the Universe! God's in His Heaven, all's right with the World."[18] The healthy-minded are extroverted and outgoing. They find that religion is natural and easy, and its practice conducive to good cheer. They tend to be unreflective and are associated with the more liberal forms of theological thinking. The religious concepts of the healthy-minded may change but the change tends to be steady, gradual, and unspectacular.

At the opposing pole of religious experience James found the "sick souls." In striking contrast to the "healthy-minded," the sick souls are impressed by the suffering and evil in the world, and pity, pain, fear, and human helplessness form the basis for the religious feelings and insights of this personality type. Although the sick souls tend to be pessimistic and introverted, they show a more thoughtful approach to life, lean towards orthodoxy, and will accept and follow a demanding theology.

The religious development of this latter type is not gradual; it is marked by ups and downs. Long periods of meditation and melancholy may be interspersed with sudden flashes of spiritual light. Visions, strong perceptions of both God and the devil, and conversion experiences are frequently associated with the sick-soul personality—along with the ability to transform suffering into insights of profound significance. In his contemplation of evil, the sick soul also develops sensitivity to the sufferings of others.

James' healthy-minded and sick soul personalities are mental constructs in the language of contemporary social thought: ideal types resting at either pole of a religious-feeling continuum. It would be difficult (if not

---

[17] William James, *The Varieties of Religious Experience* (New York: The Modern Library, 1902).

[18] *Ibid.*, p. 135.

impossible) for empirical research to isolate either a completely healthy-minded or sick-soul religious personality because each individual is a mixture of both, and some are in such good balance that it is difficult to identify characteristic traits. The healthy-minded has his conflicts and moments of doubt and despair—and the sick soul is not as pessimistic and inner-directed as he sometimes appears to be.

Several contemporary American religious groups have much to offer the personality type that requires a "healthy-minded" approach to religion and life. Christian Science, as formulated by Mary Baker Eddy, is healthy-mindedness *par excellence*. This is all the more interesting since Mrs. Eddy developed her optimistic insights out of a life that was beset with pain, suffering, conflict, and frustration. According to Christian Science, sin, death, evil, and disease are illusions that exist only in the mind of the nonbeliever.[19]

The Oxford Group movement and Moral Re-Armament, as developed by Frank Buchman, are, basically, "healthy-minded." Although these groups do not deny the reality of sin and suffering, their emphasis is upon religious activism, better interpersonal relations, and a sort of lay practice of confession. It is not a difficult or demanding religion. Those who attend and participate in Moral Re-Armament functions are said to have a good time—as one of their slogans, "Brevity, Sincerity, Hilarity," suggests.[20]

Norman Vincent Peale's "power of positive thinking" approach to religion is considered by many to be a modern application of "healthy-mindedness." Personalities who take an optimistic view and who have little concern for dogma, the tragedy of life, or the "sinfulness of man" seem to be drawn to Peale's formula for "confident living."[21]

Alcoholics Anonymous is also an essentially healthy-minded approach to a difficult personal problem and tragedy. Successful participants in this particular form of group therapy have figuratively been born again—with an optimistic and extroverted personality.

Personal Documents and Religious Identification

Allport, who maintains that the religious life is the most subjective of all areas of experience, also maintains that it has been studied with even partial adequacy only by means of the personal document.[22] The contribution that personal documents can make to understanding an individual's religious feelings and behavior will be suggested by excerpts of autobio-

[19] Mary Baker Eddy, *Science and Health with Key to the Scriptures* (Boston: Published by author, 1886), p. 414.

[20] W. H. Clark, *The Oxford Group Movement: Its History and Significance* (New York: Bookman Associates, 1951), p. 165. Also, Allan W. Eister, *A Sociological Account of the Oxford Group Movement* (Durham, N.C.: Duke University Press, 1950), p. 137.

[21] Norman Vincent Peale, *A Guide to Confident Living* (New York: Prentice-Hall, Inc., 1948).

[22] G. W. Allport, *The Use of Personal Documents in Psychological Science* (New York: Social Science Research Council, 1942), p. 38.

graphical material from a recent study of the religious "feeling"[23] which shows the variety of ways in which a religiously identified personality can be attracted to his faith. The study focuses upon typical religious personalities rather than upon those for whom religion exists "not as a dull habit but as an acute fever."

The complexity of the relationship between the individual and his faith has impressed all students who have worked with religious systems or individuals in such a context. The documents from which the illustrative excerpts are taken were written by students at a state university in the Northeast and on the Pacific Coast, as well as by mature teachers-in-service from both regions. All students and teachers are of middle-class backgrounds and Catholic, Protestant, and Jewish documents were well represented among the sample, although Methodists were about twice as numerous as any other denomination in the Protestant group.

The experimental subjects were asked to respond in writing to the question: When do you feel most religious? There was no attempt to identify, delimit, or otherwise define "religious feeling." The respondent freely described the conditions and circumstances under which he felt "most religious."

The personal statements were then returned anonymously, each respondent being asked only to indicate his religious preference—even if it were No Preference. A content analysis of the statements showed that the great majority "clustered" around one of six basic situations.

Most Religious in a Nature Situation.[24]

1. Although I have always gone to church and sunday school to learn of God, I have, somehow, felt closer to Him out of doors. Occasionally a service in church gives me a good feeling, as does reading the Bible. However, I actually feel closer to God when I am closer to nature: a deserted stretch of beach, an empty field, lots of blue sky and clear water. The reason probably is that the church is too full of people—and social—so that any communion for me would be impossible.

2. When I see a beautiful sunset it makes me think about all of the beautiful things of life and how they came about. I am very religious at this time because it makes me think of spiritual things.

3. When alone in scenic places—the big trees, ocean, forest, along mountain streams—are the times when I have the strongest religious feelings.

The Crisis Situation.[25] Religious feeling and religious experience arise out of a crisis situation for a large group of personalities. Representative of this group are those who report their most religious moments during times of combat, danger, death, or sorrow and grief. These personalities

---

[23] W. S. Salisbury, "Faith, Ritualism, Charismatic Leadership, and Religious Behavior," *Social Forces*, Vol. 34, No. 3 (March, 1956), pp. 241–45.

[24] Authors of this group of personal documents identified themselves, respectively, as 1. Episcopalian, 2. Presbyterian, 3. Methodist.

[25] Identified respectively as 1. Greek Orthodox, 2. Baptist, 3. Jewish, 4. Church of Nazarene, 5. Catholic.

might well define religion in terms of the "too-bigness" of life. To the personalities represented in the following cases religion would appear more episodic than habitual, but nonetheless real and vital when it does develop.

1. During combat in the South Pacific during World War II, I felt most religious. This extended over a period of about eighteen months. Similar feelings come about whenever any crisis arises in my family or with close friends.

2. I feel most religious at a funeral. I am a firm believer in an afterlife and during a funeral service my faith is strengthened and my feeling of death grows less.

3. I feel myself a part of the youths who feel religious in time of sorrow or grief. Somehow, in our fast way of living today, religion has become secondary. We don't seem to think about religion unless we are in very low spirits.

4. In times of crisis I feel the working of the Holy Spirit. For example, in trying to adjust to college work after many years as merely a classroom teacher, I felt His presence very real the first week here.

5. I feel most religious when some one close to me is in danger. I also turn to my religion if I have a serious problem to solve and seem to have difficulty in solving it.

Meditation and the Religious Feeling.[26]   A significant group of personalities identified their deepest religious experiences in various kinds and types of "aloneness" situations.

1. I feel most religious in individual meditation. I have found much satisfaction in quiet prayer and in reading my Bible alone. I believe that if sorrow has come to you, you can bear it alone better than with friends.

2. I feel the most religious when I am in a church where the organ is playing soft music, lights are low, no one is conversing, and I can spend some time looking at the beautiful windows and thinking about God, Jesus, the world we live in, and my part in the scheme of things.

I go to a small church where there is noise and confusion and nothing that the minister says or the things that go on lead me to a spiritual feeling or a "nearness to God."

3. I feel most religious while in church or in individual meditation. I do not enjoy an emotional sermon, and I think that is one of the biggest reasons that my church appeals to me. I like to dwell upon my religion and God while praying in a more or less quiet and "intellectual" manner.

4. I feel most religious in individual meditation because this is the time I call on God for help or guidance, or just talk with him in my own language. It is this means of self-expression that makes the difference for I can't feel too religious reading the thoughts or works of others.

5. I believe that I get my deepest religious feeling when I read the Bible and meditate over what I have read. It is only then that I gain religiously.

6. I feel most religious when I'm inside a church, usually before the service begins. This is the time when silent meditation seems to mean the most to me.

---

[26] Identified respectively as 1. Presbyterian, 2. Methodist, 3. Catholic, 4. Catholic, 5. Free Lutheran, 6. Regular Methodist, 7. Jewish, 8. Catholic, 9. Catholic, 10. Methodist, 11. Methodist.

7. I find my most religious feeling—when I feel closest to God—in individual meditation.

8. When I'm in church I usually feel quite near to God. Very often this happens at some time other than the Sunday mass.

9. It makes me feel very holy when I read the Bible. I actually get the shivers sometimes and I wish I could have lived back in the time of Christ.

10. When reading the Bible or religious books such as *How to Believe* by Sockman, or *Power of Positive Thinking* by Peale, or *The Greatest Story Ever Told* by Oursler.

11. I experience a very religious feeling while saying my prayers at night in complete darkness and quiet.

Religious Experience and the Charismatic Leader. A substantial group of religiously identified personalities is most deeply moved under the influence of, and through association with, the religious leader. This religious leader is not necessarily a formal functionary; in fact, some of the greatest have been members of the laity with no formal training. Max Weber is largely responsible for the introduction of the term "charisma" into the literature of the Sociology of Religion to define those special qualities of the individual who leads and influences largely through the power of his personality.[27]

According to Weber, the prophet of any religious movement possesses the powers of charisma, and these powers—qualities—tend to be emotional and spiritual rather than intellectual in nature. The leader has had an abiding experience of religion which he is able to convey in some measure to his followers. Billy Graham and Father Divine are contemporary religious leaders who have possessed this power in striking measure. The frontier lay preacher who had experienced the "call" and possessed the "word" was also a charismatic leader.

Both Billy Graham and Father Divine are highpowered possessors of charisma who have moved and influenced people by the hundreds and by the thousands. However, the great majority of Americans who have found their most religious moments under the inspiration of the religious leader testify in terms of their pastor, and sometimes it is merely a friend who in this case proves to be the "significant-other."

The following quotes are representative statements from personal documents of a "religious experience" by individuals who are for the most part neither highly religious nor strikingly nonreligious.[28]

1. I feel closer to God while listening to my pastor preach or by just talking to him at his home. He seems to me like a gobetween.

2. I feel most religious when listening to my pastor because he deals with the life of our Lord. In some sermons I feel as though God is present in the

---

[27] Max Weber, *The Theory of Social and Economic Organization* (New York: Oxford University Press, 1947), p. 358.

[28] Identified respectively as 1. Congregational, 2. Methodist, 3. Methodist, 4. Catholic, 5. Jewish, 6. Catholic.

church, making me feel closer to God, secure, and with a peace of mind. I also feel that the pastor's counsel is important when troubles arise. He seems to have the correct and most righteous answers to the problems.

3. We have a wonderful pastor's wife who gets down deep into my religious feeling when she conducts a worship service within a small group of church women.

4. I just feel more religious when he (the pastor) gives a talk during the Gospel. It reminds me of all the things I have done wrong in my life.

5. Listening to my rabbi tell the history of the Jews and their long and endless persecutions, I feel closer to my religion than at any other time. The idea of just listening to a man who has so much faith and understanding of a superhuman power makes me wonder. When I listen to him I never think of questioning him. Hearing him speak fills me with awe more than religion.

6. My church pastor up here at school has a way of talking to people that makes everything seem right. He cites examples which make the religion more meaningful to us. All his feelings for the church go into his sermons and the sermons are usually on problems of the day.

Priest as Mediator. Some Catholics receive their most gratifying religious experience through contact with the priest—not because of his personal and charismatic qualities but because of the special position he occupies in the administration of the sacraments, as a mediator between the individual and God, and as an interpreter of doctrine and ritual. Since he is a duly and properly ordained priest and therefore God's representative on earth, he enjoys the confidence and respect of the good Catholic. The authority and special powers which the priest holds engender a feeling of trust and security which is for some Catholics the leading source of their most cherished and abiding religious experience:

When I am in church and the priest is at the altar changing the bread and wine into the Body and Blood of Christ, I feel more strongly the presence of Christ. Don't misinterpret me and think that I don't have a religious feeling outside of church; it is that I feel more strongly religious in church.

I feel most religious when participating in the Holy Mass. I follow the Mass religiously by reading my prayer book and pondering over the various parts of the Mass while the priest reenacts that part of the life of Christ. I also enjoy and feel uplifted when he reads the Epistle and Gospel for that particular time and then explains it to the congregation, thus giving us a better conception of it.

I especially feel religious in church because the priest who is a representative of God is before us performing the services.

I feel most religious when I participate in the services of my church. The priest leads the congregation in prayer and we respond to him. In the Mass we have missals by which we can follow the priest and pray with him. Since my religion forbids it, I do not interpret the Bible. I do listen to the priest's sermons, but feel more religious when following him through the various rituals.

The special ceremonies which go with a lot of Catholic services are traditional and very beautiful. They tend to put one in a mood of prayer, and you learn to love your religion. I do think this feeling develops as one grows older. It is the outward prayer that influences inward prayer. An appreciation of the great work the priests have put in our religion because they love it makes us in turn love it and acquire great faith.

Religious Experience and the Group. One of the most common sources of the religious experience is represented by those personalities who report they feel most religious in some type of group worship or participation situation. It may be singing in the choir, or teaching Sunday School, or just the sense of being an integral, if infinitesimal, part of a great group of communicants holding like beliefs, following the same practices, and working toward common goals.

Such personalities find that the idea of "sharing," "belonging," or "fellowship," is identified with their most religious moments. A strong element of altruism, of work, of contribution for the common good is suggested in many of the autobiographical statements. In short, they are experiencing a sense of community. These documents are suggestive of the same quality of group feeling and experience that Biblical scholars have found to be characteristic of the early Christian community.[29]

1. I feel good and happy when I'm in church joining in prayer or song with the rest of the people. I seem to forget any troubles or problems I might have. When I come out of church I feel as if I had been closer to God and everything seems much brighter, at least for a while afterwards.

2. I feel most religious when I am participating in any service or organization within the church. Some inspiring anthems which I sing with the choir can mean more to me than any sermon by the minister. Perhaps that is because music of any description can move me far greater than any spoken word.

3. I feel most religious participating in the services of my church. As soon as I enter church I feel good. I just seem to forget all my troubles. It feels good just to sit back and take a part in singing, reading the scripture lesson, and prayer.

4. Participating in the services and rituals of my church gives me a feeling of security. It makes me proud to know I am part of *one* important thing—a faith of one kind.

5. I feel most religious when I am in church and especially so when teaching Sunday School classes, junior church, etc. However, there are several times a week in my everyday experience when I also feel religious. As I grow older I find my faith grows stronger.

6. I feel most religious when I am participating in the ritual of the Lord's Supper. Communion is a very special time to me and I am closer to my religious beliefs at this time. There is a fellowship at this time, a feeling of sharing with the rest of the congregation.

7. I feel most religious when I am thrown into a new situation and feel either lost or lonely. Church gives me the feeling of belonging and companionship.

8. I feel most religious when attending church and participating in the services. I feel that when I attend church it's not an ordinary act, but that I take

---

[29] Identified respectively as 1. Presbyterian, 2. Methodist, 3. Baptist, 4. Catholic, 5. Methodist, 6. Presbyterian, 7. Catholic, 8. Community Church, 9. Catholic, 10. Methodist.

a stand for faith and for a spiritual interpretation of life. It gives one a desire to do better in this everyday life and a desire to help others.

9. It is hard to describe religious feeling, and what affects one at one time may not affect him at another. For the most part I'd say I feel most religious when participating in the church service. In the church service there is the feeling of being one with a great congregation all over the world; following a ritual that has come down from the days of the Apostles. It has the power to lift up my heart and make me feel that here is help for my worries and for the troubles of the world.

10. I can readily say that when I go to church I feel as if it's the perfect end of a week—or the perfect beginning. As I listen to the reading of the Bible or participate in a hymn, I feel very reverent and it makes me feel relaxed and cleansed.

Religious Experience and Ritual. Another group of religiously identified personalities discover their finest spiritual moments in a church service that is liturgical in nature and characterized by ritual and symbolism. Most of the personalities who feel most religious under these circumstances are faithful communicants of a liturgical service.

In the American scene the largest and most liturgical church is, of course, the Catholic. There is, however, a substantial movement in some Protestant denominations and within some individual churches to bring more liturgy and ritual into the service on the ground that worship is a total experience that involves movement, sight, and hearing as well as instruction.[30]

Personalities moved by a liturgical service commonly describe their experience as "mysterious" and "wonderful." The church is "beautiful"; the service fills them with "awe" and leaves them "quiet" and "peaceful." The liturgical service is such an effective means of worship that some communicants report they are actually able to feel and experience the scenes and internalize the meanings for which the symbolic acts stand.[31]

1. I feel most religious when I have gone to confession, feel free of my sins, and anticipate receiving Holy Communion. There is a certain feeling of freedom and a sense of close association with God. I find in time of sickness or sorrow in my family that confession and Communion give me strength and hope to go on.

2. I feel most religious when entering a Catholic church, not only when attending Mass but when stopping to say a prayer. The visible reminders of Christ's birth and death increase my religious feeling. Of all the rituals of the Catholic faith, the Mass [most] increases my religious fervor because every part and movement is symbolic of Christ's life on earth.

3. When I am attending and following the Mass through means of a missal, it gives me a very close feeling to God himself. The Mass is the offering up of a sacrifice which has a deep and beautiful meaning to those who understand and participate in it. At the consecration, when the bread and wine are transformed

---

[30] Cyril C. Richardson, "Some Thoughts on the Reform of Protestant Worship," *Religion in Life*, Autumn, 1946, p. 541.

[31] Identified respectively as 1. Catholic, 2. Catholic, 3. Catholic, 4. Catholic, 5. Catholic, 6. Methodist, 7. Reform Jewish, 8. Jewish.

into the Body and Blood of Jesus Christ, it fills me with a very close feeling to God, as it does everyone in the Church.

4. I have always loved attending Mass and do it as often as I can. There is just something about the services that makes one feel so good and happy.

5. I feel most religious when I am in church participating in the services. Our services are very moving because of choir, candles, vestments, etc.

6. Often the same Sunday morning rituals become too matter of fact; that is, I recite the Lord's Prayer and Apostle's Creed as I would a lesson and do not stop to think about the true meaning. However, every so often when a special service comes along—like baptism, communion, midnight service, candlelight service—I am very impressed and I feel very close to God.

7. I feel most religious during the Yom Kippur, Rosh Hashanah and Passover holidays because I go to church services and perform all the rituals of these holidays. During the rest of the year, however, I do not follow all the rituals of my religion and I do not attend services at the synagogue. I am very much of a Reform Jew and I do not feel that it is necessary to perform all the services and rituals of my faith in order to be considered a good Jew.

8. I feel most religious during individual meditation as I do not agree with all the doctrines of my church. I interpret the Bible in my own way and enjoy reading it myself. I do, however, feel quite religious at our church services as the Ark is there and it leaves me with a reverent feeling.

It is not uncommon among college students, in their search for a more "mature" religious identification, to explore the various religious orientations that are available in their college community. The following case not only illustrates the exploratory quest but also the satisfying nature of ritual once the personality has become habituated to it.

A student who was brought up as a Baptist reached the point in her emotional and intellectual development where she was no longer willing to accept her religion at the level of *stimulus-response verbalism* alone. In her search to establish her religion on a more rational basis she visited and made some investigation into a number of churches and religions. She reported that she felt intellectually most at home in Unitarianism or with Bahai. However, her experience with an intellectual religion proved unrewarding and she found, as she indicates, that her religious needs would be best met in a situation and atmosphere that was essentially ritualistic: "I was associated with a Unitarian group this past year but the group members were a little too 'anti-religion' for my taste. They were merely a fellowship group meeting for discussion, and I found I missed being in a church singing hymns and praying."

Family Relationships and the Religious Feeling. Tillich has defined religion as dealing with the things of "ultimate concern."[32] Family relationships are so important and occupy such a high place in the hierarchy of values that some personalities are able to make an almost complete identification of family and religion. For those so oriented, the occasions of deepest religious feeling are found within the context of family relationships.

---

[32] Paul Tillich, *Journal of Religion*, Vol. 27, No. 1 (January, 1947).

For one it may be the feeling of a parent towards a child; for another that of a child towards parents and the home, or the nature and quality of the interaction and adjustment pattern between man and wife, and so on.[33]

1. A father reports "I'm not sure when I feel most religious. I think for me it is in everyday living where the teachings of religion are put to use. I enjoy going to church because I feel very close to God when I'm there, and in thinking and planning for my family I feel close to religion as I hope and pray for a good, full life with them."

2. A mother reports she feels most religious "when we attend church as a family."

3. A mother states "While religion isn't discussed much at home, we try to have it fit into our family life and hope our boys will absorb a desire for it." She adds that she feels most religious "when the family is at home and all enjoying the same thing; our Sunday evenings are often our 'family night,' whether watching T.V. or just reading individually."

4. A grandmother is most religious "Any time when I take time to evaluate the things that we are so apt to take for granted, such as normal children—both physically and mentally—a happy, well-adjusted married life and home, intimate family ties."

5. A mother: "When I look at my baby I feel most religious—gratitude, awe, wonderment at being privileged to take part in the miracle of birth and have a human being entrusted to my safekeeping."

6. A father: "I think that the time I felt most religious was in the last few weeks before my son was born."

The home and family occupy an important place in Judaism because many important rituals and practices are centered there. Because of the close identification of home and religion, many Jewish students find themselves drawn to one and reminded of the other as they leave home to attend college.[34]

1. I have never felt very religious, however, since I have been away from home, religion has come to mean more to me since it binds me closer to my family.

2. When I am alone and I realize what my parents are doing for me, I get religious and pray that nothing will happen to them. I realize then how wonderful they are and what they are doing for me.

3. I firmly believe in God and in my faith but I am not a religious person. I have respect for my religion due to tradition and knowledge of its history. On various occasions I attend the synagogue, but it is not because I truly feel religious. I will go out of *obligation to myself and my family** and because I feel it is right for me to go on certain holidays. I do not do this as a task, because if I considered it a task I would not attend.

Integration of Belief and Behavior. A number of personal documents show a religious response in not just one but in a variety of situations. A

---

[33] Identified respectively as 1. Methodist, 2. Presbyterian, 3. Presbyterian, 4. Methodist, 5. Catholic, 6. Methodist.

[34] Identified respectively as 1. Jewish, 2. Reform Jewish, 3. Conservative Jewish.
* Author's italics.

number of subjective statements were best categorized as representing the *intellectual* comprehension level of belief. In these cases the individual was a thoroughly indoctrinated and committed religious personality. He performed the necessary rituals and practices of his faith, but the rules and beliefs were not followed blindly nor taken solely on the basis of authority. Through study and meditation his religious perspective had developed until beliefs and values were thoroughly incorporated into his value system. He had thereby achieved the *intellectual comprehension* level of belief. The following cases are illustrations of this type of religious behavior.[35]

1. I do not have any special time that I feel most religious. To me, the religion I practice is my everyday living. Often when I have a spare moment, I spend it in meditation. Always morning and nightly prayer; sometime in the day a few moments spent with a periodical that I take, *Unity*, [that contains] a thought for each day. To me, religion should be practical and within a person at all times—not something donned at special times for special occasions. If I can live a respectable, kind, fruitful life, then I feel I have practiced religion. To me, ritual and fanfare do not make for righteousness.

2. The church creates an atmosphere of meditation, but too often during the formal church service my attention wanders—the extent often depends on the sermon. I enjoy the music, but often for the music's sake because I enjoy listening to the organ and to singing. I really think I feel most religious when preparing a Sunday School lesson at home, or when some question comes from the children which stimulates thoughts and the formulating of some definite idea in the religious field.

Some personal documents indicated a religious knowledge and behavior that can most appropriately be categorized as a *behavioral demonstration* level of belief. This personality type received his greatest religious satisfactions when he found himself in a position where he could apply the ethic which his faith holds up as the ideal of behavior.[36]

I feel most religious when some relative or close friend has had some disaster or tragedy and I can help them in their time of need and sorrow. Or any time I can help someone; for instance, taking baskets to the needy on Thanksgiving or boxes to elderly people at Christmas, doing for shut-ins, and the like. I also get a great deal of satisfaction doing for an underprivileged child in my classroom.

No Special Religious Feeling. It is possible to have a definite religious commitment and to adhere closely to the practices and beliefs of some formal religious system without being conscious of any special feeling or experience of religion—or of feeling more religious at one time and in one situation than at other times and in other situations. This kind of reaction to religious stimuli is most commonly found among adherents of the liturgical churches.[37]

---

[35] Identified respectively as 1. Methodist, 2. Presbyterian.
[36] Identified as Baptist.
[37] Identified respectively as 1. Lutheran, 2. Catholic, 3. Catholic.

1. I am not aware of any special feeling at any one time. Because my religious instruction as a youth was so complete, I have learned to love my religion. My religion is with me constantly. I attend church every Sunday, read my Bible every night, and pray to God regularly through the day. I feel God is with me always.

2. My religion is such an integrated part of me that I am unable to identify any special moment or moments when I feel more—or less—religious than at other times. I rarely think of my religion or what I do as being "religious." I feel my actions are controlled by early moral training and such thought is unnecessary.

3. I feel good all the time and think that life is wonderful whenever I know that I'm following the suggestions or rules of my church.

Most of the personalities who fail to recognize any feeling or experience of a religious nature are drawn from the approximately 6 percent of the American people who do not claim a Catholic, Protestant, or Jewish religious preference. The following are representative types:[38]

1. I don't believe I feel more religious at one time than another. I have never really experienced what is called religious emotion nor do I believe I am an atheist for my religious views.

2. I don't quite get the meaning of "feeling religious." I don't believe in a personal God and therefore I don't get too worked up emotionally. I accept the naturalistic theory and I don't attend any church because such a religion is not formalized.

The Basic Faiths and the Religious Experience. Some insight into the nature of the impact of the Catholic, Jewish, and Protestant religious systems upon the typical communicant of each was obtained in a recent study.[39] The study submitted a random sample of personal documents to a content analysis in an effort to describe the circumstances under which the religiously identified personality felt "most religious." Many of the excerpts which are quoted above were derived from this study, and the categories that were established as a result of the content analysis were comparable to the "religious feeling" situations already described: Charismatic Leader, Meditation, Crisis, Nature, Family. The Ritual category was more extensive, however, in that it included any kind of group behavior within a formal religious setting: various forms of low-church group interaction such as Sunday School, choir, and congregation singing, as well as high-church liturgy and ritual.

The analyzed documents were grouped under Catholic, liturgical Protestant (Episcopal and Lutheran), nonliturgical Protestant (all other Protestants), Judaism, and No Preference. For each of the faith groups the association of "religious feeling" with group interaction (ritual) is greater than or equal to any of the other categories. The primary importance of group interaction in maintaining, fortifying, and elaborating the religious

---

[38] Identified respectively as 1. No Preference, 2. Naturalism.
[39] Salisbury, *op. cit.*, p. 243.

feeling was amply demonstrated. The communicants of the most highly institutionalized and ritualistic system (the Catholic) showed the highest correlation between religious feeling and group behavior.

However, the study also showed a substantial relationship between religious feeling and the group situation among liturgical and nonliturgical Protestants, as well as among practicing Jews.[40] The association of religious feeling with the group situation, in fact, was almost as great among liturgical Protestants as among Catholics. These results can be interpreted as a measure of the greater effectiveness of the liturgical service, whether Catholic or Protestant, as compared to the representative nonliturgical service.

TABLE 1

OPINION FREQUENCY OF INDIVIDUALS IN RELIGIOUS GROUPS AS TO THEIR
DECLARED EXPERIENCE OF RELIGIOUS FEELING

Religious Feeling Associated with	Catholic	Liturgical Protestant	Non-liturgical Protestant	Judaism	No Preference ("Naturalism" Atheist, etc.)	Totals
Total number	405*	90*	344†	125	44†	1008
Total percent	100.0	100.0	100.0	100.0	100.0	100.0
Ritual	53.1%	51.1%	26.7%	38.4%	2.3%	39.9%
Charismatic Leader	10.4	12.2	16.3	6.4	0	11.6
Meditation	19.5	24.5	27.6	19.2	15.9	22.5
Crisis	6.9	4.4	7.0	8.8	6.8	7.0
Nature	4.7	5.6	12.2	6.4	25.0	8.4
Family	1.2	0	2.9	11.2	0	2.9
No Feeling	4.2	2.2	7.3	9.6	50.0	7.7

Chi-square of 132.775 with 12 degrees of freedom. Reference to Palmer O. Johnson, *Statistical Methods in Research* (Prentice-Hall, 1949), p. 361, shows this to be significant at the .01% level of confidence.
  * These cells were combined in the Chi-square analysis.
  † These cells were combined in the Chi-square analysis.
  Source: *Social Forces*, Vol. 34, No. 3 (March, 1956), p. 243.

The meditation situation—prayer, rosary recitation, Bible study, the study of religious literature, and the like—was the second most important source of the religious experience for the Catholic, liturgical Protestant, and Jewish communicant. For the low-church Protestant communicants meditation was even a slightly greater source of religious feeling than that found by the typical Protestant in group-interaction situations.

In each of the three Christian groups the influence of the religious leader is an important third source which calls forth the vital religious feeling. The leader, a "significant other," becomes a source of authority and reassurance for the individual in search of religious security.

The Charismatic Leader is most important among nonliturgical Protestant communicants and least important among the adherents of Judaism.

---

[40] See Table 2.

According to the theory and practice of Judaism, the rabbi has no ecclesiastical authority. He is a learned man who serves the congregation in an advisory capacity. Any male Jew with sufficient knowledge of the prayers and laws can conduct a religious service.[41] The leadership the rabbi exercises tends to be intellectual in nature. By contrast it would appear that the greater importance of the leader in evoking the religious feeling in the nonliturgical religious systems is based upon an appeal that is more emotional than intellectual.

The greater importance of meditation and the charismatic leader in evoking the religious feeling among nonliturgical Protestant communicants is a significant demonstration of the more individualistic nature of this branch of Protestantism.

The patterns of response which the liturgical Protestant and Catholic religious systems evoke from their communicants show a striking similarity. In the case of ritual and the charismatic leader, the liturgical Protestant pattern is virtually identical with the Catholic pattern. As far as the hold which the several religious systems have upon their respective communicants, it appears that the liturgical Protestant systems have more in common with the Catholic system than with their sister nonliturgical Protestant systems.

Judaism is distinguishable by the noticeable extent to which the highest religious feeling is identified with a family relationship and experience. These findings reflect the emphasis Judaism places upon religious observances in the home: the Passover Seder, the lighting of the candles Friday evening, and many other rituals. The impressive nature of these observances tends to integrate the family through common religious experiences so that the stability and solidarity of both institutions are thereby enhanced by this fusion.

The study also emphasizes the complex nature of the religious feeling and the variety of ways in which an individual may be attracted to and held by a particular system. Even though the largest group of respondents finds the highest expression of their religious feeling within a social context, there are several well-defined and patterned situations out of which the religious feeling may arise.

Even in the liturgical Catholic system, some "nuclear" Catholics[42] are moved primarily through contact with charismatic leadership, some through the various instrumentalities of Meditation, and some through the inspiration of a nature situation. This study also showed that some "nuclear" Catholics may follow the full letter of Catholic duties without being moved or even able to identify a "religious feeling." The same variations in behavior are found among Protestant and Jewish communicants.

---

[41] Philip Bernstein, *What the Jews Believe* (New York: Farrar, Straus, and Young, 1950), p. 5.

[42] Fichter, *op. cit.*, p. 211 ff.

A TYPOLOGY OF PARISHIONERS

The relation of individuals to their religious groups and parishes has been studied and analyzed in terms of parishioner types and categorized in typologies. The basic studies, from which typologies are constructed, seek to determine the importance of religion in the life of the individual as reflected in religious observances, in support of parish organizations and functions, and in the extent to which religious values have become an integral part of their daily living.

Catholic

Fichter has done pioneer work in this area. His typology of parishioners arose out of the intensive study which he and his staff of research assistants made of a representative parish in New Orleans.[43] The parish was subjected to an intensive study throughout one entire year. Every service and meeting was attended and studied, every Catholic family visited in its home, and intensive interview data were secured from a great many individual Catholics. It was largely from the vast amount of data gathered in this study that a typology of communicants was conceptualized to include the *saint*, the *nuclear*, the *modal*, the *marginal*, the *dormant*.

The parishioner who could live up to the ideal of spiritual perfection which is taught and encouraged by the Catholic Church would be a *saint*. This ideal of perfection is accepted without mental reservations and overtly approximated only by saintly persons.

The *nuclear* parishioner is the most active participant and the most loyal Catholic. He cooperates faithfully with the priests and parishioners of the church and attends services above and beyond the minimum requirements. He not only contributes to the support of the church; he contributes generously. He has achieved inner psychological unity by so internalizing the Catholic value system that it reflects in all his behavior. He is, in short, an "integrated Christian." Priests speak of the nuclear communicants as the most "dependable" people in the parish.

Fichter found that the "nuclear" tends to come from a "good" Catholic family and is, therefore, a born Catholic rather than a convert. He is a representative of the salaried and wage earner groups rather than the self-employed and professional groups. His relations with the clergy are spontaneous and cordial. The nuclear is orthodox in belief and "thinks with the church."

He doesn't question the relevancy or propriety that the Legion of Decency or birth control has for him. The religious institution is central, or pivotal, for him, and thus whenever sacred and secular values are in conflict he goes with the church and against the prevailing values of secular culture. The nuclears are the heart of the parish—what makes the church

---

[43] *Ibid.*, pp. 9–79.

tick—but they constitute only 10 percent of the affiliated Catholics in a typical parish.

The largest group of Catholics, which makes up 70 percent of the affiliated Catholics in the representative parish, is termed the *modal*. The modal parishioner attends mass regularly except on Holy Days of Obligation that fall during the workweek. He generally observes the laws of abstinence and is enrolled in some church organization even though he may not be very active in it. He holds a kind of aloof respect for the priests and the nuns, and his children attend the parochial schools. He chooses, however, to associate with non-Catholics of the same education, social class, and ethnic and racial background in preference to Catholics who differ from him in any of these respects. He is the ordinary or average Catholic—not the "best of Catholicism" but the "most of Catholicism."

About 20 percent of the affiliates of the parish are *marginal* Catholics. The marginal Catholic is irregular in mass attendance and may even miss making his Easter duty. His children attend the public rather than the parochial schools. His financial contributions are as irregular as his attendance, and seldom generous. He may question the authority of the priests and express disagreement with those teachings of the church which interfere with his pleasures and desires. He has a tendency to "cut the corners" of his religion and to fulfill the "easy" observances only. He is marginal in belief and observance, and is motivated primarily by secular rather than by sacred values. The church and what it stands for is peripheral to his experience and behavior.

The *dormant* Catholic—the "fallen away" Catholic—does not appear on the church rolls. According to Fichter, 36 percent of the persons baptized in the parish had disappeared as far as the records were concerned. It is this group to whom the term "leakage" is often applied. The "fallen away" Catholic has been baptized and very probably married by a priest. He may also have had his children baptized in the church and may even "ask for the priest" when dying, but for all practical purposes he is lost to the church. Because he does not join a non-Catholic denomination he is considered a dormant Catholic.

The "dead" Catholic, however, is no longer dormant if he has joined another church. He may be "dead" to the Catholic parish but "alive" to his new religion.[44]

Any of a number of causes, or complex of causes, may account for the "fallen away" Catholic. Fichter found that the more important causes include parental neglect, lack of religious training, family disorganization, mixed marriage, personality of the priest, traumatic experiences, and just plain "drifting."

The term "leakage" also applies to fallen away Catholics. Two other studies by Catholic sources indicate that the leakage found among Catholics in New Orleans is fairly representative of other parts of the country.

[44] *Ibid.*, p. 69.

The chancery of the Archdiocese of Chicago made a calculation (from a year's record of Catholic baptisms and funerals) of the number of Catholics that the archdiocese should have according to the birth and death rates of the city. A total of 1.6 million was thus calculated, but only 1,000,000 were reported by the pastors of the archdiocese. A great part of the balance that did not show up in the annual Catholic census is assumed to have become dechristianized and lost to the church.[45]

A similar calculation on the basis of baptisms and birthrate shows that there should have been approximately 40 million Catholics in the country in 1952. The number reported by the Catholic Directory of that year was only 30.4 million. Here again the leakage is something in excess of one third of all identifiable Catholics.[46]

A Gallup poll found that about as many Catholics were converting to Protestantism as Protestants to Catholicism.[47] Schnepp found that leakage considerably exceeded conversions in a well-organized urban parish.[48]

Protestant

The foregoing typology could be applied with equal validity to a typical liberal Protestant congregation. The *nuclear* Protestant attends Sunday morning services regularly, and any other special services that his church may sponsor. He very probably is a member of the adult Sunday School class, or he will teach a class or assume some responsibility in relation to the Sunday School or the youth program. He is an active member of one or more of the social ministries sponsored by the church, and he may also be a member of the committees that run and administer the church: the session, the trustees, the deacons, the deaconesses, and such.

It is not uncommon in a liberal church, however, to find modal and even marginal members on some of the ranking committees. Leadership-oriented personalities (who are not particularly religious), for example, are sometimes found on the committees that handle the business and financial affairs of the church.

If the nuclear member is a parent, family worship is stressed and church attendance as a family group—along with some sort of family worship within the home—is the rule. He believes in his religion sincerely enough to be a generous contributor, and most of the church's tithers come from this group. Religious values take precedence over secular values with the nuclear member who has sufficiently internalized these values that they are reflected in his behavior; he is something more than just a "church worker."

---

[45] John G. Milhaven, "Sociological Soundings of United States Catholicism," *America*, April 30, 1955.

[46] *Ibid.*

[47] "Conversion Poll Ends in Dead Heat," *Christian Century*, April 6, 1958.

[48] Gerald J. Schnepp, *Leakage from a Catholic Parish* (Washington, D.C.: Catholic University, 1942).

The *modal* Protestant attends church service once or twice a month on the average,[49] but this is apt to be seasonal, occurring most often during fall and winter. He attends infrequently during the summer season and is easily deterred by bad weather; and he is regularly irregular. Although he does not himself attend an adult Sunday School class, he will insist upon and expend some effort to see that his children attend.

He may be a fairly active member of some social ministry, but he will avoid positions of leadership and responsibility. He will sign a pledge during the every-member canvass and make regular contributions whether he goes to church or not. He may even be quite generous—glad to "give of his dollars" because he is "too busy to give of himself."

He is not interested in "witnessing" for Christ or supporting missions. He says, in effect, that anyone who wants to join his church or his faith should be perfectly free to do so, but should come in voluntarily and not be subjected to any kind of pressure. He tends to be ambivalent in behavior; he verbalizes the sacred values, but in cases of conflict between the sacred and secular norms, the secular wins out as often as the sacred. The typical compromise is that of following the easy observances.

The *marginal* Protestant attends church only once or twice a year; a special occasion such as Easter or Christmas marks his limited attendance at worship services. He is carried on the church rolls and may make a pledge, but his contribution is small because of the "rising cost of living" and his "other expenses." His affiliation with the church may even be limited to participation in one of the social ministries: the monthly bridge meeting of the Women's Guild, or the community church league dartball team. In any case, his relationship to the church is social and recreational rather than spiritual.

He believes that Sunday School is a good thing—that it never did him "any harm"—and he wants his children to enjoy the same experience. He is probably a "curbstone" Christian who chauffeurs his children to the church, parks and reads the Sunday paper while someone else is teaching them, then picks them up at the curb after their dismissal.

A few years ago the writer helped in the every-member canvass of the local Presbyterian Church with which he is affiliated. One individual on his list of members' names did not even recognize himself as a Presbyterian and maintained it was eight years since he had attended a service.

The marginal member is also the nominal member that the Reverend Dr. John Sutherland Bonnell said "does not really count in the advancement of Christ's Kingdom."[50] They "cannot be counted on for any form of service though they are physically and mentally equipped to serve," and Dr. Bonnell recommends that the rolls be purged of all members who are not active and "effective." Few liberal Protestant churches have been able,

---

[49] See Table 8, Chapter IV.
[50] *New York Times*, June 5, 1959.

however, to generate the courage to drop the "nominal" and "marginal" from membership and communion.

The *dormant* Protestant, like the dormant Catholic, is someone who has fallen away from his original Protestant affiliations and is Protestant only because he has not yet actively identified himself with some other religious faith. Because he is not carried on any church roll, he cannot be included in the 61 percent of Americans whom the organized sects and denominations list as members. He belongs to the substantial "unchurched" group that is found in every representative community.

Such an individual was probably born into a Protestant family that was religious enough to see that he had at least some Sunday School training and experience. The chances are that he was married by a clergyman, and even now identifies himself as a Protestant because it is popular and respectable in contemporary American culture to report a religious preference. He belongs to the great unchurched group whose Protestantism becomes manifest only in cases of religious controversy. He will, for example, line up with Protestants against Catholics in such controversial issues as state aid for parochial schools, censorship of movies and books, mixed marriages, and a U.S. representative to the Vatican.

Summary

Psychological research has identified belief and feeling dimensions of religiousness. The belief dimension is conceptualized as stimulus-response verbalism, intellectual comprehension, behavioral demonstration, and comprehensive integration levels of understanding and comprehension. Belief is also conceptualized as orthodox and unorthodox. The orthodox tends to be conservative and conventional in social behavior.

The emotional-feeling dimension of religiousness is conceptualized in terms of crisis, emotional-stimulus, and gradual awakening types of religious awareness.

The belief and feeling dimensions of religiousness are subjective in nature but tend to be related to personality traits and tendencies, while personality types, in turn, help to make the various forms of religion.

Personal documents are an important source for the analysis and understanding of personality types. Well-defined personality types gravitate toward and support religious systems that harmonize with and tend to fulfill the major or characteristic needs of their respective personality patterns. The "healthy-minded" type finds himself at home in a buoyant and optimistic religious system. The "sick-soul" personality, on the other hand, gravitates toward religious systems that tend to be "other-worldly" in outlook and concerned with the problem of "evil" and the tragedy of life.

Religion, likewise, helps to make personality. Individuals who are born into a religion tend to be molded by the beliefs, attitudes, and interaction patterns that characterize the particular religious system. Catholic communicants are conditioned to find religious experience and satisfaction within a liturgical situation. Low-church Protestants find religious experience and satisfaction in more individualistic channels: through the activities of leaders or private meditation. Jewish affiliates commonly discover religious experience in a ritualistic situation within a family context.

The ways of reacting religiously are so varied that, for example, a formal low-church Protestant may react atypically by feeling most religious in a liturgical situation; a Jew may feel most religious under the spell of a leader, and a well-adjusted practicing Catholic may not feel any personal religious feeling whatever. Attention will be given in a later chapter to the religious feelings and experiences of "third force" Protestants.

The individual relates himself to his parish or congregation on one of several levels of interest and activity, and students of religious culture have developed several typologies of parishioners. In representative Catholic or Protestant congregations a hard core of highly religious and active communicants constitute the backbone of the communion. They have been termed the *nuclear* members. They attend church regularly and faithfully, assume positions of responsibility, contribute generously, and try to realize in their behavior the ideals that are taught by their faith.

Modal members are the average communicants and constitute the biggest single category. They are not very faithful in church attendance; tend to avoid roles of leadership and responsibility, and are regular but modest contributors. The *marginal* member attends church—or a social ministry—only occasionally, and his contributions are as irregular and modest as his attendance. Religious goals and activities are peripheral in his scheme of values. The *dormant* member is a Catholic or a Protestant who is no longer active. He is unchurched and dechristianized, and is Catholic or Protestant only in the sense that he has not formally joined or become affiliated with some other religious group.

Chapter IV

The Individual as a Religious Statistic

THERE ARE A NUMBER OF WAYS in which religious involvement may be registered, and some of the indices used to measure religious interest and involvement are quantitative in nature.

Religious Affiliation: Quantitative

There is no objective or scientific enumeration of church membership in the United States. The statistics which are available are those given out by official church statisticians of the 258 organized sects and denominations within the continental United States. These reports are gathered each year and published in the *Yearbook of American Churches.*

Membership as Reported by the Denominations. The 1964 *Yearbook of American Churches*[1] reported that 1962 membership was 63.4 percent of the population, the same percentage as in 1961. The total figure of church membership for 1962 exceeded that for 1961 by 1.6 percent, but during this period the population also increased by 1.6 percent, marking the second year since World War II (1961 was the first year) that church membership had not increased at a faster rate than the population. Although the overall membership rise was an average for all the major faiths, the Catholic Church gained members at a rate of 2.3 percent and the Protestant churches at a rate of 0.77 percent.

The figures given out by the various sects and denominations are not comparable because of the differing definitions of membership and affili-

---

[1] National Council of the Churches of Christ in the U.S.A., *Yearbook of American Churches, 1964,* New York, p. 252.

ation. Most Protestant bodies report as members only persons who have attained full membership, almost all of whom are 13 years of age or over.

The Roman Catholic Church, the Lutheran bodies, the Protestant Episcopal Church, and the Moravian bodies report as members the total number of baptized persons, including infants. The Jews regard all Jews

TABLE 2
CHURCH MEMBERSHIP STATISTICS*

	No. of Bodies	No. of Churches	Members
Buddhist	1	55	60,000
Old Catholic, Polish National Catholic, Armenian Church of North America	7	348	597,372
Eastern Churches	20	1,454	3,001,751
Jewish Congregations†	1	4,079	5,509,000
Roman Catholic	1	23,412	43,847,938
Protestant	222	289,892	64,929,914
Totals	252	319,240	117,946,002
Protestant			
Baptist	28	92,242	21,643,490
Methodist	21	54,813	12,739,925
Lutheran	11	17,092	8,356,656
Presbyterian	10	14,578	4,361,344
Christian Churches (Disciples of Christ) International Convention and Churches of Christ	2	26,473	4,029,046
Protestant Episcopal	1	7,096	3,317,870
United Church of Christ‡	1	6,894	2,056,696
Church of Jesus Christ of Latter-Day Saints	1	3,780	1,682,096
Evangelical United Brethren	1	4,212	756,596
Assemblies of God	1	8,302	514,532
Reformed Bodies	6	1,594	507,751
Churches of God	11	9,570	485,010
Church of God in Christ	1	4,150	419,466
Pentecostal Assemblies	12	5,223	404,611
Seventh Day Adventists	1	3,261	335,765
Church of the Nazarene	1	4,509	323,491
Jehovah's Witness	1	4,564	286,908
Salvation Army	1	1,241	259,955
Brethren (German Baptists)	4	1,413	250,227
Spiritualists	3	419	173,001
Mennonite Bodies	12	1,746	164,440
Reorganized Church of Jesus Christ of Latter-Day Saints	1	962	159,336
Unitarians Universalist Association	1	1,043	153,689
Friends	8	1,096	128,495
Other Protestants	82	13,619	1,419,545
Totals	222	289,892	64,929,941

° Benson Y. Landis (ed.), *Yearbook of American Churches, 1964.*
† Includes Orthodox, Conservative, and Reform.
‡ New body formed by merger of Congregational-Christian and Evangelical and Reformed churches.

who live in communities having congregations as members. The Eastern Churches generally report estimates of the total number of persons within the cultural or nationality group served.[2] (The Christian Science Church does not furnish membership figures because of a regulation that forbids "the numbering of people and the reporting of statistics for publication.") According to the 1936 Census of Religious Bodies, published by the United States Bureau of the Census, there were 268,915 members of the Christian Science Church.[3] It is generally assumed that there are no fewer than that number of Christian Scientists today—and probably more.

The principle of separation of Church and State makes religion competitive in the United States. Sects and denominations vie with one another for members and in rate of growth. Protestant sources have adjusted the stated membership figures as they appear in the *Yearbook of American Churches* to include two additional categories: 1) a membership constituency that is made up of all church-affiliated persons, including infants, and 2) communicants aged 13 and over.[4]

TABLE 3
CHURCH MEMBERSHIP
CURRENT AND ADJUSTED ESTIMATES

Major Faiths	Current Reported Figures	Church-Affiliated Totals	
		Membership Constituency	Communicants Age 13 and Over
Protestant	59,822,777	87,750,000	58,500,000
Roman Catholic	35,846,477	35,846,477	21,550,000
Jewish	5,500,000	5,500,000	3,600,000
Eastern Orthodox	2,540,466	2,540,446	1,730,000
Others	478,878	478,978	320,000
Totals	104,188,698	132,115,901	85,700,000

Presbyterian Life, October 1, 1958, p. 24.

By using the "constituent membership" test for 1957, 78 rather than 61 percent of Americans would have been found to be church-affiliated. In either case the Protestant category would be a larger percent of the total of church affiliation than the current "Reported Figures" test indicates.

The Individual and Religious Preference. A number of studies of religious affiliation and preference all show that over 90 percent of the American people claim an affiliation or preference. Thus, about one-half again as many persons claim a religious identification or preference as the combined sects and denominations report upon their church rolls. Overtly, at

---

[2] Benson Y. Landis, "A Guide to the Literature on Statistics of Religious Affiliation with Reference to Related Social Studies," *Journal of the American Statistical Association,* Vol. 54 (June, 1959), p. 337.

[3] *Yearbook of American Churches, 1963, op. cit.,* p. 249.

[4] *Presbyterian Life,* October 1, 1958, p. 24.

least, the American people are eager to be associated with a formal religious group.

In 1957 the Bureau of Census sought to obtain the religious preference of the American people by asking a nationwide sample of 35,000 families the question "What is your religion?" and the replies received from persons aged 14 and over were extrapolated for the entire civilian population. It was estimated that there were 119,333,000 persons aged 14 and over in March, 1957.[5]

TABLE 4

RELIGIOUS PREFERENCE

Religion	Total	Percent of Distribution
Population (14 years and over)	119,333,000	100.0
Protestant	78,952,000	66.2
Baptist	23,525,000	19.7
Lutheran	8,417,000	7.1
Methodist	16,676,000	14.0
Presbyterian	6,656,000	5.6
Other Protestant	23,678,000	19.8
Roman Catholic	30,669,000	25.7
Jewish	3,868,000	3.2
Other Religions	1,545,000	1.3
No Religion	3,195,000	2.7
Religion not reported	1,104,000	0.9

United States Department of Commerce, Bureau of the Census, *Current Population Reports,* "Religion Reported by the Civilian Population of the United States, March, 1957."

Only the four largest Protestant families of denominations were separately tabulated. Those adhering to the Eastern Churches were included in the total of "Other Religions." Those professing a religious preference included persons who are regarded and reported as members by the particular church or sect and those who are not so regarded and reported. The total of "No Religion" and "Religion not recorded" is less than 4 percent of the total sample. The final tabulation showed that two out of three persons 14 years of age and over regard themselves as Protestant, and one out of four as Roman Catholic.

Studies of religious preferences in 1950 by the National Council of Churches of Christ[6] and in 1955 by a Gallup public opinion poll[7] showed that more than 92 percent of the general population had a religious preference. A religious experience and attitude study of a representative sample

---

[5] United States Department of Commerce, Bureau of the Census, *Current Population Reports,* "Religion Reported by the Civilian Population of the United States, March 1957," Series P-20, No. 79, 1958.

[6] National Council of Churches of Christ in the U.S.A., *Information Service,* January 21, 1950.

[7] *Public Opinion News Service,* Princeton, N.J., March 20, 1955.

of State University of New York students found that 94 percent claimed a religious preference,[8] and a similar poll of Cornell University students showed a like response. In each case approximately eight percent reported No Preference when asked for their religious identification.

Trends in Church Affiliation. According to the records the percentage of Americans affiliated with the churches has been steadily increasing since 1850[9]—from 20 percent in 1880, for example, to 63.4 percent in 1961. These figures might appear to argue that the American people today are three times as religious as they were in 1880, but the proposition is not true because statistics during the earlier period were gathered and reported on a different basis.

TABLE 5
CHURCH MEMBERSHIP AS PERCENTAGE
OF POPULATION

1850	16%	1910	43%
1860	23	1920	43
1870	18	1930	47
1880	20	1940	49
1890	22	1950	57
1900	36	1961	63.4

Yearbook of American Churches, 1963, p. 275.

A new basis for reporting members in a number of religious bodies was adopted in 1926. Before that year a few bodies reported only heads of families as members, and a few other bodies at about that time began to report all baptized persons—infants as well as adults. The figures from 1920 and earlier were not compiled on the same basis as those of 1930 and following years.

Some students of American culture maintain that the American people are neither more nor less religious today than they were a century ago. Lipset maintains that no long-term changes in formal religion, affiliation, and practice have occurred; rather, that the most striking aspect of religious life in America is its basic continuity.[10] He credits a great deal of the alleged increases in church affiliation to wide variations in statistical reporting.

Other observers maintain that even after the statistics have been adjusted there is ample evidence to show that interest in religion is more widespread in the middle of the twentieth than it was during the nineteenth century. But taken together, all the evidence indicates a broader—if not a more intense—interest in religion.

---

[8] W. Seward Salisbury, *Religion and the College Student* (Albany, N.Y.: The Research Foundation, State University of New York, 1958), p. 4.

[9] See Table 5.

[10] Seymour Lipset, "Religion in America: What Religious Revival?" *Columbia University Forum*, Winter, 1959.

It is easier to affiliate and to remain affiliated with a representative liberal Protestant church today than it was a century ago: standards for church membership are not as strict as then. Membership is easy to achieve and few members are dropped once they go on the rolls. Nineteenth century Protestantism's more demanding philosophy of membership and behavior is illustrated by the following excerpt from the session records of a Congregational church:

The session of this period [1825] rigidly enforced church discipline and the brothers and sisters of the church conscientiously preferred charges against their fellow members in order to convince them of the error of their ways. Various charges of sin were: not obeying one's husband, habitual disrespect of husband, falsehood, slander, Sabbath breaking, being unfriendly to the pastor and defective in doctrinal views, neglect of family worship and public worship, intemperance. Members proved to have committed such sins who confessed were usually restored to good standing in the church. Those confessions which seemed to lack true repentance resulted in the individual being either suspended from membership or excommunicated.[11]

Changes from this type of belief and observance will be discussed in greater detail under Secularization of Religion, but it seems obvious that one explanation for increased affiliations with formal religion is not that the American people are becoming more religious but that religion is becoming more like American culture: more secularized.

Another explanation for the increased identification with religion is advanced by Herberg,[12] who finds that religious interest increases with *mass society*—and at the expense of rural and traditional society. As the typical urban American finds himself increasingly isolated in the "Lonely Crowd" he discovers a need for "belonging." Many isolated urban individuals recover this sense in a religious group whose various "fellowship" experiences take the place of the face-to-face organization of the small town and rural community.

Herberg also maintains that some increase in church affiliation is due to the return to religion of third and fourth generation Americans. According to his theory, first and second generation Americans, anxious to avoid every possible behavior trait that might brand them as foreign, tried to disassociate themselves from the culture of their immigrant parents. In many cases this meant leaving the religious community of their parents.

Polish and Italian Catholic, Orthodox Greek and Jewish, and Swedish and German Lutheran churches were not infrequently shunned by the new generation. But now that the third and fourth generations have been almost completely assimilated into the American social and economic structure, there has been a tendency to return to the religion of their

---

[11] Elizabeth Simpson, *Mexico, Mother of Towns* (Buffalo: J. W. Clement Co., 1948), pp. 477–496.

[12] Will Herberg, *Protestant, Catholic, Jew* (Garden City, N.Y.: Doubleday & Co., 1956), p. 276.

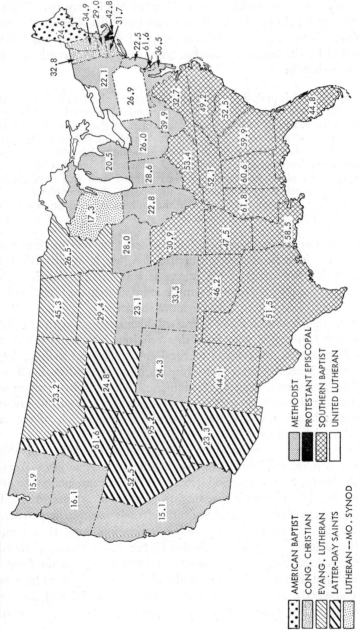

LARGEST PROTESTANT DENOMINATION WITHIN A STATE AS PERCENT OF STATE'S TOTAL REPORTED PROTESTANT MEMBERSHIP

AMERICAN BAPTIST
CONG. CHRISTIAN
EVANG. LUTHERAN
LATTER–DAY SAINTS
LUTHERAN—MO. SYNOD

METHODIST
PROTESTANT EPISCOPAL
SOUTHERN BAPTIST
UNITED LUTHERAN

Churches and Church Membership in the United States (Series C, No. 1, 1957), Bureau of Research and Survey, National Council of the Churches of Christ in the United States of America. Derived from data secured in 1952 from 114 denominations as related to the 1950 Census of Population. The 114 denominations represented 80 percent of the total of all church members reported in the United States as of that date.

REPORTED CHURCH MEMBERSHIP AS PERCENT OF TOTAL POPULATION

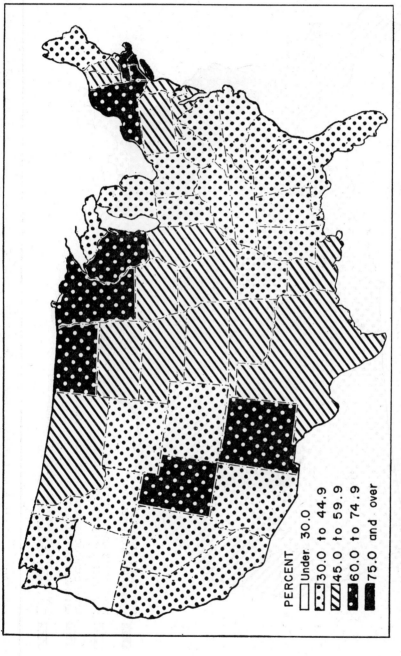

PERCENT

☐ Under 30.0
▨ 30.0 to 44.9
▨ 45.0 to 59.9
⬚ 60.0 to 74.9
■ 75.0 and over

Churches and Church Membership in the United States (Series A, No. 3, 1956), Bureau of Research and Survey, National Council of the Churches of Christ in the United States of America. Derived from data secured in 1952 from 114 denominations as related to the 1950 Census of Population. The 114 denominations represented 80 percent of the total of all church members reported in the United States as of that date.

ROMAN CATHOLICS AND ADJUSTED PROTESTANT MEMBERS RELATED TO POPULATION (LESS NEGROES)

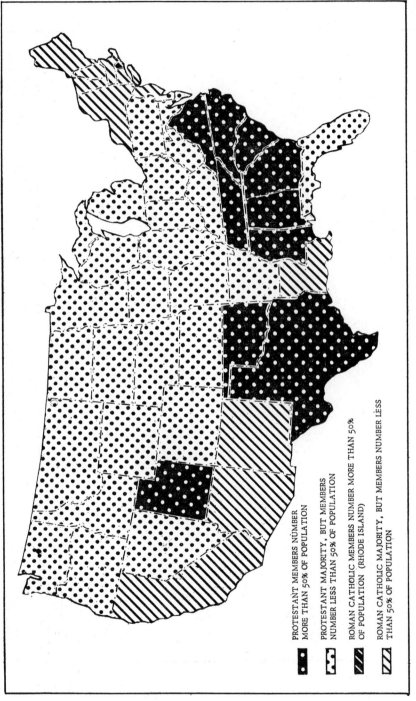

PROTESTANT MEMBERS NUMBER
MORE THAN 50% OF POPULATION

PROTESTANT MAJORITY, BUT MEMBERS
NUMBER LESS THAN 50% OF POPULATION

ROMAN CATHOLIC MEMBERS NUMBER MORE THAN 50%
OF POPULATION (RHODE ISLAND)

ROMAN CATHOLIC MAJORITY, BUT MEMBERS NUMBER LESS
THAN 50% OF POPULATION

Churches and Church Membership in the United States (*Series A, No. 4, 1956*), Bureau of Research and Survey, National Council of the Churches of Christ in the United States of America. Derived from data secured in 1952 from 114 denominations as related to the 1950 Census of Population. The 114 denominations represent 80 percent of the total of all church members reported in the United States as of that date.

ancestors—a process which Hansen has described as "children trying to remember what their parents tried to forget."[13]

The upsurge in church membership, it has been suggested, is partly due to the increase in the number of children who enter the church and of parents who follow them. Three factors, it is argued, contribute to this phenomenon: (1) An increase in the number of families with children, (2) an increase in the parents' tendency to follow their children to church, and (3) an increase in the percentage of families whose children go to church. This parade of parents into the church because of their children is said to reflect the child-centered familistic ethic of suburbia.[14]

Religious Affiliation: Qualitative

Attendance. Neither membership and affiliation reports nor statements of religious preference reveal the complete story of the importance of religion to the American people, collectively or individually. Although more than 90 percent of the American people claim a religious preference, less than half of the population attends a church service on any given Sunday.

In this connection the American Institute of Public Opinion each year conducts a sample poll of adult, civilian church attendance during the months of March, July, and December. Each person is asked "Did you attend church in the last seven days?" No more than 49 percent were found to attend church on any given Sunday. In 1959 attendance had fallen to 47 percent, where it remained for the next two years,[15] then dropped to 46 percent in 1962. Some observers interpret this relationship as a sign that the peak of national religious interest has been passed.

Attendance by Faith. Because a communicant who attends church

TABLE 6

"Did you attend church in the last seven days?"

	Yes
1954	46%
1955	49
1956	46
1957	47
1958	49
1959	47
1960	47
1961	47
1962	46

Yearbook of American Churches, 1963, p. 279.

[13] Marcus Lee Hansen, *The Problem of the Third Generation Immigrant* (Rock Island, Ill.: Augustana Historical Society, 1938), pp. 9–10.

[14] Dennison Nash and Peter Berger, "The Child, the Family, and the 'Religious Revival' in Suburbia," *Journal for the Scientific Study of Religion*, Vol. II, No. 1 (Fall, 1962), pp. 85–94.

[15] See Table 6.

every Sunday makes a greater contribution to the strength and vitality of his church than the marginal member who attends services not more than once or twice a year, the statistics of church attendance are one measure of the relative vitality and influence of any religious group. All the polls show that Catholics have the best record of church service attendance, and Jews have the poorest.[16]

TABLE 7
CHURCH AND SYNAGOGUE ATTENDANCE

	Never Attend	Attend Irregularly	Attend Weekly
Protestants	32%	43%	25%
Roman Catholics	18	20	62
Jews	56	32	12

Catholic Digest, December, 1952.

TABLE 8
WEEKLY ATTENDANCE BY GROUPS

	Percentages Attending
Protestants	40%
Roman Catholics	74
Jews	18

Yearbook of American Churches, 1959, p. 297.

Catholics attend church about twice as frequently as Protestants, and Protestants twice as frequently as Jews.

Protestants and Jews sometimes deny that church attendance is a conclusive indication of the importance or effectiveness of religion in the life of an individual. Protestants argue that Protestantism does not recognize any imperative of church attendance (as does Catholicism) and church attendance therefore is no proper basis for a comparison of religiosity.

Jews also object to citing church attendance as a measure of the effectiveness of Judaism because many of its most important services and practices are observed as a family group within the home: one can be a good Jew without consistent and regular synagogue attendance.[17]

Participation through Contributions. Some insight into the quality of church affiliation and membership can be gained through an investigation of individual contributions. Figures on per capita gifts for all purposes are available for most of the Protestant sects and denominations,[18] and, judged by these figures, the most "effective" Protestant denominations are not the largest and best known churches. The Lutheran Church–Missouri Synod and the Presbyterian Church in the U.S.A., for example, rank 17th and 20th, respectively, for total contributions but their per capita con-

---

[16] See Tables 7 and 8.
[17] William Petersen, "Religious Statistics in the United States," *Journal for the Scientific Study of Religion,* Vol. 1, No. 2 (Spring, 1962), p. 171.
[18] See Table 9.

tributions are only one-third those of the Evangelical Free Church of America and the Free Methodist Church which rank, respectively, first and second.

TABLE 9

HIGHEST PER CAPITA GIFTS FOR ALL PURPOSES

Denomination	Membership	Gift
Evangelical Free Church of America	36,705	341.09
Free Methodist	55,655	295.26
Wesleyan Methodist	46,169	239.00
Pilgrim Holiness	33,532	199.15
Brethren in Christ	7,578	193.04
Evangelical Covenant Church of America	62,389	180.19
Orthodox Presbyterian	11,994	166.69
Friends (Ohio Yearly Meeting)	6,784	156.57
Evangelical Mennonite	2,536	149.36
Church of the Nazarene	323,491	144.16
United Brethren in Christ	21,684	140.76
Church of God (Anderson, Indiana)	145,241	130.34
Pentecostal Holiness	57,366	118.84
Baptist (North American General Conference)	52,073	111.33
Mennonite (General Conference)	35,415	112.84
Presbyterian Church of the United States (South)	928,055	105.33
Lutheran Church (Missouri Synod)	2,522,095	100.51
Evangelical Congregational	30,056	90.83
Lutheran Church (Augustana)	423,664	89.37
United Presbyterian Church, U.S.A.	3,265,234	87.90

Yearbook of American Churches, 1964, p. 277.

According to this criterion it would appear that religion is more active, vital, and genuine in smaller than in larger Protestant denominations. Per capita contributions may be even more significant because of the fact that the smaller denominations draw their support from a lower economic level.

It does not, however, necessarily follow that *every* member of the high-contributing smaller denominations is more active or a better supporter of his religion and his congregation than *some* members of the larger denominations. Each large denomination can boast of tithers who are very active and highly religious individuals and to whom religion is a vital and integrated part of their lives. There is, it seems, a tendency for the larger, more "church-like" denominations to retain marginal members whose nominal and irregular contributions offset the larger contributions of the more active members.

Mobility and Participation. Mobility tends to reduce church affiliation and church attendance among Protestants. Beers and Heflin found, for example, that the movement from farm to city tends to reduce the frequency of church attendance; the more mobile the population the lower the proportion of church members.[19]

Mobile Catholics, however, were found to be better practicing Catholics

[19] Howard Beers and Catherine Heflin, "The Urban Status of Rural Migrants," *Social Forces*, Vol. 23 (October, 1944), pp. 32–37.

than the less mobile. Urban and mobile Catholics had a better record than less mobile Catholics for Easter duties, mass attendance, reception of holy communion, and sending their children to a parochial school. On the other hand, mobile Catholics were less active in parish societies. Fichter concluded that social participation and religious observance were relatively independent variables in the parish life of the urban Catholic, who also tends to think of himself as a member of the universal Catholic Church rather than as a member of this or that particular parish.[20]

Social Class and Participation. Participation and affiliation is related to social class. Among Protestants a low incidence of home ownership and low socio-economic status is correlated with low-church membership.[21] In Flint, Michigan, white collar workers and the more highly educated attended church more often than the less educated.[22] Several studies have reported evidence suggesting that upper-class Catholics are better practicing Catholics—in keeping with Fichter's finding that nuclear Catholics had more extensive education than *modal* Catholics.[23] Girls reared in homes where the father was a professional person showed a fuller understanding of Catholic teachings on sex and the family than girls whose fathers were skilled or semi-skilled workers.[24]

Sex Ratio. Women affiliate with religious groups and participate in religious activities at a higher rate than men do, and a number of studies support the following generalizations:[25]

1. More women than men attend church each week.

2. More women than men state a belief in God.

3. More women than men engage in private prayer and meditation.

4. More women than men are members of churches.

5. Women give a higher rank to religion as a source of life satisfactions than men do.[26]

The sex ratio of membership (number of males per 100 females) varies between denominations and types of denominations. Sex ratio based on the 1936 religious census showed that several denominations had some 15 percent more women than men—the smallest sex differential that was

---

[20] Joseph H. Fichter, *Social Relations in the Urban Parish* (Chicago: University of Chicago Press, 1954), pp. 94–106.

[21] David O. Moberg, *The Church as a Social Institution* (Englewood Cliffs, New Jersey: Prentice-Hall, 1962), p. 387.

[22] Basil G. Zimmer and Amos H. Hawley, "Suburbanization and Church Participation," *Social Forces*, Vol. 37 (May, 1959), p. 351.

[23] J. H. Fichter, *op. cit.*, p. 27; and George A. Kelly, *Catholics and the Practice of the Faith* (Washington, D.C.: Catholic University Press, 1946), p. 122.

[24] W. S. Salisbury, "Religion and Secularization," *Social Forces*, Vol. 36 (March, 1958), p. 204.

[25] Michael Argyle, *Religious Behavior* (Glencoe, Ill.: The Free Press, 1959), pp. 71–79.

[26] Philip Jacob, *Changing Values in College* (New Haven, Conn.: Edward W. Hazen Foundation, 1957), pp. 19–20.

recorded.[27] This group included Eastern Orthodox, Roman Catholics, Lutherans, Mennonites, and Mormons. (In the Mormon Church, with a ratio of 99.1 to 100, men are virtually equal to women in numbers.[28])

In a second group, which included Quaker, Episcopal, Presbyterian, Unitarian, Methodist, Baptist, and Congregational denominations, women outnumbered the men by 25 to 55 percent. In a third group of denominations women outnumbered men by at least 55 percent. Included in this group were the Negro Baptist and Negro Methodist churches, Assembly of God, Church of the Nazarene, Adventists, and Pentecostals. The greatest differential of all was among Christian Scientists who had more than three women for every male member.[29]

In Orthodox synagogues men are more conspicuous than women, but because Jews number membership by families, they are not bothered by a "statistical" sex differential. In Conservative synagogues, Sklare reports, women are now more numerous than men in the Friday evening service. In many Reform synagogues women outnumber men in much the same way as in representative liberal Protestant churches; they attend services more regularly and participate in more church functions than men.

Several factors contribute to the sex differential that is found among the various denominations. Denominations that are more traditional and patriarchal, and which stress family solidarity, tend to have high sex ratios. In the Mormon religion the local ward is run by the male priesthood (the worthy males) who hold the various positions of temporal and spiritual leadership, and in one study of such a Mormon community the men outnumbered the women.[30]

Denominations which have large numbers of children involved as members tend to show a high sex ratio.[31] Because the sex ratio at birth is higher for boys than for girls, and because boys have not achieved the emancipation that might permit them to reject church attendance and religion, churches that list all baptized children as members tend to have a high ratio of male members and affiliates. Conservative churches and denominations that attract a sizable proportion of their membership as adults, such as the Assembly of God and the Church of the Nazarene, generally show a low sex ratio.

Explanation of Sex Ratio. Several theories have been advanced to explain the greater affiliation and participation of women in religion. One explanation is psychological: women are innately more religious and they react intuitively to religious stimuli.

A second explanation is sociological: women are not born religious, but,

---

[27] M. Argyle, *op. cit.*, p. 78.

[28] Glenn M. Vernon, "Background Factors in Relation to Church Orthodoxy," *Social Forces*, Vol. 34 (March, 1956), pp. 252–254.

[29] M. Argyle, *op. cit.*, p. 78.

[30] G. M. Vernon, *op. cit.*

[31] T. Lynn Smith, *Population Analysis* (New York: McGraw-Hill, 1948), pp. 186–188.

because religiousness is a product of the socialization process, they learn to become religious and the differential socialization of females within the family continues after emancipation from the family as a sex-typed association. Through socialization women are conditioned to react in terms of altruism and cooperation rather than of egocentrism and competition, and therefore tend to select interaction roles with a social-emotional rather than a task emphasis.[32] Women find these roles in religious situations.

According to another theory, women can find appropriate roles for realizing their family-oriented and culture-bearer goals within religious situations. Men, on the other hand, are conditioned to seek control over their environment and to dominate a situation; to achieve their goals and find fulfillment through their own efforts.

The traditional subordination of women, conversely, makes them subject to environments and situations over which they have little or no control. They are conditioned to submission and must seek fulfillment—or "salvation"—outside themselves, and therefore find it easier and more satisfying to submit to the authority and disciplines of religion. Religion also offers women a social outlet which men experience routinely in social contacts during the working day.

Another theory explains religious differentials in terms of guilt feelings. If a function of religion is to remove guilt feelings, the theory goes, then women need religion more than men because they have more guilt feelings, and the proportion of women, in fact, rises along the continuum from Catholicism to liberal to fundamental Protestantism, reaching the highest ratio in fundamentalist Protestant sects which emphasize sin and salvation. If God is a projected father image—as Freud hypothesized—and if children prefer the parent of the opposite sex, then girls should be attracted to a deity which is presented as a fatherly male. Catholicism differs here by offering a mother figure in the Blessed Mother—so that statistically this religion should be as attractive to men as to women.

The objection to this theory, as Argyle points out,[33] is that the assumption that children prefer the parent of the opposite sex has never been confirmed. Perhaps we should be content with merely recognizing that women are consistently more interested in and active in religion, and not be too much concerned with the variety of explanations which often are contradictory or unproved.

Religion and Age. The various studies of religion and age find that adolescence is a period of intense religious interest and high religious participation. But towards the end of adolescence a decline in religious participation begins and it continues until the low point in religious interest and participation is reached—at about age thirty. Religious interest and participation revive in the late thirties and increase with advancing years.

---

[32] Fred L. Strodtbeck and Richard D. Mann, "Sex Role Differentiation in Jury Deliberations," *Sociometry*, Vol. 19 (March, 1956), pp. 3–11.

[33] M. Argyle, *op. cit.*, p. 79.

Childhood, between the ages of two and ten, is a period of religious participation for the typical child, who is taken to church with his parents or sent to Sunday School. But adolescence, from ten to 18, is a period of intense interest and participation. In Fichter's study of Catholics, for example, the life cycle peak of mass attendance and religious participation was reached during the adolescent and parochial school period.[34] The religion of the typical Protestant is likewise heightened in early adolescence, and is also marked by great intellectual doubt and emotional turmoil. It can be a period of religious awakening and renewal—or abandonment—of the faith of childhood.

The period from 16 to 30 shows steady decline in all the criteria of religious activity.[35] This is a busy time for the typical person: he leaves home, marries, has children, and becomes established in his career.[36] Horton found the decline in church participation began in the last year of high school.[37] The reduced attendance at religious services after the student has left home and become established at college has been frequently noted.[38] In one study of 1675 students, 23 percent reported they were attending church less than when at home, but 13 percent reported they were attending more.[39] Although the larger group—which tends to withdraw from religious activity—represents the dominant trend, the smaller group, that becomes more involved and committed, should not be ignored.

After the low point in religious participation is reached at about age 30, religious interest and activity gradually rise and increase with age[40]—although church attendance falls off as advanced age makes getting out and around more difficult.

The religious interest of the elderly differs in nature and in degree from the religious interest of the adolescent. In old age the intellect and the emotions are dimmed; there is no worry about the intricacies of theology nor emotional excitement about religious matters. Old people take an increasingly active part in religious practices which have long been habitual, and their belief is primarily concerned with the central fact of God and the afterlife.[41]

Summary

Americans are eager to affiliate and identify with organized religion. Affiliation can be measured both quantitatively and qualitatively.

---

[34] J. H. Fichter, *op. cit.*, p. 91.

[35] A. C. Rosander, "Age and Sex Patterns of Social Attitudes," *Journal of Educational Psychology*, Vol. 30 (1939), p. 481.

[36] M. Argyle, *op. cit.*, p. 65.

[37] P. B. Horton, "Student Interest in the Church," *Religious Education*, Vol. 35 (1940), pp. 215–19.

[38] Allan W. Eister, "Some Aspects of Institutional Behavior with Reference to Churches," *American Sociological Review*, Vol. 17 (February, 1952), p. 64 ff.

[39] W. S. Salisbury, *Religion and the College Student*, *op. cit.*, p. 8.

[40] B. G. Zimmer and A. H. Hawley, *op. cit.*

[41] M. Argyle, *op. cit.*, p. 69.

For 15 years after World War II membership in American churches grew at a faster rate than the population, until, in 1961, membership leveled off at 63 percent of the population. The growth rate of churches at that time was a little less than the population rate causing some to argue that the saturation point in church affiliation has been reached.

In various public opinion polls more than 90 percent of the American people expressed a religious preference for one of the basic faiths or denominations. Thus approximately one-third of the population claims a religious preference but is not active enough to be listed on the rolls of any denomination or church.

Although more than 90 percent of the people are members of organized religious bodies (or claim a religious preference), less than half of the American people attend church on any given Sunday. Church attendance varies with the faith. Two-thirds to three-fourths of all Catholics attend mass each Sunday; one-fourth to one-third of all Protestants attend a Sunday service, and approximately one-sixth to one-fifth of all Jews attend a weekly Synagogue service.

A higher percentage of membership is committed to the church and faith in the smaller and more conservative Protestant denominations than in the larger Protestant denominations—if such commitment can be measured in terms of per capita contributions.

Mobility influences church participation. Mobile Protestants tend to be the least active participants. On the other hand there is evidence to indicate that mobile Catholics have a higher rate of participation than less mobile Catholics.

Women are more religious than men in terms of most of the indices: belief, attendance at services, personal meditation practices, and religious activities. Most churches and denominations, accordingly, have more women than men communicants. The denominations in which men more nearly equal women in numbers tend to be traditional and patriarchal, and to emphasize family solidarity.

Religious interest and participation varies with age. Adolescence is a period of high participation and deep commitment, and adolescents tend to be conventional and orthodox. Religious interest and participation decrease after adolescence and reach a low point around age 30, when the responsibilities of parents is greatest. Interest and participation tend to increase with age.

THEORETICAL OBSERVATIONS

The disputed question whether personality makes religion or religion makes personality may be resolved by suggesting that both statements are true. *Personality* was defined as an organization of tendencies to react, and evidence was presented indicating that certain personality tendencies lead to special types and modes of religious behavior. The "healthy-minded" reaction finds expression in religious systems that are optimistic in philosophy and outlook, while the "sick-soul" tendency is predisposed towards systems that hold a pessimistic interpretation of man as a physical organism and as a social being. This latter personality type seeks out spiritual identification with religious systems that dwell upon sin and evil, predestination and punishment.

It seems obvious, therefore, that *personality* helps create and maintain religious systems—and that religious systems tend to create personality by influencing certain types of reaction, including the "religious reaction."

The Catholic religious system conditions the individual to "feel religious" through the stimulation of ritual, while Protestant reaction varies more widely—according to the various types of Protestantism. Under the impact of a theology of sin and sanctification, heaven and hell, the individual is conditioned to express the overt emotional-crisis type of religious behavior. Under the impact of the liturgical-confirmation-Sunday School complex of religious interaction the individual is conditioned to express religious feeling with restraint. Protestantism is so varied that the "religious feeling" reaction may be brought forth in such situations as Bible meditation or unstructured leadership. Participation in the Jewish religious system predisposes the individual to "feel religious" particularly in ritual situations within the context of family relationships.

Religion, it must be agreed, by creating "tendencies to react religiously," helps to form personalities.

The "significant other" is another common stimulant for religious behavior. Numerous illustrations of the charismatic leader—the minister, priest, or pastor playing the role of the "significant other" to a parishioner —are cited on pages 58 to 60. The "significant other" is not limited to the functionary; there is a case of a pastor's wife "who gets deep down into my religious feeling" (Case 3, p. 59). At other times the "significant other" is a friend, or Sunday School teacher, or parent from whom the "actor" took his cue for religious behavior.

In one sense the return-to-religion movement following World War II represents the *reference-group* phenomenon. The return to religion was (and is) a striving for a sense of belonging, especially where mobility and urbanization contribute to *anomie*. Identification with a religious group is a practical and logical antidote to the "normlessness" of the uprooted; indeed the drive to identify is so strong that not more than six to eight percent of the American people find themselves able to resist at least a nominal religious identification. The reference-group phenomenon of religious identification is one of the most compelling imperatives in American culture.

Role concepts are basic to an understanding of the religious culture. Personalities who make the religious role central and pivotal in their hierarchy of values are the key "actors" in religious interaction systems.

The "orthodox" personality (pp. 50–51) makes the religious role central and pivotal. Not only is he belief-oriented in the traditional sense, but his behavior is characterized by regular church attendance and by the emotional-feeling type of religious awakening. He gives religious satisfaction the top position in his hierarchy of values and tends to confine associational relationships within his religious in-group. He is conservative and conventional in social behavior.

The "nuclear" parishioner also makes the religious role central and pivotal, comprehensive and diffuse, focused and intense. He attends services, accepts responsibilities and participates in parish activities, contributes generously, and chooses sacred over secular values.

The marginal parishioner illustrates *role conflict*. Because he puts secular values ahead of religious values, his religious roles become incidental and peripheral to his total activity; the marginal parishioner—by his very marginality—illustrates role conflict. He is marginal *because* the sacred role competes with the secular role—always to the disadvantage of the sacred. The disagreement which such a parishioner may have with a priest over the practice of birth control is an instance of role conflict (pp. 69, 71). The golf- rather than church-oriented Sunday is often an instance of role conflict for Protestants. The "easy observances" compromise between the standards and goals of the religious community and the standards and goals of the secular community provides continuing evidence of role conflicts.

Religious behavior involves both *action* and *interaction*. Reciprocal action between personality and group underlines the importance of interaction, which has both quantitative and qualitative dimensions. Quantitative interaction (such as church attendance) is a sustaining mechanism for religious system survival because of its repetition. Qualitative interaction (emotional experiences of intensity and depth) is the *sine qua non* for vital religious systems, which would wither and disappear but for periodic renewals through widespread cases of interactive experiences in depth.

The communicant interacts in the sanctuary with the congregation functionary and with his fellow communicants. The individual also interacts with the charismatic leader, who may or may not be a functionary.

A substantial number of individuals who sought out religious identification and affiliation in recent years typify the "other-directed" personality, as conceptualized by Riesman. The desire for a sense of belonging (identification and acceptance by a respectable religious group) has a worldly rather than an other-worldly referent. Church affiliation which results from a desire to belong is usually not an experience in depth.

On the other hand, religious culture abounds with illustrations of the "inner-directed" personality whose religious orientation is at the *comprehensive integration* level of behavior. His inner-directedness is in the form of a built-in conscience, and he has so internalized the religious ethic that he behaves—as well as thinks—in terms of religious values. He is a religiously integrated Christian, or Jew.

If religion is *functional* it will contribute to the adjustment of the individual, making it easier for him to accept his position in the group and adapt to his environment. In most of the cases that have been cited the experience of religion gave the individual peace and security, or strengthened his determination to persist in the face of difficulties and adversities. However, the functional nature of the religious experience was particularly evident in the following cases:

I am a firm believer in an afterlife and during a funeral service my faith is strengthened and my feeling of death grows less. (Case 2, p. 57)

In some sermons I feel as though God is present in the church making me feel closer to God, secure, and with a peace of mind. (Case 2, p. 58)

Participating in the services and rituals of my church gives me a feeling of security. It makes me proud to know I am part of *one* important thing—a faith of one kind. (Case 4, p. 60)

When I am thrown into a new situation and feel either lost or lonely, church gives me a feeling of belonging and companionship. (Case 7, p. 60)

I feel that when I attend church it's not an ordinary act but that I take a stand for faith and a spiritual interpretation of life. It gives one a desire to do better in this everyday life and a desire to help others. (Case 8, p. 60)

I can readily say that when I go to church I feel as if it's the perfect end of a week or the perfect beginning. As I listen to the reading of the Bible or participate in a hymn, I feel very reverent and it makes me feel relaxed and cleansed. (Case 10, p. 61)

Religion, on the other hand, is *dysfunctional* for those who find that their religious experiences are negative and disturbing—or for those who are resentful of duties they are supposed to perform or because of activities in which they cannot participate. Religion for these people is more an experience of fear and frustration than of peace and security, and many become dormant church members on whom we have only limited data.

PART III

Normative Structure of the Basic Faiths

PART III WILL DESCRIBE AND ANALYZE American religious culture in terms of church-sect typologies, social institution, social system, and respective component parts.

The Frame of Reference

There have been many attempts to classify the wide range of groups that compose the religious culture of any society into typologies—or statements of the gross differences that exist between social units or phenomena.[1]

Max Weber introduced the concept of polar types of church and sect, and his writings[2] have had an important influence on American sociological thought during the past generation. Aside from the translations of his works by Talcott Parsons, Hans Gerth, and C. Wright Mills, Weber's thought regarding religious groupings is probably even better known through the work of his student, Ernst Troeltsch.[3]

H. Richard Niebuhr was the first American student of religion to

---

[1] James M. Beshers, "Models and Theory Construction," *American Sociological Review*, Vol. 22, No. 1 (February, 1957), p. 35.

[2] Max Weber, *The Protestant Ethic and the Spirit of Capitalism* (London: Allen and Unwin, 1930).

[3] Ernst Troeltsch, *The Social Teachings of the Christian Churches* (New York: Macmillan Co., 1932).

develop a church-sect typology.[4] The church construct has generally stood for a type of religious organization that accepts the social order and is at peace with it. The sect, on the other hand at odds with prevailing cultural values, develops a subculture and remains relatively isolated and insulated from society.

Sect and Church.   The analyses of Pope[5] and Wilson[6] are two significant contributions to an understanding of the sect-church dichotomy. Pope developed comprehensive criteria for the identification of a sect or a church from his intensive study of the religious and social institutions of a southern mill town, and Wilson's analyses, although studies of religious groups in England, have American counterparts so that his conclusions seem equally valid for the American situation. The following criteria for differentiating between a sect and a church draw heavily upon the studies of Pope and of Wilson:

1. The sect is hostile or indifferent to the values of secular society and the state, while the church accepts and reinforces them.

2. The sect stresses a literal Biblical interpretation of life and is otherworldly in its orientation and emphasis. The church accepts some degree of scientific and humanistic thinking in its interpretation of life and of doctrine, and worldly success as an appropriate goal and norm for behavior.

3. In the sect personal perfection is the standard, exclusiveness is emphasized, and unworthy members are expelled. The church admits to membership all who are socially compatible with it; it accepts the standards, values, and conventional morality of the prevailing culture. It is easy to get in the church, and even the apathetic and wayward are seldom expelled.

4. The sect emphasizes congregational participation and a lay ministry, while the church delegates religious responsibility to a professionally trained ministry.

5. The sect shows a principal concern for adult membership, and its worship and ethic are adult-centered. The church is concerned that religion and religious education be adapted to the needs and interests of the child.

6. The self-conception in the sect is definitive and clear: that of an elect—a gathered remnant—that possesses special enlightenment. In the church self-conception is diffuse and unfocused; doctrinal positions are not stressed.

7. The sect is suspicious of or hostile to rival sects and is characterized by a psychology of persecution. The church, characterized by a psychology of dominance and success, exhibits disdainful pity.

---

[4] H. Richard Niebuhr, *The Social Sources of Denominationalism* (New York: Henry Holt & Co., 1929).

[5] Liston Pope, *Millhands and Preachers* (New Haven: Yale University Press, 1942), pp. 122–124.

[6] Bryan R. Wilson, "An Analysis of Sect Development," *American Sociological Review*, Vol. 24, No. 1 (February, 1959), pp. 3–15.

8. Commitment tends to be total and the religious role pivotal and central in the sect. Commitment in the church is less intense for most members and the religious role is more marginal or peripheral.

Other recent studies have expanded the church-sect concept to include six more typologies: the cult, the sect, the established or institutionalized sect, the denomination, the church, and the ecclesia.[7]

Cult. The cult is a small and very loose organization which develops where there is a lack of social order and a high degree of social atomization. The cult is usually grouped around the persuasive, or charismatic, leader. The Father Divine movement, rising out of the slums of Harlem, was characterized by cult behavior in its early days.

Sect. The sect, as noted above, is a larger grouping whose members find their individual religious needs best met in a specialized system. Secondary relationships become more important. There is an increasing differentiation among members. There are various degrees and levels of leaders, leadership, and followers. In the early days the Jehovah's Witnesses, under the leadership of Judge Rutherford, began as a sect of this type.

Established Sect. The established sect is one step further along the continuum towards the polar church type. Recruitment is more selective and the membership thereby becomes more restrictive. The established sect is national rather than local or regional, but it is still segregated and isolated. Although it continues to be in conflict with some of the prevailing values of the secular society, it has achieved respectability and power. In the colonial and early national period the Methodists and the Baptists were representative of the established-sect level.

The Class Church or Denomination. The denomination is large and tends toward homogeneity; it is at peace with or accommodated to the secular culture, and is in especial harmony with the values of the social class that dominates its membership. The denomination emphasizes creed and sacraments and "right behavior." Members are "born into" a denomination and, as adults, give at least tacit assent to the formal confession of faith.

Although the Presbyterians are typical representatives of the denomination, the great majority of Methodist and Baptist congregations have by now evolved from the established-sect into a denomination.

Ecclesia. At the far end of the continuum rests the universal church or ecclesia,[8] the large, all-embracing religious association which includes all members of a society—such as the Catholic Church in medieval Europe.

Because the principles of freedom of religion and separation of Church

---

[7] Milton Yinger, *Religion, Society, and the Individual* (New York: Macmillan Co., 1957), pp. 148–155; Harold W. Pfautz, "The Sociology of Secularization: Religious Groups," *American Journal of Sociology*, September, 1955, pp. 121–128; Joachim Wach, *Types of Religious Experience* (Chicago: University of Chicago Press, 1951), pp. 187–208.

[8] Leopold Von Wiese and Howard Becker, *Systematic Sociology* (New York: John Wiley & Sons, 1932), pp. 624–628.

and State make for variation in religion, ecclesia does not and cannot exist in American culture. In such a cultural milieu any religious system must of necessity be competitive rather than universal.

American culture does however include the interclass type of religious organization, most nearly represented by the Catholic Church, which draws its members from all levels of society. Its members are scattered throughout the social structure, do not live in segregated cells or communities, and, as is true of the ecclesia and the denomination, its members are born into Catholicism, accepting their parents' religion. Not only at peace with society, the church also supports the secular powers and values. It dispenses "grace" through sacraments that can be performed only by duly ordained functionaries, and, through a comprehensive system of religious orders for both men and women, it is capable of meeting the varied religious needs of highly differentiated individuals.

The Episcopal Church, although church-like in terms of appeal, is denomination-like in terms of class affiliation. It tends to be upper-class oriented and dominated.

Recent Research on the Church-Sect Typology. In a recent study Russell R. Dynes supports the proposition that the sect tends to appeal to and be composed of persons of lower socio-economic status, while the church tends to appeal to and be composed of persons of higher socio-economic status.[9] Dynes' study also showed that when denominational status remains constant, church or sect characteristics can still be correlated with socio-economic status.

Whether the church-sect typology is as valid for mass society as it has been for the more rural and traditional society is a subject upon which students of religious culture are not agreed. Johnson, who has been concerned with the problem of church-sect analysis in contemporary culture, finds that the distinction between a sect and a church lies primarily in the different attitudes towards the social environment and concepts of salvation. He maintains that the church type is distinguishable from the sect type by its emphasis upon salvation—or justification—through a sacramental system, whereas the sect seeks salvation through adherence to a strict moral code.[10] As a consequence of these distinctive interaction systems, the church group tends to accept the social environment in which it exists while the sect group tends to reject it.[11]

Sect Analysis after Yinger. Milton Yinger classifies sects according to the way in which they react to the secular culture and the values with which they disagree; that is acceptance, aggression, or avoidance.[12]

---

[9] Russell R. Dynes, "Church-Sect Typology and Socio-Economic Status," *American Sociological Review*, Vol. 20, No. 5 (October, 1955), p. 556.

[10] Benton Johnson, "A Critical Appraisal of Church-Sect Typology," *American Sociological Review*, Vol. 22, No. 1 (February, 1957), pp. 88–92.

[11] Benton Johnson, "On Church and Sect," *American Sociological Review*, Vol. 28, No. 4 (August, 1963), pp. 539–549.

[12] Yinger, *op. cit.*, pp. 152–153.

Acceptance. Acceptance sects are those groups which believe that the causes of frustration and religious insecurity reside in the individual rather than in society, and that it is within the power of the individual through right attitude, right thought, and right behavior to establish a rapport with God and gain religious peace and security.

Aggression. An aggression sect is a religious group that, disagreeing with the behavior and values of the prevailing culture, tries through various aggressive actions to change the prevailing behavior and values.

Avoidance. Avoidance sects are those which not only disagree with the values of the prevailing culture, but withdraw, isolate, and otherwise disassociate themselves from the values and behavior of the dominant group.

The "holiness" branch of Protestantism practices various degrees of avoidance behavior. Their religion, in general, demands such a strict code of behavior that it is difficult to associate freely with the outgroup without violating some important phase of their ethical system.

Sect Analysis after Wilson. Bryan R. Wilson also has advanced a useful and fairly comprehensive classification of sects: *Conversionist, Adventist, Introversionist,* and *Gnostic.*[13]

Conversionist. Conversionist teaching and activity centers on evangelism and seeks to alter men and the world. It holds that the Bible—literally interpreted—is the only guide to salvation, and that a conversion experience and the acceptance of Jesus as a personal saviour is the test for admission to fellowship. It accuses other religious groups of diluting or betraying Christianity, and it is also hostile to clerical learning and modernism, and opposed to scientific theories of evolution. Orthodox fundamentalist and pentecostal sects are Conversionist.

Adventist. The Adventist—or revolutionist—sect predicts a drastic alteration of the world and prepares for the new dispensation. It places great emphasis upon the allegorical and prophetic books of the Bible, from which it attempts to predict the time and circumstances of Christ's second coming. It holds that conventional Christian concepts of heaven and hell are incorrect. The resurrection of the dead for judgment is central to its eschatology, as is the belief that only those who have lived up to its doctrinal and moral teachings will participate in the new kingdom.

Admission to the fellowship is not by conversion but through an understanding of the doctrine. Evangelism, furthermore, takes the form of preaching, and emotionalism and revivalism are discouraged. Comfortably established churches and the professional clergy are regarded as perversions of Biblical injunctions and opposed as anti-Christ. The Adventist sect is likewise hostile to secular society and anticipates its early overthrow. Christadelphians are one typical example of an Adventist sect.

Introversionist. The Introversionist or Pietist sect replaces the world's values with higher ones for whose realization the highest inner resources are cultivated. And although the Bible is the source of inspiration and

---

[13] Wilson, *op. cit.*

ethical insight, the letter of the Bible is regarded as secondary to its spirit. The sect considers itself an enlightened elect and develops a strong in-group morality. It is indifferent to other religious groups and movements, and does not sanction or tolerate a professional clergy. Some Holiness movements and The Society of the Truly Inspired (Amana Community) and various Holiness movements are examples of this type of sect.

Gnostic. The Gnostic sect, accepting the world's goals, offers a new or revived interpretation of Christian teaching. It regards the Bible as allegorical and complementary to its own revelation of truth, and Christ as the "way shower" rather than as the savior. Membership is predicated upon instruction and understanding, and not upon conversion. The leaders are laymen and are regarded as teachers rather than ministers.

Gnostic sects are indifferent to other religious groups and accept secular knowledge that does not contravene doctrine. Cultural standards also are accepted and utilized. The gnostic sectarian, in short, uses his special knowledge and skill for the advancement of himself and his movement.

The fellowship represented in Adventist and Introversionist sects is *gemeinschaft* in nature, while Gnostic sects reflect *gesellschaft* relationships. The Conversionist sect has both *gemeinschaft* and *gesellschaft* characteristics.

Normative Protestantism, Catholicism, and Judaism will be next considered, but some attention will also be given to atypical Protestant sects. The special importance of the functionary in religious structures will be underlined by a chapter on the clergy, and normative structure will be analyzed in terms of partial structures (See Chapter I, pp. 21–22): belief, rituals and symbolism, organization and functionaries, and values.

Chapter V

Catholicism

THE ROMAN CATHOLIC CHURCH is all-embracing. Its dogma and doctrines are definite, and comprehensive, and promulgated with assurance. The universality of the dogma and the uniformity of the worship makes the Catholic feel at home wherever he may worship throughout the world.

In spite of the uniformity imposed by one creed and one pattern of worship, parishes can vary markedly—according to the race, ethnic background, or social class of its communicants. A parish also tends to reflect the personality of its pastor and the cultural and secular values of society.

The doctrines and practices described below are based primarily upon the lectures of a number of priests over a period of years to students of Sociology and the Sociology of Religion.[1] The priests were asked to give factual lectures about their faith, touching on doctrine and belief, ritual and symbolism, organization, and special values and emphases, and the summary statements are a reflection of what they feel are the essentials of Catholic worship and practice.

Doctrine

The church and its doctrines are based, say the priests, upon the Bible—even though Catholics do not find it necessary to prove every point of doctrine with a text from Scripture[2] and upon Tradition. Tradition is

---

[1] Unless otherwise indicated, all direct quotations are taken from sociology class lectures by parish priests.

[2] J. Elliot Ross, *The Religions of Democracy* (New York: Devin-Adair Co., 1954), p. 112.

largely the experience of the Christian community during the first two centuries of the Christian Era, and it includes teachings of the Apostles which are not inscribed in Scripture.

The Deity.   There is but "one God, the Creator of all things." God is the "Supreme Being" and a "spirit," but "a real Person Who contains in Himself all that is good: all power, wisdom, holiness, beauty and goodness. Everything that calls for adoration, for praise, for love and service is found in Him."

Catholics accept the doctrine of the Trinity: "in this one God there are three persons, the Father, the Son, and the Holy Ghost." How these three Persons are separate but united in one and the same God is a *mystery*, that is, a truth revealed by God but above natural reason. Christ, the Son of God and the Second Person of the Trinity, was the fulfillment of the prophecy of the Old Testament. Christ has two natures—human and divine—and came to earth to give men grace by which they might be redeemed from sin.

The Church.   Grace is supernatural union with God in everlasting life. However, according to the Catholic doctrine of free will,[3] the individual is free to accept or to reject God's grace. Catholics include within the church all those who profess faith in Christ, partake in the same sacramental system, and are governed by lawful pastors under the Pope. The church also exists in heaven, where it is called the Church Triumphant, and in purgatory where it is the Church Suffering. On earth it is known as the Church Militant.

Sin.   Catholicism is more specific than Protestantism in its conception of sin, which it defines as "an offense against God by thought, word, deed, or omission." According to Catholic doctrine there are three categories of sin: original, mortal, and venial sins.

Original sin is the condition which men inherit from the parents of the human race, Adam and Eve. "When Adam fell from grace by deliberately sinning against God, he plunged the whole human race into a state of guilt."

Both mortal sin and venial sin are *actual* sins—or sins the individual actually commits himself. Mortal sin is so grave that it "kills" the soul in the eyes of God by depriving it of sanctifying grace—or supernatural life. A mortal sin has three characteristics: (1) Grave matter; the thought, word, deed, or act of omission must be of very great importance, (2) Full knowledge; the mortally sinful nature of the act must be realized, although willful ignorance of the gravity is not an excuse, (3) Full consent; the will must be free to assent or dissent to the act. If one of the foregoing conditions is absent, say the act is done under compulsion or fear, the act that would otherwise be a mortal sin may be, at most, only venial.

Venial sin is an offense which does not "kill" the soul, but it displeases God, weakens faith, checks the reception of grace, and deserves temporal

---

³ *Ibid.*, p. 156.

punishment here and hereafter. "Those souls go to purgatory that depart this life in venial sin, or that have not fully paid the debt of temporal punishment due to those sins of which the guilt has been forgiven." Temporal punishment will have an end, either in this world or in the world to come. The doctrine of sin is basic to an understanding and appreciation of the sacramental system of the Catholic church.

The Sacraments. The individual attains salvation by faith and by means of the sacraments, which are defined as "outward signs of inward grace instituted by Christ." The outward sign is something that can be perceived by the senses, consisting of matter and form. The matter is the substance used in giving the Sacrament, as water in baptism, and the form consists of the words used in applying the water: "I baptize thee," etc. The inward grace is the spiritual effect produced.[4]

There are seven sacraments in the Catholic religious system, each of which is believed to have been mandated by some verse or passage in the New Testament. Baptism removes the taint of "original sin," makes the individual a Christian, a child of God, a member of the church, and an heir of heaven. Baptism also forgives actual sins and takes away all punishments due to such sins. To receive baptism worthily, adults must have the beginnings of faith, sorrow for sin, and the intention of receiving the sacrament.

Baptism. Baptism by pouring is the present practice, but baptism by immersion or sprinkling is also valid. Baptism is the prerogative of the duly ordained priest, although the church recognizes baptism without "benefit of clergy" under exceptional circumstances. Baptism by blood is achieved by unbaptized persons through martyrdom for Christ. One who has faith and intends to receive baptism of water, but who dies before actually receiving it, receives "baptism of desire."

Holy Eucharist. Through the sacrament of Holy Eucharist (Holy Communion, or the Mass) the Catholic is "nourished" in his spiritual life.[5] Participation in the Mass is the highest act of worship, and the high point of the Mass is the consecration of the host when, according to doctrine, the bread and wine become the actual Body and Blood of Christ. This change is known as Transubstantiation—not a change in form or appearance but a real change in the substance of the bread and wine.

Penance. Penance is the sacrament by which mortal and venial sins committed after baptism are forgiven. This sacrament, too, has both matter and form. The matter consists of the acts of the penitent: contrition or sorrow, confession, and satisfaction. The form is the absolution pronounced by the priest: "I absolve thee from thy sins in the name of the Father, and of the Son, and of the Holy Ghost."

[4] Francis J. Ripley, *This Is the Faith: Catholic Theology for Laymen* (St. Paul, Minn.: Catechetical Guild Educational Society, 1951), p. 202.

[5] Joseph H. Fichter, *Dynamics of a City Church* (Chicago: University of Chicago Press, 1951), p. 57.

The penitent is assumed to be a reasoning person who is capable of distinguishing right from wrong. The priest exercises for the church the "forgiveness" of sin if the individual expresses real sorrow, firmly resolves to sin no more, and if he accepts the penance pronounced by the priest. The effects are the removal of mortal and venial guilt, remission of punishment, the restoration or increase of sanctifying grace, and the return to the individual of his right to Heaven—a right which is lost by even one mortal sin.

When a child is seven years old he is supposed to have reached the "age of reason" and to know right from wrong. He then makes his first confession and First Communion.[6] Responsibility for preparing the children is usually assigned to the nun in charge of the second grade.

Confirmation. The sacrament of confirmation "strengthens" the Catholic in his faith so that he becomes a "soldier of Christ." All Catholics who have reached 10 or 11 years of age (about the fifth grade) must receive this sacrament. They must be in a state of grace, properly instructed in the truths necessary for salvation, and have a good knowledge of the catechism. The sacrament is then administered by the bishop.

Matrimony. Matrimony is the sacrament which sanctifies the contract of marriage and gives a special grace to those who receive it.[7] No human power can dissolve the bond of marriage, and under no circumstances is it ever lawful for either party to marry again during the lifetime of the other. The effect is a special grace which helps them bear the difficulties of their state, to love and be faithful to one another, and to bring up their children in the fear of God.

Holy Orders. Holy Orders is the sacrament by which bishops, priests, and other ministers of the church are ordained and receive power and grace to perform their sacred duties.

Extreme Unction. As death approaches a priest administers Extreme Unction—the last rites of the Church—by annointing the five senses. The effects of this sacrament are to comfort, prepare, and strengthen the departing soul.

The clergy emphasizes the limitations of the sacramental act itself; that is, the outward sign as distinguished from the inward grace. Unless the proper inner disposition accompanies the outward manifestation, there is no resulting grace. Through the mediation of the priest and the church the individual is helped to grace, but grace cannot be imposed upon the communicant who does not cooperate in the appropriate manner.

The Six Precepts. There are, in addition to the Ten Commandments, six precepts of the church which every Catholic is obliged to follow: Mass attendance on Sunday and Holy Days of Obligation; confession at least once a year and reception of communion during Easter Tide; fasting and

---

6 J. E. Ross, *op. cit.*, p. 149.
7 John L. Thomas, *The American Catholic Family* (Englewood Cliffs, N.J.: 1956), p. 77.

abstaining on appointed days; support of the Church with proper contributions or offerings; and compliance with the marriage laws.[8] These are minimum rules; many devout Catholics attend mass and receive communion every day.

Ritual and Symbolism

Catholicism is liturgical and ritualistic. Its standardized and uniform service is presented the same throughout the world in the universal language of Latin—dramatically, colorfully, and movingly. A great deal of meaning and feeling is involved in the rendition of a Catholic service where the appurtenances of the altar and the vestments of the priest are brought to use. The Missal on which are written the prayers of the Mass, the chalice which contains the wine, and the patent that holds the host are some of the items used in celebrating the Mass.

In preparing for the Mass the priest must ritually dress himself in various symbolic garments. The *amice* is a helmet of salvation which protects him from temptation. As the priest puts on the long white *alb*, he prays that he may thus clothe himself in purity. As he ties the *cincture* he is reminded of the cords with which Christ was bound. The *maniple* worn on the left sleeve stands for the tears and toil of Christ's sacrifice. The *stole* is both the symbol of spiritual authority and of the Cross. The outer garment, the *chasuble*, represents charity because it covers all. In the ritual of vesting for mass, the priest actually and symbolically "crosses" himself a number of times.

The religious calendar is both fixed and prescribed, and certain colors are used at the altar and on the vestments in keeping with particular feast days or the liturgical "season." Purple stands for penance and mortification and is used during Advent and Lent. Green, for hope, is used after Christmas and Easter. White, for purity, is used on the feasts of Our Lord and the Blessed Mother. Red is used in honor of martyrs and black for requiems.

The special powers with which the church invests its priests as mediators between God and worshiper, and the dramatic and colorful setting in which the mass is performed make for effective and compelling ceremony. A prominent Catholic layman, in fact, once explained that although he might not like or admire a particular priest as a person, that same priest becomes something entirely different—an *alter Christus;* a representative of God on earth—when he dons his vestments and presides at the altar.

FORMAL ORGANIZATION

The Catholic Church is organized along episcopal lines and its basic unit is the parish. All Catholics living within a given geographic area are

---

[8] Robert C. Broderick, *Concise Catholic Dictionary* (St. Paul, Minnesota: Catechetical Guild Education Society, 1943), p. 88.

members of the territorial parish which is presided over by a duly appointed pastor.

The Church, however, also recognizes national—or cultural—parishes. When a sufficient number of Catholics, who speak a language different from the dominant language of a region, desire to have their own distinctive church or service they may appeal for the establishment of a national parish. (The establishment of a "national church" also requires the consent of the central authority of the church in Rome.) One small city in the Northeast, for example, that is divided into three territorial parishes, contains a French, an Italian, a German, and a Polish national church.[9]

A number of contiguous parishes constitutes a diocese which is in the charge of a bishop, who is called an Ordinary. An Ordinary has limited teaching and governing authority which is subject to review by an appropriate Roman Congregation and ultimately by the Pope. All bishops are appointed by the Pope, but each enjoys apostolic succession—a direct succession that traces back to the Apostles who were chosen by Christ himself. An archdiocese is not a combination of dioceses but simply a diocese which is headed by an archbishop, who has the same authority as a bishop. Each bishop, moreover, is the head of his diocese and is directly responsible to the Pope to whom he reports personally every three to ten years.

The title of Cardinal is honorary and bestows no territorial jurisdiction. Cardinals, who are named by the Pope and enjoy the important right of selecting the Pope's successor, may have been picked from among the clergy—or even the laity.

Monsignor is an honorary title that carries no special teaching or jurisdictional authority. An Apostolic Delegate is the representative of the Pope for ecclesiastical affairs in a particular country. A Nuncio is the diplomatic representative of the Pope in his capacity as a temporal sovereign. A Legate is the Pope's representative for some special problem or project, such as presiding at a Eucharistic Congress.[10]

The spiritual and temporal source of the Catholic Church is found at Vatican City, Rome, where the Pope resides and where the worldwide organization is administered by a number of bureaus and departments known as Congregations. Questions concerning teaching and doctrine, the meaning of canon (church) law, the advisability of new codes and rules are some of the matters that are brought before the appropriate Congregation, whose decisions, however, must be approved by the Pope. Such a decision carries the same weight within the church as a decision of the Supreme Court does within the structure of American government.

The authority of the bishop, the cardinal, and other higher functionaries is temporal and administrative as well as religious. But the lowliest

---

[9] W. Seward Salisbury, *Organization and Practice of Religion in a Small City* (Oswego, N.Y.: The Ontario Press, 1951), p. 19.

[10] J. E. Ross, *op. cit.*, p. 105.

member of the hierarchy—an assistant pastor in an obscure parish—has almost as much *spiritual* power as the highest dignitaries.

The Pope

The Pope is the supreme religious and temporal authority of the church. His religious authority has a teaching and a governing aspect, and the former aspect may be *fallible* or *infallible*. When certain conditions are met, the Pope's teaching is *infallible* and becomes binding for all the faithful. For the rule of infallibility to apply, the Pope must speak as the supreme head of the church; he must address the whole church (not just a part of it), and he must speak on a matter of faith and morals that has been revealed in Scripture or Tradition. He must also make clear his intention of using his infallible teaching authority.

The Pope's infallible authority, however, does not extend to secular subjects and it is restricted to what has already been revealed in Scripture and Tradition; the Pope, in other words, does not possess any power of new revelation, as did the authors of the Scriptures. His authority functions, rather, as a protection from error in the interpretation of what inspired authors have already uttered.[11]

Although the Pope is infallible in faith and morals when he speaks in the name of the Church, he is otherwise a mortal man and can commit sin like any other mortal. The Pope has a confessor, an ordinary priest, to whom he makes regular confessions.

The Priests

The priests are recruited from the outstanding young Catholic males who show an interest in and aptitude for the religious life.[12] They must be of good character, in good health, and stable in mind. The period of training and preparation includes two years in college, followed by six years in a seminary. Upon ordination the young priest takes vows of obedience to his lawful superiors and of celibacy. Priests who join a religious order take a third vow, that of poverty. Regular clergy (those who live by a "rule") are primarily missionaries or teachers, while secular priests deal primarily with the laity on the parish or diocesan level.

Every priest must belong to a diocese or to a religious community, and may move from one diocese to another only with the consent of his bishop and that of the bishop into whose diocese he moves. The diocese to which a priest is assigned incurs certain obligations for his support.

Religious—such as the Benedictines, Franciscans, Dominicans, Passionists, and Jesuits—may be sent from one diocese to another independently of the bishop, but no member of the regular clergy can become a pastor of a parish without the consent of the bishop of the diocese in which the

---

[11] *Ibid.*, p. 99.

[12] J. H. Fichter, *Religion as an Occupation* (South Bend, Ind.: University of Notre Dame Press, 1961), pp. 34–58.

parish is located.[13] The newly ordained secular priest is usually assigned as an assistant priest in one of the larger parishes of the diocese where he labors under an experienced pastor to gain the skill and experience that may qualify him to administer a parish as its pastor at a later date.

Aside from his regular duties, whether in a parish on the diocesan level or within a religious community, each priest is required to read from the Roman Breviary each day. This is a book of prayer and meditation composed of passages from both the Old and the New Testaments with special attention to the Psalms. This meditation takes from 30 to 40 minutes each day.[14]

Once a priest is ordained he retains the powers and obligation of the priesthood throughout his life. The proper ecclesiastical authority may for sufficient reason, however, suspend the priest and forbid him the exercise of his powers.

In 1963 the United States was divided into 17,298 parishes which were grouped into 120 dioceses and 28 archdioceses. There were 34,465 priests to serve the parishes and dioceses, 201 bishops, 31 archbishops, and 5 cardinals. In addition the work of the church had the services of 22,075 priests in religious orders, 11,968 brothers, and 177,154 sisters.[15]

Organization: The Voluntary Associations

A comprehensive complex of associations is available within the Catholic structure for laity who wish to extend their participation in the Catholic system beyond the norms of sacramental worship. These activities combine the social and the spiritual in varying degrees, and the organization and objectives of these associations are established by *canon law*, and all are subordinated directly or indirectly to the clergy. Many of these groups have counterparts within the Protestant complex of "social ministries," but others are distinct and peculiar to the Catholic religious system.

Associations are of three types: some are parochial in nature with membership and activities confined to the parish; some are interest groups that cut across parish and even diocesan lines, while others are vocational groups and restricted to persons in a particular profession or occupation.[16]

Parochial Associations. Parochial groups are categorized according to the function and emphasis of the activity.[17] *Liturgical* groups contribute significantly to the rendering of the liturgy, and choir, usher, and Altar societies that care for the sanctuary are in this category. *Sociospiritual* groups have as their chief objective the sanctification of the individual. Children of Mary, Holy Name societies, sodalities, and Nocturnal Adora-

---

13 J. E. Ross, *op. cit.*, p. 106.

14 Robert C. Broderick, *Concise Catholic Dictionary* (St. Paul, Minn.: 1943), p. 56.

15 *The Official Catholic Directory, 1963*, P. J. Kenedy and Sons, pp. 1–2.

16 J. H. Fichter, *Social Relations in the Urban Parish* (Chicago: University of Chicago Press), 1954, p. 141.

17 *Ibid.*, p. 189.

tion societies seek the greater sanctification of the member through participation in the organization and its activities.

Some groups are primarily *educational* in nature, and the Confraternity of Christian Doctrine is probably the outstanding educational group in the typical parish. The ideal organization and program for each Confraternity include:[18] teachers of religion who conduct vacation schools for rural children with no access to Catholic schools and who instruct urban children in the public schools; "fishers" who round up pupils for instruction and members for discussion clubs, who try to reclaim fallen-away Catholics, and who distribute Catholic literature; "helpers" who perform secretarial work, provide transportation, and the like, and "parent-educators" who teach religion in the home and send their children to religious instruction.

Ameliorative groups exist to do works of mercy, such as helping the poor and comforting the sick. The St. Vincent de Paul Society for men and Daughters of Mercy Society for women are representative help groups. Other groups are primarily recreational—the Boy Scouts, Girl Scouts, Brownies, and Cubs.

Interest groups that usually cut across parish lines include such organizations as Cana Conferences, retreat leagues, Knights of Columbus, Catholic Daughters, and Young Christian Workers.

The laity appears to be increasingly attracted to the various vocational organizations and groupings. In these the layman joins fellow Catholics who are pursuing the same occupation or profession for the realization of common goals within the Catholic value system. Lawyer's guilds, doctor's guilds, and nurse's sodalities are now quite common. The Catholic Rural Life Conference represents the concern of the church for farming as a vocation and way of life with Catholic values. The Rural Life Conference tries to keep the Catholic farmer on the farm, to help him appreciate his dignity as a Christian farmer, his vocation as a servant of God and as "the servant of the servants of God." The Conference also encourages non-farmers to become farmers.[19]

Sociological studies of parochial societies indicate that such groups do much for the church and mean a lot to the active participants who are, however, a relatively small proportion of the parish. Fichter reports that less than one-half of adult Catholics are even nominally affiliated with one of the parish societies, and that the active membership even much smaller. In 23 urban southern parishes there was an average of 13.2 societies, but the active membership constituted only 3.6 percent of the total parish.[20] In his northern parish study, Schuyler found that less than

---

[18] Leo R. Ward, *Catholic Life USA* (St. Louis, Mo.: B. Herder Book Co., 1959), p. 145.

[19] *Ibid.*, p. 220.

[20] J. H. Fichter, *Social Relations in the Urban Parish*, p. 157.

10 percent of the parishioners were members of and reasonably active in a lay society.[21]

Supraparochial Associations. The great suburban growth and expansion following World War II has led to the organization of many new parishes, and from 40 to 80 percent of the Catholics in these parishes are college graduates. In general the church has found that these college graduates show little interest in parish work and parish societies. They tend to be "sacramental Christians" and little else.[22]

On the other hand, voluntary associations with religious inspiration that are supraparochial in nature seem to be multiplying and meeting a spiritual need. The development of programs of Catholic Action that involve areas that the traditional parochial societies are not equipped to handle through organization or experience have proved a challenge to many of the college graduates.

These programs are constructed with the philosophy that sanctity and salvation is a round-the-clock job, and here the college graduate can make a contribution to his fellow man, his church, and to himself. The Collegium is an organization of this type. The groups organized as Collegium tackle such problems as delinquency, housing, tenancy, segregation, right-to-work proposals, and discrimination. Where appropriate, members of the Collegium will try to influence opinion and otherwise bring pressure to bear to seek a solution of a problem in terms of Catholic principle.[23]

Considerable stimulation has been given to lay organizations on the parish and the diocesan level through affiliation with the National Council of Catholic Women and the National Council of Catholic Men. The National Council of Catholic Women provides leadership and inspiration for such activities as Pre Cana Conferences, Mothers' Circles, clothing drives, and programs for foreign students.

The National Council of Catholic Men promotes and provides information for programs on such topics as the Dead Sea Scrolls, the Catholic Press, the Liturgy, the Pope, Marriage, Communism, Child Guidance, or the Apostle Paul. The National Councils also speak for Catholic men and Catholic women on such national and international issues and problems as the UN, immigration, housing, and civil liberties.[24]

Another important lay apostolic organization now functioning in the United States is the Grail Movement, which aims to unite the talents and energies of young women of every race and nation to help turn society in a "Godward direction."[25] The Movement brings young women together to live in centers of Christian life according to the spirit of the

---

[21] Joseph B. Schuyler, *Northern Parish* (Chicago: Loyola University Press, 1960), p. 229.

[22] L. R. Ward, *op. cit.*, p. 76.

[23] *Ibid.*, pp. 78–90.

[24] *Ibid.*, p. 134.

[25] *Ibid.*, pp. 107–120.

Gospel and to bring this philosophy to bear upon the structure and institutions of modern society.

One such group is the Grailville School near Cincinnati where more than fifty girls beyond high school age and education live and work together. There is a good deal of "fellowshipping" and physical and cooperative work. There are no formal lessons and no examinations. Many go on missions; others marry and carry their vision and service into the family relationship and the community where they settle. Another Grail group is the Gateway, the center of the movement in the Detroit area. The Gateway has as its goals "fostering the life of the spirit, forming a Catholic mind, building a community, and developing a Christian culture."[26]

There are a number of other important lay and action groups that endeavor to implement Catholic values. The Cana Movement and the Christian Family Movement will be discussed elsewhere.[27]

The Retreat Movement. The retreat is a voluntary religious exercise which involves a period of temporary withdrawal from the ordinary affairs of the world for the intensified practice of religious exercises. Although it may be made privately, retreats are usually made by a group of persons under the direction of a retreat master. The purposes of a retreat are the amendment of life and general spiritual progress, and an increasing number of Catholics seem to be attracted to them each year.

Weekend retreats, from Friday evening until Sunday, are the most common in this country. Persons making a closed retreat remain at the retreat house for the entire period; those making an open retreat participate only in the exercises. Many special groups make retreats together: business and professional men, teachers, students, nurses, or men or women from the same parish or place of work. The parish retreat and single days of recollection are adaptations of the retreat idea to special purposes and circumstances.

Although lay persons are not required by Canon Law to make an annual retreat (as the religious vocations are) the practice has been encouraged by the church for many centuries. It is estimated that approximately 300,000 men and 100,000 women make retreats annually in the United States.[28]

Values

Although Catholic values are immediately concerned with various aspects of faith, morals, official beliefs, and rules of conduct, they also extend into other areas of human and social relationships. Like Catholic doctrine, Catholic morality is specific, definite, and comprehensive; there is a church position on practically every personal and ethical problem that

---

[26] *Ibid.*, p. 120.
[27] See Chapter XV, Religion and the Family.
[28] *Catholic Almanac, 1960*, p. 527.

confronts the contemporary Catholic in the field of morality and human relations. The church tries to keep abreast of the changing culture by interpreting modern problems in terms of Catholic universals.

Some of the values that are of great contemporary interest are indicated below. The church puts a high value on its ideal of family life and family behavior. A definite code of boy-girl relations is kept before young Catholics as appropriate preparation for marriage. The church is positive about birth control and divorce: they are forbidden.[29]

The church also holds that the best education is that in which religious and secular education are thoroughly integrated, and the church, therefore, places great emphasis upon parochial education. Whenever and wherever possible, the parent must seek the education of his child in a parochial school.[30]

Clean and Decent Entertainment. The Legion of Decency is a contemporary adaptation of the philosophy of education and indoctrination which the church has long exercised in its *Index*. The *Index* is a listing of books which are judged by the church to be harmful to the faith and morals of the faithful, and the reading of such books is forbidden under penalty of excommunication.[31]

With the development of a highly complex and urbanized mass society served by a variety of "mass media," the technique represented in the *Index* for guarding the faith and morals of the faithful has proved insufficient and outmoded. Not only books, but movies, plays, magazines, and television have increased to bombard the representative citizen with voluminous materials that may be "good" or "bad"—or combinations of both—in terms of Catholic principles. The development of the picture presentation of plots and situations through movies and television have added a substantial group of Catholics to the public who may be influenced by materials that are immoral according to Catholic standards.

The church's answer to the problem has been the creation of the Legion of Decency, and every Catholic is encouraged to follow its recommendations as part of his responsibility of being a good Catholic. There is no machinery (or desire, apparently) to seek enforcement of its recommendations by other than moral suasion—appeals to the communicant's conscience.

Responsibility for upholding Catholic principles of faith and morality against onslaughts from the entertainment world is delegated to the Roman Catholic Episcopal Committee for Motion Pictures, Radio, and Television—a committee of bishops. The Legion of Decency operates under the supervision of this committee. A group of specialists reviews and rates the various domestic and foreign films that are shown in the United States. The ratings are A–1 (unobjectionable for general patron-

---

29 See Chapter XV, Religion and the Family.
30 See Chapter XIV, Religion and Education.
31 Broderick, *op. cit.*, p. 178.

age), A–2 (unobjectionable for adults and adolescents), A–3 (adults only), B (objectionable in part), and C (condemned). These ratings are published throughout the country for the guidance of Catholics.

Once a year, on a designated Sunday, Catholic parishioners throughout the various dioceses are given the opportunity to take the pledge of the Legion of Decency. The pledge reads as follows:

I promise to promote by word and deed what is morally and artistically good in motion picture entertainment. I promise to discourage indecent, immoral and unwholesome motion pictures, especially by my good example and always in a responsible and civic minded manner. I promise to guide those under my care and influence in their choice of motion pictures that are morally and culturally inspiring.

I promise not to cooperate by my patronage with theatres which regularly show objectionable films. I promise as a member of the Legion of Decency to acquaint myself with its aims, to consult its classifications, and to unite with all men of goodwill in promoting high and noble standards of motion picture entertainment.[32]

In its annual report for 1960 the Bishops' Committee found a substantial increase in the number of films it deemed to be morally objectionable. Of the 222 domestic films reviewed, 66 were rated A–1, 47 as A–2, 51 as A–3, 54 as B, and 3 were condemned. The percentage of films found to be morally objectionable was 24.33, an increase from 17.59 percent the previous year. (During the same year 53 foreign-produced films were reviewed and rated as follows: 14 as A–1, 8 as A–2, 16 as A–3, 10 as B, and 5 were condemned.) The bishops also criticized what they called Hollywood's "subtle and insidious introduction into a mass medium a sensational presentation of religion."[33] The bishops asked the producers to employ selfregulation to cure the evil, stating that the "explicitly stated Catholic preference" was for self-regulation rather than censorship of films.

To another standing committee, the National Office for Decent Literature, is entrusted the responsibility of evaluating comic books, magazines, and paperback books that appear for sale on newsstands—especially for their suitability for youth. The committee reported in 1960 that 39 of the magazines it reviewed were objectionable for youth. During the same period an average of 111 books a month was reviewed and an average of 52 books was found objectionable.[34]

Integration. Neither church doctrine nor polity condones racial segregation. In the eyes of the church all men are equal before God and the church, accordingly, has embarked upon a course of action that attacks segregation at both the worship and educational levels. Negroes as Catholics, and the integration of parochial schools is discussed on pp. 469–71.

---

[32] *New York Times*, November 26, 1960.
[33] *Ibid.*, November 30, 1960.
[34] *Ibid.*, November 22, 1960.

College Action.   Some of the most effective work in the interracial field has been carried on by student organizations in the various Catholic colleges. This movement began in 1933 at the College of the Sacred Heart, Manhattanville, New York. After considerable debate within the college's Catholic Action Forum a series of resolutions was adopted which gave a moral and spiritual basis for Catholic college action and have served as a rallying point for subsequent organizations and programs in other Catholic colleges throughout the nation. The following statements are known throughout the country as the Manhattanville Resolutions:

Whereas I am enjoying the privilege of a Catholic higher education, I recognize that I have certain duties and obligations toward my fellow man, among which I must consider my conduct and attitude toward the American Negro. I therefore resolve to carry out and adhere to the following resolutions:

1. To maintain that the Negro as a human being and as a citizen is entitled to the rights of life, liberty, and pursuit of happiness, and to the essential opportunities of life and the full measure of social justice.

2. To be courteous and kind to every colored person, remembering the heavy yoke of injustice and discrimination he is bearing. To remember that no race or group in America has endured the many handicaps that are his today.

3. To say a kind word for him on every proper occasion.

4. Not to speak slightingly or use nicknames which humiliate, offend, or discourage him.

5. To remember that the Catholic Church and the Catholic program of social justice have been called "the greatest hope of the colored race."

6. To recognize that the Negro shares my membership in the Mystical Body of Christ and the privileges that flow therefrom and to conduct myself in accordance therewith.

7. To give liberally on the Sundays of the year when the collections are devoted to the heroic missionaries laboring among the Negro group.

8. To become increasingly interested in the welfare of the Negro; to engage actively in some form of Catholic Action looking to the betterment of his condition, spiritually and materially.

Work for interracial justice is now centralized and administered as a subcommission in the National Federation of Catholic College Students. This organization deals with special interest fields and vital problems through a federated commission system. The Commission on Interracial Justice recommends programs of action and prepares literature and other aids for the use of regional and local interracial units. The celebration of Interracial Justice Week on college campuses has become a noteworthy activity, celebrated in 1950 by 144 colleges—several of which were located in the South.[35]

Friendship Houses.   A dramatic and significant step in the interracial movement was initiated when Baroness Catherine de Hueck founded the Harlem Friendship House in 1938. This is a lay apostolate movement

---

[35] John La Farge, *The Catholic Viewpoint on Race Relations* (Garden City, N.Y.: Hanover House, 1960), pp. 65–68.

which is devoted to the sanctification of its members and of the social environment in which they live. Staff workers live and work under the discipline of poverty, charity, and obedience, but do not take vows. Daily mass, communion, and spiritual exercises are an integral part of the community life. Other such Houses are located in the segregated sections of Washington, Chicago, and Portland, Oregon. The Houses pursue both educational and social objectives in seeking to correct discrimination and alleviate suffering. Specific activities include adult classes, forums, libraries, reading rooms, emergency assistance, clothing, and youth programs.

Interracial Councils. Under the leadership of Father John La Farge a group of distinguished Catholic laymen, white and colored, organized the first Interracial Council in New York City in 1934 and launched a specific and carefully planned program for racial justice. This movement has spread all over the country, including the South, and one of the latest councils was established in Little Rock, Arkansas.

The councils range in membership from 15 to 700; they have common principles and objectives, and coordinated operations. In 1958 the first National Catholic Conference for Interracial Justice was held in Chicago and 34 councils were represented. The second National Conference was held in St. Louis in 1960, 45 councils in attendance, and an effort to get the country's 40,000,000 Catholics to join in an active campaign to wipe out racial prejudice was started.[36] The National Conference publishes a monthly journal, *Interracial Review,* and the councils cooperate with other community organizations, including Jewish and Protestant groups, to work on problems of human relations.

Labor and the Social Order. The church has taken a great interest in the welfare of the wage-earner and is aware of technological changes and the impact and implications these changes have for the organization of society. It sees two competing forces and ideologies at work—Marxian socialism and unmitigated free enterprise—and is equally opposed to the extreme of either position. The church takes the middle ground and places a great deal of reliance upon a cooperative resolution of economic conflicts.

The position of the church has been outlined by the American bishops in *The Church and Social Order.*[37] The bishops defend the right to own private property and the right to bequeath or inherit it, but point out that ownership has a twofold aspect, one affecting the individual and the other affecting society. To deny the individual the right to own property leads to socialism or collective ownership, while denial of the social character of ownership leads to selfish individualism that repudiates responsibility for other persons and ignores the common good.

The concentration of capital with mass employment gives rise to im-

---

[36] *New York Times,* August 27, 1960.

[37] Raphael M. Huber, *Our Bishops Speak* (Milwaukee: The Bruce Publishing Co., 1952), pp. 328–29.

personal relations and lack of understanding between capital and labor. Too often, according to the bishops, an undue portion of income has been claimed by those who own or control capital, leaving the laborer wages and working conditions that are both unreasonable and unfair. The problem is one of providing equitably for the distribution of income between those who supply capital and those who supply labor.[38]

The bishops' interpretation of the Biblical injunction that the laborer "is worthy of his hire" is that of a "living" and a "saving" wage. A living and a saving wage provides sufficient income not only for an adequate standard of living for the moment, but also savings for the future—against sickness, old age, and unemployment. If individual industries alone cannot achieve these twin objectives, then it is the responsibility of society to see that this is done by invoking the principle of social insurance.[39]

Our economic life then must be reorganized not on the disintegrating principles of individualism but on the constructive principle of social and moral unity among members of human society. In conformity with Christian principles economic power must be subordinated to human welfare, both individual and social; social incoherence and class conflict must be replaced by corporate unity and organic function; ruthless competition must give way to just and reasonable State regulations; sordid selfishness must be superseded by social justice and charity. Then only can there be a true and rational social order; then only can we eliminate the twin evils of insufficiency and insecurity; and establish the divine plan of a brotherhood of man under the fatherhood of God.[40]

The church has been diligent and active in implementing this ideal of social order, and many Catholic colleges have established departments of Industrial and Labor Relations. Some outstanding priest-professors have gained national reputations for their skill and achievements as labor arbitrators. Programs of industrial and labor education and conciliation are important features for the lay apostolate in a number of dioceses.

Works of Charity. The church places charitable works high on the list of those virtues which the Catholic can perform for the succor of his less fortunate brother and the benefit of his own immortal soul. Pope Pius XI has characterized charity as the "soul of the social order,"[41] and charity has been described as a mood, a habit of mind that expresses itself in personal and social action: the bond of solidarity and the social force for the uniting of the community and all of mankind.

The religious, as individuals and as members of religious communities, are advised that they should at all times be actively engaged in charitable services and in initiating or developing programs of social action. In many dioceses Catholic charities (hospitals, homes, and various agencies)

---

[38] *Ibid.*, p. 330.
[39] *Ibid.*, p. 332.
[40] *Ibid.*, p. 342.
[41] Melvin J. Williams, *Catholic Social Thought* (New York: Ronald Press, 1950), pp. 390–92.

are, next to education, the chief drain upon diocesan funds and personnel. In granting charity Catholics are cautioned to have due respect for one's neighbor and his rights as an individual, as a member of society, and as a child of God. The Catholic effort is varied and substantial.

Summary

The Catholic Church in the United States is an integral part of the universal Roman Catholic Church headed by the Pope, with headquarters at the Vatican, Rome. The Catholic religious system places great emphasis upon creed and the sacraments, and a liturgical service rich in symbolism and ritual attracts and holds the communicant to his religion. The administration of the sacraments ordinarily requires the services of an ordained priest, an office which occupies an almost unique position in the Catholic liturgy and sacramental system as a special mediator between God and the communicant.

A well integrated and closely knit organization, thoroughly tested by time, adversity, and innumerable special problems, is one explanation of the effectiveness and influence of the Catholic Church. The church is episcopal in organization and hierarchical in administration. It is organized into parishes, dioceses, and archdioceses, and administered by pastors, bishops, archbishops, cardinals, and finally, of course, by the Pope.

A comprehensive pattern of association, spiritual and social in nature, is available to Catholics on both the parish and diocesan levels which enriches the social and religious life of the communicant, strengthens the parish, and often serves as an effective agency of Catholic action.

The Catholic interpretation of the doctrine of the infallibility of the Pope in faith and morals has led to an extensive blueprint of approved attitudes and conduct covering most problems and situations which the individual is called upon to face in the ordinary business of living.

The church's interpretation of the Christian principle of the brotherhood of man calls for the complete integration of all races within the religious and social life of the church and of the community. The hierarchy in the South has made the integration of the Negro into the Catholic sacramental and parochial structure a project of primary and immediate concern.

The church also has a philosophy of capital and labor relations. It is equally opposed to Marxian Socialism and to unmitigated free enterprise. Both the suppliers of capital and the suppliers of labor are entitled to a fair income, and owe due consideration to each other and to the wellbeing of the social order. Departments of Labor and Industrial Relations are important features of many Catholic colleges.

The church, finally, puts great emphasis upon charity, the "soul of the social order." But charity must be extended to the needy in terms of his rights as an individual, as a member of society, and as a child of God.

Chapter VI

Normative Protestantism

Variations in Protestantism

To MAKE A SUMMARY ANALYSIS of a religious faith that includes more than 200 sects and denominations is both difficult and presumptuous. When Reformation leaders removed the priest as a mediator between God and man and gave to each individual the right and duty to commune with God directly, they set in motion a philosophy of religious "organization" that could, logically, lead to as many different religious systems as there are individual Protestants.

Factors that lead to fragmentation and divisiveness are always an integral part of the Protestant structure, and, with a philosophy of individual interpretation, it is no wonder that there are more than 200 separate and distinct Protestant religious systems. However, the number of sects and denominations is misleading; there is more similarity, and more identity of belief and practice among these groups than appears at first glance. More than 80 percent of the Americans who identify themselves as Protestant belong to one of the nine denominations that claim more than a million members. And, although American Protestantism covers a wide range of belief and doctrine, these beliefs and doctrines fall largely within one of three major theological positions that are currently represented in Protestantism.

Liberalism, Conservatism, and Neo-orthodoxy pretty well cover the formal creedal allegiance of the great majority of Protestant churches and professing Protestants, and a brief outline of these positions is a logical way to begin a discussion of contemporary Protestantism. Such an introduction, however, should give some sense of continuity with the past and, possibly, offer some clues to future developments.

Liberalism, Conservatism, and Neo-orthodoxy are ideal types rather than practical realities, although some denominations are primarily oriented around one of them. This, however, is more characteristic of the smaller denominations that tend to be conservative and fundamentalist in doctrinal outlook.

But all three theological positions can be found in some denominations, generally in the larger denominations whose churches and parishes are scattered throughout the nation. Sometimes a particular parish within a large denomination will definitely lean towards one theological position while a sister church of the same denomination (not too far away) may be oriented towards another.

Conflicting theological positions within a single denomination were dramatically illustrated in the United Presbyterian Church in 1962. The New York Presbytery removed the Reverend Dr. Stuart Hamilton Merriam from the pulpit of the Broadway Presbyterian Church. Personality factors were involved, but the underlying question was said to be a clash between the theological-evangelical and the theological-liberal positions.[1] In this case the New York Presbytery, representing the liberal position, repudiated the leadership and the theological emphasis which Dr. Merriam was giving to his pastorate.

At about the same time the conservative point of view was able to impose itself upon the liberal position. The New Jersey Synod of the United Presbyterian Church refused to permit Reverend D. John Harwood Hick to be enrolled as a member of the New Brunswick Presbytery because of his refusal to affirm belief in the doctrine of the Virgin Birth of Christ. Dr. Hick, a member of the Princeton Theological Seminary and a well-known advocate of liberalism in the church, explained his position in this statement:

> The theological question at issue is whether every Presbyterian minister must affirm a biological miracle in connection with the birth of Christ, or whether this is a secondary matter about which it is impossible for some of us to be certain. I distinguish between the central Christian faith in the Incarnation, and the theologically peripheral story of the Virgin Birth, and following St. Paul, St. John, St. Mark, and most of the other New Testament writers, I do not found my belief in the Incarnation upon the Virgin Birth tradition.[2]

Nor is it uncommon to find communicants within any given church or parish who hold opposing theological opinions. Total orthodoxy of belief is impossible because of the American's lack of concern over points of doctrinal difference, and the unwillingness of most churches to hold their members to any particular doctrinal test once the member has been admitted to full communion fellowship.

---

[1] *New York Times,* May 20, 1962.
[2] *Ibid.,* March 14, 1962.

Many faithful and loyal church members, furthermore, are not particularly aware of the existence of major doctrinal positions, and religion for this type of member is more of an emotional and spiritual experience. They may verbalize doctrine and creed without necessarily assenting to it in any strict intellectual or philosophical sense;[3] they are capable of making their own modifications or interpretation of doctrine, and in so doing achieve a perfectly appropriate Protestant accommodation.

The history of Christian theology has always been the record of a continuous conversation carried on within the church, and between the church and the world in which it lives. This has been true of the Roman Catholic Church from its beginning down to the present era, and is even more characteristic of Protestant churches.

Liberalism. The Liberal Movement in Protestantism has been an attempt to rethink Christianity in forms that are meaningful for a world that is dominated by science and subject to rapid change.[4] Protestant Liberals—more than other Christian groups—stress the right of individuals to decide for themselves what is true in religion, and they react to the challenge of modernism and science by refusing to accept religious belief on authority alone. All beliefs must pass the test of reason. The Liberal, therefore, accepts Biblical criticism, discoveries in the new sciences, and human evolution.

Liberalism at the same time places major emphasis upon the *immanence* of God.[5] According to this doctrine, God dwells in the world and works through nature. This concept reduces (if it does not eliminate) the traditional distinction between the natural and the supernatural: there are no miracles in the sense of divine intrusion into the natural order.

Liberalism rests its case on the authority of Christian experience and the religious life rather than in the Bible or dogmatic church pronouncements. The supreme authority is the life of Jesus, and Liberals like to distinguish between the "Jesus of history" and the "Christ of the creeds." They are seeking, they say, "The religion of Jesus, not the theology of Paul." They stress the humanity of Jesus and maintain that the personality of Jesus is the best clue to the nature of God: God is like Jesus—not Jesus like God.

Liberals reject the traditional Christian emphasis upon the supernatural events of Jesus' recorded life: the Virgin Birth, his physical resurrection, and the others. They also reject the traditional interpretation of the Trinity; Jesus is divine in terms of character and spiritual unity with God rather than in the sense of the Nicene Creed: he was one with God in that he lived the will of God in all things.

---

[3] See Chapter III.

[4] William Hordern, *A Layman's Guide to Protestant Theology* (New York: Macmillan Co., 1957), pp. 78 ff.

[5] John Dillenberger and Claude Welch, *Protestant Christianity* (New York: Charles Scribner's Sons, 1954), pp. 217–223.

Liberalism, stressing the dignity of man, holds that man is neither naturally good nor naturally bad. What man is and what he becomes depends a great deal upon his environment, about which man can now do a great deal. Liberals therefore reject the orthodox doctrine of the fall of man and original sin.

Liberals are not agreed on immortality, either on its nature or its importance, and some even reject it. Although a minority may hold some concept of a nonpersonal immortality of the spirit,

Most Liberals hold that faith in a future life is both important and rational. They think it is important in order that men may have an adequate perspective from which to make moral judgments. They think it is rational because a God who conserves the matter and energy of the universe, so carefully that none is destroyed, would not destroy the human mind which is a much higher manifestation of creative power than either matter or energy. Liberals have given up belief in hell and in the devil; but most of them believe in heaven. However, they profess no knowledge of what heaven is like.[6]

Liberalism is also marked by:

1. A questioning spirit which tests religious beliefs according to principles of scientific inquiry. This attitude has led to the acceptance of Biblical criticism and abandonment of the concept of the inerrant or infallible Bible.

2. A tendency to erase the line between knowledge and revelation, as well as the line between the natural and the supernatural.

3. An emphasis upon the humanity of Jesus and a primary concern for social justice and the "Social Gospel."

Conservatism. The Liberal reinterpretation of Christian doctrine and belief aroused vigorous protest from many Protestants who resented the freedom that the Liberals were taking with the Bible. These "protestants," originally known as Fundamentalists because they rested their position on what they maintained were the "minimum fundamentals" upon which Christianity must be based, are now known as Conservatives. And, although the term Conservatism once included Evangelicalism as well, Evangelicalism is now not quite as literalistic and inflexible as Fundamentalism. Billy Graham is considered an "evangelical" but not a "fundamentalist."

The Conservatives use revelation as the chief defense against Liberal attacks upon fundamental beliefs of the Christian tradition. The proof of Christianity lies, Conservatives argue, in the miracles and fulfillments of prophecy recorded in the inerrant and infallible Bible, and they reject all attempts to analyze the Bible according to principles and techniques of scientific historical research. They will not accept "higher" or "lower" Biblical criticism, maintaining that only the original manuscript, inspired by God, is free from error.

---

[6] J. Paul Williams, *What Americans Believe and How They Worship* (New York: Harper & Bros., revised edition), p. 115.

Conservatives regard the supernatural as something distinct and necessarily separate from the natural.[7] They insist upon the supernatural interpretation of Jesus' life—the Virgin Birth, the physical resurrection of the body that was three days buried, the miracles—as the fundamental proofs of God's concern and activity with men.

The Conservatives include the substitutionary atonement of Jesus for the sins of man within their minimum basic beliefs.[8] The concern for salvation is likewise a central belief and the important question for each believer is "Have I been saved?" Christ's death does not save the individual unless he "accepts" Christ as his Savior.

Most Conservatives hold to a belief in the second coming of Jesus in bodily form. The Kingdom of God is not here now in the Church, nor in a perfect society that men might build; it will transpire in the manner the Bible outlined. Jesus will return to earth and, having judged the quick and dead, will rule for a thousand years. Then at Armageddon the final battle will occur between God and Satan. The saints will go to Heaven to reside there for eternity, and the wicked will be damned to everlasting Hell.

The Conservatives don't reject science—only the science that appears inconsistent with their interpretation of the Bible or incompatible with their position on Christian dogma. Some of their leaders subscribe to a theory of "Threshold Evolution" which they find entirely in harmony with their understanding of the Bible.[9]

Yet the conservative churches are quite aware of their theological position—of where they stand and the doctrines they support. They consciously identify themselves as "conservatives" and publicize services that are "Bible-centered" on "fundamental" Christianity.[10]

Neo-orthodoxy. The Liberal faith in the "Social Gospel" and the confidence that man with science (under the inspiration of God) could create a heaven on earth was rudely shaken by the Depression and World War II. The rise and development of Nazism was proof that man is not naturally good and that there is a great deal of evil throughout the world. And then the atom bomb showed that science could easily destroy the world that Liberals had looked to science to redeem.

The easy, comfortable, and optimistic outlook that was implied in Liberalism no longer satisfied an increasing number of Protestant thinkers. Critics found that Liberalism was preoccupied with the intellectual and held a watered-down concept of God that no longer had force in a world where sin and evil were everywhere in the ascendancy. Niebuhr stated that Liberalism in its extreme form taught that "a God without wrath brought men without sin into a kingdom without judgments through

---

[7] Dillenberger and Welch, *op. cit.*, pp. 226–229.
[8] Williams, *op. cit.*, p. 105.
[9] Hordern, *op. cit.*, p. 70.
[10] Case studies of Conservative churches and communicants are described in Chapter VIII, "Third-Force Protestantism."

the ministrations of a Christ without a cross."[11] What was needed, the critics maintained, was a theology that was less subjective and man-centered, and more transcendent and God-centered.

European theology had turned back towards traditional supernatural-ism by the time American Liberalism had come under attack. The thoughts of Kierkegaard and Barth provided philosophical and theologi-cal leadership for the movement. This return to historic Christian doc-trines (with such changes as seemed mandatory as a result of modern scholarship) became known as Neo-orthodoxy.

Neo-orthodoxy attacked Liberalism's faith in reason—and the belief that man in himself possesses the resources to obey the teachings of Jesus. Reliance on reason alone is arrogance; the basic truths of Christianity are a part of the divine revelation which the Christian must accept.[12] Neo-orthodoxy reaffirms many doctrines and insights of St. Paul, St. Augus-tine, Luther, and Calvin that the Liberals had either ignored or denied be-cause they had seemed not to meet the test of "scientific" reason.

While Liberalism had been content to rest its case on the humanity of Jesus, the new theology rediscovered the Jesus of Paul and the Synoptic Gospels. The Dead Sea Scrolls and other recent archeological discoveries support the proposition that Paul's gospel about Jesus is not radically dif-ferent from Jesus' gospel about himself: that God miraculously inter-vened in the world in the person of his Son, Christ; that by himself man is lost; that cure for man's sins lies in the doctrine of salvation through faith by the grace of God. Neo-orthodoxy is a reassertion of the judg-ment of God and a reaction against the comfortable theology that stresses God's love at the expense of his majesty.

Individual Protestant churches vary in awareness of the theological position which their worship and practice represent, but the preaching and worship of most of them represents the Liberal rather than the Con-servative or Neo-orthodox position. The "Social Gospel" receives a reasonable and appropriate emphasis, the minister makes more frequent references to the compatibility of religion and science than to their con-flicts, and the social ministries take a prominent part in the total pro-gram of the church. All these are liberal traits.

Neo-orthodoxy is still largely confined to the seminaries and very little conscious neo-orthodox theology has reached down to the parish level. However, those churches that are replacing social ministries with worship services, that are reserving the central position in the sanctuary for the altar rather than the pulpit, and are otherwise giving increasing attention and emphasis to the sacramental aspects of the service, are implementing neo-orthodox theology whether they realize it or not.

This analysis of Protestantism in terms of ideal creedal types tends to

---

[11] Reinhold Niebuhr, *The Kingdom of God in America* (Chicago: Willett & Clark, 1937), p. 193.
[12] Hordern, *op. cit.*, p. 132.

ignore the structural distinctions between classical Protestantism (such as Lutheranism), which retained the church as central for the "priesthood of all believers," and the highly individualistic organizations of the non-creedal sects (Anabaptists, for example, to whom such denominations as the contemporary Baptists and Mennonites owe so much).

There is no consistent pattern of worldly orientation in the creedal types. Neo-orthodoxy has been almost as closely identified with the social gospel as Liberalism. Niebuhr[13] maintained that Christian experience and tradition must remain in politics and achieve the best possible expression of the ideal. For example, neo-orthodox personalities and groups have shown they are just as completely dedicated to racial integration as the liberal personalities and groups.

Belief and Worship at the Parish Level

The preceding summarization of the three leading theological positions in contemporary Protestantism is derived primarily from the thoughts and writings of the leaders and spokesmen of official Protestantism. They are professors in the seminaries, writers whose articles appear in religious journals and the official organs of Protestantism, administrators and staff experts in the national headquarters of each denomination. Therefore, although the sources are Protestant from the top on down, it must however be observed that the philosophy and theology of Protestantism are seldom practiced or observed within Protestantism itself.

A more complete picture of Protestantism, moreover, requires some attention to the practice of religion on the parish level. How much of the doctrine and dogma is promulgated by the pastor—or accepted by his parishioners? We therefore propose to look at Protestantism at the parish level: at the Protestantism that is seen by parish pastors. The following grass roots view is also an analysis of Sociology of Religion lectures by parish pastors over a number of years. The pastors and their churches, it should also be said, tend to be liberal in theology and practice.[14]

They are theologically liberal in that they have found it possible to reconcile their religion and the Bible with the major findings of science, and, as liberals, they place considerable emphasis upon such things as the social gospel, believing it is the duty of the good Christian to help improve the social and economic conditions of his less fortunate brothers.

Episcopal, Lutheran, Presbyterian, Baptist, Methodist, and Congregational pastors gave the lectures from which the following material was gathered, but it is not assumed that all members of the respective congregations believe, accept, and internalize all the doctrines their pastors espouse. Still, a communicant can be an active and loyal member of a church and not be particularly aware of the formal creed—or completely

---

13 Reinhold Niebuhr, *An Interpretation of Christian Ethics* (New York: Harper & Bros., 1935).

14 Conservative Protestantism is discussed in Chapter 8, "The Third Force."

accept even that of which he is aware. It is assumed only (since each of the pastors has enjoyed a relatively long tenure) that the doctrines the pastors support are acceptable to the majority of the communicants.

Doctrine

Protestant churches differ "not so much in doctrine as in organization,"[15] and the various lectures, it will be seen, support this observation. Protestant churches may differ widely in liturgy and yet still agree within a broad framework of doctrine.

The Deity. There is general agreement on the concept of God: "God is a spirit, and those who would worship Him must worship Him in spirit and in truth"; "God is a creative personal spirit"; "God is a social spirit"; "God is a redeeming spirit"; "God is the creative determiner of the universe."

Liberal Protestant doctrine also provides worldly and other-worldly aspects in the concepts of the "Kingdom of God within history [social action] and the Kingdom of God beyond history [life everlasting]."

Protestants generally accept a Trinitarian doctrine which has been described as the "Universal Fatherhood of God, the Divinity of Jesus, and the Witness of the Holy Spirit." Protestant pastors at the same time are anxious to point out that their churches do not put any emphasis on Mary.

The Church. There is essential agreement on the Church, which is defined as the "whole number of believers, visible and invisible; past, present, and future." The Church is also defined as all those (and their children) "who profess Jesus Christ throughout the world."

A Methodist pastor defines the Church as "congregations of faithful men and women throughout the world where sacraments are duly administered." Another Methodist pastor sees the Church as "the redeeming and supporting fellowship of those who are searching for salvation." A Congregationalist finds the True Church to be "any group of believers bound together in Christ who are self-governing." The Church functions to make possible "the worship of God, to inspire and instruct its members, and to proclaim the Gospel to others."

Sacraments. A sacrament is defined as an "outward and visible sign of inward Grace," and as a "vehicle leading us into the presence of God," or as "a feeling that I am right with God."

Only Communion and Baptism meet the Protestant test for a sacrament: it is commanded by Jesus (as recorded in the Bible), and it in-

---

[15] Unless otherwise indicated all direct quotes are taken from lectures given to sociology classes by parish clergymen. Comparable materials can be found in authoritative articles describing the beliefs, practices, and special values of Protestant churches by outstanding spokesmen in *A Guide to the Religions of America*, edited by Leo Rosten (New York: Simon & Schuster, 1955).

A good description of the general characteristics of Protestantism, with chapters on leading Protestant denominations, is included in Williams, *op. cit.* See also Jerald C. Brauer, *Protestantism in America* (Westminster, 1953), and Herbert W. Schneider, *Religion in 20th Century America* (Harvard University Press, 1952).

volves earthly elements. (Marriage in this connection is regarded only as a "sacramental.") Episcopalians administer Communion every Sunday, Baptists report a Communion service once a month, and Presbyterians hold the service four times a year but report a widespread desire to have Communion more often.

Communion. There is a fairly wide variation among Protestants in the meaning and significance of Communion. Baptists report that they do not have sacraments but rather two Ordinances, Baptism and The Lord's Supper. And Lutherans differ from Catholics by giving both bread and wine, although they find themselves midway between the Catholic and the Protestant concepts on the nature of the sacrament. Most Protestants do not believe that the bread and wine are changed in the Communion service or that there is any "miraculous power in the acceptance of the elements. The service is helpful only as the worshiper has faith in Him."

Most Protestant churches practice "open" Communion; anyone desirous of participating in a communion service may do so even if he was not confirmed in that denomination. The Episcopalians, however, generally hold to a "closed" communion, and worshipers must be confirmed Episcopalians in order to participate. Yet a pastor of an Episcopal church once stated that he would not inquire into religious credentials and would administer Communion to anyone who came to the communion rail.

Baptism. Although Baptism is one of the two sacraments that is recognized among Protestant denominations, there is considerable variation in the meaning and significance of the service because Liberal Protestant churches generally have departed from the orthodox concept of "original sin," according to which only Baptism could remove this taint from the child and make him eligible for immediate entrance into heaven. When "original sin" is described as the "powerful bent toward willfulness and wrongdoing in every person," the importance of baptism for the salvation of souls is greatly diminished, and it is quite common in the liberal churches to speak of the baptismal rite as a "dedication." Parents "dedicate" their child to God.

The forms of Baptism likewise vary among the churches. "Pouring, sprinkling, or total immersion are equally valid" for Lutherans, sprinkling is most common among liberal denominations, and even a Baptist pastor maintains that "total immersion is not an important doctrinal point."

Sin. Although Protestants may agree that sin can be defined as a "departing in spirit or in act from the revealed will of God," they will soon disagree on what constitutes the "revealed will of God." They have nothing as specific and definite as the Catholic categories of "venial" and "mortal" sin, and the following are representative Protestant viewpoints: "Only sin separates man from God;" "There is no sin that cannot be forgiven"; "Anything that hurts personality is sin."

Salvation. Protestants retain some of the early emphasis of the Reformation reformers upon the importance of the doctrine of "justification by faith" over the doctrine of "justification by works." According to one pastor, "justification by faith"—along with the "priesthood of all believers" and the "authority of Holy Scriptures"—is the cornerstone of the Protestant tradition. A pastor compares "by faith" and "by works" to salvation by belief and salvation by action. However, he also advises that "faith without works is dead; that good works (devotion or generosity or charity) are pleasing to God." Another spokesman explains that salvation is achieved through "trusting in Christ to free the Christian from error and sin and thereby restore him to full fellowship with God and the Church."

The Bible. Protestants place great emphasis upon the Bible as the basis for their beliefs and for the practices and organization of their churches. They also profess great respect for its authority: "Where the Bible speaks we speak, where it is silent we are silent." This dependence is also expressed as confidence in the "sufficiency of the Scriptures," and one pastor maintains that the New Testament is the best guide to faith and practice when "read with the aid of the Holy Spirit." Under these circumstances the Bible can serve as a "substitute" for a creed.

Another Protestant source describes the Bible as the "inspired record of God's disclosure of Himself to man" and "the sermon takes the central place in the Protestant service because of the emphasis that it places upon Scripture."

"The Priesthood of All Believers." According to Van Dusen, Protestants differ from Catholics most importantly in the authority of the hierarchy, the attitude toward the Virgin Mary, and the reliance upon miracles.[16] A liberal Presbyterian finds that Protestants and Catholics are in essential agreement in their concepts of God and of the Trinity, but that they differ in their beliefs concerning the state of the dead and their approach to God. For in Protestantism, only Christ stands between God and man.

Protestants therefore reject the special position which Catholicism gives to the priest as a mediator and intercessor between God and the communicant, and, rather, describe their position and doctrine in this case as a "priesthood of all believers." Specifically, Protestant pastors defend their doctrine by saying: "A pastor is not different in his capacity to feel or to witness from any of his parishioners"; "All vocations are sacred"; "There is divine significance in every calling." They also speak of the "right of private judgment," "the competency of the individual soul before God," and the importance of "direct and constant fellowship between God and each believer."

Faced with the obvious question that perhaps such concepts relegate the minister to an inconsequential position, one pastor stated that "Protestants could probably get along without a minister, and some churches do." Although Protestant worship could indeed get along without the

---

[16] Henry P. Van Dusen, "What Is a Protestant?" in Rosten, *op. cit.*, p. 113.

offices of an ordained pastor, the emphasis which their service puts upon preaching makes the pastor an indispensable functionary in even the liberal churches.

Creed and the Autonomous Churches. Baptist and Congregational pastors agree that they are pastors of essentially autonomous churches. A Baptist pastor in fact reports that his church has no creed; it is a "free church," and every communicant therefore is free to believe what he wants to believe. The important thing is to follow the "dictates of one's conscience" and to gain the "experience of religion."

A Congregational pastor likewise reports that his church has no formulated Articles of Religion because each church has the right to formulate its own creed. Furthermore, there is no prescribed form of worship, and a particular church, if it desires, can have a full liturgical service. The philosophy of such autonomous churches has been stated as "in essentials *unity*, in nonessentials *liberty*, in all *charity*."

Ritual and Symbolism

Protestant churches may hold quite similar beliefs or subscribe to like doctrines and yet differ widely in ritual and symbolism. Such differences are marked—or most apparent—between liturgical and nonliturgical churches.

Liturgical Protestantism. Neither the Episcopal nor the Lutheran service has ever departed widely from the Catholic service. According to some Lutheran pastors, in fact, their opening service is really the mass in the vernacular, with the only important difference centering on the Eucharist. When the host is consecrated in the Catholic service it *becomes* the actual body and blood of Christ (*tran*substantiation), whereas in the Lutheran service the host is *symbolic* of Christ's real and substantial presence (*con*substantiation).

Both Episcopal and Lutheran church structures have the divided chancel with nothing standing "between the people and the cross." The chancel is that part of the church which surrounds the altar and is reserved for the clergy and the choir. The lectern stands on the left, the side reserved for worship and the "Word of God," and the pulpit stands on the right, reserved for sermons and the "word of man."

There is an abundance of symbolism in the liturgical service: lighted candles, the cross, the altar raised on three steps that symbolize the Trinity —to name just a few—and the pastor conducts the service in full vestment: cassock, surplice, and stole.

The church calendar also is similar to the Catholic. In the Lutheran church, 48 of the 52 Sundays of the year correspond with the Catholic liturgy, as do the symbolic black, green, purple, and red colored vestments.

Episcopalians "stand to praise, kneel for devotion, and sit for instruction." The high-church clergy is vested during the course of services, and wear the clerical collar and black suit and hat while about their daily duties in the parish and the community.

Low-church Protestantism. Low-church worship and ritual are quite different. The pulpit is centralized and raised, and tends to dominate the church. This "centrality of the pulpit" emphasizes the importance of the congregation's instruction in the Word of God—instruction which is, of course, the pastor's interpretation of the meaning of the Bible in application to individual problems and social living. An "open Bible," the low-church way of emphasizing the Bible as the total source of faith, morality, and authority, generally rests on the pulpit.

Pastors do not wear vestments while conducting a service; the plain black outer garment that is often seen is merely a "preaching robe" and has no doctrinal or creedal significance. Then too, many low-church pastors wear only a plain suit while conducting services, and go about their parish and community business dressed in the same manner as their communicants.

In the low churches also the people stand to praise and sit to be instructed, but merely bow their heads in devotion. Communion is administered by the pastor from a table in front of the pulpit, and is taken in unison by all of the congregation after distribution by the elders. Communion is "open," and grape juice is usually used in place of wine.

Plainness marks the interior of the church. The pews and the choir loft are plain; there are no statues, or pictures, or Stations of the Cross.

A trend, however, is developing among non-liturgical churches to adopt some of the practices and worship forms of the liturgical churches. It is not uncommon, for example, to find the divided chancel in new Methodist, Presbyterian, and Baptist churches, or candles and a cross on an altar which occupies the central position. A prominent Methodist pastor, explaining why he built a church which embodied many liturgical forms, said that the most important thing his people could get from a Sunday service was an "experience of worship" that arises most importantly out of the atmosphere of the church and from the liturgy—not the "instruction" delivered by the pastor in the course of the sermon. Worship is a total experience that involves sight, sound, and color, as well as instruction.

More and more Protestant pastors now wear robes during the service, and a number of low-church ministers wear the same type of clerical garb—the collar, black suit and hat—that was formerly characteristic of their high-church colleagues.

Organization

The Voluntary Associations. Protestant churches characteristically include a comprehensive group of voluntary associations within their parish programs which are known as "social ministries." The traditional pattern of worship—Sunday morning service, Sunday School, Sunday evening service, midweek prayer meeting—has been limited in most liberal Protestant churches to the Sunday morning service and Sunday School. It was partly because of this curtailment—or "vacuum"—that the social ministries developed, combining social, religious, and fund-raising activities with varying degrees of emphasis.

The pattern is similar in most of the liberal churches: women's guilds or societies, a couples' club drawn from the younger married people, a men's club meeting once a month with a supper and a program, young peoples' religious groups with frequent social activities, Boy Scouts and Girl Scouts and occasional suppers for the families of the congregation, fund-raising suppers and bazaars by one or more societies. These—and other—organizations and activities comprise the social ministries.

Although the ministries satisfy social and religious needs, and do much constructive work for the church as well, they are no substitute, according to experienced pastors, for the Sunday morning service upon which the strength and vitality of any liberal church depends. The nature and quality of the Sunday morning worship service, these pastors believe, along with the support it receives in the form of attendance and participation by the membership, is more important than any other factor.[17]

But a number of factors contribute to the rise of the social ministries at the expense of the worship services. It is partly a case of religious institutions reflecting the social climate, and in this sense the development of the social ministries could be considered an illustration of the secularization of religion.

Protestants today are not so conscious of doctrinal differences as they were a century ago—when American Protestantism was considerably more "other-worldly." Church membership and church identification required a rather strict standard of personal conduct and behavior, and a smaller proportion of the potential Protestant population was willing and able to meet this standard.

During the rise of Liberal Protestantism, in the first half of the nineteenth century, the emphasis shifted from doctrine to social activism until, ideally, the individual saved his immortal soul by good work: through serving his fellow man. It was a shift from a religion that was primarily personal to a religion that was primarily social in nature, and the introduction, then substitution, of social ministries for worship services is a logical development in the liberal tradition.

This social emphasis, however, may also be viewed as a religious reaction to the change from traditional rural society to urban mass society; from *gemeinschaft* to *gesellschaft*, from community to association, from primary group to secondary group.

In the more rural society, as we have said, religion was more of a

---

[17] W. Seward Salisbury, *Organization and Practice of Religion in a Small City* (Oswego, New York: Ontario Press, 1951), p. 23.

family affair and there was more general emphasis upon the family. Families not only went to church as a group, there was also a strong emphasis upon family worship in the home. In contrast to this situation, contemporary church organizations tend to be graded by age and sex and so, by their very nature, require participation as individuals rather than as family groups.

At the same time the development of social ministries within the church program makes church identification attractive to many people whose commitment to religion is minor and peripheral. This consideration is all the more pertinent if it is recognized that regular church attendance and worship usually require a degree of emotional and spiritual involvement that is beyond the nominally religious person. It is to these personalities that the social ministries offer an easy means of religious identification and a sense of "belonging"[18]—with the minimum of spiritual involvement. For others religious identification is an "escape from freedom"[19] into the security of conformity and convention.

In any event, some of the credit for increased church identification during the past 40 years must go to the social ministries.

Organization of the Denominations

The three basic patterns of church organization and authority—episcopal, presbyterian, and congregational—are abundantly represented among the leading Protestant churches and denominations. In the pure, episcopal form of organization, authority rests with the bishop; with elected representatives in the presbyterian, and with the open parish meeting in the congregational form. On the American scene, however, the episcopal form is noticeably subject to democratic pressures and influences, while on the other hand the congregational form is not always as democratic in practice as it is in theory. It is considerably influenced by leadership within the congregation and subject to outside pressure from the state and other organizations.

A brief description of the organization forms of the Lutheran, Episcopal, Methodist, Presbyterian, and Baptist-Disciples groups and denominations—to which four-fifths of all American Protestants belong—should present a representative picture of the power structure and authority patterns that characterize American Protestantism.

Episcopal. Although the Protestant Episcopal Church is hierarchically organized, the authority nevertheless is rather equally divided between the clergy and the laity. At the parish level the rector is in charge of spiritual matters, but a vestry elected by the parish, is in control of finance and property—and also selects the rector (whose appointment is sub-

---

18 Will Herberg, *Protestant, Catholic, Jew* (Garden City, New York: Doubleday & Co., 1956). According to Herberg the "need to belong" is the major reason for the increased interest and identification with religion.

19 Eric Fromm, *Escape from Freedom* (New York: Rinehart & Co., 1941).

ject to the approval of the bishop). Within broad limits, however, the rector enjoys tenure for life and cannot be arbitrarily dismissed by the parish and the vestry.

The United States is divided into 74 Episcopal dioceses, each headed by a bishop who has to share authority with a Diocesan Convention—a legislative body composed of the rector and an elected representative from each parish. The dioceses are grouped into a national organization which, as the General Convention, meets every three years.

The General Convention is composed of the House of Bishops and the House of Deputies, the latter body consisting of four priests and four laymen from each diocese. A presiding bishop serves as the executive officer of a third unit, the National Council, a standing body charged with the responsibility of carrying out the decisions of the General Convention. Although this type of organization would seem to place the primary authority in the hands of the professional clergy, in practice major decisions are a consensus in which clergy and lay personnel share equal authority.

Methodist. Each Methodist congregation is governed by a local committee, called the Quarterly Conference, and grouped into a District Conference headed by the District Superintendent, a clergyman, who travels among the churches to advise and counsel and assist in every way possible. District Conferences, in turn, are organized into Annual Conferences (there are approximately 100 in the continental United States) which are composed of the pastor and one layman from each church.

The Annual Conferences are geographically grouped into five Jurisdictional Conferences so as to give regional Methodism a sense of identity and common purpose with Methodism as a great national movement.

At the very top of all these organizational structures is the General Conference, composed of equal representation from the clergy and the laity. It meets once every four years to make and modify the rules and ordinances that guide and govern the church as a national organization.

The Methodist Church, evolving as it has in structure and function, is considered to be thoroughly democratic, quite political, and characteristically American. The presiding bishop of an Annual Conference for example, originally had the authority to appoint all ministers within the jurisdiction, but now the congregations of the larger churches make their own selections and the bishop can make appointments to the smaller churches only.

Presbyterian. The Presbyterian Church, not surprisingly, is also the best illustration of the presbyterian form of church organization; that form in which there is an important intermediate body with considerable power over the affairs of the church. Each local church is governed by a Session, the minister and a group of elders elected by the congregation at an annual meeting, while the Presbytery, the intermediate body, is made up of the representatives of from 10 to 30 Sessions.

The pastor and an elder from each church constitute the governing body of the Presbytery, which must approve the ministerial selection of each church, arrange for the installation or approve a resignation, or give consent to or demand a dismissal. The Presbytery also has the power to ordain ministers, to unite and to divide churches, and otherwise to promote and guard the interests of Presbyterian worship and practice within its jurisdiction. The Presbytery stands between the minister and the local congregation, giving him a measure of security against arbitrary or capricious action by the congregation. The Presbyteries of the country are grouped into 12 regional Synods which are designed to give direction and leadership to the work and development of the church.

The church's highest authority, possessing legislative, executive, and judicial powers, is the General Assembly, which can also change the Constitution of the church. All such changes, however, must receive the approval of two-thirds of the Presbyteries to become effective.

The General Assembly, like the Presbytery, is composed of equal representation of laymen and clergy, and there is no differentiation between them within this body. It votes as a unit, and a clergyman's vote—regardless of his position in the hierarchy—carries no more weight than the vote of the humblest lay member.

In connection with the presbyterian form of organization, short mention must be made of the six major groups of Lutherans. Although their organization may appear to be episcopal in form, considerable power resides (as in the sessions and Presbyteries) at the local and intermediate levels. In the Lutheran structure, local churches are grouped into Synods and Synods are organized into National Conferences.

Congregational Organization. The largest group of American Protestants—such as the Baptists, the Disciples, the Congregationalists, and the Unitarians—is organized according to the congregational principle which places a high value on the independence of the local church in matters of organization and worship. Baptists, for example, hold a doctrine of "soul competence" according to which each individual can competently deal directly with God and has no real need for the administrations of a clergyman. Such denominations also, of course, insist upon individual interpretation of the Bible.

Individualistic doctrines such as these necessarily lead to a philosophy of congregational autonomy that vests authority to hire and to dismiss, to hold property, and to modify the service and liturgy in the open church meeting. Yet despite (or perhaps as a result of) this congregationalist autonomy there are intermediate and higher units in each denomination that exercise considerable influence because democracy at the local level frequently leaves much to be desired. If, for example, all the members do not exercise their church franchise, control of the church will pass by default into the hands of a clique, or even to outside functionaries.

These churches are usually grouped into regional, state, and national associations, and the pressure and influence that, say, a State Conference can bring to bear upon a local church is considerable. Even a threat to expel is sometimes enough to prevent a local congregation from doing something that is perfectly within its congregational right to do.

Protestant churches, whether episcopal, presbyterian or congregational in organization, function in an essentially democratic process. No bishop or national secretary or other functionary can impose a policy or implement an order that does not have the support of a substantial proportion of the laymen, although from time to time a given church or conference may act in an autocratic manner. The self-correcting process, however, soon operates and brings the action and policy in accord with the will of the members.

Values

Individualism. Protestantism, although perhaps needless to say by now, places high value on individualism. The Protestant insistence that salvation is primarily determined by direct relationship between the worshiper and God, without benefit of clergy, also leads Protestants to emphasize independence and individualism in other aspects of life.

This emphasis upon individualism is reflected in a warning against conformity that Paul Tillich, a leading spokesman of the Neo-orthodox movement, gave in a commencement address:

> The future of our country would look brighter if a few graduating students at each commencement in every college and university entered their vocational life with the decision to resist the seemingly irresistible forces of conformity of present-day society.
> [He identified the three main causes of "patternization" as:] Our technical civilization as such, the intentional imposition of patterns on the masses by interest groups, the striving for security in many people, especially in the younger generation![20]

The desirability and the worth of individual choice and of following the dictates of conscience is not limited to Protestant leaders and spokesmen. Young Protestants hold this value in such high regard that they say they will "encourage" (but not "insist") their children go to church and accept Protestant religious training and affiliation.

A representative sample of college students was asked: To what extent would you bring your children up within a positive religious atmosphere? Will you take them to church and/or Sunday School regularly? Will you encourage church attendance and affiliation? Will you discourage formal affiliation or other identification with a church or sect?

More than 95 percent replied that they would make a determined effort to see that their children received religious training and became

---

[20] Paul Tillich, *New York Times*, June 12, 1957.

identified with a church. Most of them, incidentally, also chose the permissive "encourage" to the more authoritarian "take."

They seemed to be impressed with the importance of the personal and voluntary nature of the effective religious experience. They also seemed to be sensitive to, and repelled by, any indoctrination that smacked of imposition:

"I do not believe in forcing anyone to do anything against his or her will that would affect his life in later years. If you train the child right he will want to go to church and believe in God because he wants to, not because he is forced to."

"I feel that it must come from within the person. The opportuntiy must be there, though. With this procedure I feel that the religious experience will stay with them."

"I think a person should be allowed to choose their religion and yet I think they should have some religious training and guidance."

"I believe that a person should have a basic religious belief but that each person should make a personalized decision as to how closely he will follow his religion at an age when he is capable of making intelligent decisions."[21]

Gambling a Sin. Nineteenth century Protestantism was strongly opposed to gambling, considering it a sin and a vice. Church members were forbidden to gamble and were even excommunicated if they failed to amend their ways after having been brought before the Session of their church for gambling,[22] and the Puritan tradition was largely responsible for the antigambling provisions that are found in a number of state Constitutions. Where these provisions have been modified to permit pari-mutuel betting at recognized race tracks, it is usually the organized Protestant churches that bring their influence to bear against any further weakening of the principle. Protestant groups have also led the drive against the playing of bingo in charitable, fraternal, and church organizations.

One of the latest illustrations of Protestant opposition to the extension of recognized gambling involved New York City's attempt to find additional sources of revenue to meet the steadily rising costs of city services. The mayor appointed a special committee to study off-track betting to see if its legalization might help provide additional city revenue. Protestants took the traditional stand and opposed the proposal. A prominent pastor declared that

The point in the current debate over whether to legalize off-track betting centers is the fact that if it is legalized, then the bookies could be taxed. I would certainly make no apology for gambling in any form, but of the two, off-track betting is the more insidious, for it seeks only something for nothing with no reference to the interest in, or appreciation of, horses or horse racing. The

---

[21] W. Seward Salisbury, *Religion and the College Student* (Albany, New York: The Research Foundation of the State University of New York, 1958), pp. 13–14.

[22] Elizabeth Simpson, *Mexico, Mother of Towns* (Buffalo, New York: J. W. Clement Co., 1948), pp. 477–496.

Christian job is to discourage this kind of gambling and make known the sinister nature of it and the tragic end of all addicted to it.[23]

Shortly afterwards the Protestant Council of the City of New York, the official agency of 1,700 churches from thirty-one denominations, urged the mayor to abandon his proposal.

The Council said off-track betting was morally, spiritually, and economically evil. The Council contended that wagering outside the tracks would increase the number of persons gambling on horse races, lead to legalizing other forms of gambling, promote a type of gambling that frequently leads to crime, bring about problems of administration and control, and would violate the principle widely accepted by prominent criminologists that law enforcement and not legalization is the answer to the problem of gambling control.[24]

Official Protestantism maintains its traditional stand on gambling. There is no doubt, however, that many patrons of off-track betting identify themselves as Protestants. It is also interesting to note that a prominent Protestant spokesman could differentiate between types of gambling and assert that it is not quite so bad to bet if the bettor has a real interest in horses and horse racing.

Summary

The more than 200 Protestant sects and denominations in the U.S. fall into one of three major theological positions, Liberalism, Conservatism, and Neo-orthodoxy, although the majority of communicants is affiliated with a church in the Liberal category. Liberal churches, even though they may differ widely in organization and structure, are quite similar in doctrine and belief.

Their concepts of the Deity, the Church, and two sacraments (Baptism and Communion) are in essential agreement. The liberal churches agree that salvation is gained by faith, not through works. The typical layman, however, is not very clear about the nature of the distinction between faith and works—nor really much concerned with any theological point or issue. The Bible is the final authority for faith and practice, and very little consideration is given to tradition as a source of authority. The "priesthood of all believers" whereby each worshiper enjoys direct access to God, leaving no place for the priest as a special mediator, is perhaps the most important doctrine.

There is considerable difference between liturgical (high-church) and nonliturgical (low-church) Protestant services. The liturgical is rich in ritual and symbolism, and there is a tendency among some of the low-church congregations to make their services more liturgical or ritualistic.

Protestant churches, in form and theory, show a wide variation in organization; from the episcopal to the presbyterian to the congregational.

---

23 *New York Times*, November 24, 1958.
24 *New York Times*, November 27, 1958.

But in spite of their differences in form they tend to be alike in practice. Even Episcopal bishops do not administer arbitrarily; they must proceed with due regard for the desires and feelings of the local parish and its communicants. Nor does the congregational form of organization function, even on the local level, as a pure democracy. Leadership within the parish and the influence of the intermediate and higher organizations and their respective functionaries is often strongly autocratic or oligarchic.

Protestants place a high value upon the individual approach to matters of morality and behavior, but there is still substantial support for the traditional taboos against gambling and drinking. Protestants also generally line up against attempts to legalize gambling or weaken the controls that regulate the sale and consumption of alcohol.

Chapter VII

Judaism

Variation in Judaism

JUDAISM, LIKE PROTESTANTISM, acknowledges no central authority and shows an equally wide variation in doctrine and practice, variations which are fairly well crystalized in three chief divisions or forms of Jewish thought: *Orthodox, Conservative,* and *Reform.* Although this crystalization has developed in the United States within the last century, the three denominations are still in a state of flux.

Reform Judaism (which came to the United States with the German Jews, the second great wave of Jewish immigration[1]) maintains that God reveals himself to "his people" in each generation and it therefore tends to modify belief and practice in the light of reason and experience. The classic statement of Reform principles is contained in the Pittsburgh Declaration of 1885 in which the rabbis stated that they would "accept as binding only its (the Mosaic Law's) moral laws, and maintain only such ceremonies as elevate and sanctify our lives, but reject all such as are not adopted to the views and habits of modern civilization. We recognize Judaism as a progressive religion ever striving to be in accord with the postulates of reason."[2]

Reform Judaism, in short, claims authority not only to interpret but also to amend Talmudic and even Biblical Law,[3] and, by 1900, this

---

[1] See Chapter II.
[2] *Yearbook of the Central Conference of American Rabbis,* Vol. XLV (1935), pp. 198–200.
[3] Louis Finkelstein, *Religions of Democracy* (New York: The Devin-Adair Co., 1954), p. 14.

rationalistic tendency had resulted in the elimination of almost every aspect of traditional worship (except for some retention of Hebrew[4]).

Orthodoxy, on the other hand, does not deviate from the written or the oral codes, maintaining that since the Mosaic Law is the revealed will of God, it is fixed and unchanging for all time. Orthodox rabbis, accordingly, reject any modification of traditional Judaism, either in the home or in the synagogue.

The Orthodox position was strongly reinforced by the arrival of the third and greatest wave of Jewish immigration when, between 1880 and 1924, thousands of strict Orthodox Jews poured into the country from Eastern Europe and settled in the low-income areas of our large eastern cities. They brought their rabbis with them and endeavored to pursue the same strict observance of the Law they had followed in the Old Country.

But a large number found themselves unhappy with both the Reform and the Orthodox practice of their faith. As educated children of Orthodox immigrants achieved business or professional status and moved into middle- and upper-class neighborhoods, they wanted to practice a faith and a worship that was basically Jewish but that would allow them, without prejudice to their religion or economic interests, to maintain business and social relationships with the gentile world and the secular culture. Strict Orthodoxy would isolate them from the very people on whom they depended for success in life.

Reform Judaism, however, had made such sweeping changes that it looked and sounded more like liberal Protestant worship: organ music, mixed choirs (sometimes staffed by gentile singers), a sermon in English, responsive readings, and a benediction. Conservatism thus became a movement with those Jews who were friendly to "positive" Jewish tendencies, hoping that out of them an American Judaism would emerge.[5]

Distinctions between Orthodox, Conservative, and Reform became less clear in 1937 with restatement of the Reform position. In that year the Union of American Hebrew Congregations, the central body of the Reform congregations, called for the restoration of many of the traditional symbols and customs, such as the use in the synagogue of Jewish music sung by Jewish singers, and preferably by a cantor. Other changes included the Friday night candlelighting ceremony and restoration of the Kiddush, the prayer over the wine that begins the Friday evening meal.[6]

The major features of Jewish belief and practice are outlined below, and some attention is given to the differences between Orthodox, Conservative and Reform Judaism.

---

[4] Nathan Glazer, *American Judaism* (Chicago: University of Chicago Press, 1957), p. 102.

[5] *Ibid.*, p. 98.

[6] *Ibid.*, p. 104.

Doctrine

"Ethic comes first, doctrine is secondary"—and on many points of doctrine there is considerable disagreement among the rabbis. Neither in the Torah nor the Talmud, the chief sources of law and practice, is there any "imperative of faith." Judaism does not subscribe to salvation through belief ("action counts, not one's beliefs"[7]), and because it is a way of life, no mere confession of faith makes one a Jew: belief is expressed in acceptance of its discipline rather than in a verbal formula.[8]

Nature of God. The concept of the unity of God is embodied in the prayer "Hear, O Israel, the Lord our God; the Lord is One." God is a transcendental and spiritual being who has no physical or visible form,[9] but who nevertheless is "accessible" to the individual. He is a "moral being who practices what he preaches," and everything exists because of him. He is also infinite, an attribute that "finite man cannot comprehend."

Most Jewish prophets have predicted that in the fullness of time man will gain a more complete understanding of God and will inaugurate a reign of justice and peace on earth. According to the Talmud, this age of universal peace will be established by a great yet humble teacher of the lineage of David, the Messiah. But Jews agree that Jesus is not the Messiah. "Jesus may be a great teacher but he is not a prophet; he added nothing to the religion."

Although some Jews still look for the Messiah in the form of an extraordinary descendant in the line of David, others believe that the Messianic promise has been fulfilled in the state of Israel. Many Reform and Conservative Jews, however, expect the Messianic Age will come about through the gradual enlightenment of men and the work of writers and teachers. Although one rabbi lecturer has insisted that the Messianic idea is not an important doctrine in Judaism, there is general agreement that the age will be one of profound and universal faith in God, recognition of human brotherhood, and an unprecedented knowledge of the universe.[10]

Immortality. Jews are agreed on some sort of immortality but not on its exact nature. Immortality implies the endless persistence of the human personality, which finds its complete expression in reunion with God.[11] "The Jewish religion teaches the idea of immortality in the sense that the spirit of man, having emerged from eternity, returns to the eternal world after the mortal body has crumbled."[12]

There is also a general belief in the existence of the soul, reward and punishment, and a life after death. The soul lives on if the individual has

---

[7] Unless otherwise indicated all quotations are from lectures delivered by rabbis to sociology classes.

[8] L. Finkelstein, *op. cit.*, p. 4.

[9] *Ibid.*, p. 20.

[10] *Ibid.*, p. 89.

[11] *Ibid.*, p. 24.

[12] Rabbi Louis I. Newman, reported in the *New York Times*, March 29, 1959.

been good, if otherwise it ceases to exist. Immortality is a blessing to be earned and the only place one can earn it is in this world.[13]

Endless communion with God is the highest reward that man can attain and its loss is his greatest punishment. Some rabbinic authorities therefore hold that even sinful people may obtain immortal life after undergoing temporary suffering after death, and the Talmud, in fact, is the authority for the belief that punishment for even the most sinful soul is limited to one year.[14] According to one rabbi, heaven and hell are merely reference points, and some modernists profess belief in only a collective "world soul" or in the "redemption of man as a whole," and reject the idea of individual salvation or an individual savior. "The reward of the good life *is* the good life" is another "substitute" notion.

Judaism has no belief in the fall of man or original sin, and does not attribute man's backsliding to this cause. Adam was created pure and endowed with the power (free will) to choose between alternatives. Man, likewise, is born untainted and endowed with the capacity to know the difference between good and evil.[15]

Creeds of Maimonides. Maimonides, the great Jewish medieval scholar, promulgated the Thirteen Creeds which express in beautiful and majestic language the Hebrew monotheistic concept, but which are in no sense an official confession of faith. In spite of Maimonides' great influence upon Jewish thought and belief in the following centuries, many modernist Jews refuse to accept the creeds they feel are not consistent with modern science and thought.

The Thirteen Creeds

I I believe with a perfect faith, that God, blessed be his name, is the Creator and Ruler of everything that has been created, and that he alone has made, does make, and will make all things.

II I believe with a perfect faith, that the Creator, blessed be his name, is the One and Only God; his unity is unlike any other unity of which we can have any idea, and that he alone is our God, who was, is, and will be.

III I believe with a perfect faith, that the Creator, blessed be his name, is not mortal; that he is free from all accidents that are likely to happen to a mortal being, and that he has not any form whatsoever.

IV I believe with a perfect faith, that the Creator, blessed be his name, is the first and the last of all beings.

V I believe with a perfect faith, that to the Creator, blessed be his name, and to him alone, it is right to pray, and that it is not right to pray to any being besides him.

VI I believe with a perfect faith, that all the words of the prophets are true.

VII I believe with a perfect faith, that the prophecy of Moses, our teacher, peace be unto him, was true, and that he was the chief of the prophets, both of those that were before and those that came after him.

---

[13] Simon Greenberg, "Judaism," *Patterns of Faith*, E. Ernest Johnson (ed.) (New York: Harper & Bros., 1957), p. 135.

[14] L. Finkelstein, *op. cit.*, p. 25.

[15] Greenberg, *op. cit.*, p. 137.

VIII I believe with a perfect faith, that the Law, now in our possession, is the same that was given to Moses, our teacher, peace be unto him.

IX I believe with a perfect faith, that this Law will not be changed and that there will never be any other Law from the Creator, blessed be his name.

X I believe with a perfect faith, that the Creator, blessed be his name, knows every deed of the children of men, and all their thoughts, as it is said: It is He that fashioneth the hearts of them all; that giveth heed to all their deeds.

XI I believe with a perfect faith, that the Creator, blessed be his name, rewards those that keep his commandments, and punishes those that transgress them.

XII I believe with a perfect faith, in the coming of the Messiah, and though he tarry, I will wait daily for his coming.

XIII I believe with a perfect faith, that there will be a resurrection of the dead, at the time when it shall please the Creator, blessed be his name, and exalted be the remembrance of him forever and ever.[16]

Ethic

"Ethic comes first, doctrine is secondary." As has been said, and because there is no agreement on belief, what one does is more important than what one believes in Judaism. And, since a "reward of the good life is the good life," Judaism would appear to bear at least some resemblance to the Christian doctrine of salvation through good works.

The Code and Law that prescribe the behavior of the practicing Jew is derived from the sacred book and writings, of which the Torah is foremost. The Torah originally was of two parts: one written and one oral. The written Torah is the first five books of the Old Testament, which according to Jewish tradition God revealed to Moses (considered by Jews the most important person in history) on Mt. Sinai. The oral Torah is the living and growing tradition, and it interprets the basic principles of the written Torah.

At the end of the second century this oral tradition was codified and committed to writing, and became known as the Talmud. It is also referred to as the commentaries on the Torah, and is a continually growing collection of writings of sages and rabbis which have stood the test of time. By the end of the nineteenth century, the Talmud numbered more than sixty volumes.

The basic norm for conduct, upon which all branches of Judaism agree, is a corollary of the prayer, "Hear, Oh Israel, the Lord our God; the Lord is One":[17] that all men are brothers. From this comes the command to "Love thy neighbor as thyself." All branches of Judaism likewise accept the Ten Commandments, five of which deal with man's relation to God, and five with man's relation to man. Judaism holds that both these sets of injunctions are equally important. For example, the great sage Hillel taught: "Love thy neighbor as thyself, and go forth and learn," and the ethic is further prescribed in the much-quoted verse from Micah: "Love

---

[16] Salo Wittmayer Baron, *A Social and Religious History of the Jews*, Vol. VI (New York: Columbia University Press, 1958), p. 101.

[17] Deut. 6; 4.

mercy, do justly, and live humbly before God." All denominations of Judaism, it can be said, like those of Christianity, accept the Golden Rule "Thou shalt love thy neighbor as thyself."[18]

The underlying concept of the Jewish ceremonial system is that God continually reveals himself in nature, in history, and in man's daily life, and each ceremony, accordingly, in seeking to emphasize some aspect of this divine revelation becomes a special means for communion between man and God. In nonceremonial circumstances, too, a Jew is expected to recite a blessing whenever he enjoys any particular aspect of the world. When he awakes, he thanks God for having created the earth and the new day, for granting him the power of sight and the power to walk, and for the renewal of his strength in sleep.[19]

The Jews' most important moral rules, however, are found in the Torah, which the Orthodox believe is the revealed, unchanging will of God—or where "man's intellect bows to God's."

Reform Jews, at the other extreme, subject all the rules and codes to reason and experience and they ignore or discard those that do not make sense in the light of modern science and technology. Reformism emphasizes the social rather than the prophetic or legalistic aspects of the tradition.

Ritual

Rites of Passage. Every step in the life cycle has an appropriate practice or ritual for the Orthodox for whom Judaism is a highly disciplined way of life, and the rituals begin almost immediately after the birth of the Jewish child. But since the child comes into the world untainted there is no need to remove original sin and admit him to Judaism: merely being born into a Jewish household or of Jewish parents makes one a Jew and a "child of the covenant."

Boys are circumcised eight days after birth and are named during the circumcision rite. Girls are named within a week of birth, during the reading of the Torah. Thirty-one days after the birth of the first son comes a "redemption of son" ceremony.

The Jewish confirmation ceremony, *Bar Mitzvah*, by which a boy becomes an adult and responsible male and takes his proper place in the Jewish community, comes at the age of thirteen. The emotional and spiritual significance of this rite in the life of a Jewish boy is illustrated by the following personal account:

My religious training included a thorough study of the ritual of becoming a man. About six months before the actual ceremony, I was taken aside by the chief Rabbi and told that from this time on, I would be under the special tutoring of one of the assistant rabbis. It was his duty to teach me all the prayers and chants. As my Bar Mitzvah was in April I was to have a Hartorah

---

[18] Lev. 19; 18.

[19] L. Finkelstein, *op. cit.*, p. 36.

of 108 lines which would have to be sung. Before this though, there are several preliminary prayers which must be spoken. There is a different Hartorah for every month of the year and I was quite lucky to get a rather short one. My training was for two hours a day for five days a week. At first it seemed quite a chore to sit down and memorize these seemingly useless words, but after a while the entire ceremony seemed beautiful.

I cannot express my elation, as one morning I stood before the entire congregation, dressed in the traditional blue suit of the youth about to enter into manhood. I raised my head from silent meditation and started reciting the prayers. My pulse quickened, and my voice chanted in a solemn tone my adoration of God. The congregation chanted with me and pretty soon I began to feel the presence of a much higher being in my midst. I felt a love for my fellow man that I have never experienced before, a peace that can be experienced only by the righteous, while standing in awesome reverence. My whole body quivered with excitement as the Rabbi, dressed in his ritualistic vestments, placed the palm of his hand on my forehead, and blessed, in Hebrew, the covenant that I had made with God. This signified that the ceremony had ended, and that I was now a man, in the eyes of the Lord, and the community.

It was an experience that will remain with me for the rest of my life."[20]

Although girls are not confirmed in traditional Judaism, many Conservative and Reform congregations have adopted a rite of *Bath Mitzvah* for girls that is given at the age of twelve. Other congregations have established confirmation services, for both boys and girls, which come between the ages of 14 and 16. This may be in lieu of or in addition to a *Bar Mitzvah* and *Bath Mitzvah*.[21]

Marriage ceremonies are performed under a canopy, or *chuppah*. The bride circles the groom three times, and a glass is broken to remind the couple of the destruction of the Temple, that they are Jews, and that marriage has its heartaches and disappointments as well as its pleasures.

Funeral and mourning practices emphasize the continuity and solidarity of the family. The funeral is marked by simplicity. All forms of luxury, resplendent coffins, robes for the dead other than the traditional white shrouds, and floral tributes are forbidden. At the grave the family recites the *kaddish* prayer and mourners tear their garments as a sign of their loss.

After the funeral the mourners return to the home of the departed to "sit" in mourning for seven days (shivah). Mirrors are covered, jewels and other forms of ostentation are put away. A modified period of mourning then continues for another thirty days, and for twelve months the next of kin are forbidden to visit any place of amusement or to participate in any festivity. The anniversary of the death of close relatives is observed by the kindling of a special light, by attendance in the synagogue, the recital of the *kaddish,* and the giving of charity in the name of the departed.[22]

---

[20] Unpublished autobiography from the author's files.
[21] L. Finkelstein, *op. cit.,* p. 77.
[22] Leo Jung, *Essentials of Judaism* (New York: Philip Feldheim, Inc., 1957), p. 14.

The Sabbath. The Sabbath is the day in which the observing Jew withdraws from work and business and devotes himself to family, friends, and religion. Strictly interpreted, this means he will not handle any money, turn on electric lights, use a pencil or pen, engage in household work, or use any means of transportation. Therefore he must walk to the synagogue and should live within walking distance.

The Sabbath begins at sundown Friday and ends at sundown Saturday. The *kiddush*, the ceremony of sanctification at the Friday evening meal, introduces the Sabbath, and the most important service of the week is held Saturday morning. A quorum (*minyan*) of ten males above the age of thirteen is necessary for a congregational service and any male Jew familiar with the Hebrew prayerbook can lead the service. The service is in Hebrew, which is considered to be another unifying and conserving influence.

One positive feature of the Sabbath lies in the intensification of family life, spiritual contact with friends, and the opportunity to study the literature and history of the Jewish people.[23] The weekly Sabbath, moreover, is just as important and just as holy as any of the High Holy Days. Most Conservative and Reform congregations—like all Orthodox congregations—have a Friday evening service, which is usually better attended than the Saturday service. In addition to Friday and Saturday services, Orthodox and Conservative synagogues hold prayer services each day of the week.

It is difficult, if not impossible, for a Jew to carry on his business or practice his profession if he isolates himself on Saturday, and some Reform congregations, which have modified and ignored many of the rules and customs, particularly those that are difficult to follow where Jews are a minority within a dominant culture, celebrate the Sabbath on Sunday. The Reform service differs also in that it is shorter and usually in the vernacular rather than in Hebrew. And where Orthodox women sit apart or confine themselves to the home when the men are in the synagogue, Reform women take part in religion as equals of the men.

Conservative Judaism stands somewhere between the traditionalism of Orthodoxy and the modernism of Reform. Some prayers are said in Hebrew and generally there is no division of men and women in the service.

Dietary Laws. Dietary laws lie at the heart of Judaism, engendering an "abiding God-consciousness' and teaching the Jew to control his appetite by giving greater attention to spiritual values.[24]

Food that is selected and prepared according to the dietary laws is said to be *kosher,* and kosher meat must come from ruminant (cud chewing) animals that also have the cleft hoof. Only fish that have fins and scales may be eaten, and only domesticated fowl. In addition, kosher meat must

---

[23] *Ibid.,* p. 17.
[24] *Ibid.,* p. 9.

be slaughtered according to special techniques that permit the complete removal of blood from the meat. Meat and milk dishes must not be eaten together, utensils in which they are prepared, and the dishes from which they are eaten must be kept apart and washed separately. Because kosher food is quality food and hygienically prepared, many non-Jewish people patronize kosher markets and restaurants. Rabbis insist, however, that the rationale for the dietary laws is spiritual and not hygienic.

The Orthodox follow the dietary laws religiously and the Reform generally ignore them. Or a Conservative Jew may keep the dietary laws within his own home but eat nonkosher food when he is with Christian and other non-Jewish groups.

Adherence to the full letter of the Law requires discipline, sacrifice, and restraint that many Jews, orthodox in name, are apparently unwilling to accept. That this is a continuing and acute problem can be seen by the plea of a prominent Orthodox rabbi to his congregation. Charging widespread neglect of the sanctity of the Sabbath and the observance of the dietary code, he said

What is lacking today is a dedicated zeal to uphold Jewish tradition. The time has come for a widespread rededication of the Jewish spirit to God and His teachings as outlined in the written and oral law. Orthodox Judaism has never been a popular movement. It has always demanded self-sacrifice and sincere dedication. The attempt to sugar-coat Judaism through a capitulation to religious reform promises naught else than the germination of a sectarian influence completely alien to Judaism. It is the divine path we must seek in faith and not the avenue of convenience.[25]

Ritual and Symbolism

The revered traditions of Judaism, which is approximately 3000 years older than Christianity, surrounds every act and worship form with an abundance of symbolic meaning.

The Torah. The Torah, the most sacred object in Judaism, is kept in the Ark which is recessed behind a curtain in the synagogue and oriented with Jerusalem. A continuously burning light stands for the light that formerly burned in the Temple in Jerusalem.

The Torah, as has been mentioned in passing, is composed of the five books of Moses (the Pentateuch) and is written by hand on a parchment scroll. All must rise when the Torah is taken from the Ark to be read, and no irreverent or profane behavior is ever permitted in the room which contains the Torah. Nor, except for the performance of a religious service, may a Torah be moved from place to place.[26]

The word Torah has three different meanings: it is an object, the parchment roll, that is kept in the Ark; it also stands for "that which is written," the written code, and Torah also means "teaching, learning, studying." Judaism places such a high value on the Torah and learning,

---

[25] *New York Times*, Dec. 11, 1960.
[26] L. Finkelstein, *op. cit.*, p. 10.

and has done so for several thousand years of recorded history, that even in the ancient world the Jews were known as the "People of the Book."

The practicing Jew approaches the Torah with devotion and deep commitment because it symbolizes his highest ideals and hopes. It is his faith, direction, and law, and shapes his life in terms of its principles: reverence, righteousness, and compassion.

Regarded as the most holy of objects, the Torah is handled with great care and reverence, and the holy words inscribed upon the parchment are never touched by hand; a pointer is used to follow the reading. To drop a Torah, according to traditional Judaism, is an act of extreme irreverence and this irreverence must be "redeemed" by the congregation at large: by great contributions to charity or by fasting, the latter penance being discharged by successive *minyans* of ten men who fast for 40 days.

Other Sacred Objects. A number of sacred objects and garments is used by the practicing Jew in his home and on his person. The *tallis*, or prayer scarf, which is worn about the shoulders, has "prayer knots" in its fringe which remind the praying Jew of "all the commandments of the Lord." A *yarmulke*, or skull cap, is worn by the male in the synagogue during services, the head being covered out of respect for the "One above you." *Philacteries*, little boxes containing Bible verses, and tied upon the head (the seat of thought) and upon the arm (the instrument of action) during daily prayers to remind the Jew that he should be guided by love of God when he thinks and when he acts. A *mezuzah*, a small container holding verses from Deuteronomy, is attached to the doorpost to signify that a family is truly Jewish and has faith in God.[27]

The High Holy Days

The Jewish religious year has 16 holy and fast days, seven of which are of major importance and are generally observed by Jewish communities around the world. Orthodox Jews insist, however, that the weekly Sabbath is as sacred as any High Holy Day.

On Rosh Hashanah, the Jewish New Year, Jews assemble in the synagogue to reaffirm their faith, examine their past conduct, and pray for forgiveness. The *shofar* (ram's horn) is blown to reawaken their responsibility to the Lord and to call them to repentance. Orthodox and Conservative Jews observe *Rosh Hashanah* for two days, Reform Jews for one day.

The next ten days is a period of meditation. On the tenth day falls *Yom Kippur* (the Day of Atonement). This is the holiest day of the year, and the day on which the Lord judges each individual. Jews fast all day, confess, repent, ask pardon from the Lord and from their fellow man, and, in turn, freely forgive their neighbors. According to some contemporary Jewish thought, the idea of individual soul searching, repentance, and atonement derives from Judaism's basic promise that man is

---

[27] L. Jung, *op. cit.*, p. 8.

a moral being, free to choose between good and evil, and therefore accountable for his actions.[28]

Sukkot, the Feast of Tabernacles, falls in the first week of October. In ancient days it was held in celebration of the fruit harvest, when Jews built *sukkot* (temporary booths) hung with fruits and flowers. Now it is celebrated as a day of gratitude and commemorates the time that the Israelites lived in flimsy huts during their 40 years in the wilderness—wandering and homeless, yet secure in the Lord's protection.

Chanukah, which falls shortly before Christmas, celebrates the Maccabees' freeing of the Temple from Syrian conquerors who had defiled it. At its rededication oil was found to feed the holy lamp for only one day, but, miraculously, it burned for eight days. Thus, on the first day of *Chanukah* Jews light one candle on the *menorah*, and then another on each successive day. Rabbis today believe that *Chanukah* has its greatest significance as a symbol of man's continuous quest for freedom of conscience.[29]

Purim is based on an incident related in the Book of Esther: the scheming of Haman to persuade King Ahasuerus to destroy the Jews and the pleading of Esther to save them. This gayest of all Jewish holy days celebrates King Ahasuerus' decision to save the Jews and to destroy Haman, their enemy. The Book of Esther is read during synagogue service and the children twirl their noisemakers to drown out every mention of Haman's name. Contemporary rabbis find in *Purim* the age-old struggle between good and evil, and love and hate, and see it as a constant reminder to all peoples of the dangers of prejudice and discrimination.[30]

Pesach (Passover), which comes near the end of March, recalls the deliverance of the Jews from Egyptian slavery. At the traditional *seder* meals, on the first and second days of Passover, Jewish families read Exodus (the Old Testament book that tells the story of the liberation) and eat *matzot* (unleavened bread) and other symbolic foods, thereby "reliving" their ancestors' experiences. Passover is an illustrious chapter in man's perennial struggle for freedom and equality.[31]

Shavuot follows Passover by 50 days and commemorates the sacred moment at Mount Sinai when Moses received the Ten Commandments from the Lord. *Shavuot* also marks the wheat harvest of early Palestine, and Jews throughout the world decorate their homes and synagogues with greens and flowers. While Passover gave the Jews physical freedom, *Shavuot* gave them freedom of the soul.

Organization

Voluntary Associations. The associational structure of the representative Jewish congregation is very similar to that of the typical Protestant

28 Rabbi Elmer Berger, reported in the *New York Times*, Sept. 18, 1960.:
29 Rabbi Edward E. Klein, reported in the *New York Times*, Dec. 18, 1960.
30 Rabbi William F. Rosenblum, reported in the *New York Times*, March 22, 1959.
31 Rabbi Samuel M. Segal, reported in the *New York Times*, March 29, 1959.

church. There is the same proliferation of men's clubs, sisterhoods, junior congregations, youth groups, "young marrieds," "Sunday School" classes, discussion circles, adult education projects, breakfasts, brunches, dinners, suppers, and the like.[32]

Whether Jews are influenced by Protestant culture or, like Protestants, are merely reacting to the sweeping changes in the secular culture is an open question. Jews have a long history of associational relationships that are primarily social in nature within the structure of the synagogue, the center of Jewish life down through the ages. Traditionally, the synagogue had a three-fold purpose as a house of prayer, a house of assembly, and a house of study, and Jews have always regarded the synagogue as a proper place for fellowship as well.

Social relationships are an important factor in the surge of religious identification among Jews since World War II. Gordon found that denominational and theological differences were of little concern to the new congregations springing up in the suburbs.[33] These congregations not only differ very little in theology and ritual, but are strikingly similar in the associational programs they offer their congregations—so that some families find it possible to affiliate with several synagogues although each carries a different denominational label.

Another study of Jewish trends found that the Modern Orthodox, the Conservative, and the Traditional Reform congregations have two elements in common. The rabbis of each denomination were intent upon organizing and rebuilding the Jewish community around the synagogue, and in the process found themselves involved in the same complex of administrative, congregational, and community activities.[34]

The following description of the associational structure of a congregation was derived from a sociological analysis of his temple by a student in a class in sociology of religion, and is fairly representative of congregations of this size and type.

The temple that I attend is considered liberal—somewhere between Conservative and Reform in principle. The temple is a very beautiful structure with a large dome on top and four large pillars outside. The windows are stained with scenes from the Old Testament. Inside, the whole place is carpeted. The auditorium has a seating capacity of a thousand. The building includes an organ room, the rabbi's study, children's chapel, social hall for parties and plays, kitchen, gymnasium, library, Judaica shop, various lounges for social receptions, religious-school classrooms, and offices . . .

Our temple has a men's club, sisterhood, Shaariateers [couples from 30 to 60 years old], Young Marrieds club, Junior League [17 to 21 years], teenagers' club, Boy Scouts, Girl Scouts, Campfire Girls, stamp club, choral group and

---

[32] Will Herberg, *Protestant-Catholic-Jew* (Garden City, New York: Doubleday & Co., 1956), p. 206.

[33] Albert I. Gordon, *Jews in Suburbia* (Boston: Beacon Press, 1959), p. 97.

[34] Jerome E. Carlin and Saul H. Mendlovitz, "The American Rabbi: a Religious Specialist Responds to Loss of Authority," *The Jews: Social Patterns of an American Group,* Marshall Sklare (ed.) (Glencoe, Ill.: The Free Press, 1955), p. 179.

Parent-Teachers' Association. On weeknights courses are given to adults in Hebrew culture, Red Cross and home nursing, and book reviews.

The men's club and the sisterhood are the most important. They consist of the very active members of the temple and often work together. They sponsor a bulletin of temple news each week. They provide free scholarships for all children who wish to attend the religious school but cannot afford the tuition. They give Bibles to all children who are confirmed, and medals for scholarship in the religious school. The sisterhood supports a war orphan. It runs the Judaica shop and is in charge of the tea and cookies after services. The members take turns as hostesses in these after-service teas.

The sisterhood raises funds for the temple and for various charities. It has speakers and lecturers for its meetings. It sponsors card parties, bazaars, and dinners, and puts on plays. The sisterhood and the men's club formulate and assist the various activities and functions of the temple. They work through various committees. The women members are those who are at home during the day and have no children, or have children that are old enough to care for themselves. Mostly middle-aged men and women constitute the membership of the two clubs. These people have a lot of leisure on their hands and find in these clubs a new interest in life.

The Shaariateers, Young Marrieds, Junior League and teenager clubs are mostly for social purposes. They give the young people a chance to get acquainted with the Jewish young people of their age group, and to make new and dear friends. They have parties and gatherings, dancing and other functions suitable for their age level. Jewish culture is introduced to these groups through lectures and movies on various phases of Judaism. They learn Jewish songs and dances.

The stamp club, choral group, Boy and Girl Scouts, Campfire Girls, are composed mainly of children who attend the religious school.

None of the various clubs include worship services at their meetings, with the possible exception of a prayer at the beginning or a benediction at the end. The clubs, however, encourage their members to attend the worship services. Many of the people who were not members of the temple join after becoming members of the clubs. The clubs perform many services for both the temple and the community. Recently they sponsored a blood bank at our temple for the boys in Korea.[35]

The social structure of many congregations is complicated by the chapters of such national organizations as Hadassah for women and B'nai B'rith for men, organizations dedicated to various social and humanitarian projects. Hadassah combines philanthropic, Zionist, cultural and social interests through its various chapters. B'nai B'rith endorses and supports such organizations as the Anti-Defamation League, Hillel Foundation, and various charities.

In most congregations the national organizations compete with the synagogue organizations for members and for funds. It is to the credit of most congregations that they find it possible to support both the national and the local group.

Almost without exception, Jewish religious leaders reported a great upsurge of interest in religion and organizations as a result of the estab-

---

[35] Unpublished autobiography from author's files.

lishment of the state of Israel, an interest that was felt even in those congregations and groups that were officially non-Zionist.

In Conservative and Reform congregations the women's groups are more active than men's groups and include a higher proportion of their sex as members.[36] Gordon found that women outnumbered men three-to-one in Zionist organizations.[37] And, in suburban communities, women rather than men are re-establishing today's Jews as "the People of the Book," demanding study groups and classes in Hebrew language, Jewish history, Jewish ritual and ceremonies, the Bible, and even theology. Their interests even extend to home study courses taught by the rabbi or some other informed and competent teacher.[38] Part of the enthusiasm is representative middle-class behavior inasmuch as activities are appropriate forms of social behavior for middle and upper class wives, and part is due to the desire for identification.

National Organizations. The autonomous nature of Jewish congregations becomes apparent when the total number of U.S. congregations (slightly more than 4000) is compared with the approximately 1800 congregations that are affiliated with either the Orthodox, Conservative, or Reform national organizations.

Rabbis, on the other hand, show a much higher sense of identity and solidarity in that approximately 3000 are affiliated with one of the three corresponding rabbinical organizations,[39] a total that represents almost all of the rabbis holding charges. There are approximately 4000 rabbis in the United States, about 1000 rabbis without congregations, and about 1000 churches without rabbis, most of those without rabbis being quite small. (Judaism is somewhat different from Protestantism in that a rabbi may go "in and out" of religious work without prejudice, and it is not unusual for an ordained rabbi even to be gainfully employed in some secular activity and never hold a religious charge.)

Lay Organizations. The organization and division of American Orthodox, Conservative, and Reform groups is approximately as follows:

A recent report of the Union of Orthodox Jewish Congregations listed more than 700 member congregations in the United States and Canada.[40] The UOJC's women's branch had 450 affiliated sisterhoods in 21 chapters, and the National Council of Young Israel reported a membership of 20,000 families in 72 chapters.

The United Synagogue of America (Conservative) reported a membership of 508 congregations and more than 200,000 families. Its National

---

[36] Marshall Sklare, *Conservative Judaism* (Glencoe, Ill.: The Free Press, 1955), p. 139.

[37] A. I. Gordon, *op. cit.*, p. 225.

[38] *Ibid.*, p. 78.

[39] National Council of Churches of Christ in the USA, *Yearbook of American Churches, 1957* (New York), pp. 254, 268.

[40] *American Jewish Yearbook* (Philadelphia: The Jewish Publication Society of America, 1956), p. 190.

Women's League reported a membership of 160,000 women in 615 sister-hoods, while its National Federation of Jewish Men's Clubs reported approximately 30,000 members among 210 clubs. The Young People's League had 6,000 members in 70 branches, and the United Synagogue Youth had 16,000 in 240 chapters.

The Union of American Hebrew Congregations (Reform) reported 520 member congregations and 255,000 families.[41] The UAHC's National Federation of Temple Sisterhoods claimed a membership of 100,000 in 517 chapters; the National Federation of Temple Brotherhoods a membership of 55,000 in 320 chapters, and the National Federation of Temple Youth approximately 14,000 members in 380 youth groups.

The increasing and prominent part that women play in these lay organizations is considered an important aspect of the trend to the Americanization of Judaism.

Three smaller groupings were also listed in the *American Jewish Year-book*. The Union of Sephardic Congregations reported 50 congregations that ranged in membership from 20 to 500 families; the Union of Ethiopian Congregations and Rabbis claimed membership of 14,000 Falasha Jews in 37 congregations, and the Jewish Reconstructionist Foundation reported four congregations in three states.

Rabbinical Organizations. Approximately 3,000 rabbis serve American Jewish congregations and hold membership in various rabbinic organizations. The Orthodox organizations include the Rabbinical Council of America with 608 members, the Union of Orthodox Rabbis of the United States and Canada with 650 members, and the Rabbinical Alliance of America with 400 members.

Conservative rabbis are grouped in the Rabbinical Assembly of America with 600 members, and 700 Reform rabbis belong to the Central Conference of American Rabbis. The Association of Jewish Chaplains of the Armed Forces reported a membership of 525, approximately 40 percent Reform, 30 percent Conservative, and 30 percent Orthodox. (The Cantors' Assembly of America reported 191 members.)

Values

Education. It was an old Jewish custom to place a drop of honey on the open Bible when the small boy was being introduced to reading and worship, and as the boy tasted the honey the rabbi would explain how sweet and pleasant learning could be.

The traditional synagogue service requires active male participation and reciting the prayers and the Torah in Hebrew; so the practicing Jew must be literate. According to Finkelstein, the study of the Torah and the Talmud is a religious act, "a means of communion with God. Some teachers consider this study the highest form of such communion imagin-

---

[41] *Ibid.*, p. 192.

able."[42] "A student is like a seed in the ground; once it sprouts it grows towards Heaven."[43] A Talmudic maxim states that the Jew who is studying the Torah at the time for prayers need not interrupt his study to pray since he is already doing a religious exercise.

A Jewish boy at the age of 13, and through the *Bar Mitzvah* ceremony, becomes a son of the commandment and enters into religious adulthood. During the ceremony he is called to the front of the synagogue to read the Torah, and may even show his breadth of knowledge by making comments or a discourse on the Law. At least three years of study in a Hebrew school is generally required for sufficient knowledge to participate in this service, and more than 500,000 Jewish boys and girls throughout the United States attend these after-school Hebrew classes for an average of eight hours a week. There are also more than 250 full-time Jewish parochial day schools throughout the country whose curricula includes a full general education program as well as the study of Jewish religion and culture.

This interest in education is reflected on the college level, too. According to an old Jewish saying, a father will "bend the sky" to give his son an education, and studies of education in New York in 1948 and 1953 showed that one-sixth of all Jews over 18 had completed college, compared with only one-twentieth of the non-Jewish population. Recent studies in 14 cities where 10 percent of the Jewish population lives showed that 75 to 96 percent of the Jews were in "nonmanual" work compared with the 38 percent of the total United States labor force.[44]

Some of the success of Jews in fields that require higher education is probably a result of greater motivation. As a minority group subject to discrimination and as members of the latest great immigration movement, they have been forced to work hard to better themselves. That "Education has been the chief reason for Jewish survival throughout centuries of trial and tribulation"[45] would seem to be axiomatic.

A few years ago an irate citizen of Irish descent asked a political leader in New York City, also of Irish descent, why there were so many Jewish names and so few Irish names on the most recent civil service list. The political leader replied that the most important reason was that Irish boys were brought up with the philosophy that it took "pull" to get ahead, while Jewish boys had it drummed into them that it was "push" that made the difference.

The Family. Judaism places high value on family life and closely knit family ties, and Jewish children thereby gain emotional security at home

---

[42] L. Finkelstein, *The Jews: Their History, Culture, and Religion* (New York: Harper & Bros., 1949), p. 1331.

[43] Henry Cohen, "Jewish Life and Thought in an Academic Community," *American Jewish Archives*, Vol. XIV, No. 2 (November, 1962), p. 107.

[44] Hartzell Spence, "The Jews," *Look*, May 13, 1958.

[45] Arthur Levill, reported in the *New York Times*, December 18, 1960.

that enables them to surmount the pressures of a competitive and sometimes prejudiced world.

Many important religious rituals take place within the home. Prayers
are said at the beginning and end of each meal in the traditional home; the
Sabbath is welcomed at sundown Friday with the most important meal of
the week; the father chants the *Kiddush* prayer over a cup of wine and
the mother recites a blessing while lighting the Sabbath candles. Other
prayers, hymns, and recitations from the Scriptures form a ritual for the
Sabbath meal, and even many of the High Holy Days are sanctified by
rituals in the home.

The family is also integrated and strengthened through a sharp differentiation of the functions of husband and wife. Although in the Orthodox
tradition the woman has no part in the synagogue service, sits apart from
the men, and is not even confirmed, Jewish sources maintain that she
plays an essential religious role in caring for the children and by maintaining the religious codes, practices, and dietary laws within the home.

The solidarity of the home is further shown by the reluctance of Jews
to marry outside their faith.[46] Although the husband holds unilateral
power to divorce his wife under the Orthodox code, Jews insist that their
families are more stable and that theirs is the lowest divorce rate among
all the religions, including the Catholic.

Charity. According to traditional standards it is not enough to pray
regularly, to keep the Sabbath, and to observe the dietary laws; the good
Jew must also give to the poor. The ancient rabbis taught, moreover, that
it is as important to feed the gentile poor as it is to feed the Jewish poor,
and the Talmud teaches that "even one whom the community supports
must give to the poor."[47] Giving is a fulfillment of the Divine Will to the
traditional Jew and an assurance of a place in the world to come, and
Jews have an outstanding record in philanthropy.

Although many Jews give for religious reasons, there are many other
Jews whose charity and philanthropy is their only ground for Jewish
identification.[48] Although synagogues and congregations are autonomous,
giving and spending is highly organized on a national basis through the
United Jewish Appeal. Jews contribute considerably more per capita than
any comparable group in the United States.[49]

Jews also raise large sums for the poor and unfortunate within their

---

[46] Milton L. Barron, "The Incidence of Jewish Intermarriage," *American Sociological Review*, Vol. 11 (February, 1946), pp. 6–13; J. S. Slotkin, "Jewish-Gentile
Marriages in Chicago," *American Sociological Review*, Vol. 7 (February, 1942),
pp. 34–39.

[47] Morris N. Kertzer, "What is a Jew?" *Religion in America*, Leo Rosten (ed.)
(New York: Simon & Schuster, Inc., 1955), p. 66.

[48] Marshall Sklare and Marc Vosk, *The Riverton Study* (New York: The American Jewish Committee, 1957), p. 25.

[49] W. Herberg, *op. cit.*, p. 212.

own communities.[50] There are fewer Jews on public welfare rolls than any other religious or ethnic group (with the possible exception of the Mormons). Jews are also generous supporters of the Community Chest and other welfare and educational projects.

Charity, it would seem, is the common denominator that unites the religious, the non-religious, and the assimilated Jew, and many of the most far-reaching philanthropic projects in America have become identified with Jewish family names that initiated or supported such projects. Of the $70,000,000 which Julius Rosenwald gave to charity, $30,000,000 has been devoted to Negro education and welfare. The Straus brothers built hospitals and sanatoriums. For more than thirty years the Guggenheim Foundation has been giving fellowships to artists, writers, scholars, and scientists, and some of the greatest achievements in these fields are direct results of the subsidy or support of a Guggenheim fellowship. The Schiffs, Lewisohns, and Lehmans are other outstanding families that have made substantial and continuing contributions to philanthropy and charity without regard to religious affiliation. In 1957, one-third of the $60,000,-000 spent by the 116 health and welfare agencies in New York City was raised by the Federation of Jewish Philanthropies.[51]

Summary

Traditional Judaism puts the greatest emphasis upon ethic or behavior; doctrine is secondary. An Orthodox Jew is required to accept and follow 613 precepts that cover dietary laws, prayers on rising, prayers for blessings received, Sabbath strictures and observances, differentiated roles for men and women, and so on, which make religion a vital part of each waking moment. Not all American Jews, however, are traditionalist and orthodox; a large number have modified and modernized Orthodox Judaism by dropping those precepts that seem not to make sense any longer.

Two denominations have emerged from Orthodoxy as a result of modernism, Conservative and Reform Judaism, and most of the local congregations are affiliated with one of the three corresponding national organizations. However, each congregation is completely autonomous.

Doctrine is secondary perhaps because of disagreements between rabbis and sages. There is no official confession of faith, but Jews agree on monotheism and accept widely notions of immortality. Jews, of course, also accept the Ten Commandments, but these are primarily mandates for behavior rather than articles of faith.

Jewish worship is rich in ritual and symbolism and has great appeal and meaning for a religious Jew. And because of the emphasis put

---

[50] N. Glazer, *op. cit.*, p. 135.
[51] H. Spence, *Look*, May 13, 1958.

upon learning, Jews are highly literate and well represented in occupations that require extensive educational preparation. Judaism also places a high value on family worship and family solidarity, and Jewish families consequently are well integrated and stable and have a small incidence of divorce and separation.

Chapter VIII

"Third-Force" Protestantism

ONE OF THE MOST VITAL and aggressive religious expressions in American Protestantism is a group of individuals and churches which cuts across the major denominations and which Van Dusen[1] has chosen to label the "Third Force." About 5,000,000 persons are included in the several Churches of God, Adventists, Churches of Christ, various Pentecostal churches, the Church of the Nazarene, and the Assemblies of God, all of which constitute the Third Force. These churches range from the emotional Pentecostals to the sober Adventists. Most disagree with each other, and look with disapproval on each other's way of worship, but they share a common spiritual aim: a return to the intent and practices of the early Christian church.

The Third Force is not limited to the above churches, however; there are also many congregations within the major Protestant denominations that are Third Force in theology and practice. The Wesleyan Methodist Church, the Orthodox Presbyterian Church, and the General Association of Regular Baptists are of this persuasion and emphasis. (In fact, the entire theologically conservative wing of Protestantism properly belongs in this group.) Because of the sincerity of their practices, represented in both worship and in contributions, third-force churches exercise an influence that is out of proportion to their numbers.

---

[1] Henry P. Van Dusen, " 'Third Force' in American Christendom," *Life*, June 9, 1958.

Some Principles

Doctrine. The Bible is regarded by these churches as the sole guide to faith and practice, and their uncomplicated theology is based upon its literal interpretation. As Bible literalists they hold unequivocally to orthodox doctrines, and, although they prefer the term conservative, they must be categorized as fundamentalists. They accept the Bible as the inspired and infallible Word of God, the Virgin Birth, and the divinity of Christ, and the following excerpt from the Wesleyan Methodist Church Confession of Faith is a representative statement of their doctrines:

1. The Bible is the inerrant and inspired Word of God.

2. The Deity of Jesus Christ, Who was supernaturally conceived by the Holy Ghost, and born of the Virgin Mary, free from moral taint of nature and perfect in His life and conduct.

3. The expiatory death and the vicarious atonement of Christ.

4. The resurrection of Jesus Christ from the dead, and His ascension to the right hand of the Father where He now occupies the throne of His mediation.

5. Christ's second coming will be "in like manner" as He went away.[2]

Evangelism. Great emphasis is put upon evangelism—by pastors in their sermons and by visiting evangelists who are brought in once or twice a year for a series of special services. They have a philosophy and a belief that every Christian is a "witness," and therefore each member should seek out friends, neighbors, and strangers and bring them into the fold to enjoy the peace and blessings of their faith. It is a common practice for members to go out in teams perhaps once each week to "witness" for their faith.

This evangelistic emphasis also gives rise to strong missionary programs, within the continental United States and abroad, and, perhaps not surprisingly, third-force churches lead in *per capita* contributions for missionary purposes. Tithing, moreover, is not just an ideal for a few "nuclear" members; it is expected of everyone, and often the tithe is based on the member's *gross* income. It can be easily understood, then, that third-force churches lead in *per capita* contributions for all purposes.

Entire Sanctification. Seeking the ideal of a "regenerate" membership, many of the churches in this group find their authority and inspiration in John Wesley's doctrines of "entire sanctification and holiness." Their worship, too, is marked by intensity and sincerity as they seek to glorify Christ and get to "know Him as Lord and Saviour."

The doctrine of "entire sanctification" has also been known as "perfect love," "full salvation," "holiness," or "Christian perfection." It is a doctrine from the tradition and practice of Reformation pietists who, in turn, also professed to find their inspiration in the beliefs and practices of

---

[2] *The Wesleyan Methodist Church of America* (Marion, Ind.: The Wesley Press, 1958), pp. 6–8.

Primitive Christianity. Entire sanctification, according to Wesley, is an act of God by which believers are made free from original sin, or depravity, and brought into a state of entire devotion to God. It is a "work of grace wrought instantaneously in the heart of believers, upon consecration and faith, by the baptism with the Holy Spirit. The evidences of this experience to the believer himself are a pure heart and the witness of the Holy Spirit; to others, the fruit of the Spirit—love, joy, peace, long-suffering, gentleness, goodness, faith, meekness, and temperance."[3]

Entire sanctification can also be regarded as a conversion experience or spiritual rebirth in which the sinner becomes a child of God through faith in Jesus Christ. This experience frequently occurs after an evangelistic appeal when penitents are invited to come forward for prayer and a public confession of faith. Sincere third force converts talk happily of the moment, time, and circumstances in which they were "saved."

Behavior such as this is characteristic of the right wing of sanctification-holiness groups and should be distinguished from the behavior of the left-wing which (as with Holy Rollers) may include "speaking in tongues," handling snakes and fire, and going into trances.

Science and Religion.   One noted characteristic of Liberal Protestantism is its willingness to reconcile the Bible with science, accepting both "higher" and "lower" criticism: interpreting the Bible, for example, in the light of evolutionary theory. On the other hand, evolution has always been a difficult hypothesis to reconcile with conservative doctrine, and some of these latter churches reject biological evolution because it is inconsistent with the Biblical account of the origin of man. The confession of faith of the Wesleyan Church states that "Man was created by the immediate creative act of God, according to the Bible narrative, and not by the process of evolutionary transition from a lower form of animalism to his present physical and intellectual condition."[4]

In a study[5] that compared the attitudes and beliefs of orthodox- and liberal-oriented Protestants it was found that the orthodox were less inclined than the liberal to believe that science and religion are in irreconcilable conflict. Apparently the orthodox person has a confidence and assurance in this matter that the liberal does not share.

There is yet another theological stance on the science-religion controversy. One of the fundamental points of the Seventh-day Adventists is that God created the earth and all life upon it; this life itself did not evolve over vast periods of time. Seventh-day Adventists reject the evolutionary postulate, believing it is less scientific and less adequate as an explanation of

---

[3] M. E. Redfor, *The Rise of the Church of the Nazarene* (Kansas City, Mo.: Nazarene Publishing House, 1948), p. 42.
[4] *The Wesleyan Methodist Church, op. cit.,* p. 7.
[5] W. Seward Salisbury, "Religiosity, Regional Subculture, and Social Behavior," *Journal for the Scientific Study of Religion,* Vol. II, No. 1 (Fall, 1962), p. 46.

man's origin than the literal creationist view."[6] Adventists, then, hold that knowledge which is incompatible with religion is unscientific and inadequate, or, conversely, that the Bible is more truly scientific than some biological and genetic hypotheses.

Moral Code. A strict moral code sets the third force off from the majority of the community. However, they are quite willing to be different and proud to live a "separated Christian life." Their rules of conduct are norms by which the individual may measure his behavior—and also the sanction which the congregation may invoke to excommunicate the wayward brother.

These standards go back at least to the Reformation in their representation of simple values and simple living as opposed to the worldliness and profligacy of the dominant classes, and, to the degree that third-force membership is recruited from the "disinherited," this emphasis still represents a protest against the society and values of dominant groups. Most of these churches therefore have rules against ostentation in manner and dress and against alcohol and tobacco: negative rather than positive rules; not so much what the communicant should as what he should not do. The Wesleyan Methodist Church's rules of conduct are a representative statement of the moral norms of third-force churches:

> The Church stands for total abstinence and favors moral persuasion and the power of the Gospel to save men from the alcohol habit. Those who use or traffic in alcoholic beverages are not received into membership of the Wesleyan Methodist Church.

> It is the considered and prayerful judgment of the Church that secret, oath-bound societies interfere with Christian fellowship and imperil the cultivation of a deeply spiritual life. The Church holds that membership in such societies is inconsistent with our duties to God and membership in the Church.

> The Wesleyan Methodist Church insists upon modesty, simplicity and economy in dress, and discourages the wearing of jewelry and showy ornaments.

> The use of tobacco is a great evil. The Church believes that it imperils physical health, wastes the Lord's money, and is inconsistent with a Christian testimony. The Church insists that members do not grow, sell or use tobacco.[7]

These rules, however, have not always been the prerogative of conservative churches. The author vividly remembers growing up in a small-town Presbyterian church and singing (at Christian Endeavor meetings) a hymn that included the promise not to drink "cider, wine, whiskey or beer . . . or smoke the nasty little cigarette"—prohibitions which formed the basic norm of conduct for the great majority of the Protestant churches of traditional and rural America. The Wesleyans can well say:

---

[6] *Seventh-Day Adventists* (Washington, D.C.: General Conference of Seventh-Day Adventists), 1958, p. 3.

[7] *Guide to Church Membership* (Marion, Ind.: The Wesleyan Methodist Church of America).

"It is not so much that we have left the Methodist Church as it is that the Methodist Church has left us."

Case Study of a "Conservative" Denomination

The Seventh-day Adventist Church is one of America's fastest growing denominations, now numbering more than 300,000 in the continental United States. This is an increase of one-third during the past ten years, and their missionary program is, for their size, the greatest effort of any American denomination.

Doctrine. Adventists are Bible literalists and their fundamental beliefs are specific and definite. Well-indoctrinated Adventists enjoy the security of assurance, a doctrinal assurance that is—outside the Roman Catholic faith—unmatched in the Christian community. Their doctrines include the inspired and infallible Bible, the Substitutionary Atonement, and the Resurrection.

They stress the importance of "regeneration" in Christ: "Every person in order to obtain salvation must experience the new birth; this comprises an entire transformation of life and character by the recreative power of God through faith in the Lord Jesus Christ."[8]

They believe in a specific, literal second coming of Christ: "The Resurrection of the Just at the second coming of Christ will mark the 'end of the world,' but no man can know when this will be. His coming will be literal, personal, and visible to all mankind."[9]

Adventists have a unique belief on a "state" of death. "In death man rests in the grave. Until resurrection he is neither tormented in hell nor taken to heaven. He knows 'not anything.' "[10]

Adventists believe that the fourth commandment requires the observance of the Sabbath on the seventh day, which Sabbath they accordingly keep from "sundown Friday to sundown Saturday, the seventh in the cycle of the days of creation."[11] In a good Adventist community, all shops and factories, schools and colleges are closed for the Saturday Sabbath.

Moral Conduct. An Adventist is asked to live a highly moral and disciplined life according to standards derived from the Ten Commandments. They believe "That the will of God as it relates to moral conduct is comprehended in His law of the Ten Commandments: that these are great moral unchangeable precepts, binding upon all men, in every age."[12] They believe "That the followers of Christ should be a godly people, not adopting the unholy maxims nor conforming to the unrighteous ways of

---

[8] *We Believe* (Washington, D.C.: General Conference of Seventh-Day Adventists), p. 4.
[9] *Ibid.,* p. 9.
[10] *Seventh-Day Adventists, op. cit.,* p. 4.
[11] *We Believe, op. cit.,* p. 4.
[12] *Ibid.,* p. 4.

the world, not loving its sinful pleasures nor countenancing its follies."[13]
Therefore they dress simply, wear only functional jewelry, avoid ostentation, and refrain from dancing and card playing.

Health Practices. Because Adventists believe their bodies should be temples of the Holy Spirit, they value good health. They are advised "to avoid every body- and soul-defiling habit and practice"[14] and have developed rules for maintaining the body as a fitting dwelling place for the Holy Spirit. A good Adventist will not smoke, take alcohol in any form, or even drink tea or coffee. They seek out sunlight and fresh air, follow a simple diet (some are vegetarians), and discipline themselves against overindulgence. The Kellogg Sanitarium at Battle Creek, Michigan, was an early center of Adventist health and diet therapy—and Kellogg's cornflakes was one Adventist device for popularizing the simple diet.

Missionary Program. Adventists feel they have a mission to tell the gospel story to all the world and yet "not to tear down the Christian experience enjoyed in other fellowships, but in respect and appreciation for a common heritage of faith to bring to that experience the additional insights they feel are especially vital to men living in this generation."[15] Their missionary program is extensive and effective. In 1956 the Adventist Church was active in 185 countries and dealing with 748 different languages and dialects. Two hundred and forty-five missionaries were sent overseas in that year and more than $13,000,000 was spent on its overseas mission program.

Placing major emphasis upon a ministry of healing, the Adventist College of Medical Evangelism at Loma Linda, California, graduates 100 physicians and 500 nurses each year who help staff its 23 hospitals in the United States and Canada and its 92 hospitals and 84 mission dispensaries and clinics overseas. More than half a million patients are treated each year in North America, while the overseas hospitals and dispensaries care for more than a million and a half patients.

The author and his family once spent a year in Boulder, Colorado, a small, attractive, college community with two hospitals: a good, well-staffed city hospital and a Seventh-day Adventist hospital. The doctors and nurses of both hospitals were equally competent and well-trained, but in the Adventist hospital the patient enjoyed special service and personal interest in every contact with the doctors and nurses, a relationship that did not consider the religious affiliation of the patient.

Parochial Education. Six out of every ten Adventist youth are educated in schools owned and operated by the denomination, an effort and an achievement which is comparable to the Catholic school effort, and which also manifests the high value Adventists place on parochial education. More than 5000 schools are operated by the denomination, 346 of

[13] *Ibid.*, p. 8.
[14] *Ibid.*, p. 8.
[15] *Seventh-Day Adventists, op. cit.*, p. 3.

which are above the elementary level. There are 14 colleges, one university, and ten schools of nursing in Canada and the United States.

Tithing. These comprehensive missionary and educational programs take money and Adventists are able to carry these programs on only because the membership is willing and eager to contribute to the work of their church. They are the tithers *par excellence* of American Protestantism. In 1957 their per capita contribution ($212.80) was the highest of any Protestant denomination, and in contributions for benevolences their per capita contribution was more than twice that of the next highest denomination.[16]

One out of every 19 Adventists works full time for his church. They labor for love rather than for money. The workers, whether missionaries, doctors, and nurses, pastors, teachers or executives, all receive the same modest pay with living allowances adjusted to the differences in local costs of living. Their reward is primarily the satisfaction they receive for following the Adventist way of life.

Ritual and Symbolism. Although the Seventh-day Adventist service is not ritualistic or liturgical, it recognizes baptism and communion as proper rites. Baptism is by immersion and symbolizes the burial of the "old man of sin" and a resurrection of the new man reborn in Christ. It is a proper rite for those of sufficient maturity to understand its meaning. The communion service is symbolic of Christ's passion. Communion is open to all who confess Christ whether or not they are members of the Adventist Church and is held quarterly in connection with the ancient "ordinance of humility" or the washing of feet.[17]

In worship, Adventists are restrained and dignified, more intellectual than emotional. They take their Bibles to church and during the sermon the pastor makes frequent references to passages to which the worshipers turn. They frown as much upon overt emotionalism in their services as do the liturgical churches; the pastor is more teacher than preacher, and Adventists address each other as "brother" and "sister" and demonstrate a high sense of community and an in-group sense of belonging.

"Conscientious Cooperators." Adventists are patriotic noncombatants, or "conscientious cooperators." The men are classified I-A-C for the draft, eligible for duty but only in noncombat jobs. Their colleges have Medical Cadet Corps that train 1500 draft-age boys a year for medical duty. During World War II, 12,000 medical cadet corpsmen served in the armed forces.

The Adventist ideal of life, as expressed in the objectives of the College of Medical Evangelists, is "to guide in the development of a balanced sense of values as revealed in intellectual, ethical and spiritual attitudes; to engender and nurture the desire to give selfless service to mankind."

---

[16] Benson Y. Landis, *Yearbook of American Churches* (New York: National Council of Churches of Christ in America).

[17] *Seventh-Day Adventists, op. cit.,* p. 4.

Case Study of a "Conservative" Church[18]

Third-force Protestantism includes individual congregations within the major families of denominations as well as in such conservative denominations as the Seventh-day Adventists. The following is a case study of a conservative Protestant congregation, an active and effective community of worshipers and a good illustration of the "ideal" conservative church type.

The North Syracuse Baptist Church is a growing and thriving "Bible church." Syracuse has been cited as one of the three fastest growing medium-sized cities in the United States since World War II and North Syracuse, one of its suburbs, changed within a few years from a simple rural village to a typical expanding suburban area. Farm lands have been subdivided for homes, a number of new congregations have been organized and new churches built, so that the new sanctuary and adjoining educational building of the North Syracuse Baptist church is only one of several like it.

A new Catholic church and parochial school, a new Lutheran church, and a new Methodist church are located within two or three blocks of the Baptist church. And, although the church boasts a continuous life of over one hundred years, having been organized in 1847, the period of its greatest growth has coincided with the growth of the village and the suburbanization of its culture. The congregation, composed of 1,100 adult members, had an average 666 attendance at Sunday School in 1962.

Doctrines and Beliefs. The front of its weekly bulletin describes it as "A Friendly Church Where Christ Is Exalted." When the pastor was asked what he felt might be of interest to newcomers looking for a church home, he wrote "We have a program geared to meet the spiritual, social, and psychological needs of all age levels. Here you will find a hearty welcome in the warm atmosphere of Christian friendship in a fundamental, Bible-believing church." A study of the church's program and its atmosphere shows that these statements pretty accurately reflect the work and goals of the church.

In response to the query on the special emphasis of the church, the pastor listed the doctrines to which his congregation subscribes:

Regeneration or conversion
Christians should live a separated Christian life
Every Christian is a witness-personal evangelist
Bible: the final authority in faith and life
Personal, premillenial, and imminent return of our Lord and Savior, Jesus
    Christ
Bodily resurrection of the just and unjust

---

[18] Information secured by interview and participant-observer techniques.

Rewards for believers at the Judgment Seat of Christ and punishments for
unbelievers at the Great White Throne

Christian stewardship-tithing

Worship Practices. Worship services come first in the program and are
the chief means by which the congregation seeks to "glorify Christ." The
church has kept the traditional pattern of services, a Sunday morning
service, an evening gospel service, and a Wednesday evening service
called the Hour of Power-Prayer, Praise, and Bible Study.

Evangelism is emphasized through two Sunday radio broadcasts and
through a mission chapel in Syracuse for colored people. A nuclear member has reported that the church is also carrying "the word" to the Jews
of Syracuse and making a special effort to serve the foreign students at
Syracuse University. Hardly a month goes by without a special series
of services by a visiting speaker or preacher, missionary, Bible student or
clergyman with a personal evangelistic appeal. Each week two-member
visitation teams call upon newcomers and the unchurched with an evangelistic message and an invitation to worship at the Baptist church.

The congregation has been very generous in its support of missions,
and in 1958 alone raised $30,000 for the partial support of 52 missionaries
and mission organizations. Several of its members, moreover, are now
serving in the foreign mission field, and the church's goal is to raise more
for missions than they do for the local church and its program.

Many of the members are tithers and many tithe on their gross rather
than their net incomes. The pastor proudly reports there is no canvassing
or pledging at his church, and members merely place their contributions
on the collection plate with no identification. Giving is primarily a
matter of conscience between the member and God.

Religious Education. An extensive Sunday School program in the new
service building has classes for all ages: there is a men's class and ladies'
class, five couple's classes, campus and career classes for single people, and
age–grade classes for primary, intermediate, junior and senior high school
students. Attendance averages 700 each Sunday and is almost as high
throughout the summer as it is during the winter. The program also includes a Vacation Bible School, and more than 300 pupils are taught each
week during the regular public school year in a "released time" program.

The recreational and social needs of the Baptist young people are met
through graded organizations of Pioneer Girls and a Christian Service
Brigade for the boys. The church leans heavily on camp experiences for
the inspiration and education of their young people, and sends frequent
delegations to the Le Tourneau Christian Camp on Canandaigua Lake
for weekend conferences or week-long camp experiences. The costs are
kept low and any worthy youngster in the congregation will be given
financial help in meeting expenses.

Social Ministries. The church program is not limited to worship services and Bible study. It includes such social ministries as a monthly family

dinner, father and son banquet, mother and daughter banquet, women's guild, men's club and organized sports.

According to the pastor his members generally disapprove of social drinking and do not sponsor or attend cocktail parties, and, although the young people are not absolutely forbidden to engage in social dancing, the church does not sponsor or encourage dancing as desirable or proper recreation.

A good church member who attends a substantial number of the worship services, who takes some time out of the week to be a "witness" for his faith, and who participates in one or two of the social ministries does not have the time to pursue any purely secular interests and activities. He and his associates within the church constitute a self-sustaining and intimate fellowship, and achieve the ideal of living "separate Christian lives."

When the pastor was commended for the health and vigor of his church and its program, he replied that people were getting tired of the "watered-down religion" of liberal Protestantism and wanted something definite and demanding as is offered in conservative churches such as his.

Organization. North Syracuse Baptist Church is completely autonomous and has no state or national conference ties or other affiliations, although it may cooperate with other churches from time to time for missions and for fellowship. The congregation holds the power to hire and to release the pastor, and the officers of the church include the pastor, trustees, deacons and deaconesses.

One can join this particular church with a letter from a similar church, by baptism, or by "Christian Experience"—the state of an individual who has been converted and baptized by immersion but is not a member of a church.

The Pastor. A liturgical church, Catholic or Protestant, may roll on in spite of the professional leader but a conservative church is effective primarily because of the professional leader. The great success the North Syracuse Baptist Church enjoys is therefore largely attributable to the qualities of its pastor. He is in his middle thirties. He was born and brought up in New York City, had four years of college and three years of Bible seminary. He is restrained, quiet, and sincere, and works diligently and effectively. He was asked to list his three most demanding jobs in terms of time and effort, and reported them as "preparing and delivering messages, visitation and counseling, and administration."

His most important contributions to his church are his sermons and "Bible messages." He often gives as many as six different sermons or Bible talks a week, each of which is well prepared and shows considerable study, research, and knowledge of the Bible. He is not an emotional speaker but he speaks with sincerity and conviction, and his parishioners find his sermons and talks are convincing and inspiring.

He does not try to set himself off from, or above, the congregation, or wear a robe or other distinguishing vestments; he appears in the pulpit simply and unostentatiously dressed in a plain business suit, and he prefers to be called pastor rather than reverend: he tells his parishioners that pastor means "shepherd." When he was asked what personal qualities and skills were most helpful to a pastor he replied that a pastor "needs more than native ability; he needs the Holy Spirit." The pastor leads not because of education, primarily, or because of position, or because of intellectual power, although he has some fair measure of each of these qualities; he leads primarily through the intangibles of personality—an excellent illustration of the "charismatic" leader.

Inter-Varsity Christian Fellowship

The Inter-Varsity Christian Fellowship (IVCF) is properly classed in the third-force wing of American Protestantism on the basis of its doctrines and beliefs, its personal and evangelical emphasis, because it functions on campuses as an intimate sustaining fellowship, and because the religious role is key or pivotal for the members of the fellowship in-group.

History. Inter-Varsity Christian Fellowship came to the United States from England by way of Canada. The original group developed at Cambridge University in 1877 as one expression of the religious revival that permeated England between 1860 and 1880.

The group first took the name of Cambridge Intercollegiate Christian Union, then the movement spread to a number of English colleges and universities and, at the conclusion of World War I, attempts were made to unite with the Student Christian Movement. All of these failed because the SCM refused to take the same doctrinal position as the IVCF.

When the IVCF representatives posed the question: "Does Student Christian Movement consider the atoning Blood of Jesus Christ as the central point in their message?" the representative of Student Christian Movement answered "No, not as central, although it is given a place in our teaching."[19] The line between liberal and conservative Protestant student groups was drawn on this occasion and the movements have remained separate and distinct ever since.

The first IVCF Conference was held in 1919 and in 1928 the movement was brought to Canada. In 1938, at the request of interested university students in the United States, the General Secretary of the IVCF of Canada visited the University of Michigan. A group of students gathered informally and later became the first chapter of the IVCF of the United States of America.

Objectives. The Inter-Varsity Christian Fellowship constitution has a threefold purpose which it constantly strives to achieve by its campus groups:

---

[19] Charles E. Hummel, *Campus Christian Witness* (Chicago: Inter-Varsity Press, 1958), p. 2.

1. To witness to the Lord Jesus Christ as God Incarnate and to seek to lead others to a personal faith in Him as Savior and Lord.

2. To deepen and strengthen the spiritual life of members by the study of the Bible and by prayer.

3. To present the call of God to the foreign mission field and so to help all students to discover God's role for them, at home or abroad, in world evangelization.[20]

The IVCF tries to help the individual student mature in his Christian faith so as to live a total Christian life on the campus and, in turn, lead others to faith in Christ as Lord and Savior. The objective of the chapter is to maintain a united witness to Jesus Christ, as one generation of students succeeds another, so that each generation will be exposed to this vision and seek to evangelize others.[21]

Doctrine. Every officer and Bible study leader of the local campus group must subscribe to all parts of the doctrinal statement "without mental reservation"[22] if he is to be recognized by the national organization. If or when a leader no longer finds it possible to accept these statements, he must resign his leadership position. The statement of faith covers the following points:

1. The unique divine inspiration, entire trustworthiness and authority of the Bible.

2. The necessity and efficacy of the substitutionary death of Jesus Christ for the redemption of the world and the historical fact of His bodily resurrection.

3. The deity of our Lord Jesus Christ.

4. The presence and power of the Holy Spirit in the work of regeneration.

5. The expectation of the personal return of our Lord Jesus Christ.[23]

Organization. National leaders speak of IVCF as a movement rather than an organization because its policies are directed towards the creation of autonomous local groups and the development of student leadership. An effective campus chapter may be small but it must be dedicated, living and functioning as a "living organism of Christian life, and a witness of divine grace and power."[24]

The staff worker, or travelling secretary, visiting a campus is not a missionary to the students nor a Bible lecturer, but more of a spiritual coach and counselor, encouraging students to accept the ideal that the "Christian's vocation is to live to the glory of God and to proclaim the good news of salvation" and that "all wage-earning professions are, in the light of this commission, avocations."[25]

---

20 *Ibid.*, p. 50.
21 *Ibid.*, p. 7.
22 *Ibid.*, p. 77.
23 *Ibid.*, p. 79.
24 *Ibid.*, p. 5.
25 *Ibid.*, p. 4.

The number of students on any campus who can and will internalize their faith so that every other value and activity becomes secondary to religious values and activities is, invariably, small. The influence of IVCF on any campus lies not in its numbers but rather in the earnestness, sincerity, and conviction with which a small group goes about its evangelizing mission.

The United States Office of Education lists 1638 institutions of higher education which are not under Catholic or Jewish control. In 1958, IVCF had established chapters at 235 of these institutions, while informal units met on 216 additional campuses. IVCF also had 81 organized chapters and 225 informal groups in a total of 804 nurses' training institutions. Approximately 60 percent of the higher institutions—those with no IVCF chapters—offer the greatest potential for the expansion of the movement at the present time.

IVCF is incorporated as a nonprofit religious organization in the state of Illinois and it is governed by a board of directors that represents many different denominations over a wide geographic area. Sixty staff members work in the national headquarters at Chicago to help students organize and maintain fellowship groups throughout the United States. The national office has no endowment and is solely dependent for its support upon the gifts of its friends. In 1958 more than 21,000 persons contributed to its work.[26]

Summer Camps. Several summer camps are maintained by Inter-Varsity to provide intensive student leadership training during two month-long sessions. One camp is in Ontario, Canada (Campus in the Woods), another on Catalina Island off the coast of southern California (Campus by the Sea), and a third, primarily a missionary training camp, is in Upper Michigan (Cedar Campus). A year-round camp is also maintained in the Rocky Mountains at Bear Trap Ranch near Colorado Springs where monthlong and weeklong student conferences are held throughout the year. Inter-Varsity also provides a year-round schedule of weeklong conferences throughout the country for college and university students and student nurses to encourage spiritual development.

IVCF reported that several hundred students accepted Christ as Lord and Savior through its campus ministry during 1958. More than 1000 students indicated intentions of becoming foreign missionaries and about 1600 students pledged themselves to pray that God would reveal his will for their part in the worldwide mission field.[27]

Case Study of an IVCF Chapter. A chapter of IVCF has been functioning on the campus of a state college in the Northeast for the past ten years with an average of 30 students from a total student body of 3000. The group holds a meeting each week for the membership and in-

---

[26] Inter-Varsity Christian Fellowship, *Inter-Varsity's Two Thousand Mission Fields* (Chicago: 1958), p. 1.
[27] *Ibid.,* p. 2.

vited guests, and there is a considerable amount of hymn singing. (Two of the soloists of the college symphonic choir happened to be members of IVCF in one particular year.) There are also Bible readings and discussions and frequent references to the Bible are made in talks by the members and visiting speakers. And at almost every meeting some member talks about the occasion when he was "saved," and of the peace and spiritual security that came to him as a result of this experience.

The group holds 15- to 20-minute prayer meetings each day at noon in one of the student activity rooms of the College Union. (The only other comparable service is that of the Catholic Newman Club which meets each noon hour to say the Rosary.) IVCF members also get together in informal groups in their rooms for Bible study and religious discussions. The group seeks out and welcomes foreign students, several of whom have found in the IVCF their closest and most abiding campus relationships.

About half of the local chapter affiliated with IVCF because of their conservative Protestant background and the remainder joined because of the appeal of the program or the evangelizing efforts of a member. Most of the group's core members attend the Sunday services of the local conservative Baptist church, which prides itself upon its membership in the Bible Believers Fellowship, an area conference of small conservative churches. The traveling secretary visited the group twice during the year it was studied. On the first trip he spent one week working with officers, attending meetings, and counselling with students who expressed a desire to talk with him. He returned the second semester and spent three days on the campus.

This same year several members attended a regional weekend conference sponsored by Inter-Varsity, and two of the leaders attended an IVCF summer camp. During the college-sponsored Religious Emphasis Week the Newman Club, Hillel, the IVCF and other Protestant student groups conduct the program and activities. Aside from the general meeting, IVCF has its own, independent series of meetings and worship services.

IVCF is a closeknit group, somewhat removed or isolated from the social life of the college community. It is rather difficult to be an enthusiastic fraternity man or sorority girl and at the same time be active in IVCF. Some of the leaders, moreover, make themselves unpopular because of their aggressive evangelizing.

In the ten years that IVCF has been on campus two of its members have answered "the call" by becoming missionaries, one in Africa and the other in South America. Two others entered Bible seminaries and are now ordained preachers. IVCF is still a small group, and not many students become core members or active leaders, but the college community is very conscious of its presence.

Case Studies of Third-Force Personalities

Each of the following autobiographical accounts is that of a college student or of one who has had some college experience.[28] Besides illustrating the pivotal importance that religion had in their lives, these accounts also demonstrate the appeal which evangelical and fundamental Protestantism can have for reasonably sophisticated and formally educated persons.

Case 1. A girl, now a senior, reports that she was brought up as a Methodist and attends religious services more often now than when she lived home because she now attends prayer meeting and Bible study groups. She had a conversion experience in her late teens, largely through the influence of a friend, and chose the orthodox answers to questions concerning the Deity, the Person of Christ, immortality, and the Bible. She is a member of the campus IVCF.

In answering the question of what two things in life she would be proudest of accomplishing, she said "bringing souls to Jesus Christ" and "raising five children." Two lessons that she would try hardest to convey to her children are that there is "salvation only through Jesus Christ" and that they should learn "to live well with their fellow men." The three situations or experiences most vital to her life were "knowing Christ as Savior," "overcoming polio," and "going away to college." She expects religious activities to give her the greatest satisfaction that is possible in life.

Case 2. This sophomore boy was brought up as a Methodist but reports that his early religious training and experience was "incidental" rather than constructive or positive. In his teens, however, he became interested in religion and is now decidedly orthodox in his beliefs and expects the most satisfaction in the life that lies before him from religious activities. The things of which he is or could be most proud are his "religious conversion" and being a "leader of people." The things he would try hardest to teach his children are the "doctrines of Christianity" and "Christian application to everything." The experience that he did not have and would most like his children to have is an "early opportunity to accept Christ." The events of greatest importance to him were "my decision for Christ," and "college."

Case 3. This sophomore girl, an officer and leader of the campus IVCF chapter, reports her religious preference as "Evangelical Protestant" and that she experienced a religious awakening in her early teens. She feels most religious (in "direct communion with God") "through prayer, Bible reading and study, 'fellowship' with those of my own faith and with those not of my own faith to whom God has allowed me to present Him." She is quite objective in her biographical sketch about her feelings and beliefs: "Since most people would tend to identify my associations

---

[28] Case studies from author's files.

with Evangelical Protestantism as emotional, I will consent. Purity of motivation is a point which means a great deal in my own faith. To be in a right stance with God 'heartwise' is more important than to be intellectually aware of God and his gift of Jesus Christ. However, the area in which one feels the impact is the emotional. . . . The Bible tells us that man's true examination of himself comes with 'heart knowledge.' The yielding of the symbolic heart or emotional will to God in Christ is for me the ultimate identification with religion."

Case 4. Once a person has really internalized fundamentalist doctrine and religion, he is never again quite the same—as this account of a college junior suggests: "My religious experience was, on the whole, an enjoyable experience and of definite benefit to me. I went through a stage, at the age of 13, when I was a deep fundamentalist—tent meetings, revival songs, tracts in the subway. I felt it my duty to "preach Jesus" to others. During high school, this tore me apart. I am adjusting now, but I still feel inside of me that those ways are correct. I now attend the Episcopal church."

Case 5. Some parents are anxious that their children will enjoy the same religious peace and security that they have enjoyed. A mother of two, who was brought up as a Free Methodist whose religious preference is now either "Free Methodist or Fundamental Baptist," reports that she is bringing her children up in "Protestant fundamentalist beliefs" because "I really believe the Bible and its teachings. Jesus came to save the world and I accepted him as my personal savior. So I do not want the family circle broken after I die and go to Heaven. Children must have a 'something' upon which to anchor their lives."

Case 6. A mother of seven was brought up in a good Methodist home where the father conducted Bible reading for the family. She joined the Methodist church, attended prayer meeting, and young peoples' meeting (as well as Sunday services), but now attends an Assembly of God church. She takes all her children to church every Sunday and will bring them up in the Assembly of God religion because, "Having accepted Jesus Christ as my personal Savior I feel it my duty and privilege to so train my children that they may also experience this and find the faith, peace, strength, and comfort such belief brings into their personal lives. It definitely gives meaning to life. I expect them to have a good knowledge of the Bible and its teachings."

Case 7. A college male, a junior, married, member of a Baptist church that belongs to the General Association of Regular Baptists, reports he is going to church more now since "I've accepted the Lord as my Savior." He feels "most" religious during the services at his church: "I feel so at the time of our service when the pastor gives the invitation which is for anyone present that wishes to accept the Lord and be Born Again. I pray along with the rest of the congregation for those that are unsaved to come forward and to acknowledge the fact that they want to walk with Him."

He reports that he will raise any children he may have as regular Baptists. "I've answered as I have because I believe the Bible completely and have been assured of going to heaven by accepting the Lord Jesus as my Savior here on earth. I was not raised on these beliefs, but have come about them in the last two years and am eternally grateful for the saving grace that God has given us."

Case 8. Stanley Donnelly is a graduate engineer holding a responsible position in one of the major industries of the city. He is happily married, has three children, owns a nice home in one of the better residential areas of the city, and is well known and respected. He was an active lay member of the Presbyterian church and served for several years as the treasurer of the Ashland Council of Churches.

Although he was a conscientious and capable treasurer, he did not find himself in complete agreement with the business and problems that seemed to be the chief concern of the Council. Too much time was devoted, he said, to things that had little vital relation to the realities of religion. Three summers ago he and his wife began to attend the camp meetings of the Ashland Bible Conference, an organization of religious groups dedicated to a more conservative and literal interpretation of the Bible, located five miles west of the city at the foot of the mountain. He was impressed by the evangelistic sermons of two professional evangelists, but deeply moved by the message of the third speaker, a successful businessman and, at the conclusion, answered the call to come down front to be a "witness of Christ." He described his feelings and the reasons for his actions as follows:

As I listened to this speaker quote the Bible and expound its teachings, I began to realize that this was the religion for me. I was pretty smug and satisfied with myself, but it began to dawn on me that I was a sinner who could only be helped through the saving power of Christ. All I had been hearing in my church was a "liberal" and "modernist" religion—brotherly love to the exclusion of large parts of the Bible. These men could quote the Bible by the hour, from the Old Testament and the New, and it all meant the same thing: Christ is my Savior, through Him and Him alone may I secure my salvation.

Stanley drifted from the Presbyterian church and affiliated with the Baptist Tabernacle. He tells his friends that the Tabernacle and its "Bible-believers" orientation is the kind of religion that appeals to him. He reads and studies the Bible, believes strongly in the power of prayer, and prays frequently, whether at Tabernacle services or with his family at home.

Summary

Third-force Protestantism probably has no more adherents than Judaism, but because it is an active, vital, and dedicated movement, exercises an influence out of proportion to its numerical size. Its doctrines are definite and its beliefs are specific, and are based solely upon the "revealed and infallible Bible." The communicant's consequent feeling of assurance and spiritual peace is matched only in the Catholic system.

Religion is a seven-day-a-week affair for the typical communicant. He is so absorbed in religious activities and his behavior is so guided by religious values that he approaches the ideal of living a separated Christian life. Because the religious role is central and pivotal, there is no real conflict for him between the secular and the sacred; secular affairs and problems are peripheral in importance and effect.

Religion exists for third-force communicants "not as a dull habit but as an acute fever." They believe in their religion and want to share it with others, and they approach people directly and with great spiritual ardor. A local communion becomes an intimate sustaining group fellowship by the quality of the interaction of its members.

Conservative Protestantism is an interesting and challenging exhibit within the broad expanse of American religious culture. Third-force adherents are generous contributors to their local church and its missionary programs. Though the majority comes from the lower-middle class, there is some evidence indicating that many highly educated people are attracted to it.

Chapter IX

Creative Innovation and Religion

RELIGIOUS SYSTEMS are openly competitive in a social milieu of religious pluralism, and the result is that there is free enterprise in the American religious scene. An extensive variety of systems, with varying patterns of belief and worship, continually compete with each other for souls and for the allegiance of the American people. Most Americans, however, are born into their religion; they are baptized into the church or denomination of their parents and usually "join" or become confirmed in this same church when they reach the age of reason. But within the American climate of freedom the individual is always free to change his religion, or to choose no religion at all.

In keeping with free religious choice and our context of religious pluralism, a strong incentive towards religious innovation has existed throughout the historical development of American culture, and this creative innovation is the tendency for religious systems to develop new values for attitudes and behaviors which become "institutionalized" in some significant part of society. And it is the new sects that provide the most dramatic expressions of creative innovation in cultural development. Religious innovation is not, however, an attribute of the new sects alone; the "basic" faiths are equally capable of inducing cultural change. There is, for example, the Christopher movement in Catholicism, the social gospel emphasis in Liberal Protestantism, and the Reform movement within Judaism.[1]

Although religious freedom was an important factor in American colo-

---

[1] The concept of Religious Innovation is based upon the discussion in *Talcott Parsons, Religious Perspectives of College Teaching in Sociology and Social Psychology* (New Haven, Conn.: The Edward W. Hazen Foundation, 1952), pp. 28 ff.

nization, many groups who escaped from the heavy hand of an established religion imposed their own religion upon the community after they, in turn, had attained the dominant position. Several colonies even gave the dominant religion and its members privileges and considerations that were not extended to others. Pennsylvania and Rhode Island, however, were havens for religious freedom and competition.

The Revolution (to recapitulate what we have said in an earlier chapter) proved to be a victory for democracy in religion as well as government and social relations, and the movement for the disestablishment of religion by the various states was led by Jefferson in Virginia. With the acceptance of the principle of separation of Church and State, competition in religion became a reality throughout the young nation.

Such competition, within a context of pluralism, has proved to be highly beneficial to all religious groups: even churches which enjoy a privileged position in other countries flourish in the American climate of free enterprise. Evelyn Waugh finds that Catholicism is considerably more vital, effective, and dynamic in America where it must compete with all other bodies in a "free and open market" than it is in countries where it enjoys state support, protection, and special privileges.[2]

A young Lutheran pastor of our acquaintance was granted a summer scholarship by his national organization in recognition of his parish work and spent the summer studying and traveling in Norway where the Lutheran is the state church, receiving state financial support and enjoying other privileges. Our friend was surprised to find that most of the services were poorly attended, especially since his own church, functioning in a small city and in competition with a number of Catholic and Protestant churches, was thronged, active, and effective, and stood at or near the top in the areas by which parishes and congregations are commonly evaluated.[3] This pastor maintains, as a consequence of his experience, that competition is just as salutary for religion as it is for business.

Freedom and competition, however, have led to divisiveness and fragmentation, and this is particularly true in the Protestant faith. The eighteenth century was a period of doctrinal emphasis and sensitivity when many denominations split over points of doctrine. The tendency to fragment was later stimulated by the Civil War and the issues and problems that led up to it.

The Methodists and Baptists, with their emphasis upon individual interpretation of the Bible, proved a most fertile source of new religious groups. Often the points of difference seemed rather small, but to the divisive groups a little doctrinal difference justified a new church and organization. Even in 1963 the *Yearbook of American Churches*[4] listed 21 different and

---

2 Evelyn Waugh, *Life*, Sept. 19, 1949, pp. 134–8.

3 W. Seward Salisbury, *Organization and Practice of Religion in a Small City* (Oswego, N.Y.: Ontario Press, 1951).

4 *The Yearbook of American Churches, 1963* (New York: National Council of Churches of Christ in America).

independent Methodist groups, ranging from the Methodist church, with more than 10,000,000 members, to the Cumberland Methodist church, with only 65. Denominations, such as the Lumber River Annual Conference of the Holiness Methodist church, with 360 members, and the Primitive Methodist church, U.S.A., with 12,000 members, also maintained denominational identity.

Twenty-eight different Baptist groups were listed for the same year, and four were substantial aggregations of more than a million members, led by the Southern Baptist Convention with a membership of more than ten million. Doctrinal divisions are suggested by the names in the listing: Free Will Baptist, with 193,000 members; General Six-Principle Baptist, with 258 members; Primitive Baptists, with 72,000 members; Separate Baptists, with 7,000 members, and the Two-Seeds-in-the-Spirit Predestinarian Baptists, with 201 members.

A free market in religious ideas, as these examples show, encourages a proliferation of religious groupings: some groups leave their church and form their own while others may return to the fold.

Freedom to choose has also led to the creation of unique and significant religious innovations. From time to time religiously oriented individuals have found that none of the existing sects, denominations, or fragments could meet their religious needs, and a new synthesis of religious ideas or new religion has often been the result.

Out of a climate of freedom have sprung such distinctive and idiosyncratic groupings as Christian scientists, Seventh-day Adventists, and Jehovah's Witnesses which have weathered the test of time and experience, passed from the sect to the denomination stage, and are here to stay. Many Americans fall away from their identification with older churches and affiliate with these groups. This is particularly true of Christian Science and Jehovah's Witnesses.

THE MORMONS

Of all the religious innovations that have emerged throughout the historical development of American culture, none has been more dramatic, colorful—or controversial—than the Church of Jesus Christ of Latter-Day Saints, commonly called the Mormon church.

The Church of Jesus Christ of Latter-Day Saints has progressed beyond the sect into the denomination and church stage. It is highly institutionalized, has two million members and is growing rapidly, and is one of the wealthiest church bodies in the United States. The Mormon church, furthermore, is no longer primarily a phenomenon of the state of Utah; Mormons are also numerous and influential in Idaho, Washington, Oregon, California, Arizona, and New Mexico, and substantial numbers live in metropolitan areas along the eastern seaboard. In fact, many Americans seeking a source of religious truth and values have the Mormon choice continually before them; young Mormon missionaries by the thousands knock on the doors of American homes and carry their message to whomsoever will listen.

Although the Mormon religious system has a number of elements of strength, the two most distinctive are the stress upon lay leadership within a hierarchical setting and the widespread participation of the communicant in the work as well as the worship of his church.

Mormonism was a product of its time and represented a cross-section of the nineteenth century American mind.[5] Sectarianism, ecumenicism, communitarianism, and the freedom and striving that characterized the frontier all contributed to the belief and practice that became the Mormon faith. Mormonism was also an expression of the optimism of the times and a repudiation of Calvinist pessimism. The denial of human freedom that was implied in the Calvinist doctrine of predestination (and also led to Unitarianism and Universalism) contributed to the development of Mormonism.

A number of communitarian religious experiments flourished in the intellectual and religious ferment that characterized western New York during the first half of the nineteenth century. A Shaker community was located at Sodus Bay, less than 30 miles from Palmyra, New York. Jemina Wilkinson, the "Universal Friend," established her community on Seneca Lake, and a few years later (in the 1840s) John Humphrey Noyes established his perfectionist community at nearby Oneida. So many diverse movements swept this area that it has become known as the "Burned-over District."[6]

But along with divisiveness and sectarianism went a tendency toward ecumenicism, and various revival movements, constituting the "Second Great Awakening," swept through western New York at this time. These revivals tended to ignore denominational lines and to emphasize the unity rather than the variety of Protestantism. Mormonism was one of the movements in this direction.

Beliefs

Joseph Smith. Mormonism, both as a religious and as a social system, is based squarely upon the revelations of Joseph Smith, the charismatic leader and prophet whose revelations became the warp and woof of Mormon belief, organization, and values.

Smith was born in Vermont in 1805, and in 1815 his family migrated to upstate New York and established a farm near Palmyra, where Baptist,

---

[5] Thomas O'Dea, *The Mormons* (Chicago: University of Chicago Press, 1957), pp. 12–16; William Mulder, "The Mormons in American History," *Bulletin of the University of Utah,* Vol. 48, No. 11 (January 14, 1957).

[6] Whitney Cross, *The Burned-Over District: The Social and Intellectual History of Enthusiastic Religion in Western New York, 1800–1850* (Ithaca, N.Y.: Cornell University Press, 1950).

Methodist, and Presbyterian evangelists and revivalists were active. His family attended these revivals, and his mother, a sister, and two brothers were converted and joined the Presbyterian church.

Although young Joseph was highly religious and something of a mystic, none of the denominations seemed to be the answer to his religious needs. The unifying and nondenominational nature of the revivalist movements disappeared with the departure of the evangelists and soon the local churches were again bickering over converts and points of doctrine. Smith was convinced that none of the existing churches could be a sufficient repository of Christian truth.

Smith reports he was reading the Bible when he came across the verse: "If any of you lack wisdom, let him ask of God."[7] He retired to the woods on the family farm one day in the early spring of 1820 to meditate and pray, and there in a blinding light, he saw two personages "Whose brightness and glory defy all description, standing above me in the air." One spoke to him, and pointed to the other, saying "This is my Beloved Son, hear Him!" Smith asked which sect he should join and was told to join none for all were wrong. Many other things were told to him, and when "I came to myself again, I found myself lying on my back, looking up into heaven."[8]

Joseph reported his experience to a Methodist preacher, but was ridiculed, treated with contempt, and told that all visions and revelations had ceased with the Apostles. But Smith persisted in his search for religious truth and continued to meditate and pray and a second mystical experience came to him in the quiet of his bedroom September 21, 1823.

"After I had retired to bed for the night, I betook myself to prayer and supplication to Almighty God for forgiveness of all my sins and follies and also for a manifestation to me, that I might know of my state and standing before Him."[9] A figure appeared whose person was "glorious beyond description, and countenance truly like lightning." The figure said he was the angel Moroni, sent by God, and he told Smith of a book, written upon gold plates, that gave an account of the former inhabitants of this continent. Moroni said the book also contained the everlasting Gospel, as delivered by the Saviour to the ancient inhabitants.

The angel's directions took Smith to a nearby hill called Cumorah. After some digging Smith uncovered a box under a large stone, but was told by a "messenger" that the time for bringing the plates forth had not yet arrived. Smith made pilgrimages to the gold plates for four years, when, on September 22, 1827, the "messenger" told Smith that the time had come for the plates to be revealed to men.

Because of his claims of divine revelation and ministrations by angelic

---

[7] James I:5.

[8] *Joseph Smith Tells His Own Story* (Salt Lake City, Utah: Deseret New Press), p. 4.

[9] *Ibid.*, p. 7.

beings, Smith was viewed with suspicion and subjected to indignities and abuse. He sought refuge at the home of his father-in-law in Pennsylvania and, from December to February of that winter, translated the plates (said to be similar to Egyptian hieroglyphics) with the use of the Urim and Thummim (miraculous spectacles) and by the "gift and power of God." Eleven witnesses testified, in a group of three and a group of eight, that they had seen and touched the golden plates before they were "returned," and although three of the witnesses became apostates from the church, none ever repudiated his testimony. Smith shortly published a book based upon his translations from the plates and called it the Book of Mormon.

A further revelation came to Smith in answer to his prayer for guidance on baptism: a "messenger from heaven descended in a cloud of light, and having laid his hands upon us [Smith and Oliver Cowdery], he ordained us, saying: 'Upon you, my fellow servants, in the name of Messiah I confer the priesthood of Aaron which holds the keys of the ministering of angels, and of the Gospel of repentance, and of baptism by immersion for the remission of sins; and this shall never be taken from the earth.' "[10]

The Church of Jesus Christ of Latter-Day Saints believes these revelations are of the greatest importance; that the true Gospel of Christ had to be restored and the priesthood reestablished—both of which had been removed from the earth through "apostasy." Priesthood means "the power to act in the name of God," and, according to the church apologists, the authority to establish Christ's Church was restored through revelation.

Smith accordingly organized the Church of Jesus Christ of Latter-Day Saints on April 6, 1830, with six charter members, and, as commanded by his revelations, laid his hands upon each and ordained them as Elders in the church. Others were baptized later and within a year about 1500 members were brought into the church.

The church continued to grow, but wherever the Mormons settled they incurred the suspicion and animosity of the community, due in part to the radical nature of their religion and in part to the jealousy which their material achievements aroused in the hearts of the "gentile" neighbors. The covenant of the faithful called for the establishment of Zion in the western hemisphere where the faithful could await the return and rule of Christ on earth. Zion proved to be a close-knit community in which hard work and individual effort, combined with cooperation for the common good, made the Mormons highly successful in material ventures.

Within fifteen years the Mormon community moved from western New York to Kirtland, Ohio, Independence, Missouri, and Nauvoo, Illinois, struggling all the while to build the City of Zion. Their cities grew and their farms prospered, and they sent missionaries all over the United States as well as to England and the Scandinavian countries.

At Carthage, Illinois, Joseph Smith, the Prophet, and his brother Hyrum were killed by a mob. The leadership fell to Brigham Young and the deci-

---

[10] *Ibid.,* p. 16.

sion was made to migrate to Utah, beyond the reach of hostile gentiles and a hostile government. Brigham Young was not only a great religious leader but a great colonizer and pioneer as well, and the qualities that had made the Mormons a success in the settled East proved equal to the imperatives of a desert frontier. They found Utah a desert and made it "blossom like a rose."

Contemporary Belief. For several years classes in the sociology of religion have secured their knowledge of contemporary Mormon belief, worship, and practice from lectures by young Mormon missionaries assigned to the Eastern States Mission. The doctrine and belief presented was consistent and undeviating, and the following is a composite analysis.

According to the Mormons, the New World was inhabited at the time of Christ by advanced and highly cultured people, the descendants of Lehi of the house of Joseph, who, with his followers, left Jerusalem in 600 B.C., and sailed down the Red Sea and across the Indian and Pacific oceans to the western coast of South America. The people, who grew rapidly in strength and numbers in their promised land, soon divided into opposing factions under their leaders, Nephi and Laman.

The Nephites advanced in the arts and crafts, built large cities, established commonwealths, and worshipped the true God. Christ ministered among these people after his resurrection in Jerusalem. The Lamanites became a benighted, nomadic people with a dark skin, the lineal progenitors of the American Indian.

The two nations repeatedly waged wars against each other, the final struggle taking place in 400 A.D. in the vicinity of the Hill Cumorah, near Palmyra, New York, with the extermination of the Nephites. But their great prophet, Mormon, had first collected and abridged their records and engraved the history of his people on a single volume of metallic plates which was then hidden in a stone vault at Hill Cumorah.

The "pure" Church of Christ, according to the missionaries, was taken back into heaven with the death of the Apostles in the Holy Land and the annihilation of the Nephites in the New World. "We come to take away no truth that you have, but we have more truth to offer." "Our claim is a 'restoration' of Christ's Church. The Church of Jesus Christ of Latter-Day Saints is neither Catholic nor Protestant. Like Protestants and Catholics, we believe in the Trinity, the Atonement, the resurrection from the dead, and the immortality of the soul." "However, there are," say the missionaries, "important differences in the interpretation of these doctrines which make our worship and our practice a distinguishably new manifestation of the Christian faith."

Mormons are confident that science will never undo the essential concepts of the "revealed" elements of their faith. "We know these things are true," say the missionaries, "by prayer, by study, and by attending our church." Each Mormon has the test of the truth continually before him, a test which is also a means of renewal of his faith: "And when ye shall receive these things, I would exhort you that you would ask God, the Eternal Father, in the name of Christ, if these things are not true; and if ye shall ask with a sincere heart, with real intent, having faith in Christ, he will manifest the truth of it unto you, by the power of the Holy Ghost."[11]

The Sacred Books.   The Mormons have four sacred books: the *Bible*, the *Book of Mormon, Doctrine and Covenants,* and the *Pearl of Great Price.* According to the missionaries, none of them contradict the *Bible* or each other. The last three amplify and supplement points of doctrine and areas of belief where the Bible is either not clear or is lacking in information.

The *Book of Mormon* is representative of left-wing Christianity and the popular Protestantism that flourished in the early nineteenth century.[12] It rejects the doctrines of predestination, election, and original sin,[13] and it condemns infant baptism.[14]

Mormon theology leans heavily upon the doctrine of free will. Because men have been redeemed from the fall, they have "become free forever, knowing good from evil; to act for themselves and not be acted upon."[15] However, because there can be no real choice with an absence of knowledge, neither can there be guilt without knowledge.[16] *The Book of Mormon* supports the doctrine of salvation by works and states that men will be judged on this basis.

Mormonism is a religion of mastery and activism. According to the doctrine of eternal progression, human effort and constructive activity in this world will advance men toward eternal glory and even to "Godhood."[17] In one of his revelations Joseph Smith proclaimed that "Whatever principle of intelligence we attain unto in this life it will rise with us in resurrection. And if a person gains more knowledge and intelligence in this life through his diligence and obedience than another, he will have so much the advantage in the world to come."

Doctrine and Covenants include 136 revelations, all but three the revelations of Joseph Smith. *The Pearl of Great Price* includes the "Book of Moses," the "Book of Abraham," and other "inspired" writings of Smith. Whenever a question or problem arose Smith would retire to pray and meditate, and the question would always be answered by revelation. By the time of his death, at the age of 39, Smith had outlined the basic features of the faith and morality that constitute contemporary Mormon belief and practice.

The bishop of a ward, a highly successful practicing physician, showed

---

[11] *The Book of Mormon,* Moroni 10:4.

[12] T. O'Dea, *op. cit.*

[13] Joseph Smith, *History of the Church of Jesus Christ of Latter Day Saints,* B. H. Roberts (ed.) (Salt Lake City, Utah: 1902), Vol. IV, p. 546.

[14] *The Book of Mormon,* Moroni 8:5–6.

[15] *Ibid.,* 11 Nephi, 2:26.

[16] *Ibid.,* Mosiah 3:11–22.

[17] T. O'Dea, *op. cit.,* p. 56.

the great confidence and respect that Mormons have for their first Prophet when he observed: "How exciting, how miraculous to know that this wonderful religion and Church of ours is due solely to the revelations of Joseph Smith, a simple farm boy with nothing more than an elementary school education."

A New World View. The Mormon concept of the Trinity differs somewhat from the generally accepted Christian doctrine. The Father, the Son, and the Holy Ghost are three separate persons.[18] God is not a spirit, as most Christians profess to believe, but a material being. "All spirit is matter, but it is more fine or pure."[19] "God is not merely of the spirit, but is of flesh and bone and spirit. Christ is exactly like God, but the Holy Spirit has not a body of flesh and bones, but is a personage of the Spirit."[20]

God is not outside time or removed from man and the world. "As man is, God was; as God is, man may be. It is the first principle of the Gospel to know that God was once a man like us. . . . Each man possesses the potentialities of becoming like God; of going from one small degree to another, from a small capacity to a great. This is not all accomplished in this world. Man works to learn salvation and exaltation even beyond the grave."[21] Life can be an eternal progression, on and up to eternal glory.

Temple Rites. The problem of how those who have gone before may share in the new dispensation is resolved in impressive and important Temple ceremonies: vicarious rites for the dead, or baptism by living proxy which makes possible "the salvation of the dead who should die without knowledge of the Gospel."[22] By such rites are the dead enabled to progress in the afterlife—"For without them we cannot be made perfect."[23] The dead person's will in the world beyond, moreover, would be insufficient without the performance of this "earthly ordinance."[24] It is easy to understand that only Mormons in good standing are permitted to enter the "Holy of Holies" and participate in such rites.

"Sealing" of children and marriage for "time and eternity" take place only in the Temple.[25] In the marriage ceremonies, considerable attention is given to the anointing of the senses and vital organs with oil. Temple rites, according to accounts of apostates, are ritualistic, elaborate, and impressive, and in striking contrast to the informality and lack of ritual of the regular Sunday service in a typical ward chapel.

The first Temple was built in Kirtland, Ohio, but twelve are now located in the United States and various parts of the world. There are four

---

18 LeGrand Richards, *A Marvelous Work and a Wonder* (Salt Lake City, Utah: Deseret New Press), pp. 111–132.

19 *Doctrine and Covenants*, 131:7.

20 *Ibid.*, 130:22.

21 Joseph Smith, *The King Follett Discourse,* B. H. Roberts (ed.) (Salt Lake City, Utah: 1930), pp. 8–21.

22 *Doctrine and Covenants*, 128:5.

23 *Ibid.*, 128:18.

24 T. O'Dea, *op. cit.*, p. 58.

25 See Chapter XV, Religion and the Family.

in Utah, one each in California, Arizona, Idaho, Canada, Hawaii, New Zealand, Switzerland, and England, and more are being planned.

Contributions of Smith and Young. Mormons feel secure and confident in their beliefs and in the "restoration of the true church" because of the revelations their prophet received directly from God. The belief that each individual is master of his fate, and may on this earth work towards godliness, runs through all of their sacred works and is reflected in the worship and program of each local church.

Brigham Young gave practical application to the "restored" beliefs and little of importance in doctrine or morality was added after his decease. Although the doctrine of plural marriage was not promulgated publicly until 1852, several years after Smith's death, the doctrine and its practice were credited to him.

Mormon Values

Mormonism, offering a complete religious and social way of life, was a perfectionist religion in its earliest days and has remained so to the present. Its faithful are challenged to work their way to perfection through what has been termed the work, health, recreation, and education complex.[26]

Health and Recreation. A sound mind in a sound body is the first requisite of a person who desires to live happily and serve well,[27] and Mormons, maintaining that the body is the tabernacle for man's spirit, believe anything that hurts the body also harms the spirit. Because it is God's will to preserve health, intelligence, and spirituality, Mormons are forbidden to take alcohol in any form, to smoke, or to partake of tea, coffee, or other hot drinks.[28] Right living, in terms of health, extends to other dietary matters: Mormons are advised to eat herbs and fruits in season, to eat meat sparingly, and to rely primarily upon cereals and grains.[29] Since the Utah death rate is considerably below the national rate, it appears the health rules are quite largely followed.

Mormons, strong advocates of physical exercise and wholesome recreation, have from early days put a high value on play and joy while at the same time repudiating the religious pessimism and blue law orientation of the Puritan tradition. "Men are that they might have joy."[30] Sports and athletics, dancing and dramatics are important features of the socio-spiritual program of each ward. Mormons recognize the group factor in play, finding that the group not only enhances play, but is often the main motivating factor. The Mormons, in short, have spiritualized recreation.[31]

---

26 T. O'Dea, *op. cit.*, p. 143.
27 John A. Widtsoe, *Rational Theology* (Salt Lake City, Utah: 1915), p. 56.
28 *Doctrine and Covenants*, 89:5, 7–9.
29 *Ibid.*, 89:10–17.
30 *The Book of Mormon*, 11 Nephi, 2:25.
31 Rex A. Skidmore, *Mormon Recreation in Theory and Practice: A Study in Social Change* (Philadelphia, 1941), p. 5.

Education. The Mormon belief that life on earth should be a period of advancement through self-improvement and mastery leads to a great stress upon education. Joseph Smith devoted several revelations to the desirability and need for learning and intellectual development. "Seek ye out of the best books words of wisdom; seek learning, even by study and also by faith."[32] "The glory of God is intelligence, or in other words, light and truth."[33] The leaders of the early Mormon groups were reported to be noticeably above average in intelligence and education.

Utah has the highest rate of literacy of any state in the Union, and recently went ahead of Massachusetts as the birth place of distinguished men of science and of letters.[34] The ward hall is the center of both social and educational activity. Each church offers an extensive program of educational opportunities for the various levels of aptitude and interests found in its congregation. The development of hobby skills under trained teachers, discussion groups on political issues or current events, child study groups for young parents, music and dramatic training, and opportunities for participation are commonly found in the program of the ward.

One night a week the Young Men's Mutual Improvement Association meets with the Young Women's Mutual Improvement Association in a program of discussion sessions, group dancing, singing, and other forms of socializing, but always observing the Mormon prohibitions against smoking, drinking, and promiscuous intimacy between the sexes.

During their long trek across the plains, they often brought out musical instruments for singing and dancing around the evening camp fire. Nor have Mormons ever found drama and the theatre inconsistent with spiritual values. In the early days of the colony Brigham Young led the movement to build a theatre which for a long time was the largest theatre west of the Mississippi. Dramatics and dramatic festivals, dances and dance festivals, debates and orations, choruses, and sports tournaments are found in Mormon communities both large and small.

For thirty years, through the facilities of CBS and by other means, the Salt Lake City Tabernacle Choir has made Americans aware of the importance of religious music to the Mormon service.

Religion as Doing. A Mormon family devotes all of Sunday to religious activities and services. At nine o'clock the father and boys attend the weekly Priesthood meeting, presided over by the bishop, and followed by Sunday School at ten, the first meeting for the mother and daughters. It differs from the conventional Protestant Sunday School in that the first 45 minutes are taken up with a number of two and one-half minute talks by young people, many of whom are girls, and is followed by a service in which sanctified bread and water constitute the sacred

---

[32] *Doctrine and Covenants*, 88:118.

[33] *Ibid.*, 93:36.

[34] Edward L. Thorndike, "The Origins of Superior Men," *Scientific Monthly* (May, 1943); also *Science News Letter*, August 31, 1943.

elements. At 10:45 the general meeting adjourns to various age-group classes with uniform lessons for the whole church.

A second service is held in the late afternoon, primarily for adults and consisting of hymns, prayers, sacraments, and two or three speakers on assigned or chosen topics. In the evening teenagers and young adults gather for "fireside" meetings where they sing and study the scriptures. Some observers find that the Mormon atmosphere is rather informal and the talks are not impressive. The services do, however, meet the Mormon demand for widespread lay participation and act also as a training ground for young people to develop the personal and social qualities which will prepare them to serve their church in leadership positions in adult life.

The "Gathering."   Mormons meet life and solve problems with cooperation and mutuality, both of which have theological overtones. Joseph Smith's City of Zion was a "Gathering of Saints," brothers in the spirit cooperating in the flesh for the early return of Christ and the establishment of the Kingdom of God in the western hemisphere.[35] As the doctrine of eternal progression took root, less and less emphasis was given to the millennial aspect of the faith.

As Smith developed the doctrine of degrees of glory represented in the celestial, terrestrial, and "telestial" stages in the evolution of the individual, salvation became an on-going process in which life on this earth was a necessary and inevitable stage. This theological imperative gave Mormonism a strong "this-worldly" orientation. The kind of life and the nature of social relations on earth determined the individual saint's progress towards glory.

The "gathering" (or Mormon community) always involved two different, if not opposing, social processes: cooperation (mutual help and at times socialism and even communism) and individualism (capitalism, private property, and self-sufficiency). In the history of the Mormon experiment the trend towards cooperation would from time to time appear to be in the ascendancy, but always the counter trend towards independence and self-sufficiency would develop to offset the full realization of the socialistic or communistic community.

The social structure of the Mormon community at any given time was always the result of the interaction of belief and experience. The structure of the Mormon community was influenced by strong in-group loyalty and solidarity, attributable in part to religious conviction—that they were the chosen people, acting according to God's revealed will—and in part to the ever-present hostility of the non-Mormon culture, whether it was the "gentile" community in Ohio or Missouri or Illinois, or the Indians, or the federal or state governments.

In 1831, Joseph Smith revealed the Law of Consecration (or First United Order) which was based upon the Biblical teaching that the earth

---

[35] *Doctrine and Covenants,* 42:30.

is the Lord's (men merely holding the land and its resources in steward-ship) and provided that each Saint would turn his property over to the bishop. Each Saint was to cultivate his land or his business according to the principles of competition and free enterprise, but to retain only enough to meet the requirements of his family, circumstances, and "wants and needs."[36] The excess was to be turned over to the church for distribution to the landless and impoverished according to the principle of "every man according to his needs." The remainder would rest in the church treasury and be used for the common good of the religious community. Thus the plan provided for the production of wealth through free enterprise but the surplus was socialized. Saints were enjoined to live simply and frugally, to work diligently, and to share honestly in the United Order.[37]

The plan was not successful. Problems arose over the transfer of prop-erty of converts entering the Mormon community, and over the collection and distribution of the surplus. The plan, moreover, was more socialistic than the individualism and self-reliance of the individual Saints could stand. But Mormons continued to cooperate in a number of economic and business projects, in the erection of churches and temples, in contribut-ing to the support of the Church, and in 1838 Smith decreed that tithing "shall be a standing Law" for the Saints.[38]

In 1873 Brigham Young advocated another United Order where all worked together "to labor for the benefit of the whole." A number of Mormon communities tried this new type of socialism, which failed within a year. The relatively short history of Mormonism has shown that its ad-herents will cooperate voluntarily and contribute generously under central leadership, but only within the framework of individualism and self-reliance.

Cooperation. Mormons could never have survived as a community or a faith if they had not possessed a high sense of solidarity. The hundreds of communities in the Utah desert (360 at the time of the death of Brigham Young) had to cooperate to survive. Only through community-wide co-operation, for example, was it possible to divert streams from the moun-tains and to dig miles of canals and irrigation ditches to water the farm lands of each village community.

Industrialization has made American society so independent and com-plex that when the Depression hit the country in the early 1930's even rural Utah was faced with a relief and welfare problem with which the traditional relief techniques could not cope. But the church met the prob-lem by adapting basic Mormon principles to the new situation.

The local ward had kept in contact with its needy families through monthly visits of teachers under the direction of the Bishop, and relief

---

[36] *Ibid.,* 51:3.
[37] Joseph A. Geddes, *The United Order Among the Mormons: An Unfinished Experiment in Economic Organization* (Salt Lake City, Utah: 1924), pp. 31–32.
[38] *Doctrine and Covenants,* 119:3–4.

had been extended where needed from the ward storehouse of essentials kept on hand for such emergencies. The Women's Relief Society of the ward played an important role in administering this relief, and the Mormon woman served her faith by helping the needy widow or orphan.

But the Depression continued to grow and Mormons were reluctant to have the federal government step in to provide for the unemployed; reliance upon an outside source would be contrary to a principle laid down by Joseph Smith: "It has always been a cardinal teaching with the Latter-day Saints that a religion that has not the power to save people temporally and make them prosperous and happy here cannot be depended upon to save them spiritually and to exalt them in the life to come."[39]

The church reacted by doing in a bigger way what it had already been doing on a smaller scale. The Church Welfare Program, established in 1936, provided a three-fold approach to the relief and welfare problem through:

First, the distribution of necessities through a system of "work certificates"—a bishop's orders on one of the 70 storehouses maintained by the church throughout Mormon territory and cleared through the Central Bishop's Storehouse on Welfare Square in Salt Lake City. If physically able, however, the recipient had to give some service in return to preserve his self-respect.

Secondly, the program itself provided employment for church members who were out of work, especially as the industries and properties of the Church are numerous and extensive. At some time or another, the Church has fostered brickmaking, coal mining, soap making, home construction, lumber milling, and knitted underwear industries.

Thirdly, the Church holds that this program realized spiritual goals by giving "every man an intensified interest in his brother's welfare. Upon the weak and strong it places an obligation of mutual support. The strong must assist the weak; the weak must seek strength for themselves. There must be abundant charity but no almsgiving. All must produce. All must pay in some way for that which they receive. The program cannot succeed unless helper and helped in brotherhood stand shoulder to shoulder in a consecration of effort to banish the inequalities which separate them from each other and threaten their religious solidarity. Opportunity, self-support and mutual goodwill form the foundation of the program."[40]

Tithing. The welfare program is only one activity that requires large sums of money and capital. The widespread missionary and educational activities and the comprehensive building program (ward chapels and halls, temples, educational buildings) require substantial contributions from the membership. Since Smith's revelations in 1841, each Mormon is expected to obey the tithing precept and give one-tenth of his income, most

---

[39] *Helping Others to Help Themselves, The Story of the Mormon Church Welfare Program* (Salt Lake City, Utah).

[40] *Ibid.*, p. 5.

of which goes into the general church fund. In addition to the tithe, the good Mormon contributes another two percent of his income to his local ward chapel and hall.

The first Sunday in each month is a fast day in which the family forgoes two meals, and the amount of money thereby saved is donated to a special fund for the relief of the needy. Such fasting is healthful, Mormons believe, and also a form of spiritual discipline that leads along the path of *eternal progression*.

Organization

The local congregations of the Church of Jesus Christ of Latter-Day Saints are well organized, closely integrated groups of interacting personalities. The leadership is entirely lay; there is no theologically trained, specially educated, or professional leadership. Spiritual, administrative, and organizational leadership is performed by lay personnel, none of whom is paid for his services.

The church, however, is organized along both hierarchical and democratic lines in what the Mormons call a "theo-democracy." Decisions and appointments are made from above but have to be sustained by the congregation or the body concerned in an open meeting. Every young Mormon is encouraged to participate in the work of his church and it is assumed that each will work his way into positions of increasing responsibility and authority.

The opportunities to participate and to lead are abundant. In a typical ward there are approximately 200 positions of administrative and spiritual leadership, and 65 percent of all Mormons between the ages of 18 and 40 can hold one of these positions. "The genius of the organizational efforts of the Church is the universal participation in its activities."[41]

Women, although excluded from the priesthoods, play an important role in the church through their Relief and Young Women's Mutual Improvement societies. Or they may serve as missionaries. But the Mormon mother, like the Jewish mother, plays her most important religious role by maintaining a closely knit and harmonious home according to Mormon principles and values.

Geographical Organization. Each ward, varying in membership from 200 to 1800, is administered by a bishop and two counselors, and a "stake" is composed of from 4 to 15 wards, the latter being territories in which 2000 to 10,000 members reside in comparatively close proximity. There are approximately 300 stakes in the worldwide church, most of which are in the United States, Canada, Mexico, and the Hawaiian Islands. The stake is presided over by a president and two counselors with the assistance of a high council of 12 men.

The missions of the church are in scattered areas of America, Europe, and other lands where membership is low, and they are specially organized

---

[41] Stephen L. Richards, *About the Mormons* (Salt Lake City, Utah).

to take care of relatively small groups. Each mission is supervised by a president who is assisted by numerous traveling missionaries, chiefly from the stakes.

The supreme power of the church is vested in the President and his two Counselors, who constitute the First Presidency. Next to the Presidency in general authority is the Council of the Twelve Apostles. Ezra Taft Benson was an active member of the Council during the time he served as Secretary of Agriculture in President Eisenhower's cabinet. Next in authority come seven men who constitute the First Council of Seventy, then the Presiding Bishop and two Counselors. These officials, plus a Presiding Patriarch, are the 26 men who constitute the General Authorities of the Church and hold jurisdiction over its worldwide activities.[42]

The Priesthoods. A Mormon ward, counterpart of the parish or congregation, functions through two priesthoods, the Aaronic or Levitical and the Melchizedek, which include all "worthy males" "in a principle of power, of intelligence through which divine work and purpose are achieved."[43] The Aaronic priesthood is open to boys and young men between the ages of 12 and 20 and is concerned with the temporal affairs of the church. It is responsible for perpetuating the gospel and keeping the faithful in line, and is divided into three orders.

Mormon boys by virtue of their conduct and behavior can become deacons at the age of 12 and assist in passing the sacred elements at the sacramental service, running errands for the bishop, and helping in the ward building and the community.

At the age of 14, the deacon may qualify for the second order of teacher. The bishop commonly assigns two teachers to make regular monthly calls upon each Mormon family in the ward, and the teachers carry the message for the month and teach from this message. If there is any help needed they give it, or if they can not give it, they refer the family to the bishop. Finally, they encourage activity in the church's program. These calls are an important responsibility in the work and effectiveness of the church.

Through good work and appropriate spirituality, the teacher may at the age of 16 or 17 qualify for the last order of the Aaronic priesthood; that of priest. The priest has the authority and the duty "to preach, teach, expound, exhort, and baptize and to administer the sacrament."[44]

When the young Mormon has progressed through the three orders of authority in the Aaronic priesthood, he is eligible for entrance into the Melchizedek priesthood, the repository of the spiritual authority of the church. A Mormon does not ordinarily qualify for the first step in the Melchizedek priesthood, that of elder, much before the age of 20; when he

---

[42] *Ibid.*

[43] Lowell L. Bennion, *The Religion of the Latter-day Saints* (Salt Lake City, Utah: 1940), p. 147.

[44] *Doctrine and Covenants*, 20:46.

is ordained an elder he has achieved full adult status and is supposed to preach the gospel either at home or abroad. The authority of the elder includes the power to ordain deacons, teachers, priests, and elders by the "laying on of hands."

Next in the orders of the Melchizedek priesthood is the seventy, who is also charged with preaching the gospel, is assigned certain supervisory functions, and may, after years of study and service, rise to the highest order, that of high priest. The high priests are mature men usually in middle life, and hold "the keys" to the divine power. All important church positions are held by men in this category.

Missionaries. Nowhere does the Mormon religion show to better advantage than in the work, discipline, and sacrifices of its young men who are called to a mission tour of service. Mormonism has retained its acute sense of mission, believing it the function of Christ's church (of which they are the true representatives) to save the whole human family. Furthermore a Mormon, convinced he has a very fine way of life, is naturally willing and glad to share it.

Feeling it a great honor to be sent by his church on a two-year mission in an English-speaking country (a tour among non-English-speaking people is usually six months longer because of the time required for sufficient command of the language), the young man is well trained and well motivated. Twenty is considered the ideal age for by that time many of them will have had two years of college and all will be members of the priesthood. Each of the eight young missionaries who appeared before our classes over a three semester period, for example, had risen to the rank of elder.

The missionaries follow a strict regimen, live highly disciplined lives, and maintain themselves from their own savings and help provided by their families. They work in teams of two and usually rent a room or small apartment with kitchen privileges. According to mission authorities it costs an average of from eighty to one hundred dollars a month for living expenses, and thus each young Mormon contributes two thousand to twenty-four hundred dollars of his own or his family's money—as well as two years of his life—to his work for the church.

Missionaries cannot have dates. They are instructed to keep women at "arm's length" at all times and are forbidden to swim or engage in recreational activities that might lead to an accident or otherwise reduce their effectiveness. They are not permitted vacations or allowed to return home during their tour of duty. They arise early, beginning each day with prayer and meditation at six o'clock, and are expected to be out ringing doorbells by ten each morning. They dress conservatively, are always neat and well groomed and the picture of health and wholesome living. When they ring a doorbell and politely introduce themselves they gain respect for their faith, whether they gain converts or not. Every two weeks 70 to 90 young men are commissioned and depart so that approximately 5000 are always in the mission field.

In 1958 the church reported 31,817 converts had been added during the previous year through the efforts of fulltime missionaries, regular members who were not fulltime missionaries, and by stake missionaries. Stake missionaries regularly spend from 5 to 20 hours proselytizing each month. When the foreign missionary's duty is ended he returns to his home and church and takes up where he left off, whether it is a job, a business, or an educational program. Young missionaries and their families look upon this experience as education and character formation in the broadest sense, as well as a contribution to their faith and their church.

Strains and Stresses

Mormons claim that their church is one of the fastest growing in America although to outsiders the community and fellowship appear closely integrated or highly solidified in the united front they present to opposition and the gentile world. The Mormons that gentiles see most often—the young missionaries—are no doubt among the best but are they the "most" of Mormonism? Every denomination has its marginal and dormant members, its "leakage," and its backsliders. And in spite of inspired and dedicated work, the Church of Jesus Christ of Latter-Day Saints has its backsliders, the "Jack Mormons." Are these marginal and dormant members more or less numerous than in the more representative Protestant denominations? We know of no empirical study that deals with this question.

There are occasional references to "senior Aaronics" in the Mormon literature, men who fail to meet the standard of behavior required for the Melchizedek priesthood, usually for nonobservance of "The Word of Wisdom": the prohibitions against alcohol, tea, coffee, and tobacco. Only Mormons in good standing are admitted to the Temple to enjoy the important "sealing" and baptism ceremonies. Paying the tithe, keeping "The Word of Wisdom," priesthood activity, and a strict adherence to a high standard of morality are the criteria of good standing and the test of loyalty. Temple privileges have to be earned, and because they are not enjoyed by large numbers of Mormons it is possible that Mormons cannot boast a higher percentage of nuclear members than the representative Catholic parish or Protestant congregation.

Nor is there ready information on the effectiveness of conversion: how many become integrated into the Mormon community and worship, and how many apostatize, fall away, or become dormant in spirit and behavior. And, although Mormons place a high value on education, the appeal that the missionaries make is that of a literalist, strictly orthodox doctrine that has little or no intellectual overtones. We believe, but have no data to support our supposition, that the incidence of intellectual achievement is higher among Mormons who were born into the church than among those who entered through conversion.

Joseph Smith and Brigham Young hoped and planned that agriculture would remain the basis of the Mormon economy, and the Mormon religion has flourished under the conditions of rural living that characterize the farming and ranching economy of the intermountain states. Will the Mormon religion and pattern of life be as successful in meeting the religious and social needs of an increasing number of contemporary Saints who live in a typical urban environment? A recent study found that the rural Mormon was significantly more orthodox than the urban Mormon, and as Mormons became more urbanized they became even more secular and more like their non-Mormon neighbors.[45] It is no longer feasible or desirable for converts to migrate to Utah, join a Mormon community, and practice their faith as the dominant group in the community. An increasing number of Mormons will remain in urban and metropolitan areas and be "forced" to practice their religion in communities where they will be a minority and subject to the pressures of conforming to the values of the dominant culture.

From its earliest days the Mormon church has admitted Negroes to simple membership but has not permitted them to progress to the church's priesthood.[46] Negro Mormons do not have the power to baptize, cannot be married in a temple, and do not enjoy the right to bring their non-Mormon ancestors into the church through vicarious baptism. Negroes suffer these disabilities and are ineligible for full spiritual membership because, according to Mormon theology, they came into the world with the curse of Ham and Cain.

Although Mormons are criticized for this practice and belief, the church maintains that it has the right to set the qualifications for its priesthood, and that excluding Negroes is no more discriminatory than the refusal of many churches (including the Mormon) to ordain women. In answer to this charge that Mormons discriminate against Negroes, a spokesman for the church replied that "there is in this church no doctrine, belief or practice that is intended to deny the enjoyment of full civil rights by any person because of race, color, or creed."[47]

This position on Negroes is embarrassing to any Mormon who aspires to high political office and there is considerable sentiment within the church for modification of a doctrine which works against the liberal image the church would like to present to the American people. But the doctrine was established through revelation and can be removed or modified only through revelation, the prerogative of the First President of the church. Although every president since Joseph Smith has shown a reluctance to

---

[45] Wilford E. Smith, "The Urban Threat to Mormon Norms," *Rural Sociology*, Vol. 24 (December, 1959), pp. 355–61.

[46] *New York Times*, June 6, 1963.

[47] *Time*, October 18, 1963, p. 83.

exercise this power, many Mormons nevertheless anticipate that the problem will be resolved by an appropriate revelation at an appropriate time.

Mormon and Catholic Similarities

Although there has always been coolness or antipathy between the Catholic and Mormon religions, the two systems are strikingly similar in important respects. Both are hierarchically organized with leadership playing an important role at each level of organization.

Both systems are specific, definite, and unequivocal on questions of doctrine, and both are equally convinced that theirs is the only valid repository of Christian truth. For Catholics, theirs is the "True Church," while Mormons maintain the "restored" church—the Church of Jesus Christ of Latter-Day Saints—is the real and valid repository of Christian belief and fellowship as laid down in the life and teachings of Christ. Both systems, it can be seen, are marked by great assurance; each is equally convinced that its "revealed truth" and derivative doctrines are the only correct and valid ones.

Various Temple rites in Mormon worship likewise suggest certain rites or features of the Catholic sacramental system. The vicarious baptism for the dead performed in the Temple does not seem much removed in form and purpose from the Catholic doctrine of purgatory in which prayers of the living help the departed soul in its progress along the path to eternal salvation.

To Mormons as well as to Catholics marriage is a most serious and sacred experience, and when a husband and wife are sealed for "time and eternity" in the Temple, the marriage is just as binding, permanent, and indissoluble as in the Catholic sacrament of matrimony.

Both systems are equally demanding; a Mormon must fast and abstain on appropriate days much the same as a Catholic. Although a Catholic is required to contribute to the church, the Mormon is not only obliged to contribute but fails to meet the minimum obligation of his faith unless he gives at least one-tenth of his income.

Both systems are equally all-inclusive and comprehensive. The Catholic idea of what constitutes "faith and morals" pretty well covers the important areas of personal behavior; every Catholic has a well-defined blue print before him and not much is left to individual choice and discretion. The Mormon pattern of daily living is equally well outlined; the good Mormon not only knows what he is supposed to do on Sunday, but the leisure of his entire week is taken up with duties and opportunities.

And both systems are equally concerned with religious education as a bulwark against the inroads of secularization and apostasy. The Mormon pattern of seminaries and institutes, paralleling the high school and the college and university, represents the same high concern and investment of money and effort as do the Catholic elementary, secondary, and college systems.

JEHOVAH'S WITNESSES

The Witness Concept of History

All recorded history, according to the Witnesses, has been a struggle between good and evil—between the Lord (Jehovah) and Satan—and the Witnesses are, of course, the followers and supporters of the good. Abel was the first witness and Noah was the one good man whom Jehovah protected to perpetuate true religion. Unfortunately, the earth soon fell into a political state in which priestcraft and false religion ("demonism") were in command. Abraham also was a witness of Jehovah and carried on the true religion, but subsequent history was the story of totalitarian empires battling against the witnesses of Jehovah. Seven great powers (Egypt, Assyria, Babylonia, Persia, Greece, and pagan and papal Rome) constituted stepping stones from ancient to modern times. The seventh unholy and demonic power was the Anglo-American combination during World War I and II.[1]

The Witnesses believe they are the only true Christians today and that "hypocritical Christendom," composed of the traditional churches and their secular allies, is their worst enemy. The Witness does not take part in the "filthy, corrupt politics of the world. He does not go campaigning for the rival politicians of the different political systems of this dying world."[2]

Belief

The Witnesses do not accept the divinity of Christ or the doctrine of the Trinity; Jesus is an angel turned perfect man and not the second person of the Trinity.[3] On the other hand they uphold the Virgin Birth but deny the doctrine of the Immaculate Conception.[4] They differ from Catholics and Protestants in rejecting the immortality of the soul, the existence of hell or purgatory, the value of the sacraments, and the visible "Second Coming."[5]

They do, however, regard the Bible as the infallible word of God, and insist that it be interpreted literally and taken at face value. They accept science "as long as it proves the Bible. The Bible has withstood change while science is continually changing its theories and truths. As long as science seeks the truth, it will verify the Bible and scientists can never change the Bible. For example, Darwin's theory of evolution came in direct

---

[1] Watchtower Bible and Tract Society, *The New World* (New York, 1942), p. 42.

[2] Watchtower Bible and Tract Society, *Christendom or Christianity* (New York, 1954), p. 16.

[3] John H. Gerstner, *The Theology of the Major Sects* (Grand Rapids, Mich.: Baker Book House, 1963), p. 130.

[4] William J. Whalen, *Armageddon Around the Corner* (New York: The John Day Co., 1962), p. 98.

[5] *Ibid.*, p. 81.

conflict with the Bible and now scientists have refuted the Darwinian theory."[6]

Since they anticipate the end of the world (Armageddon) within their life time, Witnesses are not much concerned with contemporary society. Christ, according to the Witnesses, is the chief Theocratic Servant, and 1914 marked the entry of Jesus into the Temple where he began to judge which servants of Jehovah should be the leaders in ridding the earth of Satan in the forthcoming climatic Battle of Armageddon.[7] But true followers of Jehovah will survive the final holocaust: "Millions now living will never die."

They envision a hierarchy of the saved. An elect of 144,000 (of which all but some 13,000 have already died and been chosen) will live a spirit life with Jesus in heaven.[8] The elect date back to the Pentecost and are also known, in the literature of the Watchtower Society, as "the spiritual class," "the anointed," "the brides of Christ," and "spiritual Israelites."[9]

A lower degree of the saved are the "other sheep," or Witnesses who are faithfully following the duties and practices of their religion. After the holocaust of Armageddon the "other sheep" will live an everlasting life on earth in a reconstructed Garden of Eden where all evil—sickness, greed, pain, age—will have been banished.

Their theology and belief have been defined as a sort of unitarian fundamentalism. They worship an Old Testament God of Vengeance, Justice, and Law, a God who plans the utter destruction of the religious, political, and business classes of contemporary society.

Worship

Worship takes the form of Bible study and preaching the word, and only by constant preaching can the individual Witness hope to survive the great battle of Armageddon and gain the reward of living forever in a reconstructed Garden of Eden. Witnesses are supposed to attend several meetings each week at the local Kingdom Hall, to study the Bible and Watchtower literature at home, and to spend a number of hours each week in door-to-door calls, the average minister spending about ten hours per month in such evangelism.[10] Group Bible study classes may meet in the Kingdom Hall or in the homes of members.

Thursday is reserved for Theocratic Ministry School, which consists of instruction in Watchtower doctrine and in how to meet people and present the message. After Theocratic Ministry School there is a service meeting during which individuals may practice the preaching techniques that

---

[6] Case study from author's files.

[7] Watchtower Bible and Tract Society, *This Good News of the Kingdom* (New York, 1954), p. 16.

[8] J. H. Gerstner, *op. cit.*, p. 132.

[9] W. J. Whalen, *op. cit.*, p. 90.

[10] *Watchtower*, June 1, 1961, p. 328.

they have just heard explained. Publishers may be assigned their quotas of *Watchtower* and *Awake* to sell or distribute for the month, and other details of quotas and reports may be handled. Back calls may come up for discussion, return calls to discuss the content of literature previously left by the publisher in his round of weekly calls. The back call is often the key to a continuing interest in the Society.

A public lecture is given Sunday afternoon in Kingdom Hall, frequently by a visiting Witness on a topic such as "The Watchtower Society in God's Purpose," "You May Survive Armageddon into God's New World," or "Is Your Destiny of Your Own Making?" A second meeting follows the public lecture, and although hymns and a prayer may be included, the major portion of the meeting is given over to a question and answer recital of weekly lessons from the *Watchtower*. These discourses are largely mechanical but no more so than many of the traditional catechism rituals of the established churches.[11]

Ritual and Symbolism

Witnesses have little ritual and symbolism in the conventional Christian sense. Their Kingdom Halls are extremely plain; there are no stained glass windows, steeples, or other traditional features, and they profess to abhor images, crucifixes, and relics of saints. They do not recognize Christmas or Easter and a committed Witness goes about his regular business on even the major Christian holy days. Christmas trees, he may tell you, are sinful because they are pagan in origin.

The important annual communion, known as the Lord's Evening Meal, is held on Nisan 14. Our local newspaper carried as a news item the announcement that the Lord's Evening Meal would be celebrated April 8 at the Kingdom Hall and the public was invited. The local Hall is new, modest, neat, and adequate, and about a mile outside the city limits. I arrived as the meeting was about to start. The assembly hall was filled, there were few empty chairs. I was surprised at the number of young people and children. There were 53 adults (counting 13 and 14 year olds) and 33 children. When I expressed surprise at the number of children to the congregation leader he replied that the Jehovah's Witness was a "family religion"; that the family came, shared, and worshipped together.

The leader was a personable young man in his late twenties and from the nearby city of Syracuse. He went to the platform and began the service by announcing a hymn from the JW song book, which was sung to piano accompaniment. The leader then called upon a brother to offer a prayer from the floor, and a number of "amens" were heard at its conclusion.

This was followed by a 40-minute talk that alluded frequently to the Bible and stressed the point that only those to whom it had been revealed

---

11 W. J. Whalen, *op. cit.*, p. 107.

that they were of the "little flock" should partake of the Lord's Evening Meal. Last year (1962), said the speaker, more than one and a half million Witnesses gathered in their Kingdom Halls around the earth to celebrate the Lord's Evening Meal but only 12,714 partook of the elements. This "little flock," the speaker explained, is the "remnant" which has the heavenly "covenant" and hope, whereas the great majority has only the earthly "covenant" and an earthly hope. Referring to Bible passages to illustrate his points, the speaker pointed out that Nisan 14, which is also the Jewish Passover, occurs on the first full moon following the spring equinox.

Turning to the celebration of the communion, the speaker called upon a brother to bless the bread with a brief prayer of dedication. Consisting of two large unbroken matzoh wafers on an ordinary plate, the bread was first offered to the speaker on the platform, who refused to partake, then the plate was passed up and down each row. No one partook.

Another brother stepped forward to bless the wine, which was then poured into an ordinary drinking glass, offered first to the speaker and again refused, and passed through the congregation from hand to hand. The leader's admonitions again prevailed and no one partook of the wine.

The leader concluded the service by saying that now both covenants—the "little flock" and the "other sheep"—could go out and live and work together in "unity" in this "dying wicked old world." There was a closing song and a prayer, accompanied by "amens" as the service was brought to a close. The hall cleared rapidly.

Although the small children fidgeted and squirmed from time to time, they were amazingly restrained and quiet on the whole, and no child or adult left his seat until after the passing of the elements. The teachings and leadership of the theocracy have been effective, as can be seen from the fact that no one partook of the bread or wine at this particular service, whereas in 1938, according to the national headquarters, 52 percent of all the Witnesses who attended the Lord's Evening Meal partook of the elements. In 1961 only 1 percent of the attendance partook,[12] so that it seems the great majority of Witnesses are now satisfied to realize their salvation as "other sheep" and spend eternity as human entities in the earthly paradise.

Baptism, although it is not regarded as a sacrament, will lift the penalty of death if one is alive at the time of Armageddon. It is by total immersion and signifies that the member is now a full-fledged minister of the gospel with the power to teach, preach, and baptize.

Priesthood

The ministry is entirely lay, and the Witness who comes to the door and tells us he is a "minister of the gospel" believes he has become properly

---

[12] *Ibid.*, p. 96.

ordained through Bible study alone, scrupulously following the interpretations laid down in the books and magazines of the Watchtower Society. Preachers are known as "publishers" and have a monthly quota of books and magazines which they must put in the hands of those they contact—the "seed" which, if it falls on fertile ground and is nourished, will lead others to become witnesses for Jehovah's Kingdom. The usual contribution for a book runs between 50 and 75 cents, but the literature will be given away if the contact is unwilling to pay. Publishers therefore usually subsidize a portion of their quota from their own resources.

To be baptized and a full member a Witness must repent of his sins and answer the following two questions affirmatively:

Have you recognized yourself before Jehovah God as a sinner who needs salvation, and have you acknowledged to Him that this salvation proceeds from Him, the Father, through His son, Jesus Christ?

On the basis of this faith in God and in His provision for salvation, have you dedicated yourself unreservedly to God to do His will henceforth as He reveals it to you through Jesus Christ and through the Bible under the enlightening power of His Holy Spirit?[13]

Ideally, each Witness spends all his spare time teaching and preaching, but the average is ten hours per month. Pioneers are fulltime workers, mostly retired persons, housewives, and those who choose to make "witnessing" their life work. Any man, woman, or child who works at least 100 hours a month is a pioneer, and a special class of pioneers may work 150 hours or more. In 1961 there were more than 6000 special pioneers in foreign missions and another 25,000 in local congregations.[14] Pioneers receive only a nominal sum from the central office for maintenance and expenses.

Although a committed Witness is a dedicated preacher, we experienced difficulty in getting a member to interpret the Watchtower Society to our Religion in American Culture class until someone recommended a former high school acquaintance who had joined the group and become active in it—who lived three hundred miles away in northern New Jersey. He was invited to talk to the class and this surprising young man obtained a three-day leave from his regular job and made a 600-mile roundtrip to upstate New York to bring us his message. He gave a well-prepared and lucid interpretation of the theology and practice of the movement, the students were tremendously impressed by his sincerity and dedication, and we had difficulty getting him to accept a contribution of ten dollars "for gas"; all of which illustrates the importance given to evangelizing and the sacrifice which a good member will make to discharge his "preaching covenant" with Jehovah.

---

13 *Ibid.*, p. 95.
14 *Ibid.*, p. 158.

Subordination of Women

Women may become full members and function as ministers, but they are subordinated to men and may not hold any congregational or Watchtower Society office. They may not hold a teaching post, or deliver public lectures, or direct activities of brothers, and they must not contradict or correct brothers in Kingdom Hall meetings.[15] The male-oriented nature of the religion follows from the belief that women are weaker than men and a continual source of distraction and temptation,[16] and even if a woman is a Witness she must concede to the husband as the head of the house and allow her children to be raised in his religion if he so desires.[17]

Organization

Eighteen to 20 congregations constitute a circuit and are under the direction of a circuit servant who is supposed to visit each congregation at least three times each year. Circuits, in turn, are organized into districts.

The local organization offers considerable opportunities for leadership and participation with such offices as congregational overseer or servant (also known as presiding minister), assistant overseer or servant, Bible study servant, magazine territory servant, literature servant, accounts servant, Watchtower study servant, theocratic ministry servant, book study servant. When a congregation grows to approximately 200 members, it is the policy of the central office to split it into two congregations.

Bethel, the headquarters and center of the Watchtower Society, is an amazing complex of 700 staff people at Columbia Heights, Brooklyn, which sends orders and directions to 85 branch offices around the world. It is a small, self-contained community which provides such basic necessities as laundry and dry cleaning services, beauty and barber shops, shoe repair shop, and kitchens. A great deal of its food is produced on two farms maintained by the society, at South Lansing, New York (original site of the Gilead College), and South Murray, New Jersey. Efficient organization and the use of Witnesses has made it possible to feed a person at a cost of 54 cents a day.

The Bethel printing plant, which turns out tons of literature each week for distribution throughout the world, is operated entirely by Witnesses who work an eight hour and 40-minute day and a five and one-half day week. They receive room and board and $14 a month. *Watchtower* and *Awake* are both printed here; *Watchtower* is for the indoctrinated witness with a knowledge of the society's theology and vocabulary, and *Awake* for arousing the interest of the casual reader.

The Society does not encourage college education, and only a few are college graduates. Because of the imminence of Armageddon it is con-

---

15 Watchtower Bible and Tract Company, *Qualified to Be Ministers*, New York, p. 253.

16 W. J. Whalen, *op. cit.*, p. 203.

17 *Watchtower*, December 1, 1960, p. 735.

sidered better to spend one's time on preaching than to waste it on education.

From Sect to Church

Although the Watchtower Society has most of the characteristics of the classic sect—antagonism towards secular society and its institutions, a lay leadership, a high percentage of its recruits from the lower and lower-middle classes—it is not as sect-oriented as it used to be. Interaction patterns are not completely fixed and changes which can be interpreted as movement along the sect-to-church continuum are taking place in its pattern of organization.

A slight movement up the status ladder can also be detected among the recruits: there are more converts with a high school or college education than formerly; some congregations are moving their Kingdom Halls out of rented storefront and walk-up quarters to buildings and accommodations that are owned by the congregation, and congregations have been able to raise funds to construct a building solely as a Kingdom Hall—usually outside the city where there is plenty of room and parking space. The cars parked outside a typical Kingdom Hall today do not represent a much different range of value and appearance than those outside the typical middle-class Protestant church.

More central control and greater institutionalization of doctrine and worship are significant changes in the church's organization and interaction. In 1938, with the appointment of congregational officers by the central authority, local autonomy gave way to "theocratic" control. Full-time pioneers and circuit servants now do for the Society what bishops and various diocesan and synodical authorities do for the Catholic Church and various Protestant denominations, and although the local congregation still centers around lay leaders, both are now subject to the control and discipline of the higher authority. None of the books and articles that form the basis for belief and practice are now signed, and no national officer or other personality is identified with a doctrine or revelation that might conceivably lead to a schismatic or competing movement.

Although there is a tendency to deprecate higher education, the Gilead School for the training of pioneers has been increased from a five and one-half to a ten-month program. Singing has been reintroduced and an official hymnbook, *Songs to Jehovah's Praise*, issued. There is a tendency to use conventional church terminology: the company servant of our local congregation now speaks of himself as the presiding minister, and more sophisticated articles are appearing in *Watchtower* and *Awake*.

Witnesses have remained consistently otherworldly in emphasis although they are not noticeably bereft of material goods and live, for the most part, on the periphery of the cultural structure. It would appear that the Society has moved to a position that is not far removed from that of other Protestant fundamentalist denominations.

Values

Witnesses hold to a rather strict and high standard of personal conduct and morality. "You must be clean from immorality and loose conduct. You must be clean from drunkenness and excesses in speech and mouth, free from vulgar and obscene profanity."[18] But they condone moderate smoking and drinking and use red wine at the annual communion.

They support the conventional standards of morality concerning sex behavior and will "disfellowship" any member found guilty of adultery or other improper sex behavior. They are not, however, particularly concerned with marriage or preparation for marriage; it is more important to preach the gospel in early anticipation of Armageddon than to bother about marriage.

They are opposed to blood transfusions[19] and base their opposition on the same Bible passages upon which Orthodox Jews base some of their dietary rules. They also oppose sterilization, hypnotism, and psychiatry. If any brother or sister is disturbed or distraught, it is thought better and wiser to seek the advice and counsel of some mature member "in the truth."[20]

Although their stand for racial equality, political neutralism, and anti-colonialism makes them popular with the new African nations and the American Negro, they make no aggressive attempts for integration and tolerate segregation where it is the norm of the community. Separate congregations and Kingdom Halls are the rule in the South, and 20 to 30 percent of the United States membership is estimated to be Negro.

Secular Society

Jehovah's Witnesses are opposed to all organized or established governments of the world, including the United Nations, because the world belongs to Satan who relies upon the wicked trinity of organized religion, government, and business to help him sustain his rule. Witnesses claim only the rights of aliens, refuse to salute the flag or serve in the armed forces, and to vote or hold public offices. However, they pay taxes and obey those laws which do not conflict with "Jehovah's will."

Witnesses avoid secular groups and activities because "Association in a social way with those outside the truth is dangerous."[21] It is all right, they hold, to belong to a labor union if it is necessary to hold a job, but it is improper to become active in it. Their belief and doctrine have no place for the social gospel, and they support no colleges or hospitals.

---

[18] *Watchtower*, December 1, 1961, p. 735.
[19] *Ibid.*, January 15, 1961.
[20] *Ibid.*, September 15, 1961, p. 554.
[21] Watchtower Bible and Tract Society, *Make Sure of All Things*, New York, p. 279.

Summary

The American scene has proved to be a fertile field for creative innovation in religious thought and behavior and, given an open and expanding frontier and a free and open market in ideas, has produced such innovations as Christian Science, Mormonism, and Jehovah's Witnesses, the last two having been made case studies.

Mormonism. The Mormon development represents a cross-section of the intellectual ferment that characterized the first half of the nineteenth century, the period during which Mormonism emerged and took root. It owes something to sectarianism, communitarianism, ecumenicism, individualism, and optimism, and each of these tendencies was pronounced at some time during this period.

Sectarianism flourished, churches and denominations were doctrinally sensitive, and a great deal of splintering and fragmentation was going on within Protestantism. There was nothing unusual about the development of a new sect; the Mormons were merely one of the many that developed at this time.

The 19th was also the "century of the common man," who felt free to make his own way and achieve his own rewards unfettered by caste, class, or creed. Mormonism was one more expression of this individualism and optimism.

Mormonism gave theological expression to these social and intellectual trends. Its theology was a protest against the doctrine of predestination, the dominant note of Calvinist theology, and a protest against the aristocracy and class-consciousness of the Puritan tradition. Mormons, rejecting election and original sin, based their theological case squarely on the doctrine of free will, and they were not alone in this respect. Unitarians, Universalists, and Methodists took the same theological position, rejecting Puritan pessimism and fatalism as well, and a philosophy of mastery and self-improvement through education, study, and work became the doctrine of an eternal progression.

Communitarianism was given theological expression in the "gathering" of the chosen people, the Saints, to build the city of Zion, but not until the Saints reached Utah were they sufficiently removed from gentile hostility and aggression to give free rein to their cooperative and communistic practices.

Ecumenicism took form in the doctrine of the "restored" church, the Mormon concept of the "true church," and Mormons in this sense have remained aggressively ecumenical. Its entire missionary program is based upon the belief that man can win salvation—at least the highest levels of eternal glory—through the Mormon way alone.

Although Mormon behavior was a reflection of several social and cultural trends, the church was also responsible for some pronounced theological innovations: God is not outside time and the universe, but within it; He is of a material nature because all "spirit" is merely finer and purer matter—"As man is, God was: as God is, man may be"; the cooperation of God and men through an authoritarian church with an elaborate and extended priesthood leads to progressively greater control over the world and its creatures. These are doctrines that are quite removed from those of orthodox Christianity.

The Mormon organizational system functions in a happy combination of dissent and authority, of individualism and collectivism. Dissent was never permitted to get out of hand; splintering and fragmentation were checked through the "containment of charisma," and most of the revelations upon which Mormonism is based arose from a single source: the mystical experiences and insights of Joseph Smith. Accordingly, each president of the church is deemed to be a prophet in his own right and to have power to make revelations and pronouncements for the church as a whole (although, since Smith, this power has seldom been exercised). Mormons have, however, developed a system of checks and balances by requiring that authoritative pronouncements and decisions be sustained by the membership.

The Catholic and the Mormon systems are closely integrated, highly effective, and have important common structural characteristics. Both are good illustrations of institutionalized specificity.

There is no marked sacred-secular dichotomy in Mormonism because the Mormon way of life comprehends most of the activities and phases that are generally considered to belong in the realm of the secular. O'Dea finds the Mormon record to be a reversal of the twentieth century Protestant trend: rather than tend towards a secularization of the sacred, the Mormons have effected a "sacralization" of the secular.

The Mormons have survived by using the techniques and philosophy of individualism and collectivism, and have acquired the tradition and the skill to adjust to changing environments and changing problems. They seem as well equipped as any of the major American denominations to face a dynamic society and the unpredictable future.

Jehovah's Witnesses. All religions and civilizations, both current and historic, are perversions of the "true religion" and violations of God's will, according to Jehovah's Witnesses. They are Bible literalists and find it impossible to accept such Christian doctrines as the Trinity, the immortality of the soul, or hell and purgatory. They anticipate an early end of the world at Armageddon where the forces of good (followers of Jehovah) will triumph over the forces of evil (everything and everybody else). Various internal trends and changes, however, represent movement away from the sect and toward the church form of religious interaction.

They hold to a hierarchy of the saved: an elite "remnant," totaling 144,000, most of whom have already died, will go to heaven as spirit entities to assist Christ in ruling the universe; the great majority of Witnesses, the "other sheep," will inherit a reconstructed Garden of Eden, or earthly paradise.

Witnesses hold their meetings in unadorned Kingdom Halls where they hear lectures, study the Bible, and otherwise prepare themselves to carry their message throughout the community. They believe in a priesthood of all believers in which each member is a preacher or "publisher" who spends all or most of his spare time searching out possible members, talking to them, and supplying abundant quantities of Witness literature.

Although women may become full members, they are denied positions of leadership in local congregations and in the national organization. The national and international headquarters is in Brooklyn where a huge printing establishment turns out tons of literature, *Watchtower*, *Awake*, and special books and treatises.

Witnesses are required to maintain a high standard of personal morality, and they cite Biblical authority for refusing to accept blood transfusions. A non-militant or passive philosophy of racial equality helps make the religion attractive to Negroes.

Chapter X

The Clergy

THE CLERICAL TASK is a profession, a career, and an occupation. It is a profession since it is primarily concerned with rendering a service. It is a career since a whole life is occupied in the performing of the service. It is an occupation since it is a means of being gainfully employed.

Occupations, professions and careers have been submitted to some thorough analysis, and there are studies which deal with recruitment to the clerical profession, with programs that prepare the individual to perform the necessary roles, and with the performance of the roles themselves.

In our study of the clergy we will give some attention to all three phases. Recruitment, however, is of more than casual interest presently because all three basic faiths claim that they cannot get and train enough functionaries to meet the needs of the rapidly growing parishes and memberships.

RECRUITMENT

Catholic

Problem. The membership of the Catholic church in the United States grew 40 percent in ten years, while the number of priests increased at about half that rate, and the archdiocese of St. Paul, for example, reported a "critical shortage of priests" that would become even worse in the next three years. Each priest actively engaged in caring for the spiritual needs of Catholics in the archdiocese had 1442 under his care and, since the Catholic church considers 1000 as the greatest number that a parish priest can care for properly, the archdiocese was obviously understaffed.[1] The bishop made a report to a group of laymen concerned with the promotion of religious vocations and pointed out that the diocesan seminary graduating class would be progressively smaller in each of the next three years.

Many dioceses have the same problem, but the shortage of priests is particularly acute in the dioceses of the South and West. Many bishops seek help from the archdiocese of Boston, one of the few that produces more priests than it needs, some seek help from Ireland, and some have put on a "crash" program of local recruitment similar to that inaugurated by Cardinal Spellman in New York.

These programs have had some effect. In 1961, 134 major seminaries enrolled 15,000 men studying for the priesthood. This was an increase of 17 percent in five years but not enough to meet the needs of the rapidly growing Catholic population. A spokesman for the church reported that "we are running as fast as we can but we are still falling behind."[2]

But the Catholic problem was not caused by the lack or neglect of a recruitment program; indeed, a representative of the church has observed that no occupation or profession has a more intense recruitment system.[3] Each religious order, for example, has a vocation recruiter who works with young people and their parents, usually an outstanding example of the order (a "favorable image") who favorably represents the challenge, opportunities, and satisfactions of his order.

Motivation. They "have a vocation," the men and women, priests and religious who perform the works of service in the Catholic church, but the qualifications are set by canon law. One must have "right intentions," and the willingness and desire to serve with some degree of supernatural motivation (in psychological terms maturity, integration, and balance of personality), and "fitness," the capacity to perform the functions required by the role. The candidate must also meet certain standards of health, intellect, character, and generosity.

Men choose the priestly vocation for a variety of reasons.[4]

Since all of these men (as major rather than minor seminarians) had been accepted and retained as priestly candidates for some years, it is assumed that the reasons they gave for choosing their vocation represent a "right intention."

The greatest encouragement to the choice of a religious career comes from a functionary member of the particular order rather than from the

[1] *New York Times,* April 16, 1961.

[2] *Ibid.*

[3] Joseph H. Fichter, *Religion as an Occupation* (South Bend, Ind.: University of Notre Dame Press, 1961), p. 10.

[4] *Ibid.,* p. 24.

TABLE 10

MOTIVATION FOR ENTERING PRIESTHOOD

Reasons for Choosing Priestly Vocation	Entered Seminary at age:		
	18 or Older	17 or Younger	Total
Attracted to priestly work	10.7%	35.3%	23.9%
Surety of salvation	19.0	9.4	13.9
Strong sense of vocation	16.6	8.5	12.3
Love of God	10.2	11.1	10.7
Salvation of others	7.8	4.3	5.9

Joseph H. Fichter, S.J., *Religion as an Occupation* (South Bend, Ind.: University of Notre Dame Press, 1961), p. 24.

mother of the candidate, who ranks second in the degree of encouragement, whether it be the case of a seminarian, a brother, or a sister.[5]

TABLE 11

ENCOURAGEMENT FOR ENTERING THE RELIGIOUS LIFE

Degree of Encouragement	Seminarian	Brother	Sister
Most	Priest	Religious Brother	Religious Sister
Second	Mother	Mother	Mother
Third	Father	Father	Priest
Fourth	Religious Sister	Priest	Father

Joseph H. Fichter, *Religion as an Occupation* (South Bend, Ind.: University of Notre Dame Press, 1961), p. 22.

Characteristics and Background. The average "vocation family" has a little more than four children; 40 percent of the recruits come from families with from one to three children; only 5 percent of the candidates for the seminary and convent come from families in which they are the only child, and only 5 percent come from families with ten or more children.[6] A proportionate share of seminarians is not supplied by rural areas—as was found from studies made in the 1920's and again in the 1950's[7]—and one-fourth of the religious aspirants have a brother or sister who is also following a vocation.

These percentages are much higher than they are for the average practicing Catholic family.[8] The seminarian is a typical American youth with a normal interest in athletics; he is neither ultra-athletic nor unathletic.[9] The future religious functionary has about the same amount of participation in high school groups as does the Catholic teenager who remains a lay person, but he participates somewhat more in parish organizations.[10]

[5] See Table 11.
[6] J. H. Fichter, *op. cit.*, p. 35.
[7] *Ibid.*, p. 74.
[8] *Ibid.*, p. 50.
[9] *Ibid.*, p. 52.
[10] *Ibid.*, p. 55.

The family of the typical seminarian is middle-class. Six out of ten fathers work in white-collar occupations compared to three out of ten fathers three decades ago.[11] This change roughly represents the same de-

TABLE 12
OCCUPATIONS OF FATHERS OF SEMINARIANS

Type of Occupation	Fathers of Seminarians			Catholic Percentage
	1919–29	1950	1958*	1955
Professional	4%	6%	12%	9%
Managerial and owner	14	25	32	14
Clerical and sales	12	28.5	21	15
Craftsmen and operatives	20	22.5	17.5	41
Service and unskilled	50	18	11.5	13

* Missing percentages represent deceased or unemployed fathers. Source: Joseph H. Fichter, *Religion as an Occupation* (South Bend, Ind.: University of Notre Dame Press, 1961), p. 63.

gree of upward mobility that Catholics have experienced in the past thirty years.

The majority of religious functionaries (priests, brothers, sisters) received their early training in the parochial schools: 70 percent of the vocations attended a Catholic elementary school and 60 percent a Catholic high school. About 50 percent of all Catholic children attend a parochial school and 25 percent attend a Catholic high school.[12] Four out of five priests had been altar boys.[13]

Protestant

Problem. Protestantism does not have all the qualified ministers it needs to staff its congregations—even though the total picture of needs is difficult to obtain because of the variety of churches and types of training and experience required. Furthermore, there is no single source for statistics of ministers in training, of qualified pastors without churches, and of congregations needing pastoral leadership and able to raise the funds necessary to retain and maintain a pastor.

The discrepancy in statistics between needs and shortages was dramatized by the reaction of Protestant spokesmen to an article in the *Saturday Evening Post* which stated that enrollments in Protestant seminaries had dropped 5 percent in one year and that ministers were resigning in unprecedented numbers.[14] Protestant leaders immediately challenged both statements, maintaining that ministers were not resigning as alleged, and that seminary enrollments had in fact risen 3.6 percent during this period.

The discrepancy arose because both parties to the dispute were quoting figures based upon different seminaries and different groups of Protestant

---

[11] See Table 12.
[12] J. H. Fichter, *op. cit.*, p. 42.
[13] *Ibid.*, p. 40.
[14] *New York Times*, November 26, 1962.

clergy. During this controversy the American Association of Theological Schools reported that since 1956 its number of students had been virtually stabilized at 20,700. There was a high in 1959 and a low in 1960, but enrollments recovered and remained at the previous level. The association's figures included students working for a Master or Doctor of Theology degree as well as for a Bachelor of Divinity degree. Fifteen to 20 percent of the bachelor candidates drop out before graduation, while many graduates go into the teaching of religion, church music, church social work, the chaplaincy, and other special forms, rather than into the pastoral ministry itself.

The association is composed of 86 accredited and 40 associate schools, and it believes that fully 95 percent of all formally enrolled theological students are included in its statistics[15] (Bible colleges are not members and their theological students are not included in the association's figures). In spite of the numerical stability of enrollments, Protestant leaders however admitted that over a ten-year period they had not kept up with the increase in the total church population.

Although there is no agreement on just how many churches are without clerical leadership or on how many seminarians are needed, there is agreement that seminaries should graduate a greater number of qualified candidates. Let us take the situation of the United Presbyterian Church. Although its 9000 active ministers are not sufficient to fill present pulpits —and new churches are being established at the rate of 75 per year—360 graduates in a class of 400 went to fill posts of pastors who had died or retired, and only 40 were left for national expansion.[16] Furthermore, because the churches almost always trail industry in salary brackets and fringe benefits, anyone entering the ministry must do so in the spirit of service and sacrifice.

Liston Pope found that the chief reason for an inadequate number of ministers-in-training is poor recruitment in the churches, and several denominations have made special efforts in the past few years to attract more of their most competent young people into the ministry. The United Presbyterian Church, for one, has been making an intense effort to "get through" to qualified college people. In the summer of 1960, to stress the church's relevance, fifteen student prospects were chosen to observe its ministers work with narcotic addicts in the Chicago slums. Thirty others were sent to a "Christian Faith in a Nuclear Age" seminar with scientists at Los Alamos, N.M. The denomination also encourages Career Days in high schools when rabbis, priests, and ministers tell pupils about the challenges and responsibilities of religious vocations.[17]

Since 1955 the Methodist Church has had a special recruitment program

---

[15] The American Association of Theological Schools, *The Handbook*, Dayton, O. Communication from Jesse H. Ziegler, Associate Director, The American Association of Theological Schools.

[16] *New York Times*, November 26, 1962.

[17] *Ibid.*

that has resulted in increased seminary enrollments, but the additional graduates have not yet met the expanding needs. The needs are emphasized by recruiting officials, magazines, conferences, and a Ministry Sunday in which the choice of the ministry as a profession is encouraged by pastors and youth leaders in the local churches.

Other denominations that have increased seminary enrollments over a five-year period are the Unitarian, Congregational, United Lutheran, and Episcopal,[18] and the best known interdenominational seminaries were reported to be maintaining their enrollments.

Motivation of Seminarians. In a study of 1573 Protestant theological students Felton found that the most important single factor in the selection of the religious vocation was home training, and that the most important person influencing the decision was the minister. Over three-fourths of the students rated the minister among the three main factors that influenced their choice. The minister was first with 34.0 percent, followed, respectively, by mother at 17.4 percent, father at 11.2 percent, evangelist at 6.4 percent, college teacher at 5.8 percent, and Sunday school teacher at 5.0 percent.[19]

Background. In a study of 140 Yale divinity students, Smith found that three-fourths came from strongly religious homes, and three-fifths had one or more relatives in religious or social work.[20] The leading background factors of 306 theological students (mostly Methodist) were early religious training, participation in church youth activities, and influence of the minister. These students had above-average marks in school, and parental pressure and "religious experience" had little influence in their choice of vocation.[21]

Studies made more than a generation ago (in the 1920's) found that Protestant ministers came largely from rural communities and from families of middle- and lower middle-class status,[22] but this background is no longer so prominent. In Felton's study it was found that rural areas now supply less than their proportionate share of seminary students. Fifteen percent are sons of ministers, whose homes contribute more than twenty times their proportionate "quota" of theological students.[23]

Judaism

Problem. Empty pulpits and unmanned classrooms point up Judaism's need for rabbis and teachers—according to one spokesman a more crying

---

[18] *Ibid.*, April 16, 1961.

[19] Ralph A. Felton, *New Ministers* (Madison, N.J.: Drew Theological Seminary, 1949), p. 7.

[20] Robert O. Smith, "Personality and Cultural Factions Affecting the Religion of One Hundred and Forty Divinity Students," *Religious Education*, Vol. 43 (March–April, 1948), pp. 106–11.

[21] *Newsweek.*

[22] H. Paul Douglass and Edmund Brunner, *The Protestant Churches as a Social Institution* (New York: Harper & Bros., 1935), p. 106.

[23] R. A. Felton, *op. cit.*, p. 25.

need than either the Catholic or Protestant denominations experience. In the United States and Canada there is one rabbi for every 1800 Jews, compared to Catholicism's ideal of one priest for every 1000, the Presbyterians' one minister for every 600, and the Methodists' one minister for every 360 members.[24] The Jewish problem of need and recruitment was demonstrated by the enrollment figures for the Orthodox Seminary of Yeshiva University: in 1956 the seminary had 160 students—and only 92 in 1958 (although enrollment rose to 111 in 1959).[25]

In June 1962 the five departments of the Jewish Theological Seminary of America (Cantor's Institute, College of Jewish Music, Teachers' Institute, College of Jewish Studies, School of Judaic Literature) graduated 77 men and women, but only 25 were ordained as Rabbi, teacher, or preacher.[26]

The problem of recruitment is partly financial: qualified college-age people find that they can get fellowships for majors in the arts and sciences but not for majors in theology. Because of this, national Jewish organizations are putting on drives to raise funds for loans, grants, and scholarships so that good candidates will not be discouraged for lack of financial support.[27]

Background. In the United States all three branches of Judaism, Orthodox, Conservative, Reform, recruit candidates for rabbinical training at the college level. Representatives of the seminaries of each denomination seek out students who possess the intellectual, religious, and moral qualifications, and encourage them to enter upon rabbinical training. All three branches find that campus religious agencies, summer Hebrew camps, and young people's groups in synagogues are the chief reservoirs of rabbinical candidates.[28] One spokesman reports that most rabbis come out of congregations that have good programs of Jewish training and youth groups that are strong at the 14 to 18 age level.[29]

TRAINING

Catholic

Training for a religious vocation is carried on in minor and in major seminaries. A boy often begins his vocational training in a four- or six-year minor seminary immediately upon completion of his elementary education. (In a six-year seminary the last two years are equivalent to the first two years of college.)

---

[24] *New York Times*, February 27, 1962.

[25] *Ibid.*

[26] *New York Times*, June 4, 1962.

[27] *Ibid.*, April 16, 1961.

[28] *Ibid.*

[29] David O. Moberg, *The Church as a Social Institution* (Englewood Cliffs, N.J.: Prentice-Hall, Inc., 1962), p. 484.

A minor seminary may be organized within a diocese at the discretion of the bishop and in 1959 there were 42 diocesan minor seminaries in the U.S.A., some run as boarding schools, and some as day schools. In addition to the diocesan clergy, there are approximately 225,000 men and women who live in religious communities in the United States; more than 175,000 sisters, 10,000 brothers, and 25,000 priests, who are products of non-diocesan systems: 88 different orders of priests, for example, ranging from 12 or fewer to several thousand members.[30] The seminaries of the

TABLE 13

DISTRIBUTION OF ESTABLISHMENTS IN WHICH RELIGIOUS ORDERS
PERFORM APOSTOLIC WORKS

	Number	Percent
Elementary schools	10,372	68.7%
High schools	2,433	16.1
Colleges and universities	265	1.8
Schools of nursing	347	2.3
Hospital and sanitarium	945	6.2
Homes for the aged	326	2.2
Orphanages	279	1.8
Protective institutions	131	0.9
	15,098	100.0%

Joseph H. Fichter, *Religion as an Occupation*, University of Notre Dame Press, 1961, p. 146.

religious congregations, in fact, are about three times as numerous as the diocesan minor seminaries.

Each order of sisters maintains one or more *aspirantures* for the early training of candidates for their orders (there were 79 aspirantures in 1958). However, few candidates for a religious vocation enter training at 17, the great majority receiving their secondary school experience in a public or a Catholic high school.

Of the 45,451 priests in 1954, 63 percent were diocesan and 37 percent were religious priests. Diocesan priests are the secular clergy who live in the rectory of their respective parishes and work closely with the laity; religious priests are the regular clergy who live in their special communities and according to their rule, or *regula*.[31]

Each diocese and each order has its appropriate advanced training school or major seminary which inculcates a proper spiritual personality and trains the functionary for the special service he is to perform. The prospective functionary is trained to lead a virtuous life, to participate in some way in a community or group as a substitute for family life, to develop social relations with peers and superiors, and to perform general and specialized functions for the church.[32]

---

[30] Paul Hanly Furbey, "The Code of the Catholic Clergy," *The Annals of the Society of Political and Social Science*, Vol. 297 (January, 1955), p. 64; and *New York Times*, July 9, 1962.

[31] P. H. Furbey, *op. cit.*

[32] J. H. Fichter, *op. cit.*, p. 92.

The question frequently arises which role comes first; training to be a good seminarian, novice, or scholastic—or training to be the best teacher, preacher, nurse, or scientist. Pope Pius XII implied that they are of equal and complementary importance; that the religious vocation exists for service and that training for this service requires the best and most realistic sort of education. "The modern apostolate requires one who faces boldly the gigantic task of our age, one able to meet its dangers, overcome its spiritual destitution, competent to think for himself, and formed to maturity and judgment."[33]

A classical high school course with a concentration in Latin is preferred for the pretheological student who, at the undergraduate level, takes the Liberal Arts course that would be given in a typical Catholic college. The priestly candidate pursues a course that is strong in the humanities (but limited, according to some critics, in the laboratory and social sciences) and philosophy is usually the major. Priests are the only functionaries who are required to spend four years studying theology in a seminary or divinity school.

Most of the religious orders render their service to the church as teachers,[34] and most brothers and sisters take the courses required for certification in the states in which they will be assigned, preparation which usually carries an undergraduate major in education. Since they are frequently assigned to teaching posts before they have completed their undergraduate requirements, most finish their academic preparation as summer school or extension students, studying alongside secular students.

Protestant Training

Wide variations in the standards of preparation for the ministry exist among Protestant denominations. The usual standard for the major denominations is four years of undergraduate study, preferably with a degree in the Liberal Arts, followed by three to four years of postgraduate work —usually including a year of internship—in a theological school.

The University of Chicago Divinity School provides for an internship in a cooperating church under a competent pastor. The seminarian is given experience in preaching, youth work, and church financing, and then returns for his final year of study in residence at the seminary.[35]

Many theological students also hold pastorates in nearby small churches which make it possible for the seminarian to finance his studies while obtaining valuable practical experience. Some seminaries, recognizing the need and value of these part-time jobs run their academic program on a four-day, Monday through Thursday basis, leaving the seminarian Friday, Saturday, and Sunday to concentrate upon his parish responsibilities.

---

[33] Joseph F. Gallen, "Renovation and Adaptation," *Review for Religious*, Vol. XIV (November, 1955), p. 293.

[34] See Table 13.

[35] *New York Times*, January 8, 1961.

Most of the major denominations will issue a temporary license to promising young men who are willing to hold charges in small churches (mostly rural) that are unable to finance an experienced full-time pastor —but only after the applicant has upgraded his preparation with additional academic courses and credits.

A number of fundamentalist and conservative churches and congregations recruit their clergy from the graduates of "Bible colleges," which students can enter without a high school diploma and receive an ordination that "permits" him to hold a pastorate. However, Bible colleges are also extending their three- to five-year curriculum and are requiring more preparation. According to the secretary of the Accrediting Association of Bible Colleges, the association looks forward to having a full seven-year program of academic preparation within the next few years.[36]

Judaism

The traditional orthodox rabbi studied for the rabbinate much as the nineteenth century American studied for the legal profession. The old-time lawyer received his training by reading law cases in the office of an established lawyer where he served as an apprentice clerk. When he felt he was sufficiently prepared he would take the bar examination and, if he passed, would be admitted to the bar and the practice of law. The student rabbi similarly prepared himself by studying the *Torah*, *Talmud*, and various commentaries under the direction of a well-known rabbi. When he had mastered the thought of the *Talmud* and the commentaries he would present himself for an oral examination before a committee of rabbis and was accepted as a rabbi by the affirmative vote of this committee.

The present standard for training is a four-year college course plus four to six years at a postgraduate rabbinical school. Some orthodox rabbis receive their entire formal education in sectarian schools: Jewish elementary school, Jewish secondary school, Hebrew university, and postgraduate training at a rabbinical seminary. Reform Judaism, on the other hand, is quite anxious that the prospective rabbi get the broadest possible education and receive his prerabbinic education in the public schools and in a nonsectarian college. To become something of a specialist in one of the social or the natural and physical sciences, or in the humanities, is highly desirable.

At the rabbinical seminary the student devotes most of his four years to a study of the Bible, Talmud, Hebrew history, Midrash, Codes, and Commentaries.[37] The ideal is learning, study, and scholarship, and a rabbi can go in and out of congregational work with no particular loss of prestige

---

[36] *Ibid.*, April 16, 1961.

[37] Sidney I. Goldstein, "The Roles of an American Rabbi, *Sociology and Social Research*, Vol. 38 (September, 1953), pp. 32–37.

or stature; he does not necessarily leave his profession. As long as he is known as a learned and pious man his most important image is maintained in the eyes of the Jewish community.

ROLES OF THE CLERGY

Each of the basic faiths has invested considerable time, effort, and money in the study and analysis of the work of their clergy to discover where they succeed, where they fail, and consequently what can be done to educate and train the seminarian so that he may be able to function at maximum effectiveness in the dynamic society in which he is destined to work.

Protestant

The Protestant denominations have been particularly sensitive to the new burdens put upon their clergy as they attempt to interpret their faith to human personalities in a society that is increasingly technical, scientific, and urban. Almost every Protestant seminary is carrying on some sort of study of the work of the clergy and of the type of men who should be recruited to discharge this work.

One of the most comprehensive of these studies was that of Samuel W. Blizzard while he was a visiting professor of social science at Union Theological Seminary. Four other seminaries participated in the project: Protestant Episcopal Seminary, Alexandria, Virginia; the Louisville Presbyterian Seminary, Louisville, Kentucky; the School of Religion (Disciples), Butler University, Indianapolis, Indiana; Garrett Biblical Institute, Evanston, Illinois. Twenty-two Protestant denominations cooperated in the study and more than 1100 theologically trained clergy constituted the sample upon which the findings of the study were based.

Blizzard conceived of the master, practitioner, and integrative roles in which the clergyman functions. The master role is the clergyman's concept of the ministry as an occupation. The practitioner roles (preacher, teacher, priest, organizer, administrator, pastor) are the means or the professional skills that he may use to attain the goals of his ministry.[38] Integrative roles (evangelist, educator, father-shepherd, community problem solver, and the like) enable the clergyman to focus his attention upon the specific goals, ends, and objectives of his master role.[39]

Practitioner Roles. On the basis of the various functions which these clergy were performing in their ministries, six practitioner roles were identified. Three of these were traditional roles: preacher, teacher, priest.

---

[38] Samuel W. Blizzard, "The Minister's Dilemma," *The Christian Century*, April 25, 1956.

[39] S. W. Blizzard, "The Protestant Parish Minister's Integrating Roles," *Religious Education* (July–August, 1958), pp. 374–80.

The *preacher* role is composed of all the study, time and effort that goes into the preparation and delivery of the sermon. The *teacher* role includes the activities, Sunday School, adult classes, social ministries, and the others, where the minister acts in an "instructional" and teaching capacity. The *priest* role had to do with the special part that the clergyman plays in the liturgy and in administering the various rites of the church. The liturgical function occupies a more prominent part in the work of the minister of the churches of high ritual, such as the Episcopal and Lutheran, than it does in the work of a minister of a low church, such as the Methodist or Congregational. The priestly rites include the minister's administration of the sacraments of baptism and communion, as well as marriage and funeral services.

A Neo-traditional Role. The *pastoral* role is an old role with some new features. Traditionally concerned with visiting the various families of the congregations and calling on the sick, the pastoral role has added counseling. The pastoral role now involves and is limited to interpersonal relationships between the pastor and his parishioners in some intimate and personal situation.

Contemporary Roles. Two important roles have developed within recent years that take an increasing amount of the time and energies of the minister: the roles of *administrator* and *organizer*.

The administrator role is composed of all the things the minister does as manager of the parish, director of the stenographic and financial staff, overseer of the physical plant, and all the rest. The organizer role deals with the minister's part in planning and organizing the various socio-spiritual associations, or Social Ministries, of the parish. This involves selecting and training leaders and seeing that the various associations remain active and vital. The organizing role includes also the minister's activities in the community as a citizen and a representative of his church. The minister is trained and capable of discharging his citizenship obligations as a leader and organizer. The community expects him to be a leader and he generally accepts this role in community affairs.

Integrative Roles

The minister-informants were asked what they felt was the most important contribution that they were trying to make and did make for their faith and their parishioners, and a content analysis was made of the responses that established a primary integrative role for each minister-informant. Fourteen primary role patterns were identified. However, six of these primary patterns accounted for four-fifths of all the cases, four of them oriented to the world of people and two to the world of ideas.

People-Oriented Roles. The minister who adopts the *father-shepherd* role is a person of strength and unshakable faith; he is always near when wanted. The routine of pastoral calling: cheering the sick, visiting the aged, and comforting those in crisis and tragedy brings him close to the members of his flock. He is a loving father to his children. This role is primarily integrative for one minister in five. The minister who pursues the father-shepherd role is traditionally oriented.

The Interpersonal Relations. The interpersonal relations specialist is similar to the father-shepherd except that he is oriented towards contemporary rather than traditional values. He looks upon his ministry as a succession of conferences with people who have serious problems and believes that his most important job is to love people and to understand them. He uses psychiatric techniques in his conferences with his parishioners, and thinks of himself as essentially a lay psychiatrist. All his practitioner roles are reducible, he believes, in terms of interpersonal relations. One out of six of the minister-informants fell into this category.

The Parish-Promoter. The parish-promoter role, primarily integrative for one in seven of the minister-informants, involves the skills and techniques of the organizer and promoter and brings them to bear upon the local church system. Such a minister is an organizer of groups and a leader of leaders. He recruits leaders, trains them, and inspires them. He also brings the skills of the business man and the administrator to the church organization, and measures his contribution and his success in terms of statistics: growing attendance, number of new members, a larger budget, expanding organizations, or a growing plant.

The Community Problem Solver. The community problem solver is a minister who finds the greatest challenge to his "call" and his organizing skills in the problems of the community, either local, national, or international. He sees the demands of the "social gospel" best implemented by working towards the amelioration of such problems as crime, alcoholism, delinquency, war, and immorality. He is frequently identified with and found working for labor, reform groups, and social welfare organizations. One minister-informant in ten had this as his primary integrating role.

These four roles, oriented to the world of people, account for two-thirds of all the primary integrative roles of the total number of minister-informants.

Ideologically-Oriented Roles. Two roles are oriented to the world of ideas: the *believer-saint* and the *evangelist*. Together they account for more than one-sixth of all the roles that were primarily integrative for the minister-informants.

The Believer-Saint. The believer-saint is a traditional role and is exemplified in a minister who thinks of himself as a man of faith and who seeks for and endeavors to follow God's will. He may refer to himself in this vein: "The minister's first task is to be sure of his own health of soul." He inspires his parishioners through his saintly conduct. His personality is characterized by prayerfulness, submissiveness, and permissiveness. One in fourteen of the minister-informants was represented in the believer-saint role.

The Evangelist. The evangelist thinks and acts in terms of the "call," impelled to preach the "word" that souls may be "saved." "In my ministry I am concerned about the problem of conversion; how to present the church to the people in it and to others seeking admission." The evangelist tends to think in terms of blacks and whites: one is saved or damned. Frequently some measure of authoritarianism is evident in his relationships with his parishioners. The evangelist role was primarily integrative for one in twelve of the minister-informants.

In no one of the eight remaining role categories, accounting for 20 percent of all the primarily integrative roles, did any one role command more than 4 percent of the total.

How the Minister Views His Vocation

Another study of the work of the Protestant minister sheds additional light on the roles, conflicts, problems, and satisfactions of the liberal minister.[40] All of the informants in this study were holding charges in one-minister churches in upper New York state. This sample is a representative cross section of the medium-sized city and small-village churches in this area.

Each of the minister-informants was asked to list and to rate the three most demanding jobs in his work in terms of time and effort required. In the weighted analyses, the *preaching* role stood first and was followed closely by both the *administrator* and the *pastoral* roles. The pastoral role was interpreted to include visitation of parish members, calling on the sick, the shut-ins, and the needy. Fourth in terms of time and effort was the *counseling*, followed by the *educator* role. The educator role was broadly conceived to include the teaching aspects of the minister in his relationship with the "released time" program, Sunday School, youth activities, and preparation for confirmation and church membership.

Of lesser importance was the role of *organizer-promoter*—all the things the minister did to organize and promote the necessary parish social ministries and to recruit, train, and inspire the leadership necessary to maintain a program once it was established. The civic role appeared among the top three listed by some of the informants. Episcopal and Lutheran informants usually rated the liturgical among the important roles.

After listing the minister's three most demanding roles, each informant was asked to list and to rate what he believed are three most important duties of the minister . . . "that on which you would spend your time and energies, if entirely free to do so." In the weighted analysis of this question two roles came to the fore. The informants wanted more time to devote to preaching (a traditional role) and to counseling (a contemporary role). The role they disliked most, and what they would avoid if possible, was the administrator role.

---

[40] Unpublished study (and following cases) from author's files.

In the case of both the pastoral and the educator roles the *real* and the *ideal* ratings were essentially equal; the minister-informants found the roles were important, took time, and would continue to receive about the same degree of emphasis in their ministry. Under ideal conditions they would invest about the same proportion of their time and talent in these roles as they were already giving.

The study sought the minister's own evaluation of his vocation, and each informant was asked for any comment he cared to make on the varied duties and responsibilities of the minister, as well as on the personal qualities and skills that are helpful to a pastor in the discharge of his duties.

There was general agreement among the informants that the minister must be a "called" or "dedicated" person and that the idea of service must be implicit in his vocational choice. These are representative statements of this point of view: the minister must be "totally dedicated to the Call and the Work of the Kingdom."[41] Another said the minister must not only be "called" but must in addition continue to study to improve his background to become most effective as a "minister for Christ."[42] Another said the "pastor must be called" and "be sure of his creed,"[43] and one reported that the most important personal quality was the "desire to serve fellow church members."[44] Finally: "Pastoring requires much patience and diplomacy, and a great deal of faith. Certainly the divine must play the leading part in leadership."[45]

The informants were agreed that the pastor must have a genuine affection for people and enjoy meeting and dealing with them. "First and last he must love people";[46] "a pastor should have a genuine love for people that will keep him to the task of calling and counseling."[47] "He must be well trained, have a good personality and a love for people. A good wife is a must and can 'make or break' the pastor."[48] "I also feel that extraverted people make better priests."[49]

Problems of the Minister. Almost without exception the informants objected to the amount of time and energy that is "mortgaged" to administrative work, especially since most personalities that choose the ministry are not particularly interested in administrative work nor especially skilled in discharging administrative duties. In the smaller churches the minister finds himself doing his own secretarial work, running the mimeograph, and otherwise handling details that could be better handled by a secretary or administrative helper.

---

[41] Pastor of a Baptist church with a reported congregation of 200.
[42] Pastor of a Presbyterian church with a reported congregation of 225.
[43] Pastor of a Methodist church with a reported congregation of 400.
[44] Pastor of an Episcopal church with a reported congregation of 600.
[45] Pastor of a Lutheran church with a reported congregation of 350.
[46] Pastor of a Methodist church with a reported congregation of 300.
[47] Pastor of a Community church with a reported congregation of 350.
[48] Pastor of a Baptist church with a reported congregation of 400.
[49] Pastor of an Episcopal church with a reported congregation of 500.

The problems are too much secretarial work. Too little time for reading. Too much time spent on trivial tasks: such as handing out forms, unlocking the church, just being around at times because people expect it.[50]

Too much is expected of a pastor in this day along the lines of administration and business. His calling is to preach, teach, and train people to serve the Lord. When he has to do too many other things his power is short-circuited and he becomes less effective or ineffective for God and the Gospel of the Lord Jesus Christ.[51]

Many ministers in fact strenuously object to their involvement in administration at the expense of the two roles, preaching and pastoral, which they hold of primary concern:

I feel preaching to be a paramount concern of a pastor (a prophetic kind of preaching with a challenge to it to make the principles of Christianity a part of our daily lives). A pastor should have a genuine love for people which will keep him to the task of calling and counseling. I think it a shame to run the risk of losing sight of these things for the sake of machinery and administration. We are not won to a way of life by administration, but by hearing the word of God and being challenged to do it.[52]

Personal Qualities. The typical minister is constantly faced with so many diverse and varied duties that a proper discharge of the diverse opportunities to serve his parishioners demands a well-rounded and talented personality. No matter how effective a minister may be there are always some areas where he is not as capable or skilled as he would like to be, and ministers are keenly aware of the complex demands which the vocation puts upon them, as well as of their own limitations in meeting all these demands: "A pastor needs to know something about everything, a splendid educational background, personal and social skills, a love of his work, a love of people."[53]

The changing demands upon the pastor as he tries to play the several roles which varied situations require is brought out in the following excerpts:

A minister must be able to speak in many ways. For instance—sympathetically to the sick and needy, frankly to those who need counsel, persuasively and sternly at a sermon. Other times he must be meaningful, at other times happy or angry. He is certainly a man of many characters.[54]

The pastor must be a "quick-change artist." He must in a split second shift from the funeral mood to a "Chamber of Commerce promoter" and still be sincere.[55]

Some ministers solve the problem of trying to be a specialist in every role by limiting their contribution to the things they can do best:

[50] Pastor of a Methodist church with a reported congregation of 417.
[51] Pastor of a Baptist church with a reported congregation of 125.
[52] Pastor of a Community church with a reported congregation of 350.
[53] Pastor of a Methodist church with a reported congregation of 500.
[54] Pastor of a Lutheran church with a reported congregation of 550.
[55] Pastor of a Methodist church with a reported congregation of 319.

So varied are the needs of the Church and of the people that no one minister can meet all of them. I find one must use his gifts and abilities to the best advantage in the place he serves with primary purpose of a Christ-centered ministry always in mind.[56]

The duties and responsibilities of a pastor are many and varied. This is so much the case that no one person can do all that is expected of him and many matters of importance must be constantly by-passed. This leads to a feeling of frustration and in some cases a feeling of guilt. Breakdowns are common among the clergy today. These result from overwork—too long hours, constantly dealing with people, and usually those in trouble, having to depend so much on volunteers and volunteer giving, the frustration of work partly done and hence unsatisfactory to the one doing it, the growing complexity and pressure of life in general, personal financial difficulties, etc. To meet these pressures, a minister must have a firm faith in God, discipline himself to do his work as faithfully as possible and realize that his human limitations will not permit everything to be done as fully as its importance should demand and to accept such as a hazard of his work.[57]

In spite of the complex nature of the pastoral task, the diverse demands the task places upon the minister, and the realization of the typical minister that he cannot hope to become a specialist in all roles, most clergymen find the very complexity of the task a challenge and their work in it enjoyable and rewarding. Their work is satisfying because they receive the sort of response from their parishioners that convinces them they are rendering a real service and meeting genuine needs, and above all that their work is rewarding because they labor within the values and inspiration of the traditional man of God. They have experienced and are pursuing "a calling to serve God." These demands and values are itemized in the citations below.

Personal qualities needed:
1. Patience (lots of it)
2. Vision (beyond the limitations of the congregation)
3. Financial acumen
4. Love of people
5. Skill in developing leadership ability of laymen
6. Ability to put thoughts into cogent, understandable expression.[58]

And spiritual orientation is emphasized in this testimony:

1. What ever it is we must do—do happily and thankfully, believing that on any given moment THIS is God's work and will for you and the Kingdom.

2. Develop one's own spiritual life and practice of religion.

3. In all dealings with people, ask yourself: "What would Jesus do here?"

4. Develop the spirit of patience; take time to laugh, if need be, at one's self; don't take yourself too seriously; remain convinced of the importance of your work but remember how much you depend on everyone else for personal

---

[56] Pastor of a Methodist church with a reported congregation of 205.
[57] Pastor of a Methodist church with a reported congregation of 275.
[58] Pastor of a Methodist church with a reported congregation of 1200.

happiness and the overall success of your ministry, as well as on the Strength of God without whom you simply couldn't do ANYTHING.[59]

The Conservative Protestant Pastor

A number of ministers serving Protestant churches that were conservative in theological orientation were included in a special study, representing a Church of the Nazarene, a Wesleyan Methodist, and several Baptist congregations belonging to the General Association of Regular Baptist Churches. With the exception of one relatively large Baptist church, with 800 members, the congregations numbered less than 100 members.

The conservative ministers agreed with their liberal peers in putting the preaching role first and in giving the pastoral role a high ranking. They agreed also that administrative duties are a major drain on their time and energy and preferred to devote this time to other functions.

The conservative ministers, however, differed from their liberal peers in several important ways. They were more emphatic on the primary importance of the sermon; several spoke of the desire and need for more time "to read and study" in preparation for their "messages"; and they ranked the pastoral role second both in fact and theory. They also disagreed with their liberal colleagues in regard to counseling: only two mentioned it as an already existing role or as a desirable role.

The conservative ministers emphasize evangelism; they think of and practice the pastoral role in terms of evangelism. One informant placed "evangelistic calling"[60] as a role to which he would like to devote more time, and described it an "endeavoring to win souls." Another informant thought of education in terms of evangelism and linked "education and evangelism"[61] together as a desirable role.

Each of the conservative ministers said the experience of being "called" is a condition precedent to vocational choice. One informant reported the minister "needed more than native ability. He needs the Holy Spirit."[62]

The role pattern of the typical conservative minister shows a traditional orientation, an orientation marked by special emphasis on the Bible. They quote it extensively and give literal and fundamental interpretation to its passages. They speak of themselves and their congregations as "Bible Believers." As conservatives they preach and in their own lives practice the doctrine of sanctification. Sanctification and Bible emphasis was illustrated in the qualifications recommended by one informant:

First of all a pastor must be a saved man. By this I mean a man who has realized that he has sinned against a Holy God (Rom. 3:23, Rom. 6:23, Is. 53:6, I Jn. 1:8, 10). Next he must realize that he can't save himself—by good works or otherwise (Eph. 2:8, 9; Tit. 3:5; Gal. 2:16). Christ died for all man-

---

[59] Pastor of a Reformed church with a reported congregation of 650.
[60] Pastor of a Conservative Baptist church with a reported congregation of 60.
[61] Pastor of a Regular Baptist church with a reported congregation of 60.
[62] Pastor of a Regular Baptist church with a reported congregation of 800.

kind; which have all sinned (Lk. 10:10; I Pet. 2:24; Rom. 5:6, 8; I Pet. 3:18). Next you put faith in or commit yourself unto Christ, the only way to Heaven (Jn. 14:6; Jn. 3:16; Rev. 3:20; Jn. 1:12; Acts 16:31). Secondly, a pastor must be called of the Lord. Thirdly, a pastor must be led in every part of his life by the Lord.[63]

The Catholic Clergy

The role patterns of the Catholic clergy differ from those of the Protestant clergy. The Catholic faith makes different demands upon its priests and imposes different types of restraints. The role patterns of the two faiths also differ because the typical Catholic parish is an urban parish with a larger number of communicants than the typical Protestant church. And although there are a few large Protestant churches with a several-member ministerial staff, the representative Protestant city church is a one-minister church, whereas the typical Catholic parish will be staffed by three or four priests.

With a staff of priests to call upon it is possible for the pastor to assign various functions to his assistants, thereby taking advantage of the special skills and interests of individual priests and enjoying the benefits that accrue to a division of labor.

Mass Society and the Clergy. With the increasing urbanization and mobility of society the Catholic priest, like his Protestant counterpart, is finding that his work involves some new roles, and some traditional roles in a new setting. Furthermore, the priest finds he must serve his church in a society that is increasingly atomized and depersonalized.

Primary group relationships predominated in the more rural and traditional culture so that personality was largely a product of such an environment. In the traditional parish the *fatherly* role was of first importance. The priest was in close and intimate contact with his parishioners, seeing all and knowing all about them and their individual and family problems.

The contemporary priest, however, functions in an urban parish that is based largely upon secondary groups and associational relationships. Just a small part of what happens to the typical parishioner takes place within the parish. His job and his recreational and social activities very probably take him outside the parish and beyond the ken of the priest. The behavior patterns of the typical urban parishioner therefore are a reflection of segmentalized experience. Riesman has contrasted the goal orientations of the two personality types as "inner-directed" (as in traditional society) and "outer-directed" (as in urban society).[64]

In the traditional parish norms and values were uniform and consistent; there was one standard of conduct and behavior by which all were measured. Whether the individual did or did not internalize the culture norms

---

63 Pastor of a Conservative Baptist church with a reported congregation of 80.

64 David Riesman, *Individualism Reconsidered* (Glencoe, Ill.: The Free Press), 1954.

and values, he knew that he would be evaluated or disciplined according to the degree in which his overt behavior reflected the cultural ideal. The priest played a major part in establishing the ideals of behavior and in encouraging, or pressuring, the individual to pattern his conduct after the ideal values. The individual was free to pull himself up by the bootstraps of his own conscience—a conscience that reflected community and parish values. His was an "inner-directed" motivation.

The representative communicant of the typical urban parish is subject to the values and pressures of several subcultures—the values of the market place and of institutionalized recreation—as well as to the sacred values of the parish community. Because it is easiest for the individual to follow the crowd, reflecting the different values of the various groups with which he interacts in his daily and weekly routine, and because the overall culture places a premium on conformity and belongingness, the typical personality tends to please the particular group with which he finds himself in contact at any given time. Thus he becomes an "outer-directed" personality.

Since marketplace and other subculture values are more often than not diametrically opposed to the values of the sacred culture, the task of the religious leader becomes increasingly difficult. One of the greatest problems of the clergyman (whether Protestant, Catholic, or Jew) is the continuing effort to counteract the pull that the "outer-directed" goal or orientation has upon the behavior and values of the typical communicant. Most of the clergy's new roles, and modification of traditional roles, are attempts to adapt religious values to contemporary mass society.

Contemplative Role. Priestly roles are of two types: *apostolic* ("apostolate") and *contemplative*.[65] The apostolic role is composed of all the services, active and external with a social referent, which the priest performs for others. The contemplative role embraces the internal goal of self-sanctification and all priests, both diocesan and religious, are subject to certain obligations in furtherance of this role. They must recite the Divine Office (breviary) daily, make frequent confession, and take retreats at regular intervals. All are likewise obligated to continue the study of the sacred sciences.

Priests are enjoined to avoid participation in or attendance at activities or gatherings that are unbecoming to a man of piety. They are not to attend horse races, for example, or dances.

Apostolic Roles. A number of well-established roles are recognized in the work of the contemporary parish priest.[66] The *liturgical role* is the part the priest plays in the administration of the sacraments. Here he acts as a mediator and special pleader for man with God. No matter how much division of labor exists through role assignment in any given parish, all priests, whether the pastor or youngest curate, share two common re-

---

[65] J. H. Fichter, *op. cit.*, pp. 138–42.
[66] J. H. Fichter, *Social Relations in the Urban Parish* (Chicago: University of Chicago Press, 1954), pp. 129–36.

ligious functions: the celebration of Mass (the Holy Eucharist) and the forgiving of sins (confession or penance). A significant part of the parish priest's workweek is given up to the administration of these two sacraments alone.

Practitioner Roles. In the *administrator* role the pastor organizes and manages the community of parishioners and interacts with the curates and communicants in all the liturgical and social relationships that constitute the totality of Catholic belief and action. He is responsible to the bishop for the health and welfare of his parish, and is ex-officio president and treasurer of each parish organization. And although the pastor may delegate administrative responsibility for various groups to his assistants, he is responsible for all that goes on, or does not go on, in his parish.

The *business* role is concerned with the raising and administering of funds for the maintenance of the parish plant and program. It takes a great deal of money to maintain a modern church plant, especially since most city parishes also operate a parochial school. In addition, each parish is expected to contribute to Catholic interparish functions: diocesan services and charities. The raising of the necessary funds and supervision of their expenditure is an obligation of each pastor. He may regret the time and effort spent, and he may regret the conflict with the higher personal and spiritual values which his business role frequently imposes, but he recognizes its importance.

The priest also has a *civic* role, which includes the things he does as a citizen of the community. He stands in this role as a symbol and interpreter of Catholicism to the various nonsectarian and non-Catholic groups of the community. Priests work for the Community Chest and support civic projects such as hospitals. They participate in labor councils, and otherwise identify themselves with such worthy community projects as urban renewal and industrial development.

The *recreational* role is composed of those parish groups, functions, and relationships which are recreational or athletic in their objectives. Basketball, baseball, and bowling teams are commonly sponsored by the parish, and usually assigned to one of the younger priests.

The *ameliorative* role includes the various activities of the priest which seek to serve and to help the needy in the parish, but his activities may extend to the greater community beyond the parish boundaries. In the ameliorative role the priest may serve as an advisor to the various charitable societies of the parish. The role also includes various personal services and contributions that the priest may extend to needy individuals and families as he comes in contact with them in his parish rounds and at his work.

The *educational* role has many facets; it is teaching and instruction in the broadest sense. It includes the teaching of doctrine and the dissemination of Catholic values and Catholic morality in the pulpit, in private counseling, in the parochial school, and to public school children in the "released time" program. More and more of the representative priest's time is taken up with instruction, and especially in cases of mixed marriage. Since one-third of all Catholic marriages are mixed marriages in which Catholic nuptials are employed, the instruction burden increases. The church requires that the non-Catholic party be instructed on the obligations of a Catholic so that the non-Catholic party may enter marriage with a full realization of what it means to be a practicing Catholic and what is involved in being married to a practicing Catholic.

The *socio-spiritual* role is concerned with the advice, counsel, and instruction that the priest gives to the various groups and societies that are primarily spiritual in nature. These include the sodalities, the Holy Name Society, and various Catholic Action groups. These societies are interested in doing something over and above the minimum duties required of Catholics, and since many of the members are nuclear Catholics, they are some of the most significant groups with which the priest can work.

How the Priest Views His Vocation. A number of priests, like the Protestant ministers, were asked to rank their various roles in the order of the time and effort expended. It was found that the pastor of a typical parish spends a great deal of time in the administration of the parish plant, particularly when the plant includes a parochial school. It takes a great deal of money to maintain the material facilities and personnel of such a parish. The pastor, in addition to spiritual leadership, must be able to lead and organize his parishioners, and raise the necessary funds through contributions and various money-raising projects.

The Catholic pastor spends a greater proportion of his time in the administrative and business roles than his Protestant counterpart and the typical priest appears to be somewhat more skilled in administration than the typical minister. If not every priest on the staff of a given parish is particularly skilled in administration and business, there is at least one to whom administrative responsibilities may be assigned. Our priest-informants listed administrative duties one of the leading demands upon their time and energies.

Because of the universal, yet specific, nature of doctrine and worship, and the importance that is placed upon them, much of the priest's work is given over to dispensing the sacraments and officiating at devotions required by the liturgical calendar. Our informants reported that the priestly function makes a heavy demand upon their time. Each priest is required to say a mass each day. Hearing confessions on Saturdays and before major holy days is demanding and time consuming.

The pastoral role and the counseling role are similarly demanding. It is customary in a representative city parish to keep a priest on call at all times to meet special spiritual and temporal needs of the individual communicants as they arise. The counseling role appears to have added a modern touch to the traditional priest-communicant relationship. The priest counsels within the framework of psychological principles and techniques, and tends to be more permissive and less authoritarian than was the traditional priest. It is, apparently, a contemporary adaptation of the traditional fatherly role.

The priests reported a great deal of time was devoted to instruction; instructing engaged couples on the Catholic concept of marriage relations and marriage duties, instructing converts and school children on Catholic belief, instructing non-Catholics on their duties and obligations to their proposed Catholic spouse. Instruction is the traditional aspect of the educator role, and the church spells out in detail what a good Catholic should believe and how he should behave in the everyday business of living.

Our sample indicated there was not much difference, in terms of the time and energy required of the priest, among the priestly, the administrative, the pastoral and counseling, and the educational roles. They appeared to be equally demanding of time and energy.

Each priest, like the Protestant ministers, was asked which role he considered most important and on which he would spend the greatest amount of time if he were free to do so. They were in general agreement that they would spend more time upon the "spiritual" aspects of their vocation—the more traditional priestly and pastoral roles as opposed to the contemporary administrative, civic, counseling, and educational roles. According to the priests the latter category was necessary and unavoidable, but not as important or as satisfying as the traditionally spiritual. One priest reported his most important duty was not any one of the specific roles listed above but rather "to help give people a lift—to get them to feel close to God and Heaven."[67] A priest, pastor of a rapidly growing parish, said his biggest problem and greatest challenge was "to know when people need extra spiritual guidance for private and personal problems."[68] This pastor felt he was so removed from the great majority of his parishioners that he was unable to identify personal problems, which were the proper responsibility of a spiritual adviser. Another pastor also reported that his chief duty was his greatest problem; that "of making morality and the Ten Commandments attractive."[69]

The priests, again like the Protestant ministers, were asked to list and to comment on the personal qualities and skills needed to discharge the responsibilities of their vocation. The qualities and skills they thought most necessary were quite similar in three important respects to the qualities and skills rated by the Protestant ministers as most desirable:

1. The priest should feel "called" to the priestly vocation. They did not interpret this experience quite as literally and individualistically as the Protestant ministers, but the emphasis upon dedication and spiritual involvement was essentially the same.

---

[67] Pastor of a Catholic church with a reported membership of 2500 (two priests on the parish staff).

[68] Pastor of a Catholic church with a reported membership of 3300 (three priests on parish staff).

[69] Pastor of a Catholic church with a reported membership of 3300 (two priests on parish staff).

2. The priest should be an all-around man, broadly skilled and widely trained to meet the varied tasks and problems, expected and unexpected, that he may be called upon to discharge and solve at any time.

3. He should like people and be kindly and approachable.

The following quotations are typical and representative of parish pastors:

"Must have a love of people, patience, understanding, approachability."[70] "Kindness is the paramount virtue."[71] "Zeal, kindness, charity."[72] "The pastor must be well-versed and educated in almost every phase of life. He should have an education and training that will enable him to deal with all types of people and situations. He should not only be versed in philosophy and theology but also have a good knowledge of such other fields as business management, psychology, teaching, law, medicine. He must be prudent, sympathetic, and able to talk and meet with all people. He must be enthusiastic and have great energy and determination."[73]

An elderly priest, pastor of the same parish for over thirty years and highly revered by his parishioners who frequently refer to him as a "saint," has this to say about his vocation:

I do not say that all priests possess all these qualities [in reference to a listing of roles], but I do not think there is any calling in the world that demands as much of the individual as the priesthood. First, there must be deep personal spirituality and dedication to be on call at all times night and day; the average day begins at 6:00 A.M. and ends at midnight, this for all priests. Second, he must have a well-rounded knowledge, not only of theology but also a background of law, medicine, psychology, counseling, and almost anything you can think of, as well as being able to get things done in a community and know how to advise and where to send people.[74]

According to Fichter, two facts stand out in regard to the duties and activities of the parish priest: each priest must have some competence in each role, and the priest must conform to the needs of the parish rather than to his own interests, talents and training.[75]

The church is ideally structured to secure extensity of training and experience, and at the same time take advantage of the special skills and interests of its priests. The bishop customarily assigns the young priest first as an assistant to an experienced and capable pastor who sees to it that he gets training in the gamut of roles a priest may be called upon to perform. The work of the church in a representative diocese is so varied and com-

---

[70] Pastor of a National Catholic parish with a reported membership of 1000 (one priest).

[71] Pastor of a Catholic church with a reported membership of 3500 (two priests on parish staff).

[72] Pastor of a Catholic church with a reported membership of 700 families (three priests on parish staff).

[73] Pastor of a Catholic church with a reported membership of 1327 families (three priests on parish staff).

[74] Pastor of a Catholic church with a reported membership of 4800 (three priests on parish staff).

[75] J. H. Fichter, *op. cit.*, p. 137.

plex that any special skill a young priest has can often be used for the benefit of the church and its program. All kinds or types of administrative and teaching skills can be put to work in some area or at some level of the parochial school system. The expanding complex of social welfare services, as represented in Catholic charities, calls for special interests and skills. There is a place for the specialist in spiritual advising and counseling on the diocesan Retreat House staff, and the stirring and inspiring preacher can be shifted about the diocese as a mission preacher.

The bishop can also assign his pastors according to the particular needs of the various parishes: the priest skilled in administration and business role to the parish in debt, or about to embark upon an expansion of the physical plant; the educator to the parish with a parochial school problem, and so on. The church needs specialists, but she does not want her priests to become so specialized that they get out of touch with religion at the grassroots parish level. It is a policy, apparently, to rotate priests in specialized positions to the parish field from time to time. Such a rotation is considered good for the practice of religion at the parish level, as well as a refreshing experience for the priest himself.

There is considerable exchange of duties between priests assigned to parishes and priests given non-parochial assignments. Two out of five American parishes need weekend help from non-parochial priests (school and college teachers and chancery functionaries), and a somewhat higher percentage of parish priests, in turn, perform various non-parochial duties.[76]

The Jewish Rabbi

The status and functions of the rabbi varies with the denomination of Judaism with which he is affiliated and the congregation he serves. The three denominational positions within Judaism, Orthodox, Conservative, Reform, are three aspects of a common tradition and practice rather than three separate and distinct entities. The work of the rabbi in any given congregation depends a great deal upon the history of the particular congregation and the degree and extent to which the congregation may be modifying the customary worship and practice.

Judaism is just as individualistic as Protestantism. Since each congregation is autonomous, and since the rabbi is relatively free to take any theological position, there is no one basic role-pattern for any of the three denominational positions. A number of integrative role patterns, however, have been identified among practicing rabbis.

Orthodox Roles. Orthodox Judaism is served by two leading role patterns.[77] The *traditional-orthodox* rabbi tries to play the "scholar-saint"

---

[76] J. H. Fichter, *Religion as an Occupation*, p. 143n.

[77] Jerome E. Carlin and Saul H. Mendlovitz, "The American Rabbi: a Religious Specialist Responds to Loss of Authority," in *The Jews: Social Patterns of an American Group*, Marshall Sklare (ed.) (Glencoe, Ill.: The Free Press, 1958), pp. 382–93.

role as it was practiced in Eastern Europe where the Jews lived in relatively closed and isolated communities. The rabbi was a scholar who was an expert on the Law and the Torah; he was a saint because he practiced the full letter of the 613 precepts of the strict Jew in his daily life. He was respected for his learning *and* his behavior. He was the interpreter of the Law and the judge of the community. Since the Law was life itself, his status was unequalled within the community.

The traditional-orthodox rabbi is still found serving some Orthodox congregations in the United States. Bearded and wearing the traditional long black gabardine robe of the Talmudic scholar, he is more at home in Yiddish than in English. He strives to maintain the role of the traditional rabbi of the Old Country, and he resents and resists the various role changes that his congregation tries to impose upon him—he dislikes and resents the preaching, priestly, and pastoral functions his congregation wants him to discharge. Rabbis of this type serve congregations that are usually located in the older sections of the city.

The *modern-orthodox* rabbi serves on Orthodox congregation also and is orthodox in his conduct and belief. He speaks English well and accepts, more or less willingly, many of the modern roles introduced by the Reform and Conservative groups.

The following excerpts from a case study of a synagogue and its rabbi is typical of the work of the modern-orthodox rabbi.[78] Rabbi X serves a congregation that considers and calls itself Orthodox, and conducts a Hebrew school three days a week in the synagogue. He lists the educator, administrator, and counselor functions as his three most demanding tasks. His most important duties—those which he would give the most time if he were entirely free to do so—are education, counseling, and preaching. Although Rabbi X is orthodox in his own behavior, he spends most of his time performing services for his people that are more in keeping with Conservative and Reform than with traditional practice. Furthermore, he considers his contemporary roles the most important part of his contribution to his congregation. According to Rabbi X, the most valuable personal traits are those that characterize the "outer-directed" personality: friendliness and competency in dealing with people.

The modern-orthodox rabbi will preach, counsel, conduct services, perform rites, and concern himself with community relations. His chief interest is in organizing the educational institutions of his synagogue and his goal is the rebuilding of a traditional Jewish community around the synagogue. Orthodox in behavior, he has however given up traditional scholarship for the educator, organizer, and other contemporary roles.

Reform Roles. At the opposite pole of the belief and practice continuum are Reform Judaism and the Reform rabbi. The Reform rabbi rejects the scholar-saint role and finds himself in accord with and com-

---

[78] Rabbi of an Orthodox synagogue with a reported membership of 75 families (one rabbi).

mitted to the "protestantization" of rabbinic functions. He usually comes from a second or third generation middle- or upper-class family and has had an extensive secular education. He preaches, and both he and his congregation consider it his most important function, but he regards his message more as a "lecture" than as a sermon. He counsels because of the breadth and depth of his secular education, and he is frequently skilled as a counselor.

Because his synagogue may have the same proliferation of men's clubs, sisterhoods, junior congregations, youth groups, Sunday School classes, discussion circles, adult education projects, dinners and suppers as a well-organized liberal Protestant church, he probably has extensive administrative duties as well. He conducts services in the synagogue, performs marriages, and conducts funerals, all aspects of the priestly role. The Reform rabbis, however, consider their primary role to be that of the teacher. They teach in the sermon, in leading discussion groups and adult classes, and in the Sunday School.

A typical Reform congregation places a great deal of emphasis upon the community role of its rabbi, wanting him to be an ambassador of good will to the Christian community. One rabbi even lamented that the community role is about the only thing the representative congregation wants from its spiritual leader. "The congregants invariably imply, and often state, 'We need you as our representative among the non-Jews, to mingle with them, to speak in their churches, to make a good impression. We do not need you for ourselves. Well, for the old people, perhaps, and for the children, yes, once a week; but for the Gentiles most of all.' "[79]

According to Carlin and Mendlovitz there are three identifiable sub-roles within the overall Reform role.[80] The *intellectual Reform* rabbi stakes his claim for authority in terms of his intellectual ability and achievements. He has, he feels, the authority to speak on any subject he masters. This role is a far departure from the Orthodox rabbi who enjoys an authority based upon knowing and living a sacred law. The intellectual is probably the most common role for the Reform rabbinate.

The *social-reformer* rabbi is oriented towards liberal democratic values within a community context. He tries to show the relationship that exists between traditional Jewish and liberal democratic values. Though interested and concerned with community problems he does not neglect the synagogue, for it is the base and reference point from which he operates.

The *traditionalist Reform* rabbi is leading Reform Judaism back to the traditional values and forms which the movement originally repudiated. These rabbis look forward to a belief and practice of Judaism in which rabbis will recover the scholar-saint role.

The Conservative Rabbi. The Conservative rabbi, like the Conservative

---

[79] Alexander S. Kline, "The Rabbi in the Small Town," *Central Conference of American Rabbis Journal*, April, 1954, pp. 10–11.
[80] Carlin and Mendlovitz, *op. cit.*, pp. 393–401.

movement, holds a position between the Orthodox and the Reform. Conservatism is an attempt to keep those features of Judaism which are thought to be universally valid for all ages, while modifying or eliminating the nonessential in order to keep pace with the changing culture and new events. The two following cases are illustrations of the work of a representative Conservative rabbi in a representative Conservative congregation.

The rabbi[81] in a suburban area reports his most demanding tasks, in the order of their importance, as educational activities, family counseling, and "sermonizing." His synagogue holds a daily morning and evening prayer service, and the Saturday service includes a sermon in English. The rabbi[82] of a second Conservative congregation reports his most *demanding* duties are counseling, administration, and preaching, while his most *important* are teaching, counseling, and the pastoral. He finds a rabbi should first of all be personable and diplomatic, understanding and dedicated. The roles and personality orientation of these rabbis are attuned to an urban culture, and a far departure from the traditional.

The Conservative rabbi, concerned that the essentials be retained, believes they are inextricably bound up with a revitalized Jewish community that is centered around the religious and educational program of the synagogue. Building his synagogue up and making its program attractive, he finds he is primarily engaged in the organizer and promoter role. Furthermore, his synagogue and its program become attractive to his congregation when he does the things they expect of him; when he preaches, when he counsels, when he presides over the services and prayers, when he condones such modern trends as mixed pews, organ music, and modifications in the rituals and prayers.

In his process of making the synagogue the center of Jewish life, the Conservative rabbi finds he has sacrificed the role of scholar for such contemporary roles as preacher, pastor, priest, and organizer. For his former authority as a religious specialist he can only substitute his non-Jewish skills and secular knowledge and in fact, bases his authority and leadership upon the force of his personality.[83]

According to the Conservative rabbi the "essentials" include a significant number of the 613 precepts, the do's and don'ts of orthodox practice. He maintains a kosher table and endeavors to follow the dietary law and to keep the Sabbath holy. Although his congregation is pleased to see its rabbi a good example of correct behavior, they are reluctant to impose the same restraints and discipline upon themselves, and a Conservative rabbi will take it for granted that he cannot eat in the homes of most of his

---

[81] Rabbi of a Conservative synagogue with a reported membership of 450 families (two rabbis).

[82] Rabbi of a Conservative synagogue with a reported membership of 350 families (four rabbis).

[83] Marshall Sklare, *Conservative Judaism: an American Religious Movement* (Glencoe, Ill.: The Free Press, 1955), p. 179.

congregants. A survey of lay leaders of Conservative congregations shows that among these laymen only 37 percent maintain kosher homes.[84]

Carlin and Mendlovitz point out that modern Orthodox, Conservative, and traditional Reform rabbis have two important roles in common. They are organizers in rebuilding the Jewish community around the synagogue, and, in pursuit of this goal they find it necessary to engage in the same complex of functions—preaching, priestly, pastoral, teaching, administrative, and community.

The identity of these rabbis' goals illustrates the strong tendency of contemporary Judaism to converge upon the center. The resulting practice, traditional Judaism adapted to and at peace with the secular culture, is also a good illustration of another important trend, the "Americanization" of Judaism.[85]

Not all rabbis are happy with the evolution of the rabbi's office and the demands which contemporary role patterns make upon their time and energy. Spokesmen for both Orthodox and Conservative rabbinical groups have protested against the roles, secular and personal, that prevent the rabbi from concentrating upon the spiritual aspects of his calling.

A president of the Rabbinical Council of America (Orthodox) asks that the rabbi be relieved of such functions as business administration, fund-raising, and public relations so that he can be restored to the "position of deep spiritual authority and persuasiveness."[86] A Conservative spokesman urges that less be demanded of the rabbi and that he not be made a "jack of all trades," acting as a psychiatric counselor, a lecturer to a civic group, and a speaker at a women's auxiliary, all in one day. What the rabbi needs is the time for study and relaxation, which, according to Dr. Ginsberg, can produce the insight and understanding for spiritual leadership.[87]

The problem, according to a former president of the American Council of Rabbis, is that the contemporary rabbi overemphasizes counseling at the expense of preaching. He agrees that practical psychology has its uses but asserts that it should no longer continue to be the "overwhelming concern of the spiritual leader. Counseling is really a Christian pastoral role." Dr. Freehof urged the rabbis to stress the role of the pulpit; to preach more and counsel less.[88]

Status, Tenure, Promotion

With the ministry ranked among the learned professions for which Americans have always shown considerable respect, clergymen enjoy

[84] Nathan Glazer, *American Judaism* (Chicago: University of Chicago Press, 1957), p. 131.

[85] Will Herberg, *Protestant, Catholic, Jew* (Garden City, N.Y.: Doubleday & Co., 1955), pp. 186–213.

[86] *New York Times,* July 10, 1962.

[87] *Ibid.,* May 9, 1960.

[88] *Ibid.,* July 28, 1962.

high status in America. Various rating scales for occupations also place this among the top occupations.[89] In a national opinion poll that asked people to rank 90 occupations, the minister ranked fourteenth and the priest twenty-first, the former getting a score of 87 and the latter a score of 86.[90] In 1953, Elmo Roper took a poll in which 40 percent picked religious leaders as the group doing the most good for the country. Roper reported that "no other group—whether government, congressional, business, or labor—came anywhere near matching the prestige and pulling power of the men who are ministers of God."[91]

Catholic. The religious vocation enjoys the security of absolute tenure. All vocations, priest, brother, sister, not only involve a lifetime job and career after the taking of final vows, but also all the security which the church can offer its servants. When the priest on ordination is told "Thou art a priest forever," he becomes both the servant of his church and its responsibility. He may be moved around the diocese from position to position, and there is always something for him to do, but whether he is able to work or not his material wants and needs are the responsibility of his diocese and his bishop.

As a man of God, committed to a life of piety and sanctification with a supernatural orientation, the religious functionary is not primarily concerned with or measured by temporal values. But as a man, or woman, of God engaged in apostolic works, and as a member of a religious community, each functionary enjoys a status because of his standing in his occupation and his position within his own religious group.

Within the religious vocation the functionary enjoys the status of the particular order to which he or she belongs, and also reflects the status of the people he serves and to whom he caters.[92] The priest-professor of a college tends to enjoy higher prestige than the priest-teacher of a high school. The functionary enjoys a status that varies according to the position of leadership and responsibility that he holds in his group. The pastor enjoys more prestige than his curate, the bishop more than his director of diocesan charities, etc.

Practically every curate hopes some day to be a pastor. The length of time it takes to achieve this position varies from 5 to 35 years or more, depending upon the number of priests and parishes in the diocese, and in the very largest dioceses recently ordained priests have been advised that they may *never* reach the pastorate.[93]

Promotions are few and they come late in the career of the average priest. Promotional openings through the death of a pastor are infrequent,

---

[89] Theodore Caplow, *The Sociology of Work* (Minneapolis: University of Minnesota Press, 1954), p. 53.

[90] Bernard Barber, *Social Stratification* (New York: Harcourt, Brace and World, Inc., 1957), pp. 100–11.

[91] *Information Service*, April 3, 1954.

[92] J. H. Fichter, *Religion as an Occupation*, p. 59.

[93] *Ibid.*, pp. 166–68.

and pastors never resign. Most priests, as a result, are still assistants in a parish long after they have gained the training and experience that would qualify them to hold a pastorate. When asked the basis for promotion in their respective dioceses most curates said "seniority alone," pastors reported "achievement and seniority," while both curates and pastors mentioned "preferment by the bishop" as the third most important basis for promotion.[94] In another study the Catholic pastors in charge of medium and large parishes throughout the United States were asked what they felt had been the basis for their appointments—previous administrative experience, merit, seniority? The findings showed again that seniority was considered to be the key basis for appointment to a pastorate.[95]

The pastorate is not, however, the only avenue of recognition. In each diocese a number of offices and positions of responsibility and leadership offer priests status and recognition: the vicar general, who assists the bishop; the chancellor, who acts as executive officer; the judge of the diocesan court; the superintendent of schools; the director of charities; the editor of the diocesan newspaper; and many others. Each religious order likewise offers opportunities for temporal recognition, each community requiring a superior, a treasurer, a secretary to the superior, members of the local council, etc.

The *monsignorate* is a sort of honorary title usually granted as a reward for long years of service as pastor or diocesan official. It denotes status rather than role, and is considered a promotion.

Protestant. Appointment and tenure for the clergy in Protestantism varies according to the denomination, each having its own rules and codes. In denominations with a congregational type of organization, the recruiting and termination of services is primarily a question between the pastor and his congregation. A congregation needing a pastor investigates ministers known to be available for an appointment, and extend a "call." The minister invited is free to answer the "call" and accept, or to reject the invitation.

In the episcopal type of church organization a congregation needing a pastor appeals to the bishop, who will nominate a list of qualified ministers and the congregation will make its choice from the bishop's panel of nominees. Once hired, the pastor knows that he cannot arbitrarily be released by the congregation; he is the bishop's man and can be moved only with the consent of the bishop, who also has power to maintain a pastor with diocesan funds.

The Methodist church used to move its ministers regularly every three years, the bishop and district superintendent arranging for the movement and assignment of pastors in the annual district conventions. But this is no

94 *Ibid.*, pp. 168–71.
95 Thomas R. O'Donovan and Arthur X. Deegan, "Some Career Determinants of Church Executives," *Sociology and Social Research*, Vol. 48, No. 1 (October, 1963), p. 58.

longer the practice in established churches. A congregation and minister who are mutually satisfied with their relationships can petition the district conference to extend the pastor's appointment from year to year. It is not now uncommon for a Methodist minister to spend the greater part of his professional career in a single charge.

In churches with the presbyterian type of church organization, a higher body (a synod or a presbytery) may act as an intermediary and use its good offices to bring qualified clergymen to the attention of churches in search of a pastor.

Most Protestant clergymen, however, are employed according to free market principles and the congregational form of church organization. A minister's understanding with the congregation is usually informal and implied rather than contractual, and there is nothing to prevent his resigning his pastorate at the end of any year of service. He may leave a charge with due notice and accept service at any other church when properly "called," but the ethics of the profession of course forbid him from seeking another minister's parish until the pastorate has been formally proclaimed to have been vacated. A "good minister of Jesus Christ marches in step with other ministers and is anxious to do so."[96]

Ministers are called on the basis of their experience, record, and potential, and are paid a salary which in some measure reflects the congregation's evaluation of services rendered. Promotion means answering a call and moving to a larger church and congregation. Protestant ministers may establish a reputation in any number of ways and enhance their employability—as a preacher, as a youth leader, as a "spiritual force," or as a "pastor." The traditional path of career mobility leads from minister of a modest rural or village church to the pastorate of a large urban congregation.

The Protestant minister enjoys the status of an educated man although educational requirements differ among the denominations. The more degrees he has earned the higher his status. Clergymen also gain recognition and status by election to positions of regional, state, or national leadership in their denomination.

The Protestant minister enjoys a sort of "ex officio" status that is roughly comparable to that which his church and its communicants enjoy in the community. And, because Protestant churches are typically class-oriented, the pastor of an upper-class church enjoys a community status quite different from that of the minister of a lower-class church.

Ministers can also, through their own efforts as community citizens, achieve a status that is quite independent of their church affiliation.

Judaism. Judaism is a religion with independent and autonomous congregations. The national bodies, whether Orthodox, Conservative, or Reform, have no authority over member congregations; they are informative

---

[96] Nolan B. Harmon, "Ethics of the Protestant Ministry," *The Annals,* Vol. 297 (January, 1955), pp. 70–75.

and advisory only. The individual Jewish family likewise is free to affiliate with a congregation of its choice, or to remain unaffiliated. The unaffiliated family can always ask specific services from a congregation or rabbi and discharge its obligations by the payment of a stipulated fee or offering.[97]

A code, Principles Governing Congregational-Rabbinical Agreements, has been developed to minimize competition for placement between rabbis. Regularizing terms and conditions of employment for the welfare of both rabbis and congregations, the code calls for an initial rabbinical term of one year, and succeeding terms of three and five years each. After a rabbi has ministered to a congregation for approximately fifteen years, the relationship is deemed permanent.[98] Many rabbis have spent their entire professional careers with one congregation.

The rabbi, like his Christian counterpart, enjoys status as a member of a learned profession and a man of God. The rabbi also enjoys a community status, a reflection of the social status his synagogue and congregation have in the community.

Each rabbi enjoys additional status and prestige, according to his personal qualities and achievements. The Jewish emphasis upon learning and scholarship has led many rabbis to become experts and authorities in particular fields, and, as speakers and scholars, many have achieved regional and national reputations which are very gratifying to their congregations. One of the most important roles that many congregations expect their rabbi to play is that of interpreter of Judaism to the Christian community. The rabbi scholar can perform this role with distinction.

The rabbi, like the Catholic priest or Protestant minister, may gain a status quite independent of his synagogue affiliations through participation in community affairs as a private citizen.

Summary

The three faiths have developed professional techniques of recruitment, patterns of training, criteria of promotion, and standards for tenure for the occupation that is known as the clergy.

Catholic priests are generally recruited from high schools, usually from Catholic high schools, and are trained in minor and major seminaries. The preprofessional training of the priest is a liberal arts curriculum, with a major in theology.

The major Protestant denominations recruit from colleges. A liberal arts degree is common. Seminary training is four years and includes some intern experience, although some conservative churches are staffed by ministers trained in Bible colleges. Bible colleges usually require something less than a full undergraduate college background as a prerequisite for admittance and ordination.

---

[97] Ben Zion Bokser, "Codes of the American Rabbinate," *The Annals*, Vol. 297 (January, 1955), pp. 59–63.
[98] *Ibid.*

Conservative and Reform rabbinical students enter the seminary with a baccalaureate from a secular college, while Orthodox rabbinical students come up through parochial elementary and secondary schools and the Jewish college or university. It is still possible, however, to qualify for the rabbinate through individual study under the direction of a rabbi. In addition to mastery of the Torah and the Talmud, it is considered desirable for the rabbi to be something of a specialist in a secular subject.

The Catholic priest has life tenure, but where he pursues his profession is decided by superiors in his diocese or order. Diocesan priests look upon a pastorate as the ultimate reward for effective service in the church.

Recognition among the Protestant clergy is primarily an individual matter that depends upon the effectiveness of the minister in his successive charges. Promotion usually comes in the form of being "called" to a larger and wealthier congregation. The major denominations administer pension funds that guarantee their clergy a comfortable minimum of retirement security.

Although the initial appointment of a rabbi to a congregation is usually contractual, long-term tenure depends upon the mutual satisfaction of the rabbi and the congregation with the relationship and the services rendered. The average tenure of rabbis is longer than the average tenure of Protestant ministers.

To serve their congregations effectively, clergymen are called upon to play a variety of roles. The demands of a changing culture have added new roles to the traditional roles. This is true whether the religious functionary is a Protestant minister, a Catholic priest, or a Jewish rabbi.

Liberal Protestants have added the new roles of administrator and organizer to the traditional roles of preacher, teacher, and pastor. Counseling has arisen to give a modern touch to the traditional pastoral role. The typical Protestant minister enjoys the preaching and counseling roles, but tends to be unhappy and ill at ease in the administrator role. The conservative Protestant minister differs from his liberal peer in the greater importance he assigns to the preaching role and the greater extent to which evangelistic emphasis permeates his preacher, teacher, and pastoral roles.

The priestly and the liturgical roles are the first demands upon the time and energies of the parish priest, but the church and its priests demonstrate a characteristic ability to adapt to the demands of contemporary culture and its problems in additional roles. The proliferation of services offered in the program of the representative urban parish puts a premium upon the business and administrative skill of the pastor. The emphasis which Catholic practice puts upon instruction makes the educator role of leading importance. And counseling has grown to be as important a function of the typical priest as it is of the typical minister.

Congregations within American Judaism vary from an orthodoxy that has remained virtually unchanged for over five thousand years to a reform version that seems to have more in common with liberal Protestantism than with traditional Judaism.

The traditional-Orthodox rabbi strives to play the scholar-saint role. He is the repository of Jewish law and wisdom and a judge and interpreter of social interaction and individual behavior, as laid down in the law.

At the other pole of the continuum is the Reform rabbi, liberal in theology and modern in practice. He has adopted many of the roles of the liberal Protestant minister; he preaches, leads service, and is a counselor and an administrator. He is active in community affairs.

The Conservative rabbi stands midway between Orthodoxy and Reform. He concentrates upon making the synagogue and its program the center of Jewish education and social and religious life. The Conservative rabbi serves as an example to his congregation in his own religious life. He keeps the dietary laws and the Sabbath, and accepts many other disciplines and restraints of the Orthodox Jew. He is "more Jewish" than his parishioners, most of whom are reform in behavior.

THEORETICAL OBSERVATIONS

The sect-church continuum is illustrated in our case studies of representative religious systems. *Jehovah's Witnesses* are sectlike in that they tend to be:

1. Bible literalists.

2. Dependent upon lay leadership.

3. Adult centered and oriented.

4. Extremely emphatic in their belief that they are a gathered remnant and the "true church."

5. Largely lower class-centered.

6. Insistent upon duties and practices that tend to isolate the sect member from secular groups: the effective member is completely involved and committed. A sect-group can maintain itself only when a substantial number of its members makes the religious role central and pivotal. A sect member is socially "visible."

7. Avowedly and openly hostile to other religious groups and to secular culture and secular values; for example, "Associations of a social nature outside the truth are dangerous."

In spite of the intensity of their sect behavior, however, some minor changes in practices and beliefs represent a movement towards the "church" pole of the continuum:

1. Some of the new terms (*congregational minister* instead of *company servant*) and practices (hymns) are churchlike in nature.

2. The training period for lay leaders (Gilead) has been extended from two to ten months.

3. Some high school- and a few college-experienced persons are showing up in leadership echelons.

4. The national organization is becoming more centralized and is exerting more control over individual congregations, both at home and overseas.

Latter-Day Saints also tend to be sectlike.

1. They are Bible literalists, who have added the Book of Mormon and other material to the body of revelation.

2. They depend upon a lay leadership and widespread lay participation.

3. They have a heightened sense of the "true" church: only through Mormon conversion, baptism, and the rest can the individual be saved.

4. They are perfectionist and demanding, stressing tithing, fasting, various restraints, and health and diet rules.

They tend to be churchlike in their

1. Interpretations and practices that are adapted to the child level of interest and understanding.

2. National organization and strong international and missionary outreach.

3. Movement from a farm and rural to an urban and middle-class membership.

4. Secular and very American emphasis upon such traditional virtues as thrift, self-reliance, and conservatism.

Seventh-day Adventists tend to be sectlike in their

1. Bible literalism and their rejection of evolution and other conflicting modern ideas.

2. Heightened sense of the "true" church, with specialized concepts of heaven, hell, the state of the dead, etc.

3. Perfectionism and discipline; their strict rules on dress, diet, drinking, smoking, and tithing.

4. Hostility to certain secular values and practices. They observe the Sabbath on Saturday, oppose military service, and prefer their own parochial to public schools.

They tend to be churchlike because of

1. Comprehensive Sunday school programs adapted to child-level interest and understanding.

2. Increased formal education and training required of their ministers.

3. Their national organization and strong international and missionary outreach.

As an individual conservative church, the North Syracuse Baptist Church tends to be sectlike in

1. Its Bible literalism and orthodox doctrines, both traditionally interpreted.

2. Its high sense of being the "true" church, its evangelization and strong missionary thrust, and the duty of its members to "witness."

3. Its perfectionism and discipline. Social drinking and dancing are discouraged and tithing is encouraged. There is an almost total involvement with the ideal that leaves little time for secular associations.

4. Its autonomy; it has no binding national or regional ties.

5. Its neutrality, rather than hostility to the values and goals of secular society.

It tends to be churchlike in its

1. Comprehensive Sunday School and youth program, both adapted to various levels of interests and understanding.

2. Middle-class alignment.

Jehovah's Witnesses are the most sectlike of these illustrations. Their sectism is most apparent in their hostility toward other religious groups and to the values and goals of secular society. Latter-Day Saints, Seventh-day Adventists, and our conservative church are sectlike, and in approximately the same degree, but much less conservative than Jehovah's Witnesses. Sectism is most apparent in and by the emphasis each puts on "perfectionist" goals and the personal religious life.

Many illustrations of the sect types described can be found in the contemporary religious culture. The Oxford Group Movement and Christian Science are good examples of the *acceptance* type of sect. According to the philosophy and orientation of these groups, personal inadequacies are primarily the fault of the individual and not of society. Acceptance sects have no quarrel with society, but they place the emphasis upon individual self-analysis and improvement. The Salvation Army, too, is basically an *acceptance* type of religious group, seeking to reform and rehabilitate individuals so they can be reabsorbed into a social order the Army believes is essentially sound and constructive.

Throughout American history Quakers have functioned as an *aggressive* sect and have not hesitated to influence or change society according to their beliefs and practices in areas where they have disagreed with secular goals and practices. Quakers were the first to advocate and practice prison reform, to take a stand against slavery, to honor their treaties with Indians and otherwise treat them with consideration. And they exerted society with all the pressure and influence they could generate to adopt their solution and point of view. Currently, Quakers are active and determined to have society and societies accept their solution to the war problem.

No religious group in the past generation has more continuously and dramatically held the attention of the American people than Jehovah's Witnesses through their aggressive activities. The beliefs and activities of the Black Muslims now make them the outstanding illustration of religious aggressiveness.

Avoidance sects are illustrated by various holiness and pietistic groups. The Mennonites, particularly the Amish and to a lesser extent the Brethren, live to themselves and avoid the type of secular contacts that would tend to make them more "normal" and less "peculiar."

Seventh-day Adventists, the Salvation Army, and many conservative Protestant churches stress the need for the conversion experience to the extent and degree that they may properly be classed as *conversionist* sects. Both the Seventh-day Adventists and the Jehovah's Witnesses are *adventist* sects in that they anticipate the literal, personal, visible return of Christ to the earth and a subsequent millennium. The Latter-Day Saints are not as adventist in orientation as once they were. The doctrine of eternal progression, with its emphasis upon the improvement of the individual on earth, receives more stress from contemporary Mormonism than the doctrine of the millennium in the City of Zion concept.

All pietist groups, the Oxford Group Movement and Christian Science—but notably the Quakers, the Mennonites, and the Brethren, are *introversionist* in doctrine and practice. They stress the cultivation of inner resources; the Bible is their source of inspiration and ethical insight; they look to the spirit rather than the letter of the Bible, and find little or no need for a professional clergy.

Perhaps the most significant trend in the religious culture is the relative importance which *gnostic-like sects* have attained—offering a new interpretation of Christian teaching in which the Bible is complementary to their own revelation of truth. Membership is acquired after instruction and guidance rather than through conversion, and leaders, accordingly, are considered teachers rather than ministers. The Latter-Day Saints, Jehovah's Witnesses, Seventh-day Adventists, and Christian Scientists have strong gnostic traits in their religious systems.

Mormon missionaries have a series of six "lessons" which they offer to prospective members, an individual, small groups, or a family. New members are not brought into the church and baptized until they are completely informed and instructed on Mormon doctrine and belief.

Jehovah's Witnesses put great faith and confidence in the literature with which they shower prospective members, and a convert does not become a full member and seek baptism until he has put in long hours of supervised Bible study and of "witnessing" in the community.

Seventh-day Adventists take their Bibles to church with them. Their special beliefs require interpretation and instruction. They discourage emotionalism and look upon their ministers more as teachers than preachers.

The essence of *Christian Science* is study and meditation as individuals and in communing groups. The leaders serve to catalyze the insights that Mary Baker Eddy brought together in *Science and Health with Keys to the Scriptures*. Self-instruction is the recommended avenue to truth.

Sects thrive on such cultural forces as discontent, deprivation, and the differential distribution of wealth, power, and prestige. Contemporary American society, however, is dynamic and there is no widespread climate of economic or cultural disappointment in this economy of abundance.

The economic and social ladder is now an escalator, and everyone has been upgraded in the sense that each person shares to some measure in the increased per capita income, leisure, and access to cultural resources. It is not surprising, then, that a spokesman for a conservative denomination lists wealth and education as the two greatest dangers to his denomination.[1] Wealth and education tend to erode and dissipate the "peculiarity" on which sectary religion thrives.[2]

The history of a sect usually includes some movement along the sect-church continuum in the direction of the denomination. It is difficult for the sect to remain completely insulated from secular society because its members, consciously and unconsciously, acquire some of the values of the society. This accommodation process usually includes changes in worship and emphases that make the sect more churchlike in structure and orientation.[3] During a discussion of religious trends with a Church of the Nazarene pastor it was stated that his church is an offshoot of the Methodist. The pastor disagreed, stating that the Church of the Nazarene had *not* left the Methodist Church—the Methodist Church had left the Nazarene. The present doctrine, practices, and values of the Church of the Nazarene are, he said, those of rural culture and of the Methodist Church of the nineteenth century.

The Church of God arose from similar sources. It was organized after the Civil War by church people in protest against the increasing formalization and professionalization of the traditional churches. The dissidents formed a new fellowship, The Church of God, to carry on the "old and the true" religion.[4]

Because of the variety of personality types within the population reservoir, there are some personality needs that apparently only the sect type of religious philosophy and experience can satisfy. Sects and cults are established, according to Marty,[5] to achieve a spatial and psychological context of isolation and provide a haven from social interpenetration and complexity.

In his study of cult and sect behavior, Catton found the typical cult-prone personality is institutionally alienated but religiously intense.[6]

Economic achievement does not always assure cultural achievement. Some people may still find themselves on the cultural periphery in spite

---

[1] Claude Kendrick, "The Pentecostal Movement: Hopes and Hazards," *Christian Century*, May 8, 1963, p. 608.

[2] Thomas R. Ford, "Status, Residence, and Fundamentalist Religious Beliefs in the Southern Appalachians," *Social Forces*, Vol. 39, No. 1 (October, 1960), pp. 41–49.

[3] Earl D. C. Brewer, "Sect and Church in Methodism," *Social Forces*, Vol. 30 (May, 1952), pp. 400–408.

[4] Val Clear, "The Church of God: A Study in Social Adaptation," *Review of Religious Research*, Vol. 2, No. 3 (Winter, 1961), pp. 129–33.

[5] Martin E. Marty, "Sects and Cults," *The Annals of the American Academy of Political and Social Science*, Vol. 332 (November, 1960), pp. 125–34.

[6] William R. Catton, Jr., "What Kind of People Does a Religious Cult Attract?" *American Sociological Review*, Vol. 22 (October, 1957), pp. 561–66.

of their economic success, and it is in a sectarian religious group that such people can find the acceptance and leadership often denied them in many of the more churchlike congregations and denominations.

Sects are more other-worldly oriented than the representative church. Because of this many people find that the things of "ultimate concern," which transcend worldly things and worldly relationships, are found best within a sect context. The permissive character of belief or doctrine that characterizes worship and practice in many Protestant churches does not satisfy the religious needs of many persons. Where the church is vague and relativistic the sect, definite and specific, offers firm answers and a direct message that is readily understood.

PART IV

Religious Change

TOOLS OF ANALYSIS

SOCIETIES, EVEN TRADITIONAL SOCIETIES, are never static; all undergo degrees of change. But the more technologically advanced the society is, the greater is its rate of change.

Social change is the sum total of change in the various systems and groups which compose society at any given time, and interaction is its key factor.[1] Social systems change through interactive relations with other social systems.

Religious systems and groups are also social systems, which may change or be modified as a result of interaction with other religious systems, with secular social systems, or with individuals within a religious system.

Within any society there is always a certain amount of struggle and competition for material goods and other rewards if there is not enough to satisfy everyone's needs and desires. At the same time there is also a certain amount of cooperation and collective effort, among individuals and social systems, to the end that the cooperating individuals may better meet their needs and desires.

Anthropologists classify primitive societies as *competitive* or *cooperative* according to the extent that one such set of social relations tends to dominate the particular society. In American society, however, both of these polar forces or processes are found throughout the social fabric.

---

[1] Kimball Young and Raymond W. Mack, *Systematic Sociology* (New York: American Book Company, 1962), p. 103.

Whether American society is essentially competitive or cooperative is an issue on which social scientists do not agree.

Social scientists speak of forces and dynamic relationships that seem to characterize and to operate within a society as the social processes of change. The various competitive processes have been identified as the *oppositional*,[2] *disjunctive*, or *disassociative* processes,[3] which tend toward the fragmentation and differentiation of groups and the disintegration of society. The processes that, on the other hand, lead to the integration of groups and social solidarity are identified as *cooperative* and *conjunctive* processes.[4]

Competition is the disjunctive process in which two or more individuals or social systems compete for a common goal, with primary emphasis upon the objective and "secondary" emphasis upon the other party or social system.

Conflict is a severe form of competition in which the opposing parties seek to overcome and eliminate each other. Violence and dislike, if not hate and fear, are often involved. Direct and open antagonism between individuals and social systems, it must be said, is normative as conflicting parties or groups seek to hurt, annihilate, remove, or render the other ineffectual in their effort to gain their respective objectives.

Contravention[5] is a milder and more polite form of conflict. Here each seeks to contravene the opposing party from realization of its goal—whether the first party wishes that goal for itself or not. The parties may denounce, delay, or otherwise attempt to thwart each other. The conflict may not be direct and there may be no head-on attack or confrontation, but relations will be marked by hostility and antagonism.

Accommodation is a sort of bridging force or process between disjunctive forces and relationships, that lead to separation and differentiation, and conjunctive forces and relationships that lead to the integration of social systems and the solidarity of society. Accommodation is both a condition, or state of being, and a process. When it is a condition persons and groups formerly in conflict rest in a state of equilibrium. When it is a process working relationships are developed between individuals and social systems in conflict so as to suspend conflict and make relationships more tolerable and less wasteful of energy. Accommodation has many forms, such as compromise, toleration, secularization, which are of special significance for religious interaction and religious change. Accommodation is sometimes defined as "antagonistic cooperation."

If individuals and social relations remained at the accommodation level of interaction, there would be no *acculturation* of individuals or fusion of

[2] *Ibid.*, p. 111–13.

[3] Joseph H. Fichter, *Sociology* (Chicago: University of Chicago Press, 1957), p. 226.

[4] *Ibid.*, p. 226.

[5] *Ibid.*, p. 231.

cultures or subcultures. Individuals and social systems interacting at the accommodation stage of social relations usually, but not necessarily, proceed to the *cooperation* stage of social relations. As antagonistic cooperation diminishes, individuals and social systems find themselves interacting in terms of cooperation, which is simply the working together of individuals and social systems for the realization of common goals.

The final step in the cycle of social change is the conjunctive and integrating process of *assimilation*. Assimilation, like accommodation, is both a process and a state. As a process it can be defined as two or more personalities or social systems interacting intimately and continuously in such a manner that they become alike. Assimilation as a state is the final fusion of social systems, or of personalities as members of social systems, in which differences have disappeared.

The assimilation process may function at three levels: person-to-person, person-to-group, and group-to-group.[6] The group-to-group and person-to-group levels are of special significance for religious change, especially as the latter level of interaction includes the *conversion* process. Conversion is the type of assimilation in which an individual abandons the attitudes and values of one religious system for those of another.

---

[6] Young and Mack, *op. cit.*, p. 114.

Chapter XI

Disjunctive Processes and Relationships

COMPETITION, CONTRAVENTION, CONFLICT

AMERICAN SOCIETY, as we have noted, is dynamic, and in a dynamic society groups and individuals are continuously interacting, becoming more solidaristic, or breaking up and recombining in different cultural configurations. This differentiation, fragmentation, and recombining of groups in new cultural configurations is also characteristic of religious groups and the religious subculture.

Americans are not convinced that competition is necessarily disintegrative in their society. Traditionally considered good for business and the basis of sports, competition was also made the basis of government policy. A substantial body of opinion likewise holds that what is good for business (and sport) must also be good for religion. Cultural competition therefore is consistent with the American spirit and the American tradition: groups may interact in such a way that they fragment, then recombine in unities of interaction that are more solidaristic and more productive of individual satisfactions and values than they were before.

COMPETITION

Contemporary religious groups are very much in competition with each other and yet very little in conflict. They compete "in the marketplace"

250

for souls, prestige, and in terms of numbers or size. Most Americans, for example, are more impressed by a large church than by a small one.

Interfaith Competition

Catholics and Protestants compete with each other in most communities for the support of the uncommitted. They are sensitive of each other's success in gaining and holding adherents. They also compete in the forum of community opinion, in the effectiveness of their worship and sacramental programs, in their respective programs of social ministries, and in their concepts of the ideal education.

In this last-mentioned area the Catholic parochial system is continually being measured and compared to the Protestant concept of appropriate education: the public school. Which has the higher academic standards and can boast the higher percentage of scholarship winners? Which enjoys the best discipline—and the best athletic teams? Which handles the problems of adolescents best? Which best prepares its students to meet the problems of the modern world, and whose graduates are the most successful in the business, scientific, and professional world? Which school most truly reflects American ideals and values?

The same sort of competition exists on a "higher" plane between the respective church-related colleges. The curriculum and social and intellectual climate of the Catholic college is definitely religiously oriented. In most Proestant-related colleges, on the other hand, "protestant" individualism displaces the religious atmosphere; denominational religion is soft-pedalled or played down. The individual is largely left to make his own religious decisions and commitments.

Competition has proved to be an asset in the United States. The Catholic Church, for example, is more active, more vital, and more effective in this milieu of cultural pluralism, where it must compete to gain its support, than in any country where it enjoys a privileged position.[7]

Intrafaith Competition

Protestant churches, generally gathered into theologically liberal and theologically conservative groups of churches, also compete with each other. There is movement of communicants from liberal to conservative churches, just as there is movement from conservative to liberal churches.

There is, however, considerably more competition for souls within the groups than there is between them—more movement, that is to say, from one liberal church to another liberal church, and from one conservative church to another, than from a liberal to a conservative church or from a conservative to a liberal church. In one small city the theologically conservative group included a Church of the Nazarene, an Assembly of God

---

[7] Evelyn Waugh, "American Epoch in the Catholic Church," *Life*, September 19, 1949, pp. 134–38.

church, a conservative Baptist church, and the Salvation Army.[8] The pastors all reported a noticeable movement of marginal members from one church to another within this group.

With the decline in doctrinal sensitivity, liberal Protestant churches in most communities find they are competing for members in terms of the attractiveness of their church programs rather than in terms of a particular confession of faith or denominational label. It may be youth activities, the family program, or some other phase of the social ministries that attracts an individual or a family. Or again it may be the preaching or counselling skill of a particular pastor that attracts an individual or a family.

When church-oriented families move into a new community there is considerable "shopping around" to locate the church and congregation that best meets the social and spiritual needs of the family members. Decisions often are made on the basis of human and social relationships rather than on the denominational label of the church and the pastor. The ever-increasing mobility of the population, moreover, is one of the most important factors in the homogenization of the liberal Protestant churches.

CONTRAVENTION

Although religious groups are not in open conflict as often as they were in the past, there are numerous occasions in which one religious faith or group will try to prevent another from achieving its goals or realizing an objective. And even though the opposition may be indirect, rather than frontal, substantial antagonism and hostility may be present.

Catholic Acts that Frustrate Protestants

Because of eagerness to maintain their values, Catholics sometimes act in a manner that prevents other religious groups from realizing their own values. The attempt to control the nature and quality of what Catholics read, for example, has brought the church into frequent conflict with non-Catholic groups.

The National Organization for Decent Literature is the church agency responsible for maintaining the Catholic ideal in this area. It was so effective, in fact, that the Civil Liberties Union attacked the Decent Literature unit and accused the national organization of using blacklists and boycotts to impose a "censorship of what the American people may read." The Civil Liberties Union defended the organization's right to express its views, but maintained that Catholic parish groups made a practice of calling on booksellers and requesting that books on the prohibited list not be offered for sale. Noncompliance would result in Catholic groups refusing to buy anything from the bookseller.[9]

---

[8] W. Seward Salisbury, *Organization and Practice of Religion in a Small City* (Oswego, N.Y.: The Ontario Press, 1951).

[9] *New York Times*, May 6, 1957.

The same sort of informal censorship often results when the Legion of Decency tries to control Catholic movie-going. The controversial movie, *Baby Doll*, occasioned Catholic and non-Catholic controversy throughout the country. The church hierarchy and its Legion of Decency condemned the movie as contrary to Catholic morality, and the strongest Catholic pressures were used to prevent its showing—and to discourage attendance at theatres which, despite Catholic opposition, insisted upon showing the film.

In Syracuse, New York, Catholic influence was great enough to prevent the daily papers from carrying the usual movie ads. Thirty Protestant ministers protested what they termed a "blackout" on advertising. They maintained that the people of Syracuse had the right to see the movie and to decide for themselves whether it was moral or immoral.

The paper to which the ministers protested argued in an answering editorial that the Catholic attempt to establish its concept of morality for the guidance of the Syracuse community through informal pressure was not nearly as arbitrary and undemocratic as the current Protestant attempt to impose its anti-bingo philosophy upon all the people of the state through enforceable legislation.[10]

The lines were closely drawn and vigorously maintained on both sides, underlining the basic philosophical and practical differences of the two faiths.

Catholic emphasis upon the "cult of Mary" is also considered by many Protestants as a major obstacle to better understanding and eventual union of Catholics and Protestants within a re-united Christendom. Shortly after his call for an ecumenical council, aimed at promoting reunion with "separated communities," Pope John XXIII issued a statement that reaffirmed the position of Mary in the Roman Catholic faith. "Adoration of Jesus the Savior is always at the center of any form of devotion for His Blessed Mother," the Pope said. "It is through Mary that one goes to Jesus."

Marianism, or devotion to the Madonna, is offensive to Protestants because they feel that Catholics tend to make her the "fourth person" of the Holy Trinity. Protestants generally resist what they call the "coredemptrix" concept, and favor the "minimal" as opposed to the Catholic "maximal" role for the Mother of Christ.[11] The statement of Pope John was interpreted as an assurance to Roman Catholic zealots who feared the drive for Christian unity might weaken dogma.[12] But while the Pope's statement might allay such fears, it also stressed the doctrinal chasm that separates Catholics and Protestants and indicated the concessions that Protestants would be called upon to make if they sought union on Catholic terms.

---

[10] *Herald-American* (Syracuse, N.Y.), January 13, 1957.

[11] *New York Times*, October 30, 1963.

[12] *New York Times*, February 16, 1959.

Birth Control

Birth control is another divisive, emotionally laden question that separates Catholics on the one hand and Protestants and Jews on the other. From time to time this controversy has passed beyond the debating stage of competition (groups freely competing for community opinion in support of their values and point of view) through contravention (groups mutually opposing and thwarting each other's attempts to achieve its goals) to the conflict level of social interaction. Most religious group differences over birth control are, we believe, at the contravention level of interaction. Each group, by seeking the cooperation or support of the state for its position, threatens to impose its morality upon the community.

Catholics on the one hand, and Protestants, Jews, and secular humanists on the other, hold diametrically opposing views on the morality of birth control. Protestantism's current position approving or favoring birth control is an almost complete reversal of the position held by most Protestants a century ago. The Comstock Law of 1873, which prohibited interstate transportation of birth control information and materials, had the support of organized Protestantism. But with the approach of the twentieth century individual Protestants became sympathetic to both the philosophy and the practice of birth control. By the 1930's the position of the major denominations, as reflected in the statements of the Federal Council of Churches, had changed from outright opposition to a position of "benevolent neutrality."[13]

Since World War II birth control has been accepted by most Protestants and has become the forthright policy of the major denominations. When mothers, according to Methodist G. Bromley Oxnam, are instructed and advised to use sound scientific information so as to control parenthood and bring healthy, happy children into the family, they are using scientific means for moral ends; and when communities fail to provide proper marriage counseling, sex education, and child-spacing service they are derelict in meeting their responsibility.[14]

Bishop James A. Pike of the Protestant Episcopal Diocese of California, advises parents that they have a moral and religious obligation to practice contraceptive birth control rather than bear an unwanted child. To do less, he maintains, is to fail to "exercise the stewardship of the lives which God has committed to our charge."[15]

Protestantism at the very least stands for a policy that lets each couple decide for itself, without state or religious interference, whether and how they should practice contraception. Protestants oppose any legislation or rules against the dissemination of birth control information or birth control materials. Jews hold the same essential position as Protestants.

The stand of the Catholic Church is that contraceptive birth control

---

[13] Leo Peffer, *Creeds in Competition* (New York: Harper & Bros., 1958), p. 114.
[14] *Ibid.*, p. 115.
[15] James A. Pike, "Case for Birth Control," *Newsweek*, January 31, 1955, pp. 60–61.

is morally, and unequivocably, wrong. Sex relations that artificially prevent conception, in the Catholic view, run counter to God's purpose and violate natural law.[16] The purpose of marriage and sex first and foremost is the propagation of the species. Since contraceptive birth control is intrinsically immoral, Catholics have as much right to oppose permissive legislation as Protestants have to oppose bingo and legislation against immoral publications: so the man-on-the-street might reasonably argue.

With two such contrasting standards of morality on a specific issue, clashes and differences are bound to occur. Some clashes involved only one individual, as was the case in Albany, New York, where a Catholic hospital barred an orthopedic surgeon from treating patients because of his connection with the Planned Parenthood Association. The surgeon protested that his practice was limited to "bones and joints" and that he had nothing to do with birth control although, as an Episcopalian, he maintained the philosophy of planned parenthood as an integral part of his "basic religious beliefs."[17]

One of the most outstanding confrontations over birth control, and one in which the political power became deeply involved, took place in New York City during the summer of 1958.

The New York City Birth Control Controversy. In 1958 there was an unwritten but effective ban on contraceptive counseling in city hospitals. There was also a wide difference of opinion among professional personnel, patients, and the general public over the rightness and soundness of this policy. The issue finally was forced by the determination of a group of New York physicians to practice in public hospitals the same kind of medicine that was practiced in private hospitals and taught in the city's five medical colleges.

Dr. Louis M. Hellman officially notified the Commissioner of Hospitals, Dr. Morris Jacobs, that he was going to fit a patient with a contraceptive device at Kings County Hospital in Brooklyn. The patient was a Protestant and a diabetic, and had recently borne her third child, the second by Caesarian section. It was Dr. Hellman's diagnosis that further pregnancies would endanger the woman's life and that appropriate treatment should include contraceptive practices, a decision that was entirely acceptable to the patient and involved no violation of religious values and principles.

The patient was medically indigent. The only hospital at which she could be treated was a public hospital, and therefore the therapy she received must be within the public policy. Then, on July 16, 1958, Commissioner Jacobs made the ban official.[18]

Dr. Hellman's proposed action and Commissioner Jacob's reaction brought the long smoldering controversy into the open and caught the

---

[16] Pius XI, *Christian Marriage (Casti Connubi)*, (New York: The American Press, 1943), p. 17. Also see Chapter XV.

[17] *New York Times*, December 20, 1959.

[18] *Ibid.*, August 24, 1958.

attention of the public. Highly publicized, the controversy raged for more than three months in New York—and throughout the country.

On one side stood the Catholic Church, condemning artificial birth control as immoral for the whole community. On the opposing side stood the majority of non-Catholics—Protestants, Jews, and those with no religious affiliation—who approved of birth control (with various qualifications) and were united in protesting a policy that banned it in public hospitals. The controversy brought forth typical expressions of Catholic morality on the one hand, and of Protestant, Jewish, and secular morality on the other.

Statements were issued by the chancery office of the New York Catholic archdiocese and by the Guilds of Catholic Physicians in all of the five boroughs:

> . . . The natural law commands that the married state, as ordained by God, fulfill the function of the conservation of the human race.
>
> Artificial birth control frustrates that purpose. It is, therefore, unnatural, since it is contrary to the nature and dignity of man in the exercise of his faculties, and subverts the sacredness of marriage.
>
> However well-intentioned proponents of such practices may be, they are contributing to the harmful errors that relations in marriage are exclusively for mutual satisfaction, and that the moral law sanctions the exercise of the art itself, even though marriage's primary end be destroyed. No human authority, no medical, eugenic, or social need can give a justification to such errors. It would be extremely unfortunate if our hospitals and medical facilities, aimed for the preservation of life, should be perverted to seek for the prevention of life.
>
> Catholics cannot accept such a procedure, in or out of our hospitals, nor condone or cooperate in assisting others to this unnatural and immoral practice.[19]

The New York chapter of the Knights of Columbus, in a letter to Dr. Jacobs which it released to the press, declared "unalterable opposition" to birth control therapy in city clinics or hospitals and congratulated the commissioner on his "prompt and forthright response to a pretext which gives rights to an ignorant and indecent practice."[20]

The Protestant Council of New York City entered the controversy by asking Commissioner Jacobs to call a meeting of the hospital board to hear the Protestant view on planned parenthood. The council issued the following statement:

> There is no moral reason why a Protestant patient should be denied accepted birth control therapy by the City Commissioner of Hospitals.
>
> Parenthood is one of the major purposes of marriage. With this privilege, however, come tremendous responsibilities, particularly in the kind of world in which we live. The welfare and happiness of parents and each child are extremely important. Prayer, study, and judgment must be used in planning the number and spacing of children. It is the duty of responsible parents to

---

19 *Ibid.*, July 24, 1958.
20 *Ibid.*, August 3, 1958.

use all truth from God revealed through the church, minister, doctor, researcher, marriage counselor, and the Holy Spirit speaking directly to their conscience in planning and producing their family in order to fulfill God's highest expectations of them as parents.[21]

The president of the Freethinkers of America demanded that Commissioner Jacobs be removed from office.[22]

The New York City Board of Rabbis, consisting of more than 700 Orthodox, Conservative, and Reform rabbis, urged Mayor Wagner to rescind the Department of Hospital's policy that refused to permit birth control therapy in city hospitals:

> We as rabbis respect and defend the fundamental right of all religious groups, large or small, to formulate their particular views for their respective adherents. However, we strongly deplore and protest against the notion that patients in tax-supported hospitals who do not wish to adhere to the views of religious groups, to whom the Department of Hospitals seems to be deferring, should nevertheless be compelled by the department to do so even if, as a result, their very lives may be endangered. This most certainly is a violation of the cherished American concept of freedom of religions.
>
> Furthermore, this order contravenes another time-honored American principle—separation of church and state. Under our constitutional principles of religious liberty, government agencies may not directly or indirectly impose upon others the religious beliefs or practices of any one faith nor, as in this case, may they influence the policies of tax-supported hospitals as if they were sectarian institutions.[23]

When Mayor Wagner was asked if he would endorse a move by the Board of Hospitals to approve birth control therapy for municipal patients, he replied: "I am a practicing Catholic. As a Catholic I would be opposed to the use of contraceptives in city hospitals, but this is a question for the Board of Hospitals, and the Commissioner. This is a medical matter. I leave it to their judgment."[24]

At their next meeting, September 17, 1958, the Board of Hospitals took the ban imposed by Commissioner Jacobs under consideration. The board was composed of five prominent physicians and five eminent laymen; two were Catholics, one was an officer of the Planned Parenthood Association, and the others were known to be strongly for birth control. With Commissioner Jacobs abstaining, the board voted 8–2 to lift the ban on birth control therapy. Its resolution directed city hospitals to provide "medical advice, preventive measures and devices for female patients under their care whose life and health in the opinion of the medical staff may be jeopardized by pregnancy and who wish to avail themselves of such health services."

Without naming Roman Catholics, who oppose all artificial birth control as immoral, the board's resolution stated: "Physicians, nurses and

---

21 *Ibid.*, July 31, 1958.
22 *Ibid.*, August 3, 1958.
23 *Ibid.*, August 5, 1958.
24 *Ibid.*, August 6, 1958.

other hospital personnel who have religious or moral objections should be excused from participation in contraceptive procedures."

The resolution also said: "When there are clearly defined medical conditions in which the life or health of a woman may be jeopardized by pregnancy, it is generally recognized by the medical profession that contraceptive measures are proper medical practice."[25] The religious, medical, and civic groups who had opposed the ban hailed the reversal, but Catholic authorities were disheartened by a decision that "introduces an immoral practice in our hospitals that perverts the nature and dignity of man."

During the height of the controversy the influential Catholic lay journal, *Commonweal*, came out for moral suasion rather than law as the most appropriate means of upholding Catholic teachings about birth control:

> In seeking legislation and directives to uphold their moral tenets, Roman Catholics not only strain the limits of the community and actually lessen the persuasive force of their teachings, but they almost inevitably strengthen in the minds of non-Catholics the already present worries about Catholic power.
>
> When Catholics seem to rely more upon the power of the law rather than upon moral force and influence, they present an image of the church which does less justice to the glorious reality which it is.
>
> If Catholics were to rely on education, personal moral suasion and indoctrination in the present controversy rather than on a civil directive that embitters and alienates many people the Catholic Church would surely gain in the long run.[26]

This stand of *Commonweal* is evidence that the Catholic Church is not the monolithic institution that many non-Catholics believe it to be, and that it is possible to hold different views on how best to realize Catholic morality without being any less a good Catholic. Furthermore, these views may even be different from the views held by the hierarchy, as was true above. The Catholic Church is an organization of dynamic forces that permits wide variation and flexibility in arriving at the universally valid and binding end-goals of "faith and morals."

Protestant Acts that Frustrate Catholics

The public school has been and in some respects still is the stronghold of Protestant culture—in concepts of education, philosophy of child development, morality alike. It is only in recent years and in those parts of the nation where Catholics are a potent community and political force that the public schools have been de-Protestantized, or divested of their Protestant-oriented activities and philosophies.

Considerable attention was given to religion in the traditional public school. There was frequent reading from the Protestant, King James version of the Bible, and singing of hymns and reciting of prayers. Although such practices have largely been eliminated because of Catholic protests,

---

[25] *Ibid.*, September 8, 1958.
[26] *Commonweal*, September 12, 1958.

public schools still include other practices that are objectionable to Catholics—the way in which sex education is handled, for example.

Sex education in the public schools is usually by age and sex groups, and not by the religious faith or personal and social development and needs of the individual pupil. Education is best achieved on an individual basis, according to Catholic belief, which, moreover, maintains that sex education is the exclusive and sacred responsibility of the family, assisted by a spiritual adviser.

The many controversies and conflicts over sex education in the public school usually narrow down to disputes between Catholic parents and the school authorities. The dispute is frequently aired in the P.T.A., and Protestants invariably line up with the school's program and philosophy.

The growth of the Catholic parochial school system and the increasing burden these schools have put upon the parishes and communicants has led to Catholic pressure for public money to help defray the costs. The nature and extent to which various kinds of support might be considered as violations of the principle of separation of church and state is debatable and always controversial.

New York state amended its constitution to permit public support for transportation to parochial schools, and the necessary implementing legislation was also passed, but neither Catholics or non-Catholics have been entirely satisfied. Catholics do not regard this step as sufficient compensation for the tremendous sums the parochial schools save the taxpayer in educating children who would otherwise be the responsibility of the public schools. On the other hand, many non-Catholics are convinced that bus transportation for parochial schools is a violation of the principle of the separation of church and state, and from time to time the practice has been challenged. For example, a citizen's committee in Newtown, Connecticut, brought suit against such a state law by challenging its local option provision. Newtown had voted 1243–1218 to provide bus transportation to a school conducted by St. Rose's Roman Catholic Church.[27] The courts generally uphold laws of this type that seek to implement constitutional provisions.

Religious discrimination, or the feeling of discrimination, in business, education, and the professions is a source of hostility and mistrust on the part of the group that feels discriminated against. Since World War II a number of states have adopted legislation and established commissions to prevent discrimination because of religion, race, or color.

Overt acts of religious discrimination are not as numerous as they once were, but that discrimination still exists is shown by the cases brought before the New York State Commission Against Discrimination (SCAD) for investigation and action. Religious discrimination usually takes the form of a minority group suffering at the hands of the dominant group, but a case brought before SCAD of alleged discrimination against Catholics

---

[27] *New York Times*, October 31, 1959.

on the faculty of Queens College, a public college serving a city in which Catholics are a major religious group, is particularly interesting.

SCAD reported, after a two-year investigation into the charges, that it had found bias against Catholic faculty members. The president of the college denied, however, that it discriminated against teachers on the basis of religion, stating that the college makes no inquiries and has no records of any kind as to the religious affiliations of its staff. He maintained that SCAD had used misleading and even false statistics, acquired from anonymous sources, which it had not sought to correct or verify with college authorities.[28]

The SCAD report cited certain "manifestations" as evidence of resistance to the progress of Catholics at the college. Of a staff of 425, only 23 were Catholics; in many departments no attempt was made to solicit applications from Catholic colleges; professors in a position to recruit teachers held the opinion that Queens had cultivated a secular atmosphere in which a religiously oriented teacher would not feel at home.[29] Although the Appellate Division of the Supreme Court, which later reviewed the case, found no evidence or proof in substantiation of the charges, Catholics showed by their attitudes and actions that they nevertheless felt they were being discriminated against.[30] The situation served to intensify the solidarity of Catholics in their relations to other religious groups, and although no other religious groups were named in the investigations, it appeared that Catholics believed they were being opposed by sources of power reflecting a Protestant and a Jewish point of view.

The Bingo Controversy. The bingo controversy is an illustration of how Protestant churches, on their part, have sought the cooperation of the state in trying to impose their brand of morality upon the community.

Antigambling legislation and the many state constitutional provisions adopted in the last part of the nineteenth and the first part of the twentieth centuries had the support of the three major faiths. Catholics united with Protestants and Jews to support the passage of the federal antigambling law of 1894, and as late as 1941 Cardinal O'Connell of Boston, Protestant churches, and Jewish clergymen again cooperated to oppose Massachusetts' adoption of a state lottery as a revenue measure.

Although Protestants and Catholics joined to oppose some forms of gambling, they have basically different concepts of the morality of gambling. The official Protestant view is still the Puritan view: that all gambling whether little or great, is wrong and sinful. The Catholic view is more liberal and tolerant: although a lottery is defined as gambling, it is morally objectionable only when carried to excess; gambling is immoral when it distracts people from earning a livelihood by honest work.[31]

---

28 *Ibid.*, October 7, 1960.
29 *Ibid.*, October 5, 1960.
30 *Ibid.*, May 30, 1962.
31 *Catholic Encyclopedia*, Vol. VI (New York: The Encyclopedia Press), p. 376.

Many states have written antigambling provisions into their constitutions. In the twenties New York state had a strict and comprehensive constitutional provision but, by judicial interpretation, betting through licensed bookies at official race tracks was permitted. During the thirties the need for additional revenue and the growing indifference of the public led to a modification of the constitutional antigambling provision that permitted pari-mutuel betting at approved tracks. It was argued that people were going to gamble anyway, so why not let the state control and supervise it and use the proceeds to help support the growing welfare services it was being called upon to provide. These arguments apparently made sense to the electorate for the constitutional provision and implementing legislation were passed without difficulty. A number of tracks were authorized and constructed within a few years, pari-mutuel gambling steadily increased, and the tax revenues became a substantial source of state income.

In the thirties, with the movie industry's discovery of its great popular appeal, bingo became the most successful of the various measures the industry devised to attract the public back into the movie houses. Almost overnight, Catholic pastors throughout the nation adopted bingo as a convenient and relatively painless means of helping raise the money demanded by the rapidly growing parochial school system. The experiment proved uniformly successful. Catholics, and many non-Catholics, flocked to the "bingo nights" that were held once or sometimes twice a week in the parish hall. Not every Catholic pastor welcomed this development; some opposed it and others accepted it with reservations, but in general the church accepted bingo as a moral and proper way to raise money for worthy purposes.[32]

In New York state the question soon arose whether bingo was or was not a violation of the constitution. Judicial opinion was divided; it depended, apparently, upon the special or local circumstances under which the game was played, but Protestant church groups took the stand that bingo was always illegal and any institution that used it as a source of revenue was violating the law. The Catholic parishes that were sponsoring the game insisted that they were not violating the law. The controversy became so heated and acrimonious and aroused so much feeling in some communities that many Catholic pastors temporarily gave the game up—although still insisting that bingo as played in their parishes was not illegal.

The dispute was then carried to the legislature and the people. Those who favored bingo sought a constitutional amendment and implementing legislation that would legalize bingo and similar games of chance when all proceeds went to religious or charitable organizations. Protestant groups were likewise active—trying to influence voters and the legislature to reject the constitutional referendum and the implementing legislation. In doing

---

[32] L. Peffer, *op. cit.*, p. 101.

so they used almost the same arguments that Catholics would later use in seeking community support for their concept of birth control.

Both the Protestant Council of the City of New York and the State Council of Churches carried on intensive campaigns to defeat the proposal. They argued that legalization of bingo for the benefit of religious, charitable, and nonprofit organizations would be an entering wedge for professional gamblers; that business and professional men would be hurt because paychecks would be spent on bingo and bills would go unpaid; that those who promote games of chance have an unsatiable greed for money, would press for further liberalization of the law, and in the end circumvent all the restrictions of the state. Furthermore, in the light of the New Jersey experience, it was argued, bingo was not an efficient way to raise money anyway.[33]

The State Council of Churches was accused in the press of trying "through press agentry, pressure on legislators and other tested political means of seeking to exercise a form of control over the state." A spokesman for the Council replied that the "Protestant churches are not seeking to exert pressure on the legislators or exercise any control over the state, but they feel it to be their Christian duty to let legislators and all the people know their convictions on this matter. As Protestants we are under obligation to witness to our Christian convictions."[34]

The Protestant attempts failed; the constitutional referendum was passed and the legislature adopted the necessary enabling legislation. Anti-bingo opinion has been similarly unsuccessful throughout the nation. Most of the states and a great many communities now permit bingo.

Jewish groups kept out of the struggle and took no stand on either the desirability or the appropriateness of bingo or similar games of chance in churches or charitable organizations. Jewish authorities maintained, however, that gambling is contrary to the teachings of Judaism, and by 1959 all major national Jewish groups had officially gone on record against gambling in any form in the synagogue.[35]

Jewish Acts that Frustrate Christians

Jews are becoming increasingly articulate in their opposition to the use of public schools for the practice of Christian traditions. Christmas programs, and nativity scenes on school grounds, for example, have come under attack by Jewish groups.

A community-sponsored nativity scene, approved by the school board, was set up on an Ossining, New York, school ground and lighted immediately after the students left for the Christmas holidays. A group of Jewish citizens objected, and finally carried their protest to the state Supreme Court.

---

[33] *New York Times*, February 28, 1957.
[34] *Palladium Times*, Oswego, N.Y., February 9, 1957.
[35] *New York Times*, November 19, 1959.

The attorney for the group argued that such a display involved a use of public funds and public property, promoted a particular religion, and would have a "powerful psychological effect on the minds of children." "We believe," he said, "that the crib is quite proper providing it is shown where it belongs. There are numerous churches throughout the community where it could be properly displayed." The Supreme Court denied a request for an injunction and the mayor, appearing at the creche-lighting ceremony, described the complaints as "a lot of nonsense."[36]

Jewish groups also oppose baccalaureate graduation exercises in public schools, maintaining they are a violation of the principle of separation of church and state. The National Community Relations Advisory Council urged Jewish spiritual leaders not to participate in baccalaureate exercises in public schools and recommended that rabbis consider conducting special synagogue services to honor Jewish graduates. The Advisory Council is the coordinating agency for Jewish community councils and major Jewish groups devoted to safeguarding civil liberties and furthering intergroup relations.[37]

These attitudes of Jewish groups towards nativity scenes and baccalaureate exercises show the desire of Jews not only to maintain their identity as a religious group but also to emphasize, if not to exaggerate, how they differ from Christians and the Christian culture.

Contravention within Protestantism

The tendency for religious groups to disagree (and become disagreeable), or to denounce each other and manifest their hostilities can exist within as well as between faiths. Disagreement, antagonism, even conflict, can and does occur within Protestantism and between Protestants. Since the essence of Protestantism is individualism and dissent, this is not surprising; separatism, divisiveness, and fragmentation are normative within the Protestant tradition.

Protestants tend to separate and divide because of two major disassociative and disintegrative forces: differences in belief and differences in behavior. Protestants also tend to divide and to group around two major theological positions: liberal, and conservative or fundamentalist theology. Thirdly, Protestants tend to fall into two groups or philosophies of social action: traditionalist and progressive.

The differences between conservatism in theology and traditionalism in social action on the one hand, and liberalism and progressivism on the other, may be interdenominational in nature. Most of the larger Protestant denominations in fact carry a liberal or progressive label while most of the smaller Protestant denominations, the Church of the Nazarene, Assembly of God, and Wesleyan Methodist, lean towards the conservative and traditional poles of theology and social action. There are, however, im-

---

[36] *Palladium Times*, Oswego, N.Y., December 24, 1958.
[37] *New York Times*, June 23, 1961.

portant exceptions to this generalization. The Lutheran Church (Missouri Synod) and the Southern Baptist Convention are large denominations that are conservative and traditional in orientation. The Unitarian-Universalist Church is, as were its constituent parts, liberal and progressive.

The theological and social action differences can also be intradenominational in nature, with friction and hostility expressed and carried on under the same denominational roof. Every large liberal Protestant denomination includes a conservative wing because each denomination is much like a major political party that includes a wide range of attitudes and beliefs and represents a compromise of divergencies. Divergencies, friction, and hostility that may lie latent within a particular denomination often come to light and are aired and voiced at national meetings.

The friction and hostility that may exist within Protestantism, at certain times and over certain problems, may be more bitter and virulent than that between Protestants and Catholics, or Protestants and Jews. There are even areas of disagreement and dispute where a Protestant group may find itself closer to Catholics and the Catholic position than to some of its fellow Protestants.

Liberals Called Soft on Communism. Early in 1960 differences in Protestantism were highlighted by an allegation in an Air Force manual that Communists had infiltrated the National Council of Churches of Christ in America. The Protestant leaders against whom these charges were leveled alleged, in turn, that the manual (and conditions under which it was written and edited) was merely one step in a concerted effort of extreme economic and religious conservatives to force ministers and church councils to "stick to the gospel" and refrain from speaking out on social issues.[38]

The NCCCA takes the liberal position on social issues. It insists it is not only the right but the duty of the churches and their members to study and to comment upon issues, whether political, economic, or social, that affect human relations. But in doing so, liberal ministers act in violent disagreement with fundamentalist ministers who believe the churches should only "preach the Bible and teach Sunday School."

The two chief spokesmen for liberal Protestantism, Dr. Edwin Dahlberg, president of the NCCCA, and Dr. Eugene Carson Blake, former president of the NCCCA, defended the Association against the charges that it was infiltrated by Communists. The men, both clergymen, said the Air Force manual charges were "slanderous, biased, and venomous."[39] As a result of this protest the Defense Department withdrew the manual.

As a result of this experience, no doubt, Dr. Dahlberg stated that any prominent clergyman who takes a stand on race, disarmament, halting nuclear bomb tests, or even on strengthening the United Nations, runs the risk of being called soft on communism. Other liberals, too, complain that

---

[38] *Ibid.*, March 28, 1960.
[39] *Ibid.*, February 26, 1960.

conservatives always lump social welfare measures with communism, accusing them of an intellectual refusal to perceive or acknowledge essential differences. At any rate Drs. Dahlberg and Blake counterattacked and listed the following fundamentalists as the chief sources of attacks on the liberal clergy:

Major Edgar C. Bundy of the Air Force Reserve, chairman of the Church League of America, Wheaton, Illinois, a lecturer and pamphleteer, who led the group in the Illinois department of the American Legion that condemned the Girl Scout Handbook as un-American.

Myers G. Lowman of Cincinnati, executive secretary of Circuit Riders, Inc., organized in 1951 by thirty-three Methodist laymen to oppose Socialism and Communism in the Methodist Church.

The Reverend Carl McIntire of Collingswood, New Jersey, founder of the American Council of Churches (a small schismatic group) and editor of *The Christian Beacon,* which had often attacked the NCCCA.

Verne B. Kaub of Madison, Wisconsin, organizer of the American Council of Christian Laymen, and a pamphleteer who supported Mr. McIntire.

The Reverend Billy James Hargis of Tulsa, Oklahoma, president of The Christian Crusade, lecturer, and radio speaker. His pamphlet, *The National Council of Churches Indicts Itself on 50 Counts of Treason to God and Country,* was cited as source material in the Air Force training manual.[40]

(According to Dr. Blake support for slanderous accusations against liberal churchmen "normally comes from people who combine conservative theology with conservative economics and politics, specifically including wealthy men of the far right.")

The withdrawal of the Air Force manual incensed the fundamentalists. At large rallies throughout the "Bible Belt" the fundamentalist spokesmen insisted the charges were true. Major Bundy of the Air Force Reserve castigated Drs. Dahlberg and Blake for questioning his qualifications as a military and religious authority.

This case study in a social action controversy may serve as a convincing illustration of the wide gap that separates liberal from some conservative Protestants.

The Catholic President Controversy. A sharp division developed among Protestants during the 1960 election campaign over the desirability of a Catholic president, many conservative Protestants being sure that he would be subject to the dictates of the Pope, and liberal Protestants insisting that a close study of the inner dynamics of the contemporary Catholic Church showed no Pope could or would exert pressure that might deter a Catholic president from performing his constitutional duties in a proper manner. Two prominent liberal theologians, Drs. Reinhold Niebuhr and John C. Bennett of the faculty of Union Theological Seminary, took issue with the Citizens Group for Religious Freedom, a group of conservative Protestants that included Dr. Daniel Poling, editor of *The Christian Herald,* and Dr. Norman Vincent Peale, pastor of New York's Marble Collegiate Church,

---

[40] *Ibid.,* March 28, 1960.

which expressed fears that a Catholic president would be obligated to the Vatican.

In an earlier statement Drs. Niebuhr and Bennett had labelled some of the Protestant clergy, who were violently opposing a Catholic president, as "bigots" and members of a "Protestant underworld." Then another conservative (and generally anti-Catholic) group, Protestants and Other Americans United for Separation of Church and State, entered the controversy by deploring the "hostility and abuse" directed against Dr. Peale for stating his views on the religious issue in the presidential campaign.

Dr. Poling joined the debate by saying he supported the Washington statement of the Citizens Group for Religious Freedom as a document issued "by patriotic and worthy men with whom I am honored to be associated." Dr. Poling went on to elaborate his stand, explaining "I find myself here and now in some vital particulars of Christian faith, and in my opposition to the recognition of Red China and the admission of the Peiping Government to the United Nations, much closer to my fellow Christians of the Roman Catholic Church than I am to Drs. Niebuhr and Bennett and those others who in theology and radical social action agree with them. This I would make abundantly clear."[41]

Intradenominational Dissent and Friction. The membership of the largest Protestant denominations seldom approaches unanimity of belief or of agreement on questions of social action, a wide range of meaning being attached to the formal confession of faith to which each member has at one time subscribed. In questions of social action the membership therefore ranges from those who strongly support a particular issue to those who are definitely opposed, with a substantial number who are neutral or just don't care. The official policy of the denomination on a given issue or problem may have the support of only a bare majority or a plurality. Solidarity is a question of degree and often more apparent than real.

Disagreement and dissent, indigenous to Protestantism, often lie dormant, but from time to time an issue arises that will bring them to the surface, sometimes in angry and bitter expressions that can shake the foundations of a denomination and result in fragmentation and separatism. More often, however, differences are reduced, if not reconciled, and the denomination will continue in a working compromise of tacit divergencies.

A common pattern of dissent within Protestant denominations in recent years has been the protest of conservative member groups against some of the activities and policies of the National Council of Churches of Christ in America.

Within the Episcopal Church. A layman wrote to all the vestrymen of St. John's Episcopal Church asking them to withhold contributions from the local, state and national councils so long as these councils spoke out on social issues: "They don't speak for me. They support without exception all socialist laws. The primary purpose of the local, state, and

---

[41] *Ibid.*, September 17, 1960.

national councils is not to promote the love of Jesus Christ but more government control . . . I want to persuade the pastors to leave us poor dumb laymen to take care of politics and to concentrate on the spiritual guidance that will help us to do this."[42]

Southern Presbyterian Church. A vocal minority in the Presbyterian Church of the United States, placed before its annual general assembly a series of resolutions demanding that the southern denomination withdraw from the National Council of Churches of Christ in America. Advocates of the withdrawal directed their ire at the report of a study conference, held under National Council auspices, that urged United States recognition of Communist China and its admission to the United Nations. The National Council affirmed the right of the conference to speak for itself, but took no other action on the report.

Efforts to withdraw from the National Council have been defeated by Southern Presbyterians a number of times in recent years, but the Communist China issue this time gave the conservatives a major talking point although they were again unsuccessful. Affiliation with the National Council continued, with seven presbyteries supporting the activities and policies of the National Council and three voting for withdrawal.[43]

Friction within the Southern Presbyterian Church is not limited to social action; it extends to questions of belief as well. Fundamentalists of the Southern Presbyterian Church, who believe that Adam and Eve existed, tried to suspend the publication of an official Bible commentary that stated they were a myth. By a vote of 323–74 the general assembly supported the modernist and rejected the literalist interpretation of the story in Genesis.[44]

American Baptist Convention. The American Baptist Convention is another denomination whose conservative wing put on a vigorous drive to have the denomination withdraw from the National Council of Churches of Christ in America. Several Conservative Baptist congregations in the Midwest, led by the First Baptist Church of Wichita, Kansas (the largest in the denomination), spearheaded the drive. The board of deacons of the Wichita church voted to cut off all contributions to the denomination in protest against its council membership, an action which would constitute, according to the deacons, a "major step in getting back to basic evangelism and winning souls for Christ instead of trying to legislate for them."[45]

The conservatives at the annual meeting of the American Baptist Conference said they opposed the National Council on four points:

1. Many leaders of the National Council were identified with Communist-front organizations.
2. The resolutions of the National Council were too far to the left for most

42 *Ibid.,* March 28, 1960.
43 *Ibid.,* April 24, 1959.
44 *Ibid.,* May 15, 1962.
45 *Ibid.,* June 3, 1960.

Americans and certainly did not represent the opinion of many conservative Baptists.

3. The National Council goes all out for the one-world, one-court, one-church idea. In economics the National Council takes the extreme liberal and socialistic view towards sharing the wealth, socialized medicine, and government control.

4. The National Council had been brainwashing the younger generation into finding a common ground with all other Protestants for their beliefs instead of standing on the fundamental teachings found in the Gospel of Christ.[46]

The conservatives failed to secure enough delegate support at the annual meeting to bring about withdrawal.

The United Presbyterian Church. The United Presbyterian Church also has provided several good illustrations of dissent and controversy over doctrine within a major denomination. Broadway Presbyterian Church, New York, has long been conservative in theology and its ministers fundamentalists who adhere strictly to the Westminster Confession. By contrast, the Presbytery of New York, of which Broadway Presbyterian is a member, tends towards liberalism and has long frowned upon Broadway Presbyterian's fundamentalism—particularly since this church serves the city's intellectual centers: Columbia University and Union Theological Seminary.

After considerable deliberation the presbytery removed Broadway Presbyterian's minister, the Reverend Dr. Merriam, and the "pro-Merriam" board of elders. The presbytery charged Dr. Merriam with intolerance of contemporary theology, unsuitable evangelical approach to the needs of Columbia students, and inappropriate behavior in the conduct of church affairs. This exercise of presbyterial power led to a lengthy controversy that received great publicity both within and without the church.[47]

The wide gap between conservative and liberal theological positions within the church was further highlighted in controversies over the doctrine of the Virgin Birth. A prominent Presbyterian clergyman, the Reverend Dr. Theodore A. Gill, expressed doubts about the doctrine—further asserting that it was not an important doctrine in early Christian teaching and is peripheral even today. Conservative elements maintained that this questioning of the virgin birth made Dr. Gill unfit to head the San Francisco Theological Seminary, to which he had just been appointed, and although they made this a major issue at the next general assembly of the United Presbyterian Church, they were unable to secure enough votes to secure a vote of censure.[48]

These controversies bring into sharp focus the wide variations of theological outlook that can be found among the clergy and laymen of a large denomination.

Dissent Within the Southern Baptist Convention. The foregoing cases

---

[46] *Ibid.*, June 3, 1960.
[47] *Time*, May 18, 1962.
[48] *New York Times*, May 24, 1960.

illustrate the extent to which liberal denominations can be annoyed and frustrated by an active and determined conservative minority. But the process can work in reverse as well: a conservative denomination may be equally disturbed and frustrated by the deeds and thoughts of a liberal minority. The Southern Baptist Convention is a conservative denomination that is undergoing just such an experience.

The Southern Baptist Convention persists in holding to its traditionally conservative position and resists all attempts to liberalize its theology or its philosophy of social action. At the 1960 annual meeting of the Convention, the president declared in a public statement that he had heard of heretical teachings at one of the six seminaries the denomination maintains. "The academic freedom of professors in the seminaries ends at a certain point," he said, ". . . the point at which teaching extends beyond the traditional Southern Baptist beliefs about the New Testament."[49]

The president's statement was a reflection of the fears of many laymen and preachers that "modern," non-literal interpretations of the Bible were creeping into the denomination through teachings in one or more of the seminaries. At the same time some supporters of the seminaries feared that the professors' freedom to teach was being compromised.

The result of all this was a resolution that condemned "public statements concerning the inferiority of faculty members as inappropriate and inadvisable"[50]—proof that conservative and liberal factions are increasingly conscious of their identity and aware of the differences that distinguish them from each other.

CONFLICT

In religious interaction the most incisive illustrations of *conflict* as a process occur in the struggle between competing religious systems to secure the custody of an individual, usually a minor, and it is then that we witness the most direct, antagonistic, and punitive relations within the religious culture. Cases in point are adoptions and mixed marriages, which frequently progress to the conflict stage of relationships.

When conflict arises religious lines are clearly drawn and vigorously maintained. And if the power of the state is invoked to carry out a religious objective, all possible political pressures, powers, and countervailing powers are brought to bear by the affected religious parties.

Conflict over Adoption

When adoption involves the religious issue, the protagonists invariably are the Catholic Church on one side and an alliance of Protestantism, Judaism, and secular humanism on the other. "Lesser" interested parties

---
49 *Ibid.*, May 20, 1960.
50 *Ibid.*, May 20, 1960.

in the great majority of adoption cases are the child, the natural parents, the adopting parents, and the community.

The health, welfare, and security of a child is at stake. He needs a happy, secure home, and loving parents, but the fact is that most children up for adoption are born out of wedlock. A good adoption law will protect the rights of the natural parents—particularly the mother from hastily or precipitately signing away her child in the emotional stress that surrounds such a birth. If given time to work their problems out, the natural parents are sometimes able to legalize their relationship, live a normal family life together, and provide the care and affection that parents owe their children.

The rights of adopting parents must also be protected. When in good faith they take upon themselves all the economic, psychological, and legal responsibilities of parenthood, as well as invest a great deal of themselves in their adopted child, they should be protected from having the child arbitrarily and abruptly taken from them.

Religion becomes an issue when the natural and the adopting parents are of different religions. In light of the Catholic Church's dogmatic concepts and contention that it is the "True Church," its stand on adoption is consistent and understandable. The Catholic Church maintains that religion is a matter of *status*, not of *election*—"once a Catholic always a Catholic." Because baptism is irrevocable there can be no voluntary withdrawal from the church, and not even the explicit wish of a mother that her child be adopted by a non-Catholic couple need be honored. The church then, on these grounds, has a valid interest in the faith of its members and may properly ask that the state use its power to facilitate this interest.[51]

Judaism, like Catholicism, also maintains that religion is a matter of status rather than election, inherited through the mother, and recognizes no withdrawal from the faith.[52] But unlike Catholicism, Judaism does not seek legislation to protect its religious interests. The very position the Catholic Church takes towards adoption, in fact is inadmissible for Jews, Protestants, and secular humanists alike.

The entire process being subject to the powers of the respective states, "religious protection" laws have been passed that make religious identity the determining factor in adoption cases. The Catholic Church has vigorously supported these laws against interreligious adoptions, hoping thereby to prevent a baby baptized as a Catholic, or born of Catholic parents, from being adopted by non-Catholic parents. Laws favorable to the Catholic point of view have been passed in a number of states.

Controversy over such legislation and disputes over individual adoption cases, however, have brought Catholics into sharp and open conflict with Protestants and Jews.

The Southern Case. This case involves two foster children reared first

---

[51] L. Peffer, *op. cit.*, p. 131.
[52] *New York Times*, November 19, 1959.

as Jews and then ordered to a Catholic home. Linda and Diane Southern, 7 and 8 years old respectively, were placed in a Jewish home by their mother, who at that time said the girls were Jewish. But three years later the mother tried to get them back by asserting that she was Catholic and that the girls had been baptized as Catholics.

The Children's Court then ruled that the girls should remain in their foster homes because they had found "happiness, love and security" for the first time in their lives, and because their only recollections were of being Jewish. The court also held that the mother was "unfit to have their custody or control."

The mother, with the counsel for the Catholic Archdiocese of New York as her attorney, appealed against the ruling of the court on the ground that the Children's Court Act made religious considerations relevant and crucial—and the Appellate Division of the New York Supreme Court reversed the ruling of the Children's Court. The Free Synagogue Child Adoption Committee of New York thereupon entered the dispute and appealed the appellate court's decision on the ground that award of custody determined solely on the basis of the religion into which a child is baptized violates the principle of "separation between church and state."[53]

The Goldman Twins. Born out of wedlock to a Catholic mother who was unable to care for them, and who consented in writing that they should be adopted by the Goldmans, a childless Jewish couple, the twins were reared in the Jewish faith. Three years later the Goldmans sought to obtain legal adoption. Although the judge found that the Goldmans were good parents, and providing a good home for the twins, he refused the adoption because of the difference in religion.

According to Massachusetts law, judges in passing upon petitions for adoption are bound, "where practicable," to give controlling effect to identity of religious faith. And since a number of nearby Catholic couples had filed applications to adopt children through the Catholic Charities Bureau, the judge ruled it "practicable" to give custody of the twins to Catholics. The judge also ruled that the twins were Catholic because they had been born of a Catholic mother, although they had never been baptized.

Before the state authorities could gain physical possession of the twins, however, and carry out the ruling of the judge, the Goldmans abandoned their home and business (a clothing store in Boston) and, taking the twins with them, established a home in another state. The Massachusetts authorities were never able to locate the family, or return the twins to Massachusetts, so that the ruling of the court could be carried out.[54]

The Case of "Hildy." Hildy, too, was born out of wedlock in a Boston

---

[53] *Ibid.*, November 31, 1951.

[54] C. C. Cawley, "Outlaws: Adoption Cases," *Christian Century*, April 3, 1957, pp. 420–22.

hospital to a Catholic mother and also given, ten days after birth, to a childless Jewish couple, the Ellises, who paid the doctor and hospital bills and gave the mother $150 for incidental expenses. According to the doctor, the mother had been told that the Ellises were Jewish.

Several weeks later, declaring she had only now learned the Ellises were Jewish, the mother demanded her daughter's return so that she would be brought up as a Catholic. When the Massachusetts courts two years later ruled against the Ellises' adoption petition, Hildy had known no other parents.

The Ellises fled to Florida with Hildy, Massachusetts authorities sought to extradite the Ellises on a charge of kidnapping, and Catholic authorities and spokesmen supported—or urged—the extradition. Protestant authorities and spokesmen just as strongly opposed the extradition, and Jewish groups remained aloof from the controversy. The governor of Florida refused to extradite and some time later a Florida court granted the Ellises the adoption that had been refused by the Massachusetts courts.[55]

These cases illustrate the extent to which states may differ in the legal weight they give to "religious interest." In the Massachusetts and New York cases religious interest took precedence over all other factors; in Florida the temporal welfare of the child was the determining factor.

Adoption cases bring conflicting claims of what constitutes the good religious life into sharp focus. Catholics insist upon the primacy of the religious factor in adoption because of the church's concern for the eternal salvation of the soul: it is much better that the child live and die according to Catholic faith and morality, and achieve eternal salvation, than be temporarily happy on earth. Protestants, in contrast, stress the primacy of the child's welfare and happiness on earth, in the here and now. In the Protestant view it is the moral responsibility of the community and the parents, natural and adopting, that a child be put into the best possible home with the best possible parents, regardless of religion.

Both Catholics and Protestants seek the state's power and sanctions in support of their respective positions on adoption. Whenever either succeeds in securing its pattern of adoption legislation, it not only protects its own interests but at the same time imposes its particular ethic upon the community. Jewish groups, until recently, have refrained from seeking similar legislation, their spokesmen having taken the position that each religious group should achieve its objectives by its own efforts and not seek the legislative support of the state.

Mixed Marriages as a Source of Religious Conflict

Disputes arising from mixed marriages that end in divorce are even more frequent sources of conflict between Catholics and non-Catholics. Disputes over the custody and rearing of children, for example, as pro-

---

[55] "Fight for Hildy," *Time*, July 18, 1955, p. 38; "Hildy," *Time*, July 22, 1957, p. 65.

vided for in antenuptial agreements, often find their way into the courts for final resolution.

One such case was that of a Lutheran mother who appealed to a higher court for reversal of a ruling that gave custody of her children to the father, a Roman Catholic. The judge, who had granted the man a separation, also gave him custody of the children on the ground that the antenuptial agreement was binding.[56] The mother, through her attorney, argued that the state and federal constitutions prohibited the courts from implementing agreements that children would be raised in a specified faith.

The mother further argued that the agreement had been signed under duress—that she was pregnant at that time and her fiance (later the husband) had threatened to leave her if she failed to agree to a Catholic ceremony. Her attorney also argued that the children had been improperly awarded to the father because the mother was a "fit person on moral and other grounds." The husband, for his part, insisted that the antenuptial agreement had been "freely made and ratified."[57]

In disputes of this sort most courts refuse to treat the antenuptial agreement as a contractual relationship enforceable by law. In New York state, however, an antenuptial agreement is frequently the basis on which a Catholic may obtain a legal annulment on the basis of fraud. The courts hold that the Catholic married the non-Catholic in confidence that the children would be brought up as Catholics, and the antenuptial paper is evidence of this confidence. By not permitting the children to be so reared, it is held, the non-Catholic fraudulently led the Catholic into marriage. And "force, fraud, and duress" are the grounds for annulment under New York law.

Children involved in such adjudication are finally reared as Catholics or as Protestants—one religion gains what the other loses—but each case is a sharp instance of religious conflict.

Summary

Religious competition is part of American culture: faiths, and denominations within a faith, compete with each other, while our pluralistic culture provides a "free market" in souls. Although competition is primarily for the uncommitted, there is a small percentage of conversions which involve the falling away from one faith and adherence to another.

Faiths compete as "going institutions" for recognition of the public, and Catholics and Protestants are continually being evaluated by the public in terms of the nature and the quality of parochial as compared to public schools.

The values of religious groups differ. In attempting to maintain its values for its communicants, a religious group may interfere with or re-

---

[56] *New York Times,* February 2, 1961.
[57] *Ibid.*

strict the freedom of other groups to follow other religious values, or may even frustrate or thwart another's legitimate desires and goals.

Catholics differ from Protestants and Jews on the morality of contraceptive birth control. In their attempts to uphold the Catholic position, priests and the hierarchy sometimes follow action programs that interfere with the freedom of non-Catholics to practice it. Protestants, particularly sensitive on this issue, react definitely and positively.

The Catholic Church is definite and specific on what movies and books reflect Catholic morality, and it forbids Catholics to see improper movies or to read improper books. Non-Catholics resent and protest actions of the church which tend to interfere with their seeing movies or reading books, and making their own moral judgments.

Protestants, through their control of the public schools, in turn annoy and frustrate Catholics. Traditionally, public schools were Protestant-oriented, and are still too secular and smack too much of Protestantism for most Catholics. Catholics particularly object to the public school philosophy and practice of sex education.

Because of their opposition to nativity scenes, Christmas celebrations, and Christian baccalaureate exercises in public school programs or in public facilities, Jews annoy and frustrate Christians, who have always looked upon such activities as logical and highly proper.

Considerable antagonism and contravention occur within Protestantism itself. From time to time the conservative and liberal wings of Protestantism have shown considerable antagonism towards each other over questions of social action, conservatives, for example, finding frequent occasions for accusing liberals of being "soft" on Communism.

There is no unanimity of belief or opinion within the major Protestant denominations. The larger denominations are liberal in theology and progressive in social action, but each of them includes a conservative minority that has been highly critical of liberal policies and the liberal leadership of the NCCCA. The conservative-liberal antagonism is sufficiently deep-seated to make splintering and fragmentation an everpresent possibility.

Religious conflict in contemporary America, however, is restrained and non-violent, and the only type of conflict which a pluralistic society can tolerate.

The most hotly contested religious disputes occur in those states where Protestants are no longer the dominant, controlling group but only one of two or sometimes three religious minorities. These are the great urban states, most of which are in the Northeast, where the political balance of power is closely weighed. Gambling and birth control have been frequent sources of religious conflict in these states.

Protestantism supports the traditional Puritan view that all gambling is sinful *per se*, and has attempted to impose this concept of morality on the community. It openly and vigorously opposes the various attempts to secure permissive bingo legislation—and is opposed in this effort, in turn, by

Catholic and other non-Protestant groups. But attempts to make Protestant values prevail and endure as mandatory norms for the community have generally failed.

Adoption, mixed marriage, and divorce are other frequent sources of conflict. Where the Catholics are politically strong the Catholic Church has tried to translate its concepts of natural law into mandatory legislation for the entire community. Yet neither the Catholic nor the non-Catholic point of view has been victorious in any of these struggles; the result is a virtual standoff, and the religious issue is not always clear-cut.

Some conflict is good in a pluralistic society. Religious systems, even Christian ones, differ one from another and are forced to support their positions constructively under challenge or attack.

Chapter XII

Conjunctive Processes and Relationships

ACCOMMODATION

ACCOMMODATION is the social process that leads to the alteration of functional relationships between groups so as to avoid, reduce, or eliminate conflict and promote reciprocal adjustment. It is an important social process among religious groups. *Toleration, compromise, secularization,* and *conversion* are the types of accommodation that are most commonly involved in religious change.

In a truly pluralistic society there can never be a complete assimilation of religious groups into a common religious or secular pattern. Individuals, more subject to change, may leave their religious group, but the group lives on. Many religious groups, however, lose much of their identity and peculiarity through secularization. Even when one has moved substantially along the sect-church continuum, where differences become less evident and pronounced, the countervailing tendency to recover sect values leads to fragmentation and the reestablishment of a new religious group, highly independent and isolated.

Toleration

Toleration is both a process and a state. It is the process by which groups learn to get along with each other without necessarily accepting each other's values, and it is the state of adjustment which results when groups tolerate each other.

American society currently enjoys a very high level of toleration among

276

and between religious groups. Judaism receives its most sympathetic hearing from Protestants. Protestants and Jews participate in joint activities, talk in each other's churches, and socialize and fraternize in other ways as well.[1]

Several Lutheran pastors once were the guests of Orthodox rabbis at a post-Succoth reception in Atlantic City where they sipped sweet wine, ate *gefüllte fish*, *halvah*, and an assortment of vegetables symbolic of the Jewish harvest festival. The ministers, some of whom had never met an Orthodox rabbi, ate with gusto—all wearing white *yamulkes* or skull caps.[2]

Protestants are becoming more tolerant of Catholics. A token of this is that the use of Reformation Sunday as a traditional occasion for anti-Catholic diatribes by the Protestant clergy has recently been denounced by several Protestant leaders, Dr. Jaroslav J. Pelikan, a Lutheran scholar, advised Protestants to avoid "vicarious Pope-baiting" at their Reformation festivals and instead make the festivals an "opportunity for serious self-examination of their own reasons for existence." He went on to say that anti-Catholic sentiments are often voiced by Protestants "whose Protestantism Luther or Calvin would have a hard time recognizing."[3]

And Catholics are becoming more tolerant of Protestants. The Reverend Gustave Weigel, Jesuit scholar, has stated that Protestant-Catholic relations have never been better; that despite latent and at times overt friction the two great bodies of American Christendom are living together in more friendliness than ever before. Father Weigel found that the Catholic is now interested in the Protestant and that the Protestant is even more interested in the Catholic and Catholicism. He observed that

This new confrontation of the differing faiths has not been uncomfortable and it has been useful for both sides. Catholics are continually being invited to strictly Protestant meetings and discussions. More slowly but quite patently Protestants are being invited to Catholic gatherings either to address the group or at least to take part in the discussions.[4]

Father Weigel listed several reasons for such changes:

The United States is no longer white, Anglo-Saxon, and Protestant. It is a land of many religions, and Protestantism must take its chances "like all the others."

There has been a change in the feeling of Protestant separateness. The hope of a united church makes the Protestant look at Catholicism more sympathetically, and, as a consequence, "The Protestant wants to be a Catholic, but not a Roman Catholic."

The liturgical movement has grown. Protestant clergymen now wear vestments, de-emphasize the sermon as central to worship, and approve of more

---

[1] W. Seward Salisbury, *The Organization and Practice of Religion in a City* (Oswego, N.Y.: The Ontario Press, 1951).

[2] *New York Times*, October 17, 1960.

[3] *Time*, October 21, 1960.

[4] Gustave Weigel, S.J., "Catholic and Protestant: End of a War?" *Thought*, Vol. XXXIII, No. 130 (Autumn, 1958), p. 390.

frequent communion. The liturgy of many Protestant churches is now closer to that of the Catholic mass than it is to the form of the Puritan prayer meeting.

Catholics, for their part, have grown greatly in economic status and intellectual depth, and have gained a sense of security in numbers; they are no longer "afraid" of Protestants.

Father Weigel emphasized, however, that while the gulf of separation between Protestants and Catholics has narrowed significantly, "the Protestant is not yet ripe for conversion nor will the Catholic ever be."[5]

Compromise

Compromise is the type of adjustment between groups in which concessions are made by each in order to reduce tension and remove friction.

Reduction of Tension between Religious Groups. In some dioceses the Catholic Church has reduced the friction and tension arising over mixed marriages by progressively moving such marriages from the rectory, to the sanctuary outside the altar rail, to the high altar within the sanctuary —modifications or adjustments the church saw fit to make for reasons of its own. There is considerable sentiment within the church that the present rules on mixed marriage should be modified so as to recognize Catholic-Protestant marriages performed by a Protestant clergyman in a Protestant church. Such marriages now, in the eyes of the church, are invalid, and the children born of them illegitimate. Such a change in the marriage rules would lead, according to the brilliant young Catholic theologian, Hans Küng, to an improved interconfessional atmosphere and a more favorable climate for ecumenical action.[6]

In somewhat the same way, tension and friction over the use of public funds for parochial schools have been reduced in a number of states by providing public aid to parochial school students for transportation, welfare services, health services, and text books.

The New York state "Regents' prayer," declared unconstitutional by the Supreme Court, represented a compromise by the three faiths. The prayer, recommended for use in the public schools by the state education department, was developed in consultation with Protestant, Catholic, and Jewish representatives: *Almighty God, we acknowledge our dependence upon Thee and we beg Thy blessings upon us, our parents, our teachers, and our Country.* It was not the type of prayer that anyone of the faiths would create for worship within its own group, and at the same time there was nothing in it that was objectionable to any of the faiths.

Adjusting to the Needs of an Industrial Society. A great deal of change that takes place in religious groups is the result of adjustment to the general culture. These changes are not compromises because only the religious group changes; there is no compensating change in the general culture.

---

[5] *Ibid.*, p. 383.

[6] Hans Küng, *The Council, Reform, and Reunion* (New York: Sheed & Ward, 1962).

Yet these changes—because religious groups do not adopt traits of the secular culture—do not represent secularization either. What happens is that a religious group finds it expedient and desirable to modify its structure in order to function more effectively within the culture, some adjustment of this type being required of any system that wishes to remain an effective and vital force within a contemporary context.

The Catholic Church has shortened the breviary obligation of the priest so that he will have more time for his other duties. The Catholic priest is required to recite from the breviary, the great public prayer book of the church, each day. This is a serious obligation and is in addition to the daily mass required of each priest. The breviary is not so much a book to be read as it is a prayer to be recited. The priest is not allowed to read it to himself; he must at least form the words with his lips.

From 45 to 60 minutes each day were required to perform the breviary obligation, but in the revised breviary the time has been cut to about half. The breviary was shortened partly by reducing the rank of several feasts or observances to the category of simple feasts—the breviary prayers for feasts of higher rank take considerably longer to say. The breviary precedes the year 1100 A.D., when a major abbreviation was made in the office recited by priests, monks, and nuns throughout the church. The breviary has been shortened twice before in the twentieth century, in 1912 and again in 1955.[7]

A number of changes in the liturgy and regulations of the Roman Catholic Church have been made to better meet the spiritual needs of Catholics living and working in an urban and industrial culture. The religion has been modified but not secularized because, according to the priests, the essentials of the worship and sacramental system remain unimpaired. These modifications make it "easy for present-day Catholics to practice their faith and obtain its many spiritual blessings."[8]

Former strict rules of fast before receiving communion have been relaxed to a minimum to permit workers to receive this sacrament at noon or evening masses. Noon, late afternoon, and evening masses are celebrated, especially on Holy Days of Obligation, for the convenience of those who work in shifts in factories and offices. The liturgy of Holy Week has been revised so that most of the services are scheduled in late afternoon or evening to permit attendance by workers, school children, and family groups.

Regulations for the lenten season have been made easier, stressing acts of penance and charity rather than physical mortification through fasting and abstinence. And other fast and abstinence days, believed to have worked undue hardship on modern workers and their families, have been reduced to a minimum.[9]

---

[7] *New York Times*, May 2, 1960.
[8] *Herald American*, Syracuse, New York, November 26, 1961.
[9] *Ibid*.

Protestants, too, have felt the impact of industrialization and urbanization, and there are movements to modify its traditional patterns to better meet the needs of parishioners. A Presbyterian official warned that if Protestantism is to remain a vital force in urban life it must begin by "revolutionizing" some of its cherished customs, one being the "sacred hour" of 11 A.M. for Sunday worship. This hour, according to the official, was geared to the needs of a rural society, allowing farmers time to milk their cows in the morning. He proposed that services be held at 8 A.M. so that the "family could go to the beach, or Dad could get in some golf."[10]

Quakers likewise are considering revolutionary modifications so that their voice may be transmitted more effectively to contemporary society. In line with this, the first theological school in Quaker history is to be established at Earlham College. According to a Quaker spokesman:

> Friends from the beginning have been suspicious of theological training and the "paid ministry," but there is a growing concern for the kind of leadership which can help Friends broaden their spiritual and intellectual horizon. The purpose of a theological school would be to train and prepare men and women for the Christian ministry within the framework and tradition of Friends. There is a widespread conviction that if a school of the ministry is established it could help to focus Friends' attention and energies in such a way as to achieve greater unity internally and prepare Friends for a wider service in the Christian movement as a whole.[11]

Secularization

Secularization is the tendency or process by which sectarian religious movements become "worldly." The movement of a religious group from the sect stage of organization towards the church and denomination stage (as discussed briefly in the section on Jehovah's Witnesses) is in the direction of increasing secularization. The church and the denomination become more temporal and worldly, and less isolated and sacred, as it moves away from the sect stage of development. Secularization is also the process that transforms an isolated, sacred social structure into an accessible, nonsacred pattern of controls and interactions. Invariably, the nonsacred duties and controls are less demanding.

Commonly heard expressions, "the Americanization of the Catholic Church" or "the Americanization of Judaism," refer to changes that are essentially secular in nature. Democracy, equality for women, and liberalism are some of the major secular values that have influenced Catholicism, Judaism, and Protestantism in varying degrees. Secularization, in fact, was the most common answer given by individual Catholic, Protestant, and Jewish clergymen in our community studies to the question: What is the greatest problem of your church? To these grassroots clergymen secularization is not a theory or a concept, but a social reality.

---

[10] *New York Times*, April 8, 1960.
[11] *Ibid.*, December 5, 1959.

Methodists, for one, are moving away from sacred norms to norms characteristic of the secular culture. A recent survey conducted by Boston University School of Theology showed that they have relaxed the rigid code of behavior that once characterized members of the church. Although abstinence, for example, had been a basic tenet of the denomination over the years, the study showed that one third of all Methodists see no harm in moderate drinking of alcoholic beverages. There is also much less emphasis upon personal conduct and diligent church attendance.[12]

Presbyterians similarly are drifting in the direction of secularization, but, unlike the Methodists, have given official sanction to modification of the sacred norms. Traditionally the Presbyterian standard has been total abstinence, with no official acceptance of even moderate drinking. Recently, however, the 173rd General Assembly of the United Presbyterian Church, while encouraging voluntary abstinence, formally acknowledged the privilege of drinking in moderation: "There are many persons in our churches who in honesty and sincerity choose to drink moderately. Those who drink and those who abstain should respect each other and work constructively together in dealing with the problem of alcohol."[13]

What a change this is from the days when the youthful author and his friends used to sing the Christian Endeavor songs in which we promised not to drink "cider, wine, or whisky-beer, or smoke the nasty little cigarette."

The continuing trend of Protestant churches to substitute a program of "social ministries" for worship services is another change in the direction of secularization. The typical Protestant church at the turn of the century emphasized the worship services, the Sunday morning worship service being at least an hour and a half in length and either preceded or followed by a Sunday School hour. Then in the evening there was another service, very similar to the morning service but not as long. The third worship service in the weekly church calendar was a midweek prayer meeting. A good church family would usually attend Sunday morning service and Sunday School as a group, and be represented by some member of the family at both the Sunday evening service and prayer meeting during the week.

The Sunday morning service and Sunday School remain; however, the morning service is seldom more than an hour in length. Sunday evenings are usually limited to youth-group meetings, and women's groups, men's clubs, and family groups meet during the week but seldom oftener than once a month.

Although the social ministries include some worship features, they are more social than spiritual in nature; the focus and emphasis is more temporal and worldly than spiritual and otherworldly. No demanding duties

---

[12] *Ibid.*, June 6, 1961.
[13] *Ibid.*, May 26, 1961.

or exacting disciplines are required of a modal communicant in today's representative liberal Protestant congregation. Outside of attendance at morning service, the Sabbath is free for pleasure and enjoyment; "blue law" Sundays and behavior belong to history for most Protestants. Protestantism, in short, has adjusted to the world by becoming more like it.

Secularization in Judaism. Judaism has also felt this impact. Reform Judaism shows the greatest amount of secularization, Conservative Judaism a considerable amount, and even rabbis of Orthodox synagogues complain of the inroads secularization is making upon the practice of the faith among their congregations. As a minority faith Judaism has been influenced and modified in a culture that is predominantly Protestant-Christian, and some of the changes are compromises Jews have had to accept as the price of living and working in such a culture.

Jews have found it difficult, if not impossible, to follow the strict letter of the dietary laws and to maintain normal vocational and professional relations with the non-Jewish community. And many synagogues, because so many of the congregation are unwilling to isolate themselves from the secular society on what is often the most important business and professional day of the week, have replaced the Jewish Sabbath with the Christian Sunday.

Many of the changes in Reform Judaism were not forced by necessity, but adopted through choice. A Reform congregation and a Reform service looks and sounds much like a liberal Protestant congregation and service. The rabbi preaches and his sermon is considered by most of his congregation as the highlight of the service. The service is in English rather than in Hebrew—or if the prayer book is not in English it at least includes an English translation. Girls are confirmed. Men and women sit together during service. Women sing in the choir and otherwise participate in the service, generally being extended the same rights and privileges as men.

These changes, sometimes spoken of as the *Americanization* of Judaism, can just as correctly be described as the *Protestantizing* of Judaism, and to the extent in which these values are secular values, they are also a measure of the secularization of Judaism. The changes, therefore, that are taking place in American Judaism are brought about, directly and indirectly, by the interaction of Jewish groups and personalities with non-Jewish groups and personalities within the context of a secular culture.

In a number of areas of personal living the behavior of the Protestant, Catholic, and Jewish laity shows that the representative layman is abandoning sacred values for secular values.

Family Authority Patterns. A study that sought to confirm the hypothesis that secular values are taking precedence over sacred values found support among adherents of each of the basic faiths—as we will see from the following.

The Catholic religion teaches that the husband is the head of the family and "superior" to the wife. "The man the head, the wife the heart as

Christ is the head and the Church the heart."[14] "Since every society needs authority it is necessary that there be an authority in the family, but one that is paternal."[15]

The wife is also subordinate to the husband in the traditional Jewish family, and her subordination is underlined by the fact that the Orthodox practice does not provide for her participation in the synagogue service or study of the sacred system. Whatever influence the woman plays must be exercised through her husband.[16]

The traditional Protestant family was the old-time rural family, largely derived from the Puritan pattern. The Puritan concept of theocracy and authority was a leadership concept which, in the family context, made the father's prime position clear-cut and absolute.

Among Catholics and Jews equalitarian relationships, representing the secular value, have virtually superseded the primacy of the husband and father. Catholic and Jewish family authority patterns, furthermore, are very similar to Protestant authority patterns. Males and females of all three faiths are now in virtual agreement on the degree to which the equalitarian

TABLE 14

Family Authority Preferences as indicated by replies to the question: "If you get married and have a family, who do you expect will be the more influential in the direction and control of the family?"

	Male				Female			
	Catholic	Jew	Protes-tant	No Prefer-ence	Catholic	Jew	Protes-tant	No Prefer-ence
	N = 272	N = 47	N = 271	N = 52	N = 333	N = 112	N = 514	N = 43
Myself	24.3%	19.2%	22.9%	32.7%	3.3%	1.7%	1.9%	0%
My spouse	2.9	4.2	5.5	7.7	19.8	18.8	17.7	14.0
Both equally ...	72.8	76.6	71.6	59.6	76.9	79.5	80.4	86.0
	100.0	100.0	100.0	100.0	100.0	100.0	100.0	100.0

Source: W. Seward Salisbury, "Religion and Secularization," *Social Forces*, Vol. 36, No. 3, p. 202.

pattern is desirable; all three faiths have moved away from the sacred and approached the secular value. The Protestants moved first but now have been joined by the great majority of Catholics and Jews.

Birth Control. Catholic beliefs and attitudes towards the practice of birth control are subject to severe pressure from the secular culture. Catholic beliefs and teachings must make some difference, however, because most fertility studies show that Catholics have more children than non-

[14] Edgar Schmiedeler, *Christian Marriage, an Analysis and Commentary on the Encyclical* (Washington, D.C.: National Catholic Conference on Family Life, 1943), p. 27.

[15] National Catholic Welfare Conference, *The Father the Head of the Home* (Washington, D.C.: 1953), p. 2.

[16] David R. Mace, *Hebrew Marriage* (The Philosophical Library, 1953), p. 190; Marshall Sklare, *Conservative Judaism, an American Religious Movement* (Glencoe, Ill.: The Free Press, 1955), p. 89.

Catholics. But the differences are not as great as formerly, and in some cases have virtually disappeared.

Hamtranck, an immigrant Polish Catholic section of Detroit, had a birth rate much above the national rate in 1920, but by 1950 the rates were virtually identical.[17] The Catholic Church has therefore recognized the tendency of Catholics to reject the sacred value in this respect. A number of the hierarchy found "alarming" a report that Roman Catholic "married couples are using contraceptive birth control in about the same measures as non-Catholics."[18] The spokesman however went on to say that the Church would never allow the pressure of society to change its position against the use of contraceptives for birth control.

But the Catholic Church has officially made other adjustments to secular culture. Parts of such rites and ceremonies as baptism, marriage, and funerals, formerly in Latin, are now said in English. These changes are a concession to the education and sophistication of the communicants who are thereby encouraged to make their own interpretation of the ritual and symbolism.[19]

Another accommodation is the Catholic clergy's tendency to perform the priestly roles in a more democratic manner than formerly. The Catholic Church vests its priests with a great deal of authority and a priest can easily ensconce himself behind this authority and remain aloof from the great majority of his parishioners. Interestingly enough, in one community study it was found that those priests who led through their own personal qualities rather than by their vested authority, who met their parishioners and the public in a democratic and friendly manner, and who extended themselves over and above "the call of duty" were rewarded with greater successes in their parishes and in the respect of the community.[20]

A prominent Catholic spokesman finds that the American Catholic Church is neither a harassed minority nor a belligerent group. He believes it more prone to conservatism than to radical change and, with its generosity, activism, and optimism, probably more American than Catholic.[21]

Women in the Church. One of the most dramatic changes taking place in contemporary churches and denominations is the increasing place given to women in the administration of religion and the church. Their increasing roles and status are highlighted in the recent granting by some denominations of female ordination with full rights of the clergy.

The rising status of women, primarily a trait of the secular culture, is

---

[17] Albert J. Mayer and Sue Marx, "Social Change, Religion, and Birth Rates," *American Journal of Sociology*, Vol. LXII, No. 4 (January, 1957), pp. 383–90.

[18] Reverend Irving A. DeBlanc in an address before the National Catholic Family Life Conference as reported in the *Fresno Bee*, Fresno, Calif., June 22, 1960.

[19] *New York Times*, November 26, 1961.

[20] W. Seward Salisbury, *The Organization and Practice of Religion in a Small City* (Oswego, N.Y.: The Ontario Press, 1951), p. 18.

[21] Gustave Weigel, S.J., "Americanization of the Catholic Church," *Christianity and Crisis*, June 8, 1959.

another illustration of the secularization of religion. Women first received formal recognition in the political institution: the right to vote, to hold office, to serve on juries. It was also the political institution that legislated economic institutions into extending equality of rights to women. The impetus for increasing the status of women in religion likewise comes from the secular culture. Religious institutions, as a conserving force, confined women to different and for the most part subordinate roles within the church, and it was not difficult to find Biblical authority to justify her subordinate position.

St. Paul was widely quoted by theologians in opposition to the ordination of women: "As in all the churches of the saints, the women should keep silence in the churches. For they are not permitted to speak, but should be subordinate, as even the law says. If there is anything they desire to know, let them ask their husbands at home. For it is shameful for a woman to speak in church."[22] And there were other references to "Women being veiled in the assembly"[23] and "women not being allowed to teach."[24]

Practical objections, as well as the theological ones above, were advanced to keep women out of the ministry. It was argued that their lack of vocal power, particularly in the large churches, and their handicap in pastoral duties, especially in calls at night, limited their usefulness as ministers.

In spite of all the resistance to women in the ministry, census data showed a steady increase. Women ministers and women lawyers and judges increased at about the same rate between 1910 and 1940, but women ministers made a more rapid growth between 1940 and 1950.

A study based on denominational reports and published in 1951[25] showed that only about one half of the ordained or licensed ministers were serving as pastors of churches. More than 60 percent of the total number were in three bodies: the Church of God, the International Church of the Foursquare Gospel, and Christ Unity Science, and a little less than one tenth of the women ministers were in denominations affiliated with the National Council of Churches of Christ in America. They were not in the major Protestant denominations to any extent, being largely confined to those bodies in which the sacramental aspect of the ministry is less stressed.[26]

The movement toward ordination of women continued until midway during the 1950–60 decade two of the major Protestant denominations, the Presbyterian Church in the U.S.A. and the Methodist Church, finally extended full rights of ordination. Twice before, in 1930 and 1947, the Presbyterians had rejected the proposal. As ordained local elders in the

[22] I Cor. 14:34, 35.
[23] I Cor. 11:5.
[24] I Timothy 2:12.
[25] *Information Service*, May 31, 1952.
[26] *Ibid.*

TABLE 15

WOMEN IN SELECTED PROFESSIONS, 1910–50

	Clergy	College Presidents, Professors, and Instructors	Lawyers and Judges	Physicians and Surgeons
1910				
Number	685	2,958	558	9,015
Percent	0.5	18.8	0.4	5.9
1920				
Number	1,787	10,075	1,738	7,219
Percent	1.4	30.1	1.4	5.0
1930				
Number	3,276	20,131*	3,385	6,825
Percent	2.2	48.1	2.1	4.6
1940				
Number	3,148	19,884	4,187	7,608
Percent	2.3	26.5	2.4	4.6
1950				
Number	6,777	28,907	6,256	11,714
Percent	4.1	23.2	3.5	6.1

Source: *Information Service*, March 6, 1954.
* Probably includes some in secondary education.

Methodist Church women had been permitted to act as ministers in some churches, but it was not until 1956 that they were given unqualified rights and free movement within the various conferences.

Before the final affirmative action these churches reviewed the Biblical and theological bases for ordination and found authority sufficient to overrule their previous stands. Reference was made to the account in Genesis which states that "male and female are created simultaneously in the image of God."[27] It was also pointed out that St. Paul's statement in Galatians 3:28, "that there is neither Jew nor Greek, there is neither bond nor free, there is neither male nor female; for ye are all one in Christ Jesus," is both daring and revolutionary and more truly representative of the spirit of St. Paul.

To many theologians this new insight into St. Paul seemed more in harmony with Jesus' attitude towards women in the Gospels. Christ, unlike St. Paul, did not set down any rules; indeed, He talked with the Samaritan woman at the well, with Mary Magdalene, and others. The Bible is full of Jesus' almost continuous association with women, speaking with them, teaching them, in the home of Martha and Mary. Women were apparently in the Upper Room, at the foot of the Cross, the first at the tomb, the bearers of the news of the Resurrection—present when He broke bread and present at Pentecost. It is true that He did not choose any

---

[27] Genesis 1:26, 27.

women as Apostles, but neither did He choose any Gentiles. The national bodies of the two churches decided these arguments were sufficient Biblical and theological justifications to sanction full ordination.

The World Council of Churches also made a study of the position of women among its 168 member churches and issued the report of its findings in 1958. Forty-eight of their churches admit women to the full ministry; 9 churches ordain women to a "partial or irregular ministry"; 90 churches do not ordain women—and 21 churches supplied no definite information. Thus approximately one third of the church bodies for which information was available ordain or give women some partial status related to the ministry.[28]

In neither the Presbyterian nor the Methodist church have large numbers of women sought ordination, however. In May, 1961, five years after the permissive ruling was passed, only 30 women had been ordained as Presbyterian ministers. They worked most often in Christian education.

None of the 15 churches of the Anglican communion in the World Council of Churches ordains women. As late as May, 1955, the Protestant Episcopal diocese of New York refused to permit women to serve on parish vestries or to attend yearly diocese conventions. Shortly afterwards, however, the St. James Episcopal church of Vincennes, Indiana, appointed a woman to the post of senior warden, the key lay post in the parish.[29] Since this shattering of tradition other Episcopal parishes have also found it desirable to include women in the membership of their vestries.[30]

Even the Catholic Church has made some moves towards greater recognition and more equal treatment of women. Among other developments, Catholic sources report more coeducation in its schools, such as Fordham University's departure from its traditional policy of being strictly a male institution of higher learning. Fordham's recent expansion plans were even reported to include a coeducational unit, Thomas More College, offering traditional liberal arts and science programs to women as well as men.[31]

Judaism, too, has departed from traditional practice in a number of instances by giving women religious responsibilities and recognition in the synagogue and temple. Reform Judaism, first to confirm women and to allow them to sit with men in the synagogue and sing in the choirs, has gone furthest.

The Central Conference of American Rabbis and the Union of American Hebrew Congregations, both Reform organizations, proposed in 1955 that women be ordained as rabbis. The president of the Central Conference, Dr. Barnet Brickner, pointed out that there was no ban in Reform

---

[28] World Council of Churches, *A Report on Women in the Ministry* (New York: 1958).

[29] *Information Service*, September 10, 1955.

[30] *Herald Journal*, Syracuse, N.Y., January 20, 1962.

[31] *New York Times*, May 23, 1963.

Judaism on women in the pulpit. Noting that they were already receiving religious degrees he said: "They have special spiritual and emotional fitness to be rabbis and I believe that many women could be attracted to this calling."[32] The issue of women in the rabbinate was then renewed in 1963 when the National Federation of (Reform) Temple Sisterhoods asked the three major Reform groups, the Central Conference of American Rabbis, the Union of American Hebrew Congregations, and the Hebrew Union College–Jewish Institute of Religion (which trains students for the Reform rabbinate) to convene a conference to resolve the question of women rabbis.[33]

Conservative Judaism joined the recognition-for-women trend when one of its leading congregations, the Park Avenue Synagogue, granted women the *aliyot*, the privilege of being called to witness the reading of the Torah scroll on the Sabbath morning and to recite the blessings. A leader of the congregation said this step represents

. . . Another expression of our congregation to make Judaism traditional yet growing with modernity. . . . The mere fact that some ritual in Jewish religious life has thus far been reserved for men or for women does not imply that it is equal and fair to deny *aliyot* in our synagogue, where men and women worship together and where women serve on our board of trustees. We are extending democracy into Jewish life.

He added that this innovation demonstrated the "adaptability and viability of Jewish religious practice," and hailed it as a step that would lead to a "more meaningful public Jewish worship by both men and women."[34]

Summary

Religious groups continuously change, adjusting to each other and to the secular culture. Types of accommodation that are of particular relevance to religious change are *toleration, compromise,* and *secularization.*

A higher degree of toleration exists between Judaism and Christianity and between Catholicism and Protestantism than ever before. The conflict and tension between Catholics and Protestants over the question of state aid to parochial schools has been reduced by the compromise of permitting public support for bus transportation and welfare services to parochial school pupils.

The basic faiths have adjusted their forms and order of worship to fit the demands and exigencies of an industrial and urban culture and so that the religious needs of their communicants may more efficiently be met. Catholic masses are held in the afternoons and evenings and fasting rules have been modified so as to work less hardship and inconvenience on shift workers. Protestants are experimenting with a Sunday morning service

[32] *New York Times*, June 21, 1955.
[33] *Ibid.*, November 20, 1963.
[34] *Ibid.*, June 27, 1961.

that is earlier than the traditional 11 A.M. service, a significant departure from an hour or time of service originally keyed to the farmer's pattern of life.

Secularization is possibly the most significant trend in American religion. Through secularization the religious group becomes less sacred and less isolated, and more like and more a part of the world. The development of the "social ministries" as a substitute for the more extended pattern of worship services is a movement in the direction of secularization. Many of the modifications that Reform Judaism has made in traditional Judaism, services in the vernacular, the secular rather than kosher diet, and observance of the Hebraic Sabbath on the Christian Sunday, are similar secular adjustments.

Secularization is also reflected in the behavior of adherents. The traditional family, whether Puritan, Jewish, or Catholic, vested authority in the person of the husband and father. An equalitarian pattern has now become the dominant form in all three faiths.

The increased status and integration of women into the leadership and authority structure of religion are changes and values derived from the secular culture. Although Protestantism and Reform Judaism have gone the furthest, concessions toward the more equal treatment of women are observable even within the Catholic religious structure.

Some authorities in fact credit the great popularity of religion in the postwar years to secularization: it is not that the American people are becoming "more religious" as it is that religion is becoming more secular —more like the American culture.

COOPERATION AND ASSIMILATION

The conjunctive and integrative social processes, *cooperation* and *assimilation*, operate continuously (and importantly) within and between religious systems in American culture. Although instances of cooperation are constantly brought to public attention through the press, assimilation, according to many students of the religious culture, is the outstanding trend that characterizes contemporary religion (also known as organic union). Representative illustrations of cooperation and of assimilation follow.

INTERFAITH COOPERATION

Between Protestant, Catholics, and Jews

The National Conference of Christians and Jews is an organization of the three faiths which functions throughout the nation but is especially active in the great urban centers. It is particularly concerned with the elimination of discrimination against minority groups, and has worked closely with the various state commissions against discrimination. The Conference, often referred to as the N.C.C.J., has also accepted responsibility for improving the social climate by being a forum in which controversial issues among the faiths can be discussed, while its Institute for Religious Freedom and Public Affairs deals with the responsibilities of religious freedom. The Institute was designed "to raise the general level of public discussions and understanding among religious groups differing on issues of public concern."[1]

To be more specific, Protestant, Catholic, and Jewish groups cooperate "to bring the joint moral force of churches and synagogues to bear on problems of racial segregation."[2] The NCCCA, the National Catholic Welfare Conference, and the Synagogue Council of America jointly sponsored a First National Council on Religion and Race. Six hundred and fifty delegates from 70 religious groups attended the conference, which met in Chicago in January, 1963.[3] Brotherhood Week is another occasion for frequent expressions of cooperation and understanding. Joint statements by leaders, interfaith dinners, and interfaith choirs, each a "witness to brotherhood,"[4] are common occurrences each year throughout the country. Instances of nonformalized cooperation among the three faiths also are increasingly common.

An essay, described as "one of the first, if not the first, joint essay on religion by representatives of the three major faiths in the United States," was part of the official handbook for the White House Conference on Children and Youth.[5] The essay extolled the efforts of the Catholic, Jewish, and Protestant religions in advancing American family life.

From time to time representatives of the three faiths find it possible to come together as an informal community of scholars for mutual support and stimulation.

> The scholarly objective approach is so carefully followed at some leading centers of basic biblical studies that students of all faiths gather in them to study together. Gatherings of Catholic, Protestant and Jewish biblical scholars are not the rare events they used to be. It appears that "scholars of moderate views" have reached a substantial agreement on principles, methods, and conclusions of biblical scholarship, whatever their religious affiliations may be.[6]

Catholic and Jewish Cooperation

The American Jewish Congress hails a "new era of friendship and cooperation" in Roman Catholic and Jewish relations because of the action taken by the Vatican Council against anti-semitism. The Congress was

---

[1] *New York Times*, November 10, 1962.
[2] *Chicago Daily Tribune*, June 22, 1962.
[3] *Christian Century*, January 30, 1963, pp. 133–35.
[4] *New York Times*, March 18, 1962.
[5] *Ibid.*, February 28, 1960.
[6] Walter M. Abbott, S.J., "The Bible Is a Bond," *America*, October 24, 1959.

particularly impressed by Pope John's "serious desire to improve relations between Catholics and Jews as evidenced by the Pope's removal from Catholic liturgy of several references regarded as offensive to Jews."[7] The 1963 session of the Vatican Council continued the policy of *rapprochement* by not only condemning anti-semitism but by absolving the Jews of exclusive blame for Jesus' death, maintaining the guilt lay with all of humanity and not on the Jews alone.[8]

Protestant and Jewish Cooperation

The Jewish Reform youth group, the National Federation of Temple Youth, has proposed an extensive program of cooperation with the United Christian Youth Movement, an affiliate of the National Council of Churches of Christ. The program would include an exchange of delegates between the two groups, development of combined social action group projects in the community, development of comparative religion study programs as a means of understanding each other's faith, and exploration of community problems that concern teenagers. The Reform group announced that it would also seek to establish a similar program with the National Council of Catholic Youth.[9]

Protestants on their part are also making gestures of cooperation and understanding. Protestant children have joined with Jewish children in celebration of their *seder*[10] while, on an adult level, negative references to Jews in Protestant Sunday School texts have declined considerably in the last few years, according to a continuing study carried on at Union Theological Seminary.[11]

Protestants and Jews are frequently in a cooperative relationship in their opposition to certain measures and policies sought by the Catholic Church, the measures usually involving the principle of separation of church and state as it affects legislation and court decisions. Protestants and Jews have also found themselves in united opposition to the Catholic Church over such questions as birth control, adoption, divorce, censorship, gambling, and aid to parochial schools.[12] Relations between Protestants and Jews can be so close that in one city the council of churches listed the synagogue and its rabbi as duly accepted members of the local cooperating body.[13]

Protestant and Catholic Cooperation

Protestants and Catholics are finding more and more occasions where it is possible to associate and work together, and the NCCCA hails the "in-

---

[7] *New York Times*, November 11, 1962.

[8] *Ibid.*, November 2 and November 9, 1963.

[9] *Ibid.*, August 16, 1959.

[10] *Ibid.*, April 16, 1962.

[11] *Ibid.*, April 22, 1962.

[12] Leo Pfeffer, *Creeds in Competition* (New York: Harper & Bros., 1958).

[13] W. Seward Salisbury, *Organization and Practice of Religion in a Small City* (Oswego, N.Y.: The Ontario Press, 1951).

creasing evidence of warmer relations with the Roman Catholic Church."[14] Priests have been sent for the first time as observers to the World Council of Churches[15] and to the General Assembly of the National Council of Churches—and Protestants as observers to the Vatican's Ecumenical Council.[16]

A Catholic scholar reports that Catholics and Protestants may be using the same version of the Bible before too long because Biblical scholars of both faiths have worked together and reached a point where "a uniform translation of the Bible acceptable to both Catholics and Protestants is a real possibility."[17] Another significant example of cooperation finds Catholic and Protestant scholars writing for each other's best scholarly journals.

Dialogue

The nature and quality of the intellectual interaction between Catholics and Protestants is currently and widely spoken of as *dialogue*. Dialogue is defined as orderly conversation among adherents of various groups.

Informal Discussion. Only recently—for the first time since the Anglican withdrawal from the Roman Catholic Church—did the head of the Roman Catholic Church (Pope John XXIII) and the head of the Anglican Church (the Archbishop of Canterbury) find it possible to meet together in informal and friendly conversation.

Private discussions on theological matters are being encouraged. A Jesuit reports that Christians cannot properly fulfill their mission to the non-Christian world until they are united in faith and worship. Therefore, it is imperative that Protestant and Catholic theologians take each other's thinking seriously. They must make an effort to read and to understand each other's work.[18]

A Catholic cardinal, an Anglican priest, and a Greek Orthodox chaplain met in Washington for an *agape*—or a banquet of fraternal love. The three churchmen are reported to have discussed the question of Christian unification. The essential role that charity must play in any move toward unity was emphasized.[19]

More than half of all doctoral dissertations submitted to Roman Catholic theological faculties of Western Germany now deal with Protestant theology.[20] In earlier centuries the study of theology often separated Christians, but today it is often the element which brings Christians together regardless of its conclusions. At the personal invitation of Nathan M. Pusey,

---

[14] *New York Times*, June 9, 1962.

[15] *Ibid.*, July 28, 1962.

[16] *Ibid.*, August 4, 1962.

[17] Abbott, *op. cit.*

[18] Avery Dulles, S.J., *America*, January 24, 1959.

[19] National Catholic Welfare Conference, Bureau of Information, Washington, D.C., June 16, 1959.

[20] National Council of Churches of Christ in the USA, *Information Service*, January 7, 1961.

president of Harvard University, 150 Protestant and Roman Catholic scholars and churchmen participated in a colloquy at Cambridge on theological issues. A great deal of mutual respect and understanding was reported to have developed among the participants.[21]

Formal Catholic Steps. One of the most important steps taken during Pope John XXIII's reign was the calling of an "ecumenical council" for the universal church. The call, in the form of an encyclical (*Ad Petri Cathedram*, June 29, 1959), stated:

> . . . The council's chief business will concern the growth of the Catholic faith and the renewal along right lines of the habits of Christian people, and the adapting of ecclesiastical discipline to the needs and conditions of the present time. That event will surely be a wonderful manifestation of truth, unity, and charity; a manifestation, indeed with it is our hope that those who behold it, but who are separated from this Apostolic See, will receive as a gentle invitation to seek and find unity for which Jesus Christ prayed so ardently to His heavenly Father.[22]

The Pope gave practical emphasis to his interest in ecumenical action by creating a new Vatican Secretariat entirely devoted to matters of Christian unity.

Catholic spokesmen find that the possibilities of union with Protestantism vary according to the theological position and emphasis of the particular denomination. They take a negative view of liberal Protestantism, but find in neo-orthodoxy a school of thought in which dialogue might profitably be pursued.[23]

Orthodox Churches and Union. In his reply to a 1958 Christmas message from Pope John XXIII, Athenagoras I, the Patriarch of Constantinople and spiritual leader of all Eastern Orthodox churches, indicated he would be sympathetic to Roman Catholic overtures on unity. In April of 1960 and July of 1962 Athenagoras I made an appeal for a reunion of Orthodox, Roman Catholic, and Protestant Churches.

The Orthodox communions in the United States total approximately 2½ million members, about half of whom belong to the Greek Orthodox Church. The Orthodox communions, while adhering to the same doctrines, have no direct organizational ties. Under the leadership of Archbishop Iskovos, the Greek Orthodox Primate of North and South America, the prelates of all Eastern Orthodox churches in the United States were called together and formed a standing Conference of Orthodox Bishops as a step toward organic unity. This Conference is working towards a Pan-Orthodox Conference on a worldwide scale.[24]

Protestant Reaction to Dialogue. Many Protestants and Protestant organizations say there is a need for dialogue and that they want to engage

---

[21] *Presbyterian Life*, May 1, 1963.
[22] *Information Service, op. cit.*, February 6, 1960.
[23] Charles Stinson, *The Commonweal*, April 15, 1960.
[24] *New York Times*, April 15, 1960.

in it, and in keeping with this attitude Robert McAfee Brown has advanced certain basic conditions that should be observed if conversations between Roman Catholics and Protestants are to bring results. Each partner must assume that the other is speaking in good faith. Each should seek to understand the other's faith and should accept in humility and repentance responsibility for what his group has done and is doing to foster and perpetuate division. Each should face the issues which cause separation as well as those which create unity.[25]

Protestant observers find two emphases or approaches in the writings of Roman Catholic ecumenists. One is for unity by "absorption." The other approach is "spiritual emulation"—or praying for each other with no other purpose than the sanctification of all Christians.[26]

There were widespread expressions of satisfaction among Protestants at the announcements of Pope John XXIII's interest in the ecumenical movement. The early enthusiasm, however, has been substantially offset by expressions of doubt among various Protestants over the possibility of union with the Roman Catholic Church; few, if any, are willing to accept organic union on Catholic terms. Protestants also interpret the Catholic policy of union by "absorption" to mean that the major concessions would be made by Protestants, a misgiving that finds support in such things as a solemn high mass at St. Patrick's Cathedral for the "conversion of all non-Catholic churches to Roman Catholicism."[27]

One branch of Lutheranism, the National Lutheran Council, reported it was most "interested" in the proposed ecumenical council called by the Pope but was too involved in its own unity problem to acknowledge the papal proposal with more than a friendly nod. Another branch, the Missouri Synod Lutherans, declared "we would not consider an ecumenical council possible in the early Christian sense unless the Roman Church were willing to consider its own departure from the Word of God."

One of the major obstacles to the reunion of Christendom, according to other Protestants, is the doctrine of papal infallibility in faith and morals that was enunciated at the ecumenical council of 1870.[28]

Conservative churches and congregations are usually the most anti-Catholic of all the branches of Protestantism. The National Association of Evangelicals, representing a number of theologically conservative bodies which are not affiliated with the National Council of Churches,[29] took sharp issue with the enthusiasm voiced by some Protestants over the ecumenical council and with the Pope's invitation to non-Catholics to attend as observers.

The World Council of Churches views the various gestures of the Pope

---

[25] Robert McAfee Brown, "Rules for the Dialogue," *The Christian Century,* February 17, 1960.

[26] *Information Service, op. cit.,* January 7, 1961.

[27] *New York Times,* January 22, 1962.

[28] *Ibid.,* February 4, 1959.

[29] *Ibid.,* February 27, 1959.

and the Catholic Church primarily as changes in procedure and climate. Nothing has transpired, they report, to suggest that any of the fundamental differences which exist between the Catholic and the World Council churches have been solved. The opportunity for "dialogue" is to be grasped, but the main task in that dialogue will be "to represent the insights which God has given us together in the fifty years since our movement started."[30]

A Catholic View of Unity. An outstanding Catholic authority on Christian unity, Reverend Gustave Weigel, has said the chances for any immediate reunion between the Roman Catholic Church and the Eastern Orthodox Churches are remote—and there is even less likelihood of a union between Roman Catholicism and Protestantism. Despite the many fundamental similarities between Orthodoxy and Catholicism, Weigel found serious obstacles to union, one of the greatest being the significance and function of the Pope.

There is ingrained both in Catholics and Orthodox the unanalyzed feeling that the other party is treacherous, blind to the truth and sinfully bullheaded.

When this attitude to the partner in dialogue is deep and strong, not too much can be done. Individuals on either side may well be free of such prejudices, but they know very well that their own coreligionists are obsessed by them. Each side is demanding from the other total surrender, which, of course, neither side is willing to accept.[31]

INTRAFAITH COOPERATION

Within Protestantism

Cooperation among Protestant churches is widespread and taken for granted, and usually manifested in local councils of churches, regional councils of churches, and state councils of churches. Sometimes local councils are confined to the liberal Protestant churches, while the conservative churches remain aloof by choice or through the unwillingness of the liberal churches to accept them as cooperating groups, but more often they cooperate in combined lenten, Easter, and Christmas services, released-time programs, vacation Bible schools, and summer services—or common opposition to something the Catholics want.

On the state level, the council of churches usually meets just prior to the legislative session and takes a stand on various issues and the proposed legislation that it wants and or does not want.

Protestant Cooperation at the National Level

The largest, most extensive example of Protestant cooperation at the national level is the organization and activities of the National Council of Churches of Christ in America (NCCCA), an organization of 33 of the

---

[30] *Information Service, op. cit.,* January 7, 1961.
[31] *New York Times,* April 1, 1960.

leading Protestant and Orthodox bodies in the United States. All the large liberal Protestant bodies are members of the NCCCA, but two large conservative denominations, the Southern Baptist Church and the Lutheran Church-Missouri Synod, are notably absent.

A listing of some of the divisions and departments of the Council may give some indication of the extent and variety of the activities which the member churches have found it profitable to work at collectively:[32]

> Division of Christian Education, including a
>   Commission on Higher Education
>   Department of Youth Work, etc.
>
> Division of Foreign Missions, including a
>   Committee on Africa–Far East Office
>   Committee on Latin-America
>   Medical Missions Committee on World Literacy and Christian Literature
>   Rural Missions Committee, etc.
>
> Division of Home Missions, including a
>   Department of Town and Country Church
>   Department of the Urban Church
>   Department of Indian and Migrant Work
>   American Committee on the Christian Approach to the Jew, etc.
>
> Division of Christian Life and Work, including a
>   Department of Evangelism
>   Department of Racial and Cultural Relations
>   Department of the Church and Economic Life, etc.
>
> Broadcasting and Film Commission
>
> Department of United Church Men
>
> Department of United Church Women
>
> Department of Church World Service
>
> Bureau of Research and Survey
>
> Department of Ecumenical Relations

The NCCCA makes social action a leading concern and wherever and whenever practicable brings its influence to bear upon the relevant political body. A typical meeting of its executive body once recommended that the United States expand its nonmilitary program of mutual aid to foreign countries; agreed that the chaplaincy service should be strengthened and petitioned Congress to take the necessary steps; reaffirmed its opposition to segregated housing; requested Congress to repeal a provision of the National Defense Act requiring students to affirm they are not subversive or members of subversive organizations in qualifying for financial assistance; and authorized its representatives to testify at legislative hearings in support of the extension of minimum wage coverage to economic groups not provided for under the current legislation.[33]

---

[32] National Council of the Churches of Christ in the USA, *Yearbook of American Churches, 1959*, New York, p. 59.
[33] *New York Times*, February 27, 1959.

The NCCCA is now the clearing house through which most cooperative efforts of American Protestants are channeled. However, a number of other Protestant groups are organized at the national level to provide special services or carry on special projects. Some of them are:[34]

American Bible Society

The Associated Church Press

General Commission on Chaplains and the Armed Forces Personnel

General Association of Regular Baptist Churches

National Board of Young Women's Christian Association

National Board of Young Men's Christian Association

National Holiness Association (A coordinating agency of those religious bodies which hold the Wesleyan-Arminian theological view)

Protestant Cooperation at the International Level

American Protestants cooperate with world Protestants through the World Council of Churches which has headquarters in Geneva, Switzerland. The World Council is composed of 168 member churches of the Protestant, Anglican, and Orthodox traditions. It was founded in 1948 as the logical culmination of the increasing number of Protestant groups that had world affiliations. The NCCCA works closely with the World Council.

The nature of the work of the Council is suggested by the special divisions and departments into which it is organized. These include:[35]

Division of Interchurch Aid and Service to Refugees

Commission on Evangelism

Commission on Missionary Studies

Commission on International Affairs

The Ecumenical Review and Ecumenical Press Service.

Other Cooperative Bodies

The cooperative tendencies among Protestants on a world basis date back a full century. Among the world bodies with which American Protestants have allied themselves are the[36]

Lambeth Conference of Bishops of the Anglican Communion (organized in 1867)

Alliance of Reformed Churches throughout the World Holding the Presbyterian Order (1877)

International Congregational Council (1891)

Baptist World Alliance (1905)

Lutheran World Federation (1923)

---

[34] *Yearbook of American Churches, 1959, op. cit.*, pp. 9–13.
[35] *Ibid.*, p. 113.
[36] *Ibid.*, p. 120.

Mennonite World Conference (1925)

World Convention of Churches of Christ (Disciples) (1930)

Friends World Committee for Consultation (1937)

World Council of Pentecostal Churches (1945)

Cooperation within Judaism

Judaism is a highly independent and individualized religion. There is no official confession of faith. Jewish belief varies as widely as Protestant belief, and Orthodox, Conservative, and Reform branches of Judaism function in much the same way as various Protestant denominations. Most Orthodox, Conservative, and Reform congregations belong to respective national organizations, but each member congregation still reserves the right to act independently.

Autonomous congregations, absence of dogma, and a religion that is essentially permissive suits Judaism. The bonds that unite it are historical and traditional, common tradition and common heritage having been sufficient to maintain the continuity of Judaism for almost six thousand years in spite of persecution, diaspora, and isolation.

But now that American Judaism finds itself in a new era, in a democratic, pluralistic culture, no longer isolated and ignored but free to speak out and make its influence felt upon the social and political issues of the times, its leaders find that Jewish influence is limited by the very independence and autonomy which, within Judaism, had been an element of strength. A resolution adopted by the Rabbinical Assembly in America (an organization of 700 Conservative rabbis) called attention to Judaism's inability to make its influence felt and invited all major Jewish groups to come together in one organization that could speak for the Jewish community:

> The lack of organized unity in American Jewish life has resulted and will inevitably continue to result in confusion of counsels, unseemly competition among Jewish organizations for public attention, a confused image of Jewish policy in the mind of the American community and a weakening of the effectiveness of Jewish representation before governmental forums here and abroad.[37]

Jews were also told that "Americans are looking for a strong affirmative moral leadership" and that Jews can make their most substantial contribution in moral leadership when they organize and cooperate to speak for the total Jewish community.[38]

Thus the most individual and congregationally independent American faith finds itself moving in the direction of greater cooperation. It appears that Jews are looking for an organization which will do for American Judaism what the National Council of the Churches of Christ in America does for American Protestantism.

---

[37] *New York Times*, May 11, 1960.

[38] *Ibid.*

ASSIMILATION

Organic union is the term used in religious circles to express the assimilation of denominational groups, and is achieved when two or more denominations give up their separate corporate and religious identities and become one denomination. The issues that divide denominations, and that have to be reconciled in order to achieve organic union, are sacramental systems and the nature and authority of the clergy. We will cite some recent, outstanding examples of the movement towards unity and organic union.

Organic Union Among Lutherans

Although American Lutherans at one time were separated into as many as 150 denominations and groupings, they have always been marked by a highly developed sense of unity and identity of purpose, a solidarity based upon faith rather than upon organization. Although actually separated in organization, Lutherans have cooperated to further the work of their churches.

Three important groupings of Lutheran churches, the Synodical Conference (formed in 1872), the National Lutheran Council (1918), and the American Lutheran Conference (1930), have been delegated responsibility for services it was thought could be provided most effectively through collective action. Welfare services to refugees, American missions, student service, public relations, and the ministry to the armed services are some of the services achieved through cooperative action. In the administration of these services neither the conferences nor the council have exercised administrative or legislative authority over the synods or congregations for whom they were working.[39]

Since 1910 the movement towards organic unity—not mere cooperation—has gained strength and purpose, and, as the old barriers of speech and nationality disappeared, momentum. When the mergers now in process are completed, the number of Lutheran denominations will be reduced to 11, with all but 500,000 of the more than 8 million Lutherans in one of the three largest denominations. Also worthy of notice is the fact that most of the current mergers are a bringing together of churches with different national backgrounds.

Lutheran Church of America.   The merger of four Lutheran churches to create the Lutheran Church of America was effected in Detroit in June of 1962; it was a union of one large and three small denominations.

Before the merger the United Lutheran Church was the largest Lutheran Church in the United States, with a membership of 2½ million. It was considered the most liberal and progressive of the American Lutheran

---

[39] Frank S. Mead, *Handbook of Denominations* (Nashville, Tenn.: Abingdon-Cokesbury, 1951), p. 131.

churches. It dated back to the Colonial period, and was particularly strong in Pennsylvania.[40]

The United Lutheran Church began the merger process in 1958[41] when its National Convention approved the merger proposal. The sentiment was overwhelming; by a vote of 640 to 1 the convention approved and sent its recommendation to the 32 synods of the church. Early in 1961, 22 of the synods (the necessary two thirds) had ratified the merger,[42] and in 1963 the United Lutheran Church had qualified for the formal constitution of the new church.

The Augustana Lutheran Church, organized in 1860, was originally composed of Swedish stock. It had more than 630,000 members at the time of the merger proposal.

The Finnish Evangelical Lutheran Church, also known as the Suomi Synod, was organized in 1890. Its membership was 36,000.

The American Evangelical Lutheran Church, organized in 1894, represented Danish immigrant stock and had a membership of 25,000.

The three smaller denominations, like the United Lutheran Church, experienced no difficulty in securing authorization from their synods and congregations, and the resulting merger, the Lutheran Church of America, with over three million members, became the largest Lutheran denomination in the United States.

The American Lutheran Church. The 1962 merger of three other Lutheran denominations into the American Lutheran Church, with a membership of 2¼ million, made it the third largest Lutheran denomination. When the merger was proposed the Evangelical Lutheran Church (of Norwegian background) had a membership of 1,150,000, the American Lutheran Church had a membership of 1 million, and the United Evangelical Lutheran Church (of Danish background) had a membership of 67,000.[43]

Lutheran Church–Missouri Synod. The Lutheran Church–Missouri Synod was organized by Saxon immigrants in Missouri in 1847. The second largest Lutheran church, it refuses to cooperate with Lutheran churches that do not accept its confession of faith and concept of the ministry. The president of the Missouri Synod, reporting that his church would carry on conversations with other Lutheran bodies, said their aim would continue to be "unity of doctrine first, and that merger moves would be secondary."[44]

Lutherans have shown a tremendous record of organic union since the height of separatism around the Civil War period. The mergers represent an assimilation of ethnic and cultural groups. The primary differences that

---

[40] *New York Times*, June 29, 1962.
[41] *Ibid.*, October 16, 1958.
[42] *Ibid.*, May 24, 1961.
[43] *Ibid.*, April 23, 1960.
[44] *Ibid.*, June 20, 1962.

still divide the major denominations within Lutheranism are doctrinal, and informed spokesmen believe it will be some time before any of the three major denominations are able to effect new organic unions.

United Presbyterian Church

Two of the three major Presbyterian groups joined in organic union in 1958 when the Presbyterian Church in the United States of America and the United Presbyterian Church merged to become the 3 million-member United Presbyterian Church.

The mechanics followed the principles of organization of the respective churches. The presbyteries of each denomination first voted their approval. At the next annual meeting each church ratified the affirmative vote of its presbyteries, and the formal unifying conference took place in May of 1958.

The sentiment for unity was overwhelming and only two of the nearly 10,000 congregations involved, representing less than 500 members, defected during the first full year of union.[45] The merger, however, did not include the Presbyterian Church of the United States (the Southern Church), with 1 million members, or the smaller Cumberland Presbyterian Church.

Another uniting tendency was revealed in 1959 with an invitation of the United Presbyterian Church that nine sister denominations in the United States and Canada join it in seeking organic unity. The nine denominations were all members of the North American Area of World Presbyterian Alliance. The larger churches included were the United Church of Canada and the Presbyterian Church of the United States (Southern), each with 1 million members; the Evangelical and Reformed Church with 800,000 members, and the Presbyterian Church of Canada with 200,000 members. The Evangelical and Reformed Church replied that since it was already well on the way towards consolidation with the Congregational Christian Church (to become the United Church of Christ), it could act only as a constituent member of the parent body.

This interest the United Presbyterian Church had shown in organic union was immediately reciprocated in a United Church of Christ suggestion that the World Presbyterian Alliance and the International Congregational Council should meet "to explore their common heritage, work, and witness."[46]

The actions and tangible desires of these liberal Reformed Tradition churches give them a leading place in the ecumenical movement.

Unitarian Universalist Association

Two historic nontrinitarian Protestant churches had long been aware of essential sameness and identity of purpose. Neither the Unitarian nor the

---

[45] *Ibid.*, May 22, 1959.
[46] *Ibid.*, May 23, 1959.

Universalist believes in the divinity of Christ, but both accept his ethical teachings. The American Unitarian Association and the Universalist Church of America finally joined hands in May, 1961, in culmination of a movement that extended back almost a century.

The roots of the philosophy and beliefs of these religious systems are found in the Unitarian-Trinitarian controversy that wracked the Christian Church in the second and third centuries. The doctrine of the Trinity won out at the Council of Nicea and became the official dogma of the Christian Church. But the controversy broke out again with the Reformation, and Arminianism and Socinianism became new expressions of this old, one-Person concept of God (held by such people as Newton, Locke, and Milton). William Ellery Channing's famous sermon in 1819 was the incident that led to the break with the Congregational Church and its Calvinistic and Trinitarian doctrines, and to the formal organization of the American Unitarian Society in 1825.

Unitarians have no official creed; the individual is free to formulate and hold his own beliefs. However, some beliefs commonly held by Unitarians are the humanity of Jesus, the perfectibility of human character, the ultimate salvation of all souls; "heaven is a state, not a place," and salvation is by character: "in being saved from sin here, not from punishment hereafter."[47]

Universalists hold beliefs that are very similar to those of the Unitarians. The doctrine of universal salvation advanced by Christian agnostics of the second century was one of the inspirations for Universalism in America, and Hosea Ballou's *Treatise on Atonement* in 1805 became its rallying point. Universalist belief includes: the Fatherhood of God, God as eternal and all-conquering love, the spiritual leadership of Jesus, and the supreme worth of every human personality.[48]

Universalists and Unitarians had worked in close cooperation on a number of occasions before they took steps for organizational unity. In 1953 the two churches merged their religious education and youth organizations. In 1955 a joint commission was formed to work out the steps by which union might be effected. Delegates of the two churches voted for consolidation in the fall of 1959.

The plan for union then called for the approval of local congregations and fellowships. By the spring of 1960, 91 percent of Unitarian churches and fellowships and 79 percent of the Universalist societies had voted in favor of merger. The final step required a two-thirds vote of the governing assemblies of each denomination meeting separately. The necessary majorities were easily obtained: the annual meeting of the Unitarian Association approved union by a vote of 725 to 143, and the General Assembly of the Universalist Church by a vote of 365 to 65.[49]

---

[47] F. S. Mead, *op. cit.,* p. 201.
[48] *Ibid.,* p. 206.
[49] *New York Times,* October 30, 1959.

The movement to merge and to consolidate was not without some dissent and controversy, however, as the original statement left out any reference to Jesus or the Judeo-Christian tradition: "To cherish and spread the universal truth taught by the great prophets and teachers of humanity in every age and tradition, immemorially summarized in their essence as love to God and love to man."[50]

The two religious bodies would, in effect, be divorcing themselves from the main stream of Christendom with this statement. After considerable debate and discussion the purpose was rephrased to include a continuing identification with the Judeo-Christian tradition: "To cherish and spread the universal truths taught by the great prophets and teachers of humanity in every age and tradition, and immemorially summarized in the Judeo-Christian heritage as 'love to God and love to man.' "[51]

The constitution as finally adopted guaranteed the "independence and autonomy of local churches, fellowships, and associations," and that nothing in the constitution or bylaws "shall be deemed to infringe upon individual freedom of belief which is inherent in the Universalist and Unitarian heritages."[52] Thus the religious philosophy of the two liberal denominations was maintained, yet there was no "freezing" into creeds of their working principles. A way was left open to subject religious belief and practice to "new truth" and "fresh knowledge."

Even in union the Unitarian Universalist Association is one of America's smallest denominations. The 800 churches and lay fellowships of the United States, Canada, Mexico, and U.S. territories that constitute the Unitarian Universalist Association have a total membership of only 200,000.

United Church of Christ

The United Church of Christ is the first example of the organic union of Protestant denominations that represented different forms of organization: the presbyterian and the congregational. However the two denominations, the Congregational Christian and the Evangelical and Reformed, had long recognized their essential likeness and agreement in doctrine and belief. The final union on July 4, 1961, was the culmination of a process that had begun 35 years earlier.

In 1925 the Evangelical Protestant Church of North America united with the Congregationalists, decendants of the Pilgrims and Puritans who had broken away from their established church. In 1934 the Congregational Church united with the Christian Church, which was nearly as old as the Congregational and arose from a similar background. The two churches were also alike in eschewing denominational control. The union, in a simple amalgamation of names, became the Congregational Christian Church.

Also in 1934, the Evangelical Synod of North America and the Re-

---

[50] *Ibid.*, October 30, 1959.
[51] *Ibid.*, November 1, 1959.
[52] *Ibid.*, May 24, 1960.

formed Church united to become the Evangelical and Reformed Church. Both churches were originally composed of German-speaking settlers who traced their religious history back to the Reformation in Germany and Switzerland, and both used the presbyterian system of organization. (Local churches had defined relationships to regional and national synods.) The merged church retained these presbyterian features.

As early as 1940 the newly organized churches, the Evangelical and Reformed and the Congregational Christian, began discussions that 21 years later resulted in organic union as the United Church of Christ. The two churches were not only similar in belief and creed but complemented each other in national strength: the Evangelical and Reformed was strong in Pennsylvania and the Middle West, and the Congregational Christian was strong in New England, the Middle and Far West.

Twice during this period the uniting movement was delayed with recourse to legal action by a group of churches and individuals opposed to union. Shortly after both national bodies had approved a plan for union in 1949, a local Congregational church attacked the validity of the merger in the New York courts. Not until 1953 was the case finally dismissed by the highest state court, the Court of Appeals.[53]

The national bodies reaffirmed their plan of union but the proposed merger was again attacked, this time in the federal courts. Through the activities of a minority group, organized as "The League to Uphold Congregational Principles," four churches and ten individuals brought suit in 1957 to declare the proposal illegal. It was not until June, 1961, that the final attempt of the minority to defeat the merger was dismissed in court.

In the meantime both national bodies moved forward on the assumption that all legal attempts to thwart union would eventually fail. In 1959 a constitution was presented to the two churches that endeavored to reflect the Congregational Christian emphasis on the rights and autonomy of the local church, and the Evangelical and Reformed emphasis on the responsibilities of the local church, to other churches in the larger fellowship of the denomination. This was done by keeping the pyramidal synod structure of the Evangelical and Reformed Church at the national level while continuing the Congregational requirement that each local church be free to act for itself on all matters of policy and property. Thus a general synod would be integrated with churchwide boards, agencies, and regional synods, but the decisions of these bodies would be advisory only.

The proposal for union required that two thirds of the 33 synods in the Evangelical and Reformed Church and two thirds of all local congregations of the Congregational Christian Church must approve the union before it became official. In the final stages the sentiment for union proved overwhelming. By July 3, 1961, 32 of the 33 synods of the Evangelical and

---

[53] *Ibid.*, April 4, 1961.

Reformed Church had approved and 91 percent of all Congregational Christian churches had approved.[54]

The 800,000 members of the Evangelical and Reformed Church and the 1.4 million members of the Congregational Christian Church gave the new United Church of Christ more than two million members and made it the seventh largest Protestant church in the country. The only churches that were larger were the Methodist, Southern Baptist, United Presbyterian, Protestant Episcopal, United Lutheran, and the Lutheran Church–Missouri Synod churches.

The new church was not only stronger in numbers but also in terms of its program. The Congregational Board of Home Missions was noted for its work in church extension, evangelism, higher education, race relations, and for its colleges for Negroes in the South. The Evangelical and Reformed had strong programs for the care of the aged and orphans and was noted for its hospitals.

The union symbolized the things the two churches had in common, but at the same time protected the highly prized individuality and independence of the Congregationalist. The Congregational Christians were assured that the autonomy of local churches would be preserved and that congregations would not be bound by a general church creed. In short, the churches and their congregations were encouraged to unite by the prospect of making their Christian influences more widely felt, but no church had to do anything that its congregation was not willing to accept or support.

The Four-Church Proposal

The most comprehensive merger of Protestantism, one involving Anglican and Calvinist traditions, has been proposed and is being explored. It would be the most radical merger to date and would bring together such diverse denominations as the Protestant Episcopal Church, the United Church of Christ, the Methodist Church, and the United Presbyterian Church. Such a new church would claim a membership of approximately 20 million.

Organic union usually succeeds (or flounders) because of concepts of the ministry and the nature of the sacramental system, and within the denominations named above are found the two Protestant extremes in the concept of the ministry: ordination by bishops through apostolic succession, and the lay ministry. Union of these denominations would also involve assimilation of the three basic forms of church organization: the episcopal, presbyterian, and congregational.

Union would be a blending of two important and divergent traditions in the Protestant church: the traditional Catholic (or Episcopal), with its emphasis upon the sacraments and liturgy, and the Bible-centered Reformation churches (Presbyterian and United Church of Christ), with their emphasis upon preaching and the priesthood of all believers.

---

[54] *Ibid.*, July 4, 1961.

The Methodist Church is a product of both traditions. In organization and doctrine it is still closely related to the Anglican Church out of which it grew. It has bishops and its Articles of Religion (the official confession of faith) is very similar to the original confession of faith which John Wesley formulated from the Thirty-Nine Articles of the Church of England. But in mood and spirit the Methodist Church is closer to its nonliturgical sister churches; it stresses sanctification and holiness and emphasizes religion as experience.

The original proposal for union was made by Eugene Carson Blake, of the United Presbyterian Church, and strongly supported by James A. Pike, bishop of the Protestant Episcopal diocese of California. The Reverend Dr. Blake had a broad background of experience in denominational co-operation and organic union. He was a member of three top committees in the World Council of Churches and a past president and member of the general board of the National Council of Churches of Christ in America. As Stated Clerk (permanent executive officer) of the United Presbyterian Church he had played an intimate and important part in the merger of Presbyterian bodies.[55]

Bishop Pike was equally concerned with denominational cooperation and equally experienced. As bishop of the Diocese of California he had made church history by ordaining a Methodist minister to the Episcopal priesthood—so that he could serve as the chaplain to Episcopal students at Mills College! Bishop Pike also supported "open communion" in the parishes of his diocese and had experimented with presbyteries as the form of organization best adapted to the special mission needs of his jurisdiction.

Proponents of union argued the step was necessary to maintain an effective overseas mission program. The sins and shortcomings of denominationalism and provincialism, it was felt, were severely curtailing the effectiveness of the Christian witness to the non-Christian world. Union would also help to meet the growing challenge of the Roman Catholic Church. And since many communities had five or six Protestant churches for each Catholic church, union would help remedy the problem of over-churched communities. Furthermore, a precedent had been established when Anglican, Presbyterian, Methodist, and Congregational churches united in 1947 to form the Church of South India.

In order to find common ground on which divergent traditions could meet, the proposal would maintain continuity with pre- and post-Reformation forms: all bishops would be consecrated according to the Episcopal tradition of apostolic succession and by Presbyterian election. A minimal confession of faith would call for belief in the Trinity and the sacraments of baptism and communion.

The Reformation tradition would be followed in the recognition that God reveals Himself, and can reveal His will more fully, through the Holy

---

[55] *Ibid.*, December 5, 1960.

Scriptures. Church government would be democratic rather than hierarchical, for it is "the essence of Protestantism that decisions should generally be made by ordered groups of men under the guidance of the Holy Spirit rather than by a man who has personal authority to impose on others his decisions or judgments."[56] Ministers and laymen would share equally in church government, and a diversity of theological formulations, worship, and liturgy would be permitted and encouraged.

Opposition to Merger. Not all Protestants found the proposal desirable. Some Presbyterians saw it as a "sellout" to the Episcopalians, objecting not only to the establishment of an episcopacy but particularly to ordination by apostolic succession.[57] Nor were all Episcopalians confident that union was in the best interest of their principles. The high-church (or Anglo-Catholic) wing of the Protestant Episcopal Church told its fellow Episcopalians that merging with other Protestant denominations would jeopardize chances of reuniting with the Roman Catholic or Eastern Orthodox communions. The Anglo-Catholic faction also objected to the idea that ordination in another denomination is as valid as Episcopal ordination in the spirit of apostolic succession.[58]

It was also remembered that Episcopalians and Presbyterians had sought unsuccessfully to unite before—as recently as 1937 when Episcopalians had invited Presbyterians to explore the possibility of union. The Presbyterians accepted the invitation but the project was abandoned after eight years when neither denomination found itself willing to make necessary concessions.

Other Protestants thought the union incompatible with the essence of Protestantism, "a variety of religious experiences and expressions."[59] Methodist Bishop Wicke was "not convinced that denominationalism is an absolute evil. Fragmentation has always been both the bane and the genius of Protestantism, giving the individual the right to express himself in chaos and unity."[60] Another spokesman objected that because of the size of the proposed church it could be run only "on an authoritarian basis. That's fine for the Roman Catholic Church. I am deeply suspicious of the trend towards monolithic organizations. You see it in government and business. I regret to see it in religion."[61] And the president of the United Church of Christ protested church union under any circumstances: "Some differences were so essential that they could not be given up for the sake of unity."[62]

A Southern Baptist spokesman said the merger was a token of weakness

---

[56] *Time*, December 19, 1960.
[57] *New York Times*, May 18, 1961.
[58] *Ibid.*, July 7, 1961; September 11, 1961; January 22, 1962.
[59] *Ibid.*, May 18, 1961.
[60] *Time*, May 26, 1961.
[61] *Ibid.*
[62] *New York Times*, November 11, 1962, p. 41.

rather than strength and that Southern Baptists would shun it. Citing conservative theology and a zeal for evangelism as the hallmarks of Southern Baptist conviction, the spokesman evidently felt that neither conservative theology or evangelism would be adequately represented in the union.[63]

Support for Merger. Many influential Protestants supported the proposal for union because, as one leader put it,

It is a proposal of historic significance. We can no longer afford the luxury of our separate ways. Unification will be the most difficult task of the century. It is easier and more satisfying to live one's religious experience in a familiar context of old and accepted beliefs. But the church, or communion, or denomination, is never self-sufficient, and must not succumb to this illusion.[64]

In due course the official bodies of the four churches sat down to explore the possibilities of a four-way merger. Forty church leaders, clerical and lay, held the initial meeting in Washington, D.C., in April, 1962. After several days' discussion the group, reporting that the atmosphere and climate conducive to church unity had never been better, agreed to call itself The Consultation on Church Union. The Consultation then outlined differences that would have to be reconciled and problems that would have to be mastered before a union could be affected:

1. The grace of God could come to persons through the preaching of the gospel *and* the sharing of the sacraments. (Nonliturgical denominations had emphasized preaching, and the more "Catholic" denominations the sacraments.)

2. The problem of apostolic succession: the uninterrupted transmission of spiritual authority through bishops by the laying on of hands.

3. The variety of religious experiences and expressions as the essence of Protestantism.

4. Nontheological differences of opinion and attitude, such as Methodist disapproval and Episcopalian toleration of social drinking.

The leaders of the four denominations ended their unity talks in a spirit of "enthusiastic camaraderie"—after inviting three more church bodies to join in future consultations. These bodies were the International Council of Christian Churches (Disciples of Christ) with nearly 2 million members, the Evangelical United Brethren with 750,000 members, and the Polish National Catholic Church with 300,000 members. The Polish Catholic Church was organized in 1897 and had been in full communion with the Protestant Episcopal Church since 1956.[65] The Disciples and the Evangelical United Brethren accepted, and within a year the Consultation was a six- rather than a four-church affair.[66]

---

[63] *New York Times*, May 24, 1961.
[64] Bishop Wesley Lord, as reported in *Time*, May 26, 1961.
[65] *New York Times*, April 11, 1962.
[66] *Christian Century*, April 3, 1963.

Conversion

Conversion is the type of social change in which an individual abandons the attitudes and values of one religious system for those of another; he rejects one system and becomes assimilated into the values and behavior pattern of the system of his conversion choice. Statistics on conversions are neither abundant nor dependable: each faith has fairly accurate records on the number of converts from other faiths—but no comprehensive or accurate figures on the communicants and affiliates they lose. Because most converts come from the marginal or dormant members of another faith, who seldom come to the attention of the mother church or are even entered on its roster, such records are seldom as accurate or comprehensive as the records of converts gained.

A 1935 summarization by Douglass and Brunner of 48 research projects dealing with religious institutions found that as "between the major faiths, the Protestant, the Roman Catholic, and Jewish, relatively little transfer of adherents takes place." Furthermore, no one of the established denominations appeared to grow faster in cities than another because of superior ability or quality of church life. But because the growth of cities is chiefly due to rural migration, denominations that had large rural constituencies grew faster than those that did not.[67] This same relationship appears to hold true today: it appears that between Protestantism and Catholicism the losses and gains tend to equalize each other.

Denominations, then, seem to grow by "conservation" of members, and the most effective means by which a denomination may grow is simply by keeping the members it secures through birth. And the most fertile field for the accretion of adults is, accordingly, the reactivation of the dormant membership.

Catholic Converts. The number of converts is published each year in the church's annual directory of vital statistics, the national figure being the total of the various dioceses, with each diocese reporting the number of converts in each parish. The church reported 140,411 converts to Catholicism in the United States during 1960. Conversion was at the rate of one convert for every 281 members, although the rate varied markedly throughout the country and from parish to parish.

Both Fichter in New Orleans and Schuyler in New York City found the conversion rate in their parishes was well below this national average. The New Orleans parish averaged 8.75 converts per year,[68] or one for every 498 parishioners. A study of the churches in Mt. Holyoke in 1946 found there had been 36 converts to Catholicism—and 29 to Protestantism.[69] The

---

[67] H. Paul Douglass and Edmund deS. Brunner, *The Protestant Church as a Social Institution* (New York: Institute of Social and Religious Research, 1935), p. 66.

[68] J. H. Fichter, *Dynamics of a City Church* (Chicago: University of Chicago Press, 1951), p. 40.

[69] Kenneth W. Underwood, *Protestant and Catholic, Religious and Social Interaction in an Industrial Community* (Boston: Beacon Press, 1957), pp. 48–49.

rate of conversion to Catholicism was one for every 1,029 Catholics in the community although that same year, on a nationwide basis, the rate was one for every 260 members.

Protestant Converts. There are no comparable figures for the total of converts to the various Protestant churches in the United States. The various denominations have different ways of recording new members and converts. In answer to a request for information about converts to Protestantism, B. Y. Landis, editor of the *Yearbook of American Churches*, reported he knew of "no reliable reporting of the converts to Protestantism or converts away from Protestantism."[70]

Some Protestant denominations, however, put out information on converts. In 1960, for example, the United Lutheran Church claimed that over a six-year period it had gained four times as many converts from Catholicism as it had lost to Catholicism.[71] But this claim must be interpreted in light of the principle that denominational reports of conversion into the church are much more accurate than reports of losses through conversion to other faiths.

Judaism and Conversion. Traditional Judaism does not proselyte and for this reason, perhaps, Jewish leaders are increasingly resentful of aggressive tactics among some Christian churches to proselyte among Jews. Jewish groups have reacted to this invasion of their "vineyard" by themselves working among unaffiliated Jews and proselytizing among non-Jews. In a sermon on whether Judaism should try to win converts the prominent Rabbi Israel Goldstein said he was opposed to Christian and Jewish proselytizing:

I do not believe that Jews or Christians should actively attempt to wean people away from the religion which is their birthright, particularly when they are born into one of the great world religions which is both broad and universal.

The desires of religions to win converts is understandable but the methods are not always defensible. . . . Judaism welcomes all those who come voluntarily into its fold, but we must respect the religious commitments of our neighbors. It must be assumed that every one of the great world religions has within it the guidance and inspiration necessary for the good life.

It is the job of Judaism to make Jews more understanding of their religion and loyal to its practices. Let each religion preserve its own unique merits in its own unique way.[72]

Rabbi Arthur Hertzberg has warned that Protestant efforts to convert Jews to Christianity might impair one of the "chief glories" of Jewish-Christian cooperation, proving an embarrassment to both Jews and Christians and jeopardizing the image of America before the world. A revived Christian evangelism, reasserting its "great commission" to convert and hence to dissolve all other faiths, would not only embarrass America before

---

[70] In a letter from Benson Y. Landis.
[71] *New York Times*, April 13, 1960.
[72] *Ibid.*, November 16, 1958.

the world but would undercut our foreign policy and lend new fuel to the appeal of communism in the East.[73]

Rabbi Maurice Eisendrath, a leader of Reform Judaism, also criticized the efforts of Christian missionaries to convert members of the Jewish faith. He predicted the movement was doomed to fail: "Such missionary activities constitute a kind of religious imperialism, which, like colonial imperialism, is out of harmony with the modern era." Rabbi Eisendrath said that hope for peace and freedom in the world would be enhanced if Protestant, Catholic, and Jewish leaders in the United States broadened interfaith understanding and learned to "cooperate and to disagree agreeably where fundamental differences are at stake."[74]

Jewish leadership has reacted to Christian proselytizing pressure by organizing mission programs to bring unaffiliated Jews into active membership and by entering the missionary field for the first time—seeking non-Jewish converts to the principles and practices of Judaism. In 1959, when Judaism organized a drive to bring 2½ million unaffiliated Jews into synagogues, leaders had found that in spite of a great advance, probably no more than 60 percent of the American Jewish population had synagogue affiliation.

The project began with a four-day preaching mission in a Reform Temple in the Bronx, where only 50 percent of the borough's 525,000 Jews were members of a Reform, Conservative, or Orthodox synagogue. In addressing the first audience Rabbi Maurice Eisendrath spoke of the "spiritual hunger of the American people" and went on to say that:

> Reform Judaism has revitalized the passion for social justice which lies at the heart of the Jewish tradition, and it has created a living and relevant faith which draws upon the creativity of modern life in a democratic setting.
> The synagogue does not need us so much as we need the synagogue as the repository of all that we are as a holy people—its power to restore our identity and sense of belonging as Jews and the life-giving force which flows from God-given spiritual values.[75]

The audience was given kits containing pamphlets that dealt with various phases of Reform Judaism. The second evening was a special family service and the final meeting was a *Selihoth* service, which consists of special prayers and meditations before the Jewish holy days. Similar rallies were subsequently held in other parts of the city and other sections of the country.

For the first time in the history of Judaism a broadly representative body was organized to enter the mission field. Also in 1959 prominent laymen and clergymen from all three branches organized the Jewish Information Society. The preamble to the body's constitution reads:

---

73 *The Christian Century*, September 16, 1959.
74 *New York Times*, January 11, 1961.
75 *Ibid.*, October 24, 1959.

The purposes of the society are the propagation and dissemination by means of lectures, pamphlets, books and by such other means as may be deemed suitable of the views of God, man and the world as set forth in the basic tenets of Judaism and expanded and explained in the Hebrew Bible and in the Jewish tradition and to unite all the people of the world in a commitment to the one Universal God and the Brotherhood of Man.

A spokesman said that Judaism should open its doors and welcome those of "non-Jewish birth who are in accord spiritually and intellectually with the religious teachings of Judaism and who are not formally identified with any church or synagogue."[76]

Converts: Who, Why, How Effective. Although much of the data on converts is fragmentary and inclusive, it is clear that one of the most important factors in conversion is mixed marriage. Jewish sources claim approximately 2000 conversions each year and attribute most of them to mixed marriages: the convert is usually a "non-Jewish girl marrying a Jewish youth."[77] Jewish sources also report that the incidence of mixed marriage appears to be increasing.[78] The rabbis insist upon intensive study of Judaism by the prospective convert. The length of time involved in this study is seldom less than two months and frequently as much as a year. It is not easy to become a Jewish convert.

In the reverse direction, in his study of a New York City parish Schuyler reported a trickle of Jewish converts to the church but found that generally they are not amenable to conversion. And from his New Orleans parish Fichter reported that 75 percent of the converts came into the church via marriage. About half became Catholics at the time of marriage and the remainder after they had married Catholics.[79]

Reports differ in their evaluation of how good a practicing communicant the convert is. A Reform rabbi reported that the consensus of his colleagues is that converts to Judaism are more faithful adherents than the average Jews.[80] On the other hand Schuyler found that the statement "Converts make the best Catholics" was not borne out in his research; the converts in his New York City parish did not quite match the parish average in religious observance.[81]

The Mormons claimed more than 31,000 converts within and without the territorial United States during the first nine months of 1960, but reported they had no information to indicate "whether converts or those born into the Church are the best Saints."[82]

---

[76] *Ibid.,* June 27, 1959.

[77] Albert I. Gordon, *Jews in Suburbia* (Boston: Beacon Press, 1959), p. 143.

[78] *New York Times,* December 2, 1963.

[79] J. H. Fichter, *op. cit.*

[80] *New York Times,* October 4, 1959.

[81] Joseph B. Schuyler, S.J., *Northern Parish* (Chicago: University of Loyola Press, 1961), p. 231.

[82] Letter from Rulon J. Sperry, of the Missionary Committee of the Church of Jesus Christ of Latter-Day Saints, Salt Lake City, Utah, October 20, 1960.

Although most of the converts in the Mt. Holyoke study were from the unaffiliated, fundamentalist sects reported that a substantial proportion of their membership were former Catholics. Sixty percent of the membership of the Mt. Holyoke congregation of Jehovah's Witnesses were reported to be former Catholics.[83] A regional representative of Jehovah's Witnesses told the author that some of the "best members of the Watch Tower Society were former Catholics."

Summary

The present era is the highest point of toleration, cooperation, and goodwill ever reached among the three basic faiths and between religious groups in the history of the American people. The present feeling of solidarity and identity of purpose is due in part to the rising challenge of the two great foes of religion and its values and beliefs: communism and secularism.

The greatest exponents and apologists for communism have been and are enemies of institutional religion. Protestant, Catholic, and Jewish pastors alike protest the inroads that secularism has made upon the practices of their faiths.

There are other factors and forces leading to greater cooperation among faiths. The cooperation in religious matters is also a function of technological and scientific forces. No group is an island unto itself: every group must cooperate in some areas if it is to survive. The tendency towards cooperation and conformity is one outcome of an increasingly mature and technically sophisticated culture.

Numerous examples of cooperation between the three faiths can be cited. Protestants, Catholics, and Jews sit down together throughout the nation to solve community problems under the aegis of the National Council of Christians and Jews. Christians are beginning to recognize not only their debt but their affinity to Judaism. It is proper and intellectually sophisticated to speak—not of the Christian tradition—but of the "Judeo-Christian" tradition. More and more Protestant, Catholic, and Jewish Biblical scholars are sharing their researches and insights.

This is a period of intra- and inter-faith cooperation. Protestantism offers abundant occasions for intrafaith cooperation with its local councils, and the regional and state councils with which the great majority of Protestant churches affiliate and cooperate.

The expansion of the idea and the development of the work of the National Council of Churches of Christ in America has been notable, and this affiliation of like-minded Protestants also extends to the world scene. Practically the same denominations that belong to the NCCCA are also affiliated with and cooperate in the activities and program of the World Council of Churches.

---

[83] K. W. Underwood, *op. cit.*, p. 48.

American Judaism is characterized by considerable intrafaith coopera-tion. The leading divisions of Judaism are finding it desirable and practic-able to join together, in much the same fashion as the Protestants, to realize common ends and goals.

The spirit of cooperation extends to the idea of the bringing together of all professing Christians into one body and one organization. Discus-sions, for example, between Protestants and Catholics, which could con-ceivably lead to organic union of all Christian sects and denominations, is known as *dialogue*.

The most striking illustrations of the cooperative spirit are the numer-ous examples of organic union (*assimilation*). The first and most extensive merger of Protestant denominations in the contemporary period was that of the Methodists in 1939. Other recent mergers of major groups are those of the Lutherans and those of the Presbyterians. But the uniting spirit extends to the smaller denominations also: the Unitarian-Universalist merger brought two small, liberal churches together.

The United Church of Christ is the important last step in a movement towards union that has engaged its member churches for nearly forty years. The proposal seeking to unite the Episcopal, the Methodist, the Presbyterian, and the United Church of Christ would constitute the most comprehensive merger of Protestantism to date. Moreover, it would bring together some of the most diverse and varied elements of Protestantism. Except for the noninclusion of the conservative churches, this merger, if it is attained, would represent the nearest thing to an ultimate consolidation of Protestantism.

THEORETICAL OBSERVATIONS

Religious conflicts and tensions have been the subject of much interest and analysis, and the Herberg analysis particularly has attracted attention and received widespread support. Herberg maintains that the problems over which religious groups are in disagreement or conflict are not the primary cause of tensions because all issues tend to cross faith lines.[1] There are some Catholics and some Protestants on both sides of every issue. This is particularly the case in the controversy over birth control and public versus parochial education.

Two factors, the transformation of the nation from a one-religion to a three-religion country and the rapid upward mobility of Catholics, largely explain current tensions. In one generation Catholics have moved from a peripheral, foreign, low-class group to a nuclear, central, and middle-class position in the community. The effects of these structural

---

[1] Will Herberg, as consultant in Religion in American Culture Workshop, State University College, Oswego, New York, Summer of 1963.

changes are twofold: the long-range influence is to mitigate the conflict but the short-range influence is a sharpening of tensions.

Older Protestants, faced with the loss of their customary status and privileged position in the community, feel dispossessed. They complain about the "divisive" nature of the contemporary, three-religion community as compared to the traditional, Protestant-oriented community of their early years. Catholics, newly arrived in positions of power and influence—and suspicious and touchy—show signs of status anxiety and tend to over-compensate. Jews, the most secular group in the community and the most religious in the home, react, according to Herberg, in a manner that is basically schizophrenic.

There are important differentials in the kind and amount of group tensions and feelings. The more theologically sophisticated the group and the individual, the more understanding and the less tension. Protestant, Catholic, and Jewish theologians who are in close communication show a striking lack of antagonism and conflict. There is an important "generational" differential as well. The younger generations in all groups show markedly less antagonism and tension than their parents. Protestants, Catholics, and Jews, living side by side in a representative urban community, find one another surprisingly alike in attitudes and behavior. Neighbors, after all, think of each other as "our" kind of people.

Cooperation and assimilation, therefore, vary according to theological sophistication. The theologically sophisticated denominations, and groups within a given denomination, find it easier and more appropriate to co-operate with other faiths and with other groups. In general, it is the younger generation of any denomination that constitutes the basic support for the various types of ecumenical activity. As the assimilation and homogenization process continues it would appear, as Herberg maintains, that the tensions and conflicts will become less disturbing and less apparent.

Another contemporary researcher and observer is impressed by the trend towards cooperation and unity which he finds in the religious milieu, and he traces his analysis of this religious change to the "social sources of church unity." Some of the unifying trends that lead toward organic union and ecumenicalism are:[2]

1. The decreasing differences between country and city.
2. The decline of sectionalism.
3. Racial desegregation.
4. Compression of the American stratification system.
5. A lessening sense of ethnic differences.
6. The growth of a common culture as a result of mobility and mass communication.

The above factors, some more importantly than others, have some bearing upon the ecumenical movement, but whether they are causes, or effects,

---

[2] Robert Lee, *Social Sources of Church Unity* (Nashville, Tenn.: Abingdon Press, 1960).

is not clear. The union of several branches of Methodism, culminating in the organization of the Methodist Church in 1939, was the first substantial union of a denomination that was divided on sectional lines. On the other hand, sectional differences have kept the southern Presbyterian Church of the United States from uniting with its northern sister churches. The several large Baptist denominations, notably the Southern Baptist Convention, also tend to be regional churches.

Racial desegregation is probably a minor force in the ecumenical movement. Although the Methodist Church desegregated on the ideological plane, the persistence of its Central Jurisdiction (the organization of Negro Methodist churches) shows the difficulty of implementing this ideal on the parish and district levels. Problems of desegregation are major obstacles to the union of denominations that were originally separated as a result of the controversies that led to the Civil War.

A reduction in the outward symbols of class has tended to enlarge the boundaries that were formerly associated with the middle class. Cars, clothes, and even speech are no longer the important indices of class that they once were. The economic ladder is now an escalator that most of the population can ride. Where one third of the people in the 1930's could be properly described as ill-fed, ill-clothed, and ill-housed, not more than one fifth can be so identified in today's "affluent society." If a reduction of class differences contributes to denominational union, then the present situation is certainly favorable to ecumenicalism. On the other hand, Barry[3] believes that interdenominational union and cooperation are only expressions of class solidarity and identification in religious guise.

A lessening sense of ethnic differences was an important factor in the mergers of several Lutheran denominations. Swedish, Finnish, Danish, and Norwegian denominations of the Lutheran church family found it possible to unite perhaps partly because their memberships were now English-speaking. However, theological positions have been similar in every case of merger. The Lutheran Church–Missouri Synod, for example, has never seriously considered union.

The Lutheran Church–Missouri Synod holds to a strictly conservative theological position and practice, and shows no interest in becoming involved in union activities with any denomination that is not equally conservative. Factors other than language and theology nourish the separatist feeling. There have been occasions when Roman Catholic parishes have rejected all attempts by their bishop to form them into a "mixed" parish, even though their ethnic language has been replaced by English. Parish identification and parish loyalty alone have been sufficiently strong for the parishioners to hold out stubbornly against the will and plans of the bishop.

Our analysis defined secularization as the type of change in which religion adapts itself to the values and practices of society. We found it was

---

[3] David W. Barry, "The Fellowship of Class," *Cities and Churches*, Robert Lee (ed.) (Philadelphia: The Westminster Press, 1962), pp. 274–86.

one of the most important social processes, a process to which each of the basic faiths is to some degree susceptible.

Evidence of secularization was found in the rising status and changing roles of women, the growing tolerance or acceptance of drinking and smoking by religious systems that had previously considered such practices serious sins and vices. Protestantism's widespread substitution of "social ministries" for worship services (with the emphasis upon "social" rather than "ministries") is a secularistic change.

To Niebuhr[4] secularization is that state of social relations in which people are primarily occupied with immediate goals and generally indifferent to "the meaning of life." It is religion stripped of its historic content, and it is widespread and pervasive.

Having recognized the importance and widespread nature of secularization, it is equally necessary that we recognize a counter-movement. Although church membership statistics have recently dropped (for the first time since World War II), lay people are reported to be asking for more religion with more content; more religion "in depth," more services, Bible study, missions, retreats, and the like. Significantly, too, there is a corresponding lessening of interest in the more worldly, superficial aspects of religious practice.

---

[4] Reinhold Niebuhr, "Piety and Secularism in America," *Atlantic Monthly*, November, 1957.

PART V

Religion and Other Institutions

FUNCTIONAL ANALYSIS AS A CONCEPTUAL TOOL

STRUCTURAL FUNCTIONAL ANALYSIS is the device contemporary social scientists use to describe institutions, parts of institutions, and individuals in their social and societal context. Functions are the observable consequences that contribute to adjustment, adaptation, or integration of the society, the institution, or the individual under study. Dysfunctions are the consequences that decrease adaptation, stimulate maladjustment, or have disintegrative or destructive results for the group or the individual.[1]

Functions may also be conceptualized as *manifest* or *latent*.[2] Manifest functions relate to the *intended* and latent functions to the *unintended* consequences of a given act. The manifest function of church attendance, an approved and expected act of worship, is obviously religious. But church attendance may include a latent function, something that is social in nature; for example, it may provide the worshiper with a *social* experience that is pleasurable and satisfying. In any individual's value system it is quite possible that the latent, or social, function will be more important than the manifest, or religious, function.

---

[1] Robert K. Merton, "Manifest and Latent Functions: Toward the Codification of Functional Analysis in Sociology," in Merton's *Social Theory and Social Structure* (rev. ed.; Glencoe, Ill.: The Free Press, 1957), chap. 1.

[2] *Ibid.*, pp. 60–82.

The historic development of Western culture has seen many and great transfers of functions from one social institution to another. In the traditional American rural culture the family had important educational functions. Boys learned the skills and techniques of farming under the supervision and guidance of their fathers, and girls learned corresponding skills from their mothers. But this educational and vocational function is now the responsibility of educational or economic institutions.

A given item of behavior may perform several functions and, conversely, a single function may be served by disparate items of behavior. Social scientists term this phenomenon a question of functional alternates, equivalents, or substitutes. The worshiper who finds social satisfaction in church attendance illustrates a functional alternate. He could, and probably does, receive social satisfaction from other alternate social situations.

Functional analysis theory demands specification for not only the functional requisites of a given society but also for those functions which given parts of the whole are expected to perform in, and for, the society.[3] In broad outline the functional requisites of a social system (American society, let us say) are survival and the maintenance of homeostasis, or dynamic equilibrium, between the parts or "partial structures" of the system.

The functional needs of a social system are commonly detailed as follows:

1. Pattern maintenance: the need for appropriate behavior patterns and suitable attitudes to maintain the social system.

2. Tension management: the need to relieve the emotional tensions and strained relations which result when people interact.

3. Adaptation: the need to adapt to the environment, which may involve both adjusting to the environment and controlling the environment.

4. Role differentiation: in a complex society, adaptation requires division of labor with the necessary specialization of knowledge and duties.

5. Goal attainment. The achievement of the necessary and desired adaptation requires rational planning with norms for the allocation of scarce resources, for the distribution of tasks, etc.

6. Integration. The integration of the institutions within the system, calls for the settling of disputes, concern with the violation of the norms, with social control, the nature of authorities and their relationships.

Functional analysis seeks to determine the objective consequences of social action. It also seeks the consequences of parts, or partial structures, of the social system on the larger system, and is concerned with the extent to which the goals of the subsystems are achieved. Functional analysis, for example, would be concerned with the consequences of religious action for American society, for the church in general, for a specific church, and for the individuals who are engaged in religious interaction.

---

[3] This interpretation follows Eister's analysis. See Allan W. Eister, "Religious Institutions in Complex Societies," *American Sociological Review*, Vol. 22, No. 4 (August, 1957), pp. 387–92.

Social scientists are not agreed on the exact nature or the extent to which the several institutions contribute to the functional requirements of American society. Some social scientists see the family institution as the primary source for pattern maintenance and tension management, the economic institution as serving the adaptation need, the political institution the primary source for goal attainment, and the religious institution discharging mainly the integrative and supportive functions.

Other social scientists believe that each of the institutions serve several societal needs and that no one institution dominates any requirement. Religious, legal, and journalistic institutions are all said to share integrative and supportive functions.

Radin and Malinowski, the anthropologists, see religious institutions serving society by promoting solidarity through the provision of significant symbols, norms, and supernatural sanctions, and serving personalities (and society indirectly) by being ego-supportive, therapeutic, operative in the maintenance of self-confidence, in the reassertion of "life values," and in the reenforcement of collective sentiments in the face of such crises as famine or bereavement. In the classic theories of Durkheim, Malinowski, Radcliffe-Brown, and Radin,[4] and in the more recent interpretations of Nottingham,[5] Davis,[6] and Goode,[7] the emphasis is on the integrative, conserving, and supportive functions of religion.

---

[4] See Chapter I, pp. 12–13, for representative expressions of this anthropological school.

[5] Elizabeth K. Nottingham, *Religion and Society* (Garden City, N.Y.: Doubleday & Co., 1954).

[6] Kingsley Davis, *Human Society* (New York: The Macmillan Co., 1949).

[7] William J. Goode, *Religion Among the Primitives* (Glencoe, Ill.: The Free Press, 1951). (A functional analysis of certain primitive religions.)

Chapter XIII

Government and Religion

INTERACTIONS between religious and political institutions are numerous and complex. Within a relatively short time after settlement most of the colonies had an established church, the Puritan theocracy being perhaps the epitome of the union of church and state. By the time of the Revolution every colony except Rhode Island and Pennsylvania had an established church.

During the Colonial period an established church usually received public money for its support and its members usually enjoyed special privileges that nonmembers did not enjoy. Members of other churches were therefore relegated, because of church affiliation, to the status of second-class citizens.

The Revolution was a victory for religious democracy as well as for social and political democracy; it marked the beginning of the movement for the disestablishment of the privileged churches in all of the colonies, although the last vestiges of establishment were not removed in some states until the 1830's.

At the time the Constitution was framed the spirit of anti-clericalism and rationalism was strong. The people were not satisfied merely to disestablish religion by state action in the new state constitutions; they went one step further and sought to protect themselves from any possible establishment action on the part of the new national government by the inclusion of a protective clause in the Bill of Rights.

The First Amendment, accordingly, provides that Congress "shall make no law respecting the establishment of religion." This provision is now

322

interpreted as a guarantee that the federal government will observe and maintain, on every level of government, the fairly new principle of the separation of church and state. The First Amendment also provided that Congress shall make no law "prohibiting the free exercise" of religion. Thus, in time, the position was reached where no religion held a privileged position, and each religion enjoyed equal rights before the law.

Although the first ten amendments (the Bill of Rights) were limitations upon the coercive and restrictive powers of the national government, the above principles became national "standards" through judicial interpretation of the "liberty clause" of the Fourteenth Amendment. The Fourteenth Amendment provides that no state may deprive any person of life, liberty, or property without due process of law—liberty being interpreted by the Supreme Court to include various attributes of the religious freedom that had been guaranteed in the First Amendment. Thus the Constitution has evolved to protect individual freedom of religion from acts not only of the federal government but also from acts of the several states and their subdivisions.

Although people may take the principles of Separation of Church and State and Freedom of Religion for granted, in the assumption these principles are self-validating, it is not easy to determine just what constitutes a violation of the Separation or Freedom principles. A principle that was relatively simple to understand and apply in a stable, rural society often becomes greatly involved, complicated, and confused in an industrialized, dynamic urban society. Churches, therefore, despite their expressed allegiance to the principles of Separation and Freedom, find themselves very much interested and concerned in what the State does, whether it be the national, state, or local governments. The problem becomes all the more involved because of the "police powers," or the "reserved powers," which the federal Constitution grants to the states—powers that include safeguarding and supervising the health, safety, and morals of the community.

The police authority of the states cuts across the vital interests of the major churches. The Catholic Church, for instance, has an official position on marriage, divorce, birth control, and censorship, and would be very happy to have the state adopt its point of view and enforce its values through definitive legislation. Organized Protestantism, on the other hand, supports the traditional Puritan attitudes towards gambling and liquor, and is equally interested in winning the support of the state in making its values mandatory for all.

The major churches are also interested in and take stands on social welfare problems such as women and child labor, worker and old-age security, and aid to dependent children. They, in fact, find themselves so vitally interested in the innumerable things various state and local governments do that, as opinion-forming and opinion-influencing institutions, the churches often create the consensus upon which legislation is based.

American churches actively support the Separation principle only against those churches with whose values and objectives they disagree; most are guilty of seeking the cooperation of the State in making their values mandatory for the entire community.

Religion and War

A number of the churches have accused the national government of interfering with the "free exercise" of their religion in time of war.

The modern state cannot wage total war without the support of all its citizens, and only through conscription can it realize the maximum power of its citizenry.

Not until conscription is exacted, then, does the question of the conscientious objector (the c.o.) become a major political and social problem. The problem of the conscientious objector did not reach major proportions until World War I when, for the first time, a comprehensive program of conscription was adopted in the early stages of the conflict.

In the original proposals that Madison introduced for a federal Bill of Rights was the provision that "no person religiously scrupulous of bearing arms shall be compelled to render military service in person."[1] This concession to the conscientious objector was seriously debated but was later dropped before the Bill of Rights took its final form. Although the founders did not extend to those "religiously scrupulous of bearing arms" any specific constitutional exemption, this question was a problem of Congressional policy rather than constitutional law. Congress, with its power to raise and support an army, also has the power to deal with men whose religious beliefs prevent them from performing military service. Most conscientious objectors are communicants of the Historic Peace churches: the Mennonites, the Brethren, and the Friends (Quakers).

The Mennonites. The Mennonites are in the tradition of the Anabaptists who, escaping the slaughter that followed the Peasants' Revolt, accepted the leadership of Menno Simons, from whom their name was derived. They were for the most part simple country folk who refused to be drawn into or participate in the war system—but their attitude towards war was based upon their religious beliefs.

Mennonites are religiously opposed to force or coercion of any kind. They believe that the need for force indicates the absence of true fellowship; that a society that requires the use of force is a society of sin. Mennonites also believe that they are a group who, through the grace of Christ, has been lifted into that fellowship where the only basis for fellowship between true believers is that form of human relations which is consistent with the New Testament concept of love. Mennonites, therefore, exclude force in any form: physical force, suits at law, participation in the administration of justice, and, most importantly of all, war.

Mennonites do not have much hope for redeeming the world, which

---

[1] Mulford A. Sibley and Philip E. Jacob, *Conscription of Conscience* (Ithaca, N.Y.: Cornell University Press, 1952), p. 5.

they believe will always remain "within history." The community of "the saved" should neither assist in administering nor try to convert the world to Mennonite standards. They are proud to be known as "peculiar people" who live in isolated communities away from the mainstream of sinful, secular society. Conscientious objectors came from 17 different denominations of the Mennonite family of churches during World War II. Various degrees of orthodoxy, including the strictly orthodox Old Order Amish, were among the 17 denominations.

Although Mennonites will not participate in the things of the world because such action would make them partners in sin, their religion teaches that it is proper to obey the law. Therefore they are opposed to war, but not to conscription; they will submit to conscription for alternate public service duty, but not for armed forces duty.[2]

The Brethren. The Brethren are much like the Mennonites in their beliefs and attitude towards secular society. They claim no other creed than the New Testament and hold the principles of nonviolence, temperance, and the expression of religion through a good life. The Brethren were founded in Germany in 1708 by Alexander Mack. Then, attracted by tolerance and freedom, the first Brethren arrived in Pennsylvania in 1719.

The traditional Brethren pattern is much the same as the Mennonite. Brethren oppose conscription and refuse to bear arms. However some Brethren, unlike the Mennonites, will participate in worldly affairs, use their rights of citizenship to influence public opinion, and work for legislation for the reduction of armaments and the substitution of peaceful measures as the basis for international relations.

By World War II, however, a number of Brethren had given up the traditional peace position of their church and accepted duty in the armed services rather than in the Civilian Public Service. And those who accepted the traditional peace position of their church exercised the Mennonite interpretation.[3]

The Friends. Friends or Quakers are the best known of all for their pacifist stand but less numerous than either the Mennonites or the Brethren. The Friends were founded in England in the seventeenth century by George Fox. Because of their plain ways and nonconformist attitudes they were ridiculed by their neighbors and persecuted by the government.

When William Penn became a Friend he prevailed upon James II to discharge a debt the king had owed Admiral Penn, his father, in a grant of land in the New World. Although Penn founded his colony primarily for his persecuted coreligionists, he opened its doors equally to people of all religions. Persecuted groups, particularly the German sectaries, flocked to Pennsylvania in large numbers. Although among the last of the colonies to

---

[2] *Ibid.*, p. 19.
[3] *Ibid.*, p. 21.

be founded (in 1680) Pennsylvania in ten years boasted the largest population of all.

Quaker belief and behavior is derived from the doctrine of the "Inner Light," the spirit of God working within the informed mind and the sensitive conscience.[4] Interpreting the Bible in terms of this "Light," Friends are led to both individual and corporate belief and behavior because individual religious experiences and insights are subject to correction and testing by the experiences and insights of other Friends as revealed in their meetings. The authority of church government arose on this basis of corporate guidance, and individual Friends, once the sense of the meeting is discovered, are bound by its consensus. Leadership and experience, furthermore, have always played a major part in the development of consensus in local meetings and in the organization and control of the larger church.

Corporate discipline originally was both effective and arbitrary; a Friend who joined the army or navy was automatically expelled. But during the nineteenth century the movement was racked by dissent and division. A "liberal" point of view arose to challenge the "conservative" position. There were clashes between rural Friends and urban Friends, and between "liberals" and "conservatives." Urban Friends tended to be liberal, believing and behaving very much like liberal Protestants. Corporate interpretation in liberal Quakerism then gave way to individual interpretation, and the Inner Light could now justify any position: anarchism, or acceptance of war.

By World War I corporate discipline was no longer maintained in regard to war. A Friend could join the army and still remain in good standing in his meeting fellowship. During World War II Friends again took varying positions. There were, in fact, more Friends in the army and navy than conscientious objectors,[5] although some applied for noncombat status. Others chose alternative civilian service, and some would not even register.

Although Friends are pacifists, their religion teaches that it is proper and appropriate to enter into the affairs of the world and bring secular society the Friends' philosophy of love in terms both of human and world relations. Although present-day Friends may disagree on the correct attitude toward war, they agree on the need and desirability of supporting relief and welfare ventures.

During World War I the Friends were the only outside group permitted by the German government to carry on relief activities within the German lines. In the period between the wars, the American Friends Service Committee continued to carry on programs of help and succor to the victims of war and disaster. The Committee also distributed food and clothing on both sides during the Spanish Civil War, and to children in German-occupied France before the United States' entry into World War II.

---

[4] Howard H. Brinton, *Sources of the Quaker Peace Testimony* (Wallingford, Penn.: 1942), p. 16.

[5] M. A. Sibley and P. E. Jacob, *op. cit.*, p. 24.

Nowadays the Friends Service Committee sponsors a number of summer work camps and work projects for college students.

Always concerned for the unfortunate and the forgotten, their record includes the first organized protest against slavery in colonial America. Friends were also early leaders in working for prison reform. In recent years people of college age from various countries have been brought together in Friend-sponsored work camps to provide recreation and play facilities for underprivileged children. They have constructed water and sanitary facilities for Mexican villagers, and have carried on educational and recreational programs for Indians on reservations. They work as ward attendants in mental institutions—as involved, personal friends of patients.

Throughout the year Friends maintain comprehensive programs of conferences and seminars for high school and college students to promote the Friend philosophy and program of international relations. At the very moment when the national government, as a deterrent to war, was devoting its energy and resources to armaments and fallout shelters, the Friends sponsored a "Turn to Peace" drive,[6] an attempt to mobilize public opinion for their approach to international problems. Their approach was typical: reliance upon peaceful rather than forceful means as the basis for resolving international conflict. The Friends also pointed out that they had been running their own version of the Peace Corps in various overseas countries for the past 25 years.[7]

War and the Major Protestant Churches. The major Protestant churches had been largely indifferent to the war question; they supported the wars in which the country became involved on the ground that war was to be preferred to the likely alternatives. The churches were primarily concerned with individual salvation—until the coming of the Social Gospel.

The Social Gospel became a major concern, if not a preoccupation, of many Protestant churches in the decade that followed World War I. Its philosophy was that individual salvation would remain meaningless until the principles of love, as exemplified and expounded in the life and teachings of Jesus, was infused into the collective life of men. The Social Gospel concerned itself with such worldly problems as the maldistribution of wealth, the conditions of employment, substandard housing, and the like. War was the fruit of the "sin" of unchristian social organizations and intergroup relations. The churches began to recognize that pacificism could be an appropriate role for an individual Christian. They began to participate in the social process and, through education and propaganda, tried to "redeem" society from the "sin" of war.

None of the major Protestant churches, however, became formally pacifist in the sense and to the degree of the Historic Peace churches, but most of them took two positive positions. They condemned war and the war system as inconsistent with the teachings of Christ, and promised their

---

[6] American Friends Service Committee, *Turn Towards Peace*, Philadelphia, 1962.
[7] *New York Times*, May 23, 1962.

support to any member of their church who claimed a conscientious objector status on the basis of his religious beliefs and feelings.[8]

The Catholic Position. To be a pacifist and conscientious objector is a perfectly valid position within the Catholic religion, and a number of Catholics have been given a conscientious objector classification on the basis of religious convictions. Catholics can claim this exemption on two grounds: religious vocation and application of the "just war theory."

According to Catholic theory, God calls some people to an unworldly life; that is, monks and nuns who live a cloistered life of complete withdrawal and pursue the vocation of the "religious." Other men and women seek a life of limited withdrawal from the world in voluntary poverty and other acts of renunciation. It was men of such persuasion and experience who were granted exemption from military service on grounds of their vocational commitment.

A Catholic could also claim exemption as a result of his interpretation of the "just war theory," developed by such great Doctors of the Church as St. Augustine and St. Thomas Aquinas. The criteria for determining a just war are that it

1. Be declared by public authority,
2. Be waged by methods which distinguish between combatants and non-combatants,
3. Reasonably promise to achieve an improved moral situation,
4. Promise success at a cost that is not disproportionate to the expected benefits.

The individual Roman Catholic may determine whether a particular war is or is not a just war and may base his conduct upon this evaluation. Although this position was adopted by very few Catholics, the pacifist application of the theory was never condemned by the Roman Catholic hierarchy.[9]

Jehovah's Witnesses. The religious beliefs and practices of Jehovah's Witnesses (the Watchtower Bible and Tract Society) make them the most ardent and vocal resisters of military service.[10] A committed Witness is impelled to preach "the gospel" openly and freely; that is, the "good news of God's kingdom as having been established and not as yet come."[11] Because all political struggles and earthly wars are secondary to preaching, Jehovah's Witnesses reject both the pacifist and the conscientious objector roles.[12] They maintain the state has no right to conscript them for either military or alternate civilian service because their covenant with God would be thereby broken.

---

[8] M. A. Sibley and P. E. Jacob, *op. cit.,* p. 24.

[9] *Ibid.,* p. 29; John K. Ryan, *Modern War and Basic Ethics* (Milwaukee: The Bruce Publishing Co., 1940).

[10] See pp. 195–202, Chapter IX.

[11] Watchtower Bible and Tract Society, *This Good News of the Kingdom* (Brooklyn: 1954), p. 27.

[12] *Ibid.,* p. 24.

All Jehovah's Witnesses therefore object to conscription, including military and alternate civilian service, on vocational grounds: they are *ministers* of the gospel. The official position of the Watchtower Society, however, is that each individual Witness must decide for himself what implications Watchtower beliefs have for his personal action. Jehovah's Witnesses are not "nonresisters" like the Mennonites. They will use force to protect themselves and they never hesitate to use the machinery of government to gain their ends. They have no philosophy or concept of an "inner light," like the Friends, nor do they engage in relief work or activity. They, unlike other groups, have remained antagonistic to the Social Gospel.

The Selective Service and Training Act of 1940

The Selective Service Act provided conscientious objector classification for all conscripts who refused to accept combatant duty "by reason of religious training and belief." Classification I-A-O was for conscientious objectors who would not fight but who would accept noncombatant service in the army or navy. Medical Corps service was the type of duty to which most I-A-O's were assigned.

Seventh-day Adventist colleges, with medical corps training units in lieu of ROTC's, prepare their young men for this type of military service, and the largest group of noncombatants in the armed services was Seventh-day Adventists.[13]

The Selective Service Act provided further that conscientious objectors who object to noncombatant military service "shall in lieu of such induction be assigned to work of national importance under civilian direction." This was the IV-E classification. Work of national importance included soil and wildlife conservation in Civilian Public Service, work in mental and veterans hospitals, and public health work. Active ministers and clergymen, and theological students in good standing in their seminaries, were granted IV-D classification: unqualified exemption.

The law provided that conscientious objector status was to be determined by local draft boards, and about half of all claimants were granted such status. Any draftee could take his classification to a board of appeals if he was not satisfied with the decision of his local draft board.

Some 25,000 reported for I-A-O service with the army and navy, and almost 12,000 for duty at Civilian Public Service camps. Approximately 60 percent of those at C.P.S. camps came from the Historic Peace churches: Mennonites 40 percent, the Brethren 11 percent, and Friends 7 percent. The major Protestant denominations accounted for another 15 percent and the rest came from a wide variety of religions and beliefs.[14]

The great majority of Jehovah's Witnesses asked for IV-D classification, considering alternate civilian service as an invasion of their ministerial powers and usually choosing to go to prison rather than serve in the

---

[13] M. A. Sibley and P. E. Jacob, *op. cit.*, p. 36.
[14] See Table 16 (Denominational Affiliations of C.P.S. Men).

civilian camps. Approximately 5000 Witnesses served prison terms. This was more than three fourths of all who served in prison rather than co-operate with or accept military or alternate service.

The specific figures on conscientious objectors in World War II are admittedly less than the real number of objectors. Informed estimates give 100,000 as a round number for all conscientious objectors in World War II. This is only three tenths of 1 percent of the more than 34,000,000 registrants in the draft. Conscientious objectors were a qualitative rather than a quantitative problem.

TABLE 16

DENOMINATIONAL AFFILIATIONS OF CIVILIAN PUBLIC SERVICE MEN

Baptist, Northern	178	Friends, Society of	951
Baptist, Southern	45	German Baptist Brethren	157
Catholic, Roman	149	Jehovah's Witnesses	409
Christadelphians	127	Lutheran (nine synods)	108
Church of the Brethren	1,353	Mennonites	4,665
Church of Christ	199	Methodist	673
Congregational Christian	209	Presbyterian, U.S.A.	192
Disciples of Christ	78	Russian Molokan	76
Episcopal	88	Unitarians	44
Evangelical	50	Other churches & sects	1,695
Evangelical and Reformed	101	Unaffiliated	449
		Total	11,996

Source: Directory of Civilian Public Service (Washington, 1947), p. xviii ff.

The Supreme Court and the Free Exercise of Religion

Under the American political system the Supreme Court of the United States is the final arbiter of what behavior is or is not sanctioned under the "free exercise" of religion guarantee. Under its power of judicial review the Supreme Court not only may pass upon the acts of Congress and the President but also upon the acts of the states and their subdivisions.

What can and what cannot be done under the "free exercise" guarantee has been outlined by decisions of the Supreme Court. Freedom of religion does not include the right to engage in behavior that is considered immoral in terms of the cultural norms. A Mormon in the territory of Utah was ruled to be properly convicted of the crime of polygamy in spite of the fact that the Mormon religion at that time held polygamy to be right and proper.[15] Subsequently the Mormon Church declared the doctrine of polygamy no longer a religiously valid tenet. This action removed the final impediment standing in the way of statehood for the territory and Utah shortly after was admitted into the Union as an equal and sovereign state.

The free exercise of religion includes the right to maintain a parochial school. An Oregon statute was ruled unconstitutional which would have

---

[15] *Reynolds vs. United States*, 98 U.S. 145 (1878).

eliminated parochial schools by requiring public school attendance of every child of school age. As long as parochial schools meet the minimum standards of curriculum and instruction required by the state, the schools are free to teach religion and maintain order and discipline according to the rules and practices of their faith.[16]

Parochial schools are free to instruct their children in a foreign language if they desire. A Nebraska statute forbidding the teaching of any language but English in a private school was ruled a violation of the "liberty" guarantee of the Fourteenth Amendment.[17]

Jehovah's Witnesses have carried the torch for religious freedom. They have made their greatest impact upon the political system by the tenacity with which they have carried their cases through the courts to the Supreme Court and secured legal sanctions for behavior that is objectionable and annoying to so many of the people with whom they come in contact. The Witnesses look upon the flag salute as an act of idolatry in which the state and the flag are placed above God.[18]

The Witnesses began to attract widespread attention in the 1930's by their refusal to let their children salute the flag in public school exercises. Within a short time 17 states had passed laws requiring the flag salute of all children in the public schools. Any child who refused to participate in this exercise was subject to expulsion. The Witnesses refused to acquiesce in the rules and carried a case to the Supreme Court. The Court ruled that the flag salute did not constitute a violation of the free exercise of religion.[19] In effect, the Court said that the flag salute was an ordinary act of patriotism that did not in any real way interfere with freedom of religion.

The Witnesses were unwilling to accept this interpretation and shortly after carried a second case to the Supreme Court. The Court thereupon reversed its previous stand and declared that if Witnesses felt that saluting the flag was a violation of their religious beliefs they did not have to give the salute and could not be penalized for so acting.[20]

Witnesses are active and aggressive in carrying their "message" from door to door and in distributing their literature on public streets. Some municipalities required Witnesses to obtain the regular peddler's permit and license to carry on their proselytizing activities. Witnesses maintained that such requirements were an infringement on the free exercise of their right to disseminate their beliefs and doctrines.[21]

The freedom to distribute religious literature does not extend to minor children. A state child labor law may be enforced against the parents of minor children who require their children to distribute literature on the

---

[16] *Pierce vs. Society of Sisters*, 268 U.S. 510 (1925).

[17] *Meyer vs. Nebraska*, 262 U.S. 390 (1923).

[18] Watchtower Bible and Tract Society, *Make Sure of All Things* (Brooklyn, 1953), p. 172.

[19] *Minerville School District vs. Gobitis*, 310 U.S. 586 (1940).

[20] *West Virginia State Board of Education vs. Barnette*, 319 U.S. 624 (1943).

[21] *Cantwell vs. Connecticut*, 310 U.S. 296 (1940).

streets. The child cannot be exploited by the parents before the age of reason.[22]

Since 1938 the Jehovah's Witnesses have brought some 30 major cases involving religious liberty to the Supreme Court. In a majority of these they were successful and as a result the Supreme Court has granted the fullest expression of religion, extending it to religious groups that a majority of the citizens frequently find unpopular and objectionable.[23]

Freedom of religion does not give parents the right to forbid a child blood transfusions when the life of the child is at stake. Transferring of blood from the veins of one person to another as in intravenous feeding is an unscriptural practice because transfusions, according to Jehovah's Witnesses, are feeding upon blood and forbidden in several Biblical passages.[24]

A two-year-old child was brought to a hospital suffering from anemia. The attending physician said the child might die if he did not receive blood. The father refused to permit the transfusion saying it was "against the will of God to take blood." A juvenile court judge ordered the transfusion, overruling the parents, and the state supreme court upheld the lower court on appeal. In rendering a unanimous opinion the court said:

> Parents may become martyrs if they wish but they cannot make martyrs of their children before they reach the age of full and legal discretion when they can make that choice for themselves. Neither rights of religion nor rights of parenthood are beyond limitations. The right to practice religion fully does not include the liberty to expose a child to ill health or death.[25]

THE MILITARY CHAPLAINCY

The expansion of the military chaplaincy has complicated and compounded relations between religion and government. As the military chaplaincy has grown, important issues concerning the free exercise of religion (Freedom of Religion) and the establishment of religion (Separation of Church and State) have arisen.

Historical Development

A number of chaplains are known to have served with the Continental armies during the American Revolution. Washington was a deeply religious man and liked to believe that God was on the side of the patriots. He wanted chaplains with the army and gave them his full support. He looked upon chaplains and religious ministrations as the best antidote

---

[22] *Prince vs. Massachusetts*, 321 U.S. 158 (1944).

[23] Robert E. Cushman and Robert F. Cushman, *Cases in Constitutional Law* (New York: Appleton-Century-Croft, 1958), p. 729.

[24] Watchtower Bible and Tract Society, *Blood, Medicine and the Law of God* (Brooklyn, 1961), pp. 4–7.

[25] *New York Times*, March 6, 1962; and June 5, 1962.

against gambling, vice, and profanity, to which, as a deeply religious man, he was strongly opposed.[26]

Chaplains also served in both the Union and the Confederate armies, but the records are not entirely clear as to the exact status of all of the chaplains. Apparently some were regular army officers while others accompanied the troops as civilians. Chaplains discharged the usual religious functions and served as counsellors and comforters to the sick and the wounded. The noncombat character of the chaplain was not as clearly defined as today; some chaplains led troops in combat and were decorated for the valor they displayed. More than 2000 chaplains are known to have served in the Union armies at one time or another, with an average service of between 12 and 15 months, and sixty-six died while in service. More than 400 are on record as having served in the Confederate armies, and 25 died while on duty with troops.[27]

During World War I the early adoption of conscription led to the professionalization of the office of chaplain as well as the professionalization of the army. The Geneva Convention underlined the essential noncombatant character of the chaplain's office by defining the religious duties of the office and prescribed the behavior required to maintain a noncombatant status.

Some 2200 chaplains were appointed during the war. In addition, 150 were on duty with the regular army or the National Guard when the war broke out. A chaplain's school was organized to orient and prepare the men for the effective discharge of their responsibilities as officers as well as clergymen within the military organization. Twenty-three died while in service, 11 of whom were battle casualties. A Chief of Chaplains office was created in 1920 to recruit chaplains and to administer and supervise their work within the armed services.[28]

In the expansion of the army it was early decided that while the state had the right to conscript a man for military service it did not have the right to conscript his religion. A man should not lose the right to enjoy the benefits of his own religion upon induction into the armed services. Ideally this would require that every soldier should enjoy the ministrations of a pastor of his own denomination, but the great variety of American denominations makes it impossible to meet this ideal.

World War II

The military planners decided there should be a chaplain for every 1000 soldiers. The chaplains were recruited into the armed services according to their denominational affiliations, each denomination being granted a quota based upon the percent its members represented among the churches as

---

[26] Roy J. Honeywell, *Chaplains of the United States Army* (Washington, D.C.: Office of Chief of Chaplains, Department of the Army, 1958), chap. 3–4.

[27] *Ibid.*, chap. 6–8.

[28] *Ibid.*, chap. 10–12.

indicated in the religious census of 1936.[29] Not every denomination was able to meet its quota. In some cases this failure was due to the difficulty its clergymen had in meeting the standards established for the chaplaincy. The Army ruled that a chaplain must:

TABLE 17
CHAPLAINS
(BY DENOMINATIONAL AFFILIATION)

	Quota Percent	Quota Number	On Duty 2 Sept., '45
Roman Catholic	30.46	2,589	2,278
Methodist	11.00	935	1,200
Baptist, South	8.89	756	947
Baptist, Colored	7.20	612	84
Jewish	3.70	315	243
Presbyterian, U.S.A.	3.65	310	426
Protestant Episcopal	2.92	248	298
Baptist, North	2.66	226	412
Disciples of Christ	2.34	199	387
Lutheran, Missouri Synod	2.20	187	215
United Lutheran	2.13	181 ⎫	374
American Lutheran	2.11	179 ⎭	
Congregational Christian	2.00	170	305
Evangelical and Reformed	1.37	116	69
Latter-Day Saints	1.07	91	34
African Methodist Episcopal	.90	77	73
Presbyterian, U.S.	.88	75	138
United Brethren	.73	62	60
African M.E. Zion	.73	62	18
Churches of Christ	.63	54	30
Christian Science	.57	48	24
Colored Methodist Episcopal	.46	39	10
Evangelical	.42	36	46
Reformed in America	.37	31	43
United Presbyterian	.35	30	51
Greek Orthodox	.30	25	3
Conservative Brethren	.30	25	1
Assemblies of God	.29	25	34
Seventh-Day Adventists	.27	23	2
Church of the Nazarene	.27	23	42
American Baptist	.24	20	0*
Latter-Day Saints, Reorganized	.19	16	1
Federated Churches	.18	15	0
Christian Reformed	.16	14	17
Free Will Baptist	.16	14	0*
Salvation Army	.15	13	28
Primitive Baptists	.14	12	1
Russian Orthodox	.14	12	0
Friends	.14	12	3
Unitarian	.12	10	23
Others	7.21	613	221
Totals	100.0	8,500	8,141

Source: Roy J. Honeywell, *Chaplains of the United States Army*, Washington, D.C.: Office of the Chief of Chaplains, 1958, p. 215.

* Included among other Baptists.

[29] See Table 17.

1. Be a male citizen.
2. Between the ages of 23 and 45.
3. Ordained and duly accredited by and in good standing with some church which holds an apportionment of chaplains' appointments.
4. A graduate of both a four-year college and a three-year seminary course.
5. Actively engaged in the ministry and with three years of experience.[30]

The peace churches were unable and unwilling to meet their quotas. The relatively few ministers who could be found to serve did so reluctantly and with reservations. The fundamentalist churches and the Negro churches were under-represented. The military standards for qualification worked against the churches that were served by a lay clergy as lay clergy could not meet the three-year seminary requirement. This rule was later modified to include the "equivalent" of three years of seminary. As a result of this modification the military services permitted some outstanding religious leaders to be commissioned as chaplains, men who had shown by their experience and record that they were unusually competent and effective as lay ministers even though they did not have the benefit of formal theological training.

The Mormon, Christian Science, and Quaker churches were able to nominate ministers who possessed the "equivalent" in terms of considerable graduate education although not of a theological nature. Jehovah's Witnesses were neither willing nor able to qualify in terms of the criteria established by the chaplaincy office and the military services. All in all the military services went to great efforts to secure a panel of chaplains that would be representative of all the American denominations, and they made commendable progress towards the achievement of this goal.

Cooperation.   The chaplaincy has brought the different faiths and denominations within the Protestant and Jewish faiths in closer contact with each other. The several ways in which they come in contact with each other tend to emphasize the larger things that religions have in common.

The nature of the military organization and military camps calls for an "all-denominational" chapel. The typical chapel includes a communion rail, pulpit, lectern, ark, and movable altar that can be adjusted to the symbols of any faith. The rules require that sectarian pictures or symbols be removed or draped when not in use.[31] Thus it is possible to have a Protestant service at 9:00, a Catholic service at 10:00, and a Jewish service at 11:00. The schedule requires that each service finish on time so as not to interfere with the preparation of the chapel for the following service.

Protestant chaplains, however, have a particular problem; it is impossible to offer a service that will meet the needs of all Protestants. It is particularly difficult to offer a service that will satisfy both liberal Protestants and conservative Protestants. On most bases a general nonsectarian Protestant service is given at the Sunday morning service hour. Those denomi-

---

[30] R. J. Honeywell, *op. cit.,* p. 221.
[31] *Ibid.,* p. 229.

nations that are not satisfied with this service, which is a typically "low" service, are free to offer their particular service at another hour. On a large base the liturgical denominations, the Episcopalians and the Lutherans, and such conservative denominations as the Southern Baptist and the Lutheran Church–Missouri Synod, usually have a special service at some other hour. This may be in the post chapel, or it may be in a church of the denomination in a nearby civilian community.

On large bases it is customary to have Protestant chaplains take turns presiding over the nonsectarian service. Several years ago in the large military community at Frankfort, Germany, the author found that both a Mormon chaplain and a Missouri Synod Lutheran chaplain would from time to time preside over the general service, and in both instances would (at an earlier or later hour in the day) lead a service of their own denomination. They had no difficulty either practically or theologically in meeting this responsibility when their turn came up.

A chaplain may find himself called upon to meet the religious needs of personnel who are not only of a different denomination but of a different faith. This is particularly true at small posts and installations and in the field. The official records include the announcement of the Catholic chaplain at a small post, the only chaplain assigned because of the number of troops, who would regularly appear at the Saturday night movie and announce:

> Tomorrow is Sunday. I am a Catholic chaplain, but I will do my darndest to give the Protestants a Protestant service at 9:00 o'clock, the Jews a Jewish service at 10:00 o'clock, and the Catholics a Catholic service at 11:00 o'clock.[32]

A chaplain is not infrequently called upon to give religious comfort to the sick and perform funeral rites for the dead of faiths other than his own. The common sacrificial death of the four chaplains from different denominations on the sinking of the *Dorchester* in World War II is merely a dramatic illustration of how the military service brings religious faiths together in a common experience.

The Military Chaplaincy Office needs chaplains who can get along with their fellow chaplains of different faiths. At the School for Chaplains at Harvard, it was the practice of the school to assign a Catholic, a Jew, a liturgical Protestant, and an Evangelical Protestant chaplain-in-training to the same quarters.

Problems and Conflicts. The quota system for the selection of chaplains works against needs and desires of the small churches. Men are assigned to military units without regard to their religious affiliation. It is difficult to get enough men together for a religious service for the smaller denominations. The Office of Chaplaincy generally assigns chaplains of the Mormon, the Christian Science, the Quaker, the Jewish, and the conservative Protestant denominations on the divisional level. Soldiers of these denomi-

---

[32] *Ibid.*, p. 288.

nations then have some opportunity of seeking out a chaplain of their faith for counsel and guidance, and enough can be brought together to justify a corporative service.

During World War II an all-Greek battalion was formed. An attempt to secure a suitable Eastern Orthodox chaplain was made without success. The Nisei battalion made a phenomenal record of success and indomitable resistance. An attempt was made to secure a Buddhist chaplain to serve the religious needs of this battalion without success.

Roles of the Chaplain. Counseling is an important part of the work of the chaplain. Soldiers go to the chaplain not only for advice on personal and family problems but also for problems that arise out of their military experience. Commanding officers frequently seek the advice of the chaplain concerning individual soldiers, and seldom go contrary to a chaplain's recommendation. A chaplain's effectiveness is directly related to his personal characteristics. It is not uncommon for a chaplain to be the most influential officer in the regiment.

Formerly chaplains were frequently assigned such morale duties as recreation or health officers. This is no longer permitted. The religious duties of a chaplain are enumerated and he can be assigned only these duties. Individual chaplains may voluntarily assume recreation and even health functions when they think that such work with the men will increase their effectiveness as spiritual advisors.

Chaplains stationed at large military centers, and particularly in Europe, serve not only military personnel but often dependent families of the military and of civilians working for the military services. Many chaplains in such situations function like a regular parish pastor and organize many of the parish organizations that are found in a civilian community. The author spent a year as a civilian working for the military services stationed on three large bases in Germany. He became acquainted with several chaplains who had developed substantial and comprehensive patterns of social ministeries and parish services. There was a Catholic chaplain who had organized a married couples club, a Catholic Youth group, led a discussion group on topics of interest to Catholics, and gave religious instruction classes to Catholic children in the dependent school. A Protestant chaplain was known as a particularly good preacher and had a large following of both soldiers and dependent families at his services. He supervised a large and comprehensive Sunday School which met in the adjoining dependent school. He was familiar with the problems of dependent families living overseas within a military enclave, and spent a great deal of time in family counselling.

Role Conflicts of Military Chaplains. The military chaplain is both an officer and a clergyman. The roles that are expected of an officer are not always in harmony with the roles expected of a clergyman. A study of the conflicting roles of a sample of military chaplains shows the various ways in which they meet the conflicting claims of the military and the religious institutions upon their loyalties. The sample included chaplains of each of the three basic faiths and an equal representation from the Army, the Air Force, and the Navy. Seventeen different denominations were included in the Protestant sample.[33]

According to the findings of this study clergymen are motivated to enter the military chaplaincy more through patriotism than through religion. The chaplain is a clergyman who performs religious functions with the status, privileges, and responsibilities of an officer. The great majority (90 percent) felt that they were accepted as officers by their fellow officers, and most reported they were able to adjust to the authority of the chain of command, although approximately half said there had been occasions when they had some difficulty with their commanding officer in discharging their religious duties. However, they seldom or never went around or over their commanding officer when differences arose over how they should discharge their religious duties.

Enlisted men are the major group with whom the chaplain deals; he is faced with the problem of meeting the men as a clergyman and not letting his officer status interfere with the spiritual advisor relationship. Chaplains emphasize the counseling relationship and circumvent the officer relationship by having the men approach them informally, calling them "chaplain" rather than "sir." Chaplains ignore the general rule that officers are not to fraternize with the enlisted men. As staff officers chaplains do not have command of troops and can more easily move among the men on a friendly and fraternal basis.

Evangelism is not listed among the duties of the chaplain. There is a gentlemen's agreement that chaplains are not to proselyte. However, only 10 percent reported they had never baptized military personnel. The military chaplaincy is in fact a state-supported religious institution, but chaplains do not see in it a violation of the principle of separation of church and state. They point to the wide denominational representation among the chaplains and the complete freedom that the chaplain has to serve individual members of his faith. The total situation is, they find, more representative of the "free exercise" than of the "establishment" of religion.

The conflicting claims of idealistic religion and war is a major problem besetting the chaplain's conscience. About one fifth feel the conflict is so great that it cannot be resolved, but the majority finds it possible to resolve the conflict in a variety of ways. Many find that the war in question meets their concept of a "just war." Others find there is no conflict because the individual cannot be held responsible for the acts of the nation, the necessity for self defense obviates the antiviolence teachings of religion, and the philosophy of pacifism does not apply in the nuclear age.

---

[33] Waldo W. Burchard, "Role, Conflicts of Military Chaplains," *American Sociological Review*, October 1954, pp. 528–35.

In general, the study found that chaplains met the problem of role conflict by compartmentalization. In religious situations the chaplain is guided by religious values; in other situations by the military or the secular value.

OPPOSITION TO CAPITAL PUNISHMENT

Organized religion has shown an increasing concern with and opposition to the power of the state to impose the death penalty. Denominations representing well over half of America's Protestants and Jews have gone on record as being officially opposed to capital punishment. Although the Catholic Church has taken no official stand on the question, leading Catholic clergymen and laymen have led the fight to oppose capital punishment.

The Friends were among the first of the American churches to oppose capital punishment. Friends are still actively fighting the death sentence but have been joined by a number of Protestant and Jewish groups. The Friends maintain a continuing study of the problem and periodically issue a report giving the position of the various churches on capital punishment.

An analysis of 20 different reports and resolutions of the various churches protesting capital punishment shows that the reasons for abolition can be summarized under three heads: *retributive justice, deterrence,* and *redemptive rehabilitation.*

Retributive Justice. Punishment as retribution or retaliation is primitive and archaic. This philosophy was best expressed in the Code of Hammurabi as an "eye for an eye and a tooth for a tooth." This concept of punishment is contrary to the New Testament doctrine and philosophy of love.

Jewish circles point out that Judaism has always regarded capital punishment as repugnant to its tradition and to the most noble instincts of man. Even where the Bible prescribes such a punishment, Jewish rabbinic and ethical tradition have so interpreted this sanction as to make its application virtually impossible. Man has been created in God's image and, as such, is endowed with sanctity. His life is God-given and ends by the grace of God. No man individually or group of men collectively may take the life of another in what may seem to be just retribution to society for a heinous crime.[34]

Court decisions, because of the fallibility of individuals making them, are not without the possibility of error. In affixing any other form of penalty, an error of judgment is in a measure retrievable. This is not true of capital punishment, in which there is always a possibility that an innocent person may be put to death. Another factor which diminishes the possibility of the death penalty being an instrument of justice is the frequency with which it is evaded by those having wealth and influence,

---

[34] Friends Committee on Social Order, *What Do the Churches Say on Capital Punishment?* (West Hartford, Conn.: 1961).

while it falls disproportionately upon the poor, friendless, and those of minority races.

Deterrence. The argument that capital punishment deters others from committing homicide and other serious crimes is not borne out by the facts. Repeated studies have shown that this assumption is without foundation. In the nine states of the United States which have abolished capital punishment, the homicide rate is not greater, and in some cases lower, than in the states which retain it. The most effective deterrent is not the severity, but the swiftness and certainty of punishment. Some criminals have been set free in American society because juries have hesitated to bring in a verdict of guilty in cases where the penalty is capital punishment.

Redemptive Rehabilitation. In capital punishment the churches see man assuming God's prerogative. The death penalty makes rehabilitation through redemptive love impossible. Christians redeem through sacrificial love. A Christian view of punishment must look beyond correction to redemption. It is basic to Christian faith that redemption by the grace of God is open to every repentant sinner and that it is the duty of every Christian to bring to others by every available means the challenge and opportunity to a new and better life. Whatever may lie beyond earthly existence, to curtail life here by human edict is to cut off this possibility. For all these reasons, only God has the right to terminate life.

Death to one man as a deterrent to others is wrong. It is using man as a means to other men's ends which is contrary to Christian doctrine.

Every citizen has a personal responsibility for the corporate acts of the State. Since the individual cannot take life himself, neither can it be taken in his name.

Capital punishment is wrong because it has brutalizing and other adverse effects upon those who administer and execute the penalty, and upon society as well. The community, judge, jury, attorneys, prison staff, and relatives all suffer in some way or another.

As conservative institutions the major denominations have traditionally supported the state in imposing the death penalty for homicide and a few other particularly serious crimes. Currently, however, most of the major denominations have gone on record as opposed to capital punishment. In the nine states that have abolished capital punishment, and in those states that are considering its abolition, it appears that no small part of the public opinion against capital punishment has been created through the activities and influence of the churches.

SUNDAY CLOSING LAWS

Sunday closing laws and ordinances have become sources of controversy involving the question of the free exercise of religion in a number of states. Religions that consider Saturday as the true Sabbath find that such "blue laws" interfere with the free exercise of their religion, favor one faith over another, and are therefore both discriminatory and unconstitutional.

Jews are the chief sufferers but Seventh-day Adventists and Seventh-day Baptists have protested the restrictive legislation of several states. Orthodox Jews, who observe the Jewish Sabbath by closing their stores from sundown Friday to sundown Saturday, then remain open on Sunday, are forced to celebrate "two Sundays," if Sunday closing laws are enforced against them. Jewish spokesmen maintain that forcing Jews to observe Sunday as a day of rest is the same as compelling Jews to recognize Christianity.[35]

In Pennsylvania, the ban against Sunday sales of certain articles carried fines ranging up to $100 per article. Opponents found this penalty particularly onerous and discriminatory.[36] A New Jersey law forbade the sale of clothing, home and office furnishings, appliances, and building materials. According to the sponsors this regulation was aimed primarily at highway stores and discount houses that are open seven days a week. Jewish business men maintained that this regulation discriminated against their religion.[37]

The controversy over Sunday closing laws was especially heated in New York. The governor promised Jewish interests to use his influence to modify the law, but found the issue complex and complicated. Secular as well as religious interests were involved and concerned. Catholic interests took a stand opposing legalization of anything beyond "necessary and essential business" on Sunday. The State Council of Churches, speaking for the Protestants, supported the general principle of allowing persons observing a Sabbath other than Sunday to conduct business on Sunday.[38] The legislature of New York state met the problem by giving New York City authority to make and approve a "Fair Sabbath" law. New York City took action on this grant of power and passed a local law permitting small family-operated businesses to remain open on Sunday if the proprietor observes another Sabbath.[39]

Dissenting faiths and denominations argue that Sunday closing laws violate not only freedom of religion but, since legislation that enforces observance of the Christian Sunday is in effect providing for the establishment of religion, also the separation of church and state. A number of states have adopted permissive legislation.[40] It seems only a question of time before "blue law" legislation will have given way to the complete secularization of the Christian Sunday.

---

[35] New York Times, May 20, 1962.
[36] Ibid., October 14, 1959.
[37] Ibid., June 6, 1960.
[38] Ibid., March 7, 1962.
[39] Ibid., September 18, 1963.
[40] Ibid., March 15, 1962.

THE TAX EXEMPT PRIVILEGE

Tax exemption for property devoted to religious or charitable uses is a principle that far antedates the federal Constitution; it is a principle that has its roots in feudal theory and feudal practice. Under feudalism, society was divided into three estates; the clergy, the nobility, and the peasantry. In theory each estate performed certain services for society and enjoyed certain privileges and rights in return. The clergy, the first estate, not only maintained the religious institutions but further served the community by assuming responsibility for education and for welfare. In return for these services, the first estate not only enjoyed the privilege of special taxes, but also certain exemptions; they were not required to perform special duties or to pay the various taxes that were required of the peasantry (the third estate).

Tax exemption was brought to America as an appropriate and necessary attribute of religion. At the time of the Constitution the free exercise of religion included the tax exempt privilege. This privilege was not considered an establishment of religion because it was equally open to all religions.

Times are changing. Among the changes are the widely extended programs of services which the churches now offer. Churches are carrying on missionary activities, vacation Bible schools, youth programs, counselling services, and many other activities. The Catholic Church is doing all of these and in addition is attempting to offer a full program of education from the kindergarten to the graduate school. The search for additional funds to finance the expanded functions has led churches into a wide number of business activities.

American churches are involved in such varied business enterprises as parking lots, restaurants, apartment houses, a coal mine, a supermarket, ranches, and a cheese and dairy business.[41] Opinion differs on the wisdom or desirability of the growing wealth of the churches. Some feel that unrelated church activities have got out of hand, especially if the activities pay no taxes and have an advantage over commercial competitors. This opinion also argues that the states and federal government, ever in need of additional income, are giving it away unnecessarily by property and income tax exemptions for activities unrelated to a church's primary function.

The opposing point of view maintains that church institutions such as orphanages, hospitals, and schools, besides being nonprofit, also provide a public service which would otherwise have to be discharged by the state. Although the churches do not pay taxes on their unrelated income, they actually save the taxpayer money in the long run.

Whatever the merits of the arguments for a continuation of the tax

---

[41] Jules Loh, "Can Churches Do Business?" Rochester, N.Y., *Times-Union*, March 3, 1962.

exempt principle in this expanding field, the government is taking actions and the courts are rendering decisions that require church-operated businesses to submit to kinds and degrees of taxation. For example, the federal government will exempt from income taxation religious orders or organizations that are an integral part of a church. However, members of an order must perform sacerdotal functions or conduct religious worship to meet this test of an "integral part."

The Christian Brothers are a teaching order of men who wear clerical garb, but they are not priests and do not perform sacerdotal functions. The government held that since the order was not an integral part of a church it must pay taxes on the income of its business activities. It must do this even though all the returns from the wine-making industry of the Christian Brothers were devoted to the support of several schools which the order maintains.[42]

A printing plant, laundry, and dairy operated by church-related Harding College of Arkansas was not tax exempt according to the ruling of the Arkansas State Supreme Court. The college claimed exemption because of its status as a nonprofit corporation, and the college officials said the money earned was used to operate the school, but the state supreme court ruled that the businesses were not tax exempt.[43]

The Church of Jesus Christ of Latter-Day Saints (Mormons) is deeply involved in business enterprises. Its business activities include a sugar company, a publishing business, an insurance company, a 300,000 cattle business in Georgia and Florida, some hotels, a bookstore, and a real estate holding company. The Church owns a coal mine, 66,000 acres of farmland, citrus orchards, poultry farms, dairies, and feed lots simply to keep up its stockpiles of food at 140 storehouses across the country. The Mormons claim they have always paid the federal, state, and local taxes on any profits from each of their wholly or partially owned businesses.[44]

The extension of the religious institution into the economic area, it would appear, will continue to receive close attention and regulation by the political authority. Freedom of religion does not include the right to act in the economic sphere without the control and restraint to which all other economic institutions must submit.

POLITICAL LEADERSHIP AND RELIGIOUS AFFILIATION

The religious affiliation of public servants is always of interest and concern. Does the religious affiliation of a candidate influence the choice of the individual voter? How does the religious affiliation of an elected offi-

---

[42] Ibid.
[43] New York Times, March 21, 1962.
[44] J. Loh, op. cit.

cial affect his political acts and decisions? Does the president, for example, administer the powers of his office in terms of the values and goals of his religion? Does the legislator vote his religion?

The Presidency

The religious affiliations of the presidents have been varied but, with the exception of John F. Kennedy, all have been members of or shown a preference for some branch of Protestant Christianity.[45] The religious backgrounds of the presidents were as follows:

> Baptist: Harding, Truman
> Congregational: Coolidge
> Catholic: Kennedy
> Disciples of Christ: Garfield
> Episcopal: Washington, Madison, Monroe, William Henry Harrison, Tyler, Taylor, Pierce, Arthur, Franklin Roosevelt
> Friends: Hoover
> Methodist: Polk, Johnson, Grant, McKinley
> Presbyterian: Jackson, Buchanan, Cleveland, Benjamin Harrison, Wilson, Eisenhower
> Unitarian: John Adams, John Quincy Adams, Fillmore, Taft
> Dutch Reformed: Theodore Roosevelt

Jefferson was a member of the Episcopal Church but in later life became a deist, describing himself as "a disciple of the doctrines of Jesus" and commending Unitarianism. Lincoln attended Presbyterian services in Washington but was not a member. Hayes attended the Methodist Church but never joined it.

The presidents have reflected the predominating influence of Protestantism in the culture. Episcopalianism has claimed the allegiance of the greatest number of presidents, however, although seven of the total of nine lived during the pre–Civil War period. Since the Civil War, Presbyterianism has claimed the allegiance of the greatest number of presidential incumbents. Two of the most outstanding presidents, Jefferson and Lincoln, were nondenominational Christians.

In general the presidents seem to have been oriented towards liberal Protestantism and personally rather than denominationally religious. However, none of them has been sufficiently nonreligious to refuse to take the oath of office on the Bible. Apparently the American people feel that a sympathy toward and an affiliation with religion is a desirable and necessary qualification for high office.

Congress

Only five of the 534 members of the 87th Congress listed themselves as having no religious preference or affiliation.[46] At the same time there is no comprehensive information on how active the various congressmen are in the religious groups for which they expressed a preference. Some are

---

[45] New York World-Telegram, *World Almanac, 1961*, New York, p. 226.
[46] Table 18.

known to be prominent lay leaders in their respective churches and a few are ordained clergymen, but the religious identification of some is quite nominal. As a group they are probably not more or no less religious than

TABLE 18

RELIGIOUS IDENTIFICATION OF 87TH CONGRESS

	No.	Democrats	Republicans
Roman Catholic	98	82	16
Methodist	95	59	36
Presbyterian	73	28	45
Baptist	66	53	13
Episcopal	66	34	32
Congregational Christian	24	5	21
"Protestant"	23	12	11
Jewish	13	11	2
Lutheran	21	6	15
Disciples of Christ	13	10	3
Unitarian	6	2	4
Mormons	6	5	1
Not Listed	5	2	3
Christian Science	4	2	2
Church of Christ	4	4	0
Society of Friends	2	1	1
Evangelican Free Church	2	0	2
Universalists	2	1	1
Evangelical and Reform	2	1	1
Apostolic Christian	1	0	1
Brethren in Christ	1	0	1
Mormons (Reorganized)	1	0	1
Cumberland Presbyterian	1	1	0
Evangelical United Brethren	1	0	1
Schwenkfelder	1	0	1
Sikh	1	1	0
Seventh-Day Baptist	1	1	0
Reformed Church	1	0	1

Source: "A Congressional Directory to Aid in Legislative Action: The Eighty-Seventh Congress," National Council of Churches of Christ in America.

any other representative secular group. Religious affiliation is a desirable political asset within the cultural milieu. It would be politically disastrous in most political jurisdictions to oppose a religion—just about as serious as opposing democracy or mother love.

All three basic faiths are represented in Congress.[47] Although Catholics and Jews now have substantial representation in Congress, Protestants are still the overwhelming majority, however, and enjoy a representation considerably out of proportion to their numbers. Both Catholics and Jews are under-represented to the extent that each group has only about one half the numbers it would have if membership was secured in proportion to the total religious population of the country.

Even within the Protestant group of denominations there is a considerable disproportionate representation of congressmen. Some denominations

---

[47] Table 20.

are over-represented, some under-represented, and many small denominations are not represented at all.[48] Baptists and Lutherans are under-represented. Methodists and the Disciples of Christ have almost twice as many
members sitting in Congress as their numbers would suggest. The Presbyterians, the Episcopalians, and the United Church of Christ (Congregational-Christian and Evangelical and Reformed) have from two and one-
half to four times more members than a proportionate representation
would require.

TABLE 19
RELIGIOUS AFFILIATION OF CONGRESSMEN

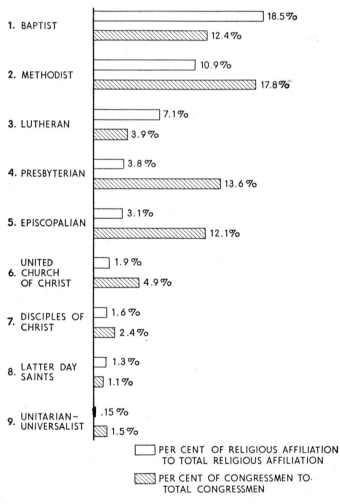

1. BAPTIST — 18.5% / 12.4%
2. METHODIST — 10.9% / 17.8%
3. LUTHERAN — 7.1% / 3.9%
4. PRESBYTERIAN — 3.8% / 13.6%
5. EPISCOPALIAN — 3.1% / 12.1%
6. UNITED CHURCH OF CHRIST — 1.9% / 4.9%
7. DISCIPLES OF CHRIST — 1.6% / 2.4%
8. LATTER DAY SAINTS — 1.3% / 1.1%
9. UNITARIAN-UNIVERSALIST — .15% / 1.5%

PER CENT OF RELIGIOUS AFFILIATION
TO TOTAL RELIGIOUS AFFILIATION

PER CENT OF CONGRESSMEN TO
TOTAL CONGRESSMEN

Congressional Directory to Aid in Legislative Action: The Eighty-Seventh Congress, National
Council of Churches of Christ in America.

---

[48] Table 19.

TABLE 20

RELIGIOUS AFFILIATION OF PROTESTANT CONGRESSMEN

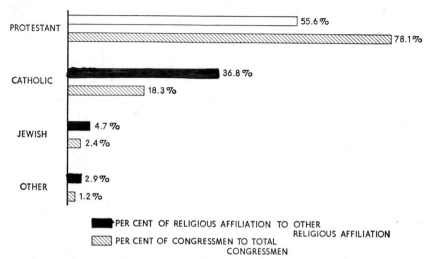

PROTESTANT — 55.6%
78.1%

CATHOLIC — 36.8%
18.3%

JEWISH — 4.7%
2.4%

OTHER — 2.9%
1.2%

■ PER CENT OF RELIGIOUS AFFILIATION TO OTHER RELIGIOUS AFFILIATION

▨ PER CENT OF CONGRESSMEN TO TOTAL CONGRESSMEN

The Unitarian Universalist Church can boast the greatest over-representation. With only fifteen-hundredth of 1 percent of the religious population of the country, they have ten times as much representation.

Religious affiliation and religious concerns are only two of the many factors that may influence the voting behavior of the electorate. Even if the religious factor were to determine the voting behavior of a group of voters, they would have to be in a plurality in any given district in order to secure the election of their man.

In states where all three faiths have strong minority representation the two major parties usually remove religion from politics by seeing to it that their respective tickets for the important state and national offices include candidates representing each of the basic faiths. In this way each party seeks to protect itself from the accusation of being partial to some faiths and prejudiced against others. Such a policy also tends to split the religious factor that might otherwise produce a religious vote.

The religious affiliation of congressmen may reflect social class status. The argument here would be that voters tend to select candidates from the upper social strata and that religious affiliation is, in most cases, incidental. Social class orientation of churches varies from community to community and from religion to religion. In some communities the Methodist or the Baptist may be the most aristocratic and influential Protestant church in the community. Traditionally, however, the Episcopal, the Presbyterian, and the Congregational churches have included a higher proportion of the educated, the successful, and the influential members of the community. These are representative values to which the typical American aspires, and by which he is impressed. It is more a vote for the American way of life than for a religious group or a religious doctrine.

The 1960 Campaign. Although the 1960 campaign broke the "only-a-Protestant-can-win-the-Presidency" belief, Kennedy had to contend with the traditional anti-Catholic bias. This proved to be particularly strong in some parts of the country. Although Kennedy won, the postelection report showed that the religious question almost caused his defeat in the closing days of the campaign.

The Fair Campaign Practices Committee is a nonpartisan, tax exempt organization endorsed by the two major national parties. During each congressional or presidential campaign it receives complaints on violations of the Fair Campaign Practices Code, accepted by both parties. After each campaign the Committee compiles a "smear study" as an evaluation of the level of the campaign.

The Committee found that most of the religious literature in the 1960 campaign was directed against Kennedy.[49] This literature came close to defeating Kennedy. A poll showed that Kennedy lost 1 million to 1½ million votes in the last three weeks of the campaign largely because of two factors: a heavy last-minute distribution of anti-Catholic literature, and adverse reaction among Protestants to a directive by the Catholic bishops of Puerto Rico ordering the faithful to vote against Governor Luis Munoz Marin. Most of the anti-Catholic literature was sent out by conservative Protestant groups. It was financed by such groups, by individual Protestants, by individual Republicans, and by individual conservatives of great wealth.

Kennedy reached his peak of popularity at the end of September, right after his Houston speech in which he declared his commitment to religious liberty and separation of church and state, and after his first TV debate with Nixon. His popularity among Protestants rose to 38 percent at that time. It dropped to 36 percent in October, and at the election had dropped to 34 percent—when 66 percent of all Protestants who went to the polls voted against him. The study showed that during the period Kennedy was losing support among Protestants, his support in the Jewish population was increasing from 79 to 82 percent. A comparison of the electoral votes won by Kennedy, strictly because Catholic votes, and the electoral votes lost, strictly because of anti-Catholic votes, shows that he gained more than he lost because of his religion. In the popular vote, on the other hand, he lost more votes than he gained by being a Catholic. The distribution of the religious vote, however, was in his favor. Religious votes gave him the electoral vote in close states, while the religious votes he lost were mostly in the states he was going to lose anyway.

Although the volume of anti-Catholic literature was "many times" greater than that circulated against Alfred E. Smith in 1928, the Committee study found that the quality of the material was substantially

---

[49] *New York Times*, February 18, 1962.

"higher" than in 1928. Thus, although religious bias was shown, it was not as arbitary or as vituperative as in the earlier campaign.[50]

During the campaign a number of Protestant clergymen expressed fears that a Catholic president would take orders from the Pope and seek in various ways to give his church a preferred position in American society. Others, including both Protestants and Catholics, predicted the president-elect would go out of his way to show his independence of ecclesiastical control and his devotion to church-state separation.

Although the popular vote was extremely close, the presidency was indisputably won by a Catholic for the first time in history. The people sat back to see whether they could detect any Catholic bias in the acts and words of the newly elected president.

The Kennedy Record. President Kennedy early went on record as opposing any United States diplomatic relations with the Vatican. On the other hand, it was an Episcopalian president, Franklin D. Roosevelt, who sent a special envoy to the Vatican, and a Baptist, Harry S Truman, who proposed sending an ambassador.

The first evidence of Kennedy's Catholic background took place on the day of his inauguration. The president-elect rested his hand upon a Douay Bible, the version used by Catholics, rather than upon a King James Protestant version.[51] Since this innovation could hardly be said to strike at the roots of the American constitutional system, it caused little comment.

The most striking and far-reaching illustration of the first Catholic president's independence of the Catholic Church and its hierarchy was over the issue of the use of federal funds in aid of parochial schools. During the campaign, Nixon, a Protestant, said that he favored letting each state decide for itself whether to include parochial schools in the federal education aid. Kennedy, on the other hand, came out squarely against any direct aid for parochial schools. He said that the use of public funds for church schools was "clearly unconstitutional."

In his actions during the first years of his administration President Kennedy showed that he was even more independent and free from Catholic pressure, and less inclined to pursue policies favored by the Catholic hierarchy, than his Protestant predecessors. Kennedy followed the stand he had taken during the campaign. The federal aid to education bill that he sponsored did not allow funds for parochial education in any form.

During the first two years it was Catholic bishops who officially protested the unyielding stand of the administration, and it was Protestant interests that praised the administration. Catholic interests would have been quite happy to have a federal aid bill that would leave the question of whether to grant aid to parochial schools up to the individual states, as had been proposed by Nixon.

Protestant interests, many of whom had been most actively opposed to

---

[50] *Ibid.*
[51] *Herald Journal*, Syracuse, N.Y., November 10, 1960.

a Catholic as president, were almost unanimous in praise of his stand. The Southern Baptist Convention, which had warned the previous year against the election of a Catholic, voted unanimously to send a telegram to the President expressing their appreciation of his stand in favor of religious liberty and the separation of church and state.[52]

Religion editors and reporters across the country rated President Kennedy's stand against the Roman Catholic bishops of the United States on federal aid to parochial schools as the top 1961 religious news story.[53] A prominent Methodist clergyman praised President Kennedy for "fulfilling every pledge, both in spirit and in letter, that he made concerning the separation of church and state."[54]

Kennedy's political acts as president, it would appear, have removed the religious question as an important factor in the selection of a candidate for the presidency of either major party. It should be possible for a member of almost any minority religious group, such as a Jew or a Mormon, to aspire to and win nomination for the Presidency.

Summary

The federal constitution requires that government and religion be kept separate, but in actual practice both institutions are much influenced by each other. The ways in which the various states implement their police powers are of concern to religious groups. Marriage, social welfare, and education are proper subjects of the police power. They are also areas in which all religious groups have some interest, and some groups have much interest.

The war power of the State is of intense concern to the Historic Peace churches, which are officially opposed to combat service. Some members of these churches refuse noncombat service but will accept alternate civilian service. Some members refuse even to render civilian service. The Catholic Church and most of the large Protestant denominations, although not officially pacifist, will support those of their members who choose the pacifist role. Some of the newer churches, Jehovah's Witnesses and Seventh-day Adventists, are officially peace churches. Jehovah's Witnesses are militantly pacifist. Individual Witnesses, although laymen, refuse to accept alternate civilian service because it interferes, they say, with their calling as "ministers."

Just what does and does not constitute freedom of religion rests with the courts. An individual cannot engage in immoral acts on the ground that such behavior is required by his religion. On the other hand, a child in the public schools cannot be required to salute the flag if such an act is considered an act of idolatry and forbidden by his religion. The political

---

[52] *New York Times*, May 26, 1961; reiterated, their approval, in the fall of 1963: *New York Times*, October 13, 1963.

[53] *Ibid.*, January 1, 1962.

[54] *Ibid.*, February 6, 1962.

authority cannot require a license as a condition precedent to public proselytizing for one's faith, nor can a state legislature legislate parochial schools out of existence by requiring all children to attend a public school.

The military chaplaincy is not considered a union of church and state; it is, rather, an attribute of freedom of religion. The various churches and denominations are now allotted a quota of chaplains based upon the percentage each denomination represents of the total religious population of the country. Thus each soldier theoretically has access to a clergyman of his faith for worship and for counsel. Some of the most striking illustrations of interfaith cooperation take place in the armed services. Facilities and materials are shared, and chaplains otherwise cooperate with each other in areas of their work that are not feasible or possible in civilian life.

An increasing body of religious opinion is against capital punishment. In those states that have abolished capital punishment, churches and church leaders have played a leading role in developing the public opinion that has brought about its abolition.

Christian domination of the culture is being challenged in a number of areas. Laws and ordinances requiring observance of the Christian Sunday are under attack. In several states Sunday closing and other "blue laws" have been modified under the pressure of non-Christian religious groups.

Churches need additional income to finance expanding church programs, and many churches have become involved in business activities as a source of revenue. The tax exempt privilege, traditionally extended to religious and charitable institutions, is under review because various units of government are also looking for additional funds to finance expanding services. In some political jurisdictions a distinction is now made between property that is devoted strictly to religious purposes and property that is managed by a religious group for profit. The tax exempt privilege has been withdrawn for the latter category and the business activities of the church have become subject to regular taxation.

Kennedy's election broke the tradition that only a Protestant-affiliated or Protestant-oriented personality could become president. Kennedy's complete independence and objectivity on all questions involving a Catholic position appears to have removed the so-called religious issue in the selection of a presidential candidate. The religious affiliation of congressmen reflects the widening scope of religious pluralism. More Jews, more Catholics, and representatives of minority religious groups are now sitting as members of Congress and participating in the lawmaking process.

Chapter XIV

Religion and Education

RELIGIOUS EDUCATION is defined as indoctrination by a faith or a denomination of its membership in its beliefs, ethics, moral code, and values. Sunday Schools, vacation Bible schools, summer camps and conferences, released time, church-related elementary and secondary schools, and church-related colleges are the principal means of religious instruction in the United States.

Sunday School

The most popular and extensive form of religious education in the United States is the Sunday School. In 1958 the 39,564,925 pupils enrolled in the Sunday Schools of the United States constituted 22.7 percent of the total population. In 1926 the comparable figure was 17.9 percent. Between 1926 and 1959 the total population increased by 53 percent, but Sunday School enrollment increased by 90 percent. Sunday School is primarily a Protestant vehicle of instruction. Approximately 90 percent of the total Sunday School enrollment of 35,850,699 was reported as Protestants.[1]

Sunday School makes the most intensive contribution to the religious education of Protestants in the 3–12 age category. A considerably smaller percent of Protestants experience the continuing influence of Sunday School at the adolescent and adult age periods.[2] Protestant denominations cooperate in many aspects of the work of the Sunday Schools, such as the

---

[1] Rolfe Lanier Hunt, "Religion and Education," *Annals,* Vol. 332 (November, 1960), p. 90.
[2] See Table 21.

TABLE 21

SUNDAY SCHOOL ENROLLMENT
BY AGE-GROUP PERCENTAGES

Sunday School Division	Age Group	Percentage of All Sunday School Pupils
Cradle roll	Under 2 years	7.2
Children's division	3–12	38.0
Youth division	12–23	19.5
Adult division	24 and over	35.3

Source: Rolfe Lanier Hunt, "Religion and Education," *Annals*, November, 1960, p. 90.

preparation of curricula for the various age groups or the training of teachers and administrators. Vacation church or Bible schools and summer camps and conferences, as agencies of religious instruction, have been developing at a rapid rate in recent years.

In 1958 a total of 108,124 vacation church schools in the United States enrolled 7,598,940 pupils under the leadership of 1,158,585 teachers and officers. Religious groups have capitalized upon the eagerness of Americans to use their increased leisure to vacation in a nature environment by developing summer camps and conferences as agencies of religious education and for the fostering of religious solidarity. In 1958 a total of 7,063 Protestant-sponsored summer camps and conferences enrolled 801,871 campers and delegates, supervised by 91,744 teachers and leaders. More than half of the children who attend camps in the United States attend church-sponsored camps.[3]

Educational leaders see vacation church schools and summer camps, which afford large blocks of time for directed and sustained effort, as better opportunities for teaching and learning than Sunday Schools.

Parochial Schools

Parochial schools exist to give the moral and religious training which some faiths, some denominations, and some parents feel is a vital and necessary part of all formal education. Parochial schools are defined as those day schools organized and administered by a church or a parish to take the place of the public school at the elementary and the secondary school level. The parochial school curriculum and experience includes all of the minimum educational materials and experiences required by state law. In addition, the parochial school is free to give as much religious and moral training as it desires and in the manner that it thinks best.

Three facts stand out in American parochial education:

1. Parochial schools teach religion. They supplement the church and the home in teaching doctrine and belief, and the philosophy and special values for which the religion stands.

2. Parochial schools help to keep the child from losing his religion, and

---

[3] R. L. Hunt, *op. cit.*

TABLE 22

ENROLLMENT IN CHURCH RELATED ELEMENTARY AND SECONDARY SCHOOLS
IN THE UNITED STATES

10 Principal Denominational School Systems	Kindergarten	Elementary	Secondary
Roman Catholic	no record	4,307,000	827,900
Missouri Synod Lutheran	1,724	149,201	8,972
Seventh-Day Adventist	—	48,824	12,104
Protestant Episcopal	3,252	12,028	17,900
Joint Synod of Wisconsin	—	21,901	—
Christian Reformed	—	31,874	6,664
Nat'l. Assn. of Christian Schools	7	8,960	7,492
Mennonite (including Amish)	88	7,568	4,325
Friends	221	4,978	5,567
Jewish	4,133	21,259	4,326

Based upon Bertha Blair's "Church Related Elementary and Secondary Schools in Continental United States," Bureau of Research and Survey *Information Service* (NCCCA, January 3, 1959); data furnished by William A. Kramer, Secretary of Schools, Lutheran Church–Missouri Synod, St. Louis, Missouri, November 29, 1960; data furnished by G. M. Mathews, Department of Education, General Conference of Seventh-Day Adventists, Washington, D.C., November 7, 1961.

parents send children to a parochial school not only to get but to keep them from losing religion. The parochial school thus insulates the child from the religious indifference and secularism of the public school.

3. The greatest support for parochial education comes from the more orthodox and the more conventionally religious of any given faith or denomination.

The Catholic Parochial Schools. The Catholic parochial school system dominates the statistics of parochial enrollment and investment.[4]

The moral and religious functions of Catholic parochial education is frequently publicized by Catholic spokesmen. The need for special education for Catholic children has been officially stated by the Catholic bishops of America as follows:

Although striking advances have been made in recent decades in helping the child physically, emotionally, and socially, his moral and religious needs have not been met with the same solicitude and understanding. The child is a citizen of two worlds. He belongs to this world, it is true, but his highest allegiance is to the Kingdom of God. It is the responsibility of parents to lead the child towards becoming a "God-centered" rather than a "self-centered" individual. Parents may do this by family prayers and rosaries, and by other religious observances and training in the home. But it would be of little avail to intensify the child's awareness of God during his pre-school years if later schooling were to rob him of these gains.[5]

Reverend James Conlan, staff member of Cardinal Hayes high school, in a sermon at St. Patrick's Cathedral defined the role of religion in Catholic schools:

---

[4] See Table 22.

[5] Raphael M. Huber, *Our Bishops Speak* (Milwaukee: The Bruce Publishing Co., 1952), p. 161.

Take heaven and hell out of the life of man, and all he has left is the space he now occupies. Laugh at the existence of original sin and man cannot be explained. Dismiss the divine virtues of faith, hope and charity, and man is a brute. Man is not merely born but created, not merely a citizen of a country but a child of God, living not merely in the "here" of space and the "now" of time, but destined to live in eternity. Man can learn these things in a God-centered school, learn them in such a way that they will influence his life, not merely add to his collection of facts.[6]

A Catholic spokesman has advocated that Catholics concentrate upon the parochial school at the secondary level if Catholics cannot afford to support both an elementary and a secondary school parochial system:

In the old days if you were going to give Catholic children a Catholic education the elementary school was the place to do it, for that was the only place that Catholics were. . . . Let us face it, the chief reason for the Catholic school system is the preservation of the faith. I, for one, have never seen a child lose its faith in the elementary grades unless the parents lost it for him. If we can only have Catholic influence around in some grades, let us have it around in the crucial years when the powers of reasoning are being strengthened, the inclination to challenge sharpened, and vocations and careers being decided. Let us have the priests and sisters around in the grades where boy meets girl; where they both meet the Reformation, the Inquisition, Communism, Darwinism, Freudianism and all the other religions and philosophies. They are much more needed there than where the boys and girls meet spelling, timetables, and long division.[7]

The Catholic Church expects parents to send their children to the parochial school whenever this choice is available, but the majority of children who attend parochial schools generally come from the more active and better practicing families of the parish. Fichter found that one of the traits differentiating the *nuclear* Catholic from the *marginal* Catholic was the factor of parochial school attendance. The nuclear Catholic accepted the precept of the Church and sent his child to parochial school; the *marginal* Catholic was generally indifferent to the advantages and values of parochial education.[8]

Trends. Approximately two thirds of Catholic children of elementary school age are attending an elementary parochial school, and approximately one half of all Catholic youth of secondary school age are attending a secondary parochial school.[9] The percentage of Catholic children attending parochial schools is steadily rising. Parochial school enrollments increased by 4 percent in one year in New York state and in that year parochial and private schools educated 23.5 percent of all elementary and secondary school children of the state.[10]

[6] *New York Times,* March 12, 1962.

[7] Monsignor George W. Casey, pastor of St. Bridget's Church, Lexington, Mass., as reported in the *Watertown Times,* Watertown, New York, Oct. 28, 1961.

[8] Joseph H. Fichter, *Social Relations in the Urban Parish* (Chicago: University of Chicago Press, 1956), pp. 28, 61.

[9] See Table 23.

[10] *New York Times,* September 18, 1960.

TABLE 23

DISTRIBUTION OF CATHOLIC STUDENTS IN EDUCATIONAL
INSTITUTIONS IN THE UNITED STATES

Educational Level	Schools	Students
Elementary School		
Parochial and institutional	10,322	4,524,393
Private	454	84,636
Protective institutions	134	15,449
Public (released time)	—	2,909,424
Secondary School		
Diocesan and parochial	1,537	623,879
Private	895	381,048
Public (released time)	—	1,119,800
College or University	282	357,764

Official Catholic Directory, 1963, New York, P. J. Kenedy & Sons, 1963.

The expansion of the Catholic parochial system has been hampered as much by the difficulty of securing proper teachers as by the cost of erecting the buildings and carrying on a modern educational program. There are just not enough sisters trained in pedagogy to staff the schools the church would like to maintain. Although the church is reluctant to depend extensively upon lay teachers, Catholic authorities estimate the needs for expansion will continue to be so great and the supply of teaching sisters so limited that by 1970 one half of all teachers in the Catholic parochial schools will be lay teachers.[11]

The rising costs of education are putting an increasing strain on the parochial schools and leaders are afraid that unless some public support is received, parochial education will be curtailed and some schools even eliminated. Catholic authorities report that the 5½ million children that attend Catholic elementary and secondary schools save the American taxpayer over 2 billion dollars each year.[12]

A Variety of Goals. According to Catholic research the children in public and parochial schools are much alike, but different from children in private schools. This does not mean that the parochial school as an educational agency is the same as the public school. The most obvious difference is the teaching of religion.[13] The representative parochial school gives the sister teaching the second grade the responsibility of preparing her children for their First Communion. Subsequently the parochial school class becomes the basis for instruction and participation in the sacraments. The children are frequently taken as a class group to confession and are encouraged to attend Sunday mass as a group.

Some parents report that they send their children to a parochial school

---

[11] *Ibid.*, May 21, 1960.

[12] National Catholic Welfare Conference, *Catholic Schools U.S.A.* (Washington, D.C., 1962), p. 1.

[13] J. H. Fichter, *Parochial School* (South Bend, Ind.: University of Notre Dame Press, 1958), chap. 4.

for reasons other than merely religious indoctrination. They send their children for better training and conditioning in discipline, to learn proper respect for authority, and because they like the emphasis upon knowledge rather than the social experience emphasis they associate with public school education. They also like the Catholic emphasis and concept of moral values, dating, and marriage relationships which is incorporated into parochial school curricula and experience.

The parochial school system does, according to Catholic studies,

. . . Resist and largely escape the increasing bureaucratization which is so much in evidence in the public school system. The parochial school is relatively autonomous from the over-bearing hierarchy of superintendents and city, county, and state school boards.[14]

Although Catholics generally support the parochial school concept, there is considerable variation among both laymen and clergy on the relative value of various aspects of parochial education and of where emphasis should be placed. As we have seen, some laymen feel that the more formal and nonprogressive type of education offered in the parochial schools is of most value. Others find the special religious training in moral conduct to be the most important single contribution of the parochial school. Some Catholic clergy would stress the secondary at the expense of the elementary level and think first in terms of the "preserving" function of the parochial school.

Catholic educators also recognize weaknesses and limitations of parochial education. A Catholic educator has warned his fellow members of religious orders in the teaching profession not to permit their roles as priests, nuns, or brothers to overawe students and thereby curb self-expression:

The religious teacher should never confuse, or allow the students to confuse his or her role in the classroom with the awe-inspiring role of a person in the religious state of life. Otherwise he or she may unwittingly foster servile respect and blind obedience to the neglect of student intiative, intellectual curiosity, and independent thinking and self-expression.[15]

It is normal and appropriate to have varying views of the nature and importance of parochial education within the Catholic religious system. The church tolerates, and even welcomes, it sometimes appears, differing views and attitudes in this area.

Jewish Education. In 1958 approximately half a million children were attending Jewish schools: fulltime day schools, weekday afternoon schools, and one-day Sunday schools.[16] The fulltime day school is the Jewish equivalent of the parochial school. It is at this school that the

---

[14] *New York Times,* July 30, 1958.

[15] Monsignor Henry C. Bezou, superintendent of schools, Archdiocese of New Orleans, in an address delivered before Annual Teachers Institute of Archdiocese of New York at Manhattan Center, New York, as reported in *New York Times,* September 10, 1961.

[16] See Table 24.

Jewish boy or girl gets his secular as well as his religious education. The curriculum includes all of the basic elements and subjects required of all children by the state, plus all of the religious instruction and training that the school desires to offer.

TABLE 24

COUNTRYWIDE ENROLLMENT IN VARIOUS TYPES OF ORGANIZED JEWISH
SCHOOLS ON ELEMENTARY AND HIGH SCHOOL LEVELS FOR 1958–59

| Type of School | Elementary School | | High School Level | | Ratio of High School to Elementary Enrollment |
	Enrollment	% of Total	Enrollment	% of Total	
Weekday afternoon Hebrew ...	228,631	51.5	16,674	38.7	7.3
Weekday afternoon Yiddish ...	5,311	1.2	309	0.7	5.8
All day schools	31,890	7.2	5,850	13.6	18.3
One-day schools	177,998	40.1	20,223	47.0	11.3
Total	443,830	100	43,056	100	9.7

David Rudavsky: "The Status of the Jewish Secondary School," *Religious Education,* Vol. LVI, No. 2, March–April, 1961, p. 105.

The weekday afternoon school, commonly known as the Hebrew School, meets two or more times after public school hours each week and prepares the boy or girl for *Bar Mitzvah* (confirmation). The study of Hebrew is an important part of the curriculum. Sunday School is a one-day affair that meets on the Christian Sunday and seeks to acquaint the student with the Jewish heritage of religion and culture.

The objectives of Jewish education, as formulated in the different curricula, are knowledge of the Bible, history, customs, Hebrew, and Yiddish; practices and participation, beliefs and attitudes, a sympathetic understanding of the Jewish heritage, and a sense of identification and belonging.

Nearly all of the schools surveyed were found to be under the direct control of local congregations. The Conservative congregations accounted for 39 percent, the Reform for 28 percent, the Orthodox for 21 percent, with Yiddish and multiple-oriented schools accounting for the rest. Nearly all of the whole-day schools were sponsored by Orthodox congregations, but Conservative congregations were found to be taking an increasing interest in them.

In 1962 Conservative leaders announced plans for the creation of 100 more all-day schools within the next ten years.[17] One hundred thirty-six of the total of 274 day schools were concentrated in New York City.[18] Approximately one half of the weekday afternoon Hebrew schools were sponsored by Conservative congregations. Reform groups were most active in the Sunday School phase of the Jewish educational program.[19]

[17] *New York Times,* May 24, 1962.
[18] *Ibid.,* November 11, 1960.
[19] Bernard D. Weinryb, "Intergroup Content in Jewish Religious Textbooks," *Religious Education* (March–April, 1960), p. 112.

Jews' own evaluation of Jewish education is just as varied as the religious positions which are included within Judaism. A poll of 1,560 Jewish community leaders revealed that 75 percent were opposed to the Jewish day school. The 25 percent who supported the day school were chiefly Orthodox and Conservative in religion. The majority opposed the day school because they felt that the public school provided their children a better preparation for life in the religiously pluralistic American society.[20]

Although Jewish schools have increased 131 percent in the last ten years, some Jewish spokesmen find they fall short of meeting real needs. The president of B'nai B'rith, a Jewish service organization, reported that Sunday Schools and afternoon Hebrew Schools were "woefully inadequate, doing little more than perpetuating a kind of juvenile Judaism that has little relationship to religious and cultural life for the student in his later years."[21]

The head of the American Zionist organization in America saw in assimilation "the greatest peril to Jewish survival" and predicted the future of Jews in America depends upon an "intensive Hebrew education which is indispensable for the preservation and development of Jewish life and Jewish tradition."[22]

On the other hand, the president of the American Jewish Congress, Dr. Joachim Prinz, maintained that Jewish life in the United States was not imperiled by anti-Semitism "but by ignorance of the American Jew about himself"; that the question of assimilation was

not a serious problem because in the context of the free American society in which we enjoy equal rights with all other Americans, it is not likely that the Jewish groups will disappear. What we are not sure of is that this Jewish survival will bring with it a vigorous and creative continuity of Jewish life.

Dr. Prinz called for a new and expanded program of Jewish education to tackle the task of "creating a meaningful Jewish life that translates mere Jewish survival into positive Jewish living."[23]

Jews are agreed that the times call for more and better Jewish education. The nature of the better education, and whether it should take the place of public education or merely supplement it, varies according to the religious orientation and philosophy of the individual Jew.

The Protestant Parochial School. Protestant denominations traditionally have been satisfied with the public school, primarily because it was Protestant-oriented. But the almost complete secularization of the public school under pressure of minority religious groups to de-Protestantize education has led some Protestants and some Protestant denominations to take an interest in parochial education for the first time.

---

[20] Alexander M. Dushkin and Uriah A. Redelheim, *Jewish Education in the United States* (New York: American Association for Jewish Education, 1959).

[21] *New York Times*, October 25, 1959.

[22] *Ibid.*, June 11, 1962.

[23] *Ibid.*, April 15, 1962.

The desire for parochial education has always been greatest among the conservative Protestant denominations. There has never been enough religion in the public school or of the right kind, to satisfy the conservative denominations. The greatest Protestant effort in parochial education has been made by the Lutheran Church–Missouri Synod and the Seventh-day Adventist Church. Because these churches are so different and definite in theology and practice they tend to remain aloof from most Protestant cooperative movements and projects.

Missouri-Synod Schools. The greatest interest in parochial education has been shown by these two denominations.[24] The time, effort, and money that these denominations have put into their parochial programs compare favorably with that of the Catholic Church. The Lutheran Church–Missouri Synod has, next to the Catholic Church, the largest number of children enrolled in its parochial schools. In 1960, 149,201 pupils were enrolled in 1,293 schools taught by 5,319 teachers. There were, in addition, 19 high schools with an enrollment approaching 10,000. The enrollment in both elementary and secondary schools has nearly doubled since World War II. The greatest growth has been in eastern, southeastern, and western parts of the United States.[25]

In the Lutheran view, faith in God and in Christ constitutes the heart of wisdom. This faith is essential for salvation but, to be genuine, it must prove itself in all the areas of life: in the family, in the church, in civic and community affairs, and in social life. Lutherans hold to a unitary concept of education, and the combination of Sunday school and public school does not meet this objective.

In the Lutheran school the pupil develops, it is said, a strictly Christian and Biblical perspective, world view, and philosophy of life. Dividing education into separate religious and secular categories does not provide the unitary education which the wholeness of truth and the wholeness of the individual demand. The Lutheran school devotes approximately the first hour of the day to direct and intensive instruction in religion. In addition, it teaches sacred music, church history and practices, and other specifically Christian or Lutheran information as part of the common school subjects. Lutheran schools aim for Christian instruction in depth: first, by imparting a thorough knowledge of Christian doctrine; second, by showing how religious belief, to be genuine, must affect all activities and areas of life; and third, by training their pupils in the Christian life which they advocate.[26]

Status of Teachers. Teachers in Lutheran schools are religiously trained and oriented. Men who graduate from one of the Lutheran teacher colleges and men teachers who pass synodically prescribed colloquies

---

[24] See Table 22.

[25] William A. Kramer, *Lutheran Schools of the Lutheran Church–Missouri Synod* (St. Louis: The Lutheran Church–Missouri Synod, 1961), p. 7.

[26] *Ibid.*, p. 15.

(tests of faith) are "ministers of religion" in the eyes of the church. Women teachers are also engaged in the ministry of the church, but they do not belong to the clergy and do not hold special membership in the Synod. Like the pastors, the teachers are formally called, installed, and dedicated to a lifelong service to the church. These teachers and "ministers of religion" are salaried for twelve months and serve the congregation the year round. Congregations often furnish a free residence for married men teachers. Otherwise, their salary is generally lower than that of public school teachers in the same community. Since they look upon teaching as a religious vocation they are willing to accept spiritual satisfaction as part of their reward and compensation.[27]

The Lutheran Church–Missouri Synod does not favor state support of parochial schools. The Missouri Synod, however, distinguishes between two aspects of the state's school program:

1. The social service program (library service, lunches, health service, transportation, etc.)
2. The teaching program (curriculum, teaching, philosophy of education)

The Missouri Synod will accept state aid for the social service program because this program does not promote the religious tenets of the church. It will not accept state support for any part of the secular program because this program, according to the Missouri Synod philosophy, must be taught in the light of the tenets of the church.[28]

In philosophy and organization the schools of the Lutheran Church–Missouri Synod have much in common with the Catholic parochial schools. In both cases the churches believe that religion and life are inextricably bound up together; that education for religion and education for life cannot be separated but must be considered together. In both cases the teachers are called and dedicated people who pursue their vocation as an act and obligation of their faith.

Seventh-day Adventist Education. Seventh-day Adventists are vigorous advocates of parochial education. Although they are a relatively small denomination, numbering some 300,000 in 1961, a substantial percent of their children attend an Adventist parochial school. Their greatest effort is at the elementary school level. In 1961, 48,824 children were attending 1,040 elementary schools taught by 2,152 teachers. In the same year 12,104 were attending 71 secondary schools taught by 1,261 teachers.[29]

Adventists are very anxious to have their children attend one of their schools. Like the Missouri-Synod Lutherans, the Adventists find that religion cannot be divorced from life; therefore, it is inconceivable to consider each separately. It follows that only that education which is pursued within a framework of religious values is appropriate.

---

[27] *Ibid.,* p. 12.
[28] *Ibid.,* p. 18.
[29] As stated in a letter from G. M. Mathews, secretary, Department of Education, General Conference of Seventh-Day Adventists, Washington, D.C., November 7, 1961.

Adventists favor parochial schools so that their children can be brought face to face with Adventists values and can learn to live and behave the way Adventists are supposed to. Adventists also want their children in parochial schools so as to protect them from the discrimination of being singled out as peculiar and different.

Adventists have strict rules of health and diet so that the body may be maintained as a worthy temple for the dwelling of the spirit. It is a plain and simple diet, primarily vegetarian, supplemented by dairy products and eggs. Adventists observe their sabbath on Saturday. They look upon dancing and movies as worldly and sinful.[30] Through experience they have found that their children learn these values and practices best in the congenial and sympathetic environment of a parochial school.

Adventist teachers are strong and active members of a Seventh-day Adventist congregation who are especially trained to integrate religious beliefs and teachings with the basic tools and other mandated minimum essentials of public education. Adventist elementary schools are small. The typical unit is a two-teacher school, usually in a rural area. It is the desire and hope of each congregation to have a parochial school even though it be a small one.

The Adventist type of education is so important to a good Adventist family that many choose to educate their children at home rather than at the public schools—if an Adventist school is not available. Several months after a new family moved into a farmhouse outside of Camden, New York, it was brought to the attention of the school authorities that the family included several children who were not attending the public school.

Upon investigation they found the mother was running a one-family school in her living room for five of her eight children and following a course of study put out by the Home Study Institute of the national office of the Seventh-day Adventist Church. The text books in use were current. The children were instructed in music and art and showed considerable skill and achievement in these areas, and when tested by the school authorities were found to be above average for the various age levels.

The public school had many events on Friday evenings and Saturdays in which their children could not participate because of their religious beliefs. Rather than have them feel left out or deprived the parents chose to go to the effort and expense of operating their own school in their own home.[31]

The Education of the Amish.   The Old Order Amish of Pennsylvania are vigorous opponents of compulsory public education, seeing in it the greatest violation of freedom of religion. If children must be formally

---

[30] General Conference of Seventh-Day Adventists, *A Quick Look at Seventh-Day Adventists*, Washington, D.C., 1959.

[31] *Herald-American*, Syracuse, N.Y., March 18, 1962.

educated they insist that this education be gained in one of their own parochial schools. "Our religious convictions direct us to stay away from secondary high school attendance. Examples and experience are the best teachers. Why should we be disturbed and molested?"[32]

The Amish are proud to be known as "peculiar people," living more or less isolated, according to the values and practices of the horse and buggy era. The women dress plainly and uniformly, and avoid jewelry and cosmetics. The men likewise dress plainly and uniformly; they wear beards and shun such modern equipment and facilities as tractors and electricity. They look upon the modern central school with its up-to-date, elaborate facilities and comprehensive curriculum as worldly, unnecessary, and in some respects downright sinful. Among other things they object to the taking of showers in groups and the wearing of gym suits, especially in the case of girls.[33]

In 1952, the Pennsylvania State Legislature made a concession to the Amish by permitting their children to leave school after the eighth grade to receive agricultural vocational training at home. This did not, however, solve the problem to the satisfaction of either the Amish or the state school authorities. In Honeydale, Chester County, Pennsylvania, eleven Amish farmers refused to send their thirteen children to the spacious Twin Valley junior-senior high school because they regarded it as too distracting, too worldly, and too far away. The parents, however, were ordered to send their children to the public school when investigation indicated that the Amish school to which their children were going did not meet the minimum five-day week, as required by law, and were being taught by an unqualified teacher who had gone only as far as the eighth grade.

The fathers were hailed into court and paid $200 in fines and costs for violation of the compulsory school attendance law. However, under a compromise worked out by the Attorney General, further prosecution of the fathers of the seventh and eighth grade pupils was halted pending an agreement on a curriculum for a two-room parochial school set up in a farm house in the Honeydale community.[34]

RELIGION IN THE PUBLIC SCHOOL

History

The public schools used to include a great deal of religious education and religious expressions of worship, but it was Protestant-oriented. This is not surprising since the public schools arose from a religious culture that was predominantly Protestant.

---

[32] *Post Standard*, Syracuse, N.Y., February 10, 1960.
[33] *New York Times*, March 31, 1960.
[34] *Ibid.*

The public school developed from the Puritan common school which had been organized by the early Puritans for religious reasons. Puritan Calvinism required that each communicant be able to read the Bible, school attendance was compulsory, and not only did the Puritan common school read and study the Bible but the whole curriculum was directed towards the teaching of the Puritan moral code. The famous McGuffey reader was made up largely of moral stories directed towards the inculcation of the Puritan value system. The public schools in the first half of the nineteenth century was virtually a Protestant parochial school. The means whereby a Protestant could worship through his religion and practice its moral values were ever present in the public school curriculum.

The first effective pressure brought against the Protestant-oriented public school came with the increase in numbers and growing political power and influence of Catholics and the Catholic Church. Catholics objected to Bible reading because it was invariably the Protestant Bible—the King James version. The Catholic Bible, the Douay edition, is not much different from the King James version but the differences are important to Catholics. Catholics objected to the comment and prayer that followed the reading of the Bible because in both instances comment and prayer tended to be individual and personal, the Protestant interpretive practices. In all important questions there is an official Catholic interpretation of the Bible and the important prayers of its religious system are found within the Missal, formal and fixed. Catholics and Protestants were not in disagreement, however, when the Bible was read without comment and prayer was limited to the Lord's Prayer.

The singing of hymns did not generally coincide with the Catholic concept of nondenominational religious expression and worship. Hymn-singing is primarily a Protestant worship practice. In fact it is possible to create different kinds of Protestant religious atmosphere just through the choice of hymns: an evangelistic atmosphere and mood—or a liturgical atmosphere and mood.

The increase in numbers and rise in political power and influence of Jewish religious and cultural groups has now led to a second attack upon religious aspects of the public school curriculum and to its de-Christianization.

American Council Report. During World War II public education was severely criticized for the scant attention given to religion in the curriculum. The American Council on Education, in cooperation with the National Council of Christians and Jews, commissioned a committee to study the problem. The report which the committee issued in 1947 became the basis for much of the developments in public schools during subsequent years.

The committee took a firm position against religious instruction (in the sense of indoctrination) in tax-supported schools, but contended vigorously for including in public school programs the objective study of religious subject matter wherever it was intrinsically related to an academic discipline. This approach to religion has been characterized as "study about religion," as opposed to teaching and learning religion in terms of "commitment and personal involvement."

The committee maintained that the intensive cultivation of religion is and always has been the function of religious institutions. To create an awareness of its importance is a responsibility of public education. At the same time the committee found general education to be a major function of the public schools, and that this includes confrontation of growing persons with spiritual values and influences in accord with their actual magnitude in the culture and the general estimate of their importance in the life of the community.

The committee recommended that religion in the various forms in which it appears today in American culture and in which it has influenced history be respectfully studied in the interest of achieving a culturally adequate education. The primary concern is to oppose the artificial separation of the sacred and the secular, the setting apart of religion from the common life. The cultural evil against which the American people protest is the nonrelevance of spiritual ideals and sanctions to everyday life, whether in business, politics, or education.[35]

Recent Developments. A survey of existing practices in 1953 found a conspicuous lack of anything approximating a uniform policy or practice with respect to the relation of religion to public education. Three overlapping and confused policies and practices were found: avoidance of religion, planned religious activities, and factual study of religion.

Avoidance of religion was most frequently and extensively found in communities which were heterogeneous with respect to religious beliefs, or where leaders of minority religious groups had made vigorous and persistent protests against practices of which they disapprove, or where educational leaders had decided to "play safe" by treating religion as lightly as possible.

Planned religious activities were widely prevalent—activities, furthermore, that could in no sense be reconciled with the rigid prohibitions set by the Supreme Court in the *Everson* and the *McCollum* cases. These planned activities were found in all types of communities and in all sections of the country, but they were most common and extensive in communities where one religious faith was dominant. Factual study of religion was more closely associated with educational leadership than with the religious composition of the population.

The survey showed that the level on which the most attention had been focused, the secondary level, was not the most controversial or the level of most concern to the community. The most insistent demands

---

[35] American Council on Education, *The Relation of Religion to Public Education*, Washington, D.C., 1947.

that came from the community for recognition of religion in the school program were concerned with religious ceremonial and symbolism to which young children are particularly responsive. The most intense forms of religious expression, the ritualistic forms, were those the public school found it hardest to avoid.[36]

In the early 1960's ritualistic practices were widely followed in the public schools. Forty to 50 percent of all public schools held Bible reading sessions. Some states permitted Bible reading, some forbade it. Where permitted it was usually limited to a few verses read in the opening exercises "without comment."[37]

Prayer in the public school varied from state to state. Thirty percent of all public schools practiced a morning devotional, usually in the form of a prayer. The Lord's Prayer was most commonly used, although some states required a nondenominational prayer similar in form and type to the Regents' Prayer formerly used in New York state.[38]

The question of the observance of religious holidays in the public schools finds religious groups divided. Holiday observance generally receives the support of Catholics and Protestants because the traditional holidays are Christian holidays. Some communities have tried to recognize the Jewish faith by providing for joint holiday observances in the public schools, for example, Christmas-Chanukah and Easter-Passover.

Ritual and the Three Faiths. Jews are the most consistent and verbal opponents of religious ceremonials and symbolism in the public schools. There is, however, no official Jewish position on any point of doctrine or ritual. Jews like to illustrate their highly developed sense of autonomy and independence by the story that the only thing upon which two Jews can agree is what a third Jew should give to charity. The best that can ever be said regarding a Jewish point of view is that "most Jews" or "most Jewish groups" believe, etc.

Jewish sources consider Bible reading a religious act, and oppose it as such. Reading from the New Testament is particularly objectionable to Jews since it is a Christian act of worship, and not only improper but discriminatory.[39]

Most Jewish groups maintain that organized prayer, whether spoken or silent, is an act of worship and therefore improper and inappropriate in the public school. Catholics and most Protestant groups find nothing objectionable in a nondenominational prayer.[40]

Jewish sources condemn what they call the "strange new hybrid religion" that they find evolving in the public schools. They refer to the

---

[36] American Council on Education, *The Function of the Public Schools in Dealing with Religion*, Washington, D.C., 1953.

[37] *New York Times*, July 1, 1962.

[38] *Ibid.*

[39] The American Jewish Committee, *Religion in Public Education, A Statement of Views* (New York, 1957), p. 16.

[40] *Ibid.*, p. 17.

attempts of educators not to offend by borrowing words and phrases from all faiths and arriving at a "lowest common denominator" of religious expression. Christmas-Chanakuh becomes the Festival of Lights and the Season of Gifts. Easter-Passover becomes the Festival of Spring. The Ten Commandments opens with "I am the Lord thy God, who brought thee forth out of [the land of Egypt] the house of bondage." Some public schools edit out "the land of Egypt." Jewish sources find these non-sectarian compromises ineffective, inappropriate, and destructive of religious training and experience in depth.[41]

Objective Teaching of Religion. In the early 1960's 20 percent of the public schools were teaching "about religion" in the various subject matter areas where religious information was relevant to the proper understanding of the discipline.[42] This approach and technique has the support of the majority of the Protestant groups, and both Catholic and Jewish groups have gone on record as supporting teaching "about religion" within their respective meanings of the concept.

A Catholic spokesman has stated that

Catholics expect the public schools to teach the regular subjects in an objective, complete and integral manner so that the students on all levels will discover for themselves the significant role of religion in human affairs, past and present. They expect the public schools to refrain from indoctrinating pupils in a doctrinaire, secularistic philosophy of life which avowedly discounts the importance of religion in all affairs.[43]

The American Jewish Committee has recommended

. . . that the schools should foster an appreciation of the impact of religion on our civilization. Such events as the Crusades, the Reformation and the colonization of America would be hopelessly distorted if religious motivations were not given proper weight. It would be equally wrong to omit the Bible from courses in literature or to ignore religious influences in the study of art.[44]

Moral and Spritual Values. Educators and the public schools have given a great deal of time and thought to programs seeking to teach "moral and spiritual values" as a secular substitute for religious training.[45] There is disagreement, however, on whether these values can be communicated through existing courses in the school program or whether there

---

[41] Leo Pfeffer, an official of the American Jewish Congress, as reported in the *New York Times,* May 8, 1957.

[42] *New York Times,* July 1, 1962.

[43] Monsignor William McManus in an address, "What Catholics Expect of the Home, Church, and School in the Religious Education of Children," delivered at the Workshop on Home, Church, and School Relationships in the Religious Education of Children and Youth, sponsored jointly by the Department of Education of the University of Chicago and the Department of Religion and Public Education of the National Council of Churches of Christ in the U.S.A.

[44] The American Jewish Committee, *op. cit.,* p. 8.

[45] National Education Association, *Moral and Spiritual Values in the Public Schools* (Washington, D.C., 1951).

should be separate courses organized specifically to teach the moral and spiritual values.

Some hold that moral and spiritual values are effective and valid only when grounded in religious sanctions. This approach is not possible in a public school. Others hold that these values are "caught" rather than "taught"; that no good teacher can operate without infusing into all her teaching, as well as into every aspect of school experience, the basic moral laws. Implicit in every teaching experience should be the inherent dignity and sanctity of the individual, the need for observing a code of fair play, and the necessity of doing unto others as one would be done by.

Catholics and most Protestants generally support moral and spiritual value programs in the public schools. Although Catholics tolerate public school programs they maintain that moral and religious training is most efficacious when it is joined with instruction in other kinds of knowledge. The best school atmosphere is, according to Catholic philosophy, the parochial school. Jews generally argue that moral and spiritual training is the proper perogative of the home and the church or synagogue, and that there is not much that can be done this way outside a context of religious sanctions.

Released Time. Religious instructions through the "released time" technique is widely used throughout the country. By means of released time children attending the public schools are given the opportunity to elect religious training under conditions consistent with the existing interpretation of the separation of church and state principles. The various denominations take advantage of released time to supplement the religious instruction and training which they give in their catechism and Sunday School programs. Approximately 2½ million children of the public elementary and secondary schools of all denominations receive religious instruction in released time programs.[46]

Disputes over the legality of programs of released time have been largely removed since the decision of the United States Supreme Court in the *Zorach* case, handed down in 1952. This decision allows released time instruction "when conducted off premises without pressure on school children to participate."[47]

The rules for released time instruction vary from state to state, but the rules of New York state are representative. In order to participate in the released time program the child must bring a written request from his parents, and the religious authorities conducting the instruction must take and report attendance to the school authorities. When taken for credit, the curriculum and examinations must be approved by the school authorities. Also, the time released from the prescribed school day must be taken at the end of either the morning session or the afternoon session. The released child must not be penalized by his absence, and no new instruction can

---

[46] *National Catholic Almanac, 1960* (Garden City, N.Y.: Doubleday & Co.), p. 485.
[47] *Zorach vs. Clauson*, 330 U.S. (1947).

be given during the time that he is excused from the public school. This time is usually given over to study hall or to individual study and consultation for the children who remain in school.

Programs of released time are maintained by most religious groups with varying degrees of emphasis. The Catholic Church makes extensive use of released time programs and finds it the best substitute for the religious instruction the public school Catholic misses by not attending a parochial school. In some cities parochial school pupils are dismissed in order to free the buildings and teachers for pupils coming from the public schools. In other communities, the Confraternity of Christian Doctrine recruits lay teachers.

The majority of the Protestant denominations in the National Council of the Churches of Christ promote a cooperative approach to the released time program, encouraging their churches to collaborate in providing personnel and facilities and in the use of common curriculum. The National Council makes a recommended curriculum available that is directed toward the interpretation of the child's experience in the public school in the perspective of the "revelation of God within the totality of man's experience."

Christian Science and Jewish groups operate released time schools in New York City. Jews, however, are divided on the appropriateness and value of released time instruction. The American Jewish Committee, which includes representatives of the three Jewish denominational positions, has gone on record opposing released time for the following reasons:

1. It threatens the independent character of the public school. Since part of the compulsory school day is released by the state on condition that the participating student devote his time to sectarian instruction, the state accomplishes by indirection what it admittedly cannot undertake to do directly; it provides a governmental restraint in support of religion.
2. It is a mechanism for divisiveness which is repeated at weekly intervals throughout the school year.
3. The normal school program is disrupted. Because classroom activities generally remain static during the released time period, children who do not participate suffer an unnecessary loss of instruction.
4. The available data indicate that many children do not reach their religious centers. Where such unexcused absences occur, the program contributes to truancy.[48]

The Mormons were pioneers in the released time concept. The Mormon system of seminaries built on church-owned properties adjacent to the public schools they serve began, in 1912, to offer weekday religious classes. In 1963, over 51,000 students were enrolled in daily classes throughout the United States and Canada in 158 released time seminaries, and another 29,000 in non-released time seminaries, giving religious instruction before and after school hours. These seminaries have been found to compare

---

[48] The American Jewish Committee, *op. cit.*, p. 15.

favorably in buildings, equipment, and qualifications of teachers with the school to which they were attached.

The seminary curriculum includes the Book of Mormon in ninth grade; the New Testament (King James version) in tenth grade; church history and doctrine in eleventh grade; and the Old Testament (King James version) in twelfth grade. The cooperating public school typically allows one-half unit of credit for the year's study of the New Testament, and another half-unit credit for the year's study of the Old Testament. Study of church history and doctrine and the Book of Mormon are usually taken without high school credit. The seminary teachers are recruited from regular high school teachers who have considerable teaching experience. They are given extra training and pay and have responsibilities in counselling and guidance.[49]

RELIGION IN HIGHER EDUCATION

Church Related Protestant Colleges

In a recent survey of church related colleges Protestant denominations reported 442 institutions of higher education.[50] This figure is a generous and optimistic statement of educational institutions that are either intimately or remotely related to the listing denomination. A variety of educational institutions is included in these figures. An analysis of the 135 institutions reported by the Methodist Church, for example, showed that only 83 are universities or four-year colleges. The remainder includes schools of theology, junior colleges, and secondary schools.[51] The figures reported by other denominations were found to be similarly all-inclusive.

In a recent year only 247 of these church related Protestant colleges received funds for current operating expenses from the sponsoring denomination. These colleges enrolled 243,153 students and received $19,200,982 from the mother denomination. The median support per student amounted to $104.05,[52] representing a small percent of the total funds needed to educate a student in an accredited institution of higher education.

The nature and amount of control of sponsoring denominations over their colleges vary widely. In some cases the relationship is historical only and in others colleges listed as denominational are autonomous and independent. The first college in Colonial America, Harvard, was founded by Congregationalists, as were most of the other colleges of the early period in New England. The United Church of Christ reports that all of

---

[49] Unified Church School System, *Announcement of Program, 1963* (Provo, Utah: Department of Education, Brigham Young University), pp. 31–57.

[50] *Information Service*, Vol. XLI, No. 3 (February 3, 1962).

[51] Board of Education of the Methodist Church, U.S.A., *Directory of Educational Institutions of the Methodist Church, U.S.A., 1962* (Nashville, Tenn.).

[52] National Council of the Churches of Christ in U.S.A., *Yearbook of American Churches, 1961*, New York, p. 285.

these New England colleges, and some in other regions, have subsequently become private independent colleges and are not consciously members of the present Congregational Christian family of colleges. These colleges exhibit varying attitudes toward their historic origins. The United Church of Christ merely notes in its Year Book, as a matter of historic record, that these colleges were Congregationally founded.[53]

The American Baptist Convention reports that 7 of the 25 colleges in its listing are completely independent and autonomous and are therefore only historically related to their denomination.[54] On the other hand the Methodist Church finds that the period in which their colleges were moving away from the church and trying to "make the best of being related is now past; and that on the part of both the church and the college there is now a renewed concern to make the relationship a meaningful one."[55]

The colleges that are church related express their religious orientation in a variety of ways. The colleges sponsored by the liberal denominations present a somewhat different pattern of curricula, regulations, and norms of behavior from that found in the typical college sponsored by conservative denominations. Within the group of liberal sponsored colleges there is considerable variation in the manner of expressing and reflecting the religious concern: through curriculum, by type of student sought and attracted, by what the college requires of the student, and by what the college leaves to the discretion of the student. The colleges sponsored by the Methodist Church, the United Presbyterian Church, the Lutheran Church in America, the Episcopal Church, and the United Church of Christ would generally express religious concern in keeping with the liberal interpretations of the Protestant faith.

The liberal colleges believe that the Christian perspective is universally associated with sound education where the search for truth is unfettered, Congregationalists, for example, maintaining that sound education requires the college to be independent of the Congregational Church. According to both traditional and contemporary Congregational theory and philosophy, responsible society is composed of three parts; church, college, and commonwealth or government. None is good enough to be in complete authority, and all are responsible ultimately to God. The college and the academic community is not a church, but college, church, and government are in continuous and creative interaction. The academic community exists for the purpose of a free inquiry into truth.

The religious character of the college is expressed primarily in the integrity and freedom of this inquiry into truth. We feel that this a more important

[53] Board of Homeland Ministries, United Church of Christ, The Meaning and Presuppositions of Church Relatedness of Congregational Christian Churches (mimeographed).

[54] As stated in a letter from Elmer G. Million, Department of Schools and Colleges, American Baptist Convention, Valley Forge, Penn., June 4, 1962.

[55] As stated in a letter from Richard N. Bender, Religion in Higher Education, the Methodist Church, U.S.A. (Nashville, Tennessee), May 23, 1962.

expression of its Christian character than the quantity of religion in its curriculum.[56]

The liberal denominations support Elton Trueblood's definition that "A Christian college is one in which the Christian perspective is accepted openly, avowedly, and unapologetically." Christianity should pervade the campus. A college does not become a Christian college just by courses in religion and chapel services.[57] The campus should be a living laboratory for the realization of a Christian community in such areas as faculty-student relationships, student government, and campus activities and facilities. The religious complexion of the college also should include Christian service to the local community.[58]

The liberal denomination sponsored colleges put a great deal of emphasis upon the liberal arts and sciences. There is a "natural affinity between the Protestant faith and liberal education."[59] The United Church of Christ advocates a nonsectarian approach to all matters of religion and recommends that the doors of its colleges be open to all students qualified for the academic program.

Race, creed, national origin, or cultural status shall never be considered as a basis for denial of admission. Our colleges shall encourage all sincere search for truth by avoiding creedal test and by insisting that different disciplines and faith groups shall be in conversation with each other.[60]

A Lutheran college reports that admission is offered to any qualified student regardless of race, creed, or color, and that in the current year Methodist students comprised the largest group. This is a tribute to the college's liberal philosophy but it is also an evidence and a consequence of the regional nature of the college. This college is located in upstate New York where Methodists are twice as numerous as any other Protestant denomination. It requires Protestant and Jewish students to take three courses in religion towards their degree, while Catholic students are permitted to substitute philosophy courses for the religious requirement.[61]

The Disciples of Christ also report that religious affiliation is not used as a criterion for the admission of students to their colleges, and that their student bodies for the most part represent the "entire spectrum of our pluralistic society."[62]

---

[56] As stated in a letter from Wesley A. Hotchkiss, general secretary, Division of Higher Education, United Church of Christ, New York, May 24, 1962.

[57] Robert Mortvedt, *The Role of the Christian College* (New York: Board of Education, United Lutheran Church in America).

[58] United Presbyterian Church of the United States of America, *The Church and Higher Education, An Official Statement*, Philadelphia.

[59] Division of Higher Education, Board of Education, the Methodist Church, *The Teaching of Religion in Church Related Colleges* (a normative statement produced by a three-year colloquium on the teaching of religion) (Nashville, Tenn.: 1962).

[60] Board of Homeland Ministries, United Church of Christ, *op. cit.*

[61] As stated in a letter from Edgar L. Sagan, director of admissions, Hartwick College (Oneonta, N.Y.), June 7, 1962.

[62] As stated in a letter from H. L. Smith, president, Board of Higher Education, Disciples of Christ, Indianapolis, Ind., May 29, 1962.

Goals and Objectives. These colleges require a varied number of hours and credits in religion, Bible, and philosophy courses. The requirements run from as little as 6 to as many as 24 hours, with the most common requirement between 9 and 15 hours. At a church related Episcopal college a student may graduate with a basic 3 hours of philosophy, 3 hours of literature, music, or art, or 3 hours of religion (Introduction to the Bible) as alternative requirements. A student may, however, major in religion with a minimum of 30 hours. Each student is required to attend Sunday chapel service on at least 9 Sundays in a term, or in lieu of college chapel may attend a church of his choice.[63]

The Division of Higher Education of the Methodist Church asks its colleges to design courses in religion that will

1. Transmit the heritage of the Hebrew-Christian tradition which has helped to shape Western culture and which points to the perennial problems of existence.

2. Make clear the role which religion plays in culture and the operation of religious presuppositions in diverse areas of life. Insights regarding how our religious presuppositions help form conclusions in law, in government, or in literature, give to the religious option a dimension which few students consider.

3. Stimulate a critical awareness of the nature of value judgments and personal commitments and, thus, prepare the student to participate positively in the theological task.[64]

The American Baptist Convention asks its colleges to provide a comprehensive program of religious life and training on the campus as well as in the local church and community, and suggests that this can be done in

1. A Department of Religion with standard courses in Bible, Christian ethics, philosophy of religion, and courses dealing with the Protestant heritage as well as our own denominational heritage.

2. Corporate worship usually in the form of voluntary or compulsory chapel, and a Christian Emphasis Program (all-year round, as well as specific emphasis once or twice a year).

3. Christian service to the local community.

4. The development of lay leadership by encouraging student participation in the church life of the American Baptist Convention as well as within the other Protestant denominations represented.

5. Encouragement of small groups for study and worship.[65]

The United Presbyterian Church advises its colleges to function in terms of three basic affirmations.

1. God, known in Jesus Christ, is Lord of all life.

2. The Christian has a vocation in the world. This means that essential worldly tasks are the result of the ordering of life by God, and are a part of the Christian's responsibility in the world.

---

[63] *Trinity College Bulletin for 1962,* Trinity College, Hartford, Conn.

[64] *The Teaching of Religion in Church Related Colleges, op. cit.,* p. 12.

[65] American Baptist Convention, *What Is a Baptist College Related to the American Baptist Convention?* Valley Forge, Pennsylvania.

3. Self-giving service. The church is called to live, not for itself, but for the world.[66]

The Board of Christian Education of the United Presbyterian Church reports that each of its colleges offers a major in the field of the Bible and religion; that most of them require six or more hours of Bible study for graduation; that in some colleges religion or philosophy may be substituted for required Bible study.[67]

Organizational Relationships. The organizational relationship of the sponsoring church and its colleges varies. Some colleges are closely tied to the church through its trustees and through contractual relationships, and others are completely independent and autonomous.

There is no uniform pattern of religious qualifications for either president, faculty, or students; the outstanding feature, rather, is the lack of religious qualifications. The United Church of Christ stresses the independence of the college from the church and seeks scholars of all persuasions of faith to join the intellectual community. The college must be independent of the church, but it is equally important that college and church be in creative communication with each other.[68]

The Disciples of Christ exercise no control over its colleges; each college is free to select its administrators and its faculty, although the Board of Higher Education of the Disciples reports that no president has been appointed to any college of its denomination without a close consultation of the trustees of the college and the Board. The Disciples also report that in the selection of a president they are more interested in the demonstrated churchmanship of the person than in his denominational affiliation.[69]

The American Baptist Convention reports there are no religious requirements for admission to a Baptist college or appointment to the faculty, but they feel that a Baptist president or dean is better equipped to work forcefully yet easily with its Board of Education.[70]

The Board of Christian Education of the United Presbyterian Church reports a number of ways in which its 45 colleges are related to the church and that this is spelled out in each individual charter. Some colleges require that a given number of trustees be members of the Presbyterian Church. Most of the colleges prefer, but do not require, that the president be a Presbyterian, and in fact about half of the presidents happen to be ordained Presbyterian ministers.[71]

The great majority of the Protestant colleges are sponsored by the large liberal denominations. The relationship of these colleges to their sponsoring

---

[66] *The Church and Higher Education, an Official Statement, op. cit.*

[67] As stated in a letter from Anne Horner, Board of Christian Education, United Presbyterian Church in U.S.A., Philadelphia, May 24, 1962.

[68] *The Meaning and Presuppositions of Church Relatedness of Congregational Christian Churches, op. cit.*

[69] H. L. Smith, *op. cit.*

[70] E. G. Million, *op. cit.*

[71] A. Horner, *op. cit.*

denominations, and the relationship of each college to its faculty and its students, is characteristically permissive. The colleges are essentially independent and individualistic, and even where the bonds between the college and the denomination are legally defined, specific, and comprehensive, there is little attempt on the part of the sponsoring denomination to arbitrarily implement its authority.

Within a broad framework of Christian affirmations colleges are encouraged to translate the Christian perspective according to their own insights and genius. For the most part students are required to do little but encouraged to do much. A student can graduate from one of these colleges a tremendously concerned and committed Christian because of his college experience. Another student can pass through the same college without being much changed by courses in religion, the chapels and convocations he has attended, or the Christian atmosphere to which he has been exposed.

Church Related Colleges of Conservative Denominations

Colleges sponsored by the conservative denominations are more demanding and less permissive, and, like their parent churches, have a confession of faith. Students are expected to accept this creed. More courses in religion and religion-related courses are required than in the liberal colleges. The rules of behavior are precise and specific; students are told what they must and what they must not do. A significant percent of the students are members of the sponsoring church and most of the faculty are not only members of the church but active in religious affairs in the college community. The following cases are representative ways in which a conservative church college implements its philosophy of education.

Augsburg College is sponsored by the Lutheran Free Church. According to the president:

All the members of the Board of Trustees are members of the Lutheran Church. Of our chief administrators, all but one are active Lutherans, and this one is an active member of the Baptist Church. A great proportion of our faculty members are active church members, and our student body is about 85–90 percent Lutheran. All of this tends to give a strong religious emphasis to our program.[72]

Hope College, sponsored by the Reformed Church in America, feels that the Christian faith is relevant to the whole of life and that the Gospel gives new depth and direction to the whole program of Liberal Arts. Faculty members must belong to some evangelical church, but not necessarily the Reformed Church of America. About two thirds of the faculty and two thirds of the student body are members of the Reformed Church. Each day begins with a twenty-minute chapel service which each student

---

[72] As stated in a letter from Bernhard Christensen, president, Augsburg College, Minneapolis, May 28, 1962.

is required to attend. The college opposes drinking, gambling, and hazing, discourages women students from smoking, and regulates social dancing.[73]

The Wesleyan Methodist Church is orthodox in doctrine and demanding of behavior. Its colleges and students are asked to conform to the confession of faith and to the same behavioral norms that are required of church members. It reports that

> The institutions under the Church's patronage and support are not permitted to employ teachers who do not accept its doctrinal views. It is considered the province of the Church to declare doctrines, and of the Church's schools to teach what the Church declares.
>
> Many of the practices allowed at other educational institutions are not permitted at Wesleyan Colleges. Fraternities, sororities, and intercollegiate athletics are forbidden. The student's physical and social well-being is not overlooked but safe-guarded. The principal emphasis is placed upon spiritual, moral and mental development.[74]

Greenville College in Illinois is one of several colleges sponsored by the Free Methodist Church. The Department of Educational Institutions of its national office reports that all of the Free Methodist colleges are Liberal Arts institutions that at the same time give a very wholesome emphasis to Christian education and the study of the Bible. All of them have daily chapel services, and attendance is required. It is expected that at least a majority of the trustees and three fourths of the faculty will be members of the Free Methodist Church.[75]

The Greenville catalog contains a statement of belief that includes the doctrine of "entire sanctification," a distinguishing feature of the Free Methodist confession. Students are expected to subscribe to this statement. The catalog also spells out the standards of conduct, requiring that

> all regularly enrolled students sign a commitment annually that they do not use tobacco or alcoholic beverages in any form. Students are not permitted to organize or to join secret fraternities. Students are required to refrain from the use of playing cards, playing billiards or games of chance, from attending theaters, dances, and other places of amusement which in the judgement of the faculty interfere with their school program or prove detrimental to the college. The college requires modesty and conservatism in dress on all occasions.[76]

The Southern Baptist Church is generally grouped with the conservative Protestant denominations. It is very active in the field of higher education, sponsoring 28 senior colleges and universities. According to the report of its Education Commission the dominant motive in education is the development of character. "Character finds its sanction only in Christian ideals."

---

[73] *Hope College Catalogue, 1961–1963*, Holland, Michigan, pp. 10–11.

[74] *The Wesleyan Methodist Church of America* (Marion, Ind.: The Wesley Press, 1961), p. 28.

[75] As stated in a letter from C. Hoyt Watson, General Education secretary, Free Methodist Church of North America, Winona Lake, Ind., May 22, 1962.

[76] *Greenville College Record, 1963–1964*, Greenville, Ill., p. 6.

In recent years the question of academic freedom on the campuses of some of its colleges has risen to plague the Southern Baptist Church. The church had this to say about denominational control:

How far should academic liberty extend? May a teacher in a Baptist institution have absolute privilege to express any opinion? The Baptist attitude is clear and historic. Liberty of thought, word, and deed is the birthright of every man. But, Baptists must insist that the teacher in a Baptist school shall contribute to the Baptist product in student life and thought. A man may teach his own ideas, regardless of their conformity to any current opinions, but he should not be unwise enough to expect Baptist salary for contravening and subverting Baptist ideals.[77]

Brigham Young University, sponsored by the Church of Jesus Christ of Latter-Day Saints (Mormon), represents the complete integration of church and college. It has a College of Religious Instruction in which each fulltime student is required to take a two-hour course in religion each semester he is enrolled. Once each week there is a one-hour devotional service at which an outstanding religious leader is the speaker. The college reports that the average weekly attendance for the academic year 1960–61 was 4,759. In this same year, 192 of the 500 fulltime faculty members held highly responsible church positions.

A large proportion of the students are active members of the church. There are three stakes, or dioceses, of the church on the university campus, consisting of 32 wards, or congregations. In 1961 the average attendance at Sacrament Meeting (worship service) at Brigham Young University was 71 percent of the membership. During this same year 85 percent of the students in these congregations were full tithe payers. Of the total students, 1,847 had previously devoted two or more years to the church as fulltime missionaries, for which they had received no financial remuneration.[78]

The Church of Jesus Christ of Latter-Day Saints provides a program of religious education for students attending institutions of higher learning that are not operated by the church. Institutes of Religion, adjacent to college and university campuses and completely operated and maintained by the church, offer formal courses in religion, a varied social program, devotional services, and a counseling program where trained personnel make their services available to students who seek their aid. In 1963, 19,000 students were taking regular classes in 39 fulltime and 96 parttime Institutes of Religion throughout the United States and Canada.[79]

The conservative church colleges are more overtly religious than the liberal church colleges. They are orthodox in doctrine and demanding and unyielding in behavior requirements. The students and the faculty inter-

---

[77] Education Commission of the Southern Baptist Convention, *Southern Baptist Campus Directory* (Nashville, Tenn.), p. 15.

[78] As stated in a letter from David H. Yarn, dean, College of Religious Instruction, Brigham Young University, Provo, Utah, June 5, 1962.

[79] *Announcement of Program, 1963, op. cit.*, pp. 34–37.

act intensively among themselves and possess many of the in-group characteristics of the early Christian community. As individuals and as groups they represent the highest embodiment of the traditional sacred pattern of values and behavior norms, and offer the greatest resistance to the secularization trend within American Protestantism.

Church Related Catholic Colleges

The Catholic Church has developed an impressive structure of educational institutions of higher learning. The *Catholic Almanac* lists 211 senior colleges and universities in addition to 33 junior colleges and a number of other specialized educational institutions.[80] One hundred and ten of these colleges are for women, 59 for men, and 42 are coeducational. Protestants are impressed by the rapid development of Catholic higher education and by the report that 96 new Catholic colleges and universities have been created since 1939—as compared to 10 by all of Protestantism during the same period.

The rationale for Catholic colleges is established in Canon Law:

From childhood all the faithful must be so educated that not only are they taught nothing contrary to faith and morals but that religious and moral training takes the first place. (Canon 1372)
The Church has the right to establish schools of every grade, not only elementary schools, but also high schools and colleges. (Canon 1375)[81]

Catholic colleges thus have a positive and a negative function. They are to teach proper religious and moral behavior, and they are to protect their students from teachings and behavior contrary to faith and morals. Catholic colleges attempt to discharge these functions. The following Catholic colleges were chosen at random to illustrate the way in which the canonical imperatives are implemented.

A Catholic Liberal Arts college for women proposes to educate its students to be valuable members of the church and of society, distinguished by minds trained to think correctly and by wills formed to standards of true moral worth. The faculty of this college believes that the central core of a truly liberal education should be theology, and 16 semester hours in theology are required: Theology 101–102, Theology of the Incarnation; Theology 201–202, Theology of the Redemption; Theology 301–302, Theology of the Mystical Body; and Theology 401–402, Theology of the Christian Life.

Students are also required to take 18 hours of philosophy, the greater part of which is made up of the thought and synthesis of St. Thomas Aquinas. Worship is stressed. Mass is offered each day. An annual three-day closed retreat is an integral part of the college calendar. All classes are suspended and the students are encouraged to focus complete attention on the privileges and obligations of a truly Christian life. Various cocurricular

---

[80] *Catholic Almanac, op. cit.,* p. 485.
[81] *Catholic Almanac, op. cit.,* p. 483.

organizations of a religious nature, such as a sodality, the choir, and the Mission Club serve to develop a deepened spiritual life and to stimulate works of charity and zeal among students.[82]

A Jesuit college for men directs its program of moral training at building the conscience of its students for the proper fulfillment of their civic, social, and religious duties. It insists upon the cultivation of the Christian virtues which operate to this end; and since religion is the only solid basis of virtue and morality, thorough instruction in its principles forms an essential part of the system. All Catholic students are required to attend classes in Christian doctrine for the equivalent of four semesters. They are also expected to attend the weekly Student Mass, are required to make an annual retreat, and are urged to receive the sacraments frequently.

Students are required to take 18 hours of philosophy as follows: Philosophy 55, Logic; Philosophy 106, Philosophy of Being; Philosophy 113, Philosophy of Man; Philosophy 126, Philosophy of Infinite Being; and Philosophy 135–136, Principles of Moral Philosophy.[83]

A Catholic coeducational university states its general objectives to be the development of learned, cultured men and women according to the principles and traditions of the Roman Catholic Church. This end is sought in part by the requirements of 10 hours in theology and 12 hours in philosophy. The theology requirements are: Theology 1 and 2, Fundamentals of Theology; Theology 3 and 4, Principles of Christian Morality; and Theology 5, Christ and His Sacraments.

Non-Catholic students do not take the above but are required to substitute Theology 15, 16, 17, and 18, Religions of Mankind, Religion and Culture, Jewish History, and Life of Christ, respectively, plus two other theology electives.

The philosophy requirements for non-Catholic students are Philosophy 1, Scholastic Philosophy; Philosophy 2, The Thinking Adolescent; Philosophy 4 and 5, The Developing Adolescent; and Philosophy 9 and 10, The Responsible Adolescent.

The Rules and Regulations of this university state that

. . . In conformity with the ideals of Christian education and conduct, the University reserves the right to dismiss a student at any time on whatever grounds the University judges advisable. Each student by his admission to the University recognizes this right.[84]

Catholic authorities take the protective function of the Catholic college seriously. The importance of their colleges in maintaining Catholic ideals and values, and the dangers which Catholic leaders see in a secular education is outlined in a statement issued by the bishop of a diocese in southeastern Kansas, warning Roman Catholic students in his diocese from

---

[82] *Bulletin of the College of New Rochelle, 1961–1962,* New Rochelle, N.Y.
[83] *Bulletin for John Carroll University, 1960–1962,* Cleveland.
[84] *St. John's University Bulletin, 1963–1964,* Brooklyn, p. 61.

enrolling in most undergraduate psychology and philosophy courses at non-Catholic colleges and universities. He charged that many of these courses constitute a form of "brainwashing" that endangers a student's faith in his church and his loyalty to his country. His directive was based, he said, upon the findings of psychiatrists who had studied the cases of those American prisoners in Korea who had defected to the enemy. The bishop found that the attitudes of the prisoners were the result of the education they had received, which were "non-religious or even irreligious."

> Here at home we have a very sneaky, sly form of brainwashing going on in our secular colleges. It is not approved by the boards of regents or by the college presidents. But it is due to individual professors of psychology and philosophy in particular, as well as some professors of sociology, history, and economics . . . the soldiers, whether Jews, Protestants, or Catholics who were well grounded in their faith were the only ones who had the intelligence and courage to remain loyal to the United States.[85]

This bishop represents the extreme Catholic position. Not all Catholics who prefer a Catholic to a secular college find the same close causal relationship between religion and patriotism and higher education that the bishop professes to see. However, most Catholics listen respectfully to the teachings of their church and go to considerable sacrifice to continue their education and development within the most favorable religious setting and environment, which is, of course, a Catholic college.

Catholic colleges also are vitally concerned that their students follow the teachings of the church on sex and marriage. St. John's University, for example, dismissed three students who violated the Catholic rules on marriage. Two were married in a civil ceremony on March 13, 1962, and the third student had been a witness. One month later, April 12, the couple was married again before a priest in a Catholic church and the same witnesses. The students were notified April 18, 1962, that they were dismissed from St. John's because the civil ceremony was "gravely sinful" and "a source of public scandal."

The students sought court action to require St. John's to reinstate them. The lawyers representing the university argued that St. John's was within its rights since the catalog explicitly said that "in conformity with the ideals of Christian education and conduct, the University reserves the right to dismiss a student at any time."[86] The Catholic college expects the Catholic student to maintain the outward forms of moral behavior taught by the church.

Organized Student Religious Groups

The three faiths have national organizations that coordinate the religious work and worship of the students of their respective faiths on various college campuses.

---

[85] New York Times, September 3, 1956.
[86] Ibid., May, 18, 1962.

The Jewish national organization is Hillel. On a large campus with a significant number of Jewish students, Hillel is served by a resident rabbi. If the Jewish group is not large enough to warrant the full-time services of a resident rabbi, a local rabbi is usually appointed to serve the local Hillel group as a part-time counselor.

The national Catholic organization is the Newman Club. Where there is a significant number of Catholic students the Newman Club is served by a full-time priest-advisor. If there are not enough students to warrant a full-time advisor, the bishop of the local diocese usually appoints a priest assigned to one of the local parishes to serve on a part-time basis as advisor to the local Newman Club. In many non-Catholic colleges the Newman Club advisor offers noncredit courses that attempt in abbreviated form to give interested Catholic students the same acquaintance with Catholic doctrine and practice as are given in formal courses in theology in the typical Catholic college.

National religious organizations that serve Protestant groups can be loosely summarized under the National Student Christian Federation (NSCF) and the Intervarsity Christian Fellowship (IVCF). The NSCF was formed in 1959 as a result of the merger of three student organizations that seemed to be dominated by the same concern and dedicated to the same objectives: the Interseminary Committee, the Student Volunteer Movement, and the United Student Christian Council. The NSCF now includes student groups that are representative of Baptists, Lutherans, Presbyterians, Episcopalians, the YMCA, Disciples of Christ, Evangelical United Brethren, and the United Church of Christ (Congregational-Christian and Evangelical and Reformed). The program of NSCF includes

1. Intercollegiate ecumenical conferences on unity, mission, and witness in higher education.
2. Planning and administering voluntary service projects. In 1960 it carried on 28 international projects and 7 projects in the United States.
3. Working with such domestic problems as the foreign student on the American college campus and interracial problems.[87]

IVCF is an interdenominational student Christian group with a theologically conservative orientation that stresses the personal experience of religion. IVCF states that it is a nationwide interdenominational student organization of college and university chapters dedicated to

1. A presentation of the relevance of the Lord Jesus Christ to college and university students.
2. Growth in Christian discipleship through individual and group Bible study, prayer, discussions, conferences, and speakers.
3. A consideration of the Christian's responsibility in world evangelism.[88]

---

[87] *Information Service*, Vol. XL, No. 10 (May 13, 1961), pp. 3–5.
[88] Inter-Varsity Christian Fellowship, *A Word About College*, 1519 N. Astor St., Chicago.

The author has been personally acquainted with a number of IVCF groups and individual members on several campuses. Both believe and practice the principles of conservative Protestantism. They meet in small groups for Bible study, prayer, and meditation. They speak with pride of those who "professed faith in Christ" as a result of personal witnessing on their part. Several have graduated to go on to serve as missionaries in the foreign field.

NSCF, on the other hand, tends to reflect liberal Protestantism both in program and in behavior. A great part of the activity on any campus deals with some aspect of the "social gospel"; that is, working in service projects, with International students, and social service work of various kinds. NSCF consistently lacks the emphasis upon the personal religious experience, with its public confession, that is invariably associated with IVCF activity. IVCF groups are usually smaller than NSCF, Newman, or Hillel groups. Although smaller in numbers they stand out for their total commitment. They also stand out by being different, and frequently find it impossible to participate in campus-wide religious activities that Hillel, Newman, and NSCF find it possible to support.

Religion in Nonsectarian Colleges

Public Colleges. Unlike the situation at elementary and secondary school levels, public institutions of higher education are growing at a faster rate than private institutions. Private institutions, until recently, enrolled the majority of students in higher education in the United States, but public institutions have been growing and currently enroll 60 percent of the students. Enrollments in public four-year colleges and universities from 1950 to 1960 rose at the rate of 83.8 percent. During this same period private institutions, including church colleges, rose at a rate of 31.8 percent.[89]

Very little has been said by the courts about religious practices in state-supported colleges and universities, even though a great deal has been said by the same courts about religion in the public schools at the elementary and secondary school level. No student is required to attend a public college, whereas elementary and secondary school attendance is compulsory. The college student is more mature and supposedly less subject to either indoctrination or "unindoctrination," as the case may be. The determination of what should be done about religion on state college or university campuses has been largely left up to the faculties and administrations of the various institutions. Public colleges represent a wide variation in what they permit, what they encourage, what they forbid, and what they discourage.

---

[89] Annual Report on the Progress of Education in the United States to the Twenty-Third International Conference on Public Education, Geneva, Switzerland. Cited in the United States Department of Health, Education, and Welfare Office of Education press release, HEW N–53, July 7, 1960.

Public colleges felt and reflected the nonsectarian movement which developed rapidly in the decades between World War I and World War II. Chapels with considerable emphasis upon the forms of religion, prayers, Bible reading, hymns, often became assemblies that had relinquished these religious aspects. In many colleges the traditional baccalaureate service, with rotation of Protestant, Catholic, and Jewish clergymen as preachers, was eliminated. Many public colleges likewise avoided all questions of religion in the curriculum as controversial and improper.

Following World War II a countertrend seems to have developed that could be interpreted as one aspect of the alleged "return to religion." According to this point of view, education is not good or adequate general education if it does not give some attention to the religious dimension. A number of projects developed throughout the country to explore the relationship of the religious dimension to both the curricular and extracurricular phases of the college program.

Teacher Education and Religion. One of the more ambitious of these projects was the five-year experimental Teacher Education and Religion project sponsored by the American Association of Colleges for Teacher Education (AACTE) and subsidized by the Danforth Foundation. This association is composed of more than 300 colleges and universities throughout the country in which teacher education and certification is an important aspect of a total program. Teacher training constitutes the largest single activity of American colleges. In 1959 almost twice as many bachelor degrees were granted with a major in Education (87,877) than in the next highest category of Business and Commerce (53,108). These fields were followed by the combined Social Sciences and by Engineering.[90]

All types of higher institutions are included in this association and participated in this project: large public and large private universities, teachers colleges and private colleges of liberal arts and sciences. It was the thesis of this project that the public school teacher did not possess an adequate general education unless he were religiously literate; that is, had some adequate concept of the place of religion in the development of American civilization as well as some knowledge about the nature and scope of religion in contemporary pluralistic society.

A study of court decisions led the sponsors and proponents to limit the scope of the project to activities, experiments, and courses that were concerned with the "reciprocal relations" between religion and culture. This was interpreted to include activities and courses about religion. Courses or activities that were taught or approached in such a way as to involve commitment were improper, at least in the public institutions.[91] The Danforth Foundation, which subsidized the project, is now known as the Danforth Teacher Education and Religion Project.

---

[90] *Statistical Abstract of the United States, 1961*, Superintendent of Documents, Government Printing Office, Washington, D.C.
[91] See Chapter XV.

Fifteen pilot institutions were selected to experiment with various activities and courses that might contribute to an understanding of the reciprocal relations between religion and the culture. The pilot institutions were chosen from various geographic regions and represented the various types of institutions concerned with teacher education: again, the large and public universities as well as the teachers colleges and the private colleges of the liberal arts and sciences.

A wide variety of activities and experiments was carried on in the pilot institutions. Some faculties made an intensive study of the question of religion and the curriculum, and some did, and others did not, recommend curricular revision on the basis of their findings. Studies were made of religious materials in elementary and secondary school text books, and courses of study were developed to compensate for what were considered to be curricular voids and limitations. A number of courses were developed and recommended as proper materials for general education, such as the Bible as Literature, Comparative Religion, Sociology of Religion,[92] Religion in American Culture, and Philosophy of Religion.[93]

The project also found that courses and experiences dealing with the contemporary religious culture possessed important special education values for teachers in training. In a typical public school elementary or secondary classroom religious questions and religious problems continually arise. The teacher who is informed about the structure and the practices of the basic American faiths is better prepared to answer questions and meet children's problems sympathetically and knowledgeably.

Variation in State College Practice. Public colleges are pretty much on their own on what they do or do not do regarding religion. There are no Supreme Court decisions specifically concerned with religion on a state college campus. Decisions and opinions in this area deal with state constitutions, state courts, and opinions of state attorneys general. A study of religious activities on state college campuses shows a wide variation in what is done and what is not done. The following data are based upon a survey made by the faculty of St. Cloud State College, Minnesota.[94] A questionnaire was sent to 256 state-supported colleges in 47 states and the District of Columbia. The survey was limited to colleges of 5,000 and under. Replies were received from 148 colleges representing 44 states. This was a 57.8 percent return on the sample.

All but 20 of the colleges reported that they had religious organizations on the campus—and 7 of the 20 had regulations against recognition of religious organizations. Religious organizations averaged slightly more than

---

[92] W. Seward Salisbury and Frank Scholfield, "Teaching Sociological Concepts by Learning about Religion," *Religious Education,* Vol. LII, No. 6 (November-December, 1957), p. 451.

[93] A. L. Sebaly, *Teacher Education and Religion* (Oneonta, N.Y.: The American Association of Colleges for Teacher Education, 1959), pp. 97–160.

[94] St. Cloud State College, St. *Cloud Bulletin, Religious Activities in Public Colleges,* Vol. 14, No. 4, May 1959, St. Cloud, Minn.

5 per campus, and only five of the religious organizations, Catholic and four of the major Protestant denominations, were found on more than half of the campuses. Some kind of interdenominational organization was found on approximately three fourths of the campuses.

TABLE 25

RELIGIOUS DENOMINATIONS REPRESENTED BY RELIGIOUS
ORGANIZATIONS ON 125 COLLEGE CAMPUSES

Denomination	No.	% of Colleges
Roman Catholic	108	84.4
Methodist	99	77.3
Baptist	79	61.7
Lutheran	76	59.4
Presbyterian	72	56.3
Episcopal	62	48.4
Congregational	15	11.7
Christian Science	13	10.2
Hebrew	12	9.4
Christian	11	8.6
Disciples of Christ	7	5.5
Latter-Day Saints	6	4.7
Church of Christ	4	3.1
Brethren	4	3.1
Assembly of God	3	2.3
Bahai	2	1.6
Orthodox	2	1.6
Unitarian	2	1.6
Church of God	1	.8
United Church of Christ	1	.8
Universalist	1	.8
Mission Covenant	1	.8
YWCA	13	10.2
YMCA	14	10.9
Inter-Varsity Christian Fellowship	28	21.9
Inter-Denominational Organizations	57	44.5
TOTAL	693	

Religious Activities in Public Colleges Bulletin, No. 4, Vol. 14 (May, 1959), St. Cloud State College, St. Cloud, Minnesota, p. 16.

Slightly less than half (48 percent) of these colleges reported that all or most of the religious organizations meet on campus; slightly more than half reported that all or most of the religious organizations meet off campus. Only about one fourth of the students on the typical college campus participated in these organizations. This is, however, a higher percent than was found to participate in religious organizations on campuses of some private colleges that are historically church related.

The religious organizations met on the average of once a week. In 115 out of 128 colleges faculty members served as advisors or sponsors for the religious organizations that are recognized by the college. In the typical college about 6 faculty members were sponsoring religious organizations. In only 17 colleges were adjustments made in the advisor's load in the light of his sponsorship of the religious organizations.

Twenty-two of 143 colleges reported that they had a campus chapel. In 13 colleges the construction of the college chapel was financed through state appropriations. Finances for the operation and maintenance of the college chapel were derived from state funds in 17 colleges. The report concluded that 19, and perhaps 20, of the colleges finance the maintenance and operation of the chapel from some source of public money. Slightly more than 40 percent of the religious organizations owned or rented their own centers or houses.

Some kind of religious emphasis week (REW) was held at 72 percent of the colleges, but 7 colleges reported that they did not sponsor a REW because of concern over the question of constitutionality. The attorney general of the state of Washington, in fact, has ruled that state university participation in Religious Emphasis Week observances was contrary to the state constitution.[95] The typical REW, however, extends over a 3 to 5 day period, and its planning and administration is typically that of a student-faculty committee.

Religion-related Courses. Slightly more than two thirds of the colleges reported that they included religion related courses in their curricular offerings. However, the religion related courses reported by 28 of the 100 colleges claiming to have such courses were restricted to courses in philosophy, ethics, cultural anthropology, and other similar courses having a dubious relationship with religion. More than one fourth of the colleges reported that they offered courses in the reading and study of the Bible. A number of course titles suggested a broader area of study than examination of Judeo-Christian teachings and traditions. The most frequently mentioned courses in this group were Comparative Religions, Religion in Contemporary America, Religious Education, or some phase or aspect thereof.

The widely varying attitudes and practices toward religion is further indicated by the following direct quotes from reporting colleges.

Religious services are not permitted on the campus (although the college does provide rooms for religious organizations meetings). Religious clubs must abide by the same policies that affect all student organizations.

We do not control the activities of our religious organizations; they are directed by clergymen of the town, men of discretion.

While this college does not recognize religious organizations on its campus, it does provide a program of spiritual guidance. Weekly, members of the clergy of each of the major faiths (Jewish, Protestant, Catholic) are available

---

[95] Mentioned in joint memorandum of the American Jewish Committee and the Anti-Defamation League of B'nai B'rith dated July 9, 1957, "Attorney General of Washington rules state university participation in Religious Emphasis Week Observances unconstitutional."

in offices on campus to meet with anyone who wishes to see them. There is a feeling that this provides the opportunity for religious guidance for those who wish it without the division that the presence of religious organizations might create.

We hold that the spiritual life of the student can be served best by his close association with the community church of his choice. Consequently, our efforts have been directed toward getting the student to the church rather than developing programs on campus which tend to shift the spiritual headquarters away from the church to the campus.

REW has not been officially discontinued but we have not had one for about three years mainly because there has been no demand for one.

We are a state college. We would cooperate [in holding REW] but could not initiate.

We have had good attendance at REW but certain groups do not wish to have their students hear religious leaders of other faiths. We operated for many years as a campus summer school where we taught the geography of the Bible but we were forced to give this up because some church leaders objected because we did not emphasize things they thought should be emphasized; others thought we colored the lessons.

The idea of having one week set apart for REW leaves me completely cold. We try to make every week Religious Emphasis Week. We hold a chapel exercise two mornings a week. The programs consist of scripture reading, music by chapel choir and a short talk by a visiting clergyman, a faculty member, or a senior.

Nonsectarian Private Universities. Courses in religion and philosophy are offered in both the large public and the nonsectarian private universities, and there is not much difference between the courses offered. Both also have the same proliferation of religious groups and organizations.

Cornell, as a representative nonsectarian university, gives a prominent place to religion. Religious activities and organizations are encouraged by the Cornell United Religious Work (CURW) and are centered in Anabel Taylor Hall, built especially as a religious center through the contribution of an interested alumnus and his wife. The building provides offices for a director, his staff, and 14 resident chaplains. It also includes a chapel, a library, an auditorium, meeting rooms, and lounges. With minor modifications the chapel can serve as an appropriate sanctuary for a Catholic, Protestant, or Jewish service.

Three fulltime staff members deal with the interfaith activities of the program. Over half of the budget (that exceeds $100,000) is contributed by the university. The member religious groups have full financial responsibility for the support of their respective chaplains and programs. "*United* [in CURW] refers not only to diverse religious groups committed to work closely together and to support a common program, also religious groups, on a united basis, working with the University to service the total University community."[96]

---

[96] Cornell (University) United Religious Work, *Where Religion and University Meet* (Ithaca, N.Y.: Cornell University).

CURW offers courses in religion which do not carry university credit. In a recent semester 400 students were enrolled in 16 courses that met one hour a week. A major in philosophy, both on the undergraduate and the graduate level, is offered in the College of Arts and Sciences, and a number of courses in religion are available in the philosophy sequence.

The Large State Universities. What is offered and what is permitted in terms of courses and activities varies according to state, but everything that is offered in the way of religious education and religious activities in private church related colleges is offered and done somewhere on some state university campus.

The School of Religion at the University of Iowa has been an integral part of the university's academic structure since 1925, operating as a department of the College of Liberal Arts. From the very beginning the School has had Jewish, Catholic, and Protestant instructors. Although they are nominated by religious groups, professors are finally selected and appointed by the University of Iowa and must have academic qualifications equal to those of faculty rank in other fields. Apart from administrative expenses, which are borne by the state, most of the School's budget is underwritten by denominational and private contributions. An undergraduate major in Religion consists of 24 hours of prescribed study plus elective study of Latin, Greek, or Hebrew.[97]

The University of Michigan coordinates courses and activities in an Office of Religious Affairs, while a vice president of Student Affairs coordinates 22 religious foundations on campus and also has the responsibility for religious counseling services.

A faculty committee selected from the College of Literature, Science and Arts is responsible for the curriculum and the intellectual aspects of religion on the campus. Eighteen hours in approved courses in religion in various departments and 18 hours in a single discipline, such as philosophy, history, or anthropology, constitute a major in Religion and Ethics.

The committee administers a lecture program, through generous university appropriations, on the beliefs and values of various religions, religious research, and related topics. Interdisciplinary thinking about religion among interested faculty members is encouraged through monthly meetings of the Faculty Colloquium in Religion. Library resources and faculty appointments are encouraged through the leadership of this committee. Altogether, religion receives generous consideration both in terms of experience and activities and intellectual inquiry.[98]

Credit programs in various religious centers around the state university are in operation at the University of Illinois and the University of

---

[97] Helen C. White, "What Place Has Religion in State University Education?" *Religion and the State University,* Erich A. Walter (ed.) (Ann Arbor, Mich.: University of Michigan Press, 1958), p. 100.

[98] *Ibid.,* p. 100–101.

North Dakota. The institutes of the Church of Jesus Christ of Latter-Day Saints are similar in operation and effect to the program at Illinois and North Dakota.[99]

RELIGION AND THE COLLEGE STUDENT

How religious are college students? To what extent has the college experience influenced the religion which college students possess? There is wide diversity on the answers to these questions. There is substantial evidence to support the proposition that the college experience has little influence upon the religious beliefs, attitudes, and behavior of students. But there is evidence that support also the proposition that the college experience modifies religious beliefs and attitudes, at least in some colleges. Furthermore, some students are so religiously involved and committed that there is nothing in a college experience that can either make them more religious or keep them from continuing to hold religious values as central and pivotal in both their philosophy and experience of life.

College Has Little Influence

The beliefs, attitudes, and behavior of college students have been widely studied. In his report, *Changing Values in College*,[100] Jacob listed 354 studies which dealt with some aspect of the impact of college and the curriculum upon the behavior of the student. Some of the best and most informative data of college students and their behavior are included in the several comprehensive studies of values that were made in the decade following World War II. Religion was one of the important values with which these studies were concerned.

In his summary of these studies Jacob found that the typical college student gave religion a relatively low rating in his hierarchy of values. The satisfactions of family and career were the dominant concerns of the typical student, followed by the satisfactions of leisure—with religion a weak fourth. On a first-second-third choice basis one comprehensive study found family and career shared the first position with a score of 89 each, leisure came next with 57, and religion had a score of 17.[101] The personal and private values of home, career, and leisure took precedence over the social values of service to the local, national, and world community for the typical student. The private values were pivotal and central while the religious and community values were marginal and peripheral.

Jacob reported there was little evidence that the values of students change as a result of their college experience. The typical student left college essentially the same sort of religious personality he was when he

---

    99 *Ibid.*, p. 101.

    100 Philip E. Jacob, *Changing Values in College* (New Haven, Conn.: The Edward W. Hazen Foundation, 1957).

    101 Rose K. Goldsen, Morris Rosenberg, Robin M. Williams, Edward A. Suchman, *What College Students Think* (Princeton, N.J.: D. Van Nostrand Co., 1960), p. 159.

entered. Neither the type of program in which the student was enrolled or the field of study in which he majored seemed to have anything to do with his values.

Jacob also reported that value patterns tend to be similar at American colleges, regardless of location, administration, size, background of student body, or character of the educational institutions. And this striking homogeneity of basic values prevailed throughout the country. On those issues on which students differed they split in about the same proportion at most institutions.[102]

Jacob was doubtful that the typical church college was more effective in developing religious awareness than the nonsectarian college, and cited the work of Espy in support of his proposition. Of several hundred teachers at church related colleges, few could recall that their own religious development had been appreciably affected by college experience, whether or not it had included compulsory chapel, required courses in religion and the Bible, and other features common to institutions with strong religious commitment.[103] By contrast half of the students at Wesleyan (a nonsectarian institution despite its name) felt that they personally had come to a higher valuation of religion during college. Against such findings it would seem that church colleges can claim no specially potent role in the business of strengthening and enlightening their students' religious perceptions.[104]

Jacob found few studies that dealt with southern colleges and Catholic colleges, and warned that his conclusions could not be considered to be representative of these institutions. He also found a lack of studies on students' evaluations of their own behavior and experience, and proposed that such data be collected and analyzed according to the techniques developed by Gordon W. Allport and his associates.[105]

Jacob found that curriculum "carryover" apparently depended upon the "value-climate" of the college community, and recommended studies to determine the nature and characteristics of these colleges whose impact upon the student apparently carried over into the individual student's value complex.

Some studies fail to find the same high degree of homogeneity in religious values among college students as was reported in the Jacob study. According to the Cornell study some college campuses are sufficiently different from other campuses as to be properly designated "religious campuses," the basis for this designation being the religiosity of the students. The criteria for religiosity of the Cornell study were students' attitudes towards religion as a major satisfaction, belief in a "divine God," the felt need for religious faith, and attendance of religious services "once a week

---

[102] P. E. Jacob, *op. cit.*, pp. 14, 55, 59.

[103] R. H. Edwin Espy, *The Religion of College Teachers* (New York: Association Press, 1951).

[104] P. E. Jacob, *op. cit.*, p. 113.

[105] *Ibid.*, p. 113; James M. Gillespie and Gordon W. Allport, *Youth's Outlook on the Future* (New York: Random House, Inc., 1955).

or more." The southern campuses (Fisk, North Carolina, the University of Texas) were found to have the highest percent of religiously oriented students. The least religious were the northeastern colleges (Cornell, Dartmouth, Harvard, and Yale), while the large middlewestern public universities (Michigan and Wayne) fell in between.[106]

A study comparing the religious attitudes and experience of a sample of students in a representative Deep South state college with a representative state college in the Northeast showed respective and significant differences in the religiosity of the students. The criteria for religiosity included a belief dimension (doctrine), a behavior dimension (church attendance), and an emotional-feeling dimension (the crisis-experience type of religious awakening). The comparisons were limited to active Protestants in both student bodies.

Active Protestants on the southern campuses proved to be significantly more regular in attendance at church services, more orthodox in belief, and more subject to the crisis type of religious awakening, and religious activities and values were more central and pivotal with them than with their northern counterparts. The southern college, in comparison to its sister institution in the North, was a "religious campus." The study concluded that the differences were more a consequence of the regional subculture than of any intrinsic difference in the college, curriculum or the student body.[107]

College Makes a Difference

The Jacob report aroused considerable interest among educators and laymen. A number of educators were disturbed by Jacob's conclusion that the typical college experience did not importantly influence or create values, many being convinced that some colleges have a positive effect upon the values that are involved in character structure. As a result of this difference the American Council on Education initiated a research study to determine the relation between intellect and character in the higher learning process. Edward D. Eddy was chosen as the director of the study and was the author of the final report.[108]

The study set out to discover the relationship between intellectual training and character influence; to determine how colleges, their students and their faculty approach the task of education; and to observe programs in operation which show signs of effectiveness. One of the assumptions of the study was that basic convictions and values are formed in the early years, and primarily in the home, but that college can modify convictions and values both for good and for ill.

---

[106] R. K. Goldsen *et al., op. cit.,* p. 159.

[107] W. S. Salisbury, "Religiosity, Region, Sex, and Social Behavior," *The Journal for the Scientific Study of Religion,* Vol. 2, No. 1 (October, 1962).

[108] Edward R. Eddy, *The College Influence on Student Character* (Washington, D.C.: The American Council on Education, 1959).

Because the study was particularly interested in securing the personal opinions and feelings of students, the participant-observer technique of securing data was emphasized, with some attention to the inclusion of more formal open-ended interviews with both students and faculty. Researchers on each campus, recent college graduates, lived with students in dormitories and fraternity or sorority houses for periods of a few days to a few weeks, attended classes and activity meetings with students, and talked with students at various times and places. A substantial accumulation of personal and illustrative data, impressions, and perceptions became the basis of the summary conclusions.

Twenty institutions, representing the variety of American colleges and universities, were chosen for the study: large universities and small colleges, church colleges and nonsectarian private colleges, state, municipal and federal colleges, men's, women's, and coeducational colleges.

TABLE 26

COLLEGES AND UNIVERSITIES COOPERATING IN THE STUDY

Name	Location	Undergraduate Enrollment°	Control	Sex
University of Arizona	Tucson, Ariz.	8,180	State	Coed
Brigham Young University	Provo, U.	10,138	Church	Coed
Colgate University	Hamilton, N.Y.	1,365	Nonsectarian	Men
University of Colorado	Boulder, Colo.	9,623	State	Coed
Cornell University	Ithaca, N.Y.	8,404	Nonsectarian	Coed
Denison University	Granville, O.	1,342	Church	Coed
Goddard College	Plainfield, Vt.	94	Nonsectarian	Coed
University of Louisville	Louisville, Ky.	6,496	Nonsectarian	Coed
Macalester College	St. Paul, Minn.	1,373	Church	Coed
United States Naval Academy	Annapolis, Md.	3,781	Federal	Men
University of New Hampshire	Durham, N.H.	3,177	State	Coed
University of Notre Dame	Notre Dame, Ind.	5,343	Church	Men
Oberlin College	Oberlin, O.	1,999	Nonsectarian	Coed
Pasadena City College	Pasadena, Calif.	8,348	Municipal	Coed
Radcliffe College	Cambridge, Mass.	1,074	Nonsectarian	Women
Saint Mary's College	Notre Dame, Ind.	951	Church	Women
Stephens College	Columbia, Mo.	1,498	Nonsectarian	Women
Stetson University	DeLand, Fla.	1,444	Church	Coed
Wesleyan University	Middletown, Conn.	742	Nonsectarian	Men
University of Wisconsin	Madison, Wis.	13,144	State	Coed

Edward D. Eddy, *The College Influence on Student Character* (Washington, D.C.: American Council on Education, 1958), p. 184.
° 1957–58 figures furnished by the individual colleges.

The investigators found a wide range of attitudes towards religion. There was nothing that could be termed a religious revival, but students were interested in religion. The most common conviction that students reported was a belief in God, but less than one third took this position. Three general attitudes towards religion were identified:

1. Religion is personal and has nothing to do with academic life.
2. A college experience cannot help but have some effect upon values, including religious values.

3. This college is interested in our beliefs; it does not destroy our convictions but asks us to examine them.

Some students equated religion with humanism and natural philosophy; religion was the same as the Golden Rule. But many wished to treat religion intellectually; to examine it and question it. They believed it had a place in the curriculum but only when taught as an academic discipline.[109]

The study concluded that some colleges definitely influenced student values and student character. It was not the product of any one factor but rather a product of the overall climate of the campus to which a number of factors contributed. Colleges that took the student beyond the intellectual and into the area of character development were marked by a high level of expectancy, requiring, or demanding, a high level of achievement and behavior from their students. These institutions were colleges of "high faculty influence." Scholars and teachers—persons of integrity and commitment—the faculty worked closely and intimately with students, frequently playing the role of the "significant other."

The curriculum of these colleges was organized to capture and hold student interest and to provide an opportunity for study in depth as well as synthesis within the framework of the goals and objectives of liberal and general education. Student responsibility was found to contribute to character development, including not only student government and joint faculty-student committees of various types but also opportunities to pursue various kinds of honors and independent study programs.

An opportunity for religious understanding and practice contributed to character growth and development as suggested above, but more than anything else the overall climate was marked by a "contagion of intimacy." Colleges of high impact tend to be limited in size and to have well-defined educational goals and internal cohesiveness.[110] Religious understanding may arise from the experience of a church related college. The Eddy report said this was the case in both the Catholic and Protestant colleges that were studied. Religious understanding may just as well arise from the experience of a nonsectarian college of high impact.

The Religiously-Oriented Student

Every campus seems to have small groups of students (one observer speaks of them as "islands")[111] who stand out because of their highly religious orientation and behavior. They are religious, it appears, not from any influence of the college, curricular or otherwise, but rather in spite of the college and in spite of their unreligious peers. The more secular the college, the more these students stand out.

These are the atypical students who give religious beliefs and activities the key and pivotal position in their hierarchy of values. Their religion has

---

109 *Ibid.*, p. 115.
110 *Ibid.*, p. 165.
111 P. E. Jacob, *op. cit.*, p. 22.

a strong emotional base and a significant percent of them report they arrived at their current orientation by means of a crisis-experience type of religious awakening.[112] Religious beliefs and values have been so internalized that they are reflected in their daily lives; they are integrated Christians.

For some years a representative state college in the Northeast has been characterized by one or more of these "islands" of highly religious students. A group of Protestants will meet each noon for a 15 to 20 minute period of prayer and meditation. They will gather in the college dining hall and precede their meal by an unobtrusive moment of silent grace. Some time during the evening, in the dormitories and rooming houses, they will gather in groups as small as two or three for Bible reading and study. The girls dress plainly and conservatively, and do not use lipstick or makeup. Leadership plays an important role in this group. When one or more student leaders are particularly committed, dynamic, and effective the group thrives. It suffers when this type of leadership is lacking.

The total of Catholic students at this college is almost as great as the total of Protestant students, but it is a small group of these Catholics that stand out for their faith and piety. They are active members of the Newman Club and meet together each noon to say the rosary, but they impress their fellow students most by their record of attendance at sacramental services. They arise early each morning to attend lower mass at the nearest Catholic church, one mile from the college. They take communion frequently, attend all the special services on the Catholic calendar, and strictly follow the teachings and moral standards of the church. Their life and behavior is wholesomely that of an integrated Catholic Christian.

Recent studies show that the highly religious student tends to be conservative, conventional, and conforming; they are more apt to conform to expected social roles and are more reluctant to countenance deviation and nonconformity.[113] Religious believers tend to compartmentalize religion and to live and to function in terms of the in-group and its values. They are more likely than others to marry within their group, send their children to a school limited to children of their faith, and to consider war an appropriate means of resolving conflict. Religious believers are more likely than others to agree with the vocabulary of prejudice.[114] They are more likely to prefer the segregated school and are less willing to grant women equal civil and political rights.[115]

Summary

Religious groups indoctrinate the beliefs and values of their faith in a variety of ways. Catholics and Protestants traditionally have relied upon

---

[112] W. S. Salisbury, *op. cit.*
[113] R. K. Goldsen *et al.*, *op. cit.*, p. 177.
[114] *Ibid.*, p. 181.
[115] W. S. Salisbury, *op. cit.*

individual instruction and catechism classes for instruction and indoctrination. The Sunday School has developed under Protestantism to become its leading source of religious instruction. Vacation Bible schools and church camps have arisen rapidly in recent years to supplement the work of the Sunday School. The Sunday School is also an important agency of religious instruction among the congregations of Reform Judaism.

A parochial school is a day school organized and run on a parish basis to provide a comprehensive experience in which religion is considered an integral part of a total and proper education. Since World War II parochial schools have been growing at a faster rate than the public schools.

Catholics dominate the statistics of parochial school enrollments. More than half of all Catholic children of elementary school age are now attending a parochial school. The Jewish parochial (the all day school) is primarily an adjunct of Orthodox Judaism although Conservative congregations are taking an increasing interest in them. Reform groups make considerable use of the Hebrew school, a one- or two-hour class meeting in the synagogue for several days each week after public school hours.

Most Protestant congregations are satisfied with the instruction and atmosphere of the public school and find no need for parochial education. Some Conservative Protestant denominations, notably the Lutheran Church–Missouri Synod and the Seventh-Day Adventists, place just as high a value and have invested just as much of their time, energy, and resources in their parochial school systems as have the Catholics.

The traditional public school was Protestant-oriented and Protestants were quite happy and at home there. The growth in power and influence of the Catholic and Jewish minority groups has brought a demand for a more rigid interpretation of the principle of separation of church and state as applied to the public schools. Such traditional Protestant practices as Bible reading, prayer, religious holidays, and baccalaureate exercises are forbidden in the public schools in a number of states and local jurisdictions where the religious population is heterogeneous. In states and communities where the population is relatively homogeneous in religion, religious practices and activities are often carried on in the public schools without regard to judicial rulings.

A number of practices have developed in the public schools to compensate for the "vacuum" created by the de-Protestantization of the curriculum. The most common include programs seeking to inculcate moral and spiritual values, teaching "about" religion, and religious instruction on "released time."

Most private colleges were originally sponsored by a religious denomination. Although colleges are still being founded and sponsored by religious denominations, public colleges and universities have grown to include a greater percent of the total college population than the private colleges.

Church related colleges, both Protestant and Catholic, generally require a minimum number of hours in religion and in philosophy and provide chapel and other religious services which students may or may not be required to attend. Some church related colleges have very definite rules for dress, behavior, and conduct, to which students are required to adhere. The colleges sponsored by the liberal Protestant denominations are more permissive and less demanding in what students have to do and in what students are free to do.

Extracurricular religious groups exist among students on all types of college campuses, church-related and public, with and without the approval and support of the faculty and the administration. Most of these student groups are affiliated with the appropriate national organization of their respective faiths: Jewish groups with Hillel, Catholic groups with the Newman Foundation. Most of the Protestant groups are affiliated with either the National Student Christian Fellowship or the Inter-Varsity Christian Fellowship.

A great deal of religion in the form of courses and activities can be found on various public colleges and universities throughout the country. Almost everything that is done in the way of religious emphasis in church related colleges can be duplicated in some public college somewhere in the United States. The amount of religious orientation and emphasis is determined to some extent by state rules and policies, but the major factor appears to be the attitude and philosophy of the particular faculty and administration.

Some public colleges, like the public schools, have felt impelled to drop the traditional devotional exercises at assemblies and baccalaureate exercises and to otherwise demonstrate overt neutrality in religious matters. More recently a countermovement has set in. Some colleges have carried on studies and initiated programs seeking to "enrich" the curriculum by giving proper attention to the reciprocal relation between religion and the culture wherever such materials are relevant to the discipline.

The religiousness of college students is always a matter of interest and concern on the part of the older generations. A number of studies have been made seeking to determine how religious college students are, and how the college experience influences students' religious beliefs, attitudes, and behavior. A summary of the existing studies suggests that the typical college student leaves the typical college with just about the same religious orientation he had when he came—and with about the same character structure and value system. He seems to have neither gained nor to have lost religion. The typical student places a higher value on the satisfactions arising out of career and family activities than on those arising out of religious activities.

On the other hand, the studies show that some colleges are colleges of "high impact." These colleges are usually modest in enrollment and can be found among the private as well as among the church related colleges. More than anything they are characterized by a "contagion of intimacy."

These colleges exert a positive influence upon the character structure and value system (including religion) of the student as well as contribute to his intellectual growth and development.

Some students are so religiously oriented that there is nothing a college can do to make them more religious or less religious. Religious values are central and pivotal in their hierarchy of values and tend to remain so throughout their college experience.

Chapter XV

Religion and the Family

WE ARE CONCERNED HERE with the consequences that religion may have for family behavior. How, for example, does being a Mormon influence the family's structure, the status and roles of its members, its relation to the community and to larger society? What influence, if any, does religion have for courtship and mate selection? To what extent does religion influence procreation—the conception and birth of children—and the early socialization of the child within the context of the family?

These are questions of importance not only for the individual in relation to his family of orientation (the family into which he is born) but also for his family of procreation (the family he forms by marriage). The answers to such questions as these are of great concern to society, for early socialization has a great deal to do with the nature and the quality of citizenship which the individual expresses as a functioning adult.

The Catholic Family

The Catholic is the appropriate family type with which to begin our inquiry. The Catholic blueprint for the family is detailed and comprehensive, and is an indication of the importance which the church attaches to family life. The church holds before each Catholic an ideal of behavior. It idealizes woman and motherhood. The tendency of the church to ascribe to Mary, the mother of Jesus, a divinity approaching that of Jesus, is seen in some Protestant circles as an important deterrent to ecumenicism.

The church spells out in considerable detail what constitutes proper family conduct. This ideal of conduct is supported by the most impressive sanctions that the church can muster. Most of the do's and don'ts are in the area of faith and morals, and therefore, binding upon all Catholics. Many are pronouncements of the popes.

The clergy spell out in considerable detail what constitutes proper relationships between the sexes. For the individual these standards begin as soon as boys and girls become aware of each other as boys and girls. They cover dating and courtship, mate selection, husband-wife relationships, the begetting and rearing of children, and the like.

A Philosophy of Sex. The church has a very definite and unequivocal philosophy of sex. There is nothing inherently evil about sex—as in the Calvinistic sense. If evil exists it must consist in exercising sexual powers contrary to the divine plan, the divine plan for sex being the propagation of the human race under conditions worthy of the human person.[1]

The divine plan calls for the exercise of sex within the Catholic concept and meaning of chastity, which is defined as the "moral virtue that controls in the married and altogether excludes in the unmarried all voluntary expression of the sensitive appetite for venereal pleasure."[2] Sex is, therefore, for procreation, not for pleasure.

Leo XIII described sins of unchastity as any conscious deliberate choice to use the sexual faculties contrary to moral law.[3] Chastity for the unmarried covers anything that is contrary to "right reason." Specifically this is interpreted to include physical union, excitation during engagement, and kissing.

The divine plan calls for modesty. The good Catholic is enjoined to practice modesty. Modesty is defined as "that habitual disposition which impels one to avoid everything which is likely to excite venereal pleasure contrary to right order either in ourselves or in others."[4]

With an ideal pattern of relations between the sexes clearly spelled out, church authorities are challenged to lead their communicants along the path of perfection. The gap which exists between the ideal and practice is often considerable. Priests continually struggle to hold the behavior of Catholics within the limits of modesty and chastity, as the church understands and defines these virtues.

Going Steady. The following cases and situations illustrate the type of current problems with which the church has to struggle to maintain its standards. The priests find "going steady" or "steady dating," which they define as "frequent, exclusive, and affectionate company-keeping of one boy with one girl," not conducive to the church's standards of modesty and chastity. Catholic young people, like their non-Catholic peers, find "going steady" the preferred dating status. But Catholic authorities are

---

[1] John L. Thomas, *The American Catholic Family* (New York: Prentice-Hall, Inc., 1956), p. 52.

[2] *Ibid.*, p. 52.

[3] Leo XIII, "Christian Marriage," in *Social Wellsprings,* Joseph Husslein (ed.) (Milwaukee: The Bruce Publishing Co., 1940), pp. 35–6.

[4] J. L. Thomas, *op. cit.*, p. 52.

agreed that going steady can lead to sin, and that it should not be followed unless there is a good chance of marriage in the near future. It can also lead to an early and ill-advised marriage and to pregnancy out of marriage.

The priests and school officials of the Roman Catholic grade schools at Peoria, Illinois, found it necessary to formulate a code covering the social behavior of pupils in 15 schools. This code forbids 6000 pupils to date, go dancing, or attend mixed parties unless they are sponsored by the schools, or to engage in mixed social activities except in chaperoned groups. The girls are forbidden to wear lipstick or other makeup. The priests said the code was established to "retain for grade school boys and girls their proper treasures of childhood, and to retard premature acceleration into social ventures."[5]

The clergy also find that going steady in high school is not the kind of relationship that leads to the Catholic ideal of marriage. It may lead, they say, to marriage between the immature or maladjusted, and it tends to restrict the adolescent's normal social activity. Parochial school authorities, however, find that their pupils are inclined to steady dating in spite of their teachings against such practices.

Steady dating is enough of a problem in some parochial schools that the authorities have imposed severe sanctions upon those of their pupils who refuse to abide by the rules against it. Four students, two boys and two girls, were dismissed from the Roman Catholic high school at Bristol, Connecticut, for steady dating after repeated warnings from the principal. The principal reported he had given the students as much time as possible to adjust to the rule, which, he said, had been in effect at the school since it was founded eight years before.

We want the students' minds on their school work and not on their girl or boy friend. Parents send their children to our school so that they can be reared in a gentle Christian environment. We do not consider steady-dating conducive to that kind of atmosphere. We want to make clear that company-keeping is a preparation for marriage and none of the students in our school have as yet reached that stage.[6]

At Sacred Heart Academy, Buffalo, New York, the school authorities imposed a steady dating ban on girls of the Third Order of St. Francis, a Catholic youth group devoted to "exemplary Christian living." Violations of the ban would lead to expulsion from the order. The principal stated that distractions from study and the moral aspect were the chief considerations for the ban, but he also observed that steady dating "often leads to marriage between couples who are emotionally disturbed and sometimes occasional forced marriages."[7]

At Catholic high schools at St. Joseph, Michigan,[8] and Allentown, Penn-

5 *New York Times*, May 17, 1957.
6 *New York Times*, February 9, 1957.
7 *New York Times*, February 8, 1957.
8 *New York Times*, March 27, 1959.

sylvania,[9] students are discouraged from going steady on pain of being barred from holding school offices, participating on athletic teams, or engaging in other extracurricular activities.

St. Francis, a small Catholic college at Loretta, Pennsylvania, found it desirable to ban "excessive" steady dating even if the couple intends to marry.[10] There appears to be no Catholic college trend towards specific prohibitions. However, Catholic colleges agree on the fundamental moral issues involved in steady dating with no likelihood for an early marriage, but disagree on the most effective way to deal with the problem on an institutional level. In the course of the ordinary educational process Catholic college authorities do their best to discourage steady dating.

Dress and Grooming. Catholic standards of appropriate heterosexual behavior extend to the way girls dress and to the amount of makeup. Girls and women are advised not to be a menace to the "purity" of boys and men by wearing short skirts or other clothes that are too tight, too sheer, or too revealing.

Miss Omaha, a candidate for Miss Nebraska in the Miss America contest withdrew when she was told she would not be permitted to reenter Duchesne College the following fall. The chief objection of the church officials who operate the school had been the bathing suit competition part of the contest. Miss Omaha withdrew, she said, so as not to jeopardize her Roman Catholic college education. At about the same time, a candidate for Miss Universe in New Mexico decided to remain in the contest although the Catholic Church had told her she would be denied the sacraments for a period unless she withdrew.[11]

Catholic educators look with disfavor upon the tendency of aging film stars to play romantic roles opposite players young enough to be their offspring. According to a survey conducted by *Extension* magazine, a national Catholic monthly publication that claims a predominantly youthful readership among its subscribers, its readers were strongly agreed that Hollywood's middleaged and older stars should "retire or quit romantic roles, especially with younger partners."[12]

Mate Selection. Catholic authorities are disturbed by the extent to which young people tend to select a mate upon the basis of romance and to the exclusion of prudential factors. Teenagers, they report, have adopted the thesis that romantic love is the "magic solution to all life's problems," and in seeking mates young people brush off such considerations as personality, similarity of backgrounds, ideals, and mutual interests as "mere censorious haggling of kill-joy elders."

In an attempt to put mate selection upon a more realistic and less romantic basis, the church has developed a series of Pre-Cana lectures that

---

9 *Oswego* (New York) *Palladium-Times,* March 19, 1960.
10 *Oswego* (New York) *Palladium-Times,* December 6, 1957.
11 *New York Times,* July 19, 1959.
12 *New York Times,* June 21, 1957.

are given each year in an increasing number of parishes and dioceses. These lectures are for engaged couples and are designed to point up the problems of married-pair living and to outline the Catholic formula for meeting these problems. A doctor, sometimes a banker or businessman, usually a successfully married couple, and a priest are representative lecturers and discussion leaders.

The doctor gives the Catholic position on the various biological and physiological problems which face the young couple. The banker or businessman discusses economic problems of the young couple; to buy or rent, credit, etc. The experienced married couple is in a position to give advice on the psychological aspects of married-pair living: husband roles, wife roles, shared roles, etc., all within the framework of Catholic ideology.

The priest speaks with authority on the religious aspects of marriage, emphasizing its sacramental and indissoluble nature. Because there are always some engaged couples whose marriage would represent a mixed marriage, the priest will usually explain what is involved when a non-Catholic marries a Catholic.

The advice of the priest extends to the wedding ceremony itself. The church is anxious to emphasize the religious nature of the ceremony and to remove the pagan and secular elements. A ceremony that includes a nuptial mass approaches the ideal. Throwing of rice is considered pagan and is discouraged in some dioceses.

Birth Control. The church has a comprehensive code governing sex relations within marriage. Sex relations are primarily for the procreation of the race.

> The essence of physical union is the communion of the male and female in the joy of procreating love. It is an act in which male and female mutually complete each other, mutually supply that which the other lacks in terms of generation. The very meaning of the act implies that each gives freely and unreservedly what they are able.[13]

The church forbids contraceptive devices that prevent the conception of children in the course of sex relations. According to the church it is as morally wrong to prevent life as it is to take it, and the prohibition of birth control has all the weight of a papal encyclical behind it. In his encyclical on Christian Marriage (*Casti Connubi*) Pius XI said:

> Since, therefore, the conjugal act is defined primarily by nature for the begetting of children, those who in exercising it deliberately frustrate its natural power and purpose, sin against nature and commit a deed which is shameful and intrinsically vicious.[14]

It is not for the individual to decide whether conception follows a marital act or not. That, according to the church, is the province of nature.

---

[13] J. L. Thomas, *op. cit.*, p. 56.
[14] Pius XI, *Christian Marriage* (*Casti Connubi*), 5th ed. (New York: The America Press, 1943), p. 17.

However, to perform the conjugal act when one of the partners is sterile, either temporarily or permanently, does not represent a deviation from the divine plan. The church therefore tolerates periodic continence, or "rhythm," because the couple places no obstacle to restrict or violate the physiological process of procreation. The process remains intact although the likelihood of procreation is obviously limited.

The couple, however, may use their knowledge of the procreative process to increase their chances of having offspring and perform the marital act only during the period when conception is most likely. Whether the couple uses periodic continence to increase conception, or to limit it, they are in neither case to interfere with the relationship between sexual union and procreation.[15] It would, however, be a violation of Catholic morality for a Catholic couple to avoid parenthood by choosing never to have sex relations when conception would most probably occur.

The development of pills to be taken orally to induce sterility on a temporary basis has created a new problem for the church, which has ruled that since this method is also a direct interference with the natural process it is forbidden to Catholics. On the other hand, a test which shows the woman's ovulation time—the period during which an egg comes into position for fertilization—may be used by Catholics to control pregnancies. This is permissible because neither the test nor the use made of the information so received interferes directly with the reproductive process.[16]

The population explosion has stimulated considerable discussion and rethinking within the church of the Catholic position on procreation and the ends of marriage. The public reaction to Dr. John Rock's controversial book, *The Time Has Come: A Catholic Doctor's Proposals to End the Battle over Birth Control*,[17] is one indication that there is considerable sentiment within the church for a more liberal interpretation of the rules concerning birth control. The following, which is said to be the position of an increasing number of Catholic prelates, priests, educators, and lay leaders concerning parenthood and its responsibilities, shows that change is already accepted by a substantial body of opinion within the church:

When a child comes into the world he must have a home to receive him, a home capable of providing him good health, and a home that is capable of developing in him the faculties of mind and heart that will enable him to take his proper place in society. This means more than food, clothing and shelter. The ends of marriage include not merely procreation but also a suitable education that opens to the child the cultural heritage of the race. The birth rate now falls within man's responsibility, and birth regulation (through rhythm) which is quite different from (contraceptive) birth control, is a normal part of the total task of the married couple. Birth regulation is the responsibility of ⸙

---

15 J. L. Thomas, *op. cit.*, p. 50.

16 *Oswego* (New York) *Palladium-Times*, July 17, 1958.

17 John Rock, *The Time Has Come: A Catholic Doctor's Proposals to End the Battle over Birth Control* (New York: Alfred A. Knopf, Inc., 1963).

the parents. Only the husband and the wife are in a position to determine the number of offspring they can properly rear and educate.[18]

A Protestant spokesman, Robert McAfee Brown, believes Catholic stress upon the proper rearing of children, and upon children brought into the world in the light of the economic and social situation, is fully in line with the Protestant view on family planning; that as far as the ends of marriage are concerned, Catholics and non-Catholics have a considerable area of agreement, although they still differ over means.[19]

Sterilization. Sterilization to prevent procreation is wrong because "man is not authorized to dispose of his own body." If natural procreation is not advisable for a married couple, the safest way for the husband and wife to satisfy their desire to have children is to adopt them. Adoption, according to the encyclical, is almost always followed by happy results and gives the adopting couple joy, peace and serenity.[20]

Therapeutic Abortion. Officially the church opposes therapeutic abortion: abortion which is necessary to save the mother's life or protect her from grave illness. This position was included in the encyclical letter, *Casti Connubi:*

> However much we may pity the mother whose health and even life is gravely imperiled in the performance of the duty allotted to her by nature, nevertheless what could ever be sufficient reason for excusing in any way the direct murder of the innocent? This is precisely what we are dealing with here. Whether inflicted upon mother or upon the child, it is against the precept of God and the law of nature: "Thou Shalt Not Kill." The life of each is equally sacred, and no one has the power, not even the public authority, to destroy it.[21]

This is also the position of the church in cases of a difficult birth where it seems to be a question of the life of the child or the life of the mother (although with the advance of medical science the physician is rarely faced with the problem of choosing between the life of the mother and the life of the child). In the increasingly rare cases where an abortion is indicated, it is usually an indirect abortion where the direct purpose of the operation is to remove a diseased condition in the mother which indirectly causes the death of the foetus. An indirect operation is permissible under Canon Law.

Artificial Insemination. The development of artificial insemination creates a moral problem on which the church has seen fit to take a stand. Pius XII declared that neither artificial insemination nor voluntary adultery may be resorted to by married couples who are sterile or who fear they may pass their defects on to their offspring. Pius XII also declared artificial

---

[18] John A. O'Brien, "Family Planning in an Exploding Population," *The Christian Century,* Vol. LXXXX, No. 35 (August 28, 1963), p. 1052.

[19] Robert McAfee Brown, "A Protestant Viewpoint," *Commonweal,* Vol. LXXVIII, No. 15 (July 5, 1963), p. 395.

[20] *New York Times,* September 16, 1958.

[21] *Casti Connubi, op. cit.*

insemination "violates the principle of natural law that no new life may be procreated except in a valid marriage. It (artificial insemination) is not included in the rights of married people and is contrary to Christian morals." Voluntary adultery is likewise condemned because "no married person may put his conjugal rights at the disposal of a third party."[22]

Child Rearing. The Catholic pattern for procreation and the rearing of children places great emphasis upon the natural and Godgiven, as opposed to man-made and acquired, techniques. The demands of procreation take precedence over the demands of personality. A Catholic spokesman urges a return to the custom of breast feeding as opposed to bottle feeding. Bottle feeding, he finds, has permitted the subordinate function of the bosom (adding to woman's beauty and attractiveness) to take precedence over the primary function. This idolatry of sexual beauty leads to confusion, distortion, and false values, and is particularly damaging to adolescents.[23]

Maintaining Catholic Values. The Cana Conference does for married couples what the Pre-Cana does for the engaged; it helps them to realize the highest personal and spiritual values by living according to Catholic ideals. The Conference is an all-day meeting held each year or oftener in many cities throughout the country. Married couples come to find out how to make their marriage a success. The meetings touch upon the basic principles of family interaction, the sacramental nature of marriage, and the physical, psychological and spiritual aspects of marriage relationships.[24]

At a typical Cana Conference husbands and fathers might be urged to help their wives by assuming their proper responsibilities as head of the home; to treat their wives as a true partner, to gain the respect of their children by being dependable, happy, helpful, and encouraging. Wives and mothers might be advised to pray with their children at their morning and evening prayers, not just listen; to supervise their children in what they see, hear, and read, on the TV, radio, or in books and magazines; to keep a watchful eye on the companions their children choose, and prevent their sons and daughters from dating too early in their youth and adolescence.

Couples are encouraged to discuss their problems and pool their experiences with other like-minded and oriented couples. The conference traditionally ends with a renewal of marriage vows before or during Benediction of the Blessed Sacrament.

The Christian Family Movement is another attempt to implement Catholic ideals in marriage and in family living with a slightly different focus. The unit of organization and activity is a small group of four to eight couples. The group observes the environment in which they live and function, evaluates this environment in terms of Christian principles, and

---

[22] *New York Times,* September 16, 1958.
[23] *New York Times,* July 16, 1958.
[24] J. L. Thomas, *op. cit.,* p. 421.

takes action to correct wrongs and shortcomings. The chaplain meets with them in their homes to bring the riches of the church. The movement, it is said, meets a need and reaches a group that up to the present has been little moved by parish and diocesan activities directed toward similar objectives.[25]

Religion and the Jewish Family

Judaism does not conceive of marriage as a sacrament in the Christian sense. However, marriage is a very religious and a very sacred experience and state. The word for marriage is *kiddushin* which means holiness, or to sanctify. To unite and live in marriage is one of the most sacred activities and holy states a Jew can experience.[26]

Importance of Marriage. Every Jew is expected to marry. Unlike Christianity, Judaism regards celibacy not so much as a state of virtue but rather as a state of sin. Rabbis are expected to marry. Traditionally men were required to marry by age 20 and to remain married until age 60. If they became widowed or divorced it was assumed that they would remarry. Mate selection was not left to chance or to the romantic interests and desires of the young people. Parents arranged to have their sons and daughters married off at an early age.[27] The *shadchan*, the marriage broker, served as a go-between to secure the most advantageous match for the son and daughter. Early marriage was encouraged even if it required subsidizing by the parents.

The importance of marriage is emphasized in the blessing recited at the circumcision rite—only eight days after birth: "May this child live to his fulfillment in religious education, to a marriage worthy of our people, and to a life of fulfillment and good deeds."[28] Traditionally, family and religion are closely integrated, and single life is considered a misfortune.

A son is highly valued and most important, and is encouraged to marry young. The emphasis and importance of children for the family is pointed up in the Old Testament stories of Jacob and Isaac. Under Old Testament times and conditions primogeniture and property considerations made a son indispensable. Jews look upon marriage without children as a disaster and do not consider marital obligations fulfilled until the couple is blessed with two children.[29]

Differentiation of Roles. In the traditional family the roles of men and women are sharply differentiated. Only the boys are confirmed (*Bar Mitzvah*) and only the confirmed males participate in the synagogue serv-

25 *Ibid.*, p. 429.

26 David H. Mace, "Jewish Point of View on Sex, Marriage, and Divorce," in *Man and Wife*, Emily Mudd and Aron Krich (eds.) (New York: W. H. Norton Co., 1957), pp. 155–62.

27 Joseph Heller, "Jewish Ways of Life," in *Jewish People, Past and Present*, Vol. II (New York: Jewish Encyclopedia Handbooks, 1948), p. 261.

28 D. H. Mace, *op. cit.*, p. 159.

29 *Ibid.*, p. 158.

ice. A *minyan* of ten confirmed males is required to conduct a service for the joint and collective saying of the prayers. In the Orthodox synagogue women sit apart from the men, and there is no imperative of synagogue attendance for women. But Jews insist that a woman has an important religious role. Her religious duty is to put her family and her children before all else and she performs this duty by staying home and caring for the home and the children.

Some of the most important rituals take place in the home where the mother is the central figure of family life. It is her responsibility to insure the observance of the dietary laws and to create the home atmosphere appropriate to the Sabbath and the festival celebration.[30]

Under their law the male enjoyed certain perogatives and occupied a superior status, but his perogatives could only be exercised within limitations that insured the woman a sense of worth and dignity. The legal norms were balanced by social and psychological (as well as religious and ethical) forces that tended to safeguard the place and person of the mother and wife. Her equal right to be honored by her children had an ancient basis in the Ten Commandments.[31]

A Philosophy of Sex. In marriage the male secured exclusive rights to a woman's sexuality; as a sexual being she became his property. To the husband the bride represented the soil in which his seed was to be planted and the means by which he might secure the children which established his "immortality." It was therefore necessary that her sexuality should belong exclusively to him.[32] If the bride proved unchaste or not a virgin, the husband could send her back to her father and demand that the things of value which the father had received as compensation for the loss of his daughter be returned.

Although her sex is her husband's exclusive property, the Talmud teaches that she may otherwise maintain a personality and identity that is her own. Outside the sexual monopoly she is not possessed by her husband and may rank as his equal or even his superior. A Jewish girl is educated and prepared from birth, both psychologically and socially, to be a wife and mother.[33] Judaism assumes that the wife should supplement her husband, not compete with him, by being a companion who shares in his life and thoughts. But, in a very modern sense, she is a person in her own right. The Talmud enjoins the husband to love his wife as himself, to consult her always, and to follow her advice.

Traditional Judaism takes a positive and healthy-minded stand on sex. There is nothing bad or sinful about sex itself; there is none of the asceticism that became the hallmark of American Puritanism. Sex is ordained of God and a blessing to both man and woman. Its exercise should

[30] J. Heller, *op. cit.*, p. 261.
[31] *Ibid.*, p. 261.
[32] D. H. Mace, *Hebrew Marriage* (New York: Philosophical Library, 1953), p. 231.
[33] *Ibid.*, p. 215.

be free and without inhibition. It can be the cord that binds two lovers for life in shared strength and shared pleasure.[34] Judaism finds abundant justification for this philosophy of sex in the sacred scripture. The *Song of Songs* is not only a poetic tribute but a glorification of the joys of sexual love, part of the birthright of the Jew and subject only to the limitations of moral restraint.[35]

Traditional Judaism, however, tolerated the double standard. The Old Testament patriarchs practiced polygyny, and in some cases the first wife would urge her husband to take a younger wife who could bear him the sons he needed to care for and maintain his flocks and herds. Polygyny was a common practice among the pastoral peoples of the Near East. Jews were only reflecting the marriage practices of the culture in which they lived. Jews have been monogamous only since 1000 A.D., and even today Jews living in Mohammedan countries are polygynous.[36]

Birth Control. Birth control is not only permissible in Judaism but mandatory when the health and welfare of the family is at stake. When conception might endanger the life of the mother, religion mandates the practice of birth control. But traditional Judaism forbade the male to use contraceptive devices. According to the Talmud the Biblical injunction to "be fruitful and multiply" is directed to males only. Men are therefore still forbidden to take any measures that might interfere with the normal process of fertilization—an injunction that does not apply to women. Women, according to rabbinic interpretation, are free to take any measure they choose to prevent conception: to conceive or not to conceive is the woman's prerogative.

Divorce. Judaism frowns on but does not forbid divorce. The Talmud teaches that it is "better for four people to be happy than for two to be miserable."[37] Originally, infidelity on the part of the husband was not unlawful; he was free to have sex relations with another woman providing he did not infringe upon another's rights over her.[38] A husband could not sin against his own marriage, but only against the marriage of another man. But this was not true of the wife.[39] Later, Jewish law finally abandoned the double standard and gave the wife the right to sue her husband for divorce on the grounds of infidelity.

In Judaism the acceptable grounds for divorce are numerous and the process relatively simple, although rabbis are under the sternest rule to discourage, postpone, and prevent divorce as long and as far as possible. The law requires mediation, cooling-off periods, and persistent legal ef-

---

[34] Herman Wouk, *This Is My God* (Garden City, N.Y.: Doubleday & Co., 1959), p. 152.

[35] D. H. Mace, *op. cit.*, p. 155.

[36] Rabbi Armand Niemand, Hillel Advisor at Syracuse University, in a lecture March 29, 1960.

[37] D. H. Mace, *op. cit.*, p. 157.

[38] *Ibid.*, p. 251.

[39] H. Wouk, *op. cit.*, p. 159.

forts at reconciliation. When these means have been exhausted, the husband, in the presence of a rabbinic court, gives his wife an ancient legal document, a bill of divorcement, and the marriage ends. A civil divorce is not a substitute for this ceremony.[40]

Religion and the Protestant Family

No single position represents the Protestant point of view on the family; almost every conceivable attitude that can be held concerning religion and the family can be found in one of the 240 sects and denominations in America which carry Protestant identification. The Protestant sects and denominations are generally agreed that marriage is not a sacrament, at least in the Catholic meaning of a sacrament, and two general positions have been identified by students of Protestantism. The conservative Protestant concept of marriage, moreover, differs from the liberal Protestant concept in several important particulars.

Conservative Protestantism. Conservative Protestantism retains the traditional concept of marriage and is not too different from the position of Orthodox Judaism as laid down in the Talmud, and the Catholic position that arises out of the doctrine of natural law. Conservatives believe that the purpose and function of marriage under God is the procreation and rearing of children. The companionate function of marriage, so emphasized by the liberals, is not included as a religious goal, and some conservatives oppose contraception altogether. Divorce is discouraged, and, where tolerated, accepted only on grounds of adultery.

Liberal Protestantism. Liberals hold a much different philosophy of marriage. Marriage, according to them, is an institution made for man, not man for the institution. Therefore this institution must meet the needs of the individual, and the extent to which any given marriage meets the physical, social, and spiritual needs of the individual, the husband and wife, becomes the basis on which it should be judged. This point of view holds that every person is a "child of God." Within the marriage bond this requires that each individual enjoy the respect of the other; that all forms of interaction must be carried on in total regard for the well-being of the other. Under this philosophy marriage, ideally, should be the instrument for excellence and the development of personality.[41]

Sex is not limited to procreation, but plays a necessary and proper part in the development of personality through the physical consummation of love and the personal and spiritual union of the couple involved. Under the personality and companionate philosophy of family, contraception is not only permitted but encouraged. Likewise, divorce is condoned when separation becomes necessary to preserve personality.

The liberal Protestant views sex as something good and desirable if it

---

[40] *Ibid.*, p. 227.
[41] Edwin E. Aubrey, "Protestant Point of View on Sex, Marriage, and Divorce," in *Man and Wife*, Emily Mudd and Aron Krich (eds.) (New York: W. W. Norton & Co., 1957), p. 137.

serves the fulfillment of man as a total being, and holds that the aim of all human relationships is to foster love. The good of any sex act always depends in some measure upon the inner meaning to the persons involved, but the sole ultimate standard is the judgment and love of God.[42]

Responsible Parenthood.   Responsible parenthood by means of birth control and contraceptive devices had become the official policy of many important Protestant denominations even before the NCCCA made its pronouncement in 1961. These denominations had been struggling with this problem for 30 years. The Episcopal, Methodist, Congregational-Christian, United Lutheran, United Presbyterian Church USA, Universalist churches, and the American Unitarian Association had all made Planned Parenthood an official policy when the NCCCA made its statement.

By the early part of 1961 the sentiment for responsible parenthood had become sufficiently crystallized among the Protestant denominations that the General Board of the National Council of Churches of Christ in America (NCCCA) issued a pronouncement on marriage and parenthood, a statement of policy that had been formally approved by the General Board or General Assembly of the NCCCA.* It expressed a substantial preponderance of opinion that there is a strong weight of ethical, moral, or religious principles in support of the policy.

The report began by pointing out that a number of churches had already given formal expression to the same basic convictions as contained in the pronouncement, but that differences of conviction made it necessary for representatives of the Eastern Orthodox churches, which take a position very close to the Catholic Church on contraception, to abstain from voting on the issue. The pronouncement considered responsible parenthood in terms of the *ends of marriage, reasons for family planning, methods of family planning,* and the *task of society.*

Ends of Marriage.   Genuine marriage is a union whereby husband and wife become "one flesh"[43] and embody a commitment to a dedicated common life. Since holy matrimony involves an occasion of God's grace, it is clear that the first duty of husband and wife is to nourish and care for the gift which God has given, a task described in Christian tradition in terms of

---

[42] Seward Hiltner, *Sex, Ethics and the Kinsey Report* (New York: The Association Press, 1953), p. 179.

* Pronouncements, however, are not binding on the member churches or individual communicants. They serve merely as a guide and help to the churches and communicants in finding God's will and doing it. If a church or an individual disagrees with a pronouncement within the context of responsible freedom it has the right to express dissent as vigorously as the occasion appears to demand. (National Council of Churches of Christ in America, *Information Service,* March 18, 1961.)

A pronouncement of the NCCCA, in short, carries as much weight and speaks for as large a group of Protestants as any one group or organization within the total structure of Protestantism. Most pronouncements probably express the view of a majority of the Protestants of the country, but regardless of the number of Protestants who support a pronouncement there are always substantial minority groups who represent one or more different positions on the particular issue in question.

[43] Gen. 2:24, Eph. 5:31.

sanctification and mutual perfection. These considerations emphasize the spiritual character of the basic purpose of marriage, which can be served through parenthood, companionship and vocation:

1. Parenthood is a divinely ordained purpose of marriage.[44] It is participation in God's continuing creation, which calls for awe, gratitude, and a sense of high responsibility.

2. Mutual love and companionship rooted in the need of husband and wife for each other have also been ordained of God,[45] although Christians differ in regard to sanctions for the sexual expression of marital companionship. Although most of the churches of the NCCCA hold such expression right and necessary within the marriage bond, and independently of procreation, all agree that Christian marriage should be free from sensuality and selfish indulgence, and that mutually accepted periods of continence can be of value in a common life of Christian discipline.

3. Vocation, or the service of the couple in society, is another high purpose through which the "two become one." Just as vocation may enjoin celibacy upon those to whom the gift is given,[46] so the calling of the couple may in certain circumstances enjoin family limitations.

Responsible parenthood, in the first instance, means to weigh the claims of procreation in relation to the total purposes of marriage and the situation of the family in society. For most couples the new knowledge of human reproduction and of means to avert conception affects ethical decisions regarding parenthood. But the responsibility, to be exercised in prayer and trust, has deeper roots.

Reasons for Family Planning. Within the purposes of marriage, ordained by God, there are a number of considerations concerning parenthood which need to be taken into account in trying to determine the number and frequency of pregnancies. These include:

1. The right of the child to be wanted, loved, cared for, educated, and trained in the "discipline and instruction of the Lord."[47] The rights of existing children to parental care have a proper claim.

2. The prospect of health of a future child if medical and eugenic evidence seem negatively conclusive.

3. The health and welfare of the mother-wife, and the need for the spacing of children to safeguard it.

4. The social situation, especially when rapid population growth places dangerous pressures on the means of livelihood and endangers the social order.

The parents need to remember, however, that having children is a venture in faith that requires courage and a measure of confidence in God's goodness.

Methods of Family Planning. Most of the Protestant churches hold contraception and periodic continence to be morally right when the motives are right. They believe that couples are free to use the gifts of

---

[44] Gen. 1:28.
[45] Gen. 2:18.
[46] Mt. 19:11.
[47] Eph. 6:4.

science for conscientious family limitation, provided the means are mutually acceptable and noninjurious to health. Periodic continence (the rhythm method) is suitable for some couples but is not inherently superior from a moral point of view. The general Protestant conviction is that motives, rather than methods, form the primary moral issue, provided the methods are limited to the prevention of conception.

Protestant Christians are agreed in condemning abortion or any method which destroys human life except when the health or life of the mother is at stake. The destruction of life already begun cannot be condoned as a method of family limitation.

Voluntary sterilization is another means of family limitation, but because medical science cannot guarantee that the procedure is reversible it presents the Christian conscience with special problems. Responsible parenthood is seen by many as a day-to-day process of decision making which sterilization may negate. On the other hand, where reasons of health or the obligations of parenthood argue the use of the most effective means of family limitation, sterilization represents one sure method now available.[48]

Task of Society. While responsible parenthood is the moral obligation of husband and wife, the concept also has implications that society assist parents in the exercise of their duty. For example, family planning requires access to appropriate medical information and counsel for most couples. Legal prohibitions against the impartation of such information and counsel therefore violate both the civil and religious liberties of many Protestant and other citizens. Their right to means they approve in conscience does not infringe the right of others to refrain from using such means. Legislation or institutional practices that impair the exercise or moral and professional responsibilities of family-serving professions should be opposed.[49]

Religion and the Birth Rate

Studies of the fertility of adherents of the three basic faiths show that in general Catholics have a higher birth rate than Protestants, while Jews have the lowest birth rate of all.

The birth rate differential was first emphasized in empirical studies that were carried on during the 1920's and 1930's. Notestein found that class for class, Catholics are more fertile than Protestants.[50] Stouffer found that the fertility of Catholics in urban Wisconsin surpassed that of non-Catholics.[51]

The three basic faiths show a characteristic inverse association between

---

[48] *Information Service, op. cit.*

[49] *Ibid.*

[50] Frank W. Notestein, "Class Differences in Fertility," *Annals*, CLXXXVIII (November, 1936), p. 33.

[51] Samuel A. Stouffer, "Trends in the Fertility of Catholics and Non-Catholics," *American Journal of Sociology*, XLI (September, 1935), pp. 143–66.

fertility and occupational status: the higher the occupational status of the father, the lower the birth rate.[52]

A study of the men listed in the 1926–27 edition of *Who's Who in America* found the Jews to have the lowest number of children per family and the Mormons the highest number. Catholics were second highest, and Protestants showed considerable variation within the middle range. There was less difference between the family size of Congregationalists and Jews than between the Congregationalists, Baptists, and Lutherans.[53]

TABLE 27

AVERAGE NUMBER OF CHILDREN OF MEN LISTED IN
1926–27 EDITION OF *Who's Who in America*

Religion of Father	
Jewish	2.6
Congregationalist	2.7
Baptist	3.1
Lutheran	3.1
Catholic	3.3
Mormon	5.3

Ellsworth Huntington & Leon F. Whitney, *The Builders of America*, New York, William Morrow & Co., Inc., 1927, p. 342.

Following World War II the birth rates of all three faiths rose, but the same relative relationships continued. The Catholic birth rate was 25 percent higher than the Protestant birth rate, and Jews had the lowest rate—18 percent lower than the Protestant birth rate.[54]

Convergence and Divergence in Birth Rates. A recent trend towards the convergence of the birth rates of Catholics and Protestants has, however, been noted from time to time by various researchers. Stouffer pointed out that although Catholics in Wisconsin had a higher birth rate than Protestants, the rate was declining faster for Catholics than for non-Catholics. He attributed this greater decline to the impact of urbanization upon Catholics; that Catholics were reacting the same way that Protestants had reacted in the previous generation.[55]

This trend became particularly pronounced by the mid-1950's. Not only were the birth rates of Catholics and Protestants approaching each other, but in some categories the rates actually coincided.

A study of a national sample of married women taken in 1957 showed the relative spread in the mean number of children born to Catholic and Protestant women 15 to 44 years of age to be considerably less than between the older group of Catholic and Protestant women, those 45 years and older.[56] A recent survey of a national sample of white married women

---

[52] F. W. Notestein, *op. cit.*

[53] See Table 27.

[54] P. K. Whelpton and C. V. Kiser, "Social and Psychological Factors Affecting Fertility," Vol. 1, *The Household Survey in Indianapolis*, The Milbank Memorial Fund, New York, 1946, pp. 6–8.

[55] S. A. Stouffer, *op. cit.*

[56] See Table 28.

between the ages of 18 and 39 found no significant difference between the birth rates of Catholics and Protestants.[57]

Some of the latest evidence uncovered suggests that the most recent development may once again be in the direction of divergence of birth rates. This trend began during the later years of the 1950–60 decade. A Detroit study showed that younger couples in both Catholic and Protestant groups were having more children, but that the increase was more rapid in the Catholic group.[58] The extent and importance of this trend await verification by further studies.

Social Class, Faith, and Fertility. The fertility differentials between upper-class Catholics and upper-class Protestants are consistently greater than the fertility differentials between lower-class Catholics and Protestants. During the early 1930's a study found the differences between the size of families of Catholic businessmen and Protestant businessmen were greater than between unskilled Catholic and unskilled Protestant laborers.[59]

TABLE 28

MEAN NUMBER OF CHILDREN BORN TO MARRIED WOMEN, ACCORDING TO MOTHER'S AGE AND SOCIO-RELIGIOUS GROUP

Socio-Religious Group	Women Aged 15–44	Women 45 and Over
Non-whites	2.66	3.21
Catholics	2.28	3.06
White Protestants	2.13	2.69
Jews	1.75	2.22

Table adapted from Table 40 in *Statistical Abstract of the United States*, 1958. Data obtained from Current Population Survey by the Bureau of the Census in March, 1957.

During the late 1930's a study found Catholic couples "of college status" were 35 percent more fertile than Protestant couples of comparable education. On the other hand, the fertility rate for Catholic couples of grammar school status was only 3 percent higher than for Protestant couples of the same limited education.[60] In a study of the attitudes and behavior of college students residing in the Northeast in 1955, the daughters of Catholic professionals reported they desired and expected a significantly greater number of children than daughters of Catholic skilled and semiskilled workers were reported as desiring and expecting. No comparable differences were found in the attitudes of daughters of Protestant professionals and daughters of Protestant skilled and semiskilled workers.[61]

---

[57] Ronald Freedman, P. K. Whelpton, and Arthur A. Campbell, *Family Planning, Sterility, and Population Growth* (New York: McGraw-Hill, Inc., 1959).

[58] Gerhard Lenski, *The Religious Factor* (New York: Doubleday & Co., 1961), p. 216.

[59] F. W. Notestein, *op. cit.*

[60] P. K. Whelpton and C. V. Kiser, "Social and Psychological Factors Affecting Fertility," *Milbank Memorial Fund Quarterly*, XXI (July, 1943), pp. 271–77.

[61] W. Seward Salisbury, "Religion and Secularization," *Social Forces*, Vol. 36, No. 3 (March, 1958), p. 203.

This differential is the consequence, it would seem, of the acceptance by upper-class Catholics of the Catholic teaching that procreation is the end and objective of sex relations and that contraception should not be practiced. The religious factor more than offsets the factor of class. They are "good Catholics" in spite of class status.

Jewish fertility rates consistently run somewhat lower than the overall Protestant rates. However, Rosenthal reports that Jewish fertility rates are very similar to the rates of Episcopalians, Congregationalists, and Presbyterians, and that Jews represent about the same social class pattern as Episcopalians, Congregationalists, and Presbyterians in education, occupation (white collar), and residence (urban). Fertility rates here are more a consequence of social class, and particularly residence (urban), than of religion.[62]

Religiousness and Fertility. The degree of religiousness seems to have a positive effect upon the birth rate. In all three of the basic religious groups those who attend church regularly have larger families than those who do not. This relationship proved most marked in the Catholic group where those who attended Mass every week had had 2.22 children on the average while those who were less regular had had 1.88. Among Protestants the comparable figures were 1.90 and 1.75.[63]

Recent rises in family size have affected all segments of the population, but are most marked among active Catholics. During the measured period, active Catholics showed an increase of five children for every ten families. Marginal Catholics and active and marginal Protestants all showed an increase of approximately three children for every ten families during the same period.[64]

The more religious are more conventional and conservative in other aspects of sex and marriage relationships. Both the more religious Protestants and the more religious Catholics were found to be more opposed to "trial marriage" situations than were their less religious counterparts, the nominal Protestants and the nominal Catholics.[65]

Mixed Marriage

How widespread is mixed marriage? How does the fact that one is married to someone of a different religion affect one's behavior, both religious and secular? These questions are of concern and interest to sociologists. Each of the basic faiths is officially opposed to marriages across faith lines. The clergy of each faith are fond of repeating the saying that

---

[62] Erich Rosenthal, "Jewish Fertility in the United States," *American Jewish Yearbook, 1961* (Philadelphia: American Jewish Publication Society), p. 4.

[63] G. Lenski, *op. cit.,* p. 229.

[64] *Ibid.*

[65] W. S. Salisbury, "Social Correlates of Religious Orthodoxy," *Abstracts of Papers, Fifty-Fifth Annual Meeting, American Sociological Association,* New York University, New York City, 1960, p. 11.

"a family that prays together stays together." In fact Canon Law forbids a Catholic to marry a non-Catholic.[66]

As a practical matter the Catholic Church has found that in a democratic society, characterized by religious pluralism and mobility, it is difficult if not impossible to enforce the canon against mixed marriage. But, although marriage to a non-Catholic is forbidden, and this "mixture," according to Catholic theory, is an *impediment*[67] to marriage in the first place, it can be removed if both the non-Catholic and Catholic party agree to and sign the Antenuptial Agreement. A valid mixed marriage may then be created.

The non-Catholic party by this action agrees that the marriage can be broken only by death; that his (or her) spouse shall be permitted the free exercise of religion according to the Catholic faith without hindrance or adverse comment; that all children born shall be baptized and educated only in the Catholic faith; and that no marriage ceremony other than that by the Catholic priest shall take place. The non-Catholic also agrees to accept the teaching of the Catholic Church concerning birth control and to respect the other religious principles and convictions of the Catholic spouse.

The Catholic party promises to practice his (or her) religion faithfully and to induce his life partner to seriously investigate the teachings of the Catholic Church in the hope that such investigation will lead to conversion.[68]

In spite of the clergy's admonitions against marrying outside one's faith there is a great deal of it on the American scene; there has, in fact, been a gradual and steady increase in mixed marriages since 1910.

Studies by the Catholic Church show that approximately one third of all Catholic marriages are valid mixed marriages. In addition to valid mixed marriages, another 10 to 18 percent of Catholics contract a marriage that is not sanctioned by Catholic nuptials as outlined above.[69] In an analysis of Catholic mixed marriages throughout the nation several trends stand out:

1. A high rate of mixed marriages where Catholics are a small proportion of the population. In Raleigh, North Carolina, where Catholics are only 2 percent of the population, 76 percent of Catholic marriages are mixed marriages.[70]

2. Few mixed marriages where large Catholic minorities remain highly

---

[66] J. L. Thomas, *op. cit.,* p. 152.

[67] C. S. Mihanovich, G. J. Schnepp, and J. L. Thomas, *A Guide to Catholic Marriage* (Milwaukee, Wisconsin: The Bruce Publishing Co., 1955), p. 139.

[68] Judson T. Landis and Mary G. Landis, "Mixed Marriages," in *Sex Ways in Fact and Faith*, Evelyn M. Duvall and Sylvanus M. Duvall (eds.) (New York: Association Press, 1961), pp. 86–87.

[69] J. L. Thomas, *op. cit.,* p. 154.

[70] *Ibid.,* p. 155.

solidified and isolated in national parishes. Mexicans in Texas live in such communities and have a very low rate of mixed marriage.[71]

3. A higher rate of mixed marriages among the upper socio-economic groups . . . 19.3 percent among the higher, and 8.5 percent among the lower.[72]

4. A high rate of mixed marriages among both Catholics and Protestants where both are large groups, where both are well distributed up and down the social class ladder, and where both associate freely with each other along class lines in spite of differences of faith.

A study of the marriages of the parents of several thousand Michigan State University students showed that 23 percent of the Catholics had married outside of their faith. These marriages were contracted during the 1920's and early 1930's. The families were primarily residents of Michigan and centered in the upper-middle class.[73]

A study of the religion of the parents of students in the State University of New York showed Protestants represented almost as high a rate of mixed marriage as Catholics. The students were a representative sample from ten colleges in the state university system and came from a middle-class socio-economic background with some representation from the upper-middle and lower-middle classes. Both the Protestant and the Catholic were large minority, but not dominant, groups. The marriages studied were largely contracted in the 1930's. A marriage between a couple, one with a religious faith identification and the other a No Preference identification, was rated a mixed marriage. Of the 740 families in which one or both of the parents were Catholic, 40.9 percent represented a mixed marriage. Of the 984 families in which one or both parents were Protestant, 34.9 percent represented a mixed marriage.[74]

In Iowa in 1953, 27 out of every 100 marriages represented a marriage outside the Catholic faith. Only 23 out of every 100 Catholic "first" marriages represented mixed marriages compared to 42 out of every 100 Catholic "second" marriages—the great majority of second marriages being invalid in terms of Catholic faith and morals. In contrast, 92 percent of all male Protestant marriages and 91 percent of all female Protestant marriages were within the faith.[75]

The mixed marriage differential between Protestants in Iowa, as compared to Protestants in New York state, is an important consequence of the Protestant numerical dominance in Iowa. In Iowa there are relatively few Catholics for Protestants to marry, while in New York there are almost as many Catholics as Protestants.

[71] Ibid., p. 156.

[72] Ibid., p. 158.

[73] J. T. Landis, "Marriages of Mixed and Non-Mixed Religious Faith," American Sociological Review, Vol. 14 (June, 1949), pp. 401–407.

[74] See Table 29.

[75] Loren E. Chancellor, and Thomas P. Monahan, "Religious Preference and Inter-religious Mixtures in Marriages and Divorces in Iowa," American Journal of Sociology, Vol. 61 (1955), pp. 233–239.

TABLE 29

RELIGION OF PARENTS

	Number	Percent
Both Catholics	430	25.7
Both Jews	150	8.9
Both Protestants	641	38.3
Both No Preference	68	4.1
Mixed Catholic and Protestant		16.0
Father Catholic; Mother Protestant	124	7.4
Father Protestant; Mother Catholic	145	8.6
No Preference and Christian		6.0
Father No Preference; Mother Protestant	61	3.6
Father No Preference; Mother Catholic	31	1.8
Mother No Preference; Father Protestant	8	.5
Mother No Preference; Father Catholic	1	.1
Jewish and Christian		1.0
Father Jewish; Mother Catholic	6	.4
Father Jewish; Mother Protestant	3	.2
Mother Jewish; Father Catholic	3	.2
Mother Jewish; Father Protestant	3	.2
Totals	1,674	100.0

W. Seward Salisbury, *Religion and the College Student,* The Research Foundation, State University of New York, Albany, 1958, p. 34.

Jewish Intermarriage. Jews show a greater tendency than Catholics or Protestants to marry within their group. Some early studies found that 95 percent of Jews married within their faith,[76] and only 9.1 percent of the marriages of the parents of New York college students (one or both parents being Jewish) represented a mixed marriage.[77] A more recent study shows that the mixed marriage rate among Jews is increasing and that third generation Jews have a mixed marriage rate ten times greater than that of first generation Jews.[78] First generation (foreign born) Jews showed an intermarriage rate of 1.4 percent, second generation 10.2 percent, and third generation 17.9 percent. Even this rate, however, is considerably lower than that of Catholics or Protestants. Rabbis view the rising rate with concern, seeing in it an indication of increasing assimilation and secularization of Jews and a threat to the survival of the Jewish religion. Jewish spokesmen report that 99 percent of the rabbis refuse to perform a marriage ceremony which represents a mixed marriage. This, it is claimed, is a definite change of policy from the 1920's and 1930's when many Reform and some Conservative rabbis would officiate at such marriages.[79]

Attitudes toward Mixed Marriage. College students in secular institu-

---

[76] Milton L. Barron, "The Incidence of Jewish Intermarriage in Europe and America," *American Sociological Review,* XI:1 (February, 1946), pp. 11–12; J. S. Slotkin, "Jewish-Gentile Intermarriage in Chicago," *American Sociological Review,* VII:1 (February, 1942), pp. 34–39.

[77] See Table 29.

[78] Erich Rosenthal, *American Jewish Yearbook, 1963* (Philadelphia: American Jewish Publication Society).

[79] Rabbi Armand Niemand, *op. cit.*

tions are generally tolerant of mixed marriages. When asked if they would be willing to marry someone of a different faith, all other factors being equal, a substantial proportion reported they would. More than 50 percent of Michigan State University students reported they would marry out of their faith. There was little difference between the stands taken by Catholics and Protestants on this question.[80]

Even among students attending a Catholic college, a substantial number reported they were willing to marry a non-Catholic. Thomas found that 33 percent of the boys and 40 percent of the girls would do so.[81]

By the middle 1950's a number of Protestant denominations took cognizance of the growing number of mixed marriages in which the Protestant party signed the antenuptial agreement and made the customary concessions to the Catholic religion. Several denominations issued reports and statements advising their members not to marry a Catholic if the antenuptial vow was a condition for marriage.

Religiousness and Mixed Marriage. Devout Protestants and Jews are more reluctant to enter into a mixed marriage with a Catholic than the nominally religious, and highly religious Protestants are significantly less willing to enter a mixed marriage than the nominally religious Protestants —39 percent as compared to 73 percent. Highly religious Catholics likewise are less willing to marry outside their faith than the nominally religious (69% to 92%).[82] Only 12 percent of Jewish girls from devout families (in a California sample) were willing to marry outside their faith, compared to 60 percent from families indifferent to their religion.[83]

The devout Catholic, however, is significantly more willing to enter into a mixed marriage than his counterpart, the devout Protestant; the comparative figures are 69 percent and 39 percent.[84] In California, Catholics proved to be the most willing to marry outside their faith—72 percent —but at the same time were the least willing to change their faith.[85]

It is interesting to note the change that has taken place in many Catholic parishes regarding the nature and locale of the wedding ceremony. Formerly the mixed marriage ceremony was usually performed in the rectory —not in the church. The first modification of this rule permitted the wedding to take place within the church—but outside the communion rail and the sanctuary. In many parishes the ceremony is now performed in the sanctuary before the high altar, only the nuptial mass being omitted from

---

[80] J. T. Landis and Mary G. Landis, *Building a Successful Marriage* (New York: Prentice-Hall, Inc., 1948), p. 138.

[81] J. L. Thomas, "Factor of Religion in the Selection of Marriage Mates," *American Sociological Review*, XVI (1951), pp. 487–489.

[82] W. S. Salisbury, *Abstracts, op. cit.*

[83] J. T. Landis, "Religiousness, Family Relationships, and Family Values in Protestant, Catholic, and Jewish Families," *Marriage and Family Living*, XXIII:4 (November, 1960).

[84] W. S. Salisbury, *Abstracts, op. cit.*

[85] J. T. Landis, *Marriage and Family Living, op. cit.*

the otherwise religious ceremony. (The nuptial mass is said only when both parties are Catholics in a state of grace.) This modern modification is an attempt, apparently, to impress upon both parties, and particularly the non-Catholic party, the sacredness of marriage, the importance which the church places upon the marriage relationship, and its indissoluble nature.

Devout Catholics, moreover, are more willing to marry non-Catholics because they can expect the marriage to be conducted according to standards laid down by their church. They feel, apparently, as if they would have very little to lose and a great deal to gain.

Sex Ratio and Mixed Marriage. In both the Catholic and the Protestant faiths there is a tendency for more females than males to marry outside their faith. A Catholic bishop's study on mixed marriage found that 60 out of every 100 Catholics entering into a mixed marriage were females.[86] Fichter found the sex ratio even more disproportionate in his study of Catholics in New Orleans where 73 out of every 100 Catholics entering a mixed marriage were females.[87]

Lutherans report that almost twice as many Lutheran women as men enter into a mixed marriage. However, they also report that when the mixed marriage is between a male and a female from the same socio-economic class, the number of men who enter into such a marriage is equal to the number of women. Women outnumber men in those mixed marriages in which the husband is from a higher socio-economic class than the wife.[88]

Conversion. Studies show that mixed marriages affect the religious lives of the couple in one of three patterns: the respective spouses may try to continue the worship and practice of their respective religions in their customary manner; one or both may drop out of their church; one may give up his faith and convert to the faith of the other. The predominant pattern seems to be a falling away from religion.[89]

The Catholic Church is well aware of the dangers which mixed marriages present to the Catholic faith. Church sources report that the Catholic spouse runs a far greater risk than usual of losing his religion beliefs, or practices, or both. Children are often brought up in religious confusion, or with no religion.[90]

Children of mixed parentage have a lower average record for mass attendance, monthly communion, and Easter duties than children from an

---

[86] Bishops' Committee on Mixed Marriage, *A Factual Study of Mixed Marriages* (Washington, D.C.: National Catholic Welfare Conference, 1943).

[87] Joseph H. Fichter, *Dynamics of a City Parish* (Chicago: University of Chicago Press, 1951), p. 107.

[88] United Lutheran Church in America, *A Study of Mixed Marriages in the United Lutheran Church in America*, New York, p. 4.

[89] J. T. Landis and M. G. Landis, *Sex Ways in Fact and Faith, op. cit.,* p. 88.

[90] Joseph B. Schuyler, *Northern Parish* (Chicago: Loyola University Press, 1960), p. 264.

entirely Catholic home.[91] The church has found that it is much better that the Catholic parent be the mother than the father, for in cases where the mother was non-Catholic twice as many in the family missed mass and were irregular in the reception of the sacraments, and seven times as many were brought up as Protestants, than in homes where the mother in a mixed marriage was Catholic.[92]

Information on conversions as a result of mixed marriages varies, and differences in reports vary because the samples upon which studies are made often vary. Some of the studies made by churches tend to bias in their favor because not all of the marriages of their communicants are recorded. Quite often nominal members enter an interfaith marriage and have the ceremony performed by some one other than their own clergyman. Many such marriages never become a part of the statistical record of the parish, and there is no evidence to indicate whether a marriage or a conversion has taken place.

Studies of the marriages of parents, reported by their children, have some merit in that the record is reported by someone intimately acquainted with the marriage and the relationship but someone who does not, directly or officially, represent a particular faith. In a study of the marriages of parents in Michigan, one third of the parents involved in a mixed marriage converted to the faith of their spouse. There was no difference between Catholics and Protestants in the respective rates of conversion (56 percent parents turned Catholic and 57 percent turned Protestant).[93] And in a large eastern seaboard Catholic parish only about 18 percent of the mixed marriages resulted in the conversion of the non-Catholic party,[94] according to a study conducted by the Catholic Church.

TABLE 30
CONVERSION AMONG MIXED MARRIAGE PARENTS

Faith of Parent	Number	Conversions	Percent
Protestant Father	148	23	15.6
Catholic Father	127	24	18.9
Protestant Mother	127	28	22.1
Catholic Mother	151	35	23.2
Jewish Father	9	1	11.1
Jewish Mother	6	1	16.7

W. Seward Salisbury, *Religion and the College Student* (Albany, N.Y.: Research Foundation, State University of New York, 1958), p. 35.

In a New York state sample there was little difference between the Catholic and Protestant rate of conversion, whether male or female, al-

[91] Paul H. Besanceney, S.J., "Unbroken Protestant-Catholic Marriages Among Whites in the Detroit Area," *American Catholic Sociological Review*, Vol. 32, No. 1 (Spring, 1962), pp. 3–20.

[92] J. L. Thomas, *Indiana Catholic Record*, Indianapolis, March 16, 1956.

[93] J. T. Landis, "Marriages of Mixed and Non-Mixed Religious Faith," *op. cit.*

[94] Gerald J. Schnepp, *Leakage from a Catholic Parish* (Washington, D.C.: The Catholic University of America Press, 1942), p. 91.

though in both faiths women converted at a higher rate. The Jewish sample was too small to offer any valid comparisons with other faiths.[95] The Lutherans seem to have the greatest "holding power" of the major Protestant denominations in terms of Protestant-Catholic marriages. The United Lutheran Church even claims that in cases of mixed marriages four times as many Catholics convert to the Lutheran religion as Lutherans convert to Catholicism.[96]

Some indirect evidence of the impact of mixed marriage upon the Catholic faith is gained by comparing the statistics contained in the *Official Catholic Directory* for 1961 with the statistics contained in the 1960 Directory. From 1951 to 1961 baptized Catholics increased by 13,470,021, a gain of 47 percent. This made the Catholic Church the fastest growing religion in the country. But in 1961, there were 511 fewer weddings than in 1960, a drop of 30,923 in infant baptisms, and a decrease of 14,571 in the number of conversions.[97] An important causal factor in these differences is believed to be the increase in invalid mixed marriages: those not sanctioned by Catholic nuptials.

Religion and Divorce

Each of the basic faiths places a great deal of emphasis upon the religious nature of marriage; each takes the Biblical injunction "What God has joined together, let no man put asunder" seriously and, accordingly, opposes divorce. However, the opposition to divorce varies from the absolute prohibition of divorce by the Catholic Church to the reluctant acceptance of divorce by some Protestant and Jewish bodies after all other means of maintaining family relationship and a constructive marriage have been exhausted.

The Catholic Church holds that a valid, consummated marriage cannot be dissolved by divorce. According to Catholic teaching the essential qualities of a marriage are unity and indissolubility.[98] And, whereas the major Protestant groups do not encourage divorce, they will accept it when they find that some conditions are so destructive to human values, of the husband, wife, or children, that divorce becomes the more Christian alternative.

In recent years many Protestant churches have adopted more liberal stands on divorce. Until recently the Episcopal Church's stand on divorce was almost as absolute and unyielding as that of the Catholic Church. In a recent statement the Methodist Church has said:

Divorce is not the answer to the problems that cause it. It is symptomatic of deeper difficulties. The church must stand ready to point out these basic problems to those couples contemplating divorce, and help them to discover

---

[95] See Table 30.
[96] United Lutheran Church, *op. cit.*
[97] *Time*, May 12, 1961.
[98] Mihanovich, Schnepp, Thomas, *A Guide to Catholic Marriage, op. cit.*

and, if possible, to overcome such difficulties. As a Christian Church and as ministers, we are obligated to aid, by counsel, those persons who have experienced broken marriage and to guide them so that they may make satisfactory adjustments.[99]

The stand of the American Lutheran Church is similarly a representative Protestant point of view:

The legal dissolution of a marriage sometimes is the lesser of evils. Adultery and willful desertion have long been held to be valid grounds for which a Christian may seek or suffer a divorce. . . . Cruel, calloused, consistent or continuing selfishness, the very opposite of the divine principle of love, can as fully wreck the inward unity of marriage as do adultery or physical desertion. . . . A study of Jesus' entire ministry, an understanding of human nature, and a realization that regardless of the legal decision of guilt each party bears some responsibility for the failure of the marriage, require of the church that it follow an evangelical rather than a legalistic approach to the problems of divorce.[100]

Judaism, as we have seen,[101] permits divorce only after all other remedial and conciliatory measures have been taken and failed.

Religious and Civil Divorce. Because religious and civil divorce, annulments, and separations are often confused, it is necessary to distinguish between them. The available data are statistics of civil divorce, civil annulments, and civil separations.

A Catholic may contract a perfectly valid *civil* marriage, and yet not be married in the eyes of the church because the marriage was not in accordance with Catholic law. But this same marriage may be recognized as a perfectly valid religious and civil marriage by any one of a number of Protestant denominations, then later be dissolved by a civil divorce. Yet the Catholic party will not have broken the Catholic divorce prohibition because his marriage was never recognized by the church. It is also important to recognize that many Catholics, who are parties to civil divorce and civil annulments, may have acted contrary to the teachings of the church, in effect having excommunicated themselves so that they no longer are Catholics in good standing.

Religion and Divorce Rates. Religion makes a difference in divorce rates. In general, available studies indicate that Catholics have internalized the teaching of their church so as to show a significantly lower divorce rate than that of Protestants. Jewish marriages are about as stable as Catholic marriages.[102] In Iowa, in 1953, Catholic divorces were less than half the divorce rate of the general population: Catholic marriages accounted for

---

[99] John C. Wynn, "What the Churches Say Today," *Sex Ways in Fact and Faith, op. cit.,* p. 58. Taken from a statement of the American Lutheran Church approved at Blue Island, Illinois, October, 1956.

[100] *Ibid.,* p. 59.

[101] See p. 408–9.

[102] Table 31.

TABLE 31

PERCENTAGES OF MARRIAGES ENDING IN DIVORCE,
ACCORDING TO RELIGION OF SPOUSES

	24,184 Cases°	2,654 Cases†
Both Catholic	5.0%	7.7%
Both Jewish	5.0	3.3
Both Protestant	8.0	10.0
Both No Preference	18.0	18.2

° Composite of Bell's Maryland study, Weeks' Washington study, Landis' Michigan study: Howard M. Bell, *Youths Tell Their Story*, American Council on Education, Washington, D.C., 1938, p. 21; H. Ashley Weeks, "Differential Divorce Rates by Occupation," *Social Forces*, March, 1943, p. 336; Judson T. Landis, "Marriages of Mixed and Non-Mixed Religious Faith," *American Sociological Review*, June, 1949, p. 401.

† From a California sample in Judson T. Landis' "Religiousness, Family Relationships, and Family Values in Protestant, Catholic and Jewish Families," *Marriage and Family Living*, November, 1960.

18 percent of all first marriages but for only 7 percent of all first divorces.[103]

Religion is certainly a stabilizing factor in marriage. Marriages in which the parties are religiously identified, whether Catholic, Protestant, or Jewish, show a much lower rate of marital dissolution than marriages in which both parties claim No Preference in religion.[104]

It is apparent, however that Catholic marriages show a degree of dissolution that can no longer be considered rare.[105] In Ohio, from 1944 to 1950, 8 percent of all divorces were by persons professing to be Catholic in religion.[106]

A distinction should be made at this point between first and second marriages. First marriages are usually performed by the clergy, and subsequent marriages are as frequently performed without benefit of clergy as with. In 1948, 81 percent of all first marriages were performed by clergy. In the same year, among remarriages, only 55 percent of the grooms and 51 percent of the brides were married by clergy. Civil marriages predominate among divorced Catholics who remarry.[107]

The low rate of recorded dissolutions (absolute divorces and annulments) does not necessarily mean that marriages of the lower divorce group may be happier than the group with higher divorces. There is some evidence to indicate that desertion may be higher among Catholics than among non-Catholics and that desertion may offset the higher divorce rates of other groups.[108] In his California study Landis found that children

---

[103] Chancellor and Monahan, *op. cit.*, p. 239.

[104] J. T. Landis, "Marriages of Mixed and Non-mixed Religious Faith," *op. cit.*, p. 401.

[105] Chancellor and Monahan, *op. cit.*, p. 239.

[106] Paul Jacobson, *American Marriage and Divorce* (New York: Rinehart & Co., 1959), p. 101.

[107] *Ibid.*, p. 59.

[108] T. P. Monahan and W. M. Kephart, "Divorce and Desertion by Religious and Mixed Religious Groups," *American Journal of Sociology*, Vol. 59 (March, 1954), p. 464.

of Catholic parents and children of Protestant parents found little difference in the "happiness rating" of their respective parents.[109]

Mixed Marriage and Divorce. Mixed religious marriages in general show a higher incidence of divorce than marriages between couples of the same religious faith. No Preference marriages have about the same high rate of dissolution as do mixed marriages.

It makes a difference in Protestant-Catholic marriages whether the wife is a Protestant or a Catholic. Divorce rates have been found to vary from as low as 6.7 percent when the wife is Catholic, to as high as 20.6 percent when the wife is Protestant.[110] A later study shows the same trend; that the survival rate of the marriage of Catholic wives and non-Catholic husbands is higher than the survival rate of the marriages of non-Catholic wives and Catholic husbands, but the differentials are not as great as in the earlier studies.[111]

The causal factors are complex and interrelated and vary with the individual couple. It may be easier for the Catholic wife and mother to live up to the requirements of the antenuptial agreement than for the Protestant wife and mother. Approximately three fourths of all divorce actions in the United States are initiated, and won, by the wife. The Catholic wife would be restrained by her religious commitment from divorcing her husband. No comparable religious sanctions would operate to inhibit the Protestant wife from initiating divorce proceedings.

TABLE 32

PERCENTAGE OF MIXED MARRIAGES (WITH CHILDREN)
ENDING IN DIVORCE

Religion of Spouses		
Catholic-Protestant		14.1%
Protestant Husband, Catholic Wife	6.7%	
Catholic Husband, Protestant Wife	20.6%	
No Preference Husband, Catholic Wife		10.0%
No Preference Husband, Protestant Wife		19.0%

Judson T. Landis, "Marriages of Mixed and Non-Mixed Religious Faith," *American Sociological Review*, June, 1949, p. 401.

Religion and Child Training

The influence of religion upon child training is another important question. To what extent may the Catholic pattern of authority in religious beliefs and behavior—faith and morals—be reflected in a more authoritarian philosophy of child training? Conversely, to what extent is the Protestant individualistic theology reflected in more individualistic and permissive patterns of child training and parent-child relationships?

---

[109] J. T. Landis, in *Marriage and Family Living, op. cit.*

[110] See Table 32; see also Chancellor and Monahan, *op. cit.*; p. 239.

[111] Lee B. Burchinal and Loren E. Chancellor, "Survival Rates Among Religiously Homogamous and Interreligious Marriages," *Social Forces*, Vol. 41, No. 4 (May, 1963), p. 353.

Lenski, on the basis of the Detroit studies, maintains that religion makes an important difference in the type of training the child receives and the type of personality he develops. The Detroit studies sought to measure the degree of intellectual autonomy (thinking for oneself) and intellectual heteronomy (obedience to the dictates of others) found in the various socio-religious groups.

Jews and Protestants were found to be more likely than Catholics to value intellectual autonomy above intellectual heteronomy at all class levels. The upper-middle class was more likely than the lower-working class to value intellectual autonomy, and the biggest differences between socio-religious groups were found at the highest status levels.[112]

Patterns of discipline were studied and measured. The attitude towards and use of physical discipline, such as spanking, and symbolic discipline such as scoldings, withholding of privileges, and the like, was studied. White Protestants valued symbolic discipline more than white Catholics at the middle-class levels, and white Protestants more than white Catholics and Negro Protestants at the working class levels. Here again the differences between socio-religious groups were greatest at the higher class levels. These data bear out the more authoritarian nature of Catholic child training. These data show, also, that an ethnic as well as a religious and a social class variable may contribute to an authoritarian pattern of child training.[113]

TABLE 33

PERCENTAGE OF MOTHERS ADVOCATING PHYSICAL PUN-
ISHMENTS FOR TEN-YEAR OLD CHILD ACCORDING TO 1953
SURVEY

Socio-Religious Class	Percent	Cases
Middle class		
White Protestants	9	55
White Catholics	26	43
Working class		
White Protestants	24	70
White Catholics	46	67
Negro Protestants	47	19

Gerhard Lenski, *The Religious Factor* (New York: Double-day & Co., 1961), p. 209.

Leisure time activities of a hypothetical 14-year-old child in representative Protestant and Catholic families were studied and measured. The activities and program were dichotomized in terms of present-oriented and future-oriented goals. The data showed that Protestant families tend to stress future-oriented activities more than Catholic families. Future-oriented activities tend to develop the habits and skills that contribute to success in the world of work.[114]

---

[112] G. Lenski, *op. cit.*
[113] *Ibid.*, p. 209.
[114] *Ibid.*, p. 208.

Religion and Sexual Activity

In each of the basic faiths sex attitudes and sex relations are cast within a framework of religious values and goals. According to the Kinsey reports religion has some effect upon the frequency of sex activity, whether the activity is premarital sex relations or sex relations within the marriage bond.

Kinsey found there was little or no difference between the frequency of sex relations among Protestants, Catholics, and Jews.[115] Landis found no significant difference between the reported virginity of Protestant, Catholic, and Jewish families in his study of California college students.[116] Regardless of how explicit, definite, and comprehensive the teachings regarding sex of one faith, compared with the teachings of any other faith, the overall impact of such teachings upon behavior was essentially the same. However, the degree of religiousness of individuals within each of the faiths importantly affects the amount of sexual activity. The more devout, the more religiously active, the more orthodox are less active sexually than the less devout, less religiously active, and the unorthodox.[117] This differential is particularly marked in the case of the devout and religiously active women.[118]

The sexual activity of Orthodox Jews is less than that of any other religious group. This has been attributed to the pervading asceticism of Hebrew philosophy.

Within Catholicism there is a striking disparity between the low sexual activity of active Catholics compared to the high sexual activity of inactive Catholics. The "more literal" of the Protestant groups tend "to make sex appraisals which are close to those of the Talmud and of Catholic natural law"; that is, appraisals that control and limit sex activity.[119]

Summary

Religious attitudes and values importantly shape the personality of religiously oriented individuals who enter into a marriage relationship. These attitudes and values have important consequence for the organization and behavior of marriages formed and families created.

Each of the three basic faiths emphasizes aspects of family life and family relations that distinguish it from the others. The comprehensive faith and morals of the Catholic faith provides a blueprint of conduct that touches the important phases of family life. Catholic morals are supported by an effective system of sanctions.

Preparation for marriage begins at the pre-adolescent stage with a positive philosophy of heterosexual relations. The Catholic Church discourages

---

[115] Alfred C. Kinsey, Wardell B. Pomeroy, and Clyde E. Martin, *Sexual Behavior in the Human Male* (Philadelphia: W. B. Saunders Co., 1948), p. 486.

[116] J. T. Landis in *Marriage and Family Living, op. cit.*, p. 348.

[117] Kinsey, Pomeroy, and Martin, *op. cit.*, p. 486.

[118] *Ibid.*, p. 485.

[119] *Ibid.*, p. 485.

early dating and "going steady" until shortly before the couple is in a position to marry. The religious and sacramental nature of marriage is stressed. One of the six precepts of the practicing Catholic is to obey the marriage laws. Children must be baptized, confirmed, and educated according to Catholic principles.

The church teaches that the primary objective of sex is for procreation, and it forbids birth control by any means which interferes with natural processes. A consummated valid marriage is indissoluble. Divorce is forbidden.

The contemporary Jewish family is the product of 5000 years of law, custom, and modifications to meet the conditions of a changing environment. Many of the important religious rituals are centered in the home. The Jewish wife and mother plays an important role in maintaining religion in the home. The proper celebration of the High Holy Days and the maintenance of the dietary laws are her responsibility.

Traditionally the roles of the husband and wife were highly differentiated, with the husband in a superior position. He was the master, she was the servant. She was confined to the household. He alone possessed the right to divorce. In practice, however, the wife enjoyed a position of dignity and respect. In contemporary society the Jewish wife and mother, like American wives generally, is equal to her husband. The unilateral authority of the husband to divorce no longer holds for the great majority of American Jews. The right to initiate a divorce is now shared by the wife.

Attitudes towards sex, birth control, and child training are individualistic and quite similar to the philosophy and practice of Protestantism.

Protestant marriage and family values and practices are as varied as Protestant theological beliefs. Some Protestant denominations support as definite and absolute a pattern of marriage codes and behavior as does the Catholic Church. The great majority of Protestant denominations permit and encourage an individualistic interpretation of the principles of Christian marriage. There is no recognizable, consistent, and uniform stand on such issues as courtship and dating as is found in Catholicism. Most Protestant denominations permit the individual couple to practice birth control to achieve the ends of Christian marriage according to the dictates of their Christian consciences. When the needs of spouses and children seem to require it, divorce is condoned and remarriage accepted.

Religion affects fertility. Catholic birth rates are consistently higher than Protestant birth rates, and Jewish birth rates are lowest of all. The greatest differentials in birth rates are found at the higher social and economic levels. The long-time tendency for Catholic and Protestant birth rates to converge appears to have been checked and to be offset by a new divergence trend.

Religion affects the divorce rate. Catholic and Jewish divorce rates are consistently lower than Protestant divorce rates. Each of the basic faiths has shared to some extent in the general increase in divorce since World War II.

Marriages between Catholics and Protestants are increasing. The insistence of the Catholic Church that the conditions of the antenuptial agreement be met disposes Catholics to be more favorably inclined towards such marriages than Protestants. Active Protestants are more reluctant to marry a Catholic on terms that the Catholic Church demands. It appears there are few mixed marriages between individuals who are strongly and actively religious in their respective faiths. Catholic authorities find mixed marriages tend to lead to a weakening of the faith in the case of the spouse, and especially in the case of the children.

Religion makes some difference in child training. Catholic child training patterns differ from Protestant and Jewish child training patterns in placing greater emphasis upon external authority. Protestant and Jewish patterns are more permissive and place greater responsibility upon the individual.

The more devout and orthodox, whether Protestant, Catholic or Jew, have fewer sexual experiences both within and without marriage than do the nominally religious.

Chapter XVI

Religion in Representative Subcultures

THE CHURCH IN RURAL AREAS

RURAL AND URBAN are not precise terms or as clearcut distinctions as formerly between country living and city living. The lines of demarcation between rural and urban are blurred and becoming less distinguishable. According to the United States census, rural populations are all those people who live in the open country and in centers of population up to 2500. Urban populations are all the people who live in population centers of 2500 or more.

In the nineteenth century those living in the open country were farmers, and the small communities categorized as rural served as market and trading centers for the surrounding farming economy. Rural philosophy and rural values dominated these village centers.

The application of science and technology to agriculture has made it possible for a smaller and smaller proportion of the people to be gainfully employed in farming to produce the necessary food and fiber for the nonfarmers. Not only has the proportion of farmers declined but an increasing number of people not engaged in farming have made their homes in the open country.

In recognition of this phenomenon census statistics of rural population are now recorded as rural farm and rural nonfarm. By 1957 the census showed 64 percent of the American people to be urban, 24 percent rural nonfarm, and 12 percent rural farm.[1] The rural church has been profoundly influenced by the changes that have taken place in farming and by the changed pattern of life in the country, both among farmers and non-farmers.

The distinctions between rural and urban churches are blurring just as the distinction between rural and urban living is less pronounced. Rural type churches can be found in the cities just as some urban type churches may be found in the country.

In the horse and buggy days, the villages and hamlets designated as rural population were culturally rural as well. Most of these villages were service and trading centers for agriculture and the farming population. These villages bought the farmers' products and provided him with his essential goods and services. The country village of Phelps, upstate New York, just prior to World War I was one of these villages. It contained several blacksmith shops where the farmers brought their teams in on rainy days to be shod, hardware and feed and fertilizer stores to provide the farmer with his necessary supplies, produce companies to buy his products, and grocery stores to sell him staples and take his surplus butter and eggs in trade. The biggest industry also was farmer-related, a food processing plant. The village had five churches, four Protestant and one Catholic. At least half the church members and affiliates were farmers and farm families who drove in as a family group to church and Sunday School.

Rural population includes a large number of people who choose to live in the open country, are not engaged in farming, and may commute anywhere from ten to 100 miles each day to their place of employment, usually a nearby city. All of these changes of working and living have some bearing upon rural religion and the country church. The rural areas most influenced are those near the metropolitan areas. More remote areas and some other areas, notably the South, are less influenced; here religion is more traditional and less changed.

Rural Protestantism

The traditional Protestant church was a rural or a small village church. The rural church was the dominant church since the greatest proportion of the people were living in a rural culture. It was not until the decade of 1910–1920 that urban population caught up with and surpassed rural population.

The traditional Protestant church served the religious needs of people living within the context of a *gemeinschaft* society. People were born and grew up in a social milieu of community and communality. Everyone knew everyone else. All activities in which the citizens participated took place within the context of communality.

In the traditional church the congregation gathered to worship, to

---

[1] United States Department of Commerce, Bureau of the Census, *Current Population Reports*, Series P-20, No. 79, February 2, 1958, table 3, p. 7.

hear the Word preached, and to receive the sacraments on behalf of the community.[2] The emphasis was personal and otherworldly. A self-respecting rural or village church could boast a pattern of worship services that included a good hour-and-a-half Sunday morning service, the minister being expected to preach one hour or 45 minutes of this service. Sunday School either followed or preceded the service, and Sunday evening was given over to a second service at which the minister preached another sermon. The midweek prayer meeting constituted the fourth worship service.

Rurality of the Denominations. The Catholic, Lutheran, Congregational, Presbyterian, Episcopal, and Unitarian churches are overwhelmingly urban although each denomination has strong rural followings in some regions. Shortly after World War II, Catholics were 85 percent urban, Episcopalians 83 percent, Presbyterians 75 percent, Congregationalists 70 percent, Lutherans and Methodists 65 percent.[3] Northern Baptists were 75 percent urban while the Southern Baptists were 60 percent rural. The predominantly rural denominations have been the United Brethren, the various Mennonite groups, the Friends, and the Churches of Christ.[4]

Rural churches have been affected by the continuing migration of their

TABLE 34

RELIGIOUS DISTRIBUTION BY RURAL AND URBAN RESIDENCE

	National Percent	Farm	To 2,500	2,500 to 10,000	10,000 to 100,000	100,000 to 500,000	500,000 & Over
National Sample (Cases: 12, 421)	100.0%	16.4%	8.9%	20.4%	20.8%	13.5%	20.0%
Roman Catholic	19.7	8.5	6.1	13.9	20.8	18.4	28.3
Methodist	17.6	22.8	12.9	24.5	19.1	10.5	10.2
Baptist	11.6	21.9	10.5	22.7	19.3	14.8	10.8
Presbyterian	7.9	16.2	8.2	26.3	20.5	12.5	16.3
Lutheran	6.2	25.3	9.5	19.6	20.1	10.6	14.9
Episcopal	4.8	7.8	10.0	20.5	23.0	18.5	20.2
Jewish	4.4	0.7	0.0	4.2	9.0	9.4	76.7
Congregational	3.1	19.1	9.5	22.9	32.0	7.2	9.3
Latter-Day Saints ...	1.5	27.4	15.1	35.8	11.7	7.3	2.7
Christian Scientist ...	1.1	12.1	5.0	17.0	17.7	22.0	26.2
Other	22.1	—	—	—	—	—	—

Information Service, National Council of Churches of Christ in America, March 15, 1948, p. 5.

people to urban areas. Between 1924 and 1930 rural churches in 11 denominations, including the Catholic, declined in total numbers, in membership, and in Sunday School attendance.[5]

Some of the distinguishing characteristics of rural religion and rural

---

[2] Gibson Winter, *Suburban Captivity of the Churches* (New York: Doubleday & Co., 1961).

[3] See Table 34.

[4] Stuart A. Queen and David B. Carpenter, *The American City* (New York: McGraw-Hill, Inc., 1953), p. 289.

[5] H. Paul Douglass and Edmund de S. Brunner, *The Protestant Church as a Social Institution* (New York: Harper & Bros., 1935), p. 4.

churches—their characteristics, problems, and modifications to meet changing conditions—follow below.

Internal Characteristics of Rural Churches. Rural churches are handicapped by lack of size and tend to be small. Indiana has 5000 rural churches, an average of one for every 350 rural residents, with an average membership of 127.[6] Thus, only one out of three rural residents is affiliated with a church—a proportion considerably less than the national norm, according to which 60 percent of the people claim a church affiliation. Extreme isolation accounts for the low proportion of membership in some rural areas.[7]

The proportion of church members in any rural community tends to increase with the size of the community.[8] Vidich and Bensman found that the four Protestant churches in an upstate New York village of 1700 had a total membership of approximately 600, about half of which were active members.[9] As a result of his studies of rural churches in Kentucky, Kaufman reports that a rural church needs a membership base of at least 300 to provide an effective program.[10]

Many rural areas are overchurched, and, as competition increases, averages for Sunday School membership and for finances further decline.[11] Protestant leadership therefore developed the larger parish movement to meet some of the problems of small rural churches. The larger parish is interdenominational in scope. Several churches in a given rural area are combined in a single parish to secure the program and services that a single church and congregation could not afford. With the larger parish several ministers with specialized talents and skills become available to each congregation on some sort of a rotation basis.[12]

The most effective rural churches offer three or four services a week, along with an adequate program of educational and recreational activities to supplement the religious services.[13] Village churches have a more adequate program of services than open-country churches. Seven out of eight village churches had at least one Sunday service, while less than two

---

[6] J. E. Losey, *The Rural Church Situation in Indiana* (Lafayette, Ind.: Purdue University, A.E.S., E.C.–153, September, 1957), p. 6.

[7] John A. Hostetler and William G. Mather, *Participation in the Rural Church* (University Park, Pa.: Pennsylvania State University, A.E.S. Paper No. 1762, Journal Series, October, 1952), p. 5.

[8] A'Delbert Samson, *Church Groups in Four Agricultural Settings* (Bozeman, Mont.: A.E.S. Bulletin 538, March, 1958), p. 16; William G. Mather and T. C. Scheifele, *The Rural Churches in the Central Pennsylvania Synod of the United Lutheran Church in America* (University Park, Pa.: Pennsylvania State University, Department of Agricultural Economics and Rural Sociology, 1951), p. 20.

[9] Arthur J. Vidich and Joseph Bensman, *Small Town in Mass Society* (Princeton, N.J.: Princeton University Press, 1958), p. 227.

[10] Harold F. Kaufman, *Religious Organization in Kentucky* (Lexington, Ky.: A.E.S. Bulletin 524, 1948).

[11] Edmund de S. Brunner, *Village Communities* (New York: George H. Doran Co., 1927), p. 73.

[12] Mark Rich, *The Larger Parish* (Ithaca, N.Y.: Cornell Extension Bulletin, 1939).

[13] A. D. Samson, *op. cit.,* p. 21.

fifths of the open-country churches reached this goal.[14] The same relationships were found in Pennsylvania and in Missouri. Only one fourth of the rural Missouri churches conducted a fulltime service each week.[15]

The typical rural church is served by a minister with substantially less formal training than the minister of the typical urban church. Four fifths of urban white Protestant ministers were college graduates, or had seminary training, while less than half of the rural ministers enjoyed as much formal education and training.[16] And, as might be expected, the open-country church has a greater number of ministers who are serving their congregations on a parttime basis. In Missouri 14 percent of the open-country churches had a fulltime minister, as compared to 63 percent of village churches with a fulltime minister.[17] Indiana reported that two out of three rural churches have a minister on a parttime basis.[18]

Many rural churches are near enough to a college or to a Protestant seminary to secure a college student or a seminarian-in-training on a parttime basis. Seminary faculties and seminary students look upon such an experience as a practical and effective way to train a minister and at the same time contribute to his economic support.

The effective rural church adapts its program to the needs of its constituents, which usually are the social and economic needs of the whole community. Felton found the most effective rural churches were those that promoted activities such as soil conservation, land ownership, and health clinics.[19] The Washington Prairie Evangelical Lutheran Church of Decorah, Iowa, one of the four outstanding rural churches of America (according to the *Christian Century* study) made conservation of the soil a moral issue.[20] The 4-H club and other community organizations were extended the use of the parish hall, and church and congregation maintained a close identification with community problems and projects.

The able and forceful pastor of the Olive Chapel (Southern) Baptist Church of Apex, North Carolina, another of the four outstanding rural Protestant churches, preached the stewardship of the soil as a cardinal Christian virtue. This church, too, also concerned with community problems, made itself the center of community life.[21]

---

[14] John H. Kolb & E. de S. Brunner, *A Study of Rural Society* (New York: Houghton Mifflin Co., 1946), p. 524.

[15] Lawrence M. Hepple, *The Church in Rural Missouri, Part V: Rural-Urban Churches Compared* (Columbia, Mo.: A.E.S. Research Bulletin 633E, July, 1959), p. 291; Melvin W. Sneed & Douglas Ensminger, *The Rural Church in Missouri* (Columbia, Mo.: A.E.S. Research Bulletin 225, June, 1935), p. 65.

[16] E. de S. Brunner & J. H. Kolb, *Rural Social Trends* (New York: McGraw-Hill, Inc., 1933), p. 226.

[17] M. W. Sneed and D. Ensminger, *op. cit.*, p. 65.

[18] J. E. Losey, *op. cit.*

[19] Ralph A. Felton, *A New Gospel of the Soil* (Madison, N.J.: Drew Theological Seminary, 1952).

[20] Thomas A. Tripp, "Making 'Great' Rural Churches," *Christian Century*, Vol. 68 (January 24, 1951), pp. 109–10.

[21] *Ibid.*

A high sex ratio is usually associated with a strong Sunday School program in which adult as well as children's classes are featured, and the effective rural church can boast a high sex ratio. Each of the four outstanding rural churches had a higher than average number of men per women among their active communicants. Weak churches in rural Missouri had a low sex ratio—12 percent fewer men in their congregations than their sister congregations of the same denomination in urban areas.[22]

Environmental Factors Contributing to Effective Rural Churches. Economic prosperity leads to church strength. As the economy improves the churches gain strength and all-around effectiveness.[23] On the other hand, economic depression and poverty lead to weakening and devitalization of rural churches. "Soil erosion means soul erosion."[24]

Homogeneity leads to strong rural churches. Each of the four outstanding rural churches drew its communicants from a geographic area that was largely homogeneous and bound together by strong ties of ethnicity and culture.[25] In each case the culture was strongly religious. There were strong in-group feelings and traditions.

The Evangelical and Reform Church of New Knoxville, Ohio, and the Trinity Lutheran (Missouri-Synod) Church of Freistatt, Missouri, were settled as German-speaking cultural groups and maintained German language services until recently. The Evangelical Lutheran Church at Decorah, Iowa, was settled 100 years ago as a homogeneous Norwegian community. The same close relationship that is found in Judaism between religion and ethnic identity is found in the Decorah Evangelical Lutheran congregation.

Stability of population contributes to strong rural churches, and stable rural population is a reflection of a sound and prosperous agriculture. In a prosperous agricultural community a high proportion of farm operators are owners,[26] who generally have a high morale and sense of community identity. Some young people leave the community for the challenge of urban occupations and urban living, but a substantial number remain to carry on the family farming business and to give continuity to community religious institutions.

Rising educational levels also contribute to strong rural churches; the higher level of education the greater the percentage of church affiliation. This holds true in rural as well as urban communities. There is, however, a tendency for local congregations to be overly represented in the higher

---

[22] Milton Coughenour and Lawrence M. Hepple, *The Church in Rural Missouri, Part II: Religious Groups in Rural Missouri* (Columbia, Mo.: A.E.S. Research Bulletin 633B, September, 1957), p. 63.

[23] H. F. Kaufman, *op. cit.*, p. 27.

[24] Emerson Hynes, "The Parish in the Rural Community," in C. J. Nuesse and Thomas J. Harte (eds.) *The Sociology of the Parish* (Milwaukee: The Bruce Publishing Co., 1951), p. 126.

[25] T. A. Tripp, *op. cit.*

[26] *Ibid.*

TABLE 35

CHURCH MEMBERSHIP AND ATTENDANCE OF 800 OKLAHOMA FARM FAMILIES BY
STANDARD OF LIVING QUARTILES

	Richest Families	Upper Inter- mediate	Lower Inter- mediate	Poorest Families
Husband church member	74.0%	53.0%	41.0%	23.5%
Husband attends church	77.9	65.3	54.5	40.5
Wife church member	88.0	72.4	57.5	33.0
Wife attends church	85.9	74.5	58.5	43.0

Rockwell C. Smith, *The Church in Our Town* (New York: Abingdon-Cokesbury Press, 1945), p. 46.

social and educational levels and underrepresented in the lower social and educational levels.[27] Church-type Protestant denominations tend to be dominated by the agricultural and professional elite of the community.[28]

The Sect in the Rural Community. The rural religious culture includes both sect-type and church-type religious groupings. Extensive data is available from two states showing the relative incidence and the characteristics of both sect-type and church-type religious groupings. The Montana study of rural churches distinguishes between fundamentalist and nonfundamentalist churches[29] and the Missouri study between the sect-type and the church-type of religious groupings.[30] The criteria for sect-type and church-type in the respective states are essentially similar.

Sect-type congregations are smaller in size than church-type congregations but have more worship services per week than church-type congregations. In the rural churches of Missouri only 39 percent of the church-type congregations held worship services each week, compared to 62 percent of the sect-type congregations. Church-type congregations, however, had more social, educational, and recreational organizations and made greater use of the church facilities than did the sect-type church.

TABLE 36

AVERAGE NUMBER OF CHURCH MEMBERS IN FUNDAMENTALIST
AND NONFUNDAMENTALIST CHURCH GROUPS BY LOCATION

	No.	Funda- mentalist	No.	Non- funda mentalist
Open Country	7	16	2	128
Village (to 500)	6	35	13	92
Town (500–2500)	13	22	16	196
City (2500 plus)	6	65	5	200

A. Delbert Samson, "Church Groups in Four Agricultural Settings in Montana," University of Montana, AES Bulletin 538, March, 1958, p. 35.

---

[27] See Table 35.
[28] A. J. Vidich and J. Bensman, *op. cit.*, p. 238.
[29] See Table 36.
[30] See Table 37.

TABLE 37

MEAN MEMBERSHIP OF RELIGIOUS GROUPS BY LOCATION,
CHURCH-TYPE, AND SECT-TYPE

	Church	Sect
Open country (to 200)	92	51
Small village (200–1,000)	143	39
Large village (1,000–2,500)	238	62
Small city (2,500–5,000)	376	57

Lawrence M. Hepple, "The Church in Rural Missouri," University of Missouri, AES Bulletin 633E July, 1959, p. 289.

The sect-type minister has less formal education than the church-type minister. In Montana the sect-type minister had an average of 14.2 years of formal education compared to 18.2 years for the church-type minister.[31] In Missouri 76 per cent of sect-type ministers had no college education whatsoever.[32]

More sect-type than church-type ministers are parttime ministers—engaging in other kinds of work than clerical for income. In Montana 40 percent of the sect-type ministers supplement their income by other work, as compared to only 3 percent of the church-type ministers. In Missouri 48 percent of the church-type ministers in open-country parishes and 89 percent in small city parishes are fulltime ministers compared to 24 percent of sect-type ministers in open-country parishes and 48 percent in small city parishes. However, a higher percent of sect-type than church-type ministers serve only one congregation.

Sect-type churches are most active in forming new congregations, but once established show little vitality in membership growth. The conditions that call forth and maintain sects are found in both rural and urban areas. The chances are 1 in 4 that a rural church will be a sect-type church, and 1 in 3 that a small city church will be a sect-type church.[33]

The Rural Catholic Church

Although the Catholic membership is primarily urban, 8000 out of 15,000 churches are located in rural areas.[34] Shortly after World War II 8 percent of the membership was rural farm, and another 6 percent rural nonfarm. These percentages and relationships are changing. If current trends continue the number of Catholic farmers will soon be outnumbered by the number of Catholic nonfarmers living in rural areas. The rural parish, however, more than reproduces itself; few urban parishes do. Since rural Catholics are a constant source of recruitment for urban church parishes, the church therefore has a twofold interest in her rural parishion-

[31] A. D. Samson, *op. cit.*, p. 37.

[32] L. M. Hepple, *The Church in Rural Missouri, Part III: Clergymen in Rural Missouri* (Columbia, Mo.: A.E.S. Research Bulletin 633C, December, 1958), p. 160.

[33] L. M. Hepple, *op. cit.*, Bulletin, 633E, p. 297.

[34] D. Ensminger, "The Rural Church and Religion," *Rural Life in the United States*, Carl Taylor (ed.) (New York: Alfred A. Knopf, Inc., 1949), p. 126.

ers: for their own social and spiritual well-being, and as a source of recruitment for the urban church.

The National Catholic Rural Life Conference, organized to meet the needs of rural Catholics, is "dedicated to the ideal that our nation's greatness springs from the qualities of physical and spiritual strength fostered by rural living." The conference seeks to make the material and spiritual advantages of life in the countryside available to more than just a few families, and reports the further objective of "working for the spiritual and material welfare of the families of farmers, rural tradesmen, professional and retired people living in the country, and in the small towns."[35]

To accomplish these objectives the National Catholic Rural Life Conference has developed a program that seeks to:

1. Care for underprivileged Catholics living on the land.
2. Keep on the land Catholics that now live there.
3. Increase the number of Catholics living on the land.
4. Improve the spiritual, social, and economic well-being of rural parishioners.

St. Joseph's Church of Bremen, Iowa, has been cited as an illustration of the Rural Life program.[36] In this parish 40 families banded together to reverse the forces that wreck rural family life. Parish-centered 4-H clubs and parish clubs for married couples were organized. The parish encourages and sponsors neighborhood cooperation through the cooperative marketing of crops and the cooperative buying of supplies. Moreover, the parish does not limit its activities to farm families alone; it seeks to uncover and develop job opportunities for parish members not engaged in farming.

The 4-H club functions somewhat as church-affiliated Boy Scout and Girl Scout troops do in an urban parish. The 4-H clubs are dedicated to the all-around development of rural boys and girls in a rural setting, emphasizing "head, hand, heart, health." Rural opportunities and rural values are stressed and encouraged. *Catholic Rural Life*, the official voice of the Catholic Rural Life Conference, is published monthly at Des Moines, Iowa.

Summary

The traditional rural church was a Protestant church. Its organization and program was geared to the needs of a *gemeinschaft* community. Certain of the Protestant denominations, notably the Southern Baptist, the Mennonites, the Friends, and the Churches of Christ, are primarily rural churches.

The rural church is feeling the effect of the impact of science and industrialization upon farming as an economic activity and farming as a

---

35 *Ibid.*

36 "Bremen Bucks the Trend," *Catholic Rural Life*, Des Moines, Ia., December, 1958.

way of life. It takes fewer farmers to produce the necessary food and fiber for the nation. In some regions there are more nonfarmers than farmers living in rural areas.

The typical rural church does not have enough members and resources to maintain a completely trained fulltime minister and to offer an adequate program of services and social ministries. The most successful rural churches provide a program that meets the spiritual and social needs of their members. Successful rural churches are found arising out of an environment of economic prosperity with a homogeneous and stable population that is also marked by a rising level of education.

The social and spiritual welfare of rural Catholics is the concern of the National Catholic Rural Life Conference. Rural Catholic churches are encouraged to offer programs that meet the social and economic, as well as the spiritual needs, of Catholic farmers. The rural Catholic parish is a feeding ground for urban Catholicism.

URBAN RELIGION

The urbanization of the country continued during the first half of the twentieth century, and has been particularly pronounced since World War II. The farming population has continued to decline. In 1960, 70 percent of the people were classed as urban. The leading trend within the urban areas was the great postwar movement to the suburbs. In 1958, 59 percent of the population was concentrated in 168 metropolitan areas. A metropolitan area is any city with a population of 50,000 plus its surrounding satellite communities. Between April 1950 and July 1958, the suburbs next to these metropolitan areas grew at an annual rate of 3.7 percent. This was a rate of growth almost three times greater than that of the central city, and more than double that of the country as a whole.[1]

The churches of the representative American city were located and built in terms of the ecological pattern of the city, and the congregations, the programs, and vitality of churches have changed as the ecological areas in which they have been located have changed.

The typical American city of the latter part of the nineteenth century was geared to a horse and trolley pattern of transportation. Close to the central business and commercial center of the city was located the class A residential area: the homes of the wealthy. The business and professional men living here were within easy carriage distance of their businesses and offices, and their churches, the aristocratic downtown churches, were erected in or near their residential areas. The typical city had an industrial district near which lived the industrial workers, and the churches of the

---

[1] Truman B. Douglass, "Ecological Changes and the Church," *The Annals of the Academy of Political and Social Science*, Vol. 332 (November, 1960), pp. 80–88.

industrial workers were located in their residential areas, within walking distance of their homes. The typical city had one or more middle-class residential districts, with churches appropriate to the spiritual and social needs of the neighborhood.

The continuing industrialization of society, with the increased use and dependence upon the automobile, has caused great growth and expansion in the representative American city. The business and commercial area expanded outward to invade the "Class A" residential areas. This area became a zone in transition. The upper classes left their original homes to build new homes and form new neighborhoods in country areas, outside the city limits.

The big Victorian homes of the wealthy became rooming houses or were split up into low-cost apartments, and eventually demolished to make way for new business and commercial structures. The zone in transition typically became a slum and the area of greatest social disorganization. It is currently included in the term "inner city" and is the most frequent subject for urban renewal. These changes have had important consequences for city churches, particularly the Protestant churches.

Urbanization and the Three Faiths

The relative urbanization of the basic faiths is shown in a study by the Bureau of Research and Study (National Council of the Churches of Christ in the United States of America) of the distribution of Protestants, Catholics, and Jews between metropolitan and nonmetropolitan areas.[2] Jews and Catholics are primarily urban, while more of the numerical strength of Protestantism is in the small cities, villages, and open country.

TABLE 38

URBANIZATION OF THE THREE FAITHS

	Metropolitan	Nonmetropolitan
Number of counties	277	2,797
Population (millions)	85½	65
Percent of population	57%	43%
Percent of members (all faiths)	61%	39%
Percent of all Protestants	46%	54%
Percent of all Roman Catholics	75%	25%
Percent of all Jews	98%	2%
Percent of Protestant churches	29%	71%
Percent of Roman Catholic churches	50%	50%

Information Service, National Council of Churches of Christ in America, March 28, 1959, p. 1.

The nature and location of the churches in any given city is related to the numbers and distribution of affiliates and communicants of the three faiths. Protestants and Protestant churches dominated the religious map of the representative American city in the nineteenth century. Today Catho-

[2] See Table 38.

TABLE 39

Religious Affiliation,* New York City (1957)
(Population in Thousands)

	Total	Protestant		Roman Catholic		Jewish†		Other		Unaffiliated‡	
New York City	7,795	1,040	13.4%	2,075	26.6%	2,060	26.4%	172	2.2%	2,448	31.0%
Bronx	1,424	140	9.8	414	29.0	502	35.2	32	2.2	336	23.8
Brooklyn	2,602	306	11.7	603	23.2	884	33.9	57	2.2	752	29.0
Manhattan	1,794	324	18.0	423	23.6	316	17.6	40	2.2	691	38.6
Queens	1,763	240	13.6	553	31.4	347	19.7	39	2.2	584	33.1
Staten Island	212	30	14.1	82	38.6	11	5.2	4	2.2	85	39.9

Source: Leland Gartrell, *Religious Affiliation, New York City and Metropolitan Regions*, Department of Church Planning and Research, Protestant Council of the City of New York, p. 9.
* Members enrolled in the various religious institutions. (The Jewish figure is a cultural count.)
† Jewish cultural count.
‡ Excludes unaffiliated of Jewish background.

lics comprise from one third to two thirds of the population of our large cities. Two thirds of America's 5½ million Jews live in or adjacent to ten of the largest cities: New York, Los Angeles, Philadelphia, Boston, Chicago, Newark and environs, Cleveland, Washington, D.C., Baltimore, and St. Louis. Protestants, however, constitute the highest proportion of the suburban population and in many suburbs are in the majority.[3]

The "inner city" is that part of the city next to the central business district. In a dynamic and growing city the inner city becomes a zone of transition, an area of social disorganization, and the most frequent object of urban renewal. In the nineteenth century the inner city was the stronghold of Protestantism and was dotted with Protestant churches. As the technological revolution increased in tempo, most Protestant denominations found they were losing ground as a result of population movements and changes in the inner city. Protestants were moving out and the recent immigrant groups, primarily Catholics and Jews, moved in to take their places. In New York City, while 200,000 people were moving into the area below 14th Street, 17 Protestant churches were moving out.[4]

In New York City, Catholics and Jews are twice as numerous as Protestants. Catholics are more numerous than Protestants in all five boroughs of the city; Jews outnumber Protestants in three boroughs and are approximately equal to Protestants in Manhattan, and are outnumbered by Protestants only in Staten Island.[5]

Population changes and movements are further emphasized by a look at the ethnic distribution of Protestants. In all the boroughs of New York City, Negro Protestants and Puerto Rican Protestants outnumber white Protestants. In the Bronx, Negro and Puerto Rican Protestants are three times as numerous as white Protestants; in Brooklyn Negro Protestants alone outnumber white Protestants. It is only in the more suburban bor-

TABLE 40

PROTESTANT AFFILIATION, NEW YORK CITY (1957)
(Population in Thousands)

	Total Pop.	White		Non-white		Puerto Rican	
New York City	1,040	500	48.1%	442	42.5%	98	9.4%
Bronx	140	35	25.1	62	44.2	43	30.7
Brooklyn	306	140	45.7	140	45.8	26	8.5
Manhattan	324	116	35.8	181	55.9	27	8.3
Queens	240	183	76.1	55	22.9	2	1.0
Staten Island	30	26	86.7	4	13.3	—	—

Leland Gartrell, *Religious Affiliation, New York City and Metropolitan Regions.* Department of Church Planning and Research, Protestant Council of the City of New York, p. 9.

---

[3] Albert I. Gordon, *Jews in Suburbia* (Boston: Beacon Press, 1959), p. 6.

[4] Ross W. Sanderson, *The Church Serves the Changing City* (New York: Harper & Bros., 1955), p. 238.

[5] See Table 39.

oughs of Queens and Staten Island that white Protestants are clearly in the majority.[6]

Urban Protestantism

The Metropolitan Church. The twentieth-century American city may include several types of Protestant churches. Some cities can boast of one or more "metropolitan" churches located "downtown," perhaps even occupying the same site as the original church or churches. But their memberships are now drawn from throughout the city. They feature brilliant and well-known preachers and offer extensive programs of social ministries, age- and sex-graded, and other services from the hands of specialists.[7] These services may include such modern features as psychiatric or marriage counseling. It is a wealthy church because of its endowment and the nature of its membership.

The people living in the neighborhood of a metropolitan church may be from an entirely different class than the membership. For this reason some of these churches have developed a program of spiritual and social services for people who live around the church. But, although the church may even appropriate money to carry on such services and programs, there is no attempt to socialize between the old membership and the people for whom the services were developed. Some metropolitan churches are therefore serving dual and triple constituencies.[8]

The Neighborhood Church. Another characteristic church in the twentieth century American city is the neighborhood church. It is located in a portion of the city where enough people live nearby to support it, but where less growth occurs than in the suburbs. The areas these churches serve are undergoing little change; the populations are fairly placid and constitute communities that are really neighborhoods. Usually people come to church from within a mile, and the neighborhood church carries on in a traditional Protestant fashion. It has a representative program of social ministries but does not have the staff, or organization, or such frills as the psychiatric counseling of the metropolitan churches.[9]

Not every Protestant church that finds its neighborhood engulfed by a class of people entirely different from its membership reacts by becoming a metropolitan church. Some move out and follow their membership into the suburban areas. As early as 1876 a recorder noted the closing of one Protestant church as "owing to the moving away of the class of the

---

[6] See Table 40.

[7] Stuart A. Queen and David B. Carpenter, *The American City* (New York: McGraw-Hill, Inc., 1953), p. 292.

[8] Gibson Winter, *The Suburban Captivity of the Churches* (New York: Doubleday & Co., 1961), p. 85.

[9] National Council of the Churches of Christ in the USA (Department of the Urban Church), *Toward Better City Churches*, Ross W. Sanderson (ed.), New York, 1955, p. 34.

population in this quarter whose needs are met by such a church."[10] Some carry on as a dying church, at a gradually diminishing tempo, with fewer and fewer members.

The Mission Church. In some instances Protestantism continues to serve the area by maintaining mission churches, supported in part if not entirely by the parent denomination. Mission churches are either static or diminishing in size. However, if growing and dynamic, the church soon reaches the point where it is self-supporting and self-sufficient and loses its mission status. Mission churches are as often a "holding" as an evangelizing operation.

The Inclusive Parish. A more recent reaction of Protestantism to the zone in transition and the area of social disorganization is the development of the inclusive parish, represented by the East Harlem Protestant Parish (EHPP) in New York City,[11] and the West Side Christian Parish in Chicago. EHPP was established to meet the social and spiritual needs of a "crime infested slum area." A quarter million Italians, Puerto Ricans, and Negroes were living within one square mile. The area was plagued with probems of racial discrimination, inadequate housing, juvenile delinquency, alienation from meaning in work, and problems in the use of leisure time. Less than 25 percent of the residents had active affiliations with any church.

The pagan character of the community, the previous withdrawal of Protestant forces from the area, and the need for depth and variety of missionary resources made an inclusive geographical parish organized on the basis of neighborhood need a necessity. From the beginning the parish has received united Protestant support. It has been supported by the American Baptist, Congregational Christian, Methodist, Presbyterian (USA), Reformed Church in America, Evangelical United Brethren, and Evangelical and Reformed churches.

The parish employs a variety of facilities: four main parish centers, two clubrooms for work with two street clubs, two apartments on 100th Street that house a medical clinic, a storefront headquarters for work with drug addicts, an office in a former store where there is a federal credit union, a legal aid clinic, and a library, and a farm and wooded retreat center in the country north of Peekskill. The larger parish is not the only religious organization in the area. Seven other churches, nine storefront churches, and three Catholic parishes are active here.

Chicago's West Side Christian Parish is an inner-city organization established, like EHPP, to minister to the needs of the various residents within the parish boundaries. Located in the near west side of Chicago, the parish was designed to meet the challenge offered by the presence of a great mass of transient and "minority" peoples, overwhelmed by inadequate

---

[10] Howard G. Hageman, "The Theology of the Urban Church," *The City Church,* May–June, 1959.
[11] George W. Webber, "EHPP: Emerging Issues," in *Cities and Churches,* Robert Lee (ed.) (Philadelphia: The Westminster Press, 1962), pp. 162–76.

housing facilities and insufficient incomes, and characterized by a depressing overtone of apathy. The parish has carried on an appropriate religious and social program from three modest church centers. It maintains a counseling center and a youth center, and has taken an active part in promoting a comprehensive plan for urban renewal within its parish boundaries.[12]

The "Storefront Church." Storefront religious groups are typically found in the socially disorganized areas of large cities and are generally housed in smaller secular buildings. The storefront church is usually, but not always, Protestant; it may be cultic in nature. If Protestant it usually represents the fundamentalist type of religion from which the major denominations tend to stand aloof. Storefront churches differ from denominations and ecclesia by the more limited education of their clergy, the lower economic stratification of their congregations, by the unconventional and unsophisticated nature of their theology, and by their unpretentious meeting places.[13]

In his analysis of storefront groups Eddy identified three types: the transitory local group, emotional in character and without strong interchurch affiliation, such as a primitive Pentecostal group; the "charismatic" type, built around the leadership and personality of a single individual, as illustrated by the House of Prayer of Daddy Grace; the type based upon a myth that unifies people socially by giving them a distinct ritual and belief. The Church of God and Saints of Christ, commonly known as the "Black Jews," would belong in this last category.[14]

The Suburban Church. The suburban church serves the suburban community. Removed from the central city, the community is largely residential, with a local community consciousness, but most of its residents are closely related to the central city.[15] It should be distinguished from an industrial suburb or a satellite city. From 1870 to 1950 numerous, decentralized congregations moved to the suburban and satellite areas. Losses from the urban white collar and the working classes were offset by gains among this new suburban middle class.

Some observers find most of what is good in Protestantism in the suburban church while others see weaknesses and shortcomings. Suburban Protestantism is seen by some as the homogenization of Protestantism because the similarities among denominations are more evident than the differences. The Church, it is said, is disturbed at finding itself too readily at home in a one-class community. More negatively, the dominant churches tend to change the typical suburb into a middle-class ghetto.

---

[12] Chicago's West Side Christian Parish, City Church Study Kit Number 2, Department of the Urban Church, National Council of the Churches of Christ in the USA, New York.

[13] G. Norman Eddy, "Store-Front Religion," *Religion in Life*, Vol. 28 (Winter, 1958–59), pp. 68–85.

[14] *Ibid.*

[15] *Toward Better City Churches, op. cit.*

The suburban Protestant church is frequently characterized by denominational irrelevance. Many pastors of these churches annually received, by transfer from congregations of *other* denominations, three or four times as many members as they received by transfers from congregations of their *own* denominations. Denominational loyalty is low. Convenience, the Sunday School, the general excellence and reputation of the church, even parking facilities, appear more important in the choice of a church than the family's previous denominational affiliation.[16]

In his study of the Congregational Christian Church, Fukuyama found that only one out of three members was originally a Congregational. Among the previous affiliations were:[17]

Methodist	18%
Presbyterian	15
Baptist	11
Lutheran	8
Catholic	2

At Park Forest, a suburb of Chicago, Whyte reported the reasons for choosing a church in this order of importance: pastor's personality, skills and qualifications, the Sunday School, convenient location, the denomination, the music.[18]

The Urban Catholic Church

The Catholic church is not a class church like most Protestant churches. Any given Catholic church tends to cut across class lines because of the organization of the parish. The basic parish is a geographical and inclusive parish. All Catholics in a designated geographical area belong to this parish and are the responsibility of the parish pastor. Racial and ethnic parishes, which might encompass all of the particular race or ethnic group within a given area, are the only exception to this rule. The geographic, or inclusive, parish is a class church only to the degree that all the Catholics within a given parish happen to be of a certain social class, and this situation is seldom found in central city parishes.

Two comprehensive studies of parishes are available for information and generalizations on the functioning of the Catholic church in the American city: Fichter's study of a representative New Orleans parish,[19] and Schuyler's study of a representative parish in New York City.[20]

The New Orleans parish is located in the Riverside neighborhood and has within its boundaries a population which is approximately 75 percent

---

[16] Douglass, *op. cit.*

[17] *Ibid.*

[18] William H. Whyte, *The Organization Man* (New York: Doubleday & Co., 1956), pp. 417–21.

[19] Joseph H. Fichter, S.J., *Southern Parish: Dynamics of a City Church* (Chicago: University of Chicago Press, 1951).

[20] Joseph B. Schuyler, S.J., *Northern Parish: A Sociological and Pastoral Study* (Chicago: Loyola University Press), 1960.

white and 25 percent Negro. In religious identification this population is 52 percent Catholic, 42 percent Protestant, 2 percent Jewish, and 4 percent Other or Unknown. Seventy percent of the Negroes are Protestant and 60 percent of the whites are Catholic.

Within the parish boundaries are eight white churches, of which one (St. Mary's) is Catholic, and 22 Negro churches, of which one (St. Benedict's) is also Catholic. The Negro churches are generally small or of the storefront sect type with a parttime pastor.

St. Mary's is a parish of ethnic diversity. Present parish membership is primarily of German, French, Irish, and Italian background, with smaller numbers of English and Spanish descent. The Germans and the French came into the neighborhood over a hundred years ago, at the time the parish was organized. The Irish settled between 1850 and 1900, and the Italians from 1900 on.

Only the two Catholic churches are in any sense biracial. A few Negro Catholics can be found attending services in St. Mary's, and a few white Catholics attending services at St. Benedict's. Aside from worship, the two churches are completely separate and independent in organization.[21]

The communicants at St. Mary's cut across all class lines. A few families from the highest social class belong to the parish. However, a smaller percent of the parish is gainfully employed in the professional and managerial occupations than is found in the non-Catholic white group. The highest and lowest classes are underrepresented among St. Mary's parishioners; the concentration is strongly lower middle class.

Our Lady of Mercy parish is located in the heart of the upper Bronx, New York City. Within the parish boundaries live second and third generation descendants of German, Irish, Italian, and Central European immigrants.

Like the New Orleans parish, just slightly more than half of the residents are identified as Catholics. Jews account for 24 percent, Protestants 10 percent, Other 2 percent, and None or Unknown 9 percent of the population.[22]

Approximately 1000 of the 4700 Catholic families residing within the parish belong to or attend other Catholic churches. Seven hundred of these families are members of Our Lady of Mount Carmel parish, a national parish for Italians. Two hundred and seventy families (about 5 percent of all Catholics living within the OLM parish boundaries) attend other Catholic churches adjacent to Our Lady of Mercy parish, but this number is offset by an approximately equal number of Catholics who live just outside the parish boundaries but attend Our Lady of Mercy parish.

The parish cuts across all class lines represented in the community but, compared with the neighborhood, it is somewhat underrepresented in the professional and managerial occupations and overrepresented by manual

[21] J. H. Fichter, *op. cit.,* chap. 3.
[22] J. B. Schuyler, *op. cit.,* chap. 6.

TABLE 41

Types of Occupations by County, Neighborhood, and Parish

	Bronx County	OLM* Neighborhood	OLM* Parish
Professional & managerial	20.8%	25.9%	14.6%
Craftsmen & operatives	35.4	28.0	26.2
Clerical work & sales	29.0	34.6	39.6
Manual labor & domestic service	14.8	6.8	19.5

Joseph B. Schuyler, S.J. (*Northern Parish*, Chicago: Loyola University Press, 1960), p. 134.
* Our Lady of Mercy parish.

labor and domestic service.[23] There are few significant differences between the educational background of the residents of the borough or county, the residents of the neighborhood, and the parishioners.

The above cases show that the urban church is able to function effectively at the parish level in spite of a variation in the social class structure of the parish. Both of the above parishes include some parishioners from the upper classes as well as some from the lower classes. Both parishes likewise are composed primarily of descendants of European immigrants who have achieved varying degrees of upward mobility. At the same time neither parish is a demonstration of complete religious integration of the classes for each has a number of families residing within the parish boundaries who belong to, and worship at, a nearby racial or ethnic church.

Rossi has pointed out that the Catholic parish is a client member-oriented organization as compared to the typical Protestant class church, which is member-oriented.[24] The priest-communicant is the important relationship in the Catholic system because the emphasis is upon worship, and the priest the indispensable mediator. Social relations are incidental and secondary.

This is quite different from the Protestant class church where social relations are frequently determinative both for initial and continuing affiliation. Although the Catholic system provides a number of parish societies to perform acts of piety and charity, and for the furtherance of public worship, membership or participation is wholly voluntary. The number of parishioners who take an active part in these organizations is small, a fact deplored by the priests. Fichter found that only 3.6 percent of all parishioners 14 years old or over were members of a parish society, attended at least one third of the meetings, and otherwise played an active role in the organization.[25] Catholics worship but do not socialize.

The Suburban Catholic Church. The Catholic church, like the Protestant church, has felt the influence of mobility and the redistribution of population. Large numbers of Catholics have joined the postwar trek to

---

23 See Table 41.
24 Peter Rossi, *Why Families Move* (Glencoe, Ill.: The Free Press, 1955), p. 30 ff.
25 J. H. Fichter, *Social Relations in the Urban Parish* (Chicago: University of Chicago Press, 1954), p. 157.

the suburbs and many Catholic parishes in the central city have been deci-mated by these withdrawals. In a number of cases the church has found it possible to redirect the facilities and services represented in these central city parishes for the benefit of new arrivals, Negro migrants from the South and Puerto Ricans. The church has well-established programs and parishes for Puerto Ricans both in New York and Chicago.

The rapidly growing suburbs are just as marked by the organization and development of new Catholic churches and parishes as they are by new Protestant churches and congregations. The Catholic church has invested considerable thought and effort in an analysis of suburban Catholicism and finds administering to the needs of the new suburbanites is both a challenge and an opportunity.[26]

The suburban church is more of a class church than the traditional inner city parish. The families comprising the parish are relatively homogeneous. They are largely the grandchildren and great grandchildren of immigrants who have achieved substantial economic and social success. The bread-winner enjoys a representative upper-middle class income. The educational level is high; college and graduate degrees are common.

The suburbanite is typically a good Catholic. Catholic spokesmen re-port that the record of "observable religious" practices have never been surpassed by as large a group. Suburban Catholics not only attend services but support and demand parish organizations and activities. A "good parish" is one where lots is going on; a "poor parish" one where nothing goes on.

The suburban parish is "child-centered," with the child under the super-vision and control of the parochial school five hours a day. The child is educated, trained in the social graces, and given a sex education appropriate to Catholic philosophy and morality, and provided with recreation by the parochial school.

The suburban milieu puts different, and in some respects greater, de-mands upon the priest and the priestly role. He is no longer the only edu-cated or "best educated" man in the community.[27] Intellectually sophisti-cated parishioners feel free to disagree with the clergy on matters that less educated parishioners would accept on authority. Parishioners are not so much impressed by the priest's learning as by his competence in perform-ing the various functions that comprise the round of priestly duty in a suburban community.[28]

Catholics are not isolated but fully assimilated and accepted in suburban secular culture and come in close contact with secular practices such as divorce, birth control, and premarital sex that are in direct conflict with Catholic teaching. Parish clergy are challenged to maintain Catholic

---

[26] Andrew M. Greeley, *The Church and the Suburbs* (New York: Sheed and Ward, 1959).

[27] *Ibid.*, p. 55.

[28] *Ibid.*, p. 73.

spiritual and moral values in this highly materialistic and scientific culture. They come to grips with the problem of maintaining Catholic absolutes and universals with programs that seek to involve Catholic communicants: the Liturgical Movement, Catholic Action, the Catholic Family Movement, and others.[29]

The Liturgical Movement puts emphasis upon the liturgy in employing and recognizing the "fundamental religious intuitions"; that is, the creating father in heaven, the regenerative powers of water, reverence due sacred places, and the importance of sacred seasons.[30]

Catholic Action seeks to involve the talent and energies found in the suburban parish and employ them constructively in such socially desirable projects as economic planning, urban renewal, and intergroup relations. The Catholic Family Movement is similarly pointed towards the maintenance and renewal of Catholic ideals of family responsibility and sex relations.

Urban Judaism

Judaism is primarily an urban religion[31] and all denominational types are found within the central city, from the small and strictly Orthodox synagogues to the large Conservative or Reform temples, modernistic in construction and design, and with extensive adjoining facilities to meet the social and educational needs of a congregation of several hundred families.

Although 2500 of the 4000 Jewish congregations carry an Orthodox identification, there is a wide variation in both the religious practice and the ecological distribution of Orthodox congregations and synagogues. The strictly Orthodox congregations and their synagogues are generally found in or near areas of first settlement. The extreme illustration of Orthodoxy is the Hasidic Jewish community of the Williamburg section of Brooklyn.[32] Here Hasidic women cut off their hair upon marriage and wear unbecoming wigs. Pallid scholars, dressed in black and with side curls dangling under the brims of fur-trimmed hats, walk silently along the sidewalks.

Other Orthodox congregations have moved to the suburbs where they are building synagogues adapted to their needs.[33] These congregations participate in the economic and professional life of the secular society but at the same time find it possible to follow Orthodox rules in the home and on the Sabbath.

Conservative and Reform temples are located throughout the city and reflect the wealth and size of the respective congregations.

Suburban Judaism. Jews participated actively and prominently in the

---

[29] *Ibid.*, p. 58.
[30] *Ibid.*, p. 172.
[31] See Table 38.
[32] *New York Times*, July 2, 1962.
[33] *Ibid.*, April 28, 1957.

great movement to the suburbs that followed World War II. In a study of 89 suburbs that included a Jewish congregation, Gordon found that the center of gravity in Jewish religious life has shifted from the home to the community.[34]

Park Forest, a suburb of Chicago, is one of these communities. The following analysis of Park Forest and its Jewish community is offered as a representative case study of the transfer of religion from the home to the synagogue and temple in a typical newly developed middle-class suburb.[35] Park Forest was planned and developed as a combination of garden apartments and single-family homes, and the great bulk of the families that moved into the apartments and houses were veterans. The families were young, the men about 35 and the wives about 30, with one or two children of school age. The gainfully employed head of the family was typically a business or professional man.

A number of these young families were Jewish in background and had been brought up in a Jewish neighborhood in the central city, typically in a working class area. Their parents had come to the United States as part of the third great Jewish immigration movement, from 1890 to 1924, the influx from Eastern Europe.

These young couples tended to be upper-middle or middle class depending upon whether the breadwinner represented a professional and business or a subprofessional type of occupation and income. They overwhelmingly pursued the middle-class style of life according to the class and culture patterns of "young moderns." Most of them had moved up one or two steps on the social class ladder when compared to the pattern of life from which they had come, or with their parents in the areas of second and third settlement in the inner city.

These young Jewish couples not only lived *like* other Park Foresters but lived *with* them. They were not isolated or segregated into a Jewish neighborhood or community but were scattered throughout the "garden apartments" and the single family home area. They were socially accepted. However the young couples were not entirely satisfied with their life in the community because their children lacked the religious experience and associations that would give them a Jewish identity.

The Catholic and Protestant children with whom the Jewish children played attended church and Sunday School. The Jewish children wanted to know what their religion was and why they did not go to Sunday School like their friends—Park Forest had no synagogue or temple. This was no hardship for the parents because they were not interested in following the rituals and disciplines characteristic of the Jewish community in which they had grown up, but the desire of the parents to give their chil-

---

[34] A. I. Gordon, *op. cit.*, p. 95.

[35] Herbert J. Gans, "The Origin and Growth of a Jewish Community in the Suburbs: A Study of the Jews of Park Forest," in *The Jews: Social Patterns of an American Group*, Marshall Sklare (ed.) (Glencoe, Ill.: The Free Press, 1958), pp. 205–48.

dren the social and the psychological security which the children seemed to need led to the organization of a community Sunday School.

The majority of the parents wanted the Sunday School to give their children not religion (Judaism) but identity (Jewishness). The parents wanted religion and culture to be taught so that their children would grow up identifying themselves as Jews, but not the type of training and indoctrination which would require the parents to keep the rituals in the home and to attend services in a temple or synagogue. The resulting Sunday School was community sponsored and oriented. It taught the things upon which all Jews could agree whether they were of the Orthodox, Conservative, or Reform background.

The nondenominational Sunday School was a *child-oriented* religious experience and a substantial departure from *adult-oriented* traditional religion where children were trained and taught to think and to behave as adults. The boys and girls were educated for adulthood and adult responsibilities. At his *Bar Mitzvah*, at age 13, the boy takes his place alongside the other men in the congregation as a responsible Jew in the adult community. The community Sunday School sought to make the children happy in the knowledge of their Jewish identity. There was little or no emphasis upon the disciplines and responsibilities of traditional Judaism.

As Park Forest grew so did its Jewish population. The number of Jewish families who were not satisfied with the minimum of Jewish religion and culture represented in the community Sunday School increased and began to agitate for the organization of a congregation in Park Forest. Within five years of the establishment of the community Sunday School, a congregation was organized. Forty percent of the now 600 Jewish families contributed to the erection of the edifice and the support of the congregation.

The denominational position of the congregation was described as "Eastern European Reform." Although the rabbi hired had been raised as Orthodox, he was Reform in practice. The congregation was permissive towards the deprivational practices in the home—the kosher diet, for example—and maintained a quasi-Conservative array of ceremonies, Hebrew readings, and responsive chanting at services. Women took the leadership in the social and educational organizations of the temple.

The establishment of the temple crystallized the sentiment for a more traditional type of Jewish indoctrination than that offered at the community Sunday School. The rabbi and the congregational leaders organized a competing congregational Sunday School where children were taught not as children but as adults in miniature. The emphasis was upon specific congregational loyalty rather than diffuse religious affiliation.

In spite of the more traditional emphasis in the training of their children, the parents of the congregation continued to avoid religious activities and religious services. Religious-cultural activities ran a poor second to social activities. Friday night services were attended by only some 50 to 75 of approximately 600 persons represented in the 240 families of the congregation. Even so, the social hour following the service was thought to be the biggest attraction. The temple and its organizations function for the majority of participants as a source of social relations.

Adults are religious in terms of their children and their parents. They will attend the *Yahrzeit* service for their next of kin, show up at a *Bar Mitzvah*, and on the High Holy Days, but will otherwise turn out only for social meetings.

Through formal organizations in the temple and community schools, the typical middle-class Jew in the suburban community retains the identity he secured informally while growing up in continuous association with others in a neighborhood totally or predominantly Jewish. Social organizations give to the second and third generation suburban Jew the sense of identity and belonging that the first generation Jew received through the informal associations in the all-Jewish neighborhood in the inner city. Jewish religious institutions seem to be taking on the associational and bureaucratic characteristics of a *gesellschaft* society.

Summary

The changing ecological structure of the American city is influencing and modifying the organization and practice of religion of each of the basic faiths. Protestant churches tend to be class churches and to reflect the values and attitudes of the areas in which they are located. The metropolitan church, the neighborhood church, the mission church, and the storefront church are representative types of churches in the typical American city.

The Protestant suburban church is middle-class oriented and child-centered. The Protestant suburban church is more marked by its general Protestantism than by its denominational relevance.

Urban Catholicism is served by national as well as geographic parishes. The geographic parish serves the various Catholics within the parish boundaries and tends to cut across class lines. The urban parish is less of a class church than the Protestant church. The national parish serves a particular ethnic group and generally reflects a more homogeneous constituency than the geographic parish.

The suburban Catholic church is more of a class church. Like the suburban Protestant church, its parishioners are largely white-collar, business, or professional families. The suburban Catholic parish tends to be child-centered. Parish organizations and ministries occupy a more prominent place in the program than in the representative inner city Catholic parish.

Judaism is almost entirely urban. Orthodox, Conservative, and Reform congregations are all found within the typical large city. Suburban Judaism bears many resemblances to suburban Protestantism. It is child-centered and, like its sister Protestant suburban churches, denominationalism is relatively irrelevant. Congregational affiliation is a leading avenue for identification. Parents seem to be more concerned that their children gain a Jewish identification than religious training and indoctrination.

STRATIFICATION AND RELIGION

On the basis of an extensive study of the numerous scattered studies of social class, Moberg reports that the leading Protestant denominations may be ranked from high to low in the following approximate order: Episcopal, Unitarian, Congregational, Presbyterian, Christian Science, Friends, Methodist, Disciples of Christ, Lutheran, Baptist, Mormon, Eastern Orthodox, Assemblies of God, Pentecostal, Holiness, and Jehovah's Witnesses.[1]

Warner finds a similar pattern of denominational stratification: Episcopalians and Unitarians generally rank higher than the Methodists and the Baptists, while Congregationalists, Presbyterians, and Christian Scientists are centered in the middle class.[2]

Several generalizations stand out from the various studies and reports:

1. Protestant churches tend to be class churches. Few congregations draw from all the social classes in the community.

2. Every community has stratification among its churches, but there is a great variation among communities. All of the classic studies of small town and small cities amply document religious stratification: West, *Plainville*;[3] Kaufman, *Prestige Classes in a Rural Community*;[4] Vidich and Bensman, *Small Town in Mass Society*;[5] Hollingshead, *Elmtown's Youth*;[6] Davis *et al.*, *Deep South*;[7] Lynd and Lynd, *Middletown*;[8] Warner, *Yankee City*,[9] and many others.

Great variations are found among communities. Some Episcopal churches draw their members from a lower level of the class structure than certain Baptist or Methodist congregations in the same community.[10] In the South the Methodist church often enjoys a position like that of the Episcopal church in most other communities. There are some communities in the Northeast where a Baptist church includes the greatest share of the persons and families of

---

[1] David O. Moberg, *The Church as a Social Institution* (Englewood Cliffs, N.J.: Prentice-Hall, Inc., 1962), p. 459.

[2] W. Lloyd Warner, Marchia Meeker, and Kenneth Eells, *Social Class in America* (New York: Harper & Bros., 1960), p. 96.

[3] James West, *Plainville USA* (New York: Columbia University Press, 1946).

[4] Harold F. Kaufman, "Prestige Classes in a Rural Community," Cornell AES Memoir 260, Ithaca, New York, 1944.

[5] Arthur J. Vidich and Joseph Bensman, *Small Town in Mass Society* (Princeton, N.J.: Princeton University Press, 1958).

[6] August Hollingshead, *Elmtown's Youth* (New York: John Wiley & Sons, 1949).

[7] Allison Davis, Burleigh Gardner, and Mary Gardner, *Deep South* (Chicago: University of Chicago Press, 1948).

[8] Robert S. and Helen M. Lynd, *Middletown* (New York: Harcourt, Brace & Co., 1929).

[9] W. Lloyd Warner and Paul S. Lunt, *The Social Life of a Modern City* (New Haven, Conn.: Yale University Press, 1941).

[10] D. O. Moberg, *op. cit.*

wealth and prestige. In other communities a Presbyterian church may occupy this position.

3. Religious organizations decline in influence among the most privileged and among the most disadvantaged. The strength of most churches lies among the middle classes.[11] Church membership is proportionately higher among persons employed as business, professional, and white-collar workers than among skilled and unskilled laborers, and more farm owners and managers than tenants and laborers also are members.[12]

4. Sects are a continuing force in the religious culture and derive most of their following from the lower social and economic strata of the community.

If the congregation has an ideology and ritual which are informal, emotional, and make a literal interpretation of the Bible, the chances are good that almost all the people in the church will be from the lower half of society, and probably from the lowest part.[13] In a middle western city, on a five step class structure, 100 percent of the Free Methodists and 87.5 percent of the Gospel Tabernacle were in the upper lower class, and 12.5 percent of the latter sect in the lower lower class.[14] Sects substitute religious status for social status. Sect members' needs for recognition and belonging are gained within their own group.

Sects cannot be explained entirely or primarily on the basis of economic determinism. Kahl cites statistics of changes in the labor force between 1910 and 1950 showing that the American economic proletariat is now a much smaller percent of the gainfully employed than formerly.[15] Economic determinism it would seem, should therefore have caused sects to diminish in numbers and vitality, but this has not happened. Assemblies of God increased from 148,000 in 1936 to 505,000 in 1958. The sect church in a representative village or small city on any given Sunday will have just about the same pattern of modern and up-to-date cars parked outside as will be found in the middle-class churches of the community. The pentecostal and holiness groups have not diminished in evangelizing zeal nor have the high status churches taken up the slack.[16]

We propose to cite some of the studies upon which the generalizations concerning social class and religion have been made, and to indicate some of the limitations of sociological knowledge in this area. A number of factors contribute to the social class position that a particular individual or family may occupy in a community or social group. Social class has a reputational and an objective as well as a subjective dimension.

The personal prestige or lack of prestige which the individual enjoys among other members of the community constitutes the reputational

---

[11] Liston Pope, "Religion in the Class Structure," *The Annals of the Academy of Political and Social Science*, Vol. 256 (March, 1948), p. 90.

[12] D. O. Moberg, *op. cit.*

[13] W. L. Warner, M. Meeker, and K. Eells, *op. cit.*, p. 96.

[14] *Ibid.*, p. 95.

[15] Joseph A. Kahl, *The American Class Structure* (New York: Rinehart & Co., 1957).

[16] Truman B. Douglass, "Ecological Changes and the Church," *Annals of the Academy of Political and Social Science*, Vol. 59 (November, 1960), p. 83.

dimension. This prestige is evidenced in the respect that his neighbors have for him and the deference with which he is held.

The objective dimension of social class includes the things and possessions that can be objectively measured. The individual's occupation, his home, its location, how much it is worth, and how he cares for it give him a high, average, or low rating in the community. The interaction pattern, friends and groups with whom the individual or family maintains intimate social relations—or "who-invites-whom-to-dinner," are significant indications of social position.

Values define the ends of life and the approved means of approaching them. When people are largely in agreement about the things they consider good, important, or appropriate, they are pretty sure to occupy about the same social position in their community.

Most of the studies of religious behavior and social class are in terms of only one of the above variables of social class. One variable is strongly indicative, but no conclusive evidence of social class. These studies are, therefore, an indication of the general social class orientation of denominations but by no means the complete story of the correlation of religious behavior in terms of social class.

Eminence and Denominational Affiliation. A study of the religious affiliation of the men listed in *Who's Who in the East* showed the Unitarian Church far overshadowed other Protestant denominations when compared on the basis of men of eminence per 100,000 male church members. The Episcopal, Congregational, and Presbyterian churches shared second ranking, and considerably outranked the Methodists and the Baptists.[17]

Occupation and Religion. Several studies of religious affiliation and social class are based upon occupation—an important criterion of social class. It is one of the three factors upon which Warner constructed his Index of Social Status formula.[18] An intensive study of church membership in Madison, Wisconsin, showed that almost half of the membership of the Unitarian church came from families in which the breadwinner was a professional. About one third of the Episcopal church membership was from the professional classes, but less than one tenth of the Lutheran membership were professionals.[19]

Another much-quoted source of social class orientation of the major denominations is based upon four polls taken in 1945 and 1946 by the American Institute of Public Opinion. Data were secured from approximately 12,000 cases. Approximately one third of the Episcopal, Presbyterian, and Congregational samples enjoyed a business and professional

[17] B. Davis, "Eminence and Level of Social Origin," *American Journal of Sociology*, Vol. 59 (July, 1953), pp. 11–18.

[18] W. L. Warner, M. Meeker, and K. Eells, *op. cit.*, pp. 121–129.

[19] Louis Bultena, "Church Membership and Church Attendance in Madison, Wisconsin," *American Sociological Review*, Vol. 14 (June, 1949), p. 386.

status as compared with one fifth of the Methodist and one eighth of the Baptist and Lutheran samples.[20]

The denominations showed a similar variation in the proportion of the respective samples who were college graduates—between 20 and 25 percent of the Presbyterian, Episcopal, and Congregational samples, about half that percentage for the Methodists and Baptists, and one third percentage for Lutherans.[21]

Social Class of Catholics

In his summary analysis of religion and social class Moberg reported that Catholics rank just above Baptists and below the other major Protestant denominations.[22] The Public Opinion Poll studies support this generalization. Catholics have a slightly higher percent of their members in business and professional occupations than Baptists and Lutherans but are outranked by the other major Protestant denominations.[23]

TABLE 42

OCCUPATIONAL CATEGORIES IN MAJOR RELIGIOUS BODIES, 1945–46*

	Business and Professional	White Collar	Urban Manual Workers†	Farmers
Entire Sample	19%	20%	44%	17 %
Catholic	14	23	55	8
Jewish	36	37	27	0.6
Methodist	19	19	39	23
Baptist	12	14	52	22
Presbyterian	31	21	31	17
Lutheran	13	18	43	26
Episcopalian	32	25	36	7
Congregational	33	19	28	20

* Figures pertain to "the principal breadwinner" in the case of each family interviewed and where the interviewee was not personally employed.

† This category includes urban manual workers of all grades of skill, and also incorporates a diverse group of "service occupations" that are primarily manual in character (such as domestic servants, policemen, firemen). A great deal of variation is repersented within each of the categories in this table, and their relative class status varies from community to community.

Source: Liston Pope, "Religion in the Class Structure," *Annals of the American Academy of Political and Social Science*, March, 1948, p. 87.

Catholics also have approximately the same percent of members who are college graduates as Baptists and Lutherans and are again outranked by the other major Protestant denominations. Catholics approximately equal Lutherans in the percentage of members who have less than a high school education, but rate below the Baptists in this category. All three denominations are outranked in educational achievement by the other major Protestant denominations.[24]

[20] See Table 42.
[21] See Table 43.
[22] D. O. Moberg, *op. cit.*
[23] See Table 42.
[24] See Table 43.

TABLE 43

Educational Levels in Religious Bodies, 1945–46

	High School Incomplete (or less)	High School Graduates (or more)	College Graduates
Entire Sample	52%	48%	11%
Catholic	57	43	7
Jewish	37	63	16
Methodist	49	51	12
Baptist	65	35	6
Presbyterian	37	63	22
Lutheran	56	44	8
Episcopalian	35	65	22
Congregational	29	71	21

Liston Pope, "Religion in the Class Structure," *Annals of the American Academy of Political and Socal Science,* March, 1948, p. 87.

In his analysis of the data of the Detroit area study Lenski found that white Protestants had achieved an occupation and income somewhat higher than that of the white Catholics. White Protestants and white Catholics had the same percent of their membership in the lower-working class (25 percent) and about the same percent in the lower-middle class (25 percent and 27 percent). But white Catholics had somewhat less representation in the upper-middle class and somewhat greater representation in the upper-working class.[25]

TABLE 44

Percentage of Respondents in Various Classes by Socio-Religious Group* (1957)

	Upper-middle†	Lower-middle†	Upper-working‡	Lower-working‡	Totals Percent	Totals Cases
Jews	43%	30%	9%	17%	99%	23
White Protestants	19	25	31	25	100	259
White Catholics	12	27	35	25	99	220
Negro Protestants	2	10	19	69	100	94

* Gerhard Lenski, *The Religious Factor,* Doubleday & Co., Garden City, N.Y., 1961, p. 73.
† Upper-middle class respondents are those in which the family head was a businessman, a professional man, a clerk, or a salesman with an income of $8,000 or more in 1957. Respondents in similar occupations but earning less tha n$8,000 were classified as lower-middle class.
‡ Upper-working class respondents are those in which the family head was a manual or service worker who himself earned at least $5,000 in 1957. Those in families whose head was in a similar occupation but earned less than $5,000 were classified as lower-working class.

There has been considerable interest among research sociologists concerning the validity of the Weberian thesis for contemporary American culture. Weber argued that Protestantism made virtues of those qualities which made for capitalist success, and that it was no accident that capitalism had made its greatest advances where Protestantism was most strongly entrenched. Luther and Calvin sanctified work and made virtues of in-

---

[25] See Table 44.

dustry, thrift, and self-denial. The Protestant Reformation gave divine sanction to the drive to excel. Catholicism on the other hand had a more other-worldly emphasis. Since the good Catholic was not so stimulated to worldly success, he was also not as high an achiever as his Protestant counterpart.

Sociologists are concerned to discover whether the Protestant ethic is operative today; whether the traditional virtues have been sufficiently internalized among Protestants so as to make them more successful than Catholics economically and occupationally. The evidence is conflicting. Catholic congregations are changing, faster in some areas and regions than in others, so that the differential rates and kinds of change suggest the inadvisability of comprehensive generalizations on the basis of empirical data secured from Catholics living within limited geographic and ecological areas.

The universality of Catholic doctrine and worship has prevented the Catholic Church from becoming class-bound, and differentiation in Catholic parishes tends to follow ethnic rather than class lines. The ethnic working class church of first and second generation Europeans is rapidly giving way to the middle-class Catholic parish. This trend is well illustrated in Oswego, New York, a small city of 25,000. Four of the seven Catholic churches were established as ethnic, national parishes. Each of the four is now English speaking but has retained its original constituency, many of whom have risen to middle and upper-middle class status through business and professional success. Weber's "Protestant ethic" is not confined to Protestants in this city.

Lenski cites his Detroit data on occupational achievement of white Protestants as compared to white Catholics to show that the Weberian thesis is operative there.[26] In another analysis of the Detroit area data, Mayer and Sharp find that most Protestant denominations exceed Catholics in economic standing and they look upon their findings as partial validation of the Weberian thesis. However, they also found that the very highest achievers were Jews, followed by Episcopalians,[27] the most like Catholics in philosophy and doctrine of all the Protestants. Guerin and others found that Protestants expressed greater job satisfaction and had fewer problems on the job than Catholics. They concluded that this greater involvement may reflect a Protestant focus on achievement that stems from the Protestant ethic.[28]

Other studies disagree with the proposition that Protestants are more

---

[26] Gerhard Lenski, *The Religious Factor: A Sociological Study of Religion's Impact on Politics, Economics, and Family Life* (New York: Doubleday & Co., 1961), pp. 75–119.

[27] Albert Mayer and Harry Sharp, "Religious Preference and Worldly Success," *American Sociological Review*, Vol. 27, No. 2 (April, 1962), p. 218.

[28] Gerald Guerin, Joseph Veroff, and Sheila Feld, *Americans View Their Mental Health* (New York: Basic Books, Inc., 1960), p. 244.

highly motivated than Catholics to earthly success. Mack, Murphy, and Yellin found little evidence that the Protestant ethic is participated in less by Catholics than by Protestants.[29]

In a study of high achievement motivation based upon a nationwide sample, Veroff and Feld found that high achievement motivation was most prevalent among Jewish men, and more prevalent in Catholic than in Protestant men.[30] In another study of the occupational status of Iowa grooms from 1953–57, Kenkel and Burchinal reported that Catholic grooms represent higher status levels than Protestant grooms or grooms with no religious identification.[31] They point out that their data seems to refute Lenski's conclusion that status-related differences are increasing between white Catholics and white Protestants, and that Lenski's conclusions may be applicable only to Detroit and other metropolitan areas. In other words, their data for Iowa grooms suggest that Lenski's conclusion is not appropriate for Iowa and other similar areas dominated by small and middle-sized cities.

In a nationwide study of the influence of religion on the career plans and occupational values of college graduates Greeley found that Catholics were as likely as Protestants to go on to graduate school, to choose an academic career, to specialize in the physical sciences, and to plan a life of research. Nor were there any indications that Catholics were less inclined than Protestants to economic rationality.[32]

Bressler and Westoff tested the hypothesis that among Catholics a Catholic education is negatively related to achievement values and subsequent economic success. They reported that the hypothesis is completely rejected; that available evidence fails to sustain the hope or the fear that a Catholic education magnifies religious differentials in the economic or other secular areas of American life.[33]

These varying reports point up the complex nature of human and religious behavior and suggest the possibility of unidentified intervening variables. There is considerable current evidence that the Catholic religion has consequences for primarily religious behavior, but that otherwise Catholics are motivated by secular values and committed to the secular culture.

---

[29] Raymond W. Mack, Raymond J. Murphy, and Seymour Yellin, "The Protestant Ethic, Level of Aspiration, and Social Mobility: An Empirical Test," *American Sociological Review*, Vol. 21 (June, 1956), pp. 295–300.

[30] G. Guerin, J. Veroff, and S. Feld, *op. cit.*

[31] Lee G. Burchinal and William F. Kenkel, "Religious Identification and Occupational Status of Iowa Grooms, 1953–1957," *American Sociological Review*, Vol. 27, No. 4 (August, 1962), pp. 527–32.

[32] Andrew M. Greeley, "Influence of the 'Religious Factor' on Career and Occupational Values of College Graduates," *American Journal of Sociology*, Vol. 68, No. 6 (May, 1963), p. 658.

[33] Marvin Bressler and Charles F. Westoff, "Catholic Education, Economic Values, and Achievement," *American Journal of Sociology*, Vol. 69, No. 3 (November, 1963), p. 233.

Stratification and the Jews

Jews fall in about the same position as Christian Scientists, with the Orthodox Jews somewhat lower and the Conservative and Reform Jews somewhat higher. Jews also have about the same distribution of their membership in the upper-class national norms as Episcopalians, the Presbyterians, and the Congregationalists.[34]

The relative position of Jews in the social class structure varies from city to city. In Detroit, for example, on a four-point class typology, Jews had more than twice the concentration of membership in the upper-middle class (the top category) as Protestants, and more than three times greater than Catholics.

Even more striking were the relative concentrations for the three groups between the middle classes and the working classes.[35] Among Jews the concentration was 73 percent in the middle classes and 26 percent in the working classes, among Protestants 44 percent and 56 percent, and among Catholics 39 percent and 60 percent. Jews had almost twice the proportion of membership in the middle classes as Protestants, and considerably more than twice the proportion of Catholics.

Occupation is one of the important factors that contribute to class determination. In terms of national norms Jews have the highest proportion of their membership engaged in the business and professional category and are quite similar in this respect to Episcopalians, Presbyterians and Congregationalists.[36] Jews are most different from the other major Protestant denominations in that less than 1 percent of their membership are gainfully employed as farmers.

In terms of educational achievement—high school graduates or more—Jews show about the same percent as Presbyterians and Episcopalians, with the Congregationalists having the highest proportion of all the major denominations. In the percent of college graduates Jews are somewhat above the Methodists, but lower than the Episcopalians, Presbyterians, and Congregationalists.[37]

The occupation with the highest percentage of affiliation for Jews is that of businessman.[38] Occupational distribution varies from city to city. In Madison, Wisconsin, Episcopalians had 36 percent of their heads of families gainfully employed as professionals as compared to 16 percent for Jews.[39]

The rapid rise of Jews in the occupational and class structure during the first half of the twentieth century is the consequence, according to

[34] See Table 42.
[35] See Table 44.
[36] See Table 42.
[37] See Table 43.
[38] See Table 42.
[39] L. Bultena, *op. cit.*

Glazer,[40] of Jewish religious and cultural values. The Jewish values of foresight, sobriety, and deferred gratification were maintained among the newly arrived immigrants even when there was no immediate prospect of going into business or entering the professions. Jews did not drink. Students were docile and willing to accept today's restraints for tomorrow's rewards. Workers stayed out of jail.

Nonmanual occupations were expanding greatly during the period of the greatest Jewish immigration, and unskilled manual work and farming were employing a progressively smaller proportion of the labor force. Between 1910 and 1950 the proportion of the population engaged in nonmanual work rose from 21 percent to 38 percent. The individual had to possess the proper social and psychological traits to take advantage of this opportunity for occupational upgrading. Jewish immigrants possessed the necessary traits. While Americans in general became more markedly middle-class in occupational structure, Jews became even more so.

Summary

Protestant churches tend to be class churches. A composite of the various studies of religion and class indicates that the Episcopal, Presbyterian, and Congregational churches tend to be upper and upper-middle class oriented. Methodist, Lutheran, and Baptist denominations follow in that order. Class orientation varies with the community and the region; in any given community it is quite possible for the membership of the Baptist church to represent the highest position in the class and power structure in the community.

Sects are more lower-class oriented. They tend to draw the bulk of their membership from the lower-middle and the upper-lower classes.

The strength of any congregation is in its middle-class membership. Although upper and lower classes may be formally affiliated with particular churches they tend to be less active than the middle-class membership.

Nationally, Catholics appear to rank just above the Baptists on this general social scale and below the other major Protestant denominations. In one generation the Catholic population has moved from a predominantly lower class, peripheral, and immigrant group status to become a nuclear, middle-class, and assimilated segment of the total population. Recent studies of class orientation and behavior disagree on the extent to which Catholics have achieved middle-class status, but the differences are probably the consequence of a differential rate of mobility represented in the various regions from which the samples were chosen and the respective studies made.

In general Jewish communicants represent a class status just below the Episcopalians, Presbyterians, and Congregationalists, and just above the

---

[40] Nathan Glazer, "The American Jew and the Attainment of Middle-class Rank," in *Jews: Social Patterns of an American Group*, Marshall Sklare (ed.) (Glencoe, Ill.: The Free Press, 1960), pp. 138–46.

Methodists, Lutherans, and Catholics. Orthodox congregations are drawn from a somewhat lower class and Conservative and Reform congregations from a somewhat higher status level.

THE NEGRO AS A RELIGIOUS SUBGROUP

Negro religion reflects their minority status. Because of their high "visibility," Negroes are most marked as a minority group and suffer correspondingly.

Characteristics of Negro Religion

Denominational Affiliation. Negroes are primarily Protestant, and most Negro Protestants belong to one of the five major Negro denominations:[1]

National Baptist Convention, United States of America, Inc.	5,000,000
National Baptist Convention of America	2,668,799
African Methodist Episcopal Church	1,166,301
Christian Methodist Episcopal Church	392,167
African Methodist Episcopal Zion Church	770,000

The 1957 study of religious preference, based upon a sampling of the population by the Bureau of the Census, showed about the same proportionate preference of Negroes for religious denominations as had been reported in the statistics of membership by the various denominations:[2]

Catholic	7%
Baptist	61
Methodist	17
Other Protestant	10

Characteristics of Negro Religion. Although the racial church has some distinguishing characteristics, it is more like than different from the white church. The Negro left his original religion behind in Africa. The religion of the slave was the white man's religion, with some modifications.

Americans generally are religious, Southerners are more religious than the rest of the nation, and Negroes are more religious than white Southerners. The caste system forces the Negro to be an "exaggerated American."[3]

Negro religion differs from white religion in three important ways.[4]

---

[1] National Council of Churches of Christ in the U.S.A., *Yearbook of American Churches, 1962*, New York, pp. 249–54.

[2] United States Department of Commerce, Bureau of the Census, *Religion Reported by the Civilian Population of the United States: March 1957*, Current Population Reports: Population Characteristics, Series P–20, No. 79, February 2, 1958.

[3] Gunnar Myrdal, *American Dilemma* (New York: Harper & Bros., 1944), p. 863.

[4] Robert Lee and Ralph L. Roy, "The Negro Church," *Christian Century*, Vol. 74, (October 30, 1957), pp. 1285–87.

1. Negro religion is more literalistic in theology. Negroes can find in their historic past a close cultural identification with the literal Bible. The Biblical account of Moses leading the children of Israel out of bondage, the prophets crying out against the incompatibility of riches and the Kingdom of Heaven, and the Pauline doctrine of free grace all strike a responsive chord among a discriminated minority.

2. The church plays a more salient part among Negroes than among whites.

3. Negro religion is marked by freedom of emotional expression and by great emphasis upon spirituals and gospel hymns.

These have been and to some degree are still the major features that set Negro religion apart from white religion. On the other hand, there are many similarities. Among Negroes, as among whites, females attend religious services more frequently than males, the middle-aged and the old attend more than the youth, and the uneducated and lower and middle classes more than the upper classes.[5]

Urbanization. Negro religion has been modified by the continuing migration of Negroes from the rural South to the urban areas of the North and West. The Negro population of the 30 largest northern, midwestern, and western cities more than doubled in 1940–50. In 1950, 63 percent of the Negroes lived in urban areas and only 37 percent in rural areas.[6] This is the continuing pattern of migration.

The northern migration of Negroes has led to an increase in Catholic and in sectarian churches, and to a decrease in the numbers and membership of independent Methodist and white-affiliated Methodist churches, and in Episcopal and Presbyterian churches. The Negro Baptist Church, however, seems to be holding its own.[7]

In an intensive study of the Negro community in Chicago, Drake and Cayton[8] found that class for class the Negro church was not much different from the white church. Five percent of the Chicago Negro community belonged to the upper class. The churches of this upper class were the same as for the white upper class: Episcopal, Congregational, and Presbyterian predominantly, and the services were similarly restrained and intellectually oriented.

Sixty-five percent of the Chicago Negro community were rated as lower class, but the religiously oriented segment of the lower class was a woman's world inasmuch as less than one third of lower-class church members were men. It was estimated that approximately one third of the church-oriented people in the lower class belonged to large lower-class churches, one third to churches dominated by upper-class persons, and one third to storefront churches.

---

[5] G. Myrdal, *op. cit.*

[6] J. Oscar Lee, "Religion Among Ethnic and Racial Minorities," *Annals of the Academy of Political and Social Science*, Vol. 332 (November, 1960), p. 115.

[7] E. Franklin Frazier, *The Negro in the United States* (New York: The Macmillan Co., 1949), p. 353.

[8] St. Clair Drake and Horace R. Cayton, *Black Metropolis* (New York: Harcourt, Brace & Co., 1945), p. 613.

The middle class comprised 30 percent of the Negro community. The typical middle-class church was a large Baptist or Methodist church. It tended to be a "mixed type" church in that it incorporated both lower-class behavior (shouting and verbal "amens") and such middle-class features as a restrained service and a sermon with some degree of ethical content. Although shouting and "amens" continue to be heard in many middle-class churches, a smaller number, mostly older people, appear to engage in such expression.[9] Many upwardly mobile Negroes seek membership in churches with a more restrained service.

The storefront church is an adaptation of the small rural church to city life. In Chicago, 75 percent of nearly 500 churches in the Negro community were storefront churches. Their members, limited in education, often impoverished, find status and security in the "oldtime religion," its emotional outlets, and the warmth of fellowship found in the face-to-face associations of the small church. This type of person finds himself isolated and lost in the mass of numbers in the large church.[10] Many of the storefront churches are affiliated with various Holiness and Pentecostal denominations.

Cults. Although cults attract a relatively small part of the Negro population, the dramatic nature of cult behavior and activity makes them a noticeable part of the Negro religious culture. Cults are primarily an urban phenomenon—a reaction to the frustration and problems of urban life.[11] Many lower-class migrants, forced to live in slum areas in a milieu of social disorganization, are drawn to some of the more radical forms of religious expression that the various cults represent. The Spiritual and Spiritualist cults accounted for 10 percent of all the churches in the Chicago Negro community.[12]

The Spiritualist religion is an eclectic religion, borrowing its hymns from the Baptists and Methodists, and appropriating altars, candles, and statues from the Catholics. It offers healing, advice, and "good luck" in return for a prayer and the price of a candle or holy flower. It provides colorful robes for its preachers and "mediums." The Spiritualist does not condemn card playing, dancing, policy numbers, ward politics, or the "sporting life."[13]

Father Divine's Peace Mission developed during the depression years, and local congregations—"Heavens"—are found throughout the cities of the Northeast and the Midwest. Divine's Peace Mission involves "faith healing" and "sanctifications," but it is also interracial. About ten percent

---

[9] Ruby Johnson, *The Religion of Negro Protestants* (New York: Philosophical Library, 1956), pp. 3–15.

[10] E. F. Frazier, *op. cit.*, p. 355.

[11] Wilson Record, "Extremist Movements Among American Negroes," *Phylon*, No. 17 (First Quarter, 1956), pp. 17–23.

[12] S. C. Drake and H. R. Cayton, *op. cit.*, p. 414.

[13] *Ibid.*, p. 642.

of the "angels" (nuclear followers) are white. There is no racial discrimination but it is a Negro-dominated group. An angel must

> . . . Refrain from stealing, [from] refusing to pay just debts, indulging in liquor in any form, smoking, obscene language, gambling, playing numbers, racial prejudice or hate of any kind, greed, bigotry, selfishness, and lusting after the opposite sex.[14]

Another popular type of cult consists of religious groups that in protest against racial injustice take the form of a complete rejection of the white world through an escapist program of Negro nationalism. Three important nationalist groups, the Moorish Temple of Science in America led by Noble Drew Ali, the Universal Mutual Improvement Association led by Marcus Garvey, and the Black Muslims of America led by Elijah Muhammed, have flourished among American Negroes during the first half of the twentieth century.

The Moorish Temple of Science and the Universal Mutual Improvement Association reached their peaks during and shortly after World War I. Both groups lost followers and languished with the loss of their leader. The Black Muslims have been the dominant nationalist group since World War II.

All black nationalist groups have three characteristics in common:[15]

1. A disparagement of the white man and his culture
2. Repudiation of Negro identity
3. An appropriation of Asiatic culture symbols.

At the peak of its influence the Moorish Temple of Science numbered from 20,000 to 30,000 followers with temples located in Detroit, Harlem, Chicago, Pittsburgh, Philadelphia, and a number of cities in the South. The movement lost its momentum when its leader, Noble Drew Ali, died or was killed during an internal struggle for power.[16]

The Universal Mutual Improvement Association, led by Marcus Garvey (the "Black Moses") and sponsored by the African Orthodox Church, was more of a political than a religious movement. Garvey wished to resettle a large group of his followers in Africa, but aroused the distrust of Negro social and intellectual leaders who subsequently worked against his movement. He was eventually convicted of using the mails to defraud and was deported. He died in obscurity in London in 1940 but lives on as a symbol of Negro nationalism.[17]

A Black Muslim is an American Negro, a follower of Elijah Muhammad, who is believed to be the messenger of Allah commissioned to wake

---

[14] Arthur Huff Fauset, *Black Gods of the Metropolis* (Philadelphia: University of Pennsylvania Press, 1954), p 64.

[15] C. Eric Lincoln, *Black Muslims in America* (Boston: Beacon Press, 1961), p. 50.

[16] *Ibid.*, p. 53.

[17] Edmund David Cronon, *Black Moses: The Story of Marcus Garvey and the Universal Negro Improvement Association* (Madison, Wis.: University of Wisconsin Press, 1955).

the sleeping Black Nation and rid it of the white man's age-old domination. Black Muslims are taught they are not Negroes, or Africans, but Asiatics: Christianity is the white man's religion, Islam the religion of Asiatics.

Members pray five times a day, facing the East; observe dietary laws, and keep the body clean. Emotionalism is frowned upon. All Muslims are forbidden to gamble, smoke, drink liquor, overeat, or buy on credit. Men are urged to hold steady jobs and are expected to give a fixed percent of their income each year. Some contribute as much as one third of their income. The movement demands an entirely separate Black Economy.[18]

A study of the constituency of the movement shows that

1. The membership is young; most are between the ages of 17 and 35. The small group of older people are predominantly ex-Garveyites or ex-Moorish Temple Science Muslims. It is activist, directed to the youth, and worldly in orientation.
2. Membership is predominantly male.
3. The membership is essentially lower class. They live and build their temples in the heart of the Negro ghetto. A survey in the early years of the movement (1930–34) found an overwhelming number of members were recent migrants from the rural South. In 1959, however, rural migrants did not form quite as great a proportion of the membership.
4. The membership is predominantly ex-Christian. Most of the youthful members were born into and had some affiliation with a Christian church before becoming Black Muslims.

The movement is nationwide. It is estimated that approximately 100,000 Black Muslims are worshiping in temples that range from New England to San Diego and from San Francisco to Miami.[19]

In a study of five prominent Negro cults Fauset found four compulsions that operate to attract members: "the supernatural, the personality of the leader, relief from physical and mental illness, and race consciousness."[20] The last two are functions of the adjustment to the northern environment. The folk Negro finds that cults give a new meaning to life: "faith healing" becomes a cure for both physical and mental ills, and "holiness" and "sanctification" help resolve the moral conflicts created by the free and easy ways of the city.[21]

The lower-class Negro church has been criticized by practically all Negro leaders for not being concerned with the real moral problems of the Negro population and following the principle that the poorer its members and the more in need they are of concerted efforts to improve their lot in this life, the more other-worldly its theology and emphasis tends to be. The lower-class church is also accused of being out of touch with current social life in the field of morals and preaching puritanical morals

---

[18] C. E. Lincoln, *op. cit.*, pp. 17–21.
[19] *Ibid.*, pp. 22–25.
[20] A. H. Fauset, *op. cit.*, p. 121.
[21] E. F. Frazier, *op. cit.*, p. 21.

that have little effect on the bulk of the Negro population.[22] The social and economic upgrading of the Negro and the direct action policies of religious leaders such as Martin Luther King suggest that the traditional theology of other-worldliness is becoming a less dominant feature of Negro religion.

Social Functions of the Negro Church

Social Protest. The Negro church has served as a substitute for political organization and, in the South, has been the outstanding agency by which Negroes have struggled to gain civil rights. Reverend Martin Luther King's leadership of the Negro churches of Montgomery, Alabama, to break segregated seating on city buses is only one illustration of the church acting as an agency of social protest.

Symbol of Group Identification. As Negroes have risen in the social class structure and gained in civil rights, the church has increasingly become a symbol around which they can best maintain a sense of pride and common identity. The racial church has been welcomed by Negroes even in areas where physical separation in worship was not demanded.[23]

Leadership Opportunities. In many communities the racial church has been the only available channel through which the Negro could exercise leadership on the basis of character and ability.[24] Negroes have a higher ratio of ministers than the general population although they lack a proportionate share in all other professions.[25] In a study of 570 rural churches in 17 counties in the rural South, Felton found that nearly half of the adults held some church position.[26] The Negro minister has held the historical role of leader in the community. He has been described as the "most unique personality developed on American soil—a composite of the roles of leader, politician, orator, boss, intriguer, and idealist."[27] He has held a virtual monopoly on leadership, but this is changing. He now has to share leadership with teachers, doctors, lawyers, business and other professional men. Even so, he still has the greatest contact with the masses of people.[28]

Personality Function. The Negro church has been a leading avenue for self-expression, emotional escapism, and personal adjustment. It has served Negroes as the center for face-to-face relations, for communication, for recreation, and for psychological, as well as physical, escape from their troubles.[29]

---

[22] G. Myrdal, *op. cit.*, p. 22.

[23] Charles S. Johnson, *A Preface to Racial Understanding* (New York: The Friendship Press, 1936), p. 153.

[24] J. O. Lee, *op. cit.*, p. 115.

[25] David Moberg, *The Church as a Social Institution* (Englewood Cliffs, N.J.: Prentice-Hall, Inc., 1962), p. 450.

[26] Ralph A. Felton, *These My Brethren* (Madison, N.J.: Drew Theological Seminary, 1950), p. 38.

[27] R. Lee and R. L. Roy, *op. cit.*, p. 1286.

[28] J. O. Lee, *op. cit.*, p. 115.

[29] R. Johnson, *op. cit.*, p. 153.

Social Control. The church has enlisted the Negro's deepest loyalties, has set up and defined the norms of moral conduct, and provided the necessary discipline to enforce its rules of behavior. The church has been a stabilizing influence in an urban area often characterized by disorganization and anomie. By supporting the *status quo*, by placing the emphasis upon the hereafter, by protesting against the sins and vices of the lower class Negro, the church has been a conservative influence in the urban community. The church, then, has been the chief source of social control in the Negro world, a force which whites took no notice of except as their interests were affected.[30]

SEGREGATION AND THE CHURCHES

The present movement to do away with segregation (an ultimate ideal) has stemmed mainly from the churches.[31] By the mid 1950's all major bodies in the North and the South had issued statements officially adopting the principle of desegregation.[32] The churches have found, however, that it is one thing to verbalize the ideal on a national level and something quite different to implement it at the parish level. The typical communicant in any given church tends to reflect the mores of the community in questions of segregation and racial relations.

Catholic Church

The Catholic Church has taken great strides in the movement towards complete integration, and in the South has shown great courage in battling, sometimes almost alone, the segregation complex.

Reverend John LaFarge, the Jesuit authority on the Negro, reports that four types of segregation have been practiced in the church. *Traditional segregation* comes down from slavery; it permitted Negroes to worship in white churches, but forced them to sit separately. In *compulsory segregation* Negroes are restricted to separate churches. *Theoretical or planned segregation* is sanctioned by the rationalization of whites about the Negroes' pride in having their own institutions and maintaining group identity. *Voluntary segregation* is segregation based upon the real desires of minorities to be separate from the majority.[33]

LaFarge identifies several integration policies in the church. In minimal integration the Negro is integrated only into "essential" activities of worship and remains segregated in "nonessential" activities. In another policy all church institutions are open to Negroes in a definite but incomplete

---

[30] E. F. Frazier, *Black Bourgeoisie* (Glencoe, Ill.: The Free Press, 1957), p. 117.

[31] Anson Phelps Stokes, *et. al.*, *Negro Status and Race Relations in the United States, 1911–1946* (New York: Phelps Stokes Fund, 1948), p. 50.

[32] D. Moberg, *op. cit.*, p. 451.

[33] John LaFarge, S.J., "Caste in the Church, II: The Roman Catholic Experience," *Survey Graphic*, No. 36 (January, 1947), pp. 61–62.

break with biracialism since the racial parish and compensatory segregation remain in the diocese. Integration is complete when all forms of
Catholic life are subject to the free choice of the communicants and there
is no special parochial school. Complete integration is the official policy in
most northern dioceses.[34]

Numbers. The Catholic concern for the Negro since World War II
is reflected in the rapid increase in the number of Negro Catholics. In the
decade ending in 1955, 8 percent of all Catholic conversions were
Negroes.[35] In 1961 the Church claimed 653,217 Negro members, compared
to 389,111 in 1950.[36] The growth is greatest in the large cities to which
Negroes migrate. A survey in Philadelphia showed that the Negro membership of Catholic churches increased 55 percent during a five-year
period. Negroes report that the Catholic Church is the most interracial of
the major denominations. The urbanization of the Negro has brought him
into close contact with Catholics, leading to mutual understanding and appreciation.[37] Negroes also are increasing in the Catholic priesthood. In
1950 there were 37 Negro priests, in 1961 there were 120.[38]

Integration in New Orleans. The Archdiocese of New Orleans has
taken an active and dramatic part in the church's integration movement.
New Orleans has a large concentration of white and a significant minority
of Negro Catholics. Forty percent of New Orleans is Catholic. About half
(600,000) of all the Catholics in the South live in the archdiocese, and of
these 68,490 are Negroes, roughly one tenth of all the Catholic Negroes
in the country.[39]

In the Catholic religious structure the integration-segregation question
lies in the realm of faith and morals. It is the province of the hierarchy to
make the proper rules and the duty of the laity to follow them. Following
World War II Archbishop Joseph Rummel of New Orleans decided the
time had arrived for the church to take positive steps towards the implementation of the Catholic ideal, but he ran into tremendous opposition on
the part of his own parishioners. In 1949 he caused a stir when he ordered
"white" and "colored" signs removed from the pews of Catholic churches.
Now although Negroes attend mass with white parishioners, generally
they are not welcomed with enthusiasm.

In 1956 Archbishop Rummel issued a pastoral letter in support of the
Supreme Court decision on desegregation in the public schools, declaring
that segregation is "morally wrong and sinful." Probably no Catholic
prelate in the United States has ever been subjected to more vilification for
taking a moral position. After this declaration on segregation his name was

---

[34] *Ibid.*, pp. 104–106.

[35] Francois Houtart, "A Sociological Study of the Evolution of the American
Catholics," *Social Kompas*, No. 2 (January–April, 1955), pp. 189–216.

[36] *The National Catholic Almanac, 1962* (New York: Doubleday & Co., p. 492.

[37] R. Lee and R. L. Roy, *op. cit.*

[38] *Catholic Almanac, op. cit.*, p. 74.

[39] *Ibid.*, p. 492.

booed at a meeting of the White Citizens Council, and later the same night a cross was burned on the lawn of his residence. Some Catholic priests even refused to read his pastoral letter.

Shortly after, the Archbishop stated that the parochial schools would be integrated "at the earliest possible opportunity and definitely not later than when the public schools are integrated." There were 80,473 children in the elementary and secondary schools of the archdiocese in 1958 of which 12,276, or 14 percent, were in Negro schools. (Many of the Negro children, however, and some of the white were non-Catholic.[40]) A group of white Catholic laymen opposed to the integration of Catholic diocesan schools then appealed to the Pope but were strongly rebuked by the Vatican.[41]

In October, 1955, a Negro priest was assigned to say mass at St. Cecilia Mission at Jesuit Bend, Louisiana, because no white priest was available. The white parishioners refused to allow the Negro priest into the church and told him that a Negro could not say mass in St. Cecilia. Archbishop Rummel told the parishioners that since they had violated the laws of the church, and because there was a shortage of priests, he was closing the mission. The agitation subsided but the mission was not opened until some time later and, at the opening service, a white priest celebrated the mass.[42]

In New Orleans, priests did not confine their integration activities to the parochial school system. The Reverend Jerome Drolet, a Roman Catholic priest, was jeered by picketing parents as he accompanied a Methodist minister and his daughter from a desegregated public school.[43]

In April, 1962, the Archbishop made specific his promise to desegregate the parochial schools under his jurisdiction; he ordered desegregation for the fall term and provided a period for Negro pupils to register for transfer to an integrated parochial school. A Catholic parishioner, Mrs. B. J. Gaillot, Jr., a leader in the militant anti-integrationists, made headlines by flouting the decrees of the Archbishop. The Archbishop thereupon threatened the extreme sanction of excommunication for "disobedience" and inciting others to disobedience of the rules and laws of the church. Only a token number of the Negro students in the parochial schools took advantage of the opportunity to seek a transfer to an integrated parochial school.[44]

The Archbishop does not stand alone in his feeling for integration. Many priests give integration wholehearted support. Reverend Joseph Fichter, of the Department of Sociology of Loyola University (New Orleans) has written books and actively worked against segregation. The

---

[40] *New York Times*, July 8, 1959.
[41] *Time*, April 27, 1962, p. 46.
[42] *New York Times*, July 8, 1959.
[43] *Ibid.*, November 30, 1960.
[44] *Ibid.*, April 14, 1962.

Reverend Louis J. Twomey, also on the Loyola faculty, is a widely known labor priest who has helped to desegregate unions in the area.[45]

The Protestant Churches

The various Protestant churches are struggling with the integration ideal. Each of the major denominations has gone on record supporting integration at the national level—and each has experienced varying degrees of difficulty, and success, in achieving integration at the congregational and parish level. Pope estimates that 10 percent of Protestant churches are interracial and that this is a fivefold increase over a ten-year period.[46]

The Methodist Church. The Methodist Church has the largest number of Negro communicants of all the Protestant churches: approximately 600,000 Negroes are in predominantly white Protestant denominations, of which 393,000 are in the Methodist Church. All but 26,000 of the Negro Methodists are represented in the Central Jurisdiction of the Methodist Church.[47]

When the Methodist Church was organized in 1939 it was divided into five geographic and one central jurisdiction. The geographic jurisdictions were composed of all the white Methodist churches in the respective areas into which the country was divided. The Central Jurisdiction was composed of all the Negro congregations, regardless of where they might be located. This segregation of Negro congregations was demanded as a condition precedent to merger by the white Methodist congregations of the South.

Each jurisdiction is self governing and elects its bishops and members of boards and agencies. The Central Jurisdiction gives Negro churches and Negro leaders opportunities for leadership that they would seldom achieve as a minority group in a jurisdiction dominated by whites. As representatives of the Central Jurisdiction, Negro leaders have had the opportunity to sit on the national councils and committees of the Methodist Church and participate in the formation of policy.

Under a policy of total integration the Central Jurisdiction would be abolished and the Negro congregations throughout the country would be absorbed into an appropriate geographic jurisdiction. The 1957 quadrennial General Conference took a step in this direction by adopting a plan providing for the voluntary withdrawal of Negro congregations from the Central Jurisdiction and admission into the regional geographic jurisdiction. In four years only six Negro congregations, all in the North, had transferred out of the Central Jurisdiction and into the geographic jurisdiction.

By 1960 it was apparent that neither the white nor the Negro congregations were ready for integrated jurisdictions. The quadrennial confer-

---

45 *Ibid.*, July 8, 1959.
46 Liston Pope, *The Kingdom Beyond Caste* (New York: Friendship Press, 1957).
47 *New York Times*, April 29, 1960.

ence therefore accepted a report recommending that the Negro nongeo-graphic Central Jurisdiction remain intact. Supporters of the report argued that to eliminate the Central Jurisdiction by legislation would be harmful to the church and "disastrous" to Negro Methodists, who would be suddenly set adrift. There were hints, also, that if the Central Jurisdiction were abolished and integrated jurisdictions mandated, some of the southern church groups would withdraw from the denomination. Instead, Methodists were urged to create through education and experimentation the "spiritual and psychological climate" in which an inclusive Methodist Church might become a reality.

Although the General Conference failed to mandate integration, 74 bishops of the Methodist Church in a "state of the church" message reaffirmed the church's position on race relations: "To discriminate against a person solely on the basis of his race is both unfair and unchristian. There must be no place in the Methodist Church for racial discrimination or enforced segregation."[48]

The General Conference also rejected a proposal that would have required the immediate integration of all divinity schools when it was shown that some divinity schools of the church in the South were not ready to take this step without a more extended period of preparation.[49]

Methodists could, however, point to an experimentation in integration at the local level that had achieved considerable success. Volunteer family groups of two Methodist churches in Huntington, Long Island, exchanged churches for three months. Fourteen adults and ten children from the Bethel African Methodist–Episcopal church on Park Avenue, Huntington, and 24 adults and 12 children from the Methodist church on West Neck Road, Huntington, became associate members of the other church. Most of the exchange members were matched as to church activities, choir-singer, Sunday school teacher, trustee, or club member. At the end of the period both groups declared the experiment a success and found the experience particularly valuable for the children involved.[50]

The Baptists. Baptists generally divide on questions concerning integration, whether in the public schools or in the church, according to whether they live and grew up in the South or in the North. The Southern Baptist Church consistently pursues a policy that would continue the separation of the races for the near and predictable future. In 1956, during the controversy over the desegregation of the Clinton, Tennessee, schools, a poll of Southern Baptist ministers in Tennessee showed that only 39 percent favored integration of the schools.[51]

At about the same time, Reverend Gardner C. Taylor, a leader in the American (Northern) Baptist Convention, became the first Negro to be

---

[48] *Ibid.*, April 28, 1960.
[49] *Ibid.*, May 3, 1960.
[50] *Ibid.*, May 6, 1960.
[51] *Ibid.*, December 16, 1956.

chosen President of the New York City Protestant Council of Churches. The Council represents about 1700 churches of 31 denominations and approximately 600,000 members throughout New York. Dr. Taylor had been outstandingly successful as the pastor of the 10,000-member interracial Concord Baptist church in Brooklyn.[52]

The Presbyterians. The United Presbyterian Church of the United States of America, the largest denomination within the Presbyterian family of denominations, has demonstrated its interest in the integration of the races through its selection of leaders. The two leading candidates for Moderator of the General Assembly were both outstanding advocates of racial integration.

The Reverend Edler G. Hawkins, pastor of St. Augustine Presbyterian church, the Bronx, had made church history by being the first Negro to be chosen the moderator of the Presbytery of New York. In 1960 he was selected to be one of the two nominees for position of national moderator.[53] His opponent was the Reverend Dr. Herman L. Turner, pastor of the only United Presbyterian (Northern) Church in Atlanta, Georgia. Dr. Turner was a chief advocate for the "Atlanta Manifesto" in which, for the first time, white Protestant ministers in the South banded together to urge free and open communication between Negroes and whites in questions concerning civil rights and racial equality. Dr. Turner won the post by the narrow margin of two votes, 471–469. The General Assembly chose Reverend Hawkins as vice moderator.[54]

Unlike the Methodists, the United Presbyterians did not have to contend with a large group of Southern Presbyterians over the integration issue. The great bulk of Southern Presbyterians were members of the autonomous Presbyterian Church of the United States, the southern branch of Presbyterianism.

The Protestant Episcopal Church. The Protestant Episcopal Church, like the Methodist Church, is nationwide in scope and representation. There is no independent southern denomination, as is found in the Presbyterian and the Baptist families of denominations, to absorb and channelize an Episcopal expression of the southern mores of race relations. The Episcopal Church has to pursue a policy of moderation and gradualism in race relations or run the risk of a schism within its ranks.

The Episcopal Church, like the Baptist, Methodist, and Presbyterian, has had greater success with integration among its northern than among its southern constituents.

The bishop of the Episcopal diocese of Long Island issued a pastoral letter stating there should be no room for bias in the diocese. He reported that the diocese already had 12 Negro priests and 60 Negro layreaders serving parishes and missions, and four Spanish speaking priests were

---

[52] *Ibid.,* July 10, 1959.
[53] *Ibid.,* February 2, 1960.
[54] *Ibid.,* May 19, 1960.

ministering to the Puerto Rican population of Brooklyn. As Negroes and Puerto Ricans prospered they were moving out of their racially homogeneous parishes in the central city into the suburbs. The bishop's letter was directed to the suburban parishes where Negro and Puerto Rican families were seeking affiliation with all-white congregations.[55]

This diocese also found that it is easier to verbalize integration than to implement it. The diocesan officials were accused by the New York City Commission on Human Relations of practicing discrimination in St. John's Episcopal Hospital. The hospital was alleged to be segregating patients in its policy for the occupancy of semi-private rooms.[56]

A group of liberals dissatisfied with the slow pace of integration within the Episcopal Church organized the Episcopal Society for Cultural and Racial Unity. The Society gave its support to "sit-ins" and "kneel-ins" as appropriate measures of Christian passive resistance to segregation and discrimination. Within a few months the Society claimed membership in all but 12 of the 102 dioceses of the Episcopal Church. The Society urged its members to resign any church institution that was racially exclusive and recommended that the clergy should decline to perform baptism, confirmation, or celebration of the eucharist where segregation was practiced.[57]

The conservatives within the Episcopal Church consider the members of the Society for Racial Unity "extremists."[58] The executive body of the Protestant Episcopal Church issued a document which, among other items, included a statement expressing sympathy for the Negro sit-in movement. The bishop of the Alabama diocese of the Episcopal Church called upon the National Council to repudiate the statement. The National Council refused to take such action.

Interfaith Cooperation. The integration-segregation problem has received considerable interfaith and interdenominational support. The Atlanta Manifesto was signed by 309 Atlanta clergymen representing 17 Protestant and Jewish denominations. The manifesto urged the community to obey the law (the desegregation decree) and to keep the public schools open.[59]

Discrimination in private housing had become a pressing problem for the expanding Negro community in Syracuse, New York. The three faiths decided to take the leadership in meeting this problem and jointly supported an "open occupancy" covenant. Parishioners of the three faiths were urged to sign these covenants at their respective churches. By this covenant the property owner goes on record promising that whenever he

---

[55] *Ibid.*, May 17, 1959.
[56] *Ibid.*, July 13, 1962.
[57] *Ibid.*, January 11, 1961.
[58] *Ibid.*
[59] *Ibid.*, November 23, 1958.

decides to sell his home he will make it equally available to all buyers without regard to race or creed.[60]

In many communities it is customary for the three faiths to make it a point to celebrate a Race Relations Sunday on the same day, and to scan social tensions in the light of the brotherhood principles common to the churches of the Judeo-Christian tradition.[61]

Summary

Negroes are primarily Protestant in religion although they have joined the Catholic Church in growing numbers in the northern cities. Over 60 percent of Negroes are affiliated with a Baptist denomination. Negroes have been forced to express their religion within the context of a caste system, and their religion tends to be more literalistic, more emotional, and more important to them than religion is to whites generally.

The migration of Negroes from the rural South to the cities has progressed to a point where approximately two thirds of all Negroes are urban dwellers. Well over half of urban Negroes are forced to live at lower-class levels and standards. The lower-class Negro church is a woman's world; only one third of the membership is male.

Some Negroes are attracted to the variety of cults that flourish in urban areas. But the cults are more spectacular and dramatic than significant since only a small part of the Negro population is affiliated with them at any given time. The Father Divine Peace Movement and the Moorish Temple of Science were at their peak of influence just before and after World War II. In recent years the Black Muslims have come to the front as an active, ardent, and sometimes violent protest movement. The Black Muslims are separatists who repudiate and wish to withdraw from the white culture and all white contacts. Black Muslims are young, male, lower-class, and ex-Christians.

Religion performs a number of social functions for Negroes. It is an agency of social protest, an agency of social control, a symbol of group identification, and it provides numerous opportunities for leadership experience and personality development.

Although the Christian churches have been struggling with the problem of segregation, the major denominations have found it easier to give lip service to integration than to practice it. The Catholic Church, particularly in the South and in New Orleans, has taken the leadership in trying to implement integration in the sanctuary and in its parochial schools.

The leading Protestant denominations have gone to considerable efforts to encourage integration at the national level and among their member churches. Recently prominent churchmen of all denominations have taken public stands supporting the efforts of Negroes to secure equality of treatment and opportunity in both economic and social fields.

---

[60] *Herald-Journal*, Syracuse, N.Y., February 21, 1960.
[61] *New York Times*, February 4, 1961.

THEORETICAL OBSERVATIONS

Functional Analysis of Religion

Functional analysis (determination of the consequences of social action) may be in terms of society, of a social system within the greater society (a church, a denomination, etc.), or in terms of an individual. Specifically, religion (a unit or unity of behavior religious in nature) may be found to be functional (have consequences that contribute to the adjustment, adaptation, or integration) for society, for a religious system, or for an individual.

Religion and Society. Religion has been variously reported to be functional for society in that it helps people to define the goals and purposes of life, provides a standard of morals, serves as a watchdog over the mores, and acts as a critic of society.[1] All of these consequences serve to integrate society and create social solidarity.

Religion has been variously reported to be dysfunctional in that it tends to exercise a conservative and even reactionary influence on the social order.[2] As a conserving institution, it inhibits new approaches to social problems. It has given its support to reactionary governments, held women in positions of subordination, and sanctioned segregation. The conflict of religion and science has at times worked against the rational solution of social problems.

Religion is said to be dysfunctional in emphasizing the other-worldly to the neglect of the worldly and social reform: the biblical injunction to "render unto Caesar the things that are Caesar's and unto God the things that are God's" has been construed to tolerate and to countenance injustice.

Religion and the Churches. Various activities and patterns of interactive relationships, religious in nature, have been reported to be functional within a religious system (that is, a congregation or a denomination); to have a comprehensive program adapted to the psychological, social, and spiritual needs of the various age, sex, and intellectual categories found within the religious system; to have a program of worship and practice in terms of historic theological content; and to have a membership large enough to provide an adequate and comprehensive program, but not so large that the individual member is lost in the mass.

Various patterns of behavior that are religious in nature have been found to be dysfunctional for a religious system: Where bureaucratization and over-institutionalization of the church or denomination take precedence over the critic and the "witness" (the stand-up-and-be-counted) functions; and where man-centered mores take precedence over God-

---

[1] David O. Moberg, *The Church as a Social Institution* (Englewood Cliffs, N.J.: Prentice-Hall, Inc., 1962), pp. 175–77.

[2] J. Milton Yinger, *Religion, Society and the Individual* (New York: The Macmillan Co., 1957), pp. 209, 359.

centered ideals (for example, the "inactive" integrationist ministers of Little Rock).[3] Competitive religion that leads to over-churching and the consequent withering away of already weakened congregations is dysfunctional.

Religion and the Individual. Religion is functional for the individual when it leads to his greater integration, adjustment, adaptation to the social environment, and to the greater development of his powers and potential for service and fulfillment. Religion is functional for the individual when it relates him to the transcendental and the supernatural, provides a pathway to discovery of and adjustment to God, and helps to define the true nature and scope of religion.[4] Religion that leaves the individual with a feeling of peace and security, that provides a therapy for disturbed persons, that offers a rationale of and compensation for the problems of "evil" is functional.[5]

Religious beliefs and practices are dysfunctional that leave the individual more with a feeling of fear and frustration than peace and security, that impose guilt feelings with no compensatory values or experiences, that create neurotic personalities, that act as a crutch at the expense of initiative, or that serve as an "opiate" rather than a stimulus to self-analysis and personal development.

Religion's Contribution to Societal Equilibrium. Operational religion contributes substantially to pattern maintenance. Herberg's thesis that the three basic faiths stand more than anything else for common values, best expressed as the American Way of Life, is pattern maintenance *par excellence.*

Religion may serve as an instrument of *tension management.* Many individuals find relief from the emotional tensions and frustrations of modern society through their involvement in a religious system. Many people also find the "guide-to-confident-living" type of religion an effective antidote for their tensions. Pluralism in religion acts as a tension remover. Religion is a safety valve—one of the few areas in which the individual does not have to conform in patterned ways but rather is free to select the discipline by which he chooses to pattern his behavior.

Churches and denominations are important sources of societal integration and social solidarity. Their conserving and supporting functions give stability and validity to the social order. Since the sects either challenge or ignore the prevailing values they are neither integrative nor do they contribute to social solidarity.

Transfer of Functions. The functional analysis of religion takes on added meaning in the light of the historic development of the church in

---

[3] Ernest Q. Campbell and Thomas F. Pettigrew, "Racial and Moral Crisis: The Role of Little Rock Ministers," *American Journal of Sociology,* Vol. 64, No. 5 (March, 1959), p. 509.

[4] D. O. Moberg, *op. cit.,* pp. 162–164.

[5] J. M. Yinger, *op. cit.,* pp. 78–80.

Western civilization. In medieval society the church enjoyed a monopoly over a number of important functions that are today shared with, or the prerogative of, other institutions. Under the feudal organization of society the church was responsible for social welfare. It was a repository, holding the responsibility for learning, science, and education, and enjoying important political powers and duties. These were all in addition to the purely religious function of providing services and "saving souls." In the implementation of the separation of church and state principle the church was divested of all but its spiritual functions.

In the evolution of American society there has been a widespread transfer of functions among and between the various social institutions. In the terminology of theoretical sociology transfer of functions involves questions of functional alternatives, equivalents, and substitutes. Basic needs have been met but within a different social context.

In theory American society has accepted the separation of church and state principle. Church is separate, supreme, and unfettered in the religious sphere; the state is separate, supreme, and unfettered in the political sphere. However, in the American political system an agency of government, the Supreme Court, acting as the umpire of the federal system, decides what is properly and solely the prerogative of government.

But what is theoretically correct is practically impossible, for the state is in the "religious business" and the churches are in business for profit. American churches have never been as privileged or received as much public support, or official recognition, as they receive as participants in the comprehensive chaplaincy system that is incorporated throughout the armed services. Clergymen are recognized as officers, housed, and compensated; chapels are constructed and religious supplies provided—all at public expense. This is not an "establishment of religion" but rather an "establishment of religions." The mitigating factor is that no one denomination is favored over the others; all are supported equally.

On the other hand the churches are literally "in business." Throughout the country churches and denominations are getting deeply involved in the production of goods and services for a profit. It is a twentieth century return to the position held by religion and the church during the medieval period when the church, as a feudal lord, exercised economic as well as spiritual functions.

The transition from the medieval period, when education was the responsibility of the church, is now complete. In theory, education is the responsibility of the state. In practice, however, education was never completely divorced from the church; the churches are in fact moving back into the "education business."

As the public schools are increasingly divested of any materials or exercises suggesting religion or a religious philosophy of life, even Protestants are unhappy. No one of the faiths is now satisfied with the religious indoctrination and atmosphere that can be offered after public school hours, over the weekend, or by "released time" techniques. Protestants, as well as Catholics and Jews, are setting up parochial schools where secular education is not separated from but integrated with religion.

Although public colleges are expanding faster than church related colleges, the tendency to offer courses in religion or about religion is increasing in spite of the separation of church and state principle. It is possible for young Americans to become religiously knowledgeable in two quite different institutional environments.

Religion as Multi-Functional Behavior. Religion and family are interwoven and interdependent. Religious behavior and family behavior are frequently multifunctional. For many persons the "things of ultimate concern" are never far removed from the family; familial acts are also religious acts.

The family religious relationship is nowhere more emphasized than in Judaism. According to Jewish teaching the mother is performing her highest religious duties by remaining in the home and caring for her children and her husband. The home is the site of some of the most important religious customs and rituals (the kosher diet and the ceremonial Friday evening meal, to name just two). Periodic prayers and services for a departed family member are a family duty.

Family and religion are also closely integrated in a good Catholic family. Various items of behavior may have a religious function and a family function. A good Catholic family will pattern its eating habits to conform to the Catholic rules for fasting. In a good Catholic family sex behavior is consistent with Catholic teaching concerning procreation and birth control. Sex relations are religious as well as familial acts.

Religion and the home are closely integrated in a good Protestant family, although rites and practices within the home are as varied as Protestantism itself. There are no particular dietary laws in most Protestant systems, and the most common rites and practices would include blessings, family prayers, and Bible reading.

Both Protestantism and Judaism surround sex relations and procreation with religious values and connotations and both condone and advocate birth control in the realization of religious ends.

Religion is diffuse and pervasive. It defies neat classification and compartmentalization. A given item of behavior may serve several functions, including a religious one. Conversely, differing items of behavior within widely differing institutional contexts may have a religious function.

It is quite possible there is neither more religion nor less religion than there used to be in American society, but rather that religion is more diffused and less intense.

Chapter XVII

Concluding Observations

The Basic Faiths

Catholicism. The Catholic community in America is experiencing the adjustments caused by the rapid upward mobility of its constituents when in one generation it has moved from a peripheral, foreign, and low-class group to a nuclear, central and middle-class group. This movement was dramatically brought to the attention of the American people by the achievements and contributions of the Kennedy family who currently represent an aristocracy of wealth, social prestige, and public service. This rapid movement upward of Catholics removes strains and tensions within the Catholic group, and with other groups, but at the same time tends to create new intragroup and intergroup strains and tensions.

Through the widespread dissemination of the reports and deliberations of Vatican Councils I and II a more accurate picture of the internal structure of the church has become common knowledge. Contrary to a popular stereotype the Catholic Church is not a monolithic organization ruled by a rigid hierarchy exercising detailed control over the beliefs and conduct of each parishioner. Rather, within the fundamentals of faith and morals the community of Catholics includes an amazing variety of opinion and behavior.[1] The deliberations of the councils represent an attempt to adapt an institution 20 centuries old to the demands and needs of a nuclear age barely 20 years old. The problem of streamlining the church has focused

---

[1] The difference in belief and the variety of opinion among American Catholics is underlined in Jon Victor's article, "Restraints on American Catholic Freedom," *Harper's*, December, 1963, pp. 33–39.

public attention upon the wide range of opinion which exists between conservatives and progressives within the church hierarchy.

The proposed changes in the structure of the church have great significance for American Catholics and for the Protestants and Jews with whom Catholics interact secularly—and even religiously. Although ecumenicalism, the union of Catholic and Protestant Christians, seems remote and unattainable in the near future, some of the changes already made (and others suggested within the structure of the church) will reduce tensions between Catholics and Protestants and bring both into closer secular, if not spiritual, communion. The proposed modification of the marriage laws of the church to recognize mixed marriages performed by Protestant clergymen, and the issue as legitimate, would remove an important source of tension and conciliate many Protestants and Protestant groups.[2]

The removal from the liturgy of phrases offensive to Jews by the late Pope John, and the virtually unanimous agreement of the hierarchy at Vatican Council II that the responsibility for Christ's death rests with all of "sinful humanity" rather than with Jews alone has put the church squarely against anti-Semitism and opened the door for the best relations ever between Catholicism and Judaism.

Proposals seeking a decentralization of authority within the structure of the church are in the spirit of Protestantism and Judaism, and viewed with favor by both groups. A proposed reformulation of the doctrine of papal infallibity from something like "Once the Pope says it, that's it" to "Once the Pope says it, we already believe it"[3] would emphasize the consensual, as opposed to the hierarchical, nature of Catholicism. The proposed transfer of authority from the Roman *Curia* to national episcopal conferences of bishops (collegiality) is the sort of home-rule approach to government that is popular among Americans. Recommendations for the increased participation of laymen in the administration and control of the Catholic religion and parish, including the restoration of the diaconate, would release an important reservoir of talent and dedication, and further contribute to the Americanization of the Catholic Church.

Although there is no sure indication of how many of the reforms proposed by the progressive wing of the church will finally be accepted and become official policy, the mere discussion of the proposals does much to conciliate and foster friendly relations with non-Catholics. While it appears doubtful that any sizable group of Protestants will be absorbed by the Catholic Church in the foreseeable future, it is quite possible that the new configuration of religious systems within the secular power structure will increasingly find some Protestants taking stands on social and political

---

[2] Hans Küng, *The Council, Reform, and Reunion* (New York: Sheed and Ward, 1962).

[3] *New York Times*, October 11, 1963.

issues more closely allied to the Catholic position than to the stands of Protestants of the conservative right.

Protestantism. Protestantism is marked by doctrinal cleavage between the traditional orthodox (fundamentalists) and the liberals and modernists. The traditional orthodox take belief on authority, accept the Bible literally, and are more concerned with otherworldly goals and personal salvation than with social issues here and now. The modernists make a complete reconciliation of belief with science and history, emphasize ethics rather than salvation and rationalism rather than revelation. Doctrinal cleavage also separates different denominations (Third-force Protestantism is a stronghold of traditional orthodoxy) and is also found within the major Protestant denominations (where traditional orthodoxy generally occupies a minor position in both numbers and influence).

Neo-orthodoxy is a significant intellectual movement within Protestantism, differing from liberal Protestantism in doctrine and dogma but like it in social class orientation and humanitarian concern.

The ecumenical movement in Protestantism is definite and substantial. Where the nineteenth was a century of particularity and fragmentation, the twentieth is characterized by a trend towards cooperation and organic union. Whether the unity movement is a demonstration of the inherent and essential strength of Protestantism (as is claimed by proponents) or more a reflection of Protestant weakness (as opponents claim) is not clear in the mid-1960's. Both liberal and neo-orthodox Protestantism find it possible to support ecumenicalism at the consultative stage. Who joins whom, or who joins something different, and the subsequent relations of the joining segments to Catholicism, are matters of conjecture. Conservative and fundamentalist Protestantism have shown little interest in ecumenicalism.

The ecumenical movement is a demonstration that religious systems of belief seldom operate as single and separate entities for extended periods. They are subject rather to complex interpenetrations, conflicts, and reformulations that result in continually shifting realignments and configurations.[4]

Judaism. Judaism parallels Protestantism in doctrinal cleavage. The Orthodox are the fundamentalists of Judaism and the Reform the liberals and modernists. A convergence towards the center (Conservatism) is noted. The Orthodox are tending to be somewhat less literal and rigid in doctrine and practice while many Reform congregations are restoring worship practices they had previously given up.

Leaders throughout Judaism have expressed concern that secularization and assimilation are posing a greater threat to Jewish religious and cultural survival than Nazism. Reform has for the first time taken an interest in

---

[4] Robin M. Williams, Jr., *American Society* (2d ed., rev.; New York: Alfred A. Knopf, Inc., 1960), p. 468.

parochial education, and leaders of Orthodox, Conservative and Reform Judaism more than ever speak out against mixed marriages.

Judaism has risen from the status of a minority religion functioning in the shadow of a Protestant-oriented and dominated ethos to a position of equal status in a three-religion country. The widespread acceptance of this new status is demonstrated in the commonly heard expression, "our Judeo-Christian tradition." The changed relationship is reflected in the tolerance and the nature and the degree of cooperation that is shown between Judaism and Catholicism and between Judaism and Protestantism. Cooperation and understanding appear to vary with theological sophistication, however. The greater the theological sophistication of the individual or the group, the better the understanding and appreciation of other faiths.

The change from a position of subordination to one of equality has both strengthened and weakened the internal cohesion and solidarity of Judaism. Whether strength or strain will predominate in the long run is another subject for speculation.

Sects and Cults. Sects and cults flourish in a period of rapid social change when value systems are disturbed and under threat. They are another expression of the "religious fecundity"[5] of American society. Sects and cults tend to be uneroded, unexposed, withdrawn, and in every particular provide a counter-current to the mid-century religious revival and the movement towards union and cooperation.[6]

Institutional Themes

Religion as "Belonging." Theologians and social scientists have done a great deal of theorizing about the status of religion and the church in contemporary culture, about religious trends, and the meaning and significance of trends that they identify. One interpretation that has attracted a great deal of attention and received considerable support sees the "return to religion" as primarily a drive to secure a feeling of "belonging." Herberg has offered this thesis in terms of the following closely connected assertions:

1. That in the course of the past generation, America has been transformed from a *Protestant* nation into a *three-religion* country.
2. That this has come about largely through the replacement of the ethnic group by the *religious community* as the primary source of self-identification and social location in American society.
3. That the new role of religion as a vehicle of identification and belonging has been a major factor in the marked upsurge of religiousness that has been underway in this country in the past 15 years.
4. That this new role of religion as a vehicle of American identity and

---

5 Willard L. Sperry, *Religion in America* (New York: The Macmillan Co., 1946), p. 77 ff.

6 Martin Marty, "Sects and Cults," *Annals of the American Academy of Political and Social Science,* Vol. 332 (November, 1960), pp. 125–34.

belonging makes for an increased evacuation of historic religious content in favor of a kind of generalized religiosity or religion-in-general.

5. That what has been emerging in this country is a kind of "common faith," or overarching superreligion, defined by the American Way of Life, of which the three major conventional religions are seen as varying expressions, and in terms of which they are understood and validated.[7]

Marty, the Protestant theologian, interprets the phenomena in the same vein. He finds that particular religion is being replaced by "religion-in-general" and sees an "erosion of particularity" leading to a corresponding "smoothing of the edges of Witness."[8]

To the sociologist Williams, religious affiliation founded on the desire to "belong" constitutes a functional reversal;[9] the means-ends becoming the ends-means. The sense of belonging is the end, and the religious expression itself is merely the means to this nonreligious end: "belonging." The ends-means analysis is further validated when the drive for "social acceptance" becomes the motive for affiliation.

Pluralism and Secularism. A second common observation is the dual existence of religious pluralism and secularism, and the feeling that somehow the two behavior constellations are related to each other. Parsons[10] sees secularism as a sort of loyal opposition to the religious point of view and argues that the right to religious pluralism and secular orientation is now a fundamental institutionalized right in American society. Parsons would here seem to support the "safety valve" function of religion, modifying it only by making secularism one of the emotional-releasing choices open to the individual.

To Williams a heterogeneous society (religious pluralism is one aspect of heterogeneity) is a secular society and a homogeneous society a sacred society.[11] The variety of religious groups composing a heterogeneous society works against the acceptance of the value complex of any one religious system. A homogeneous society gives religious sanctions to its integrating values even though these values are not religious in any formal or traditional sense.

Russian Communism is a sacred society in the sense that the Communist ideal of life is followed as a religion: the approved way of "striving for the highest." It could in like fashion also be argued that American society is a sacred society. If the "American Way of Life" is the common faith of the three religions then American society is a sacred society. This would then be another example of the "sacralization of the secular."

---

[7] Will Herberg, as workshop consultant for Religion in American Culture, State University College, Oswego, N.Y., summer of 1963.

[8] M. Marty, *The New Shape of American Religion* (New York: Harper & Bros., 1959).

[9] R. M. Williams, *op. cit.*, p. 429.

[10] Talcott Parsons, *Structure and Process in Modern Society* (Glencoe, Ill.: The Free Press, 1960).

[11] R. M. Williams, *op. cit.*, p. 369.

Both Reinhold Niebuhr[12] and Will Herberg[13] see the religious pluralism and secularism phenomenon as an indication that American society is both the most religious and the most secular of cultures. Marty[14] also finds religion serving as merely one aspect of the general culture, neither in tension with it nor exercising a critical function towards it. Religion is available to the individual, along with secularism, as an acceptable value system for group identification. The religious choices available are largely man-centered and not demanding. On the other hand authentic religion, God-related and with historic content, is demanding of the individual and in a continual state of moral tension with the general culture.

Intrinsic Religion. Intrinsic religion is a readily identifiable type of the religious culture. A number of social analysts and theologians have noted both the existence and importance of this type of religious emphasis and behavior on the contemporary scene. Religious behavior that emphasizes the "private and personal" character of religion, in which religion is experienced in depth and where religious values are internalized and validated in behavior, is intrinsic religion. Parsons maintains that American society is witnessing a revival that is religiously genuine because intrinsic religion is the principle feature of American religious patterns.[15]

The behavioral implications of Tillich's theology are also found to be in support of intrinsic religion. Tillich's "ultimate concern"[16] is interpreted in terms of the "religious experience." In his analysis of American society Williams finds intrinsic religion of central importance and lists it as a common value characterized by nonempirical referents and moral respect.[17]

In his research studies and general observations of religious groups, the author also is impressed by the evidence of intrinsic religion in the religious culture. Almost without exception, religious feelings and experiences in depth are a significant part of the nuclear parishioner's resources. Intrinsic religion appears to be the inescapable common residual without which no religious group can long maintain itself; it is the hard core of those who have not only experienced religion in depth but have also internalized its values.

Cultural Themes

Religion is both a unifying and an individualizing force, and an important expression of the strain towards consistency within American society; but it serves to unify on a cultural rather than on an organizational

---

[12] Reinhold Niebuhr, "Piety and Secularism in America" *Atlantic Monthly*, November, 1957.

[13] W. Herberg, *Protestant, Catholic, Jew* (Garden City, N.Y.: Doubleday & Co., 1955), p. 287.

[14] M. Marty, *The New Shape of American Religion, op. cit.*

[15] T. Parsons, *op. cit.*

[16] *Ibid.*

[17] R. M. Williams, *op. cit.*, p. 367.

level. Religion is a unity of diffuse convergence rather than an established, centrally controlled system of beliefs and practices.[18] It is a unifying force at the value and symbol level of abstraction.

Religion, through the various rubrics, also represents and reflects the strain towards variety. This is true not only of the sects but also of the basic faiths: a synagogue is still a synagogue and in no sense a Protestant church; a Catholic sanctuary is still a Catholic expression of religion, and the religion practiced there is something quite different in form and matter from what goes on in a Protestant service.

The underlying cultural themes bend the religious structure towards individualism and pragmatism, and towards ethical and humanitarian concern.

---

[18] *Ibid.,* p. 359.

Bibliography

Bibliography

Chapter I: Introduction

CHAPIN, STUART F. *Contemporary American Institutions*. New York: Harper & Bros., 1935.
   Research data on the structure and functions of American institutions. One of the standard works in the field.

GLOCK, CHARLES Y. "The Sociology of Religion," *Sociology Today*. MERTON, ROBERT K.; BROOM, LEONARD; and COTRELL, LEONARD S., JR. (eds.), New York: Basic Books, Inc., 1959.
   What the author believes are the significant theoretical, empirical, and procedural problems that are being studied and that require study in the sociology of religion.

HERTZLER, J. O. *American Social Institutions*. New York: Allyn and Bacon, Inc., 1961.
   Systematic analysis of basic social institutions.

KLAPP, ORRIN E. *Ritual and Cult: A Sociological Interpretation*. Washington, D.C.: Public Affairs Press, 1956.
   The social consequences of ritual and symbolism.

LEE, ROBERT. "The Sociology of Religion: Some Basic Problems and Prospects," *Religion In Life*, Vol. 30 (Spring, 1961), pp. 268–78.
   A summary and interpretation of the current status of the sociology of religion.

MALINOWSKI, BRONISLAW. *Magic, Science and Religion and Other Essays*. Glencoe, Illinois: The Free Press, 1948.
   Myth and ritual interact: myths justify rituals, while rituals reenact and bring myths to life. Emphasizes the functional role performed by myth in integrating culture and maintaining social organization.

MARETT, R. R. *The Threshold of Religion*. London: Methuen, 1914.
   An anthropological interpretation of the origin and development of religion. Finds that a belief in an impersonal supernatural force (mana) precedes a belief in spirits.

MOBERG, DAVID O. *The Church as a Social Institution*. Englewood Cliffs, New Jersey: Prentice-Hall, Inc., 1962.
   A systematic interdisciplinary approach to the sociology of religion in America.

491

MORRIS, RUDOLPH E. "Problems Concerning the Institutionalizing of Religion," *American Catholic Sociological Review*, Vol. 17 (June, 1956), pp. 98–108.
 Problems arising out of the institutionalization of personal religious experience.

RADCLIFFE-BROWN, ALFRED R. *Religion and Society*. London: Royal Anthropological Institute of Great Britain and Ireland, 1945.
 Finds religion and religious rites the means by which the group adjusts to crisis situations, reinforces the sense of group identity, and thereby contributes to the survival of society.

RADIN, PAUL. *Primitive Religion: Its Nature and Origin*. New York: The Viking Press, 1937.
 Sees primitive religion arising primarily from man's emotional responses to threatening situations.

TYLOR, EDWARD B. *Primitive Culture*, 7th ed. New York: Brentano, 1925.
 Primitive religion found to be rooted in the belief that man could control nature by supernatural means if he used the proper techniques.

WACH, JOACHIM. *Sociology of Religion*. Chicago: University of Chicago Press, 1944.
 The first major sociology of religion in English. A summary of the findings of theologians, anthropologists, and social scientists in the interrelation of religion and society in different cultures and ages.

WILLIAMS, ROBIN. *American Society*. New York: Alfred Knopf, Inc., 1960.
 Keen sociological analysis of institutions in American society from a functionalist viewpoint.

YINGER, MILTON J. "Some Consequences of the Scientific Study of Religion," *Religious Education*, Vol. 52 (September–October 1957), pp. 350–54.
 Sees the long-range effect of the scientific study of religion as constructive for the religious institution and for the religiousness of the mature personality.

—— *Religion in the Struggle for Power*. Durham, N. Carolina: Duke University Press, 1946.
 Discusses religion as a source of values which regulates the development of modern culture.

Chapter II: The Historical Development of the Three Basic Faiths

DILLENBERGER, JOHN, AND WELCH, CLAUDE. *Protestant Christianity*. New York: Charles Scribner's Sons, 1954.
 The development of Protestant Christianity from the Reformation to the present.

ELLIS, JOHN TRACY. *American Catholicism*. Chicago: University of Chicago Press, 1956.
 A general survey of the development of the Catholic Church from the days of the colonial missions to the present by an outstanding Catholic historian.

FERM, VERGILIUS. *The American Church of Protestant Heritage*. New York: Philosophical Library, 1953.
 Twenty-one articles about American Protestant churches, each chapter written by a member of the religious body in question.

GLAZER, NATHAN. *American Judaism*. Chicago: University of Chicago Press, 1957.
 An historical survey of the Jewish religion in America. Considerable attention to contemporary scene, the Jewish religious revival, the reasons for it, and the extent to which it expresses religious and spiritual as well as social needs.

HALL, THOMAS CUMING. *The Religious Background of American Culture*. New York: Frederick Ungar Publishing Co., 1959.
 A history of the background of contemporary religious culture, including the European as well as the American record. Puritanism is equated with "the Anglo-American Dissenting Mind."

HANDLIN, OSCAR. *Adventure in Freedom: Three Hundred Years of Jewish Life in America*. New York: McGraw-Hill Co., 1954.
 The historic evolution of the Jewish community in America seen as but a part

of the general epic of immigration and adjustment of the various European ethnic and religious groups in this country.

HANLEY, THOMAS O., S.J. "The Emergence of Pluralism in the United States," *Theological Studies*, Vol. 23, No. 2 (June, 1962), pp. 207–32.
The development of pluralism, embracing the Catholic as well as the several Protestant groups in the post-Revolutionary period, with especial attention to the Maryland situation.

HOPKINS, CHARLES H. *The Rise of the Social Gospel in American Protestantism, 1865–1915.* New Haven, Connecticut: Yale University Press, 1940.
The contribution of the Social Gospel movement to liberal Protestantism.

HUDSON, WINTHROP S. *American Protestantism.* Chicago: University of Chicago Press, 1961.
The historical development of Protestantism. Author finds that Protestantism has been more transformed by its American experience than Catholicism or Judaism.

HUGHES, PHILIP. *A Popular History of the Catholic Church.* New York: The Macmillan Co., 1949.
A history of the Catholic Church from the early days of primitive Catholicism to the present.

LANDIS, BENSON Y., editor. *A Rauschenbusch Reader: The Kingdom of God and the Social Gospel.* New York: Harper & Bros., 1957.
Selections from the greatest exponent of the main stream of the Social Gospel movement.

MAYER, F. E. *The Religious Bodies of America*, 2nd ed. St. Louis: Concordia Publishing House, 1956.
A thorough and comprehensive treatment of American religious groups; their history, organization, and teaching.

MEAD, FRANK. *Handbook of Denominations in the United States*, 2nd rev. ed. Nashville: Abingdon Press, 1961.
Alphabetically arranged data on 255 religious bodies in the U.S. giving history, doctrine, organization, and present status.

MYERS, GUSTAVUS. *History of Bigotry in the United States.* New York: Random House, 1943.
Bigotry is frequently found to arise from a religious context.

OLMSTEAD, CLIFTON E. *History of Religion in the United States.* Englewood Cliffs, New Jersey: Prentice-Hall, Inc., 1960.
A history of religion which emphasizes the influence of political, economic, and social forces upon the development of American religious institutions.

SMITH, JAMES WARD, AND JAMISON, A. LELAND (ed.). *Religion in American Life*, Vol. I, *The Shaping of American Religion.* Princeton, New Jersey: Princeton University Press, 1961.

———— "Religious Perspectives in American Culture," *Religion in American Life* series, Vol. II. Princeton, New Jersey: Princeton University Press, 1961.
Essays in the history and current status of the major denominations by specialists. Emphasis is upon the intellectually respectable phases of the American religious scene.

SMITH, TIMOTHY L. *Revivalism and Social Reform in Mid-Nineteenth Century America.* New York: Abingdon Press, 1957.
Offered as a "new slant on the origins of the Social Gospel."

SPERRY, WILLARD. *Religion in America.* New York: The Macmillan Co., 1948.
The history and current status of American churches and denominations; an interpretation.

STEPHENSON, GEORGE M. *The Puritan Heritage.* New York: The Macmillan Co., 1952.
The planting and early development of Puritanism in America; detailed chapters on eighteenth century religious awakening and nineteenth century revivalism.

SWEET, WILLIAM W. *Story of Religion in America.* New York: Harper & Bros., 1939.

———— *The Baptists, 1783–1830*. New York: Henry Holt Co., 1931.
A collection of source materials.

———— *The Congregationalists*. Chicago: University of Chicago Press, 1939.
A collection of source materials.

———— *The Methodists*. Chicago: University of Chicago Press, 1946.
A collection of source materials.

———— *Religion in Colonial America*. New York: Scribner's & Sons, 1942.

———— *Religion in the Development of American Culture, 1765–1840*. New York: Scribner's Sons, 1952.
Selected titles from the dean of the historians of American Protestantism.

Chapter III: Religion and Personality

ALLPORT, GORDON W. *Becoming, Basic Considerations for a Psychology of Personality*. New Haven, Connecticut: Yale University Press, 1955.
An attempt to correlate and interpret psychology's views on human welfare and religion.

———— *The Individual and His Religion*. New York: The Macmillan Co., 1950.
An interpretation of the significance of religion from the psychological point of view. Said to be the most important psychological study of religion since William James.

ARGYLE, MICHAEL. *Religious Behavior*. Glencoe, Illinois: The Free Press, 1959.
A summary and critique of the sociological and psychological studies of American and British religion.

BOISEN, ANTON T. *Religion in Crisis and Custom*. New York: Harper & Bros., 1955.
Thesis: "Religious experience is rooted in the social nature of man and arises spontaneously under the pressure of crisis situations." Religion of crisis is localized at times of individual stress: birth of children, marriage, illness.

BROWN, DANIEL G., AND LOWE, WARNER L. "Relgious Beliefs and Personality Characteristics of College Students," *Journal of Social Psychology* (February, 1951), pp. 103–29.

CLARK, WALTER H. *Psychology of Religion*. New York: The Macmillan Co., 1958.
An inquiry into the psychological aspects of religion, its effects upon human behavior, the problem of faith, conversion, prayer, ritual, the practice of mysticism, and the relationship of religion and psychotherapy.

DREGER, RALPH M. "Some Personality Correlates of Religious Attitudes as Determined by Projective Techniques," *Psychological Monographs*, Vol. 6, No. 3 (1952).

DUNLAP, KNIGHT. *Religion: Its Functions in Human Life*. New York: McGraw-Hill, Inc., 1946.
Religion seen as the consequence of psychological processes and individual needs.

FERM, ROBERT O. *The Psychology of Christian Conversion*. Westwood, N.J.: Fleming H. Revell Co., 1959.
Interprets Christian conversion in terms of a unique experience.

FICHTER, JOSEPH H., S.J. "The Profile of Catholic Religious Life," *American Journal of Sociology*, Vol. 58 (1952), pp. 145–49.
The life cycle and religious participation.

FREUD, SIGMUND. *Civilization and Its Discontents*. Trans. JOAN RIVIERE. New York: Jonathan Cape and Harrison Smith, 1930.

———— *The Future of an Illusion*, Trans. W. D. ROBSON-SCOTT. London: Horace Liveright and The Institute of Psycho-Analysis, 1928.

———— *Moses and Monotheism*. Trans. KATHERINE JONES. New York: Vintage Books, 1955.
The founder of psychoanalysis found religion primarily negative in nature: an escape from reality and a search for a father image. According to Freud, religion sustained inadequate institutions, prohibited critical thinking, prevented the development of an adequate institution, and fostered an infantile fixation.

FROMM, ERICH. *Psychoanalysis and Religion.* New Haven, Connecticut: Yale University Press, 1950.

    In studying neurosis, the author discovers he is studying religion. Maintains that Freud was not necessarily "against" religion, nor Jung necessarily "for" it.

GILLILAND, A. R. "Changes in Religious Beliefs of College Students," *Journal of Social Psychology* (February, 1953), pp. 113–16.

GREGORY, W. E. "The Psychology of Religion: Some Suggested Areas of Research of Significance for Psychology," *Journal of Abnormal and Social Psychology* (April, 1952), pp. 256–58.

HARMS, ERNEST. "The Development of Religious Experience in Children," *American Journal of Sociology,* Vol. 50 (September, 1944), pp. 112–22.

    Stages in the religious experience and education of children.

JAMES, WILLIAM. *The Varieties of Religious Experience.* New York: The Modern Library. Originally published by Longmans, Green & Co., 1902.

    A classic in the psychology of religion.

JOHNSON, PAUL E. *Personality and Religion.* Nashville: Abingdon Press, 1957.

    Author arrives at a dimensional view of personality that he calls "dynamic interpersonalism." Based upon a study of the psychology of four stages of life: infancy (after Sigmund Freud), childhood (after Kurt Lewin), youth (after Henry Stack Sullivan), maturity (after Gordon Allport).

JUNG, CARL G. *Modern Man in Search of a Soul.* Trans. W. S. SELL and C. F. BARNES. New York: Harcourt, Brace & Co., 1933

———— *The Integration of Personality.* New York: Rinehart & Co., 1940.

    Jung, although an early associate of Freud in the development of psychoanalysis, found religion making a more positive contribution to personality. Religion, according to Jung, performs a positive function by helping the individual to achieve self-realization.

LIU, WILLIAM T. "The Marginal Catholics in the South: A Revision of Concepts," *American Journal of Sociology,* Vol. 65 (January, 1960), pp. 383–90.

    A critique of Fichter's marginal member concept based on research findings.

McCANN, RICHARD V. "Developmental Factors in the Growth of a Mature Faith," *Religious Education,* Vol. 50 (May–June, 1955), pp. 147–55.

MacIVER, R. M. (ed.). *Moments of Personal Discovery.* New York: Harper & Bros., 1952.

    Thirteen educators, theologians, and scientists describe the time, the circumstances, or the experience that led them to their "moment of personal discovery." Many such moments prove to be religious in nature.

MAVES, PAUL B. "Conversion: A Behavioral Category," *Review of Religious Research,* Vol. 5, No. 1 (Fall, 1963).

    Conversion is a behavioral science category, not a theological one, and needs to be studied by behavioral scientists.

STRUNK, ORLO, JR. (ed.). *Readings in the Psychology of Religion.* Nashville: Abingdon Press, 1959.

    A collection of 49 readings, including excerpts from such authorities as Hall, James, Allport, Freud, Otto.

TOCH, HANS, AND ANDERSON, ROBERT. "Religious Belief and Denominational Affiliation," *Religious Education,* Vol. 55 (May–June, 1960), pp. 193–200.

    Denominational affiliation shows little relationship to beliefs about God, Jesus, the Bible, the church, or theology.

VERNON, GLENN M. "An Inquiry into the Scalability of Church Orthodoxy," *Sociology and Social Research,* Vol. 39 (May–June, 1955), pp. 324–27.

    A scale developed for ranking the orthodoxy of members of the Church of Jesus Christ of Latter-Day Saints.

WIEMAN, HENRY N. *Man's Ultimate Commitment.* Carbondale, Illinois: Southern Illinois University Press, 1958.

    Out of a professional experience extending over 50 years, a well-known psychologist develops a philosophy of creativity which is equated in terms of ultimate commitment (religion).

Chapter IV : The Individual as a Religious Statistic

American Jewish Yearbook. New York: The American Jewish Committee.
Articles and statistical information interpreting Jewish culture and institutions.

BULTENA, LOUIS. "Church Membership and Church Attendance in Madison, Wisconsin," *American Sociological Review,* Vol. 14 (June, 1949), pp. 384–89.
Based upon an intensive sociological study of 18 Protestant churches.

BUREAU OF RESEARCH AND SURVEY, NATIONAL COUNCIL OF CHURCHES. *Churches and Church Membership in the United States.* New York, 1956–58.
Five series of bulletins summarizing the churches and church membership in a number of religious bodies by counties, states, and regions. Based on data from the 1950 Census of Population.

CANTRIL, HADLEY. "Educational and Economic Composition of Religious Groups: An Analysis of Poll Data," *American Journal of Sociology* (March, 1943), pp. 574–79.

CUBER, JOHN F. "Marginal Church Participants," *Sociology and Social Research,* Vol. 25 (September–October 1940), pp. 57–62.
Church participation in Detroit.

LANDIS, BENSON Y. "A Guide to the Literature on Statistics of Religious Affiliation with References to Related Social Studies," *Journal of the American Statistical Association,* Vol. 54 (June, 1959), pp. 335–57.
An analysis and survey of the bibliography of religious statistics by the editor of the *Yearbook of American Churches.*

———— *Yearbook of American Churches.* New York: National Council of Churches.
Most comprehensive and authoritative summary of denominational statistics on churches, church membership, religious education, clergymen, finances, etc., as reported by more than 250 religious groups.

Official Catholic Directory. New York: P. J. Kenedy & Son.
Annual religious statistics of the Catholic Church.

PETERSEN, WILLIAM. "Religious Statistics in the United States," *Journal for the Scientific Study of Religion,* Vol. 1, No. 2 (Spring, 1962), pp. 165–79.
A critical evaluation of the distribution of the population by the techniques of claimed church membership and stated religious preference.

Part III : Normative Structure of the Basic Faiths

CLARK, ELMER T. *The Small Sects in America,* rev. ed., New York: Abingdon-Cokesbury Press, 1949.
A seven-place typology of American sects developed with the use of historical, social science, and theological data.

COUGHENOUR, C. M. "An Application of Scale Analysis to the Study of Religious Groups," *Rural Sociology* (September–December, 1955), pp. 197–211.
Church-type and sect-type religious groups differ significantly in the extent of suborganizational development: Sunday Schools, women's organizations, youth organizations, men's clubs, young adult organizations, and older adult organizations.

DYNES, RUSSELL R. "Church-Sect Typology and Socio-Economic Status," *American Sociological Review,* Vol. 20, No. 5 (October, 1955), pp. 555–60.
Empirical study that finds the economic factor central in sect orientation and affiliation.

HAMMOND, PHILLIP E. "Contemporary Protestant Ideology: A Typology of Church Images," *Review of Religious Research,* Vol. 2 (Spring, 1961), pp. 161–69.
A typology incorporating an ideological and a community-individual dimension.

JOHNSON, BENTON. "On Church and Sect," *American Sociological Review,* Vol. 28, No. 4 (August, 1963), pp. 539–49.
   Sect is distinguished from church primarily in terms of the acceptance or the rejection of the social environment.

NIEBUHR, RICHARD H. *The Social Sources of Denominationalism.* New York: Henry Holt & Co., 1929.
   An interpretation of the development and growth of religious bodies in which social class and social change are seen as central and causal.

POPE, LISTON. *Millhands and Preachers.* New Haven, Connecticut: Yale University Press, 1942.
   An outstanding illustration of the effective use of the church-sect typology in the analysis and interpretation of the churches of Gastonia, North Carolina.

TROELTSCH, ERNST. *The Social Teachings of the Christian Churches.* Trans. OLIVE WYON, 2 vols. London: Allen and Unwin, 1931.
   One of the classical works in the sociology of religion. Church-sect typology central to the analysis.

WILSON, BRYAN R. "An Analysis of Sect Development," *American Sociological Review,* Vol. 24, No. 1 (February, 1959), pp. 3–15.
   An attempt to distinguish and characterize distinctive types of the sect, and to determine the specific elements and combinations of elements which promote or retard sect development.

Chapter V: Catholicism

America. National Catholic weekly review published by the Jesuits of the United States and Canada.

(The) American Catholic Sociological Review. The official, quarterly publication of the American Catholic Sociological Society.

COGLEY, JOHN (ed.). *Religion in America.* New York: Meridian Books, 1958.
   Essays on the role of religion in a free and pluralistic society.

Commonweal. Weekly journal edited by Catholic laymen.

CROSS, ROBERT D. *The Emergence of Liberal Catholicism in America.* Cambridge: Harvard University Press, 1958.
   Variations in American Catholicism and the growing importance of the "liberal wing" of Catholic thought and action.

DEPLOIGE, SIMON. *The Conflict Between Ethics and Sociology.* St. Louis: B. Herder Book Co., 1938.
   A Catholic criticism of positivism and a defense of Thomistic theology and ethics.

ELLIS, JOHN TRACY. *Perspectives in American Catholicism.* Baltimore: Helicon Press, 1963.
   Twenty-three topical essays by one of the outstanding authorities on the historical development of American Catholicism.

FICHTER, JOSEPH H., S.J. *Dynamics of a City Church.* Chicago: University of Chicago Press, 1951.
   An intensive sociological study of a representative Catholic parish in New Orleans.

—— *Social Relations in the Urban Parish.* Chicago: University of Chicago Press, 1954.
   A theoretical analysis of the Catholic parish: the interaction of priests and parishioners. Based upon an empirical study of a New Orleans parish.

HUBER, RAPHAEL M. *Our Bishops Speak.* Milwaukee: The Bruce Publishing Co., 1952.
   Official pronouncements of the bishops of the American Catholic Church on social questions.

MERTON, THOMAS. *Seeds of Contemplation.* New York: Dell Publishing Co., 1953.
   A Roman Catholic monk presents modern Catholic mysticism in its most persuasive form, exerting a wide influence upon Protestants as well.

MOODY, JOSEPH N. (ed.). *Church and Society: Catholic Social and Political Thought and Movements, 1789–1950.* New York: Arts Inc., 1953.
   An extensive symposium on Catholic political and social thought.

NUESSE, C. J., AND HARTE, THOMAS J. (eds.). *The Sociology of the Parish.* Milwaukee: The Bruce Publishing Co., 1951.
   An informative collection of essays on various aspects of the Catholic parish.

ONG, WALTER J., S.J. *Frontiers in American Catholicism.* New York: The Macmillan Co., 1957.
   Essays on the interaction of Catholic ideology and culture: business, humanism, technology, and Catholicism.

ROSTEN, LEO (ed.). *Religions in America.* New York: Simon and Schuster, 1963.
   The original *Look* magazine series of 19 articles on religious groups and denominations, plus facts, figures, tables, charts, articles, and comprehensive reference material on churches and religious groups. An excellent profile of the faith of America.

SCHUYLER, JOSEPH B., S.J. *Northern Parish.* Chicago: Loyola University Press, 1960.
   A sociological and pastoral study of an urban New York City Catholic parish.

SPITZER, ALLEN. "The Culture Organization of Catholicism," *American Catholic Sociological Review,* Vol. 19 (March, 1958), pp. 2–12.
   Catholicism viewed as a continuum from formal to folk culture: formal and universalistic Catholicism transcends the social environment while folk culture reflects the social environment.

WARD, LEO R., C.S.C. *Catholic Life, U.S.A.: Contemporary Lay Movements.* St. Louis: B. Herder Book Co., 1959.
   A "grass roots" portrayal and analysis of important Catholic lay movements.

WILLIAMS, MELVIN J. *Catholic Social Thought.* New York: Ronald Press, 1950.
   Expands on the theme that charity is "the soul of the social order."

Chapter VI: Protestantism

CARTER, P. A. *The Decline and Revival of the Social Gospel: Social and Political Liberalism in American Protestant Churches, 1920–1940.* Ithaca, New York: Cornell University Press, 1956.
   Traces the response of the church to the attacks upon the social gospel in the twenties, and its revival in relationship to the ecumenical movement and the New Deal.

Christian Century. A nondenominational Protestant journal published weekly by the Christian Century Foundation. A liberal Protestant point of view is generally represented.

COBB, JOHN B., JR. *Varieties of Protestantism.* Philadelphia: Westminster Press, 1960.
   Nine types of Protestantism are identified and examined: two of "reformation" Protestantism, one stemming from Luther, the other from Calvin; two types of "churchly" Protestantism, the "liturgical" and the "authoritarian"; two types of "individualistic" Protestantism; three types of "liberal" Protestantism.

HORDERN, WILLIAM. *A Layman's Guide to Protestant Theology.* New York: The Macmillan Co., 1957.
   Orthodoxy, Fundamentalism, Liberalism, and New-orthodoxy explained in the light of the historical development of Christian thought. Because of their influence and importance, the theologies of Karl Barth, Emil Brunner; Reinhold Niebuhr, and Paul Tillich are discussed separately.

JOHNSON, F. ERNEST. *Patterns of Faith.* New York: Institute for Religious and Social Studies, 1957.
   Interpretive essays on Liberal Protestantism, Classical Protestantism, Roman Catholicism, Judaism, and Naturalistic Humanism by outstanding authorities of the respective religions.

KEGLEY, CHARLES W., AND BRETALL, ROBERT W. (eds.). *Reinhold Niebuhr, His Religious, Social, and Political Thought.* New York: The Macmillan Company, 1956.
Contains interpretive and critical essays.

——— *The Theology of Paul Tillich.* New York: The Macmillan Co., 1952.
Fourteen religious and theological authorities interpret the mind and thought of Tillich.

MARTY, MARTIN E. *The New Shape of American Religion.* New York: Harper & Bros., 1959.
The hope of Protestantism lies in the theological renaissance and a remnant that is interested in the "recovery of integrity of membership and clarity of witness."

MAY, HENRY F. *Protestant Churches and Industrial America.* New York: Harper & Bros., 1949.
A study of the stand of five major denominations, Presbyterian, Congregational, Baptist, Methodist, Episcopal on social problems in the nineteenth century.

McLEAN, M. D. "Diagnosing Patterns of Religious Belief," *Religious Education,* Vol. 43 (November–December, 1948), pp. 343–49.
Religious concepts: three types of orthodoxy, three types of liberalism, and three types of nontheistic humanism, defined and identified.

MIXTER, RUSSELL L. (ed.). *Evolution and Christian Faith Today.* Grand Rapids, Michigan: William B. Eerdmans Publishing Co., 1959.
The present status of evolutionary theory and its relation to Christian faith and doctrine, as interpreted by 13 biological and physical scientists.

MYERS, DONALD B. *The Protestant Search for Political Realism, 1919–1941.* Berkeley: University of California Press, 1960.
Political factors in the development of Neo-orthodoxy.

NIEBUHR, REINHOLD. *An Interpretation of Christian Ethics.* New York: Harper & Bros., 1935.
A major early work of the central figure in the development of a more critical and less optimistic Social Gospel.

SCHNEIDER, HERBERT W. *Religion in 20th Century America.* Cambridge: Harvard University Press, 1952.
Author examines religion in its cultural context. Scholarly and interesting.

TILLICH, PAUL. *Systematic Theology.* Chicago: University of Chicago Press, 1951.
The author, an outstanding representative of the neo-orthodox position in Protestantism, states his purpose is to present the method and structure of a theological system written from an apologetic point of view and carried through in a continuous correlation with philosophy.

WEBER, MAX. *The Protestant Ethic and the Spirit of Capitalism.* Trans. by TALCOTT PARSONS. London: George Allen and Unwin, Ltd., 1930.
A classic study in which the attitudes and values of Calvinist Protestantism were found to be closely associated with the rise and development of capitalism.

WILLIAMS, J. PAUL. *What Americans Believe and How They Worship,* rev. ed., New York: Harper & Row, 1962.
A descriptive survey, partly historical and partly contemporary, of the major religious groups in the U.S. Especially good chapters on the major Protestant denominations.

Chapter VII: Judaism

COHEN, ARTHUR A. "Why I Choose to be a Jew," *Harper's,* 1959, pp. 61–66.
Argues that the present generation of American Jews is the first generation of Jews in centuries who are free to choose to believe as Jews. Young Jewish scholar explains his faith in the God of the Old Testament who has chosen the Jews as a special instrument to bring all men to redemption.

Commentary. Published monthly by the American Jewish Committee as a journal of significant thought and opinion on Jewish affairs and contemporary issues.

FINKELSTEIN, LOUIS J.; ROSS, ELLIOT; AND BROWN, WILLIAM ADAMS. *The Religions of Democracy*. New York: the Devin-Adair Co., 1954.
Essays on Judaism, Catholicism, and Protestantism in creed and life by a leading theologian and authority of each of the three faiths.

GORDON, ALBERT I. *Jews in Transition*. University of Minnesota Press, 1949.
The author, for 15 years a rabbi in Minneapolis, tells the story of the Jews in one community. A sociologically oriented study from which the non-Jew may gain a new respect and understanding of the American Jew.

HERBERG, WILL. *Judaism and Modern Man*. New York: Farrar, Straus and Young, Inc., 1951.
A systematic attempt to bring into focus the fundamentals of Jewish faith in the light of modern life and thought.

LEARSI, RUFUS. *The Jews in America*. Cleveland: The World Publishing Co., 1954.
A solid history and reference with considerable attention to the modern problems of American Jews.

PLAUT, W. GUNTHNER. *The Rise of Reform Judaism*. New York: World Union for Progressive Judaism, Ltd., 1963.
A source book of its European origins. The men who established Liberal Judaism speak for themselves, through their journals and pamphlets, their books and sermons, their petitions and resolutions.

SKLARE, MARSHALL. *Conservative Judaism: An American Religious Movement*. Glencoe, Illinois: The Free Press.
Conservatism seen as an American adaptation of Orthodoxy.

—— (ed.). *The Jews: Social Patterns of an American Group*. Glencoe, Illinois: The Free Press, 1960.
Describes the actual day-to-day beliefs, practices, and social organization of the Jews. Almost every aspect of Jewish life is covered: the demographic, the religious, the communal, the psychological, and the cultural.

SKLARE, MARSHALL, AND VOSK, MARC. *The Riverton Study: How Jews Look at Themselves and Their Neighbors*. New York: The American Jewish Committee, 1957.
Many nonreligious Jews find in charitable activities the one means of expressing Jewish identification.

WAX, MURRAY. "Ancient Judaism and the Protestant Ethic," *American Journal of Sociology*, Vol. 65 (March, 1960), pp. 499-555.
Elements of the Protestant ethic in ancient Judaism.

VORSPAN, ALBERT. *Giants of Justice*. New York: Thomas Y. Crowell Co., 1960.
Great American Jews of this century and their contributions to social justice.

WOUK, HERMAN. *This Is My God*. Garden City, New York: Doubleday & Co., 1959.
A revelation of facts and insights about Judaism by an outstanding novelist.

Chapter VIII: "Third-Force" Protestantism

BREWER, EARL D. C. "Sect and Church in Methodism," *Social Forces*, May, 1952, pp. 400–408.
Methodism has, from its sect beginnings in the early national period, moved substantially along the continuum towards the church type of religious organization and behavior.

CLEAR, VAL. "The Church of God: A Study in Social Adaptation," *Review of Religious Research*, Vol. 2 (Winter, 1961), pp. 129–33.
Stages in the evolution of a church from a sect; from dissent to accommodation.

ECKARDT, A. ROY. *The Surge of Piety in America*. New York: Association Press, 1958.
An analysis and appraisal of the revival of folk religion in contemporary Protestantism.

GOLDSCHMIDT, WALTER R. "Class Denominationalism in Rural California Churches," *American Journal of Sociology*, January, 1944, pp. 348–55.

Social class similarity a more important force than theological likeness in determining religious group affiliation.

HERNDON, BOOTON. *The Seventh Day*. New York: McGraw-Hill, Inc., 1960.
An interpretation of the theology and history of the Seventh-Day Adventists by an observer who is not a church member.

HOLT, JOHN B. "Holiness Religion: Cultural Shock and Social Reorganization," *American Sociological Review*, October, 1940, pp. 640–47.
Rural migrants suffer "culture shock" when they move to the city and readjust through the mechanism of holiness religion.

HUMMEL, CHARLES E. *Campus Christian Witness*. Chicago: Intervarsity Press, 1958.
A brief history of the Intervarsity Christian Fellowship movement, and a manual telling how an Intervarsity Fellowship may be organized and maintained on a college campus.

MCLOUGHLIN, JR., WILLIAM G. *Modern Revivalism*. New York: Ronald Press, 1959.
An account of the last three great revival movements in America, which the author calls "modern revivalism." Charles Farney, D. L. Moody, Billy Sunday and Billy Graham illustrate the periods.

MITCHELL, DAVID. *Seventh-Day Adventists*. New York: Vantage Press, 1958.
A sympathetic interpretation of a "Faith in Action." Who these people are, what they believe, what their critics say about them, and how they reply.

MUELDER, WALTER G. "From Sect to Church," *Christendom*, Autumn, 1945, pp. 450–62.
The Church of the Nazarene and some Pentecostal groups move from dissent to accommodation, from social ostracism to social acceptability, and otherwise reflect change that represents movement along the continuum from sect to church.

RADFOR, M. E. *The Rise of the Church of the Nazarene*. Nazarene Publishing House, 1948.
How the holiness principle in Christianity is implemented in the organization and development of the Church of the Nazarene.

SCHREIBER, WILLIAM I. *Our Amish Neighbors*. Chicago: University of Chicago Press, 1962.
A sympathetic account of the Ohio Amish. Author sees the Old Order Amish in America as the last refuge of German peasantry.

SMITH, C. HENRY. *The Story of the Mennonites*, rev. ed. Mennonite Publication Office, 1950.
A history of the Anabaptist movement and the Mennonites in Europe and America.

VAN DUSEN, HENRY P. " 'Third Force' in American Christendom," *Life*, June 9, 1958.
Van Dusen calls attention to the strength and vitality of conservative Protestantism.

WHITLEY, OLIVER R. "The Sect-to-Denomination Process in an American Religious Movement: The Disciples of Christ," *The Southwestern Social Quarterly*, December, 1955, pp. 275–81.
The church-sect typology as a measure of change.

Chapter IX: Creative Innovation and Religion

BRADEN, CHARLES S. *Christian Science Today*. Dallas: Southern Methodist University Press, 1958.
Developments in the doctrine, teaching, and organization of Christian Science since the death of Mary Baker Eddy in 1910.

——— *These Also Believe*. New York: The Macmillan Co., 1949.
Study of modern American cults and minority religious movements.

——— *Spirits in Rebellion*. Dallas: Southern Methodist University Press, 1963.
The rise and development of the New Thought movement. Christian Science is seen as one of the main streams of the movement.

CANTRIL, HADLEY. *The Psychology of Social Movements*. New York: John Wiley & Sons, 1941.
Includes an interpretation of Father Divine's movement and the Oxford Group.

CLARK, WALTER H. *The Oxford Group: Its History and Significance*. New York: Bookman Associates, 1951.
A psychologist's interpretation of the development of the "Buchman" movement.

COHN, WERNER. "Jehovah's Witnesses as a Proletarian Movement," *The American Scholar*, Vol. 24 (Summer, 1955), pp. 281–98.
Reflects behavior characteristics of socially isolated and culturally peripheral individuals and groups.

COLE, MARLEY. *Jehovah's Witnesses*. New York: Vantage Press, 1955.
A sympathetic account of Jehovah's Witnesses in their worldwide activities. Traces their origin back to Bible times and covers the modern organization through a 75 year period from the early Pastor Russell days to the present.

EISTER, ALLAN W. *Drawing Room Conversion*. Durham, North Carolina: Duke University Press, 1950.
A sociological study of the Oxford Group Movement in relation to the historical period in which it appeared.

GERSTNER, JOHN H. *The Theology of the Major Sects*. Grand Rapids, Michigan: Baker Book House, 1963.
Comparative analysis of the theology of Seventh-Day Adventists, Jehovah's Witnesses, Mormons, Christian Science, and others.

HINCKLEY, GORDON B. *What of the Mormons?* Salt Lake City: Church of Jesus Christ of Latter-Day Saints, 1947.
A brief history of the Mormons written by an official of the Church of Jesus Christ of Latter-Day Saints and published by the church.

HOSTETLER, JOHN A. "Old World Extinction and New World Survival of the Amish: A Study of Group Maintenance and Dissolution," *Rural Sociology*, September–December, 1955, pp. 197–211.
The Swiss and German origins of the Amish Mennonites, the early history of the sect, its dissolution in Europe, and its survival in America.

HOWARD, PETER. *The World Rebuilt*. New York: Duell, Sloan & Pearce, Inc., 1951.
The story of Frank Buchman and the achievement of moral rearmament.

JOHN, DEWITT. *The Christian Science Way of Life*, with *A Christian Scientist's Life* by Erwin D. Canham. Englewood Cliffs, New Jersey: Prentice-Hall, Inc., 1962.
An explanation of the practice and the impact of contemporary Christian Science by two prominent members of the Church of Christ, Scientist.

McMURRIN, STERLING M. *Philosophical Foundations of Mormon Theology*. Salt Lake City: University of Utah Press, 1959.
An exploration of the intellectual and rational sources of Mormon belief and practice.

NELSON, LOWRY. *The Mormon Village*. Salt Lake City: University of Utah Press, 1952.
How Mormon religious values influence social behavior; based upon sociological studies of several Mormon villages.

O'DEA, THOMAS F. "Mormonism and the Avoidance of Sectarian Stagnation: A Study of Church, Sect and Incipient Nationality," *American Journal of Sociology*, November, 1954, pp. 285–88.
The Mormon religion defies easy classification.

——— *The Mormons*. Chicago: University of Chicago Press, 1957.
A study of the history, doctrine, and present-day Mormons. Considers the strength and weakness of the Mormon Church, the Book of Mormon, and the role played by Mormonism in the U.S.

STROUP, HERBERT H. *The Jehovah's Witnesses*. New York: Columbia University Press, 1945.
A scholarly analysis based upon empirical research.

WHALEN, WILLIAM J. *Armageddon Around the Corner: A Report on Jehovah's Witnesses.* New York: The John Day Co., Inc., 1962.

A popular interpretation based upon observation, interviews, and correspondence in which the author says he seeks neither to whitewash nor to attack.

WIDTSOE, JOHN A. *Evidences and Reconciliations.* Salt Lake City: The Bookcraft Co., 1960.

A Mormon apologetic: the Bible, Revelation, salvation, family, freedom *versus* organization in the church, etc.

WISBY, HERBERT. *Soldiers Without Swords: A History of the Salvation Army in the U.S.* New York: The Macmillan Co., 1956.

A study of the Salvation Army in relation to other institutions; its significance for social history, social work, and organized religion.

YOUNG, KIMBALL. *Isn't One Wife Enough?* New York: Henry Holt & Co., 1944.

A sociological study of the institution of plural marriage among Mormons: how it began, how extensive it was, what people both within and without the community felt about it, how it was eradicated.

Chapter X: The Clergy

CUMMING, ELAINE, AND HARRINGTON, CHARLES. "Clergyman as Counselor," *American Journal of Sociology,* Vol. 69, No. 3 (November, 1963), pp. 234–44.

A study based upon a sample of 61 churches in Syracuse, New York, that included 45 percent of the Roman Catholic, 40 percent of the liturgical, 47 percent of the other Protestant, 48 percent of the fundamentalist, and 37 percent of the Jewish churches.

DENTON, WALLACE. *The Role of the Minister's Wife,* Philadelphia: The Westminster Press, 1962.

A sociological and psychological study based upon personal interviews, counseling experience, and questionnaires.

DONOVAN, JOHN D. "The American Catholic Hierarchy: A Social Profile," *American Catholic Sociological Review,* Vol. 19 (June, 1958), pp. 98–112.

American bishops tend to come from Irish or German backgrounds, and to be one of several children. The family quite often has other representatives in religious vocations.

FELTON, RALPH A. *New Ministers,* Madison, New Jersey: Drew Theological Seminary, 1949.

Background and attitude factors of 1700 divinity students from 57 Protestant seminaries.

FICHTER, JOSEPH H., S.J. *Religion as an Occupation: A Study in the Sociology of Professions.* South Bend, Indiana: University of Notre Dame Press, 1961.

A study of the 250,000 fulltime professionals in the American Catholic Church in which the author seeks to compare the Catholic Church as an employer with other secular employers. Recruitment, training, tenure, etc., are examined from the standpoint of scientific sociology.

GOLDSTEIN, SIDNEY I. "The Roles of an American Rabbi," *Sociology and Social Research,* Vol. 38 (September–October, 1953), pp. 32–37.

His roles are many. His congregation expects the rabbi to be a teacher and a scholar, an educator, a preacher, a prayer leader, a pastor, an organizer, an administrator, and an ambassador of good will to the non-Jewish world.

GUSTAFSON, JAMES. "An Analysis of the Problem of the Role of the Minister," *Journal of Religion,* Vol. 34, No. 3, 1954.

A competent analysis of the institutional and organizational framework within which the minister must understand his role.

HAGSTROM, WARREN O. "The Protestant Clergy as a Profession: Status and Prospects," *Berkeley Publications in Society and Institutions,* Vol. 3 (Spring, 1957), pp. 1–12.

HULME, WILLIAM E. *The Pastoral Care of Families.* Nashville: Abingdon Press, 1962.

In this study of pastoral counseling the author uses the life cycle of the family, from courtship to old age, as a basic outline.

Journal of Pastoral Care. A quarterly devoted to articles, news, and reports on various aspects of the pastoral role.

LEIFFER, MURRAY H. *The Layman Looks at the Minister.* New York: Abingdon-Cokesbury Press, 1947.
    An analysis and interpretation of 1000 Methodist laymen to a questionnaire as to what they liked and disliked about ministers.

MICHAELSON, ROBERT S. "The Protestant Ministry in America: 1850 to the Present," in H. RICHARD NIEBUHR AND DANIEL D. WILLIAMS, *The Ministry in Historical Perspective*, New York: Harper & Bros., 1956.
    A Protestant view of the development and nature of the Christian ministry. Study made at the request of the American Association of Theological Schools as part of a survey of theological education.

MOORE, EDWARD R. *Roman Collar.* New York: The Macmillan Co., 1951.
    Autobiographical account of priestly work in the archdiocese of New York over a 30-year period. Answers the question: "What does a priest do?"

NIEBUHR, H. RICHARD; WILLIAMS, DANIEL D.; AND GUSTAFSON, JAMES M. *The Advancement of Theological Education*, New York: Harper & Bros., 1957.
    A survey of the needs and problems of Protestant training for the ministry.

OATES, WAYNE E. *The Christian Pastor.* Philadelphia: Westminster Press, 1951.
    The pastor's role as "problem solver." How a representative pastor in a representative parish may meet the various demands upon his time and his talents.

Pastoral Psychology. A monthly devoted to the practical synthesis with spiritual and religious values of the principles and dynamics of counseling, dynamic psychiatry, and psychology.

SMITH, LUKE M. "The Clergy: Authority Structure, Ideology, Migration," *American Sociological Review*, June, 1953, pp. 242–48.
    Sacramental churches are differentiated from instrumental churches in terms of role expectations of the clergy.

SMITH, ROBERT O. "Personality and Cultural Factors Affecting the Religion of One Hundred and Forty Divinity Students," *Religious Education*, Vol. 43 (March–April, 1948), pp. 106–11.
    In the majority of cases the family and relatives were strongly religious or engaged in religious or social work.

WAGONER, WALTER D. "The Ministry: Image and Reality," *Christian Century*, Vol. 77 (April 20, 1960), pp. 464–66.
    Five reasons why many of the more thoughtful Christian students fail to enter the seminary.

WILSON, BRYAN R. "The Pentecostal Minister: Role Conflicts and Status Contradictions," *American Journal of Sociology*, Vol. 64 (March, 1959), pp. 494–504.
    The status of the Pentecostal minister is contradictory because of the lack of consensus among those for whom his role has significance.

Chapter XI: Disjunctive Processes and Relationships

BARON, SALO W. *A Social and Religious History of the Jews*, Vol. V, *Religious Controls and Dissensions*, New York: Columbia University Press, 1957.
    Controversies and disagreements in the historical development of Judaism.

BLANSHARD, PAUL. *American Freedom and Catholic Power*, Boston: Beacon Press, rev. ed., 1958.
    Blanshard offers documentary evidence to support his charges against the Catholic Church.

COWAN, WAYNE H. (ed.). *Facing Protestant-Roman Catholic Tensions.* New York: Association Press, 1960.
    Leading Catholics and Protestants suggest how to think clearly about the issues.

DOUGLASS, TRUMAN. "Ecological Changes and the Church," *The Annals of the American Academy of Political and Social Science*, Vol. 59 (November, 1960), p. 83.
    Sees the church as the most conservative of human institutions. Although the

churches speak boldly for liberal reform, they lag behind government, the armed services, and industry in implementing liberal programs.

HAGER, DON J.; GLOCK, CHARLES Y.; AND CHEIN, ISADOR (eds.). "Religious Conflict in the United States," *Journal of Social Issues*, Vol. 12, No. 3, 1956, pp. 1–67.
   Six articles describing and analyzing the tensions and conflicts between Protestants, Catholics, and Jews.

HERTZBERG, ARTHUR; MARTY, MARTIN E.; AND MOODY, JOSEPH N. *Outbursts That Await Us*. New York: The Macmillan Co., 1963.
   The differing responses of Protestant, Catholic, and Jew to the areas in which religion and culture interact.

KANE, JOHN J. *Catholic-Protestant Conflicts in America*. Chicago: Henry Regnery Co., 1955.
   A Roman Catholic sociologist surveys and analyzes the issues that divide Catholics and Protestants.

MOORE, EDMUND A. *A Catholic Runs for President*. New York: Ronald Press Co., 1956.
   A description of the 1928 presidential campaign in which Al Smith, the Democratic candidate and a Roman Catholic, was defeated.

O'NEILL, JAMES. *Catholicism and American Freedom*. New York: Harper & Bros., 1952.
   A Catholic layman answers the charges brought against the Catholic Church by Paul Blanshard.

PFEFFER, LEO. *Creeds in Competition*. New York: Harper & Bros., 1958.
   Author sees the competition of the basic faiths over such issues as the separation of church and state, public *versus* private schools, family values, etc., as a creative force in American culture.

ROY, RALPH LORD. *Apostles of Discord*. Boston: Beacon Press, 1953.
   A study of organized bigotry on the fringes of Protestantism, seen in the light of many denominational struggles.

SCHARPER, PHILIP (ed.). *American Catholics: A Protestant-Jewish View*. New York: Sheed & Ward, 1959.
   Six essays describing the images of Catholics commonly held by non-Catholics.

SIMON, MAURICE. *Jewish Religious Conflicts*. London: Hutchinson's University Library, 1950.
   The history of internal divisions in Judaism.

SUGRUE, THOMAS. *A Catholic Speaks His Mind on America's Religious Conflict*. New York.
   A Catholic minority view of religious conflict in post-World War II America.

UNDERWOOD, KENNETH. *Protestant and Catholic*. Boston: Beacon Press, 1957.
   An intensive study of Catholic-Protestant relations in Holyoke, Massachusetts, during the period when the majority of the population was changing in religious affiliation and identification from Protestant to Catholic.

Chapter XII: Conjunctive Processes and Relationships

BARNES, ROSWELL P. "The Ecumenical Movement," *The Annals of the American Academy of Political and Social Science*, Vol. 332 (November, 1960), pp. 135–45.
   The ecumenical movement is primarily the result of an internal dynamic arising from religious convictions, but it is also in part a response to social forces and historical developments. It is more inclusive than the major Protestant denominations in the American tradition and broader than the organizations which promote cooperation among the churches.

BILHEIMER, ROBERT S. *The Quest for Christian Unity*. New York: Association Press, 1952.
   A survey of American Protestantism in the last half century, with special attention on the ecumenical hope and achievement.

BLISS, KATHLEEN. *The Service and Status of Women in the Church*. London: SCM Press, Ltd., 1952.
    The role and status of women in the churches, and women members of the World Council of Churches.

BROWN, ROBERT McAFEE. *The Spirit of Protestantism*. New York: Oxford University Press, 1961.
    A study of the spirit of Protestantism that points the way for a more realistic and fruitful dialogue between Protestant and Catholic.

FELTON, RALPH A. *Cooperative Churches*. Madison, New Jersey: Drew Theological Seminary, 1947.
    A survey among village and country churches of various kinds of church co-operation.

KAGAN, HENRY ENOCH. *Changing the Attitude of Christian Toward Jew*. New York: Columbia University Press, 1952.
    A sociopsychological approach to the problem of religious conflict and mis-understanding.

KÜNG, HANS. *The Council, Reform and Reunion*. New York: Sheed & Ward, 1962.
    Theme: There can be no possibility of reunion between the Church of Rome and her "separated brethren" that is not preceded by radical reform of Catholicism at its center and throughout its length and breadth. Proposals for reform include papal infallibility, Mariology, reform of the liturgy, reexamination of clerical celibacy, laws of marriage, and the *Index*.

LAUER, ROSEMARY. "Women and the Church," *The Commonweal*, December 20, 1963.
    A review of some recent changes in the attitude of the Catholic Church toward the position of women in the church, and a plea for a modification of the Aristotelian-Thomistic interpretation of woman's proper role and status.

LEE, ROBERT. *The Social Sources of Church Unity*. New York: Abingdon Press, 1960.
    Social factors contributing to the movement towards church union.

MORRISON, CHARLES C. *The Unfinished Reformation*. New York: Harper & Bros., 1953.
    Denominationalism is attacked. The achievement of a united church is sought.

MUELDER, WALTER G. "Institutional Factors Affecting Unity and Disunity," *The Ecumenical Review*, 8 (January, 1956), pp. 113–26.
    A sociological analysis of the institutional factors that promote unity and disunity.

PFAUTZ, HAROLD W. "The Sociology of Secularization: Religious Groups," *American Journal of Sociology*, Vol. 61, No. 2 (September, 1955), pp. 121–28.
    The movement of Christian Science from the *sect* type to the *institutionalized sect* type of religious organization seen as a function of the secularization process.

ROSENTHAL, ERICH. "Acculturation without Assimilation: The Jewish Community in Chicago, Illinois," *American Journal of Sociology*, Vol. 66, No. 3 (November, 1960), pp. 275–88.
    By voluntary segregation in a high-status area Chicago, Jews endeavor to retain Jewish identity.

SALISBURY, W. SEWARD. "Religion and Secularization," *Social Forces*, Vol. 36, No. 3, (March, 1958), pp. 197–203.
    An empirical study: the typical religiously identified personality shows a high degree of secularization in terms of selected sacred values.

Chapter XIII: Government and Religion

The Experience of the American Service Committee in Civilian Public Service. American Friends Service Committee, 1945.
    One of the "historic peace" churches shares its experience with the conscientious objector camps during World War II.

BARON, SALO W. *Modern Nationalism and Religion*. New York: Harper & Bros., 1947.
    Traces the development of nationalism in the principal countries of the world and its relation to Catholicism, Protestantism, and Judaism.

DAWSON, JOSEPH MARTIN. *America's Way in Church, State, and Society*. The Macmillan Co., 1953.
  The genesis and progress of the principle of the separation of church and state, and how it has affected life in the United States.

EBERSOLE, LUKE E. *Church Lobbying in the Nation's Capitol*. New York: The Macmillan Co., 1951.
  Organization, personnel, and financial resources of the Protestant and Catholic groups which lobby in Washington.

——— "Religion and Politics," *Annals of the American Academy of Political and Social Science*, Vol. 332 (November, 1960), pp. 101–11.
  Religious groups participate in a wide variety of political activities but are not organized in political parties or machines.

GLOCK, CHARLES Y., AND RINGER, BENJAMIN B. "Church Polity and the Attitudes of Ministers and Parishioners on Social Issues," *American Sociological Review*, April, 1956, pp. 148–56.
  The differing attitudes of the church, the clergy, and the laymen on social issues give rise to a church practice that is a resultant of forces which are at times conflictive and at times supportive in nature.

HONEYWELL, ROY J. *Chaplains of the United States Army*. Washington, D.C.: Office of the Chief of Chaplains, Department of the Army, 1958.
  The rise and development of the chaplaincy in the military services.

MOEHLMAN, CONRAD H. *The Wall of Separation Between Church and State*. Boston: The Beacon Press, 1951.
  A Protestant-oriented study of the religious clause of the First Amendment.

NIEBUHR, REINHOLD. *Christianity and Power Politics*. New York: Charles Scribner's Sons, 1948.
  Discusses the relationship between religion and other institutions.

PFEFFER, LEO. *Church, State, and Freedom*. Boston: The Beacon Press, 1951.
  The competing claims of religion, government, and freedom in a pluralistic society, as seen by a spokesman for Judaism.

SHIELDS, CURRIN V. *Democracy and Catholicism in America*. New York: McGraw-Hill Book Co., Inc., 1958.
  How a political scientist views the religious-political relationship.

SIBLEY, MULFORD A., AND JACOB, PHILIP E. *Conscription of Conscience*. Ithaca, New York: Cornell University Press, 1952.
  The story of the American state and the conscientious objector during World War II.

STOKES, ANSON PHELPS. *Church and State in the United States*, 3 vols., New York: Harper & Bros., 1950.
  An exhaustive and scholarly study of the subject; valuable reference book. Carefully annotated and indexed, extensive bibliography.

Chapter XIV: Religion and Education

BRESSLER, MARVIN, AND WESTHOFF, CHARLES F. "Catholic Education, Economic Values, and Achievement," *American Journal of Sociology*, Vol. 69, No. 3 (November, 1963).
  Catholic education does not magnify religious differentials in the economic or other secular areas.

BROWN, NICHOLAS C. (ed.). *The Study of Religion in the Public Schools*. Washington, D.C.: The American Council on Education, 1958.
  The report of a conference on religion and public education, based upon six prepared papers and the discussion that followed.

CRAGON, MILLER M. "The Religious Influence of the Parochial School," *Religious Education*, Vol. 16, No. 3 (May–June, 1961), pp. 180–84.
  Regular religious instruction in the parochial school may lead to superior religious knowledge but not necessarily to higher behavior standards and improved

attitudes. The parochial school may supplement but cannot replace the home in the development of religious attitudes and ethical behavior.

CUNINGGIM, MERRIMON. *The College Seeks Religion.* New Haven, Connecticut: Yale University Press, 1947.
    An historical account of the place given to religion in American colleges and universities.

DIRKS, J. EDWARD. "Should Religion Be Taught in Tax-Supported Colleges and Universities?" *The Christian Scholar* (Winter, 1962).
    A statement published by the Commission on Higher Education of the National Council of Churches of Christ in the USA.

DUNN, WILLIAM KAILER. *What Happened to Religious Education?* Baltimore: Johns Hopkins Press, 1958.
    A scholarly analysis of the decline of religious teaching in the public elementary school from 1776 to 1861.

EDDY, EDWARD R. *The College Influence on Student Character.* Washington, D.C.: The American Council on Education, 1959.
    An organized attempt to assess influences on character in a college setting, based on a study of 20 colleges and universities.

FICHTER, JOSEPH H., S.J. *Parochial School.* South Bend, Indiana: University of Notre Dame Press, 1958.
    An empirical study of a parochial school and a matched public school. The differences and similarities in curricula, procedures, and outcomes are pointed out.

GAUSS, CHRISTIAN (ed.). *The Teaching of Religion in American Higher Education.* New York: The Ronald Press, 1951.
    Directed to teachers and administrators who are interested in the place which religion should occupy; and how it can be taught in American colleges.

GILLESPIE, JAMES, AND ALLPORT, GORDON W. *Youth's Outlook on the Future.* New York: Doubleday & Co., 1955.
    Religious beliefs and activities of American youth found to be more representative of self-referent than of social-referent values.

GOLDSEN, ROSE K.; ROSENBERG, MORRIS; WILLIAMS, JR., ROBIN M.; AND SUCHMAN, EDWARD A. *What College Students Think.* Princeton, New Jersey: D. Nostrand Co., 1960.
    An analysis and interpretation of what college students think about such subjects as love, marriage, education, religion, society, and life goals. The report of the extensive, eleven-university study of student values, conducted by the Cornell University Department of Sociology.

HEALEY, ROBERT M. *Jefferson on Religion in Public Education.* New Haven, Connecticut: Yale University Press, 1962.
    A careful delineation of Jefferson's views; views which are often cited by advocates of different and even contradictory positions.

JACOB, PHILIP E. *Changing Values in College.* New Haven, Connecticut: The Edward W. Hazen Foundation, 1957.
    Report of a study that sought to determine what changes occur in students' patterns of value during college, with particular emphasis upon the extent to which such changes stem from exposure to various types of social science instruction in the "general curriculum."

JACOBSON, PHILIP. *Religion in Public Education.* New York: The American Jewish Committee, 1960.
    The arguments for and against released time, use of the Bible, prayer, ceremonials, and other topics that involve the question of the separation of church and state.

JOHNSON, F. ERNEST (ed.). *American Education and Religion: The Problem of Religion in the Schools.* New York: Harper & Bros. (for the Institute for Religious and Social Studies), 1952.
    The problem of religion in the schools. A series of addresses by religious, lay,

and educational leaders, representing both public and private institutions of lower and higher learning.

KANE, JOHN J. "Church and Laity among Catholics," *The Annals of the American Academy of Political and Social Science*, Vol. 332 (November, 1960), pp. 50–69.

Discusses the responsibility of Catholic parents for sending their children to Catholic schools.

LA NOUE, GEORGE R. *Public Funds for Parochial Schools?* Studies of Church and state by the Department of Religious Liberty of the National Council of Churches of Christ in the USA, 1963.

A resource document dealing with the historical and legal background of the issue, and the question of public policy.

LOUISELL, DAVID W., AND JACKSON, JOHN H. "Religion, Theology, and Public Higher Education," *California Law Review*, Vol. 50, No. 5 (December, 1962).

A study made for the Commission on the Study of the Place of Religion in the Curricula of State Universities, sponsored by the University of Minnesota and the Religious Education Association, 545 W. 111th St., New York City.

Religion and the Schools. Bureau of Publication, Teachers College, Columbia University, New York, 1963.

The pros and cons of the question of public funds for parochial schools; religion in education in legal perspective.

Religious Education.

The bimonthly journal of the Religious Education Association. A platform for the free discussion of issues in the field of religion and their bearing on education.

SANFORD, NEVITT (ed.). *The American College: A Psychological and Social Interpretation of the Higher Learning.* New York: John Wiley & Sons, 1962.

Articles on impact of college education, role perceptions of teachers and others that apply to modern social theory and personality theory.

SHAVER, ERWIN L., *et al.* "Weekday Religious Education," *Religious Education*, Vol. 51 (January–February, 1956), pp. 18–70.

A study of 152 released time programs, and constitutional and other problems concerning weekday religious education, by Protestant, Catholic, and Jewish educators.

SNAVELY, GUY E. *The Church and the Four-Year College.* New York: Harper & Bros., 1955.

The history of the relations of churches and colleges in the United States.

STROMMEN, MERTON P. *Profiles of Church Youth.* St. Louis: Condordia Publishing Co., 1963.

A report of a four-year study of 3,000 Lutheran high school youths in the church; their beliefs, values, family relationships, conflicts.

TAYLOR, MARVIN J. (ed.). *Religious Education.* New York: Abingdon Press, 1960.

A symposium dealing with the methods and techniques of the agencies that provide Protestant, Catholic, and Jewish religious education.

WHITMAR, SAFARA A. "Protestant Forfeiture in Education," *Christianity Today.* Washington, D.C., May 11, 1959.

Most church related Protestant colleges were founded in the nineteenth century, but since 1900 Catholic and tax-supported colleges have dominated the statistics of organization and growth.

Chapter XV: Religion and the Family

BARRON, MILTON L. *People Who Intermarry.* Syracuse: Syracuse University Press, 1947.

A study of intermarriage in a New England industrial community.

BOSSARD, JAMES H. S., AND BOLL, ELEANOR S. *One Marriage: Two Faiths.* New York: The Ronald Press, 1957.

The significance of interfaith marriages, attitudes of various churches, and the problems relating to husband, wife, and children.

BOUMA, DONALD H. "Religiously Mixed Marriages: Denominational Consequences in the Christian Reformed Church," *Marriage and Family Living*, Vol. 25 (November, 1963), pp. 428–32.

In a strong ethnic church (Dutch) 41 percent of marriages found to be religiously heterogeneous, but church gained three members for every two lost through intermarriage.

DUVALL, EVELYN AND SYLVANUS (eds.). *Sex Ways in Fact and Faith*. New York: Association Press, 1961.

Reviews the Biblical and historical bases for Christian views on sex and marriage. Presents the latest denominational pronouncements on such matters as divorce, remarriage, mixed marriage, and family limitation.

FERRÉ, NELS F. S. "A Christian Theology of Family Life," *Religion in Life*, Vol. 33 (Winter, 1963–64), pp. 90–98.

The Christian family should be evaluated in the light of Christ, as the Incarnate Love of God. Christian love should be implemented in terms of the three aspects of family living: the physical, the intellectual, the spiritual.

HEISS, JEROLD. "Premarital Characteristics of the Religiously Intermarried in an Urban Area," *American Sociological Review*, Vol. 25 (February, 1960), pp. 47–55.

The intermarried report a lesser early tie to religion, lesser early family integration, and greater emancipation from parents at time of marriage.

KELLY, GEORGE A. *Birth Control and Catholics*. Garden City, New York: Doubleday & Co., 1963.

The Catholic philosophy of birth control and parenthood, written for Catholic married couples.

LANDIS, JUDSON T. "Religiousness, Family Relationships and Family Values in Protestant, Catholic, and Jewish Families," *Marriage and Family Living*, Vol. XXIII, No. 4 (November, 1960).

A study of the religious backgrounds and religious values of 3000 university students.

LEIFFER, MURRAY H. "Mixed Marriages and the Children," *The Christian Century*, Vol. 66, No. 4 (January 26, 1949), pp. 106–108.

A study of 305 families of mixed Catholic-Protestant parenthood found that the mother is more important than the denomination in determining the allegiance of the children.

LENSKI, GERHARD. *The Religious Factor*, Garden City, New York: Doubleday & Co., 1961.

How Catholics, Jews, Negro Protestants, and white Protestants of Detroit differ in political and economic values, in competition for economic advancement, and in the patterns of family life. A result of the research carried out by the Detroit Area Study of the University of Michigan.

LOCKE, HARVEY J.; SABAGH, GEORGE; AND THOMAS, MARY M. "Interfaith Marriages," *Social Problems*, Vol. 4 (April, 1957), pp. 329–33.

MACE, DAVID R. *Hebrew Marriage*, New York: Philosophical Library, 1953.

A sociological study of marriage and the family, based upon the evidence of the Old Testament and upon anthropological and archeological discoveries.

MARTINSON, FLOYD M. *Marriage and the American Ideal*. New York: Dodd, Mead & Co., 1960.

A sociological interpretation of American marriage in which the special values that distinguish Catholic, Protestant, and Jewish marriage and family relationships are emphasized.

MAYER, JOHN E. *Jewish-Gentile Courtships*. Glencoe, Illinois: The Free Press, 1961.

A study of the factors influencing a group of persons living in the New York metropolitan area to enter into a mixed marriage.

McCORMICK, RICHARD A., S.J. "Conjugal Love and Conjugal Morality," *America*, Vol. 110, No. 2 (January 11, 1964), pp. 38–42.

A re-evaluation of the Catholic position in terms of total marital commitment.

Pike, James A. *If You Marry Outside Your Faith*. New York: Harper & Bros., 1962.
A prominent Protestant clergyman offers counsel on mixed marriage, based on an extensive counselling experience.

Reuss, Carl F. "Research Findings on the Effects of Modern-Day Religion on Family Living," *Marriage and Family Living*, Vol. 16 (August, 1954), pp. 221–25.
Research studies summarized and interpreted.

Rock, John. *The Time Has Come: A Catholic Doctor's Proposals to End the Battle over Birth Control*. New York: Alfred Knopf, Inc., 1963.
The author sets out to prove that Roman Catholicism and birth control ("the pill") are reconcilable through a reinterpretation of natural law.

Shanks, Hershel. "Jewish-Gentile Intermarriage: Facts and Trends," *Commentary*, Vol. 16 (October, 1953), pp. 370–75.
A summary of studies made between 1937 and 1950 shows that between 5 and 10 percent of all marriages involving Jews were intermarriages.

Slotkin, J. S. "Jewish-Gentile Intermarriage in Chicago," *American Sociological Review*, Vol. 7 (February, 1942), pp. 34–39.
The premarital characteristics of those who marry within their faith compared with those who marry across faith lines.

Thomas, John L., S.J. *The American Catholic Family*. Englewood Cliffs, New Jersey: Prentice-Hall, Inc., 1956.
An interpretation of the Catholic family within the frame of reference of the Catholic concept of marriage by a sociologist who is also an authority on the Catholic family.

—— "The Factor of Religion in the Selection of Marriage Mates," *American Sociological Review*, Vol. 16 (August, 1951), pp. 487–91.
An empirical study of mixed marriage between Catholics and non-Catholics, based upon an extensive sampling of Catholic parishes in the East and Middle West.

Willits, Fern K.; Beales, Robert C.; and Bender, Gerald W. "Interreligious Marriage among Pennsylvania Youth." *Marriage and Family Living*, Vol. 25 (November, 1963), pp. 433–38.
Religious endogamy exceeded exogamy for all major groups (Roman Catholic, Protestant, and no affiliation) except for nonaffiliated males. Rates of exogamy high for individual Protestant denominations.

Chapter XVI: Religion in Representative Subcultures

The Church in Rural Areas

Blackwell, Gordon W., et al. *Church and Community in the South*. Richmond, Virginia: John Knox Press, 1949.
A summary and analysis of studies of southern communities. Considerable attention is directed to the role and status of the church in the community.

The Church in Rural Missouri, Midway in the 20th Century, College of Agriculture, University of Missouri, Agriculture Experiment Station Series.
Part I. Lawrence M. Hepple, "Introduction," Research Bulletin 633A (September, 1957).
Part II. Milton Coughenour and Lawrence M. Hepple, "Religious Groups in Rural Missouri," Research Bulletin 633B (September, 1957).
Part III. Lawrence M. Hepple, "Clergymen in Rural Missouri," Research Bulletin 633C (December, 1958).
Part IV. John S. Holik and Lawrence M. Hepple, "Index of Religious Group Action," Research Bulletin 633D (January, 1959).
Part V. Lawrence M. Hepple, "Rural-Urban Churches Compared," Research Bulletin 633E (July, 1959).
Part VI. George T. Blume and Lawrence M. Hepple, "Spatial and Social Relationships," Research Bulletin 633F (September, 1960).
Part VII. Lawrence M. Hepple and C. Milton Coughenour, "What Rural People Think of Church," Research Bulletin 633G (February, 1961).

The most complete and extensive study of rural religion in the post-World War II period.

DOUGLASS, H. PAUL, AND DE S. BRUNNER, EDMUND. *The Protestant Church as a Social Institution,* New York: Harper & Bros., 1935.
This is the most comprehensive study of the Protestant Church to appear between World War I and II. Particularly strong in rural church structure and trends.

ENSMINGER, DOUGLAS. "The Rural Church and Religion," in CARL C. TAYLOR, *et al., Rural Life in the United States.* New York: Alfred A. Knopf, Inc., 1949.
What sociological studies have discovered concerning the nature and structure of the rural church.

FELTON, RALPH A. *A New Gospel of the Soil.* Madison, New Jersey: Drew Theological Seminary, 1952.
Discusses 16 rural churches and their outstanding contributions to community improvement.

HOSTETLER, JOHN A., AND MATHER, WILLIAM G. *Participation in the Rural Church,* Agricultural Experiment Station Paper No. 1762, Journal Series (October, 1952), Pennsylvania State University, University Park.
A summary of a number of studies. Church participation is discussed in terms of sex, age, length of residence, tenure, income, social class, education, and occupation.

HYNES, EMERSON. "The Parish in the Rural Community," *The Sociology of the Parish,* C. J. NUESSE AND THOMAS J. HARTE (eds.), Milwaukee: The Bruce Publishing Co., 1951.
The place and characteristics of the rural Catholic parish in the United States.

JUDY, MARVIN T. *The Larger Parish and Group Ministry.* New York: Abingdon Press, 1959.
How the larger parish can serve the needs of a changing rural society.

LOOMIS, CHARLES P., AND BEEGLE, J. ALLAN. *Rural Social Systems,* Englewood Cliffs, New Jersey: Prentice-Hall, Inc., 1955.
See Chapters 12 and 13: "The Nature and Function of Religion," and "The Character of Religion."

RICH, MARK. *The Rural Church Movement.* Columbia, Missouri: Juniper Knoll Press, 1957.
An account of the historical periods, important concepts, and dominant leaders of the rural church movements in the United States.

SAMSON, A'DELBERT. *Church Groups in Four Agricultural Settings,* Montana Agricultural Experiment Bulletin 538 (March, 1958), Montana State College, Bozeman.
────── *Church Pastors in Four Agricultural Settings,* Montana Agricultural Experiment Bulletin 539 (April, 1958), Montana State College, Bozeman.
A study of the religious structure in communities serving varied types of agriculture: livestock ranching, dryland wheat farming, irrigated agriculture, diversified mountain. Fundamentalist and nonfundamentalist church groups compared.

SMITH, ROCKWELL C. *The Church in Our Town.* New York: Abingdon-Cokesbury Press, 1945.
An evaluation of the place and the work of the rural and village church in a community composed of small town people and farmers.

WEST, JAMES. *Plainville U.S.A.* New York: Columbia University Press, 1946.
A sociological study of a traditional rural community. Especially see chapter 4: "Religion."

Urban Religion

FOSSELMAN, DAVID H. "The Parish and the Urban Community," *The Sociology of the Parish* (ed. C. J. NUESSE AND THOMAS J. HARTE), Milwaukee: The Bruce Publishing Co., 1951.
Variability of the urban Catholic parish, life history of the downtown parish, social characteristics of urban parishes.

GORDON, ALBERT I. *Jews in Suburbia*. Boston: Beacon Press, 1959.
   A summary and discussion of what is happening to Jews in suburbia: their family life, their children, their religious values and practices. Based upon a study of Jewish communities in more than 80 suburban areas in the United States.

GREELEY, ANDREW M. *The Church and the Suburbs*. New York: Sheed & Ward, 1959.
   Changes and emphases brought about in the suburbanization of the Catholic Church.

KINCHELOE, SAMUEL C. *The American City and Its Church*. New York: Friendship Press, 1938.
   Problems arising out of the growth of urban population; what the churches can and should do for city people.

KLOETZLI, WALTER. *The City Church: Death or Renewal*. Philadelphia: Muhlenberg Press, 1961.
   The impact of rapid social and physical change on eight protestant urban parishes.

LEE, ROBERT (ed.). *Cities and Churches*. Philadelphia: The Westminster Press, 1962.
   Thirty-two readings by various authorities on the problem of meeting the religious needs of Protestants in urban environments.

SANDERSON, ROSS W. *The Church Serves the Changing City*. New York: Harper & Bros., 1955.
   An analysis and survey of some instances where American Protestantism is effectively ministering to urban residents in areas of underprivilege.

SHIPPEY, FREDERICK A. "The Variety of City Churches," *Review of Religious Research*, Vol. 2 (Summer, 1960), pp. 8–19.
   Seven typologies of city churches, evaluated, and a new classification offered.

WINTER, GIBSON. *The Suburban Captivity of the Churches*. New York: Doubleday & Co., 1961.
   An evaluation of the Protestant religious development in metropolitan areas.

Stratification and Religion

BURCHINAL, LEE G., AND KENKEL, WILLIAM F. "Religious Identification and Occupational Status of Iowa Grooms, 1953–1957," *American Sociological Review*, Vol. 27, No. 4 (August, 1962), pp. 526–32.
   Catholic grooms reflect a higher social and economic status than Protestant grooms.

FRAZIER, FRANKLIN E. *Black Bourgeoisie*. Glencoe, Illinois: The Free Press, 1957.
   Rise of the Negro middle class in the United States, with corresponding modifications in religious values and religious behavior.

GLAZER, NATHAN. "The American Jew and the Attainment of Middle-class Rank," in *The Jews: Social Patterns of an American Group* (ed. MARSHALL SKLARE), Glencoe, Illinois: The Free Press, 1960.
   Jewish economic and social advantage in the form of superior education and a higher proportion of self-employed persons attributed to the practice of "deferred gratification," a traditional Jewish value.

GREELEY, ANDREW M. "Influence of the 'Religious Factor' on Career and Occupational Values of College Graduates," *American Journal of Sociology*, Vol. 68, No. 6 (May, 1963).
   An empirical study showing no indication that Catholics are any less inclined to economic rationality (the "Protestant ethic") than Protestants.

HOLLINGSHEAD, AUGUST. *Elmtown's Youth*. New York: John Wiley & Sons, 1949.
   A sociological study of a small midwestern community, with emphasis upon the relation between social class and behavior of the youth of high school age. See chapter 10: "Religion and Religious Behavior."

HURVITS, NATHAN. "Sources of Middle-Class Values of American Jews," *Social Forces*, Vol. 37 (December, 1958), pp. 117–23.
   The class factor in the Americanization of Judaism.

KAUFMAN, HAROLD F. *Prestige Classes in a Rural Community*. Cornell University, A.E.S. Memoir 260, Ithaca, New York, 1944.

One of the outstanding social class studies of a rural community. Religious and educational institutions play a prominent part in the pattern of interactional relationships.

MACK, RAYMOND W.; MURPHY, RAYMOND J.; AND KELLIN, SEYMOUR. "The Protestant Ethic, Level of Aspiration and Social Mobility: An Empirical Test," *American Sociological Review*, Vol. 21 (June, 1956).

Whatever influence the "Protestant ethic" may have on the Protestant or Catholic subculture is overridden by the general ethos.

MAYER, ALBERT, AND SHARP, HARRY. "Religious Preference and Worldly Success," *American Sociological Review*, Vol. 27, No. 2 (April, 1962).

A study offering some support for the Weberian thesis of the "Protestant ethic," and also presenting important modifications.

OBERHAUS, VICTOR; SCHROEDER, W. WIDICK; AND ENGLAND, CHARLES D. "Church Participation Related to Social Class and Type of Center," *Rural Sociology*, Vol. 23 (September, 1958), pp. 298–308.

The church and class relationship in a midwestern rural area.

VEROFF, JOSEPH; FELD, SHEILA; AND GURIN, GERALD. "Achievement Motivation and Religious Background," *American Sociological Review*, Vol. 27, No. 2 (April, 1962), pp. 205–18.

High achievement motivation scores, derived from thematic apperceptive measures administered in a nationwide sample survey, were most prevalent in Jewish men, and more prevalent in Catholic than in Protestant men. The inconsistency of these findings with previous findings is interpreted in terms of the high economic status and restricted geographic locale of the population from which previous samples were drawn.

VIDICH, ARTHUR J., AND BENSMAN, JOSEPH. *Small Town in Mass Society*, Princeton, New Jersey: Princeton University Press, 1958.

Class, power, and religion in a rural community. Contends the central fact of Springdale's history (name given to Upstate New York community) is the community's growing dependence on forces originating in the larger society and especially in the more urbanized segments of that society.

The Negro as a Religious Subgroup

CRONON, EDMUND DAVID. *Black Moses: The Story of Marcus Garvey and the Universal Negro Improvement Association*. Madison, Wisconsin: University of Wisconsin Press, 1955.

Portrayal of the Negro leader who was one of the most controversial, loved, and criticized personalities of the turbulent 1920's.

DRAKE, ST. CLAIR, AND CAYTON, HORACE R. *Black Metropolis*. New York: Harcourt, Brace & Co., 1945.

The most comprehensive sociological study of the Negro community in a large city (Chicago). See Chapter 15: "The Power of the Press and Pulpit."

FAUSET, ARTHUR HUFF. *Black Gods of the Metropolis*. Philadelphia: University of Pennsylvania Press, 1944.

Some Negro religious cults in urban areas of the North.

FRAZIER, FRANKLIN E. *The Negro in the United States*. New York: The Macmillan Co., 1949.

An institutional and functional approach, scholarly, with extensive footnotes, and an exhaustive classified bibliography. See Chapter 14: "The Negro Church."

GUNNAR, MYRDAL (with the assistance of RICHARD STERN AND ARNOLD ROSE). *The American Dilemma*. New York: Harper & Bros., 1944.

The classic study directed by the Swedish social scientist of the history and the current status of the Negro in American life. The scope and nature of the contemporary problem (the "Dilemma") is emphasized. See Chapter 41: "The Negro Church."

JOHNSTON, RUBY. *The Religion of Negro Protestants*. New York: Philosophical Library, 1956.

The development, nature, and variety of Negro Protestantism.

Lincoln, Eric C. *Black Muslims in America*. Boston: Beacon Press, 1961.

A sociologist's account of the Black Muslim movement in the United States, touching on forerunners, origins, doctrines, and leaders.

Loescher, F. S. *The Protestant Church and the Negro*. New York: Association Press, 1948.

Interracial problems and practices of the Protestant denominations in the United States; a pattern of segregation.

Mays, Benjamin E., and Nicholson, Joseph W. *The Negro's Church*. New York: Institute of Social and Religious Research, 1933.

Based on a firsthand study of 609 urban and 185 rural churches widely distributed in 12 cities and 4 country areas. Covers training of ministers, number and size of churches, finances, membership, etc.

Ottley, Roi. *New World A-Coming*. Boston: Houghton Mifflin Co., 1943.

A popularly written interpretation of the fads and fancies of Negro Harlem. See Chapter 7, "I Talked with God," for an early account of the Father Divine movement.

Pope, Liston. *The Kingdom beyond Caste*. New York: Friendship Press, 1957.

A discussion of the relation of the Christian Church to the question of race and to the concept of democracy, by the dean of Yale University Divinity School.

Index

Index

519

Witnessing for Christ, 71, 158, 164, 168, 172

Women
  in Catholicism, 283, 287, 399–401
  and church participation, 86
  clergy, 51, 284–87
  explanation of sex ratios, 87–88
  in Judaism, 87, 124, 283, 287–88, 406–9
  in Protestantism, 283–87
  subordination of, 87, 189, 200, 283, 408
"The Word," to possess, 30, 58

World Council of Churches, 287, 292, 294–95, 297

World Presbyterian Alliance, North American area, 301

Worship services, 165, 281

Wouk, Herman, 408, 409, 500

Wynn, John C., 423

Y

Yahrzeit, 453

Yarmulke, 147

Yarn, David H., 377

Yearbook of American Churches, 74, 75

Yellin, Seymour, 460

Yiddish schools, 358

Yinger, Milton J., 8, 16, 97, 98, 477, 478, 492

Yom Kippur (Day of Atonement), 62, 147

Young, Brigham, 181, 184, 185, 187

Young, Kimball, 247–49, 503

Z

Zimmer, Basil G., 86, 89

Zion, City of, 180, 186

Zorach Clauson, 368

This book has been set on the Linotype in 10 point Janson, leaded 1 point. Part and chapter numbers and titles are in Garamont and Garamond. The size of the type page is 27 by 47 picas.